IMPORTANT:

HERE IS YOUR REGISTRATION CODE TO ACCESS
YOUR PREMIUM McGRAW-HILL ONLINE RESOURCES.

For key premium online resources you need THIS CODE to gain access. Once the code is entered, you will be able to use the Web resources for the length of your course.

If your course is using **WebCT** or **Blackboard**, you'll be able to use this code to access the McGraw-Hill content within your instructor's online course.

Access is provided if you have purchased a new book. If the registration code is missing from this book, the registration screen on our Website, and within your WebCT or Blackboard course, will tell you how to obtain your new code.

Registering for McGraw-Hill Online Resources

TO gain access to your McGraw-Hill web resources simply follow the steps below:

(1) USE YOUR WEB BROWSER TO GO TO: **register.dushkin.com**

(2) CLICK ON **FIRST TIME USER**.

(3) ENTER THE REGISTRATION CODE* PRINTED ON THE TEAR-OFF BOOKMARK ON THE RIGHT.

(4) AFTER YOU HAVE ENTERED YOUR REGISTRATION CODE, CLICK **REGISTER**.

(5) FOLLOW THE INSTRUCTIONS TO SET-UP YOUR PERSONAL UserID AND PASSWORD.

(6) WRITE YOUR UserID AND PASSWORD DOWN FOR FUTURE REFERENCE.
KEEP IT IN A SAFE PLACE.

TO GAIN ACCESS to the McGraw-Hill content in your instructor's WebCT or Blackboard course simply log in to the course with the UserID and Password provided by your instructor. Enter the registration code exactly as it appears in the box to the right when prompted by the system. You will only need to use the code the first time you click on McGraw-Hill content.

TOANK you, and welcome
to your McGraw-Hill
online Resources!

*YOUR REGISTRATION CODE CAN BE USED ONLY ONCE TO ESTABLISH ACCESS. IT IS NOT TRANSFERABLE.

0-07-297827-9 T/A BRANNIGAN: ETHICS ACROSS CULTURES, 1E

MCGRAW-HILL
ONLINE RESOURCES

REGISTRATION CODE

5kec6-tmgk-9xqk-4bi7

ETHICS ACROSS CULTURES

The McGraw-Hill Companies

Mc Graw Hill Higher Education

ETHICS ACROSS CULTURES: AN INTRODUCTORY TEXT WITH READINGS
Published by McGraw-Hill, a business unit of The McGraw-Hill Companies, Inc.,
1221 Avenue of the Americas, New York, NY, 10020. Copyright © 2005 by
The McGraw-Hill Companies, Inc. All rights reserved. No part of this publication
may be reproduced or distributed in any form or by any means, or stored in a database
or retrieval system, withough the prior written consent of The McGraw-Hill Companies, Inc.,
including, but not limited to, any network or other electronic storage or transmission,
or broadcast for distance learning.

Some ancillaries, including electronic and print components, may not be available
to customers outside of the United States.

2 3 4 5 6 7 8 9   FGR/FGR   0 9 8 7 6 5 4

ISBN 0-7674-2418-2

Editor-in-Chief: Emily Barosse
Senior Sponsoring Editor: Jon-David Hague
Editorial Coordinator: Allison Rona
Senior Marketing Manager: Zina Craft
Project Manager: Roger Geissler
Senior Production Supervisor: Tandra Jorgensen
Interior Designer: Victoria Kuskowski
Cover Designer: Preston Thomas
Art Editor: Emma Ghiselli
Compositor: G&S Typesetters
Printer: Quebecor Fairfield
Cover Printer: Phoenix Color
Cover Image: Liubov Popova (1889-1924). *Still Life.* Museum of Fine Arts,
    Gorky, Russia (c) Erich Lessing/Art Resource, NY

Library of Congress Cataloging-in-Publication Data
    Brannigan, Michael C.
        Ethics Across Cultures: An Introductory Text With Readings/
            Michael Brannigan
            p. cm.
        Includes Index
        ISBN 0-7674-2418-2
        1. Philosophy   2. Social Ethics   I. Title
        B724.B72   2004
                                                        174.2-dc21

ETHICS
ACROSS CULTURES

AN INTRODUCTORY TEXT WITH READINGS

MICHAEL C. BRANNIGAN

CENTER FOR PRACTICAL BIOETHICS,
KANSAS CITY, MISSOURI

Boston   Burr Ridge, IL   Dubuque, IA   Madison, WI   New York   San Francisco   St. Louis
Bangkok   Bogota   Caracas   Kuala Lumpur   Lisbon   London   Madrid   Mexico City
Milan   Montreal   New Delhi   Santiago   Seoul   Singapore   Sydney   Taipei   Toronto

CONTENTS

PART TWO: THE QUEST FOR UNIVERSAL MORAL STANDARDS IN THE WEST 57

PART FOUR: CAN ETHICS SAVE THE WORLD?   395

A web of national and international suspicion has accompanied President George W. Bush's January 2004 announcement for a more aggressive exploration and eventual American colonization of Mars. Yet one advantage in contemplating an effort of this scale may well lie in its vantage point. That is, from the perspective of the Red Planet, the fourth planet from the sun, the planet after whom the Romans named their god of war, our world is one planet – indeed, one planet among many.

Yet our planet does not bear witness to this truth. The dawn of the 21st century rides in the wake of perhaps the most brutal century in human history, taking the bloodiest toll on this planet's life. And in the lingering aftermath of September 11th, 2001, dark clouds fill the skies as disparate worldviews continue to collide. Our technologies remind us that horrific events across the globe compress both spatial and temporal dimensions and underscore the indelibly brutal fact that there is no safe haven anywhere in the world.

We need to understand, now more than ever, these dimensions of space and history. We need to know more about other cultures, about "the other," about our world as one planet. That is what this book is all about. It is an invitation to view the world as one global community. In doing so, it summons us to face its core, underlying question: Are there moral standards, principles, and values that are universal, which traverse spatial and temporal borders? Do we accept this summons? How we respond is absolutely critical. There is simply too much at stake, in fact everything: our futures, our world.

In order for us to even begin to confront this challenge, we need to seriously examine the values, principles, beliefs, behaviors, and rules of other cultures besides our own. And in learning more of "the other," we cannot help but gain further insight into ourselves, who we are, our values, what gives our lives meaning, what makes us happy, what we are committed to live for, what we are willing to die for.

This is no easy task. Learning more about other cultures and their values is indeed daunting for it challenges us to reexamine deep-rooted assumptions. As a culture, we Americans are increasingly ruled by our own material needs, so that our self-bestowed right to purchase and consume may in essence "consume" any possibility for recognizing our fundamental connectedness with "the other." Despite the lessons of September 2001, do we still pay sole tribute to our nation or group without the need for global accountability? Are we committed to the wellbeing of Americans first and foremost? What about the wellbeing and interests of "others," those outside of our immediate circle of concern, the "stranger" in other countries, of other faiths, other cultures? Are we imprisoned in a paralysis of national and cultural self-interest? Can we afford to remain partial to "our own kind"?

In this uncertain world, one thing is crystal-clear: We can no longer afford to return to business as usual. As one planet, one global community, we can hopefully transcend the rigid lines of national and cultural boundaries, so that (whether it was Diogenes or Socrates who first stated it) the assertion "I am a citizen of the world" rings true.

ACKNOWLEDGEMENTS

This book would never have seen the light of day without Ken King, the ever-present pilot who always encouraged me onward. Nor would this book have stood on its own without the steadfast, supportive, and learned voice of Jon-David Hague. I am especially grateful to Jon-David for his faith in the project from start to finish. (He himself bears witness to the rich fruit that comes about when cultures engage one another.) And there are others on the McGraw-Hill team to whom I owe special thanks, particularly Allison Rona and Roger Geissler for their expert advice and constant support, Marty Granahan for her professional and highly competent assistance with permissions, and Preston Thomas for his creative insight and ingenuous choice of artwork for the cover.

My assistant Casey Bajack has played an invaluable role in painstakingly obtaining the necessary permissions for the readings, in providing her never-ending support, and in doing an all-around great job orchestrating the work of our Institute for Cross-Cultural Ethics, whose mission this book embodies.

Erin Ryce's keen vision, artistry, and third eye in detecting the heart of the cases at the end of the book lend an especially unique quality to the work. Darlene Veghts provided her graceful vision and help with copyediting. Christy Cusick-Sarver's conscientious work at our college library enabled me to locate various sources. The following readers provided their most insightful comments and critique:

Maurine Stein—Prairie State College
Maud H. Chaplin—Wellesley College
Mark A. Ehman—Barry University
Kerry Edwards—Red Rocks Community College
Katherine Shamey—Santa Monica College
Robert Ferrell—University of Texas at El Paso
Felicia W. McDuffie—Young Harris College
Clarence H. Guy   University of Arkansas at Little Rock

Moreover, a host of colleagues both here and overseas have taught me invaluable lessons in cross-cultural dialogue: Kazumasa Hoshino, Akira Akabayashi, Shin Ohara, Tomoaki Tsuchida, Naoko Kakee, Jim Heisig, Veena Rani Howard, Rama Rao Pappu, Kunio Aoki, Gen Ohi, Alireza Bagheri, Zhimin Chen, King-tak Ip, Sujatha Byravan, Kalpana Chittaranjan, Stella Gonzalez-Arnal, Martin Makinde, Bushra Mirza, Zhang Youyun, Ricardo Castro Gonzelez, Masahiro Morioka, Bob Kisala, Paul Swanson, David Kum-Wah Chan, Serguei Chebanov, Laura Shanner, Zhang Qi, Surinder Bhardwaj, Michael Fetters, Nahoko Yamada, Charlotte Harrison, Timothy Liau, Robert LeFlar, Lorren Timberman, Amitai Etzioni, Ron Takaki, Gabriela Tymowski, Matthew Cannon, Ruth Landau, Ahmad Al-Akhras, Brian Schrag, Sahin Aksoy, Gilbert Pollet, Robin Wang, Noriko Hashimoto, Austin Kutscher, Diane Chavis, Gregory Pence, Ruth Macklin, Tom Murrin, Cole Puvogel, Michael Myers, Robert Carter, Carl Olson, Frank McCluskey, Paul Churchill, Shabbir Mansuri, Joe Cunneen, numerous others, and many esteemed colleagues here at La Roche College.

As for family and friends, words fall thoroughly short; I will always owe them my deepest, heartfelt tribute. This is particularly so with my wife Brooke who, as always, has tolerated and put up with me through her tireless patience and support.

Michael C. Brannigan is the Vice President of Clinical and Organizational Ethics at the Center for Practical Bioethics, based in Kansas City, Missouri. He was formerly Executive Director of the Institute for Cross-Cultural Ethics as well as Professor and Chair of the Philosophy Department at La Roche College. Along with numerous scholarly articles on ethics, Asian thought, and cross-cultural studies, his books include *Cross-Cultural Biotechnology, Healthcare Ethics in a Diverse Society, Ethical Issues in Human Cloning, Striking a Balance: A Primer in Traditional Asian Values,* and *The Pulse of Wisdom: The Philosophies of India, China, and Japan.* Born in Fukuoka, Japan, and raised in Newport, Rhode Island, he received his Ph.D. in Philosophy and M.A. in Religious Studies from the University of Leuven, Belgium. He has lectured widely on ethics, applied ethics, and intercultural perspectives, and has received various national and international awards. His other interests include athletics, music, and the martial arts. He and his wife Brooke, and their affably eccentric dog Seamus, are now discovering the richness of America's Heartland.

DEDICATED TO MARISA, MATT, AND DANNY—
MY DEAR NIECE AND NEPHEWS.
MAY THEY AND THEIR KINDRED NEVER LOSE TOUCH WITH
AND ALWAYS SEEK TO RECONNECT WITH THEIR
JAPANESE, IRISH, ITALIAN, BELGIAN, SIOUX, FRENCH,
ENGLISH, AND CHEROKEE ROOTS.

INTRODUCTION

I know you believe you understand what you think I said, but I am not sure you realize that what you heard is not what I meant.
(ANONYMOUS)

Like many if not most of us, I suspect that I was a product of lust. Most likely my Japanese mother and my father, a GI of Irish descent stationed in Japan during the Korean War, did not deliberately set out to conceive me through their post-nuptial rendezvous. Nevertheless, due to their tryst I saw the light of day in the Japanese port town of Fukuoka. And for over fifty years in marriage, Misae Kimura and Tom Brannigan have intimately sustained, at times evenly tolerated, and seldom resented each other's companionship. There is a lot more to their chemistry than desire. They continue to understand each other in a special, nonquantifiable capacity. The moral of the story? Even between cultures as distant and disparate as Japanese and Irish, intercourse on a deeper level is possible.

What reasonable grounds do we have for asserting this? To begin with, mere perceptions won't do. During World War II, when the Japanese imperial air forces hoped to turn the tide in Japan's favor after its decisive defeat at the Battle of Midway, they resorted to aerial suicide attacks on American aircraft carriers, battleships, and destroyers. After 9/11/01, we perhaps now have less difficulty visualizing those Zero fighter planes equipped with high explosives and aimed at leviathan vessels that first appeared as tiny specks and grew larger on a vast ocean. And needless to say, during that time from October 1944 to the war's end in 1945 these flying coffins bewildered the Americans. The Yanks called them *"baka"* planes, *baka* being the Japanese word for "idiot." Yet an endless line of young Japanese men fervently volunteered to fly these idiot planes and to give their lives for their parents, country, and Emperor. The first official mission was

1

named the *Shimpu* Unit. *Shimpu* means "divine wind," in memory of two failed attempts in 1274 and 1281 by Mongols to invade Japan. (The name *kamikaze* for these missions came about much later and lacked the solemn tone of *shimpu*.)[1] Terrifying hurricanes, a blessing from the spirits, devastated the invading fleets.

In the same way, Japanese were again hoping for another miracle from the gods. To illustrate, the Japanese 201st Air Group was selected as the first unit from which to solicit volunteers for the suicide missions. The unit was stationed in the Philippines, preparing for the Americans' impending attack on Okinawa. Without hesitation, every member of the 201st volunteered. On October 25, Admiral Onishi, the brains behind the suicide strategy, addressed twenty-four young pilots as they lined up before their first historic attack:

> *Japan is in grave danger. The salvation of our country is now beyond the powers of the ministers of state, the General Staff, and lowly commanders like myself. It can only come from spirited young men such as you. Thus, on behalf of your hundred million countrymen, I ask of you this sacrifice, and pray for your success. . . . You are already gods, without earthly desires. . . . I shall watch your efforts to the end and report your deeds to the Throne. You may all rest assured on this point. . . . I ask you all to do your best.*[2]

No doubt, Japanese views of these suicide missions differed radically from the perceptions of Americans.

As another example, consider the ancient Hindu practice of *sati*. *Sati* refers to the wife who deliberately immolated herself in order to accompany her deceased husband. It was the ultimate bodily commitment and expression of devotion to her husband. What Westerner would not be horrified witnessing a Hindu widow throw herself upon the funeral pyre of her husband in order to meet her fiery end along with her partner? And while we shake our heads in disbelief, we may also cast moral aspersions on such practice. However, adherents justify the action in light of traditional Hindu teachings surrounding a wife's duty to her husband as well as views of karma and the eternal soul, or *atman*. Indeed, the etymology of the Sanskrit term *sati* is revealing. It finds its origin in words pertaining to "being," "virtue," and "truth."[3] Thus in this way the widow manifests herself as "being true" in the most radical and violent fashion.

The list of examples is unending. Can we even begin to fathom the ancient Chinese custom of footbinding in which the ideal form of beauty for women consisted in having 3-inch-long feet? What about the now virtu-ally extinct Taliban regime that strictly forbade women from showing any parts of their bodies in public? In Kabul, Afghanistan, where the Taliban held reign, they punished offenders through public executions held in what had formerly been the sports stadium. What about the practice of female genital excision that continues to affect millions of young girls each year in certain areas of East and West Africa and in parts of India, Malaysia, and Yemen? Many critics instead prefer to call this female genital "mutilation." Yet the Arabic term for "excision" literally means "purification."[4]

For an example closer to home, consider the ritual among the Puerto Ricans and Cubans who belong to the Santeria religion (a blend of ideas from Catholicism and East African beliefs) that consisted in distributing vials of mercury throughout their houses in order to ward off illnesses and disease. Until recent laws prohibited the practice, many bodegas throughout New York City sold these small vials of mercury. Such in-stances, along with countless others, illustrate obvious differences in be-liefs and perspectives. Though the practicing culture condones as well as encourages such customs, outside cultures often find them distasteful and morally reprehensible.

Can we make sense of these differences? Why do these kinds of dis-agreements exist? Though the answers are indeed complex, one thing is certain. It is both simplistic and wrong to find the solution in one single reason, particularly if that reason has to do simply with the notion of "cul-ture." To reduce everything to "culture" obfuscates the problem, since the meaning behind culture is not all that clear. Are we thinking of culture in a geographic sense, such as the culture of India being Indian culture? Or do we mean a distinct body of beliefs? If so, since India comprises Hindu and Christian as well as Muslim beliefs, we can say that India consists of Hindu, Christian, and Muslim cultures. And how broadly do we define this body of beliefs and practices? That is, there are subcultures within cultures so that, in a sense, these subcultures constitute their own cultures. Within Hindu tradition, there are various subschools and sects such as the Jains. The Jains, especially with their strict interpretation of the Hindu teaching of *ahimsa,* or nonviolence, therefore constitute a separate culture. This is distinct from Hinduism's orthodox school of Advaita Vedanta. In any case, the notion of culture remains elusive.

This problem regarding cultures and subcultures is all the more clear in a few of the opening scenarios in the text. For instance, Chapter 8 on Bud-dhism begins with the tragic drama of the Aum Shinrikyo cult, led by the infamous Shoko Asahara, the megalomaniac who believes that he is the new Buddha. Chapter 9, Confucianism, opens with a vignette about the painfully bizarre custom of binding the feet of young girls. Chapter 11 on Islam commences with the assassination of Egyptian President Anwar Sadat. These scenarios are not meant to offer conventional and acceptable representations of Buddhism, Confucianism, and Islam. They are not meant as exemplary models of these teachings. If so, in the apt words of one reviewer, it would be "like introducing an American to Islam via Osama bin Laden. It's going to leave a bad taste in people's mouths."[5] Rather, these scenarios intend to illustrate how devotees of these teachings can distort them in extreme and violent ways. These examples show us how beliefs can be twisted to suit any purpose. The believers thus form their own subcultures within the culture, firmly convinced that their interpretations are authentic. In this way, they thereby legitimize their actions. Indeed, all of the opening scenarios in the text are intended to prick the reader into realizing that any set of teachings—any of the ethical systems, values, and tenets that the book presents—can assume many different guises. Some of these manifestations make sense. Some are a bit off the mark. And others pervert a culture's core convictions.

Moreover, we need to bear in mind that the various patterns of behavior and customs in cultures are not strictly identical to what we think of as basic moral principles. Practices and moral principles are not identical. Even though facts often demonstrate certain values and these values reflect principles, there is still an important distinction between facts and principles. Moreover, in our perception, understanding, and assessment of these different practices, our sentiments, that is, our feelings and emotions, often play a leading role in how we view these practices. Feelings of repulsion or attraction toward certain customs no doubt influence how we *think* about these same customs. This is natural. Yet proper evaluation requires that we not permit our visceral reactions to cloud over our reasoning about both these behaviors and the cultures in which they occur.

In order to minimize these sorts of difficulties that we face in properly understanding and evaluating the variety of cultural expressions and the values they may reflect, I propose the following set of minimal requirements in order to construct a feasible starting point for our study. Here are five prerequisites for studying ethics across cultures. First, let us be clear from the start that we need to be extremely careful about making generalizations regarding other cultures. We usually generalize by virtue of classifying and categorizing. In a sense, generalizations are unavoidable since it is a method of organizing information. What we need to watch out for are premature or hasty generalizations, that is, claims or conclusions arrived at without sufficient evidence, in which case generalizations tend to ignore external similarities as well as internal discrepancies. There are certainly similarities among Indians and Americans, and there are also dissimilarities among Indians themselves such as among Indian Muslims, Indian Hindus, and Indian Christians. In making hasty and unfair generalizations, we mistakenly cast a monolithic net over a culture and its rich abundance of values and perspectives. In turn, this also requires that we exercise restraint so that we do not force similarities and symmetry where they do not exist. In principle, it may make sense to discover common ground among apparently different cultures and traditions. But we can only do this if such common ground actually exists, and only if the similarities far outweigh the differences.

Second, let us bear in mind that any discussion of "ethics" outside of Western traditions naturally takes on a hue that is distinct from Western approaches. For instance, we cannot assume that teachings regarding morality are systematically presented. Nor can we even assume that we all share a common discourse, as seen in the opening quote. Classical Chinese had no terms for "moral," "rights," and "autonomy." As for Japan, only after the Meiji Restoration (1868) did the Japanese invent a term for "rights," *kenri*. However, *kenri* may be translated as "rights," but it does not necessarily pertain to rights in the same way that we think of moral rights. This compels us to approach non-Western traditions in a prudent and qualified fashion. To be sure, these traditions underscore values and encourage as well as discourage certain behaviors. Yet the absence of both a more systematic approach and a shared language does not preclude the presence of "ethics" in the broader sense as an understanding of right and wrong. This means that we need to avoid slipping into a "self-referential tendency" in which we impose our own standards for understanding and evaluating another culture.[6] This tendency occurs when we study and evaluate other viewpoints without applying any degree of self-critical analysis so that we unfairly assume that our standards are universally sound.

Third, we need to cast aside a bifurcating view of cultures. This view distorts issues so that we think of cultures as being either absolutist or relativist in their moralities. To assume that a position is one or the other is misplaced. The spectrum of moral postures cannot be reduced simply to these two positions, for there are usually many positions in between. For instance, the moral position of soft universalism acknowledges the existence of some universal values while admitting that these same values are not literally manifested in the same ways in all cultures. Soft universalism acknowledges universal moral standards while remaining flexible as to how these standards are applied. When studying various cultural values, we therefore need to wear multicolored lenses so that we avoid a strict black-and-white reductionism.

The fourth requirement underscores what we said above in that we ought not to confuse specific behaviors and practices with moral principles. The practice among some elderly Eskimos of withdrawing from the village and freezing to death is not identical to a certain moral principle. We need to see the practice for what it is—as an action. There may well be certain moral values and principles behind the act, but the act still remains distinct from the principle it may or may not reflect. Identifying actions with principles is conceptually wrong and dangerous, since by falsely associating certain actions with certain principles, we thus view the act in the most confined way. For example, we can mistakenly identify the above action of elderly Eskimos with the principle that at times there is a moral obligation to commit suicide. It takes a good bit of study and understanding to recognize that apparently disparate practices may actually reflect similar principles. On this account, we also need to be cautious so that we do not reify ideas, hypotheses, concepts, and principles. Reification occurs when we take these ideas, hypotheses, and so on, out of their contexts and then view them as fixed entities. These ideas then become static and no longer assume their naturally dynamic quality. For instance, we need to avoid reifying the term "ethics" in a way that is divorced from its temporal, spatial, and cultural contexts.

The fifth and perhaps most critical requirement is this. We need to keep in mind that an explanation for a specific practice is not equivalent to its moral justification. Explaining why a particular custom occurs is one thing. Morally justifying that custom is another. Reasons as to why female genital excision continues to occur will include factors such as traditional practice as well as beliefs pertaining to women, virginity, and marriage. Ethical justification is more demanding. It requires close and strict investigation of these reasons, an exacting examination of underlying principles, and a critical analysis of the logical and philosophical consistency between these practices and their reflected principles. It also applies various ethical theories to further test the moral legitimacy of such practices, for example, by considering consequences of such actions in view of calculated benefits and harms. To illustrate, even though one reason for the practice of female genital excision is that it has been the prevailing cultural custom and tradition, further analysis questions whether this appeal to tradition is in itself morally satisfying. That is, by itself respect for tradition does not offer a sound enough premise to establish the act as being morally justifiable. In like manner, this appeal to tradition may explain why footbinding has endured for so long in China. Yet this reason does not necessarily justify the practice. The confusion of explanation with justification is common. It is also perilous, for it short-circuits further inquiry and examination. It minimizes levels of critical analysis that are necessary for sound ethical reasoning.

These five requirements constitute a necessary starting point for our study of various cultures and traditions and our accompanying quest for any possible grounds for universal moral standards. This quest is in turn collective and interdisciplinary. That is, at the very least it requires that we avoid studying these cultures only through the lens of isolated disciplines. For far too long, academic disciplines have remained territorial and segregated. The possibility for cross-cultural dialogue can only take shape through a cross-disciplinary effort, though one that still respects the essential integrity of each discipline.

Studying ethics across various cultures is indeed filled with challenges and obstacles. Perhaps its greatest challenge to us lies in demanding that we do not fall prey to the two fundamental tyrannies that we need to free ourselves from in order to live morally. The first is the false notion that only the local is real. The second is the equally false idea that only the moment matters. These are the tyrannies of space and time. Seriously studying other cultures' values with the aim of cultivating cross-cultural sensitivity and understanding—what this book is ultimately about—demands that we free ourselves from these two self-imposed prisons so that we can authentically be with others as well as with ourselves.

■ NOTES

1. See Ivan Morris, *The Nobility of Failure: Tragic Heroes in the History of Japan* (New York: Meridian, New American Library, 1975), p. 289.

2. Rikihei Inoguchi and Tadashi Nakajima, *Shimpu Tokubetsu Kogekitai no Kiroku (Records of the Divine Wind Special Attack Force)* (Tokyo, 1963), pp. 48–49; cited in Morris, p. 287.

3. Catherine Weinberger-Thomas, *Ashes of Immortality: Widow-Burning in India*, trans. Jeffrey Mehlman and David Gordon White (New Delhi: Oxford University Press, 2000), p. 20.

4. This was pointed out to me by a female Muslim student. See Michael Brannigan, "Is Cross-Cultural Discourse Possible?" *Sensabilities* 2, no. 2 (Spring 1999): 12.

5. My thanks to Professor Kerry Edwards, Red Rocks Community College.

6. See Brannigan, 12–14.

PART ONE

DIVERSITY

AND

ETHICS

THE CASE FOR CULTURAL DIVERSITY

■

FEMALE GENITAL EXCISION OR MUTILATION?

Egyptian author Nawal El Saadawi was six years old when she was circumcised. "Strangers" seized her at night. She well remembers the sound of that knife, her pain, and her startling discovery.

> *I strained my ears trying to catch the rasp of the metallic sound. The moment it ceased, it was as though my heart stopped beating with it. I was unable to see, and somehow my breathing seemed also to have stopped. Yet I imagined the thing that was making the rasping sound coming closer and closer to me. Somehow it was not approaching my neck as I had expected but another part of my body. Somewhere below my belly, as though seeking something buried between my thighs. At that very moment I realized that my thighs had been pulled wide apart, and that each of my lower limbs was being held as far away from the other as possible, gripped by steel fingers that never relinquished their pressure. I felt that the rasping knife or blade was heading straight down towards my throat. Then suddenly the sharp metallic edge seemed to drop between my thighs and there cut off a piece of flesh from my body.*
>
> *I screamed with pain despite the tight hand held over my mouth, for the pain was not just a pain, it was like a searing flame that went*

through my whole body. After a few moments, I saw a red pool of blood around my hips.

I did not know what they had cut off from my body, and I did not try to find out. I just wept, and called out to my mother for help. But the worst shock of all was when I looked around and found her standing by my side. Yes, it was her, I could not be mistaken, in flesh and blood, right in the midst of these strangers, talking to them and smiling at them, as though they had not participated in slaughtering her daughter just a few moments ago.[1]

At least two million young women and girls in Africa, the Mideast, and Southeast Asia are circumcised each year. Here, we come face-to-face with one of the most heated cross-cultural ethical issues. Female genital circumcision, or what we will refer to as female genital excision, lays bare the unrelenting tension between, on the one hand, the need to tolerate various cultural customs out of respect and, on the other hand, the urge to criticize these customs on the basis of some alleged universal standards of right and wrong. Critics, especially in the West, usually label the practice with the more inflammatory term "female genital mutilation" and demand its outright prohibition, placing it on a par with child and woman abuse. At the same time, supporters invoke reasons like the tradition of maintaining family honor. These supporters have, in turn, accused Western critics of being preoccupied with an exaggerated notion of individual rights. Yet numerous grassroots movements in African, Arab, and Asian countries are staunchly opposed to the practice. Not all those in cultures that practice female genital excision necessarily support it.

Have we in the West inflated the issue? Quite a few African and Arab feminists seem to think so. They also point out that in doing so we have lost sight of more pressing issues like women's education, legal rights, and inheritance laws.[2] Are we at a moral impasse? Should we permit female genital excision on the grounds of its long-standing tradition in certain cultures even if we ourselves are seriously opposed to it? If we do so, would we be taking a giant step toward discrediting the possibility of any universal moral standard? If we concede that prevailing practice dictates morality, have we not eliminated dependable standards for morality? Or should we take active measures to intervene in certain cultures and thereby outlaw what we may believe is a barbaric and unjustifiable practice?

■ DOES THE FACT OF DIVERSITY
LEAD TO ETHICAL RELATIVISM?

Overwhelming evidence from anthropology and ethnography shows that different cultures exhibit different behaviors and hold different beliefs. This is indisputable. One culture approves behavior, such as cannibalism, polygamy, or female infanticide, that another culture condemns. What can we reasonably infer from this? First of all, does the fact of cultural diversity necessarily lead to what is known as cultural relativism? Note that the two notions are not the same. Cultural diversity underscores the prominent fact that cultures differ in practices and in beliefs. Cultural relativism goes further. In its broadest form, cultural relativism claims that cultures differ not only according to their practices and beliefs, but also with respect to their moral rules. It then goes on to state that these moral rules are strictly dependent upon a culture's own beliefs, customs, and practices.

Note that we use the term "rules" and not "principles." The two are distinct. Moral *rules* are concrete expressions of underlying moral principles. Moral rules are therefore derived from moral principles and are of the second order. Moral *principles* are of the first order. It remains to be seen whether cultures truly differ in their moral principles.

Cultural relativism can be defined even further. For instance, the anthropologist Melford Spiro distinguishes three types of cultural relativism: descriptive, normative, and epistemological.[3] The descriptive type basically acknowledges what we have referred to above as cultural diversity, namely, that diverse cultures have different practices and beliefs. As we said, this is self-evident. The normative type maintains that the moral positions maintained within cultures are legitimate for that culture. The epistemological form of cultural relativism is more radical. It runs deeper in that it even questions the likelihood of different cultures to understand each other and to engage in cross-cultural discourse. The ramifications of this are far-reaching, for if cross-cultural discourse is not possible, then judgments about others' behaviors and customs lack sufficient grounds.

We face this question. How does the fact of diversity among cultures impact upon ethics? That is, in light of cultural pluralism, what ethical choices do we have? Consider some options: moral absolutism, moral relativism, moral nihilism, and moral skepticism. If we adopt moral absolutism, that means we believe that there are definitive, true moral rules and codes that apply to all peoples at all times. These immutable moral rules and beliefs constitute objective moral standards and they are exceptionless. Thus when cultures disagree about these standards, it is because their vantage points and premises are simply wrong. Or we can choose to be moral relativists. We will examine this more closely below. Put briefly, moral relativism basically acknowledges that morality is solely contingent upon different moral contexts. It therefore denies the idea of any universal and objective moral standard. If we chose to be moral nihilists, we go further and assert that morality is essentially meaningless. There is no morality and no need for morality. This outright rejection of morality differs from relativism, since, contrary to what some critics of relativism allege, relativism does not reject morality. Or we can embrace moral skepticism. Moral skepticism accepts the relativist thesis and then goes on to conclude that we can never genuinely know anything objective about morality. That is, we can have no real knowledge of moral principles. This is similar to Spiro's epistemological relativism.

Again we ask: What can we conclude in view of the fact of cultural diversity? In the opinion of many philosophers, the bewildering array of different cultural practices and customs leads not only to cultural relativism but to ethical relativism as well.[4] Ethical relativism has also been called moral relativism. For our purposes in this text, they are interchangeable terms. Now what more precisely do we mean by moral or ethical relativism? Here is the definition offered by a staunch defender of moral relativism, the philosopher Gilbert Harman:

> Moral right and wrong (good and bad, justice and injustice, virtue and vice, etc.) are always relative to a choice of moral framework. What is morally right in relation to one moral framework can be morally wrong in relation to a different moral framework. And no moral framework is objectively privileged as the one true morality.[5]

He stresses two features in this definition. First, when it comes to making any sort of moral judgment, our judgment is *only valid* in relation to the "moral framework" we find ourselves in.

> For the purposes of assigning truth conditions, a judgment of the form, it would be morally wrong of P to D, *has to be understood as elliptical for a judgment of the form,* in relation to moral framework M, it would be morally wrong of P to D. *Similarly for other moral judgments.*[6]

Suppose that Amena believes that female genital excision is morally justified. Moral relativists would argue that it is only justified within

Amena's own moral framework, that is, her values, rules, and principles, which Harman also refers to as "moral coordinates." If Frances disagrees with Amena, her disagreement is valid only within Frances's own moral framework. This being the case—that moral validity only works within one's own moral circle—the second feature logically follows: There are no privileged moral circles.

> There is no single true morality. There are many different moral frameworks, none of which is more correct than the others.[7]

Therefore, even though female genital excision may be morally wrong for Frances but not for Amena, neither Frances nor Amena is objectively right or wrong. In this way, relativism rejects the absolutist posture along with its implied attitude of moral elitism. In other words, the relativist refutes the notion that any one individual, group, or culture can know what is right and wrong for all other peoples and cultures.

Harman's two features of moral relativism are expressed in a succinct way by another philosopher, John Cook. Cook, however, rejects relativism. Nevertheless, he goes on to describe the relativists' "fully developed argument" in this way:

> If we had acquired our moral views in the way we acquire scientific views, namely, by means of a rational fact-finding procedure, then we could criticize other cultures wherever their morality differs from ours, just as we criticize, for example, the idea that illness is caused by witchcraft. But we do not acquire our moral views by discovering objective moral facts. (This becomes obvious when we realize that moral principles differ from culture to culture, for this state of affairs would not exist if there were a realm of objective moral facts everyone can discern — as everyone can discern that the sky is blue.) Moral principles are acquired, not by any rational process, but by the causal process of "enculturative conditioning," that is, they are impressed upon us in subtle ways by the culture in which we are raised. We do not, therefore, have any grounds — any good reasons— for holding the moral views that we do hold. And that being so, it is a mistake to think that our moral views are both (a) known by us to be true and (b) apply to people of other cultures who don't share our moral views.[8]

Ethical relativism therefore maintains that (1) any moral judgment we make is purely dependent upon our own specific moral framework and

(2) is valid only within that framework. We can act morally or immorally only on the basis of moral principles and rules established by our own culture. Whereas an absolutist might claim that "Cannibalism is wrong, period," a relativist would qualify this and state, "Cannibalism is wrong only *within a specific moral framework* that is unique to a culture." In other words, "Cannibalism is not *absolutely* wrong." Morality and the assertion of moral rules and principles is in essence arbitrary and comes from "enculturative conditioning," and not from inductively reasoning from facts as in science. This means that different cultures have different moralities.

Therefore, there are no universal moral principles, no objective moral standards that hold true for all cultures at all times. Note the radical nature of this conclusion. It does not simply admit that there are differences in the way *similar* moral principles are applied in different cultures. For example, numerous customs demonstrate how the same principles can be applied differently. Whether Westerners shake hands with each other or Japanese bow to each other, they both reflect the underlying principle of respect. Instead, ethical relativism maintains that, because of a real variance in moral rules, principles, and practices, and because morality must therefore be culture-bound, we can only conclude that *no* universal moral standards exist, even that of respect for other persons.

CROSS-CULTURAL DISCOURSE

Let us look more closely at the option of moral skepticism, or what amounts to epistemological relativism. Our original question bears repeating: Does the fact of cultural diversity necessarily lead to ethical relativism? This question carries even more weight when we consider the difficulties involved in intercultural communication. With well over three thousand languages spoken worldwide, how reliable can our understanding be of another culture that speaks a radically different language? How accurate is our translation of that language? This leads us to the problem concerning cross-cultural discourse. Communication requires dialogue. But before we can dialogue with others we must be able to converse, to engage in discourse of varying levels. Can we genuinely engage in cross-cultural discourse?

Philosopher Willard Quine mounts a persuasive attack against the possibility of genuine cross-cultural discourse.[9] Assuming that language governs the way we view things (what is known as the Sapir-Whorf hypothesis), he points to what he calls an "ontological relativity" in that we cannot comprehend different cultures' ways of understanding the world if these cultures speak radically different languages. For example, in my attempt to understand a translation from its original Pali text of the *Nasadaya*, the celebrated hymn that deals with the creation of the universe, how can I adequately comprehend the ancient Hindu worldview that the text espouses? How can I impartially translate any Pali text? My point of departure will always be my own language and culture with its accompanying ideas and concepts. Will I not impose these?

Any answer bodes ill if moral judgments are analogous to this linguistic predicament. Just as we are inherently faced with difficulties in translating and interpreting a text in another language, how are we to make moral assessments of behaviors outside our own cultural circle? Are such differences irreconcilable? We seem stuck in our various cultural circles that encompass the spatial (social) and the temporal (historical).

Yet, as difficult as proper translation may be, that does not preclude the possibility of genuine communication. After all, there is an objective reality, a world, a given, just as there *is* a *Nasadaya* hymn that we all seek to make sense of. Moreover, linguists themselves will point to the interaction among languages, what Henry Rosemont Jr. calls the "linguistic web." [10] No language is an island. Indeed, when it comes to moral rules and principles, cross-cultural communication *is* possible. This means that there may well be a universal understanding of ideas concerning things like respect for others, justice and equity, truth-telling, and altruism, as well as prohibitions against cruelty, theft, and unnecessary harm.

DO CULTURES REALLY DISAGREE WITH EACH OTHER MORALLY?

This issue of cross-cultural discourse relates directly to the meaning behind disagreement. That is, genuine disagreement can occur only if we share a common discourse. If you ask me whether I believe in God, and I answer "No," you then claim that you disagree because you yourself believe in God. Do we truly disagree with each other? It would have behooved me to reply to your question with another and ask you what you mean by "God." If you mean an ancient man in the heavens staring down on earth below, I can then confidently reply "No." Furthermore, I can only interpret your definition of God if I already share some ideas with you, so that I know what you mean by "ancient man," "heavens," and "earth below." In which case, now that I understand your idea of God, we can begin to disagree. (We will further examine the components of disagreement in our next chapter where we discuss the role of critical thinking in moral reasoning.)

Suppose you and I come from radically different cultures with very different worldviews. According to Quine's thesis, if our worldviews are completely different, then we can share no language. Even if we use similar terms, what these terms mean for each of us would be different. We could not assume any affinity between our terms and their concepts. In which case we cannot be in real disagreement because we lack a basis upon which to disagree. We would each dwell in our own solipsistic, linguistic, and moral Babel.

Yet this view makes little sense, for intercultural communication does occur in varying degrees. The fact that we can translate Pali texts into English, and so on, testifies to this. In which case, there are no solid grounds nor logical basis for claiming that some cultures' worldviews are *completely* alien to others. The act of making the claim is inconsistent with the claim itself. How could I make this claim unless I knew enough about the culture that is allegedly so different? And if the culture is so radically different, how could I know anything about it?

■ WEAKNESSES IN ETHICAL RELATIVISM

ARE CULTURES ALL THAT DIFFERENT?

Let's return to our question. Does cultural diversity necessarily lead to ethical relativism? Consider the strength of evidence: Ethical relativism has the support of evidence in that different cultures have different and often conflicting moral rules. What does that really mean? So-called "honor killings" continue to be practiced in some Arab cultures. (Keep in mind that although some Arabs perform these "honor killings" and feel justified in doing so, the majority of Arabs do not.) In Arab cultures, it is of the utmost importance for family honor that a daughter remain a virgin until marriage. If it is discovered that her virginity has been violated, this incurs terrible dishonor upon her family and spouse. In fact, if she became pregnant as a result, in some instances the daughter's own male relatives have killed her in order to restore the family's honor. Most Americans would without hesitation condemn the practice. On the other hand, many Arabs in some countries would consider this morally acceptable. On the basis of this, can we assert that there is a clear *moral difference* between Americans and Arabs?

According to relativists, convention and custom determines the scope of morality, and the full scope of morality encompasses principles, rules, and

practices. If this is correct, then the two cultures are indeed morally different. But that is the case only if we accept the relativist premise that the nature of morality is purely culture-bound. *But accepting this from the start
begs the question, since we need to somehow prove that this is the case.*

Let us pursue this further using what phenomenological analysis refers
to as *epoche*, that is, a bracketing of presuppositions in order to view the
matter with less subjectivity. In this case, let us apply what we can call
a *moral epoche*. This means putting aside or "bracketing" our own moral
beliefs and dispositions, including the relativist premise as well as religious
moral teachings. This also means that we now need to dig deeper and
ask: Why do some condone this practice? This of course requires understanding reasons for the practice. What *moral rules* does the practice express? Furthermore, what *moral principles* underlie the rules? Clashing
moral rules do not denote a genuine moral disagreement. Yet if it turns out
that the underlying moral principles, the foundational component in
ethics, are radically different, then we do have a moral difference. All this
means that the nature of morality is much more complex than simply a
matter of convention and socially accepted practices. It consists of fundamental principles. And these principles generate moral rules within specific
contexts. Practices are then those types of actions that conform to these
rules.

Note the quandary we now find ourselves in. It is illogical to beg the
question and assume the relativist premise that morality is merely a matter of socially condoned or prohibited conduct. By the same token, why
should we accept the need for distinctions among practices, moral rules,
and moral principles as done above? The quandary lies in this. No matter
where we start from, we still start from some vantage point. As much as
we may attempt to bracket moral presuppositions, we never start from nor
do we arrive at a totally objective perspective.

Another consideration concerns the way we depict other cultures' practices. In many instances, we will describe a practice in a way that already
begs the question. For example, when we refer to the traditional custom
among Eskimos of abandoning their elderly so that they freeze to death, we
may call it "murder." And on this basis we may conclude that our culture
and the Eskimo culture have different moralities. But *is* such a practice
among the Eskimos "murder"? It is construed as such if done in our own
culture. Nevertheless, one must understand the rationale behind the Eskimos' practice in order to more properly assess it. Among the Eskimos, it
is regarded as an act of "sacrifice" in order to help conserve already-scarce

resources within the community. Unless we make a concerted effort to understand an apparently disparate practice, we may slip into what Cook calls the "Projection Error":

> *It [the Projection Error] occurs when, having witnessed (or perhaps read about) certain actions of an alien people, one misconstrues their actions because of the following circumstances: (a) one is ignorant of the actual motivation of those people, and (b) their actions appear similar in some way to actions of a sort that might occur in — or that one is familiar with from — one's own culture. . . . The error itself consists of thinking, on account of their similarity, that the actions of an alien people are actions of the* same *sort as actions that might occur in — or that one is familiar with from — one's own culture.*[11]

In this same vein, Cook refers to the Dyaks of Borneo who are headhunters. The Dyaks collect the skulls of enemy villagers, whether men, women, or children, steered by the belief that these skulls possess magic that will protect them against their enemies. Is this Dyak practice "murderous"? No doubt, if this occurred in the United States, it would be called that. Moreover, would this cause us to conclude that the morality of the Dyaks is different from the morality of Americans? Do the Dyaks have *completely different moral values* than we do?

Why would we assume that the fact of cultural diversity necessarily leads to moral diversity? We would do so if we equated moral rules with moral principles. Different cultures and societies do have different and often conflicting moral rules: "Humans should not eat meat" versus "It is permissible, even good, for humans to eat meat." Due to this diversity regarding moral rules, cultural relativism makes sense. However, we need to recall the crucial distinction between rules and principles. *Moral principles* are general axioms of the first order such as the Buddhist principle of "respect for all sentient creatures." *Moral rules* are codes that seek to apply these axioms to concrete situations. They are therefore of the second order. An example would be the moral rule "Humans ought to refrain from eating meat." This rule is an application of the general first order principle "Humans ought to respect all sentient creatures."

This means that diverse moral rules do not necessarily translate to diverse moral principles, or genuine moral difference. Moral rules may vary, but that does not necessarily mean that first order moral principles vary as well. Moral rules and codes reflect the culture's application of more general moral principles. Disagreement among moral codes in no way compels us to conclude that there is disagreement among moral principles. One therefore wonders whether cultures are all that different when it comes to acknowledging fundamental moral principles since conflicting moral rules can still reflect the same moral principle. Whether one is urged to eat meat or to not eat meat, the rules still reflect an elemental respect for sentient beings.

WHY CONCLUDE THAT THERE ARE
NO OBJECTIVE STANDARDS?

Suppose different cultures do, in fact, exhibit different first-order principles. In other words, for the sake of argument, suppose that among cultures there is genuine moral diversity. What if one culture believes it is important to respect all sentient beings while another culture does not. Here we have a clear moral disagreement between two cultures. What can we conclude from this disagreement?

Logically, it makes no sense to infer from this that there must be no objective standards whatsoever to evaluate the moral legitimacy of each culture's principles. Give the fact of moral disagreement, why would we thereby conclude that neither position is objectively correct or incorrect? Deducing such a conclusion from the premises does not follow. (As we will see in the next chapter, a valid argument must pass certain tests in order for the conclusion to necessarily follow from the premises.)

Ethical relativism claims that there are no objective, universal standards and that there is no objective "truth" in ethics. Morality is purely culture-bound, and we cannot make any objective claims or pass any legitimate judgment beyond our own culture. Yet, what we are now stipulating is that moral diversity in and of itself does not logically lead to the above claim. In other words, the fact that two cultures disagree concerning moral principles does not at all mean that there are no universal moral principles. All we can logically conclude is that they disagree, pure and simple. One culture could be mistaken. They could both be mistaken.

Matters of Belief and Matters of Fact What lies at the core of all this is the ever-present tension between what is subjective and what is objective, between what is *believed* to be the case and what *is* the case. Many Sudanese believe that the practice of genitally excising young girls and women is justifiable, while most Americans believe that it is not. This disagreement says nothing about whether female genital excision *is* morally justifiable or not. It simply points to a disagreement in beliefs. Just because we believe something to be true does not mean that, in reality, it is true. If so, this becomes an insidious form of moral subjectivism, so that moral positions are merely matters of taste. Morality is reducible to what each person believes it to be, an absurd conclusion with dangerous consequences.

In turn, believing that something is the case may help to *explain* why it is practiced. But it does not *justify* the practice. Here indeed is the critical distinction between explanation and justification. (We will examine this distinction more closely in the next chapter.) Unfortunately, we often confuse the two. One thing is certain. The content of a belief is not the same as facticity, or what is. And the fact that two cultures have opposing beliefs about the morality of female genital excision does not at all mean that one position is not wrong. To confuse *belief* with what *is* leads to the pernicious notion that opinion is all that matters, a common error we can easily make because we tend to pursue the path of least resistance, particularly in matters of morality where close scrutiny and critical self-examination are especially important.

WHAT WOULD BE THE CONSEQUENCES?

Cross-Cultural Judgments as Meaningless For the sake of argument, suppose we accept ethical relativism. What would be the consequences?[12] One serious consequence is that we would have no grounds whatsoever for making objective, moral evaluations of other cultures and societies and their practices. We would not be able to offer any transcultural moral critique. We would be precluded from making valid moral judgments of practices, beliefs, and rules of other cultures. We would not be able to either condemn or praise practices alien to our own culture. Our circle of moral judgment would be limited to those acts, beliefs, and rules within our own culture. We could certainly pass judgments on other practices, but our judgments would be objectively meaningless.

This meaninglessness of cross-cultural moral judgments makes sense when we consider the numerous instances of ethnocentrism throughout human history, such as those Roman Catholic missionaries in the New World who viewed the native inhabitants as barbaric and pagan. But what about the practice of female genital excision, which seems to be deplored by the majority of cultures? Nonetheless, according to relativism, Americans and numerous human rights groups can condemn the practice of female genital excision, but their condemnation would essentially carry no weight because it would lack any reference to any objective standard.

The same goes for judgments made by other cultures about our own. America is the wealthiest country in the world, yet recent statistics have cited America as also being the stingiest, giving away the least percentage of its wealth to poor countries. Other cultures have criticized our own as being enslaved to consumerism. For instance, there is the scathing critique by the Thai Buddhist monk, Sulak Sivaraksa, which represents that of millions of Buddhists throughout Southeast Asia. If we take relativism seriously, Sivaraksa's critique lacks any merit and is essentially meaningless. The implications of relativism, most likely not at all what well-wishing relativists had intended, shield ourselves and others from vital external critique.

Internal Reform as Groundless Another consequence of ethical relativism follows from the above. The sole arbiter of morality within any given culture would be that culture's beliefs and practices. In the words of the anthropologist Ruth Benedict, "Morality . . . is a convenient term for socially approved habits."[13] The circle of moral evaluation is simply and ineradicably confined to each individual culture. The only standards are the standards within each culture. And these standards determine what is right and wrong *only* for that culture. In this respect, individual cultures are like moral monads, self-enclosed and self-standing with respect to their moral rules and beliefs. This is a spatial relativism in that, as far as moral evaluation and judgment goes, only the local is real and worthy of evaluation.

Yet this imparts some profound difficulties. If each culture is its own sole determinative standard for right and wrong conduct, then what justifies measures for internal reform? Upon what grounds can we challenge the norms of our own culture? According to the implications of relativism, we should not swim against the tide of our own cultural norms, since our culture sets the norms of right and wrong. The moral standards are strictly culture-bound. This, in theory, squelches any attempt to reform the prevailing perspectives within one's culture. If the prevailing practice accepts donning white sheets and seizing and whipping African Americans, it is considered wrong to challenge this.

Equally plaguing is another puzzle: How do we even establish what constitutes the "norm" in a culture? Must this be the opinion of the majority? Of those in power? If so, the efforts of reformers who critique their culture's norms, beliefs, and values are spurious and without any meaningful grounds. Moreover, in such a climate the law rests upon no solid basis, thus setting up a state of affairs where laws that are perceived to be unjust need to be changed. Yet, resting upon how laws are established, there may be no adequate grounds for challenging these laws. Thus, according to ethical relativism, not only would we lack grounds for criticizing other cultures, but we would not be able to criticize our own as well.

Another problem lies in the notion of "culture." Given the claim that each culture establishes for itself its own moral rules and principles, what do we mean by "culture"? What constitutes a culture? And what about subcultures within a culture, such as minority groups within the American culture? We can extend this further. Subcultures can exist within subcultures. When we think of American Hispanics, do we mean those from South America, Spain, Cuba, or elsewhere? Irish Americans belong to various organizations and clubs, each with their own sorts of rules and rituals. These are types of subcultures. And an Irish American can be opposed to abortion, as a Catholic, yet be tolerant of the law that permits it, as an American citizen. How do we draw parameters as to what constitutes a culture? If we define culture with the broadest stroke, we can each consider ourselves to be, in a sense, independent cultures. Given this, moral relativism essentially can lead to a sort of moral anarchy, in that each individual, in a sense construed as a unique "culture unto him- or herself," sets the standard for his and her own morality. Norman Mailer calls this "absolute relativity," wherein each one of us is the arbiter of our own morality. If moral standards are basically arbitrary, then the possibility of any moral constraint becomes nebulous. Our moral circle becomes more confined.

A Matter of Tolerance? What about the idea that ethical relativism nurtures the value of tolerance? This strength can turn into its weakness. According to ethical relativism, there is no objective basis for passing moral judgments on other cultures' practices. We therefore need to be tolerant of these practices. But suppose a particular culture does not value tolerance at all.

In this case, the consequences of ethical relativism logically conflict each other. Consequence A is that a culture's practices are morally right for that specific culture. Consequence B is that we must be tolerant of and therefore not intervene in any other culture's practices. Here's the problem: Cultivating tolerance can clearly clash with cultures that do not see the need to cultivate tolerance. To be tolerant of intolerance can only lead to disaster. The two consequences are inconsistent with each other. Furthermore, tolerance can make sense for the relativist only if the relativist already assumes it as a universal value to cultivate. Yet ethical relativism precludes the notion of viable universal values because it denies universal principles.

John Cook adds an interesting qualifier to this, by arguing that we need to be careful to avoid a blanket assertion that moral relativism necessarily leads to this logical contradiction. For him, relativism does not promote the *principle* of tolerance. Nor does it militate against the *principle* of intolerance. Rather, it works to combat ethnocentrism. Doing so would definitely place relativism in an illogical box since it would then mean that relativism does hold a certain *principle* to be absolute, namely tolerance.[14] Relativism does not advocate that we must "tolerate" other cultures' behaviors if by "tolerance" we mean "overcoming one's moral objection to something in a quite particular way: by finding a morally acceptable excuse or justification for the conduct in question." [15]

Yet this qualifier only makes sense depending upon how we view and interpret what it means to be tolerant. If tolerance simply means refraining from moral judgment altogether, then the above argument of logical inconsistency seems valid. In any case, this inconsistency does exist as a possible consequence.

Temporal Relativism This means that any claims regarding moral improvement or moral regression are meaningless. We cannot make valid moral judgments across time-lines. During the Medieval period, prisoners in parts of Europe, were often tortured as a way of testing their guilt or innocence. Today, European countries have outlawed this practice. Yet, according to ethical relativism, these countries cannot legitimately claim their current policies represent any advance over past practices. Such a claim would only make sense according to some objective standard that transcends temporal and historical parameters.

In America's history, African Americans were viewed in many southern states as having inferior status to persons. Many believed that they were "nonpersons" and therefore without any legal or moral rights. Today, even though this perspective is no longer the norm in the South, does this mean that we have "advanced" in moral sensitivity? When we apply this to the ideology of the Nazi regime just slightly four generations ago, such a posture is evidently embarrassing because most reasonable persons would admit that Germany's Third Reich had diminished in moral sensitivity. Yet, according to relativism, can we say that the Nazi perspective was morally "regressive"? Can we say anything? Accepting ethical relativism would mean that judgments passed at international tribunals such as at Nuremberg and Tokyo have no legitimate basis in morality. Temporal relativism means that we cannot pass any judgment historically regarding either moral improvement or moral regress. Simply put, without an objective, universal moral standard, such claims are meaningless.

■ STRENGTHS IN ETHICAL RELATIVISM

Let us now consider the strengths of ethical relativism — what appears to be the most popular option in the face of cultural diversity. Ethical relativism is indeed appealing to many of us. It is perhaps the most prevalent moral position among contemporary adults in the West. It is certainly the most popular posture of my students. What accounts for its appeal? Why do we often resort to relativist axioms like "Each to his or her own" and "It's all relative"? One reason has to do with our resistance against any form of moral absolutism such as ethnocentrism. We are all too familiar with efforts past and present at ethnic cleansing. Another reason seems to be the decline of the authority of religion in the modern era, particularly in Western cultures. This decline of meaningful religious authority represents for many of us the erosion of order. Relativism is also appealing because we ourselves tend to pursue the path of least resistance, and when it comes to our personal moralities, relativism requires the least amount of critical self-examination. It suggests a convenient leap from acknowledging the realm of what "is," facticity, to the realm of what "ought to be," morality. For instance, since it *is* the case that many students cheat on their exams, then we can more easily rationalize to ourselves that we *ought* to cheat on exams. Indeed, the human mind has the capacity to rationalize just about anything, so belonging to the relativist camp offers us an uncritical comfort zone. Along with these factors, there are certain strengths in the relativist position that further explain our attraction.

EVIDENCE

Relativism seems to have the backing of solid evidence. It is plainly true that different cultures exhibit different practices. Social behavior and practices are no doubt culture-bound, and cultures also seem to differ in their moral rules. Note again the distinction we are making between moral rules and moral principles. By moral rules, we mean the specific application in concrete circumstances of more basic and underlying moral principles. In Japan, it is morally acceptable to cremate the dead. This has been the common practice for centuries, not only because of the purificatory power in fire, but also because cremation conserves ground space, a scarce resource in a small, overpopulated country. When Christian missionaries first journeyed to Japan, they were no doubt shocked by this practice because it violated the Christian practice of burial. Here we had an obvious clash in moral rules between the Christians and Japanese as to how to treat the dead, though the moral principle of showing respect for the dead may be the same in each case. In any case, cultural diversity is a fact.

CORRECTIVE

Ethical relativism is a corrective against moral absolutism. As stated above, moral absolutism is the position that states that certain moral standards, rules, and principles must be adhered to without exception. It is thereby inflexible in the application of these principles. By setting forth exceptionless moral principles and rules, absolutism imparts an imperialistic moral tone. A moral absolutist presumes to have some monopoly on the moral truth, and goes on to impose that "truth" on all others.

The relativist position opposes this moral imperialism. It is moral hubris to assume that we are necessarily in touch with moral certitude and that all others who disagree with us are thereby mistaken. This implies the accompanying belief that all of our practices are therefore justifiably grounded on some set of absolute principles. But this implication makes little sense, because it is abundantly clear that many of our practices are culturally derived.

TOLERANCE

Ethical relativism, because it rejects moral absolutism, thereby rejects any stance that reflects moral elitism or moral superiority, such as ethnocentrism. In doing so, it appears to uphold the value of tolerance, in the sense of having an open-mindedness and a willingness to entertain diverse perspectives. This is particularly so in the face of past and present expressions of ethnocentrism and cultural chauvinism. Witness the cultural and spiritual elitism that accompanied periods of colonization and missionary zeal throughout human history. Witness the continued sentiments of Western cultural superiority over less "civilized" societies.

There is no more fundamental fact than that of disagreement. What is crucial is how we deal with it. (We will address this again in our next chapter.) Tolerance is valuable in that it enables us to live with others who hold different beliefs and values. In advocating tolerance, ethical relativism reminds us that our moral positions may well reflect our own personal biases as well as those of our culture.

■ ARE THERE BETTER OPTIONS?

The weaknesses in ethical relativism clearly outweigh its strengths. Even though this does not necessarily mean that the theory is false, it still compels us to inquire into whether there may be more reasonable moral alternatives than ethical relativism or moral absolutism. In our philosophical quest for what is true, we stand in need of options that make more sense and that can better withstand critical inquiry. That is what this book is all about.

A more viable and sensible option must be one that avoids the two extremes of relativism and absolutism. It would assert that there *are* universal moral principles, yet these principles need to be flexible in terms of how they are applied in varying circumstances. This idea of flexible universal principles is similar to William Ross's notion of *prima facie* principles, principles that are to be usually heeded, although in certain situations some principles may give way to other principles. That is, these principles are not annulled nor abandoned. They are instead overridden by other principles.

Moral absolutism and moral relativism are not the only options. On the one hand, moral absolutism is clearly inflexible. It contends that there are universal principles that can only be applied in one correct way in every culture. Therefore, moral rules that flow from these principles are rigidly applied regardless of different cultural contexts. For instance, when we apply the moral rule of informed consent in the United States, we stipulate that the consent needs to be signed. Must this be an absolute rule? What about Chile or the Philippines, where the signing of forms is resisted because of fears of invasion of privacy and confidentiality with negative consequences for family members as well?

On the other hand, the weakest link in moral relativism lies in its purported attempt to describe the nature of morality. For the relativist, morality turns out to be based upon whatever are the accepted practices, customs, beliefs, and values of a culture. Thus, morality is equated with the customary. But is that all there is to morality? Both intuition and real experience have shown that prevailing practices are not necessarily the litmus test of what we ought to do. What we *do* (the realm of facticity) and what we *ought to do* (the realm of morality) are not the same. Granted, there is some power in the force of custom. What we have been taught and the ways we have been taught certainly influence our personal morality. But is not our own morality more than the result of cultural conditioning? What are the sources of morality? Herein lies our quest, the search for universal moral standards that we can rely upon.

■ NOTES

1. Nawal El Saadawi, *The Hidden Face of Eve: Women in the Arab World,* trans. and ed. Dr. Sheriff Hetata (Boston: Beacon Press, 1982), pp. 7–8.

2. Sandra D. Lane and Robert A. Rubinstein, "Judging the Other: Responding to Traditional Female Genital Surgeries," *Hastings Center Report* 26, no. 3 (1996): 36.

3. Melford Spiro, "Cultural Relativism and the Future of Anthropology," *Cultural Anthropology* 1 (1986): 259–86.

4. Keep in mind that the theory of cultural relativism does not necessarily *disprove* moral absolutism. However, as the philosopher Gilbert Harman tells us, the "rejection of moral absolutism . . . is a reasonable inference from the most *plausible explanation* of the range of moral diversity that actually exists." Gilbert Harman and Judith Jarvis Thomson, *Moral Relativism and Moral Objectivity* (Cambridge, MA: Blackwell, 1996), p. 10.

5. Ibid., p. 3.

6. Ibid., p. 4.

7. Ibid., p. 5.

8. John W. Cook, *Morality and Cultural Differences* (New York: Oxford University Press, 1999), p. 11.

9. See Willard Quine, *Word and Object* (Cambridge, MA: MIT Press, 1960), and *Ontological Relativity, and Other Essays* (New York: Columbia University Press, 1969).

10. Henry Rosemont Jr. discusses this need for a "universal grammar" in "Against Relativism," in Gerald James Larson and Eliot Deutsch, eds., *Interpreting Across Boundaries: New Essays in Comparative Philosophy* (Princeton. NJ: Princeton University Press, 1988), p. 46–47.

11. Cook, p. 93.

12. James Rachels succinctly discusses consequences in his *Elements of Moral Philosophy,* 4th ed. (New York; McGraw-Hill, 2003), pp. 21–23.

13. Ruth Benedict, "Anthropology and the Abnormal," *Journal of General Psychology* 10 (1934), cited in Cook, note 3, p. 180.

14. Cook, pp. 24–28.

15. Ibid., p. 27.

CRITICAL THINKING AND MORAL REASONING

■

BIFURCATING THE WAR IN IRAQ

After three weeks of intensive fighting in March and April 2003, the coalition forces of the United States and Great Britain easily toppled Saddam Hussein's brutal regime in Iraq. Soon after the victory, major U.S. news networks showed faces of Iraqis jubilant over their vanquished dictator. Nevertheless, questions still remain: How will the victors establish law and order among a disordered populace? Who will manage the new government? How will democracy be gradually implanted among the Muslims? A less popular question: Though we've won the war, have we really won? Have we truly taken a significant step forward in what started out as our war against the terrorist group al-Qaeda, led by the infamous Osama bin Laden whose whereabouts are still unknown? Now that we've broadened the enemy to include terrorism in general, this question is all the more crucial.

How does this relate to our chapter on critical thinking, especially as it pertains to ethics? An old cliché, one that we often prefer to ignore, is that the first casualty of war is truth. Along these lines, we can also assert that, when it comes to moral conflict, the first casualty is critical thinking, the ability to examine issues with precision, logic, comprehension, and sensitivity. In light of this, here is the first rule in ethics: Never abandon critical thinking, the willingness to wade through the mud of moral battles, sift through numerous arguments, and ensure that their premises are grounded in logic. To illustrate, let's take the recent war in Iraq.

Upon critically examining the prevailing discourse throughout the war that had been presented to us by administration officials as well as major news media, we cannot help but detect some egregious fallacies in logic. One flagrant fallacy is what is called "bifurcation." This is the splitting up of complex issues in a way that unfairly simplifies matters, distorts the facts, and thus presents us with a misleading choice of "either/or." Here are examples.

When well-known newscaster Connie Chung scolded Democratic Representative Mike Thompson on October 7, 2002, for challenging President Bush's claim that Iraq posed an immediate threat to the United States, she insinuated that any challenge to the Commander-in-Chief implied supporting Saddam Hussein. In so doing, she also embodied the current tendency among major news networks to uncritically endorse the war in Iraq. Instead of informing the public with varying and conflicting viewpoints, the major networks such as ABC, CBS, and NBC acted more like official cheerleaders of the administration's war. As of this writing, these networks still continue to swamp viewers with commentary from generals, military strategists, government officials, and up-close interviews with troopers on the ground. As we follow their action our attention is drawn to the siege and its aftermath rather than to whether or not we should have conducted the siege in the first place. Major networks have underrepresented dissenting voices.

When we look back and think critically about the news coverage—from the arms inspections to the American invasion, triumph, and its wake—the reporting seems to have been selective rather than balanced. For instance, there was very little follow-up among major news media after the London *Observer*'s groundbreaking March 2, 2003, story of U.S. operatives who deliberately intercepted telephone conversations and e-mails of UN delegates representing the so-called Middle Six nations (Chile, Mexico, Pakistan, Guinea, Cameroon, and Angola). The spying was conducted in order to gather information on the delegates' views regarding the work of UN arms inspections teams and whether or not they would support an American-led preemptive attack or else a more prolonged inspection effort by a UN team.

Another example of bifurcation was the stream of ultimatums posed by President Bush to Saddam Hussein. President Bush's March 17 ultimatum to Saddam Hussein, issued in defiance of the UN Security Council's current strategy, framed alternatives to the dictator in a way that, should Saddam Hussein in turn flout the ultimatum, he becomes the culprit, the cause of any further devastation in Iraqi as he commits his "final mistake." In so

doing, those who offer the ultimatum relieve themselves from accountability. By virtue of such ultimatum, the "real cause" of the devastation of
Iraq, the deaths of numerous innocents, and the destruction of precious ar-
tifacts is Saddam Hussein, on account of his refusal to accept the ultimatum. Under the veneer of a reasonable choice, the ultimatum reveals an undercurrent of righteousness amidst a rising tide of national hubris.

Bifurcation also shows itself in the conventional thinking and argument
that because countless Iraqis hate Saddam Hussein, they will embrace their
American liberators. This is skewed logic at its worst. It discounts the fact
that we are also the uninvited occupiers of their land. It overlooks that time
in history when our American troops stood by and did little to squelch the
brutal suppression of uprisings that occurred in southern Iraq in 1991 right
after the Gulf War. It disastrously applies President Bush's "either with us
or against us" fallacy to the Iraqi people, and in so doing it underestimates
the power of Iraqi patriotism against a common enemy—us/U.S. There is
an Arab saying: "I and my brother against our cousin. I, my brother, and
our cousin against the foreigner."

Another example of bifurcation lies in the administration's doctrine of
preemptive war. Now having been set in motion by the war, the doctrine
establishes an insidious precedent. It presupposes that we either attack now
or else be attacked in the future. Critical thinking compels us to ask: Is this
reasoning based upon irrefutably clear and compelling evidence of a serious and imminent threat? From the evidence that has so far been mounted,
not claims but solid evidence, the answer is a resounding "No." If this is
true, then such reasoning may instead shamefully exploit what are understandable public fears of any type of reenactment of 9/11, a day that remains so profoundly traumatic that we lack a suitable name for it other
than the date. Yet despite the lack of convincing evidence, the war discourse
coming from both government officials and major news media still insists
upon puffing up Saddam Hussein's alleged link to al-Qaeda while deflating
long-range negative repercussions of our invasion. It ignores the deep ideological differences between Saddam Hussein and Osama bin Laden. Bin
Laden has even referred to Saddam Hussein as an infidel, since Hussein is
out for his own personal power. In contrast to Hussein's megalomania, bin
Laden's has to do with seeking what some have called a "pan-Arab theocracy." Yet the impression we get from official administration sources and
from news media is that, by virtue of their common enemy—the United
States—they are inextricably linked.

Referring to this notion of preemptive war, Pulitzer Prize–winning historian Arthur Schlesinger claims that "the Bush doctrine is a doctrine of

preventive war, which makes America the self-appointed world's judge, jury, and executioner."[1] Schlesinger goes on to remind us that "anticipatory self-defense" was the same rationale behind the Japanese attack on Pearl Harbor. Looking at this critically, one can't help but consider the irony! We now have become the perpetrators of infamy upon the innocent Iraqi people. The moral of the story? We cannot surrender our critical thinking. And this becomes all the more vital when, as in war, our collective moral struggle is at its extreme.

■ WHAT IS CRITICAL THINKING?

Moral reasoning requires critical thinking. Yet what is critical thinking? To begin with, critical thinking is more than simply the ability to reason. The ability to reason is no doubt needed in order to make moral decisions, but it is not all that is needed. In other words, reasoning is a *necessary* condition, but not a *sufficient* condition. Indeed, reasoning is a double-edged sword. We can wield it for good or for bad. There are quite a few psychopathic murderers who possess rather keen reasoning skills. Psychopaths are habitual liars. They know what they want, and they manipulate others in ways to get it. We can use reason purely for purposes of self-interest, or we can use it to bring about the good of others. The human mind has the capacity to rationalize to itself any and all human actions. Thus, we need more than the ability to reason. We need to reason *well* and properly.

This is where critical thinking skills come in. Applying sound critical thinking skills can help to ensure that our reasoning is valid and sound. These two concepts—valid and sound—are important. First, our reasoning is *valid* when our conclusions or claims follow logically from our premises. Using our opening remarks about the war in Iraq, here is an example of valid reasoning:

Premise 1: All wars are morally justifiable wars.
Premise 2: The armed conflict in Iraq is a war.
Conclusion: Therefore, the armed conflict in Iraq is a morally justifiable war.

Here, the conclusion necessarily and logically follows from the premises. That is, if we are to assume that the premises are true, the conclusion must follow. Note also that we are here referring to claims that are prescriptive moral claims, that is, claims with moral weight. This differs from descriptive claims that have no moral weight. This distinction between descriptive and prescriptive claims is discussed in the article "Moral Reasoning" at the end of this chapter.

As we can see, however, there is more to this line of reasoning. Can we assume the premises to be true? Our reasoning must also be *sound*. And it is sound when our argument is not only valid, but our premises are based upon solid evidence. That is our ideal. We need to strive to achieve sound positions in our thinking, positions that are both logically constructed and based on the facts. Is it true that "All wars are morally justifiable"? There is a "just war" tradition that stipulates certain conditions that must be met in order for a war to be morally justifiable.[2] Does the recent war with Iraq meet these conditions? No doubt, the second premise is true. Our invasion of Iraq initiated the war in Iraq. Nevertheless, the conclusion can be *sound* only if we can establish enough evidence to support both premises. Only then does the conclusion truly follow from the premises. Only then do we have our ideal—a sound position.

In any case, in order to achieve this ideal, *as a necessary starting point, we still must at least ensure that our reasoning is valid.* That's the bottom line, what this chapter is all about. And determining the validity of any argument or position is no easy matter. There are quite a few rules that in turn have sub-rules, and so on. Learning these rules takes time, and the more complex the issue is, the more complex the reasoning becomes. The above example is exceedingly artificial and unreal because it is overly simplistic; there is much more to the war in Iraq than this proposition. The rest of this chapter will highlight certain ingredients in critical thinking that should enable us to reason more clearly when it comes to moral matters.

▪ FALLACIES: WHAT SHOULD WE AVOID?

Let us now examine some fallacies that we typically encounter when attempting to reason about moral issues. When it comes to reasoning properly, fallacies are troublesome stumbling blocks. They are flawed ways of reasoning. Fallacies represent severe defects in reasoning and an absence of critical thinking. We need to avoid fallacies at all costs.

AD HOMINEM

One of the most offensive fallacies occurs when we judge a particular perspective, belief, or position on the basis of how we think or feel about the person who holds that belief. This is termed *ad hominem*, which is Latin for "toward the person." With respect to the values and beliefs of cultures, we can allow our biases about that culture to influence how we reason about that culture's beliefs. Basically, what this pares down to is that we judge the culture instead of its beliefs. Or we judge another person instead of that person's beliefs.

If I am more favorably disposed toward "white" cultures than toward other cultures, then I may already prejudge African beliefs on this basis. I may discredit their beliefs as "primitive" or "unsophisticated" on the basis of my own personal prejudices. Though I may pretend to seriously evaluate their positions, I am actually motivated by my prejudices. This is totally illogical. Even worse, it is dangerous because it provides grounds for racism, our worst enemy. In similar fashion, as our chapter on Islam indicates, there are varieties of Muslim positions. For example, note the tensions among Sunnis, Shiites, and Sufis throughout the history of Islam. Yet after September 11, 2001, we may tend to think of Muslims as being of one cloth, brand them as essentially militarists or extremists, and proceed to evaluate their beliefs and values in terms of how we feel about Muslim extremists. This fallacy constitutes one of the most insidious forms of reasoning.

APPEAL TO IGNORANCE

Another common fallacy occurs when we offer as sufficient evidence for a particular position (A) lack of evidence to the *contrary* of that same position (Z). This is called "appeal to ignorance," or argument from ignorance, that is, ignorance of any evidence to the contrary. Simply put, lack of evidence to the contrary does not suffice as evidence. For instance, is there any sound basis to infer the existence of a universal moral standard? From this text, we discover that no one has yet proven that there exists *no* foundation or infallible authority for a universally binding morality. However, this does not logically lead us to conclude that there must therefore *be* a universal moral standard. Asserting this commits the argument from ignorance.

> *Premise:* No one has yet proved that there is no source or authority for a universal morality.
> *Conclusion:* Therefore, there is a universal morality.

Or, to take the situation in Iraq:

> *Premise:* No one has yet proved that the Iraqis do not harbor weapons of mass destruction.
> *Conclusion:* Therefore, the Iraqis must be harboring weapons of mass destruction.

Reasoning in this way is fallacious. It is all the more absurd when we realize that one can simply respond to the above conclusions: Neither has anyone proved that there *is* a source for a universal morality. And neither has anyone proved that the Iraqis *do* have weapons of mass destruction. In which case, the argumentation becomes circular. We go in circles with our claims and counterclaims.

APPEAL TO THE MAJORITY

For many of us, the majority opinion constitutes the litmus test of whether something is morally right or wrong. This is logically absurd. Aside from the logistical problem in precisely determining and assessing this "majority" opinion, a deeper problem lies in our assuming that what most of the people prefer carries moral weight.

Critical thinking and moral reasoning require that we gather, in the best way we can, all the relevant facts in the situation. Do the majority necessarily possess sufficient details and knowledge concerning a moral issue or controversy? Do most people know facts about global warming? Do most of us know the relationship among an excess of chlorofluorocarbons (CFCs), our ozone layer, and protection from solar heat? Why would we assume that most people have gathered all of the relevant facts?

While gathering the facts, we also need to seriously reflect upon relevant concerns and issues. Can the majority of people engage in serious reflection? Why assume that most people have given serious thought to issues in global warming? Another way to think of the majority is the social norm. We are often influenced by the social norm in our society, and this norm becomes so strong a voice that it becomes our own uncritically accepted frame of reference as to what is right and wrong. So an American social norm that endorses individual freedoms will influence views of sports utility vehicles (SUVs), CFCs, and global warming. In contrast, a social norm of Confucianism that stresses collective well-being may view these differently.[3]

Critical thinking requires that we be as impartial as we can. We need to "bracket" and put aside whatever vested interests or biases we may have, and not allow them to influence or detract from our reasoning about the issues.[4] Is the majority necessarily impartial? Are Irish Americans impartial regarding the continuing conflict in Northern Ireland? What about the Irish? Are Jewish Americans impartial as to the Israel-Palestine struggle? What about Arab Americans? Why would we assume that most people are able to bracket their biases? Admittedly, we all look at an issue from our own perspective so there is always a taint of subjectivity in the way we see and understand things. Nevertheless, thinking critically requires that we not allow our biases to unduly influence us.

In the United States, the television media assume a powerful voice in constructing the social norm. In fact, television not only represents values but also generates values. TV commercials orient us toward buying, for example, SUVs, and consumerism becomes the norm. What is important to keep in mind is that even though we may think that the social norm reflects the majority view, this is not necessarily the case. For instance, although commercials often portray Americans as typically affluent, upper middle class, and suburban, consider the numerous pockets of poverty scattered throughout the United States. All of this points to one significant rule of thumb in moral reasoning: When making moral decisions, do *not* rely upon majority opinion.

APPEAL TO TRADITION

If we justify actions because they happen to be the traditional practice, then we commit the gross error of assuming that what is traditional is necessarily morally justifiable. Slavery in the South was the social norm and the traditional practice for quite some time up until the late nineteenth century. As we saw in Chapter 1, many defend the practice of female genital excision because it has been the long-standing traditional practice in particular cultures. The fact that it has been a traditional practice may help *explain* why it continues to be a custom. However, in no way does this necessarily *justify* the practice.

As we said earlier, there is a prominent difference between explanation and justification. Appeals to tradition such as family honor may help explain the persistence of "honor killings" in certain Mideast cultures. And there is the Hindu "traditional" practice of *sati*, the "voluntary" self-immolation of a widow on her husband's funeral pyre. The Chinese practice of footbinding was traditional and thus commonplace for centuries. Polygamy still continues to be the traditional practice in quite a few African and Muslim societies. We in the West resort to a "natural law" tradition that helps explain our customary practice of monogamy. However, in and of itself, the appeal to tradition does not necessarily justify the practice. Moral justification requires a critical examination of reasons, assumptions, and evidence supporting particular claims. For example, I may bemoan what I feel to be the surging tide of relativism in our culture and fear that we are becoming morally bankrupt. This fear by itself is not an adequate reason for refuting ethical relativism. Nor is it a good reason for believing in some universal moral standards. Justification cannot rest upon feelings. Moral justification requires in-depth examination that weighs the various arguments, their premises and assumptions in the light of putative moral principles.

Closely aligned with this fallacy is the appeal to authority. This could be the authority of tradition, the authority of leaders, teachers, books, and so on. This occurs when we accept their authority as the *final* word on a subject. This type of inflexibility allows for no exceptions. It is harsh, unbending, and ultimately dangerous in its application.

APPEAL TO FEELINGS

Ours is a culture that thrives on immediate gratification of desires. Yet overvaluing the role of feelings leads us to undermine the role of reason and critical thinking. This is not to say that feelings play no role in moral reasoning. In fact, throughout Western intellectual history feelings have been given short shrift, an undeserved subordinate role. Feelings have been viewed as dangerous and threatening. Even worse, as we shall see in our chapter on feminist ethics, feelings have been mistakenly associated with women, whereas men have been linked with the capacity to reason. This skewed view of gender difference continues to contribute to a long-standing history and practice of male dominance and patriarchy in many cultures, including our own.

Nevertheless, just as there can be a tyranny of the intellect (an excess and uncritical overdependence upon intellect, reason, and logic), there can also be a tyranny of feelings. This exaggerated importance of feelings when it comes to moral reasoning is perhaps a reaction to centuries of excess in the other direction. Put simply, if feelings and desires become the arbiter of what is morally acceptable and what is not, then the result is moral chaos. We then justify anything we do on the basis of our feelings and desires about things. In Robert James Waller's 1992 novel *The Bridges of Madison County*, discussed in our chapter on deontology, are Francesca and Robert justified in their affair on the basis of their feelings toward each other? When we discuss the environment, are we justified in treating nature as essentially "disposable" if it suits our immediate desires?

The main problem with feelings as the litmus test for moral decision making is that our actions then become ultimately solipsistic. We become trapped in the prison of self and self-interest. "So what if our present lifestyles have any bearing on future generations? Let them take care of their own problems." We can only be moral if we are able to free ourselves from this prison, if we are able to consider the interests of others on an equal par with or more important that our own.

ABSOLUTIZING RULES

Our chapters will examine various moral rules and principles such as Aquinas's natural law theory, Kant's deontology, Mill's utilitarianism, Hindu *dharma*, and the Buddhist Eightfold Path. However, we need to be careful to avoid thinking of moral rules as being absolute, that is, applied literally in every given situation at all times and in all cultures. Moral rules such as telling the truth are general rules of thumb, often referred to as prima facie, that we apply to specific circumstances and that we generally ought to follow. However, absolutizing these rules can prevent us from looking closer at circumstantial facts and details that we also need to consider in order to arrive at a morally appropriate resolution. For instance, in our deontology chapter's case of Billy Budd, unbending allegiance to law and duty can come at a high price, namely, sacrificing humaneness and compassion.

If we absolutize moral rules, they become inflexible, and we end up stacking the deck toward a predetermined resolution that does not allow for exceptions. In this way, we essentially become slaves to the rule. In our chapter on Hindu ethics, consider Arjuna's plight in the *Bhagavad Gita*, where his strict duty as a warrior clashes with his sensitivity to others' suffering. Morality is not always so rigid, and moral judgments require flexibility. We need to think beyond the cocoon. This is all the more important when we consider other cultures and their particular value systems.

DOUBLE STANDARDS

We engage in double standards when we apply certain rules and principles in a particular case that involves others, while at the same time we do not apply the same rules and principles to ourselves when we act in a similar fashion. This is one of the most common faults in critical thinking. It not only means being selective in how we apply rules and principles; it also betrays a fundamental moral hypocrisy in our judgments of others.

For instance, we Americans may claim that Muslim women are as a whole terribly oppressed because of how they dress, assuming that wearing clothes that cover nearly the entire body does not allow for freedom of expression. Thus, we may apply the principle of respecting individual and personal freedom of expression. Yet, in a subtle way, could we not issue the same critique to many American women who freely choose to buy into fashions and styles that still serve the interests of a male-dominated culture in which women continue to be viewed as sexual objects rather than as individual persons? Whose interests are being served when women wear stiletto heels, which are undeniably unhealthy for the posture?

Our willingness to engage in double standards rests again upon what we said earlier about the human mind and its ability to rationalize anything to itself. Our capacity to justify anything to ourselves is all the more evident when it comes to matters in which we invest a good deal of emotional energy in particular positions and beliefs. Feminists often point out double standards in varying levels of tolerance or approval regarding the sexual behavior of young adult men as opposed to young adult women. Critical thinking is required to keep our mind and reason on the right course.

To illustrate, consider one of the clearest policy statements that underscore universal moral principles: the United Nations' Declaration of Human Rights, formulated on December 10, 1948. Here is a clear instance of an international effort to delineate universal ethical principles, principles that cross cultures and borders. It is an explicit condemnation of practices like slavery, genocide, racism, torture, wrongful imprisonment, and intimidation. The Declaration is cited in full at the end of this chapter.

When we examine this Declaration, we wonder whether we as a nation uphold these same principles. Or do we commit double standards when it comes to their application? Indeed, it seems as if many countries actually violate these principles, even the United States. Officials of Amnesty International have pointed out that the United States exhibits a "widespread pattern" of rights violations. According to officials, in the United States

> *police forces and criminal and legal systems have a persistent and widespread pattern of human rights violations. . . . Across the country thousands of people are subjected to sustained and deliberate brutality at the hands of police officers. Cruel, degrading, and sometimes life-threatening methods of constraint continue to be a feature of the U.S. criminal justice system.[5]*

BIFURCATION

Here is a vital formula in moral reasoning: Complex issues do not lead to simple answers. Unfortunately, we tend to seek clear-cut, straightforward answers. It would be much easier if we could simply cast an ethical template over decisions, deeds, and issues. Because we seek this sort of simplicity, we are often drawn to those extreme positions that offer a black-and-white resolution. And this is why many of us find ethics and philosophy to be exceptionally difficult and frustrating as we discover the issues to be rather complex. Nonetheless, reducing a complex issue into an oversimplified format, so that we in turn view the options as *either* for one position *or* for the other, is outright distortion. Presenting things in a false either/or way is called bifurcation, perhaps one of the deadliest fallacies in moral reasoning.

Political leaders are certainly not immune to bifurcation. Note these statements by President George W. Bush in his "war against terror": "Now is the time to draw a line in the sand against the evil ones."[6] In the next statement, he extends his campaign both geographically and historically when he says, "Across the world and across the years, we will fight the evil ones, and we will win."[7] This dualistic thinking, this either/or approach, spells disaster in the long run. It dangerously oversimplifies an extraordinarily complex issue. It also distorts the nature of the struggle by presenting a universe of two principles: good and bad. This leaves no room for reasoned dissent, nor does it leave room for other alternatives.

Certainly there are issues that are quite clear-cut. Practices such as slavery, racism, torture, sexism, murder, rape, genocide, and fraud are definitely wrong and surely merit our total opposition. Unfortunately, things are often not so simple. One group's "freedom fighting" is another group's "terrorism." We may oppose the outright sexism expressed by the Taliban, yet still remain sexist ourselves whenever we perpetrate the objectification of women through pornography.

HASTY JUDGMENT

We often pass judgment on an issue before we adequately understand it. As we said above, we need to make an all-out effort to understand the issues and the relevant details in the best way we can. Of course, it is impossible to completely understand the issues because this would require knowing all of the facts; we can't possibly know all of the facts because there are always facts that have not yet been uncovered. Nevertheless, we need to know and understand the facts sufficiently enough before we make a moral evaluation.

This is all the more critical when it comes to evaluating other cultures. All too often, we will leap to premature conclusions about other cultures' practices before sufficiently understanding them. We may think that the

Eskimos are coldhearted in their treatment of the elderly since they allow the elderly to leave the village on their own to then freeze to death so that they are not a burden to the group. Or we may conclude that Chinese women are thoroughly oppressed because women are not generally considered within the framework of the Confucian Five Cardinal Relationships. Or we may judge that the Muslim concept of *jihad* has to do only with waging war against the enemies of Islam. In many respects, we often view the other culture through the lens of our own culture. Why? Because we mistakenly assume that the lens we use represents a universal frame of reference. Or else we may assume that it is the only right frame of reference, and all others that sway from it are in error.

■ STEPS TO MORAL REASONING

Given the above, the following is a brief outline of the necessary steps to sound moral reasoning. Throughout all of these steps, we need to ensure that we avoid the above fallacies. In addition to these steps, refer also to the article "Moral Reasoning" at the end of the chapter.

STEP ONE: KNOW THE FACTS

We need to sift through as much detail and evidence as we can regarding an issue. We place a high premium upon being well-informed. The more informed we are about an issue, the better position we are in to more properly evaluate it. Furthermore, when we examine evidence, we need to consider the sources of our information. Are the sources biased? Media sources tend to be naturally biased in view of competition for ratings and for news that "sells." What about our own biases? Am I only reading sources that support my own feelings? Are these the "facts" because I want them to be the facts? Because they serve my own interests? Am I thinking as impartially as I can? Am I selecting only the facts that support my position?

STEP TWO: VIEW THESE FACTS
FROM VARIOUS PERSPECTIVES

Keep in mind that the facts are often presented to us within various frames of reference. We need to make an earnest effort to understand as well as we can these other frames of reference. This is especially critical in our journey through various cultures. We are not entitled to evaluate the beliefs and practices of other cultures unless we make an effort to understand those beliefs and practices. All too often, particularly with other cultures, we end up evaluating their beliefs and practices from *our own* frames of reference. We often make the spurious assumption that our values and principles, that is, our own frames of reference, are universal and absolute. In doing so, we impose our own values and principles upon these other cultures. We challenge this assumption from the start.

STEP THREE: IDENTIFY THE MORAL ISSUES

What are the key moral issues at stake? We need to be sure that we are on the right track. We must ensure that we know what the moral issues are. This means distinguishing considerations that are moral from those that are nonmoral. This also means knowing what constitutes moral values and nonmoral values as well as distinguishing between descriptive claims and prescriptive claims. This is discussed further in the "Moral Reasoning" article included at the end of the chapter.

STEP FOUR: IDENTIFY FACTORS THAT ARE MORALLY RELEVANT

In applying the above rule, we need to distinguish between those factors and details that are morally relevant—that is, relevant to moral resolution—and those factors that are extraneous. Have I left out morally relevant details? Who are the stakeholders? Who are the decision makers? Who will be affected by the decision? Do they have a role in the decision?

STEP FIVE: CLARIFY THE VARIOUS WAYS THE ISSUE CAN BE RESOLVED

What are the various ways to resolve the moral conflict? What ethical theories can be reasonably applied to the issue? Here we can test the legitimacy of these theories. What theories make logical sense? What avenue seems to offer the most reasonable approach?

STEP SIX: CHOOSE THE BEST MORAL OPTION

Applying the various moral theories and rules to the issue, which decision or action makes the best sense? Which option is the most reasonable?

In summary, moral reasoning in the area of cross-cultural ethics is exceptionally demanding. This is because we need to view an issue through diverse lenses, from various frames of reference. This requires that we understand our own frames of reference. It also requires that we understand frames of reference that are foreign to us. This is no easy task. We have to somehow listen to different voices and wear different lenses. We need to make the best effort we can to know and understand perspectives that are unfamiliar. Herein lies our challenge in examining ethics across cultures. Only if we face this challenge in the proper frame of mind can we make a good start on this journey.

■ NOTES

1. *Newsweek*, March 22, 2003.

2. The traditional criteria for a just war are the following: (1) There must be a just cause, namely acting in self-defense and to redress a suffered injury. (2) War must be declared by a legitimate authority. (3) War can only be the last resort, after all other options have been exhausted. (4) The intent must be to establish peace and not to inflict unnecessary suffering. (5) There must be a reasonable chance of success. (6) The means must be proportional to the end. That is, excessive force must not be used to bring about the desired end. (7) Combatants must be discriminated from noncombatants. Noncombatants can never be the intentional targets.

3. See the discussion in Vincent Ryan Ruggiero, *Thinking Critically About Ethical Issues*, 5th ed. (Mountain View, CA: Mayfield, 2001), pp. 16–20.

4. The term "bracketing" refers to a phenomenological method, originating with the German philosopher Edmund Husserl (1859–1938), to enable one to arrive at a more respectable level of objectivity.

5. "Amnesty Finds 'Widespread Pattern' of U.S. Rights Violations," *New York Times*, October 5, 1998, p. A11.

6. Remarks in a ceremony at the Federal Bureau of Investigation's headquarters, the Edgar Hoover Building, Washington, D.C., October 10, 2001.

7. Statements in his Thanksgiving Day speech to troops at Fort Campbell, Fort Campbell, Kentucky, November 21, 2001.

MORAL REASONING

■

NINA ROSENSTAND AND ANITA SILVERS

Astrid has a problem. Her good friend Gina asked to borrow money. Astrid is aware that Gina needs the money—but at the same time Astrid suspects Gina may find it difficult to repay the loan, and Astrid knows it will trouble their relationship if Gina doesn't. Unfortunately, Astrid is also convinced that refusing to make the loan will strain the relationship, too. So she isn't at all sure what she should do.

Astrid is pondering a moral issue. Moral questions arise all the time—whenever we wonder what we or others ought to do or what is right or proper or fair or appropriate. You may perhaps have the idea that mortality is "just a matter of personal opinion" and that there isn't much of a place for reasoning when it comes to moral issues. But you can—and do—reason about moral issues. You consider options, weigh consequences, think about what is right and wrong, and make a decision. When you try to figure out what you should do, you employ moral reasoning.

DESCRIPTIVE AND PRESCRIPTIVE MORAL CLAIMS

Fortunately, moral reasoning is basically no different from reasoning about matters of other kinds, except for one thing: Moral arguments all contain conclusions that are value judgments, judgments that evaluate something. "I shouldn't lend Gina money" is a value judgment; it assigns a negative value to a course of action. "I should lend Gina money" assigns a positive value to the action. Moral philosophers often use the term **prescriptive claim** interchangeably with "value judgment," and we'll often use that terminology as well, for reasons that will become clear shortly.

A prescriptive claim (value judgment) like " I shouldn't lend Gina money" is quite different from a claim like "Gina has brown hair " If you say that Gina has brown hair, you're merely stating what you take to be a fact. A claim of that sort, which does not assign a value to things but instead just asserts what you take to be a fact, is said to be a **descriptive claim.**

Here are some descriptive claims

Gina is twenty-seven.
The steaks are frozen.
Yo-Yo Ma plays the cello.
The president has never been divorced.

Here are some prescriptive claims

Gina shouldn't ask people for money.
It is wrong to eat meat.
Children should be taught to appreciate music.
The president ought to be able to be divorced if she wants to be.

Moral prescriptive claims characteristically dictate or specify—that is, pre-scribe what actions we should take or avoid, what ends each of us should seek to bring about by our actions, or what kind of person each of us should try to be. Thus, moral reasoning is distinguished from other kinds of reasoning by the fact that the conclusions it reaches (or tries to reach) are moral prescriptive claims, or value judgments. All the prescriptive claims in the example above are moral prescriptive claims.

Distinguishing moral prescriptive claims from other prescriptive claims Not all prescriptive claims assign moral values to things. For example, if we com-plain that the coffee is bitter or maintain that dogs make better companions than cats, we are making value judgments (prescriptive claims) that have noth-ing to do with moral issues. To take another kind of example, if we assert that Gina is beautiful, or that Beethoven's Ninth Symphony is stirring, or that Tom Cruise is a better actor than Keanu Reeves, or that the 2001 Lexus is a work of art, then we are making aesthetic evaluations. Later in this chapter we take a look at evaluations (prescriptive claims, value judgments) of the aesthetic va-riety, but here we are focusing on moral evaluations.

One general point to keep in mind is that prescriptive claims typically em-ploy key words such as "good," "bad," "ought," "should," "right," "wrong," "proper," and "improper." These particular words often—but not always—signal a moral evaluation. For example, if somebody tells you that you ought to keep your promises, that's a moral judgment. But if he or she says you ought to keep your knees bent when you're skiing, he or she is merely giving you practical advice.

Getting an "ought" from an "is": Descriptive premises and prescriptive claims
It has been said that no claim about plain fact—that is, no description—can imply a claim that attributes a moral value or a moral obligation. In other words, we cannot legitimately infer what *ought (morally) to be* the case from a claim about what *is* the case. Using the terminology from the previous sec-tion, we can put it this way: No prescriptive conclusion can follow from set of purely descriptive premises. For example, consider the following argument:

1a. Mr. Jones is the father of a young child. Therefore, Mr. Jones ought to contribute to his child's support.

We hear such claims often in the context of everyday life, and we are often per-suaded by such conclusions. But we should beware, for the conclusion doesn't follow from the premise; it is, in other words, a **non sequitur.** Jumping to such conclusions is a common phenomenon that philosophers generally refer to as **the naturalistic fallacy.** Let us take a closer look. The premise of this argument states a (nonmoral) fact, but the conclusion is an "ought" claim that prescribes a moral obligation for Mr. Jones. As the philosopher David Hume pointed out, there is nothing in a purely descriptive statement of fact that implies a moral duty—the concept of duty is added to the statement by our sense of right and wrong.

However, this seems to lead to an unacceptable situation, for shouldn't we, on the basis of facts and statistics, be able to make policies about social and moral issues? If we know that child abuse is likely to create a new generation of adults who will also practice child abuse, shouldn't we then have the right to state that "Child abuse should be prevented by all means" without being ac-cused of committing a non sequitur? The answer is that of course facts and sta-tistics can be used to formulate social and moral policies, but not the facts and statistics *by themselves:* We must add a premise to make the argument valid. In this case the premise is the moral statement that "Child abuse is wrong. " Adding this statement may seem trivial, and you may object that this evalua-tion is already given with the word "abuse," but the fact is that our moral sense, whether it is based on feelings or reasoning or both, is what allows us to proceed from a set of facts to a conclusion about what ought to be done. Let us return to Mr. Jones:

1b. *Premise:* Mr. Jones is the father of a young child.

   Premise: Parents ought to contribute to the support of their young children.

   Conclusion: Therefore, Mr. Jones ought to contribute to his child's support.

The result is now a valid deductive argument. Now, in a real-life dispute about whether Mr. Jones has an obligation toward his child, an argument like ex-ample 1b is not likely to convince anyone that Mr. Jones has this obligation if he or she doesn't agree with the premise that parents should take care of their children. But the fact the argument is valid does help clarify matters. It may be an undisputed fact that Jones is a parent, but it may not be as undisputed that parents ought to take care of their young children under all circumstances. In other words, if you disagree with the conclusion, you need not start disagree-ing with the factual claim of the first premise, but you can enter into a discus-sion about the truth of the second premise. It is important to be able to enter into such discussions apart from the case of Mr. Jones, for otherwise it would be too easy for us to let our thinking be prejudiced by the facts presented in the first premise.

Let us consider a few additional examples:

2a. Sophie promised to pay Jennifer five dollars today. So Sophie ought to pay Jennifer five dollars today.

It is perfectly natural to want to see this as a convincing argument as it stands. But, in keeping with our strategy, we require that an "ought" claim be explicitly stated in the premises. In this case, what would you say is the missing premise? The most obvious way of putting it is "One ought to keep one's promises." If we add the required premise we get this:

2b. Sophie promised to pay Jennifer five dollars today. One ought to keep one's promises. So Sophie ought to pay Jennifer five dollars today.

If it seems to you that the second premise is not really necessary in order for the conclusion to follow, that is probably because you accept that making a promise involves a moral duty to keep the promise. In that case, the second premise would just be true by definition, but even so, there is no harm in stating it. And suppose it is *not* true by definition? Not all implicit moral evaluations are; and if they are not, then adding the premise is absolutely necessary in order for the argument to the valid. Consider this example:

3a. It is natural for women to have children. Therefore, women ought to have children, and those who try to avoid having children are unnatural.

The trouble with this argument is the concept of "natural," a very ambiguous word. There are several hidden assumptions behind this argument, and one of these—which we'll call the missing premise here—is the following: "What is natural is morally good, and going against nature is evil." We might also say, "What is natural reveals God's intentions with his creation, and if one goes against God's intentions, one is evil (or sinful)." This also explains the concept of "unnatural" for although "natural" in the premise looks completely descriptive, "unnatural" in the conclusion has a judgmental slant. If we add the missing premise, the argument will look like this:

3b. It is natural for women to have children. What is natural is morally good, and going against nature is evil. Therefore, women ought to have children, and those who try to avoid having children are unnatural.

Now the argument is valid, but you may not want to agree with the conclusion. If so, although in some sense it is, overall, "natural" for females to have offspring, you may want to dispute the premise that what is natural is always morally good. After all, many "natural" things, such as leaving severely disabled individuals to fend for themselves or scratching oneself in public, are considered unacceptable in our culture.

Whether an "ought" claim can ever follow directly from an "is" claim has been a controversial issue among philosophers; some point out that a statement such as "An open flame can burn you, so stay away from the campfire" makes an unproblematic transition from an "is" to an "ought"; other philosophers point out that there is a hidden premise that is taken for granted: that getting burned is bad because it hurts.

CONSISTENCY AND FAIRNESS

A common mistake made in moral reasoning is inconsistency—treating cases that are similar as if they weren't that way. For example, suppose Moore announces on the first day of class that the final in the class will be optional "except," he says, pointing at some person at random, "for the young woman there in the third row. For you," he says, "the final is mandatory."

The problem is that Moore is treating a student who is similar to the rest of the class as if she were different. And the student will want to know, of course, why she has been singled out: "What's so different about me?" she will wonder (as she drops the course).

A similar sort of problem occurs if Moore gives two students the same grade despite the fact that one student did far better in the course than the other. Treating dissimilar cases as if they were similar isn't inconsistent; it just involves a failure to make relevant discriminations.

As you have probably foreseen by now, when we treat people inconsistently, the result is often *unfair*. It is unfair to the woman in the third row to require her alone to take the final; alternatively, it would be unfair to the rest of the class to make the final mandatory for them and to make it optional for the woman in the third row. From the perspective of critical thinking, what is so troubling about unfairness is that it is illogical. It is like saying "All Xs are Y" and then adding, "Some Xs are not Y."

This doesn't mean, of course, that if you have been treating people unfairly, you should *continue* to treat them unfairly on the grounds that it would be inconsistent for you to change your policy. There is nothing illogical in saying, in effect, "I treated the Xs I encountered to date wrongly, but now I will not treat the Xs I encounter wrongly." People sometimes adhere to a bad policy simply on the grounds that it would be inconsistent of them to change, but there is no basis in logic for this idea.

Not all cases of consistency result in unfairness. For example, let's imagine that Parker approved of the Korean War and opposed the war in Vietnam but is unable to point out any relevant differences between the two cases. This isn't a matter of unfairness, exactly; it's just inconsistency on Parker's part.

When are two or more cases sufficiently similar to warrant our calling somebody inconsistent who treats them as if they were different? The answer is that there is no hard-and-fast rule. The point to keep in mind, however, is that the burden of proof is on the person who appears inconsistent to show that he or she is not is not treating similar cases dissimilarly. If, when challenged, Parker cannot *tell* us what's different about Vietnam and Korea that justifies his difference in attitude between the two, then we are justified in regarding him as inconsistent.

Imagine, that Carol is a salesperson who treats black customers and white customers differently: She is, let us imagine, much more polite to customers of her own racial group (we needn't worry about which group that is). Can Carol explain to us what is so different about black and white customers that would justify her treating them differently? If not, we are justified in regarding her practices as inconsistent.

Suppose, however, that Carol thinks that skin color itself is a difference between blacks and whites relevant to how people should be treated, and she charges us with failing to make relevant discriminations. Here it would be easy for us to point out to Carol that skin color is an immutable characteristic of birth like height or eye color; does Carol adjust her civility to people depending on those characteristics?

It isn't difficult to perceive the inconsistency on the part of a salesperson who is more polite to customers of one group; but other cases are far tougher, and many are such that reasonable people will disagree about their proper assessment. Is a person inconsistent who approves of abortion but not capital punishment? Is a person inconsistent who, on the one hand, believes that the states should be free to reduce spending on welfare but, on the other, does not think that the states should be able to eliminate ceilings on punitive damages in tort cases? No harm is done in asking "What's the difference?" and because much headway can be made in a discussion by doing so, it seems wise to ask.

UNIVERSAL DECLARATION OF HUMAN RIGHTS

GENERAL ASSEMBLY OF THE UNITED NATIONS

Preamble

Whereas recognition of the inherent dignity and of the equal and inalienable rights of all members of the human family is the foundation of freedom, justice and peace in the world,

Whereas disregard and contempt for human rights have resulted in barbarous acts which have outraged the conscience of mankind, and the advent of a world in which human beings shall enjoy freedom of speech and belief and freedom from fear and want has been proclaimed as the highest aspirations of the common people,

Whereas it is essential, if man is not to be compelled to have recourse, as a last resort, to rebellion against tyranny and oppression, that human rights should be protected by the rule of law,

Whereas it is essential to promote the development of friendly relations between nations,

Whereas the peoples of the *United Nations* have in the Charter reaffirmed their faith in fundamental human rights, in the dignity and worth of the human person and in the equal rights of men and women and have determined to promote social progress and better standards of life in larger freedom,

Whereas *Member States* have pledged themselves to achieve, in co-operation with the United Nations, the promotion of universal respect for and observance of human rights and fundamental freedoms,

Whereas a common understanding of these rights and freedoms is of the greatest importance for the full realization of this pledge,
Now, therefore,

The General Assembly
proclaims

THIS UNIVERSAL DECLARATION OF HUMAN RIGHTS as a common standard of achievement for all peoples and all nations, to the end that every individual and every organ of society, keeping this Declaration constantly in mind, shall strive by teaching and education to promote respect for these rights and freedoms and by progressive measures, national and international, to secure their universal and effective recognition and observance, both among the peoples of Member States themselves and among the peoples of territories under their jurisdiction.

Article 1. All human beings are born free and equal in dignity and rights. They are endowed with reason and conscience and should act towards one another in a spirit of brotherhood.

Article 2. Everyone is entitled to all the rights and freedoms set forth in this Declaration, without distinction of any kind, such as race, colour, sex, language, religion, political or other opinion, national or social origin, property, birth or other status.

Furthermore, no distinction shall be made on the basis of the political, jurisdictional or international status of the country or territory to which a person belongs, whether it be independent, trust, non-self-governing or under any other limitation of sovereignty.

Article 3. Everyone has the right to life, liberty and security of person.

Article 4. No one shall be held in slavery or servitude; slavery and the slave trade shall be prohibited in all their forms.

Article 5. No one shall be subjected to torture or to cruel, inhuman or degrading treatment or punishment.

Article 6. Everyone has the right to recognition everywhere as a person before the law.

Article 7. All are equal before the law and are entitled without any discrimination to equal protection of the law. All are entitled to equal protection against any discrimination in violation of this Declaration and against any incitement to such discrimination.

Article 8. Everyone has the right to an effective remedy by the competent national tribunals for acts violating the fundamental rights granted him by the constitution or by law.

Article 9. No one shall be subjected to arbitrary arrest, detention or exile.

Article 10. Everyone is entitled in full equality to a fair and public hearing by an independent and impartial tribunal, in the determination of his rights and obligations and of any criminal charge against him.

Article 11. (1) Everyone charged with a penal offence has the right to be presumed innocent until proved guilty according to law in a public trial at which he has had all the guarantees necessary for his defence.

(2) No one shall be held guilty of any penal offence on account of any act or omission which did not constitute a penal offense, under national or international law, at the time when it was committed. Nor shall a heavier penalty be imposed than the one that was applicable at the time the penal offence was committed.

Article 12. No one shall be subjected to arbitrary interference with his privacy, family, home or correspondence, nor to attacks upon his honour and reputation. Everyone has the right to the protection of the law against such interference or attacks.

Article 13. (1) Everyone has the right to freedom of movement and residence within the borders of each state.

(2) Everyone has the right to leave any country, including his own, and to return his country.

Article 14. (1) Everyone has the right to seek and to enjoy in other countries asylum from persecution.

(2) This right may not be invoked in the case of prosecutions genuinely arising from non-political crimes or from acts contrary to the purposes and principles of the United Nations.

Article 15. (1) Everyone has the right to a nationality.

(2) No one shall be arbitrarily deprived of his nationality nor denied the right to change his nationality.

Article 16. (1) Men and women of full age, without any limitation due to race, nationality or religion, have the right to marry and to found a family. They are entitled to equal rights as to marriage, during marriage and at its dissolution.

(2) Marriage shall be entered into only with the free and full consent of the intending spouses.

(3) The family is the natural and fundamental group unit of society and is entitled to protection by society and the State.

Article 17. (1) Everyone has the right to own property alone as well as in association with others.

(2) No one shall be arbitrarily deprived of his property.

Article 18. Everyone has the right to freedom of thought, conscience and religion; this right includes freedom to change his religion or belief, and freedom, either alone or in community with others and in public or private, to manifest his religion or belief in teaching, practice, worship and observance.

Article 19. Everyone has the right to freedom of opinion and expression; this right includes freedom to hold opinions without interference and to seek, receive and impart information and ideas through any media and regardless of frontiers.

Article 20. (1) Everyone has the right to freedom of peaceful assembly and association.

(2) No one may be compelled to belong to an association.

Article 21. (1) Everyone has the right to take part in the government of his country, directly or through freely chosen representatives.

(2) Everyone has the right of equal access to public service in his country.

(3) The will of the people shall be the basis of the authority of government; this will shall be expressed in periodic and genuine elections which shall be by universal and equal suffrage and shall be held by secret vote or by equivalent free voting procedures.

Article 22. Everyone, as a member of society, has the right to social security and is entitled to realization, through national effort and international co-operation and in accordance with the organization and resources of each State, of the economic, social and cultural rights indispensable for his dignity and the free development of his personality.

Article 23. (1) Everyone has the right to work, to free choice of employment, to just and favourable conditions of work and to protection against unemployment.

(2) Everyone, without any discrimination, has the right to equal pay for equal work.

(3) Everyone who works has the right to just and favourable remuneration ensuring for himself and his family an existence worthy of human dignity, and supplemented, if necessary, by other means of social protection.

(4) Everyone has the right to form and to join trade unions for the protection of his interests.

Article 24. Everyone has the right to rest and leisure, including reasonable limitation of working hours and periodic holidays with pay.

Article 25. (1) Everyone has the right to a standard of living adequate for the health and well-being of himself and of his family, including food, clothing, housing and medical care and necessary social services, and the right to security in the event of unemployment, sickness, disability, widowhood, old age or other lack of livelihood in circumstances beyond his control.

(2) Motherhood and childhood are entitled to special care and assistance. All children, whether born in or out of wedlock, shall enjoy the same social protection.

Article 26. (1) Everyone has the right to education. Education shall be free, at least in the elementary and fundamental stages. Elementary education shall be compulsory. Technical and professional education shall be made generally available and higher education shall be equally accessible to all on the basis of merit.

(2) Education shall be directed to the full development of the human personality and to the strengthening of respect for human rights and fundamental freedoms. It shall promote understanding, tolerance and friendship among all nations, racial or religious groups, and shall further the activities of the United Nations for the maintenance of peace.

(3) Parents have a prior right to choose the kind of education that shall be given to their children.

Article 27. (1) Everyone has the right freely to participate in the cultural life of the community, to enjoy the arts and to share in the scientific advancement and its benefits.

(2) Everyone has the right to the protection of the moral and material interests resulting from any scientific, literacy or artistic production of which he is the author.

Article 28. Everyone is entitled to a social and international order in which the rights and freedoms set forth in this Declaration can be fully realized.

Article 29. (1) Everyone has duties to the community in which alone the free and full development of his personality is possible.

(2) In the exercise of his rights and freedoms, everyone shall be subject only to such limitations as are determined by law solely for the purpose of securing due recognition and respect for the rights and freedoms of others and of meet-

ing the just requirements of morality, public order and the general welfare in a democratic society.

(3) These rights and freedoms may in no case he exercised contrary to the purposes and principles of the United Nations.

Article 30. Nothing in this Declaration may be interpreted as implying for any state, group or person any right to engage in any activity or to perform any act aimed at the destruction of any of the rights and freedoms set forth herein.

PART TWO

THE QUEST FOR
UNIVERSAL MORAL
STANDARDS IN THE WEST

3

ARISTOTLE AND AQUINAS

■

HAVING A CHILD VIA CLONING

Francis and Maureen tried desperately for the three years they have been married to have a child, but to no avail. For Francis, a teaching tennis professional who had once been a top-ranked tennis player, number one on his university team, singles state champion and all-American, his life-long dream was to raise a son or daughter who would excel in tennis. Maureen was also a star player on her university team as well as a champion swimmer.

After a visit to an infertility clinic, they discovered that Francis was sterile. He was an ardent bicyclist who also spent more than enough time relaxing in a hot tub after workouts, and, apparently, the combination of the two rendered him sterile. A crisis eventually ensued in their marriage. Now that their dream of having their own child was shattered, they decided to look into alternatives.

Maureen suggested that they adopt, but Francis was dead set against the idea. Not only was it costly, but it would entail all sorts of time, effort, and bureaucratic hassle. Most important, the child would not be biologically theirs. A physician friend suggested that Maureen be artificially insemi-nated with the sperm of an anonymous donor, a procedure known as AID. Maureen did not like the idea of having a stranger's sperm injected into her egg, and Francis rejected this since the child would not be "his."

It was then that one of Francis's tennis students, a geneticist who worked at the infertility clinic, suggested that he might want to consider a procedure known as somatic cell nuclear transfer (SNT), otherwise known as cloning. This procedure has not yet been tried with humans, but the geneticist knew of an Italian physician, Severino Antinori, who was actively involved in human reproductive cloning research in Europe. Antinori claimed that within a few years he would successfully produce the first human clone. Hundreds of couples have already volunteered to be subjects for his research. Coincidentally, he was scheduled to be the guest speaker at a conference on reproductive technologies in nearby Chicago. The geneticist could arrange a meeting with Antinori.

Francis and Maureen agreed, and upon meeting Antinori they were impressed as he explained the process of SNT. This would entail extracting an egg from Maureen, enucleating her egg (taking out the nucleus), and replacing it with the nucleus of a cell from the skin of Francis. The result would be an embryo containing the genetic makeup of Francis. If successfully implanted into Maureen's uterus, she would then bear the fetus and eventually give birth to a child who would virtually be genetically identical to Francis. Excited about the prospect, Francis and Maureen signed up on the list of Antinori's research subjects. If successful, Francis would have his biological connection, and Maureen would bear their child. Their marriage would stay intact, and Francis could pass on his own genetic legacy in athletics.

■ ARISTOTLE, TELEOLOGY, AND VIRTUE

Philosophers have inherited a reputation of "having both feet firmly planted in the air." We could never say the same for Aristotle (384–322 BCE). The most gifted of Plato's students in Plato's Academy, he disagreed with his teacher when Plato asserted that the essence of reality lies in some abstract world of Forms or Ideas. Aristotle held, in contrast, that the source of meaning comes from concrete, physical reality. Aristotle was a scientist who studied botany, physics, biology, and astronomy along with politics, psychology, aesthetics, rhetoric, and poetry. His knowledge was so comprehensive that it was said that he knew all there was to know during his time. He later became personal tutor to the son of King Philip the Great of Macedonia, Alexander, who later conquered much of the world. Aristotle no doubt inherited this empirical interest from his father, who happened to be Philip's personal physician. In any case, Aristotle's rift with Plato eventually led him to establish his own school called the Lyceum, its primary emphasis being philosophical reflection on the natural sciences.

Aristotle believed that the profound metaphysical truths sought by philosophers could only be reached through serious study of the sciences. He thus taught his students to be *engaged in the world* and to learn from this engagement. This is particularly the case in ethics. For Aristotle, ethics originates from our encounter in the real world and with each other, the world of experience. Ethics is not a matter of abstract theoretical rules and principles that we simply apply to our life experience. Ethics is grounded in our life experience.

Relationship is a key notion here, for the individual does not exist alone as a private, independent entity. The individual exists in *relationship with others.* This explains Aristotle's natural interest in politics. The term "politics" comes from the Greek term *polis* and refers to the city-state, incorporating the idea that each individual is a member of the city-state. The individual is thereby fundamentally relational, a member of a wider community. For Aristotle, any understanding of ethics must be based upon this idea. Therefore, ethics intrinsically deals with how we as individuals relate to each other. Ethics is necessarily concrete and practical. This is why today there is a renewal of interest in Aristotle. Aristotle reminds us that ethics has little to do with merely following abstract principles and rules. It is not so much a question of *doing* the right thing, but rather of *being a good person.* Ethics has to do with cultivating good character.

TELEOLOGY AND HAPPINESS

How do we cultivate good character? We do so by fulfilling our human nature. What does this mean? As a start, Aristotle tells us that all things in nature, including humans, have their own specific end and purpose. The Greek term for this specific end is *telos.* All things in nature have a specific *telos.* This idea that all things are meant to pursue their end is called teleology. Seeds are meant to grow into flowers and trees. Infants are meant to grow into adults. Talents must be nurtured. Bodies need to become healthy bodies. By exercising their specific functions and pursuing their appropriate ends, things in nature thus acquire their own excellence. Excellence is the realization of natural capacities.

What is the *telos* for a human being? Aristotle points out that humans are by nature *rational animals.* We share with other animal species basic instincts and desires such as the instinct for survival and the desire for pleasure. At the same time, Aristotle believed that as humans we also have the unique capacity to reason, to be rational. Because of this, we can exercise some control over our instincts and desires. Our end or purpose is therefore to fulfill our human nature as rational animals by properly exercising our reason. This in turn constitutes human excellence. Moreover, Aristotle asserts that *only in this way can we be genuinely happy.* Let us explore more closely this connection between pursuing our nature and being happy.

The notion of happiness is critical in understanding Aristotle's ethics. In his classic work and first systematic treatise on ethics in the Western world, *Nicomachean Ethics*, Aristotle tells us that we all ultimately seek happiness, the Greek term for which is *eudaimonia*, literally meaning "wellbeing." This happiness is an *intrinsic* good that we seek in that we seek it for its own sake. This intrinsic good is distinct from all other goods or goals that are *instrumental*, that is, goods that we desire in order to attain some other good. Since it is an intrinsic good, happiness is our ultimate goal.

We need to be clearer about this distinction between intrinsic and instrumental good. An intrinsic good is good in and of itself. Happiness is what we seek for its own sake and not in order to attain anything else. On the other hand, steps we take to achieve this ultimate good are instrumental. For instance, why do students take courses in ethics? Is it to fulfill a curricular requirement? Is it to gain more understanding of ethics? Is it because it suits their schedule? Whatever the reasons, they are taking a course in ethics because they have another goal in mind. Therefore, taking this course is an instrumental good. Why do students pursue college degrees? Since it is in order to achieve another goal, obtaining a degree is an instrumental good. The same can be said for all other goods or goals that we pursue, except for happiness.

However, we have different views about what constitutes happiness. What does Aristotle mean by "happiness"? Many of us associate happiness with pleasure. Yet, when we examine the nature of pleasure, especially physical pleasure, we see that it does not endure. In fact, this temporary quality to pleasure makes us desire it even more. If pleasure were permanent, there would be no need to desire it. Because feelings of pleasure are temporary, they cannot be an intrinsic good and cannot be identical to happiness. Happiness, on the other hand, is an enduring condition; it is permanent. Indeed, we can admit that we seek pleasures in order to become happy, so that pleasures are instrumental goals and goods, not intrinsic. In other words, while it may be the case that happiness incorporates feelings of pleasure, feelings of pleasure do not in themselves constitute happiness.

In the same way, happiness is not the same as the possession of material wealth, high social status, good health, or sound reputation. In the case of

Francis and Maureen, nor is happiness identical to having one's own biological child. And as an instrumental good, it certainly does not guarantee happiness. These goods may be pleasurable, but they are not identical to happiness. Happiness is a condition, a state that is in-and-of-itself desirable. As Aristotle states in his *Nicomachean Ethics*:

> An end pursued in itself, we say, is more complete than an end pursued because of something else. . . and hence an end that is always choiceworthy in itself, never because of something else, is unconditionally complete.
> Now happiness more than anything else seems unconditionally complete since we always choose it because of itself, never because of something else.[1]

Thus happiness is neither pleasure nor material nor social gain. It is not something temporary. It is a condition, a state that is enduring. Happiness has to do with inner peace, personal well-being, and, as we shall soon see, balance.

VIRTUE AND THE GOLDEN MEAN

We pursue happiness in our own ways. Yet Aristotle tells us that there are still some necessary conditions for happiness. Just as all things in nature achieve their excellence through pursuing their natural end or *telos*, so it is the case with humans. We can acquire excellence only when we realize our true natures as rational animals, when we properly exercise our reason throughout our lives. Aristotle gives this human excellence another name—virtue. Herein lies the heart of Aristotle's ethics. His prescription for genuine happiness is to live virtuously. Only by living virtuously can we attain happiness. This relationship is described further in the reading from Aristotle at the end of this chapter. Alan Donagan in his article also discusses this important link between happiness and virtue. Furthermore, living virtuously requires that we make a habit of practicing virtue. In this way we cultivate good character. Therefore, only a person of good character can be truly happy. Given this, what then are the ingredients of living virtuously?

Throughout our lives we tend to slip into two extremes: deficit and/or excess. Due to the overpowering force of our desires, we lean toward the extremes of either not enough or too much. Consider sexual desire, one of the most powerful forces in our lives. As natural as it is for us to have sexual desire, such desire can take us over. It can compel us to act in ways that throw reason and caution to the wind. We can be driven to excess in uncontrollable, even harmful, ways. On the other hand, the complete repression of sexual desire is also unhealthy and harmful. Either way, excess and deficit are destructive and lead to the opposite of virtue, namely vice.

Virtue lies in avoiding these extremes. As Aristotle puts it, virtue is the "golden mean" between the extremes and requires that we exercise our reason in balanced fashion. In the case of sexual desire, virtue lies in channeling this desire in reasonable, moderate, and appropriate ways. Virtue is thus all about living reasonably. In the following chart, philosopher W. T. Jones nicely cites various virtues in light of their steering a path between the two extremes of excess and deficit:[2]

Activity	Vice (excess)	Virtue (mean)	Vice (deficit)
Bodily actions (eating, drinking, sex, etc.)	Profligacy	Temperance	"Insensitivity"
Giving money	Prodigality	Liberality	Illiberality
Claiming honors	Vanity	Pride	Humility
Social intercourse	Obsequiousness	Friendliness	Sulkiness
Retribution for wrongdoing	Injustice	Justice	Injustice

Aristotle distinguished two types of virtues: intellectual and moral. Intellectual virtues consist in exercising our reason in two distinct ways. First, we reason in order to live practically in our day-to-day lives. This type of intellectual virtue requires us to live sensibly through practical reason, or what Aristotle terms *phronesis*. This form of intellectual virtue is thereby practical in nature. Second, we reason for the purpose of discovering higher truths. We exercise our reason so that we may contemplate higher, more theoretical truths and principles such as the idea of the Good. This intellectual virtue comes about when we exercise our more philosophical dispositions, and this type of virtue is thereby more philosophical in nature. The exercise of both practical and philosophical wisdom requires us to cultivate a disposition to be virtuous in these ways by making such virtues a habit. In other words, as with moral virtues, making a habit of these virtues will engender proper dispositions, and such dispositions will cultivate good character.

Moral virtues, our main concern in this chapter, have to do with how we behave and how we conduct our lives. Though these two are distinct, they still share the common denominator of balance, or finding the mean between the extremes. Moral virtues are the centerpiece of Aristotle's ethics, and they come about only with habitual practice. Indeed, the Greek word for habit is *ethos*, and so we see the link with ethics.

Again, the aim in Aristotle's ethics is to cultivate good character, and this can happen only by practicing virtue as a habit. Through habitual acts of virtue, we cultivate the condition of virtue in that we become virtuous persons. Repeated actions lead to a condition. An act is thereby distinct from a condition. One act of virtue does not make a virtuous person. We can become virtuous only by making virtue a habit so that acting virtuously becomes second nature. Repeated acts of virtue lead to the condition of virtue, and the condition of virtue is synonymous with good character.

EXAMPLE: THE VIRTUE OF COURAGE

Consider the virtue of courage. The deficit of courage, cowardice, exists when our fears overwhelm us in ways that paralyze us so that we cannot act appropriately in a given situation. Suppose that while walking along the Ocean Drive in Newport, Rhode Island, I spot a swimmer struggling in the sea about 30 meters off a stone jetty. As far as I know, there is no one else around. The swimmer obviously needs help. However, I fear being pulled under by either the current or the swimmer if I were to approach the swimmer. Even though I am a strong swimmer, and though my fears are natural enough, I have allowed them to overcome me, and the swimmer drowns.

On the other hand, suppose that I immediately leap into the water without thinking. I do not consider that the coastline is packed with dangerous, unseen rocks and has a treacherous undercurrent. My head hits a sharp rock, I am stunned, and before I know it, I am being pulled out to sea, weak and unable to save the victim. The swimmer drowns, and I barely make it back to shore. Or let us suppose that I do not hit a rock when I dive into the water, and I manage to rescue the swimmer. Either way, regardless of the consequences, I have acted in a way that was foolish. I have not demonstrated courage.

The virtue of courage requires that we face our fears and, *through reason*, not allow them to overcome us. By acting reasonably, I act in the best way I can to save the victim while putting myself at risk. Courage requires that I avoid either extreme of cowardice or foolishness, deficit or excess. This judicious use of reason is what Aristotle called "practical wisdom," the Greek term being *phronesis*. *Phronesis* requires that we take into consideration all relevant factors before we act in a given situation. Are Francis and Maureen exercising *phronesis* in their efforts to have a child?

The above example is instructive in a number of ways. First, it illustrates how *phronesis* demands the careful exercise of reason according to the particular situation. Second, it reminds us that the practice of virtue must become ingrained. That is, virtue must become a habit. In this way, only the *habit* of exercising virtuous acts will cultivate virtuous character. And here is where happiness comes in. For Aristotle, the genuinely happy person is only one who is virtuous. As he tells, happiness is the "exercise of reason in accordance with virtue." This is because the virtuous person is one who has actualized her potential and purpose, her *telos*. She has done so by living a reasonable and balanced life and has deliberately made a habit of practicing virtue.

WEAKNESSES IN VIRTUE ETHICS

To begin with, Aristotle claims that humans are "rational animals" since they possess the unique capacity to reason. Yet, is it true that the ability to reason is unique to humans? We are now finding out that other animal species are capable of some degree of thinking. Chimpanzees, for example, are able to solve various kinds of simple problems and thus demonstrate that they can reason to some extent. This challenges Aristotle's assumption about the special character of being human. This kind of "speciesism" in Aristotle is all the more evident since he links the Good, that is, the intrinsic good of happiness, to being human. Why preclude other animal species? In which case we ask: What *is* the distinctive quality of being human? If it is not necessarily the ability to reason, then what is it? Passion? Other creatures experience desires, but do they experience passion? Passion is the driving force of creativity. Are creativity, art, and culture distinctive qualities of being human?

A second flaw appears to lie hidden in the notion of the golden mean. Just how morally convincing is the "golden mean"? It strikes us as certainly sensible and practical, but not necessarily moral. Can a wicked person can still exercise sound, practical, common sense in acting out his wickedness? In other words, wicked persons can still act reasonably by way of avoiding extremes. How morally useful is the maxim of avoiding extremes?

STRENGTHS IN VIRTUE ETHICS

Aristotle follows in the tradition of Socrates and Plato when he emphasizes the importance of living virtuously. And he goes one big step further by taking up this theme and systematizing it. His greatest monument to ethics lies in his insistence that good character is what really matters. The most important thing is to be a good person. This is in contrast to modern philosophical theories that emphasize doing the right thing. For Aristotle, as long as we cultivate good character, we will be more prone to doing what is right. Therefore, there is a natural unity between being and doing. However, if we emphasize doing the right thing, following the proper principles, adopting the right rules, we risk diminishing the crucial importance of character.

Let's put it another way. A person can do the right thing in a situation without necessarily being a good person or cultivating good character. A physician may tell the truth to a dying patient in accordance to the rule in the Patient's Bill of Rights that patients are entitled to know the truth about their medical condition. Yet, mechanically following the rule does not at all mean that the physician is exercising the virtue of honesty.

Is Francis exercising virtue by insisting upon his own biological progeny? He feels he has a right to his own child, and he may base this upon the idea of self-determination, known as the principle of autonomy. Yet what about his character? Maureen is willing to consider adoption. There are millions of children who are without parents and need a home. Despite this, Francis wants his own blood link. Is there any virtue in this? Is he being self-centered?

Along these lines, Aristotle assumes that there is a natural link between who we are and what we do. An honest person will most likely tell the truth. By stressing good character, what the contemporary philosopher Bernard Mayo refers to as an "ethics of Being," an "ethics of Doing" will naturally proceed. Therefore, we find a unity of character in Aristotle's ethics in that we place our emphasis upon *being* rather than *doing*. Mayo points this out:

> It is obvious that a man cannot just be; he can only be what he is by doing what he does; his moral qualities are ascribed to him because of his actions, which are said to manifest those qualities. But the point is that an ethics of Being must include this obvious fact, that Being involves Doing; whereas an ethics of Doing ... may easily overlook it.[3]

This unity between being and doing incorporates another type of unity—the unity between the individual and the community. Recall that for Aristotle, each individual is a member of the city-state, the *polis*. Each individual is therefore part of a community. Furthermore, this individual-community is situated within a specific context, a specific time and place. It would therefore be wrong to think of each individual as some private entity. This solipsistic way of viewing persons regards them as atomistic so that individual behavior is viewed as having no effect upon others. Hence, another rich feature in Aristotle's ethics is that it compels us to think of each individual as part of a collective whole, as part of a social and historical context.

■ AQUINAS AND NATURAL LAW

The brilliant medieval theologian and philosopher Thomas Aquinas (1225–1274) assumes a natural relationship between religion and morality. Religious moral teachings assume a universality by appealing to some sort of divine law, the deviation from which comprises what is called "sin." This is especially evident in Aquinas's teaching concerning natural law. According to his theory of natural law, an act is right or wrong contingent upon whether or not that act deviates from what is viewed as "natural." An act is thereby only justified if it is natural and thus conforms to the natural moral law. Consider the opening case of Francis and Maureen. Many interpreters of Aquinas claim that any form of asexual reproduction is "unnatural" in Aquinas's sense. For this reason, it would be morally unjustified for Francis and Maureen to have their child through human reproductive cloning. At the same time, other interpreters of Aquinas may find this issue less problematic, depending upon how one conceives of the notion of "natural." Aquinas would certainly not go to the extreme of, for example, Christian Scientists, who claim that any medical intervention whatsoever is unnatural. As another example, many cultures have viewed homosexuality as immoral on the grounds that that it is "unnatural." For these cultures, heterosexual relationships are natural and intended for the primary purpose of procreation. Homosexuality is thereby often viewed as a breach of this natural law. Oxford University law professor John Finnis, who specializes in Aquinas and natural law theory, argues that homosexuality undermines the "natural" state of heterosexual marriage and that this, in turn, threatens the stability of the family. According to Finnis, homosexuality is not oriented toward procreation, which is a natural aim in marital expression of mutual love.[4] On the other hand, University of Guelph philosopher Michael Ruse points out the arbitrary quality of the notion of "natural," in which case the morality of homosexuality cannot rest upon biological grounds of what is natural. According to Ruse, if anything, since homosexuality may aesthetically offend people, for these people it is a perversion. But this does not make it immoral.[5]

Even though the idea of natural law did not originate with Aquinas, his interpretation of it became the authoritative posture in Roman Catholic moral teachings for well over three hundred years. His influence upon Protestant theologians has also been far-reaching. For instance, contemporary Protestant theologians such as Stanley Hauerwas and James Gustaf-son owe much to Aquinas's work. Nevertheless, the idea of natural law dates back to early Greek and Roman philosophers such as the Stoics's Epictetus (ca. 50–130) and Marcus Aurelius (121–180) who believed in an innate purpose to nature, one that we need to live in harmony with. They made a virtue of accepting nature's laws, laws that are universal and that change with neither time nor place. Moreover, Cicero (106–43 BCE) noted that what especially distinguishes us from animals is our capacity to dis-cern this universal purpose, this Law, through the "gift of reason." As Ci-cero states, "For those creatures who have received the gift of reason (*ratio*) from Nature have also received right reason (*recta ratio*) and therefore they have also received the gift of Law (*lex*), which is right reason applied to command and prohibition."[6]

We have seen that Aristotle also has a sort of natural law theory with his concept of *telos*, when he tells us that all things in nature have a chief purpose and design, and we need to act in ways that are in harmony with this end. He believed in an ultimate force, or principle, behind the order and perfection that is evident throughout all of nature, and he called this ultimate source the First Principle.

These ideas undergo significant modification in the hands of Thomas Aquinas. Alan Donagan discusses some of these in his Aquinas Lecture. He describes how Aquinas transformed some of Aristotle's ideas, particularly his idea of teleology and happiness. Aquinas was profoundly influenced by the "Philosopher," Aristotle, and his teleology. But whereas Aristotle designated the ultimate source of this natural order to a First Principle, a philosophical idea, Aquinas assigned this role to God, the Christian view of God as creator. After all, Aquinas, a Dominican monk, was first and fore-most a devout Christian. The personal creator God is for him the divine architect. Therefore, following the natural law is following the will of God. Under this theological mantle, the law of nature now assumes a more im-perative tone.

NATURAL LAW AND NATURAL INCLINATIONS

Aquinas asserts that we ourselves can rationally intuit this natural law (*lex naturalis*). That is, as asserted above by Cicero, it lies in our nature as ra-tional creatures to have this innate capacity. As Aquinas states:

> [Each human being] has a share of the Eternal Reason, whereby it has a natural inclination to its proper act and end: and this partici-pation of the eternal law in the rational creature is called the natu-ral law.[7]

This is a key passage. First of all, note the "natural inclination" that we have to our own "proper end." This means that we have the innate capacity to understand natural law because we possess natural inclinations in such a way that we inherently know our true ends. What Aquinas further asserts is that on account of this natural instinct, we possess an inherent moral sense of what is right and wrong. He refers to this innate sense as *synderesis*, a term that designates an instinctual "spark," a sense of right as being that toward which we naturally strive, and wrong as being that which we naturally seek to avoid. While we naturally and instinctively pursue the good, we also naturally avoid that which is not good, that which is harmful. As he goes on to state in his *Summa Theologica*:

> *the first principle for the practical reason is based on the meaning of good, namely that* it is what all things seek after. *And so this is the first command of law, "that good is to be sought and done, evil to be avoided."* All other commands of natural law are based on this.[8] [emphasis added]

Here again, we find a key statement in which Aquinas does two things. Recall that in Aristotle's version of the natural law, he claimed that all things pursue their end, called *telos*. In the above statement, Aquinas goes one step further. Not only does he take up Aristotle's teleology, but he also designates that this end to which all things strive is essentially good. The proper end we naturally pursue is good. At the same time, we naturally avoid the opposite of what is good. We can call this Aquinas's first-order principle.[9]

His second move follows naturally in view of our nature as rational creatures. Namely, all other rules regarding natural law follow from the above first principle. We can call these inferred rules Aquinas's second-order principles. Subsequently, we can also arrive at even more specific third-order or fourth-order rules. All of this hinges upon our ability as rational beings to think deductively. Just what are these more specific rules of natural law? As we said, the fundamental, first-order principle is that we are naturally inclined to seek the good and to avoid evil. From this natural inclination, Aquinas deduces six inclinations that we have as humans. Philosopher James Fieser nicely summarizes them as follows:

- to preserve our lives
- to reproduce through sexual union between man and woman
- to educate our children

- to think rationally
- to know God
- to engage with others socially [10]

Consider the natural inclination, according to Aquinas, of reproducing through heterosexual intercourse. This is an inclination that is deduced from *synderesis*. That is, our natural sexual desires are naturally aimed at what is our proper end or good. And what constitutes this proper end is the continuation of our progeny. Thus, the natural desire for heterosexual intercourse aims for this proper end. From this natural inclination of heterosexual reproduction, we deduce the critical natural law: We ought to engage in heterosexual intercourse within legitimate contexts (i.e., marriage) for the purpose of having children. The syllogistic reasoning is evident:

> *Major premise:* All acts that aim for our proper and good end are acts that we should do.
> *Minor premise:* Acts of heterosexual reproduction are acts that aim for our proper and good end.
> *Conclusion:* Therefore, we should engage in acts of heterosexual reproduction.

But the reasoning does not stop there. Otherwise, we would all feel justified in randomly going out and having sex with any person as long as the person is of the opposite sex. This kind of behavior would be harmful to others and to society in general. Therefore, our natural intuition leads us to this reasoning:

> *Major premise:* All acts that harm our proper and good end are acts that we should not do.
> *Minor premise:* Acts of heterosexual reproduction outside of the legitimate contexts (i.e., outside of marriage) are acts that harm our proper and good end.
> *Conclusion:* Therefore, we should not engage in acts of heterosexual reproduction outside of the legitimate contexts.

Therefore, as a second-order natural law rule, we ought to only engage in heterosexual reproduction within the confines of marriage. The logical construct behind Aquinas's natural law formulations is evident. In this

way, Aquinas proposes six second-order natural rules that have been deduced from our six natural inclinations:

- We should act in ways that preserve human life.

- We should engage in heterosexual reproduction within legitimate contexts.

- We should educate our children.

- We should cultivate our reasoning and critical thinking.

- We should worship God.

- We should cultivate social harmony.[11]

All other specific rules of natural law follow from these. In any case, according to Aquinas, God implants in us this innate spark of moral consciousness, this *synderesis*. God, the creator and architect of the universe,
therefore endows us with an innate sense of what is right and what is
wrong. God endows us with an innate knowledge of natural law.

NATURAL LAW AND GESTATION

To show the far-reaching effect of Aquinas's natural law theory in Roman
Catholic moral thought, note the official Catholic positions regarding
artificial means of contraception and abortion. The Catholic Church condemns these practices on the grounds that they violate natural law and
specific rules of natural law that we should act in ways that preserve life.
Since, according to Catholic teachings, life begins around the time of conception and since there is the natural law that requires us to acts in ways
that preserve life, any intervention in fetal life or in gestation that interferes with life is immoral. Abortion as the deliberate destruction of fetal
life and prohibition of birth is therefore wrong. Artificial means of birth
control are also wrong because they are the intentional interference with
the natural process of gestation.

What about artificial insemination either with the husband's sperm
(AIH) or with the sperm of an anonymous donor (AID)? The official Catholic position considers these to be problematic. Why is this the case since
these techniques are performed in order to bring about life, not to end it?
Remember that another natural law teaching is that intercourse must be
heterosexual and within the legitimate parameters of marriage. The official
Catholic position further stipulates that this heterosexual intercourse must
be via natural means. Artificial intervention such as in artificial insemina-

tion is thereby illicit, even if the husband's sperm is used. Needless to say, this specific natural law rule prohibits any form of asexual reproduction, especially human reproductive cloning.

In all of this, we need to be careful. Not all scholars of Aquinas and his natural law theory accept the official Catholic interpretation. Furthermore, we need to avoid the impression that interpretations of Aquinas's theory necessarily lead to the conservative posture as apparently reflected in the official Catholic stance.[12] For example, University of Leuven's prominent moral theologian Louis Janssens's views on conjugal and sexual morality challenged official, mainstream positions and laid some of the groundwork for insights regarding marriage that came out of Vatican II. Nonetheless, within the development of Catholic moral theology, natural law became interpreted in more static ways so that transgressions of natural law were viewed in terms of concrete actions apart from their contexts. Thus, any act interfering with the process of gestation was viewed *in itself* as wrong. Yet, as Catholic moral theologian Franz Bockle reminds us, this view of natural law becomes rigid, inflexible, and extraneous to the human person, and is not at all what Aquinas intended. By disregarding the force of reason within the person, this view becomes too legalistic and violates the spirit of Aquinas's teaching that, according to Bockle,

> the natural moral law is accordingly nothing more than the intrinsic, structural law of reason controlling human actions, whereby reason subordinates its self-determination and self-assessment to the demands of unlimited good. In this self-determination by reason and free will subject to the demands of good lies the imago Dei of the person and thus the basis of dignity.[13]

Along these lines, not all Catholic theologians agree with the official Catholic position regarding *in vitro fertilization* (IVF). Although many would affirm Pope John Paul II's (Karol Wojtyla) more holistic view of sexuality in that it is not solely relegated to biological features, many also feel that Wojtyla's view does not go far enough. For example, Bockle argues that the Pope's position still forces an unnecessary link between a couple's mutual expression of love and their conjugal act, thus imposing upon this link a "procreative value." Such a position thereby rules out the legitimacy of any medical intervention such as IVF.[14]

Through his extensive analysis of Catholic views regarding conjugal morality, moral theologian Joseph Selling asserts that even though Catholic moral teachings have been more or less associated with the official position, this dominant position has not been universally operative. Various other perspectives have come into tension with this official view especially within the past century. He claims that four distinct models of conjugal morality have evolved in Catholic thought: the natural, unitive/procreative, intimacy, and personalist models.[15] While there is no need here to go into detail regarding these models, the aim is to impress upon the reader that the so-called official position in Catholic moral teachings continues to be challenged by Catholic moral theologians. For instance, according to Selling, the first *"natural model* of conjugal life (and human sexual expression) presumes that there is a pre-determined blueprint that dictates what is to be considered 'natural,' 'normal,' or in general 'morally acceptable.'"[16] Selling argues that this model does not genuinely represent Catholic Christian teachings. Both Selling and Bockle tend to place more emphasis upon the personalist model of marriage and sexual morality, a view that continues to gain further support in Catholic theology. Yet whether the models are personalist, intimacy, or unitive/procreative, they all work to counter a rigid determination of natural law as applied to conjugal morality. This illustrates all the more the tension within Catholic moral teachings when it comes to various issues, particularly more recent controversial ones such as human cloning and same-sex marriages.

What's Wrong with Human Cloning? There are two types of human cloning. The first is human embryonic cloning, also called therapeutic cloning. This is the cloning of a human embryo for purposes of research with the embryo. The method behind this is somatic cell nuclear transfer (SNT). This entails the removal of the nucleus of a somatic cell and implanting that same nucleus (in vitro) into an enucleated cell from an embryo. Hopefully, under proper conditions, this new cell will develop into an embryo. The primary intention here is to extract the embryonic stem cells (ES cells) in order to study these stem cells in light of the potential for these cells to regenerate into any tissue type in the human body. This kind of research, part of what is called regenerative medicine, carries the potential for the alleviation of numerous degenerative disorders and diseases such as Parkinson's, Alzheimer's, and heart diseases.

Despite this potential, however, the Catholic Church is officially opposed to this type of research. The principal reason lies in the fact that these stem cells can only be extracted by destroying the embryo, or more technically the pre-embryo, or blastocyst. Because the official Catholic belief, along with that of many other Christian and religious denominations, is that human life begins in and around the time of conception, this manipulation of the blastocyst constitutes an unwarranted destruction of life. In short, this violates the natural law of the preservation of human life and the avoidance of any unnecessary harm to human life. This type of cloning remains a thorny issue among all who adhere to this natural law belief. There are currently attempts by scientists to skirt this difficult issue by extracting adult stem cells from other body parts and thus not deliberately induce harm to the embryo.[17]

When we examine human reproductive cloning, the issue becomes even more volatile. Human reproductive cloning is precisely what Francis and Maureen are considering in order to have their own biological child. It means applying the technique of SNT so that an embryo is formed, and that embryo is then implanted into a woman's uterus, with the intention of producing a full human being. According to many natural law theorists, not only does this entail the initial manipulation of human life (the embryo), but it also violates the natural law that requires that we reproduce only through natural, heterosexual means. For many critics, this distorts the natural process of human procreation. Theologian Gilbert Mileander claims that with reproductive cloning, instead of procreating another human being, we "manufacture" another human being and view that human being as a product and not a gift.[18]

Although human reproductive cloning has not yet been achieved, scientists (like Severino Antinori) in privately funded research centers are competing with each other in order to produce the first human through SNT. In the United States there continues to be a federal ban against government funding for both types of cloning. Yet this ban leaves the door open for private companies to pursue this research without federal monitoring. Many commentators believe that it is simply a matter of time before we see the first human clone. This issue will undoubtedly remain one of the thorniest issues of this century. And the most vocal opposition comes from those who adhere to a natural law perspective.

NATURAL LAW AND SAME-SEX MARRIAGES

On April 25, 2000, after a barrage of public demonstrations, debates, and political wrangling, Vermont legislators passed the Civil Unions Bill. The bill allows gay and lesbian partners to enter into so-called civil unions that would be equivalent to legal marriage. Gay couples in these unions would therefore have the same legal rights and protections as all married couples. This occurred four months after the state's supreme court ruled in *Baker v. Vermont* that homosexual couples are entitled to the same legal rights as married heterosexual couples. All of this represents a land-mark for gay and lesbian rights. After similar struggles in Hawaii and Alaska, Vermont is the first state to officially grant such legal rights and recognition.

This victory for gay rights activists is not without intense opposition. Conservative religious groups continue to staunchly oppose same-sex mar-riage. Their key argument is that same-sex marriage defiles the institution of marriage, an institution that joins together a man and a woman. There-fore same-sex unions are unnatural. Furthermore, critics argue that same-sex marriage would lead to the erosion of a stable social order, a society that rests upon family stability. These critics cite statistics that between 6 and 14 million children in the United States have gay or lesbian parents.[19] Numerous antigay groups such as Christian Coalition and Focus on the Family as well as the official Catholic and Mormon churches will no doubt continue to speak their voice. Moreover, these groups have far-ranging po-litical clout in that Congress passed the Defense of Marriage Act (DOMA) shortly after Clinton took office. This act legally defines, under federal law, marriage as the legal union between a man and a woman. This means that if a state like Vermont officially legalizes same-sex marriage, that same union is not legally recognized across state lines.[20] Even though proponents of same-sex marriage tasted their initial victory in Vermont, the battle is far from over. With outspoken religious groups raising the flag of natural law in their defense, there continues to be a strong current of antigay sen-timent throughout the country.

WEAKNESSES IN NATURAL LAW

Aquinas's list of six natural inclinations appears somewhat contrived in that it supports Aquinas's own moral agenda. The list is restricted. For in-stance, where is the natural inclination for sexual pleasure in and of itself, apart from any need or desire to procreate? What about the natural incli-nation to form intimate friendships? Or the natural inclination to express oneself creatively? In addition, why does Aquinas regard certain inclina-tions as "natural"? Why is the inclination for reasoning and critical think-ing natural? Would this not be more of a matter of socialization and accul-turation? And why is the desire to know God a natural inclination?

Another flaw is that Aquinas fashions his idea of natural law, an idea that has normative force, based upon what he considers to be the facts of our human natural inclinations. In other words, we learn what we *should do* based upon what *is* the case, our natural inclinations. Is it justified to make claims about what we ought to do based upon what is? Is it reasonable to leap from *is* to *ought?* Influenced in this regard by the Scottish philosopher David Hume (1711–1776), British philosopher Jeremy Bentham (1748–1832) argues that this tendency to leap from *is* to *ought,* particularly common among natural law theorists, is unwarranted. For instance, *if* we do have a natural inclination to reproduce through heterosexual intercourse, then why is it morally imperative that we do so? Using this same logic, *if* we do have a natural inclination to enjoy sex, then we *should* do so. This, of course, is contrary to Aquinas's moral teaching since he already precludes this as a natural inclination, evidence again of his moral agenda.

To illustrate further, consider the British philosopher Thomas Hobbes's (1588–1679) view of human nature. He performed the most radical revision of Aquinas's natural law theory. Whereas Aquinas believed that we have a natural inclination to seek the good, Hobbes argued that we are naturally self-absorbed and self-centered. According to Hobbes, we possess an innate desire for self-preservation at all costs. For this reason, we have to form a social contract. Otherwise we would kill each other off. He states that *"homo est lupus hominis,"* "man is a wolf to man." Now *if* it is true that we are creatures who are naturally self-seeking, does that therefore mean that we *ought* to be self-seeking? Hardly. What all this means is that inferring what we ought to do based upon what are believed to be the facts needs to be carefully formulated and logically supported.

STRENGTHS IN NATURAL LAW

At first glance, Aquinas's notion of *synderesis* appears vague. The idea that we should pursue our proper end, entailing that we seek the good and avoid evil seems very general to the point of appearing useless. However, Aquinas does have something specific in mind. His concept of *synderesis* essentially means that seeking the good and avoiding evil lies in our natures. This is insightful, for it means that any inclinations we have that are "evil" and that will induce harm to ourselves and to others are not natural to us. By our very natures, we pursue the good. If we behave otherwise, then other factors such as socialization account for such behavior. In stark contrast to Hobbes, Aquinas has a positive view of human nature. Furthermore, in Donagan's Aquinas Lecture, we read that Aquinas transforms Aristotle in a way that exceeds Aristotle's view of happiness and thus lays the ground for even more optimism.

■ NOTES

1. Aristotle, *Nicomachean Ethics,* trans. Terence Irwin (Indianapolis, IN: Hackett, 1985), 1097a32–1097b2, p. 14.

2. W. T. Jones, *The Classical Mind* (New York: Harcourt, Brace & World, 1952, 1969), p. 268; cited in Christina Sommers and Fred Sommers, eds., *Vice and Virtue in Everyday Life,* 4th ed. (Fort Worth, TX: Harcourt Brace, 1997), p. 294.

3. Bernard Mayo, "Virtue or Duty?" in Sommers and Sommers, eds., *Vice and Virtue in Everyday Life,* p. 312.

4. John M. Finnis, "Law, Morality, and 'Sexual Orientation,'" *Notre Dame Law Review* 69 (1994): 1049–76.

5. Michael Ruse, "Is Homosexuality Bad Sexuality?" in Michael Ruse, *Homosexuality: A Philosophical Inquiry* (Oxford: Blackwell, 1988), pp. 179–92.

6. Cicero, *The Republic and the Laws,* trans. Clinton Walker Keyes (Cambridge, MA: Loeb Classical Library, 1938), I.x.33.

7. Aquinas, *Summa Theologica,* 1a2ae, 90.2, cited in James Fieser, *Moral Philosophy through the Ages* (Mountain View, CA: Mayfield, 2001), p. 58.

8. Aquinas, *Summa Theologica,* 1a2ae, 94.2, cited in Fieser, p. 58.

9. See the analysis in Fieser, pp. 58ff.

10. Fieser, p. 60.

11. Fieser, p. 60.

12. Reviewers' comments were especially helpful in pointing this out.

13. Franz Bockle, "Nature as the Basis of Morality," in Joseph A. Selling, ed., *Personalist Morals* (Leuven, Belgium: Leuven University Press, 1988), p. 48.

14. Ibid., p. 55ff.

15. See Joseph A. Selling, "Evolution and Continuity in Conjugal Morality," in *Personalist Morals,* pp. 243–64.

16. Ibid., p. 254.

17. There is a full-fledged effort by researchers in Pittsburgh along these lines. The collaboration of Pittsburgh's scientists, researchers, clinicians, business partners, and academicians may well establish Pittsburgh as a world center in regenerative medicine.

18. See Gilbert Meilaender, "Begetting and Cloning," in Michael C. Brannigan, *Ethical Issues in Human Cloning* (New York: Seven Bridges Press, 2001), pp. 77–81.

19. David Goodman, "A More Civil Union," *Mother Jones* (July/August 2000), p. 51.

20. Ibid., p. 78.

NICHOMACHEAN ETHICS

ARISTOTLE

BOOK I

ALL HUMAN ACTIVITIES AIM AT SOME GOOD

Chapter 1.   Every art and every scientific inquiry, and similarly every action and purpose, may be said to aim at some good. Hence the good has been well defined as that at which all things aim. But it is clear that there is a difference in ends; for the ends are sometimes activities, and sometimes results beyond the mere activities. Where there are ends beyond the action, the results are naturally superior to the action.

As there are various actions, arts, and sciences, it follows that the ends are also various. Thus health is the end of the medical art, a ship of shipbuilding, victory of strategy, and wealth of economics. It often happens that a number of such arts or sciences combine for a single enterprise, as the art of making bridles and all such other arts as furnish the implements of horsemanship combine for horsemanship, and horsemanship and every military action for strategy; and in the same way, other arts or sciences combine for others. In all these cases, the ends of the master arts or sciences, whatever they may be, are more desirable than those of the subordinate arts or sciences, as it is for the sake of the former that the latter are pursued. It makes no difference to the argument whether the activities themselves are the ends of the action, or something beyond the activities, as in the above-mentioned sciences.

If it is true that in the sphere of action there is some end which we wish for its own sake, and for the sake of which we wish everything else, and if we do not desire everything for the sake of something else (for, if that is so, the process will go on *ad infinitum,* and our desire will be idle and futile), clearly this end will be good and the supreme good. Does it not follow then that the knowledge of this good is of great importance for the conduct of life? Like archers who have a mark at which to aim, shall we not have a better chance of attaining what we want? If this is so, we must endeavor to comprehend, at least in outline, what this good is, and what science or faculty makes it its object.

It would seem that this is the most authoritative science. Such a kind is evidently the political, for it is that which determines what sciences are necessary in states, and what kinds should be studied, and how far they should be studied by each class of inhabitant. We see too that even the faculties held in highest esteem, such as strategy, economics, and rhetoric, are subordinate to it. Then since politics makes use of the other sciences and also rules what people may do and what they may not do, it follows that its end will comprehend the ends of the other sciences, and will therefore be the good of mankind. For even if the good of an individual is identical with the good of a state, yet the good of the state is evidently greater and more perfect to attain or to preserve. For though the good of an individual by himself is something worth working for, to ensure the good of a nation or a state is nobler and more divine.

These then are the objects at which the present inquiry aims, and it is in a sense a political inquiry. . . .

THE SCIENCE OF THE GOOD FOR MAN IS POLITICS

Chapter 2. As every science and undertaking aims at some good, what is in our view the good at which political science aims, and what is the highest of all practical goods? As to its name there is, I may say, a general agreement. The masses and the cultured classes agree in calling it happiness, and conceive that "to live well" or "to do well" is the same thing as "to be happy." But as to what happiness is they do not agree, nor do the masses give the same account of it as the philosophers. The former take it to be something visible and palpable, such as pleasure, wealth, or honor; different people, however, give different definitions of it, and often even the same man gives different definitions at different times. When he is ill, it is health, when he is poor, it is wealth; if he is conscious of his own ignorance, he envies people who use grand language above his own comprehension. Some philosophers, on the other hand, have held that, besides these various goods, there is an absolute good which is the cause of goodness in them all.* It would perhaps be a waste of time to examine all these opinions; it will be enough to examine such as are most popular or as seem to be more or less reasonable.

Chapter 3. Men's conception of the good or of happiness may be read in the lives they lead. Ordinary or vulgar people conceive it to be a pleasure, and accordingly choose a life of enjoyment. For there are, we may say, three conspic-

_____

*Plato

uous types of life, the sensual, the political, and, thirdly, the life of thought. Now the mass of men present an absolutely slavish appearance, choosing the life of brute beasts, but they have ground for so doing because so many persons in authority share the tastes of Sardanapalus.[†] Cultivated and energetic people, on the other hand, identify happiness with honor, as honor is the general end of political life. But this seems too superficial an idea for our present purpose; for honor depends more upon the people who pay it than upon the person to whom it is paid, and the good we feel is something which is proper to a man himself and cannot be easily taken away from him. Men too appear to seek honor in order to be assured of their own goodness. Accordingly, they seek it at the hands of the sage and of those who know them well, and they seek it on the ground of their virtue; clearly then, in their judgment at any rate, virtue is better than honor. Perhaps then we might look on virtue rather than honor as the end of political life. Yet even this idea appears not quite complete; for a man may possess virtue and yet be asleep or inactive throughout life, and not only so, but he may experience the greatest calamities and misfortunes. Yet no one would call such a life a life of happiness, unless he were maintaining a paradox. But we need not dwell further on this subject, since it is sufficiently discussed in popular philosophical treatises. The third life is the life of thought, which we will discuss later.

The life of money making is a life of constraint; and wealth is obviously not the good of which we are in quest; for it is useful merely as a means to something else. It would be more reasonable to take the things mentioned before— sensual pleasure, honor, and virtue—as ends than wealth, since they are things desired on their own account. Yet these too are evidently not ends, although much argument has been employed to show that they are. . . .

CHARACTERISTICS OF THE GOOD

Chapter 5. But leaving this subject for the present, let us revert to the good of which we are in quest and consider what it may be. For it seems different in different activities or arts; it is one thing in medicine, another in strategy, and so on. What is the good in each of these instances? It is presumably that for the sake of which all else is done. In medicine this is health, in strategy victory, in architecture a house, and so on. In every activity and undertaking it is the end, since it is for the sake of the end that all people do whatever else they do. If then there is an end for all our activity, this will be the good to be accomplished; and if there are several such ends, it will be these.

Our argument has arrived by a different path at the same point as before; but we must endeavor to make it still plainer. Since there are more ends than one, and some of these ends—for example, wealth, flutes, and instruments

---

[†]A half-legendary ruler whose name to the Greeks stood for extreme mental luxury and extravagance.

generally—we desire as means to something else, it is evident that not all are final ends. But the highest good is clearly something final. Hence if there is only one final end, this will be the object of which we are in search; and if there are more than one, it will be the most final. We call that which is sought after for its own sake more final than that which is sought after as a means to something else; we call that which is never desired as a means to something else more final than things that are desired both for themselves and as means to something else. Therefore, we call absolutely final that which is always desired for itself and never as a means to something else. Now happiness more than anything else answers to this description. For happiness we always desire for its own sake and never as a means to something else, whereas honor, pleasure, intelligence, and every virtue we desire partly for their own sakes (for we should desire them independently of what might result from them), but partly also as means to happiness, because we suppose they will prove instruments of happiness. Happiness, on the other hand, nobody desires for the sake of these things, nor indeed as a means to anything else at all.

If we start from the point of view of self-sufficiency, we reach the same conclusion; for we assume that the final good is self-sufficient. By self-sufficiency we do not mean that a person leads a solitary life all by himself, but that he has parents, children, wife and friends and fellow citizens in general, as man is naturally a social being. Yet here it is necessary to set some limit; for if the circle must be extended to include ancestors, descendants, and friends' friends, it will go on indefinitely. Leaving this point, however, for future investigation, we call the self-sufficient that which, taken even by itself, makes life desirable and wanting nothing at all; and this is what we mean by happiness.

Again, we think happiness the most desirable of all things, and that not merely as one good thing among others. If it were only that, the addition of the smallest more good would increase its desirableness; for the addition would make an increase of goods, and the greater of two goods is always the more desirable. Happiness is something final and self-sufficient and the end of all action.

Chapter 6.   Perhaps, however, it seems a commonplace to say that happiness is the supreme good; what is wanted is to define its nature a little more clearly. The best way of arriving at such a definition will probably be to ascertain the function of man. For, as with a flute player, a sculptor, or any artist, or in fact anybody who has a special function or activity, his goodness and excellence seem to lie in his function, so it would seem, to be with man, if indeed he has a special function. Can it be said that, while a carpenter and a cobbler have special functions and activities, man, unlike them, is naturally functionless? Or, as the eye, the hand, the foot, and similarly each part of the body has a special function, so may man be regarded as having a special function apart from all these? What, then, can this function be? It is not life; for life is apparently something that man shares with plants; and we are looking for something peculiar to him. We must exclude therefore the life of nutrition and growth. There is next what may be called the life of sensation. But this too, apparently, is shared by man with horses, cattle, and all other animals. There remains what I may call the active life of the rational part of man's being. Now this rational part is twofold; one part is rational in the sense of being obedient to reason, and the other in the sense of possessing and exercising reason and intelligence. The active life too may be conceived of in two ways, either as a state of character, or as an activity; but we mean by it the life of activity, as this seems to be the truer form of the conception.

The function of man then is activity of soul in accordance with reason, or not apart from reason. Now, the function of a man of a certain kind, and of a man who is good of that kind—for example, of a harpist and a good harpist—are in our view the same in kind. This is true of all people of all kinds without exception, the superior excellence being only an addition to the function; for it is the function of a harpist to play the harp, and of a good harpist to play the harp well. This being so, if we define the function of man as a kind of life, and this life as an activity of the soul or a course of action in accordance with reason, and if the function of a good man is such activity of a good and noble kind, and if everything is well done when it is done in accordance with its proper excellence, it follows that the good of man is activity of soul in accordance with virtue, or, if there are more virtues than one, in accordance with the best and most complete virtue. But we must add the words "in a complete life." For as one swallow or one day does not make a spring, so one day or a short time does not make a man blessed or happy. . . .

Inasmuch as happiness is an activity of soul in accordance with perfect virtue, we must now consider virtue, as this will perhaps be the best way of studying happiness. . . . Clearly it is human virtue we have to consider; for the good of which we are in search is, as we said, human good, and the happiness, human happiness. By human virtue or excellence we mean not that of the body, but that of the soul, and by happiness we mean an activity of the soul. . . .

BOOK II

Moral virtues can best be acquired by practice and habit. They imply a right attitude toward pleasures and pains. A good man deliberately chooses to do what is noble and right for its own sake. What is right in matters of moral conduct is usually a mean between two extremes.

Chapter 1. Virtue then is twofold, partly intellectual and partly moral, and intellectual virtue is originated and fostered mainly by teaching; it demands therefore experience and time. Moral virtue on the other hand is the outcome of habit, and accordingly its name, *ethike*, is derived by a slight variation from *ethos,* habit. From this fact it is clear that moral virtue is not implanted in us by nature; for nothing that exists by nature can be transformed by habit. Thus a stone, that naturally tends to fall downwards, cannot be habituated or trained to rise upwards, even if we tried to train it by throwing it up ten thousand times. Nor again can fire be trained to sink downwards, nor anything else that follows one natural law be habituated or trained to follow another. It is neither by nature then nor in defiance of nature that virtues grow in us. Nature gives us the capacity to receive them, and that capacity is perfected by habit.

Again, if we take the various natural powers which belong to us, we first possess the proper faculties and afterwards display the activities. It is obviously so with the senses. Not by seeing frequently or hearing frequently do we acquire the sense of seeing or hearing; on the contrary, because we have the senses we make use of them; we do not get them by making use of them. But the virtues we get by first practicing them, as we do in the arts. For it is by doing what we ought to do when we study the arts that we learn the arts themselves; we become builders by building and harpists by playing the harp. Similarly, it is by doing just acts that we become just, by doing temperate acts that we become temperate, by doing brave acts that we become brave. The experience of states confirms this statement, for it is by training in good habits that lawmakers make the citizens good. This is the object all lawmakers have at heart; if they do not succeed in it, they fail of their purpose; and it makes the distinction between a good constitution and a bad one.

Again, the causes and means by which any virtue is produced and destroyed are the same; and equally so in any part. For it is by playing the harp that both good and bad harpists are produced; and the case of builders and others is similar, for it is by building well that they become good builders and by building badly that they become bad builders. If it were not so, there would be no need of anybody to teach them; they would all be born good or bad in their several crafts. The case of the virtues is the same. It is by our actions in dealings between man and man that we become either just or unjust. It is by our actions in the face of danger and by our training ourselves to fear or to courage that we become either cowardly or courageous. It is much the same with our appetites and angry passions. People become temperate and gentle, others licentious and passionate, by behaving in one or the other way in particular circumstances. In a word, moral states are the results of activities like the states themselves. It is our duty therefore to keep a certain character in our activities, since our moral states depend on the differences in our activities. So the difference between one and another training in habits in our childhood is not a light matter, but important, or rather, all-important.

Chapter 2.   Our present study is not, like other studies, purely theoretical in intention; for the object of our inquiry is not to know what virtue is but how to become good, and that is the sole benefit of it. We must, therefore, consider the right way of performing actions, for it is acts, as we have said, that determine the character of the resulting moral states.

That we should act in accordance with right reason is a common general principle, which may here be taken for granted. The nature of right reason, and its relation to the virtues generally, will be discussed later. But first of all it must be admitted that all reasoning on matters of conduct must be like a sketch in outline; it cannot be scientifically exact. We began by laying down the principle that the kind of reasoning demanded in any subject must be such as the subject matter itself allows; and questions of conduct and expediency no more admit of hard and fast rules than questions of health.

If this is true of general reasoning on ethics, still more true is it that scientific exactitude is impossible in treating of particular ethical cases. They do not fall under any art or law, but the actors themselves have always to take account of circumstances, as much as in medicine or navigation. Still, although such is the nature of our present argument, we must try to make the best of it.

The first point to be observed is that in the matters we are now considering deficiency and excess are both fatal. It is so, we see, in questions of health and strength. (We must judge of what we cannot see by the evidence of what we do see.) Too much or too little gymnastic exercise is fatal to strength. Similarly, too much or too little meat and drink is fatal to health, whereas a suitable amount produces, increases, and sustains it. It is the same with temperance, courage, and other moral virtues. A person who avoids and is afraid of everything and faces nothing becomes a coward; a person who is not afraid of anything but is ready to face everything becomes foolhardy. Similarly, he who enjoys every pleasure and abstains from none is licentious; he who refuses all pleasures, like a boor, is an insensible sort of person. For temperance and courage are destroyed by excess and deficiency but preserved by the mean.

Again, not only are the causes and agencies of production, increase, and destruction in moral states the same, but the field of their activity is the same also. It is so in other more obvious instances, as, for example, strength; for strength is produced by taking a great deal of food and undergoing a great deal of exertion, and it is the strong man who is able to take most food and undergo most exertion. So too with the virtues. By abstaining from pleasures we become temperate, and, when we have become temperate, we are best able to abstain from them. So again with courage; it is by training ourselves to despise and face terrifying things that we become brave, and when we have become brave, we shall be best able to face them.

The pleasure or pain which accompanies actions may be regarded as a test of a person's moral state. He who abstains from physical pleasures and feels pleasure in so doing is temperate; but he who feels pain at so doing is licentious. He who faces dangers with pleasure, or at least without pain, is brave; but he who feels pain at facing them is a coward. For moral virtue is concerned with pleasures and pains. It is pleasure which makes us do what is base, and pain which makes us abstain from doing what is noble. Hence the importance of having a certain training from very early days, as Plato says, so that we may feel pleasure and pain at the right objects; for this is true education. . . .

Chapter 3.   But we may be asked, what we mean by saying that people must become just by doing what is just and temperate by doing what is temperate. For, it will be said, if they do what is just and temperate they are already just and temperate themselves, in the same way as, if they practice grammar and music, they are grammarians and musicians.

But is this true even in the case of the arts? For a person may speak grammatically either by chance or at the suggestion of somebody else; hence he will not be a grammarian unless he not only speaks grammatically but does so in a grammatical manner, that is, because of the grammatical knowledge which he possesses.

There is a point of difference too between the arts and the virtues. The productions of art have their excellence in themselves. It is enough then that, when they are produced, they themselves should possess a certain character. But acts in accordance with virtue are not justly or temperately performed simply because they are in themselves just or temperate. The doer at the time of performing them must satisfy certain conditions; in the first place, he must know what he is doing; secondly, he must deliberately choose to do it and do it for his own sake; and thirdly, he must do it as part of his own firm and immutable character. If it be a question of art, these conditions, except only the condition of knowledge, are not raised; but if it be a question of virtue, mere knowledge is of little or no avail; it is the other conditions, which are the results of frequently performing just and temperate acts, that are not slightly but all-important. Accordingly, deeds are called just and temperate when they are such as a just and temperate person would do; and a just and temperate person is not merely one who does these deeds but one who does them in the spirit of the just and the temperate.

It may fairly be said that a just man becomes just by doing what is just, and a temperate man becomes temperate by doing what is temperate, and if a man did not so act, he would not have much chance of becoming good. But most people, instead of acting, take refuge in theorizing; they imagine that they are philosophers and that philosophy will make them virtuous; in fact, they behave like people who listen attentively to their doctors but never do anything that their doctors, tell them. But a healthy state of the soul will no more be produced by this kind of philosophizing than a healthy state of the body by this kind of medical treatment.

Chapter 4.   We have next to consider the nature of virtue. Now, as the properties of the soul are three, namely, emotions, faculties, and moral states, it follows that virtue must be one of the three. By emotions I mean desire, anger, fear, pride, envy, joy, love, hatred, regret, ambition, pity—in a word, whatever feeling is attended by pleasure or pain. I call those faculties through which we are said to be capable of experiencing these emotions, for instance, capable of getting angry or being pained or feeling pity. And I call those moral states through which we are well or ill disposed in our emotions, ill disposed, for instance, in anger, if our anger be too violent or too feeble, and well disposed, if it be rightly moderate; and similarly in our other emotions.

Now neither the virtues nor the vices are emotions; for we are not called good or bad for our emotions but for our virtues or vices. We are not praised or blamed simply for being angry, but only for being angry in a certain way; but we are praised or blamed for our virtues or vices. Again, whereas we are angry or afraid without deliberate purpose, the virtues are matters of deliberate purpose, or require deliberate purpose. Moreover, we are said to be moved by our emotions, but by our virtues or vices we are not said to be moved but to have a certain disposition.

For these reasons the virtues are not faculties. For we are not called either good or bad, nor are we praised or blamed for having simple capacity for emotion. Also while Nature gives us our faculties, it is not Nature that makes us good or bad; but this point we have already discussed. If then the virtues are neither emotions nor faculties, all that remains is that they must be moral states.

Chapter 5.   The nature of virtue has been now described in kind. But it is not enough to say merely that virtue is a moral state; we must also describe the character of that moral state.

We may assert then that every virtue or excellence puts into good condition that of which it is a virtue or excellence, and enables it to perform its work well. Thus excellence in the eye makes the eye good and its function good, for by excellence in the eye we see well. Similarly, excellence of the horse makes a horse excellent himself and good at racing, at carrying its rider and at facing the enemy. If then this rule is universally true, the virtue or excellence of a man will be such a moral state as makes a man good and able to perform his proper function well. How this will be the case we have already explained, but another way of making it clear will be to study the nature or character of virtue.

Now of everything, whether it be continuous or divisible, it is possible to take a greater, a smaller, or an equal amount, and this either in terms of the thing itself or in relation to ourselves, the equal being a mean between too much and too little. By the mean in terms of the thing itself, I understand that which is equally distinct from both its extremes, which is one and the same for every man. By the mean relatively to ourselves, I understand that which is neither too much nor too little for us; but this is not one nor the same for everybody. Thus if 10 be too much and 2 too little, we take 6 as a mean in terms of the thing itself; for 6 is as much greater than 2 as it is less than 10, and this is a mean in arithmetical proportion. But the mean considered relatively to ourselves may not be ascertained in that way. It does not follow that if 10 pounds of meat is too much and 2 too little for a man to eat, the trainer will order him 6 pounds, since this also may be too much or too little for him who is to take it; it will be too little, for example, for Milo but too much for a beginner in gymnastics. The same with running and wrestling; the right amount will vary with the individual. This being so, the skillful in any art avoids alike excess and deficiency; he seeks and chooses the mean, not the absolute mean, but the mean considered relatively to himself.

Every art then does its work well, if it regards the mean and judges the works it produces by the mean. For this reason we often say of successful works of art that it is impossible to take anything from them or to add anything to them, which implies that excess or deficiency is fatal to excellence but that the mean state ensures it. Good artists too, as we say, have an eye to the mean in their works. Now virtue, like Nature herself, is more accurate and better than any art; virtue, therefore, will aim at the mean. I speak of moral virtue, since it is moral virtue which is concerned with emotions and actions, and it is in these we have excess and deficiency and the mean. Thus it is possible to go too far, or not far enough in fear, pride, desire, anger, pity, and pleasure and pain generally; and the excess and the deficiency are alike wrong; but to feel these emotions at the right times, for the right objects, towards the right persons, for the right motives, and in the right manner, is the mean or the best good, which signifies virtue. Similarly, there may be excess, deficiency, or the mean, in acts. Virtue is concerned with both emotions and actions, wherein excess is an error and deficiency a fault, while the mean is successful and praised, and success and praise are both characteristics of virtue.

It appears then that virtue is a kind of mean because it aims at the mean.

On the other hand, there are many different ways of going wrong; for evil is in its nature infinite, to use the Pythagorean phrase, but good is finite and there is only one possible way of going right. So the former is easy and the latter is difficult; it is easy to miss the mark but difficult to hit it. And so by our reasoning excess and deficiency are characteristics of vice and the mean is a characteristic of virtue.

"For good is simple, evil manifold."

Chapter 6.   Virtue then is a state of deliberate moral purpose, consisting in a mean relative to ourselves, the mean being determined by reason, or as a prudent man would determine it. It is a mean, firstly, as lying between two vices, the vice of excess on the one hand, the vice of deficiency on the other, and, secondly, because, whereas the vices either fall short of or go beyond what is right in emotion and action, virtue discovers and chooses the mean. Accordingly, virtue, if regarded in its essence or theoretical definition, is a mean, though, if regarded from the point of view of what is best and most excellent, it is an extreme.

But not every action or every emotion admits of a mean. There are some whose very name implies wickedness, as, for example, malice, shamelessness, and envy among the emotions, and adultery, theft, and murder among the actions. All these and others like them are marked as intrinsically wicked, not merely the excesses or deficiencies of them. It is never possible then to be right in them; they are always sinful. Right or wrong in such acts as adultery does not depend on our committing it with the right woman, at the right time, or in the right manner; on the contrary, it is wrong to do it at all. It would be equally false to suppose that there can be a mean or an excess or deficiency in unjust, cowardly or licentious conduct; for, if that were so, it would be a mean of excess and deficiency, an excess of excess and a deficiency of deficiency. But as in temperance and courage there can be no excess or deficiency, because the mean there is in a sense an extreme, so too in these other cases there cannot be a mean or an excess or a deficiency, but however the acts are done, they are wrong. For in general an excess or deficiency does not have a mean, nor a mean an excess or deficiency. . . .

Chapter 8. There are then three dispositions, two being vices, namely, excess and deficiency, and one virtue, which is the mean between them; and they are all in a sense mutually opposed. The extremes are opposed both to the mean and to each other, and the mean is opposed to the extremes. For as the equal if compared with the less is greater, but if compared with the greater is less, so the mean state, whether in emotion or action, if compared with deficiency is excessive, but if compared with excess is deficient. Thus the brave man appears foolhardy compared with the coward, but cowardly compared with the foolhardy. Similarly, the temperate man appears licentious compared with the insensible man but insensible compared with the licentious; and the liberal man appears extravagant compared with the stingy man but stingy compared with the spendthrift. The result is that the extremes each denounce the mean as belonging to the other extreme; the coward calls the brave man foolhardy, and the foolhardy man calls him cowardly; and so on in other cases.

But while there is mutual opposition between the extremes and the mean, there is greater opposition between the two extremes than between extreme and the mean; for they are further removed from each other than from the mean, as the great is further from the small and the small from the great than either from the equal. Again, while some extremes show some likeness to the mean, as foolhardiness to courage and extravagance to liberality, there is the greatest possible dissimilarity between extremes. But things furthest removed from each other are called opposites; hence the further things are removed, the greater is the opposition between them.

In some cases it is deficiency and in others excess which is more opposed to the mean. Thus it is not foolhardiness, an excess, but cowardice, a deficiency, which is more opposed to courage, nor is it insensibility, a deficiency, but licentiousness, an excess, which is more opposed to temperance. There are two reasons why this should be so. One lies in the nature of the matter itself; for when one of two extremes is nearer and more like the mean, it is not this extreme but its opposite that we chiefly contrast with the mean. For instance, as foolhardiness seems more like and nearer to courage than cowardice, it is cowardice that we chiefly contrast with courage; for things further removed from the mean seem to be more opposite to it. This reason lies in the nature of the matter itself; there is a second which lies in our own nature. The things to which we ourselves are naturally more inclined we think more opposed to the mean. Thus we are ourselves naturally more inclined to pleasures than to their opposites, and are more prone therefore to self-indulgence than to moderation. Accordingly we speak of those things in which we are more likely to run to great lengths as more opposed to the mean. Hence licentiousness, which is an excess, seems more opposed to temperance than insensibility.

Chapter 9.   We have now sufficiently shown that moral virtue is a mean, and in what sense it is so; that it is a mean as lying between two vices, a vice of excess on the one side and a vice of deficiency on the other; and as aiming at the mean in emotion and action.

That is why it is so hard to be good; for it is always hard to find the mean in anything; it is not everyone but only a man of science who can find the mean or center of a circle. So too anybody can get angry—that is easy—and anybody can give or spend money, but to give it to the right person, to give the right amount of it, at the right time, for the right cause and in the right way, this is not what anybody can do, nor is it easy. That is why goodness is rare and praise worthy and noble. One then who aims at a mean must begin by departing from the extreme that is more contrary to the mean; he must act in the spirit of Calypso's advice,

"Far from this spray and swell hold thou thy ship,"

for of the two extremes one is more wrong than the other. As it is difficult to hit the mean exactly, we should take the second best course, as the saying is, and choose the lesser of two evils. This we shall best do in the way described, that is, steering clear of the evil which is further from the mean. We must also note the weaknesses to which we are ourselves particularly prone, since different natures tend in different ways; and we may ascertain what our tendency is by observing our feelings of pleasure and pain. Then we must drag ourselves away towards the opposite extreme; for by pulling ourselves as far as possible from what is wrong we shall arrive at the mean, as we do when we pull a crooked stick straight.

In all cases we must especially be on our guard against the pleasant, or pleasure, for we are not impartial judges of pleasure. Hence our attitude towards pleasure must be like that of the elders of the people in the *Iliad* towards Helen, and we must constantly apply the words they use; for if we dismiss pleasure as they dismissed Helen, we shall be less likely to go wrong. By action of this kind, to put it summarily, we shall best succeed in hitting the mean.

Undoubtedly this is a difficult task, especially in individual cases. It is not easy to determine the right manner, objects, occasion and duration of anger. Sometimes we praise people who are deficient in anger, and call them gentle, and at other times we praise people who exhibit a fierce temper as high spirited. It is not however a man who deviates a little from goodness, but one who deviates a great deal, whether on the side of excess or of deficiency, that is blamed; for he is sure to call attention to himself. It is not easy to decide in theory how far and to what extent a man may go before he becomes blameworthy, but neither is it easy to define in theory anything else in the region of the senses; such things depend on circumstances, and our judgment of them depends on our perception.

So much then is plain, that the mean is everywhere praiseworthy, but that we ought to aim at one time towards an excess and at another towards a deficiency; for thus we shall most easily hit the mean, or in other words reach excellence.

THE TWO TELEOLOGIES

ALAN DONAGAN

There are at least two different ways in which human beings explain one another's actions. One, the most common, is by treating the action to be explained as behavior with a purpose, and a purpose as an end to be brought about. When we know what somebody proposed to bring about when he acted in a certain fashion, and why he believed that so acting was, in his situation, the way to bring that end about, we can claim so far to understand his action. Philosophy furnishes us with a word for such explanations: the word 'teleological.' Human action is characteristically directed to *telē*, or ends; and a *telos* is an event of a certain kind to be made to happen, or (less accurately, I believe) a state of affairs of a certain kind to be brought about. Sometimes this event is fairly simple, such as at last getting in your first serve in a tennis game, after an ignominious string of failures; sometimes it is highly complex, such as living a happy life.

A second way of explaining human actions, although less common, is nevertheless familiar. You have match point in a tennis game against an opponent to whom you mostly lose, and he makes a nearly impossible return which only you are in a position to see. With much inward grief, you have to call "In!" You are not a moral masochist. Giving calls against yourself in such situations is not one of your purposes in life. And yet we understand your doing it, even if, in your shoes, we should not have. How do we understand it? Perhaps, to begin with, in terms of fairness and sportsmanship. But what lies behind the rules of fairness and sportsmanship? Is it not simply that your opponent is somebody to whom you owe the truth, miserable wretch though he is for bringing that return off? You acted for his sake, not to realize any purpose of your own.

The phrase "for his sake" is inescapably teleological. It signifies that on account of which your action was done. You did what you did, not for any outcome it might have produced, but out of concern for your opponent. You were certainly not concerned to concede him the point. If his return had been in and neither he nor you had seen it, you would not have repined at all. Yet, for his sake, you regarded cheating as out. Your opponent was the end of your action in a way quite different from that in which any purpose you had might have been.

Even so, is not the fundamental sense of 'telos' the first: that of an event to be made to happen? Not for St. Thomas, as we shall see. But that is not immediately evident in his language, as it was to be in the language of his great successor, the blessed John Duns Scotus. Scotus distinguished *finis,* an end (that is *telos*) from what he called *finitum,'* literally an 'ended,' namely, that which stands to an end as that which is brought about stands to what brings it about.

> [A] *finitum* depends for its being upon a *finis* as [essentially] prior [Scotus declared] just to the extent that the *finis* as loved moves an efficient [cause] to confer being on it.

And so, he proceeds,

> a corollary follows, which should not be passed over in silence, namely, that a certain opinion about the *finis* is a *falsa imaginatio.* [That opinion is] that the final cause of a being is the last operation [in causing it], or the object brought about through that operation.[1]

His line of thought, I take it, is this. Sometimes, as in official or productive activity, the end of an action is either the last operation performed (such as the granting of an official permission), or is something produced by that operation (such as a finished product turned off an assembly line); but in neither case do the actions that lead up to the end depend on it as essentially prior to them, for it is prior to them only as something thought by the agent or designer. By contrast, when the end of an action is essentially prior to it, it cannot be either an operation that forms part of it or something produced by it. It can only be a pre-existent thing that is loved by the agent, and for the sake of which he acts. And an ultimate end must be essentially prior to any action of which it is the end.

It is evident that the two kinds of *telos* disclosed by these examples are connected with two different conceptions of morality. Events to be brought about are *telē* of the kind that are recognized in consequentialist conceptions of it, and persons are *tele* of the kind that are recognized in conceptions of it as a limit to be observed in trying to realize our purposes.

Anybody who, like myself, is interested in these two kinds of *telos* will be refreshed by St. Thomas's treatment of the ends of human action in both his moral philosophy and his moral theology. For, unlike most of our contemporaries, he did not embrace one of the two kinds of *telos* and ignore the other. Nobody has reaffirmed more emphatically than he the Aristotelian doctrine that "all men agree in seeking an ultimate end, which is happiness (*beatitudo*)."[2] Nor has anybody confessed more passionately than he the Mosaic and Christian faith that "the end of human life and society is God."[3] And God is not, as some process theologians would have us believe, an event to be brought about.

Unfortunately, I have not enough learning to investigate St. Thomas's teleology of human action thoroughly and systematically. At best, I can lead you on a free ramble through some things he wrote about it in the two of his works with which I am least unfamiliar: the two *Summae*. Even here, when the mountain air makes breathing hard for me, I shall retreat to the valleys of more recent philosophy. However, as you will see, that is not because I think any philosopher to have done better that St. Thomas on the questions I shall consider. My hope is that I may irritate somebody better equipped into providing us with something more systematic.

THE TWO TELEOLOGIES IN ST. THOMAS

St. Thomas's commitment to both of the kinds of teleology I have distinguished is evident in what he had to say about the difference between the relation of intellectual creatures to what he referred to as "the ultimate end of the whole of things" and that of non-intellectual ones. "Only the intellectual creature reaches the very ultimate end of the whole of things through his own operation, which is the knowing and loving of God: whereas other creatures cannot attain the ultimate end except by a participation in its likeness" (*Summa contra Gentiles* III, 111, 1). Here, while the ultimate end of the whole of things is unmistakably God, presumably the operation by which intellectual creatures reach that end is also an end for them. God is indeed the being for whose sake they act, but the operation by which he is attained is an event they aim at bringing about.

Although the cheerful remark I have quoted from the *Summa contra Gentiles* seems clear enough, it must be acknowledged that some philosophers have found it difficult to conceive how any existing being can be an end. For example, Sir David Ross, the great British Aristotle scholar of the first half of our century, wrote, in another connection, the "an end is an object of desire, and an object of desire is something that does not yet exist."[4] If Ross were right, attaining an end could not be anything except bringing it into existence. And so it would be nonsensical to describe God, who exists now and always, as an end to be attained by rational creatures in one way, and by non-rational creatures in another.

Before we dismiss Ross's objection as fatuous, which I think it is, we should acknowledge that St. Thomas himself, when he wrote about the end of human life, as distinct from the end of the whole of things, usually referred to it as something not yet existing which we hope may be brought into existence. For example, in *Summa contra Gentiles* III, 25, 7, he wrote that

> a thing has the greatest desire for its ultimate end. Now, the human intellect has a greater desire, and love, and pleasure, in knowing divine matters than it has in the perfect knowledge of the lowest things, even though it can grasp but little concerning divine things. So, the ultimate end of man is to understand God, in some fashion.

Here the ultimate end of human beings in this life is presented as an object of desire that does not yet exist. And a little later in the same chapter St. Thomas went on to identify it with *felicitas*, the commonest equivalent in the *Summa contra Gentiles* of Aristotle's *eudaimonia*. Apparently, whatever his opinion may have been about the ultimate end of the whole of things, he agreed with Ross that the ultimate end of human beings in this life is to attain a state they have not yet attained.

How are such pairs of passages as these to be reconciled? One way would be this. The ultimate end of everything in each order of being—inanimate things, plants, brute animals, rational animals and separate substances—is to attain a state it is not in; and since those states are definable only by reference to God, God is the ultimate end of the whole of things in the sense that he and he alone is that by reference to which the ultimate ends of all things are defined. What is wrong with this will be evident to you. It is that there must be some reason why the ultimate ends of all things can be defined only by reference to God; and that reason must yield a deeper sense in which God is the ultimate end of the whole of things than that their specific ends can all be so defined. What is that deeper sense?

St. Thomas's first answer to this question in *Summa contra Gentiles* was metaphysical. An end is a final cause. From this it follows that

> the end holds first place over other types of cause, and to it all other causes owe the fact that they are causes in act: for the agent only acts

for the sake of the end. . . . Therefore the ultimate end is the first cause of all (III, 17, 9).

And the first cause of all is, of course, God: the first cause, and the first agent. Now, St. Thomas continues,

> an end that is produced by the action of an agent cannot be the first agent; it is, rather an effect of an agent. Therefore, God cannot be the end of things in this way, as something produced (*constitutum*), but only as something pre-existing (*praeexistens*) to be obtained (III, 18, 3).

The ultimate end of human action, or of action of any other kind, cannot be something that does not yet exist, if that end is, as all good Aristotelians believe, the ultimate final cause. Hence we must distinguish between the end of an action, which exists before it, and what St. Thomas calls the 'obtaining' of that end. *Obtaining the end is not the end.* Nor does 'obtaining,' as St. Thomas uses it here, stand for any kind of exclusive ownership or dominion.

Of course, this line of thought does not find favour with many metaphysicians today. And on this point I imagine that most of us here, including many who would call themselves Thomists, stand with the majority of our contemporaries. If we accept, as I do, St. Thomas's doctrine that God is something like the final cause of things as that is conceived in Aristotle's metaphysics (of course that is not all he is), it is not for Aristotle's reason, that the universe has a final *natural* cause. For what reason then? I believed that St. Thomas gets at it in an observation about the ends of productive actions generally.

> [T]he ultimate end of any maker, as a maker, is himself; it is for our own sakes that we use things made by us, and if sometimes a man makes a thing for some other purpose, this has reference to his own good, either as useful, or delectable, or right (*honestum*).

Now, what holds for all makers holds for God.

> God is the productive cause of all things. . . . Therefore, he himself is the end of all things (III, 17, 8).

This argument implies that creatures as well as God may be ends. Later in the third Part of *Summa contra Gentiles* St. Thomas went on to draw that conclusion when he came to address himself to the foundations of morality. Rational creatures excel all others not only in the dignity of their end, but also in the perfection of their nature.

> In perfection of nature, only the rational creature has dominion over its acts, freely moving itself to doing them (*ad operandum*). Other creatures are moved to the activities (*opera*) proper to them rather than move [themselves to them] (III, 111, 1).

Among creatures, only the intellectual ones (St. Thomas uses the words 'rational' and 'intellectual' interchangeably in this connection) are principal agents, as distinct from instruments.

> What is moved only by another has the nature (*ratio*) of an instrument: but what is moved *per se* has the nature of a principal agent. Now, an instrument is wanted, not for its own sake (*propter seipsum*), but so that a principal agent may use it. Hence all the careful work that is devoted to instruments must be referred to the principal agent as end; but what is done for the principal agent, either by himself or by another, is for his sake (*propter ipsum*), inasmuch as he is a principal agent. Therefore intellectual creatures are treated by God as things cared about (*procuratae*) for their own sakes. . . . (III, 112, 1).

To this, St. Thomas added a parallel argument: namely, that intellectual creatures are ends—things cared about for their own sakes—not only as principal agents, but also as attaining what they do through their own efforts.

> [W]henever things are ordered to any end, if any among them cannot attain the end through their own efforts (*per seipsa*), they must be subordinated to those that attain it and are ordered to it for their own sakes. . . . Now . . . God is the ultimate end of the whole of things. An intellectual nature alone attains to God in himself, that is, by knowing him and loving him. . . . Therefore the intellectual nature is the only one in the universe that is wanted (*quaesito*) for its own sake, and all others for its sake (III, 112, 3).

Moreover, creatures of intellectual nature are wanted for their own sakes as individuals. "A rational creature," St. Thomas declared, "stands to divine providence as governed and provided for for his own sake, not only for the sake of his species, as other corruptible creatures are" (III, 113, 2).

That rational beings as such are ends, creator and creature alike, is the foundation of the moral law. "Law is nothing but a certain reason and rule of operation (*ratio et regula operandi*)" (III, 114, 3). In governing themselves according to that reason and rule, human beings "participate in a certain likeness of divine providence" (III, 114, 2). But "the end of every law, and above all of divine law, is to make men good," and what makes a human being good is "possessing a good will" (III, 116, 3). A person of good will wills, first of all, "to cling to God. . . . through love," and next, to love his neighbors (III, 116,1 and 117, 1). That he do so, St. Thomas pointed out, is the sense of what St. Matthew's gospel recognizes as the two fundamental commandments on which the whole Mosaic Torah hangs (III, 116, 6 and 117, 7).

In explaining the reason of these commandments—that is, why they are laws—St. Thomas makes it clear that the first holds because God is an end: "the will is good because it wills a good object, and especially the greatest good, which is the end" (III, 116, 3). However, he does not make it as clear that the same is true of the second. Indeed, the reason he gave for it is easily mistaken for an anticipation of Hume's.

> [T]here ought (*oportet*) to be a union in affection among those for whom there is a common end [he wrote]. Now men share in common the one ultimate end which is happiness. . . . So, men ought to be united with each other by a mutual love (III, 117, 1).

And he continued,

> [I]t is natural to all men to love each other. A sign of this is that by a certain natural instinct, a man comes to the help of any man in need, even one he does not know. . . . Therefore, mutual love is prescribed for men by the divine law (III, 117, 6).

Unlike Hume, however, St. Thomas saw in natural instinct not a substitute for a requirement of practical reason, but a sign that such a requirement underlies it.[5] And his assertion that happiness (*beatitudo*) is the ultimate end shared by all men must be understood in the light of his doctrine that happiness itself presupposes a pre-existent end.

The structure of morality as St. Thomas presents it in *Summa contra Gentiles* accordingly seems to be this. God, the first cause and first agent, is the ultimate pre-existing end of the whole of things, before all produced ends (*fines constituti*). Rational creatures also, by the providence of God, act for their own sakes. But what their own sakes require is that they obtain the ultimate end of the whole of things by loving and understanding it. A necessary condition of their doing that is that their wills be good: that is, that they will according to law. Law is reason and rule. And reason and rule require, first of all, that they love God, and secondly, that they love their neighbors—all other rational beings. The Mosaic Torah lays down in detail what these fundamental commandments imply.

However, *Summa contra Gentiles*, written between 1258 and 1264, is one of St. Thomas's earlier works. In the later *Summa Theologiae*, written between 1266 and 1273, morality is treated much more elaborately, and at first sight, differently. The morality of *Summa contra Gentiles* is unmistakably a deontology based on a distinctive teleology of pre-existent ends; that in *Summa Theologiae* is for the most part a theory of virtues and vices based on a theory of right reason. Yet, despite the obvious differences of subject, differences of doctrine turn out to be largely in emphasis.[6]

A brief survey must suffice. That the treatise *de Lege* in *Summa Theologiae* (I-II, 90-97) expands the treatment of moral law in the earlier *Summa*, but without contradicting it, is as far as I know, not seriously questioned. What is called in *Summa contra Gentiles* "divine law," that is, the reason and rule of operation in which human beings participate in a certain likeness of divine providence, is now called "natural law (*lex naturalis*)" (*ST* I-II, 91, 2). And, as in *Summa contra Gentiles*, all the moral precepts of the Mosaic Torah are declared to be contained in the natural law, and to be summed up in the two *prima et communia praecepta*, 'Love God' and 'Love your neighbor' (*ST* I-II, 99, 1 ad 2; 100, 3). The additions to Mosaic moral teaching made by Christianity are declared to be few, and chiefly to be a matter of forbidding internal acts not forbidden in all cases by Moses (*ST* I-II, 107, 4).

That both God and human beings are recognized to be pre-existent ends in *Summa Theologiae* is equally evident. As for as morality is concerned, it is explicitly laid down that all morality arises from love of the pre-existent ends, God and human beings. St. Thomas commented on St. Paul's at first sight surprising assertion that "If there is any other commandment it is comprised in this saying: "Thou shalt love thy neighbor as thyself,'" that

> [T]he whole of the law is summed up in this single
> commandment . . . as the end to which, in a certain sense, all the com-
> mandments are directed. For when one loves one's neighbor for God's
> sake, then this love includes the love of God also (*ST* I-II, 99, 1 ad 2).

I shall therefore assume that, early and late, St. Thomas thought of morality as a matter of law (law itself being understood as a matter of reason), and of law as resting on a teleology of pre-existent ends.

4

KANT'S DEONTOLOGY

■

BILLY BUDD

"God bless Captain Vere!" These were Billy Budd's last words as he stood over the deck, a noose around his neck. Moments later he was hanging from the yardarm, his neck snapped from his weight. The crew watched, crestfallen. Everyone loved the gentle and kindhearted Billy. Though he was simple and uneducated, he was a hard worker and a trustworthy sailor. He possessed no mean bone. Why was he executed?

The year is 1797, and the ship is the British vessel *Bellipotent*, part of a large fleet in the Mediterranean. On the previous day, Billy's superior officer, the master-of-arms John Claggart, a cruel human being and the only man on the ship who felt malice toward Billy, brought Billy before the captain, "Starry" Vere, and accused Billy of conjuring up a mutiny. Claggart's timing was deliberate. Some months earlier, there were two separate mutinies in the British fleet, one especially menacing known as "the Great Mutiny." Author Herman Melville says of this latter uprising: "To the British Empire the Nore Mutiny was what a strike in the fire brigade would be to London threatened by general arson."[1] The British navy could not afford another disruption. It was imperative that Captain Vere maintain strict order on his ship and squelch any potential disobedience.

Billy is innocent of the charge, though he did know that some of the crew were not happy with Captain Vere's leadership. Some of them questioned the captain's state of mind. Lately, he has been acting strange. In any case, stunned by Claggart's false accusation, Billy is taken totally off guard. Billy has never been articulate in speech, and when he becomes upset, he finds it especially difficult to express himself. Claggart's charge shocks Billy, and, unable to speak and feeling powerless, he lashes out at Claggart. Billy is extremely powerful and sometimes does not know his own strength. Claggart crumbles in a heap, dead from Billy's blow. Vere, the event's sole witness as well as the ship's captain, arranges an immediate hearing in order to settle the matter. He convenes a "drumhead court" consisting of the first lieutenant, the sailing master, and the marines' captain. They hold court in the quarterdeck cabin where the event occurred. In what ensues, Melville gives us one of the most poignant accounts of the tension between law, in this case military law, and morality. Melville's *Billy Budd: Sailor* remains a classic in its own right. Since it is exceptionally rich in meaning, we include a portion of it at the end of this chapter.

Captain Vere is the first to speak and renders his account of what occurred in his cabin: Claggart's accusation of mutiny on the part of Billy, Billy's striking Claggart, and Claggart's death. Honest by nature, Billy admits that the Captain's account is correct, although he denies the charge leveled against him by Claggart. "It is just as Captain Vere says, but it is not as the master-at-arms said. I have eaten the King's bread and I am true to the King." Captain Vere himself admits that he believes that Claggart's accusation is false: "I believe you, my man." Billy also tells the court that he had absolutely no intention of killing Claggart.

> *"I am sorry that he is dead. I did not mean to kill him. Could I have used my tongue I would not have struck him. But he foully lied to my face and in presence of my captain, and I had to say something, and I could only say it with a blow, God help me!"*

Again Vere responds, "I believe you, my man." And when asked about whether he knew of any "incipient trouble" among some of the crew, Billy denied knowing so, his loyalty to his fellow sailors prevailing.

We now venture into the trial's most critical moments. Vere insists before his officers that the sole consideration in this event must be Billy's actual deed and that speculations as to his various motives are irrelevant. Just as Claggart's motives for bringing false accusation against Budd cannot be fathomed and are immaterial, Billy's intent behind striking Claggart is just as irrelevant. What counts is Billy's act—nothing more, nothing less. "The prisoner's deed—with that alone we have to do."

Moreover, sentiment and compassion on the part of the officers are also beside the point. Vere himself feels for Billy, for he is extremely fond of Billy and recognizes that Claggart was a cruel, vicious, and evil man. Yet

Vere maintains that feelings like compassion are "scruples that may tend to enervate decision." Vere argues that the court must put all such scruples aside and conduct their *duty* as officers of the King's navy. Vere instructs his officers that they must do what the law requires and not be influenced by either their feelings or their "private conscience":

> "But the exceptional in the matter moves the hearts within you. Even so too is mine moved. But let not warm hearts betray heads that should be cool. . . . But something in your aspect seems to urge that it is not solely the heart that moves in you, but also the conscience, the private conscience. But tell me whether or not, occupying the position we do, conscience should not yield to that imperial one formulated in the mode under which alone we officially proceed?"

Vere clearly makes his case. Although Billy intended neither the death of Claggart nor mutiny, motives need to be set aside in order to focus upon his deed. He acted in a way that resulted in the death of his superior officer. Even if Claggart had not died, the act of striking an officer still constitutes the most serious offense under military law. For Vere, the issue is clear-cut, with only two alternatives: Either condemn Billy or set him free. And even though the sailing master suggests a third option of clemency, Vere points out that, given recent mutinies, a lenient sentence would be misread by the crew. For Vere, the heart of the matter lies in performing one's duty in obeying maritime law. And according to this law, killing a superior officer warrants execution without delay. Vere's argument sways the court, and Billy is sentenced to hang. Early next morning, Billy is executed before the entire crew. In Melville's unforgettable depiction of the scene, note the execution's impact upon the crew.

> The prisoner was presently brought up, the chaplain attending him. . . . Brief speech indeed he had with the condemned one, but the genuine Gospel was less on his tongue than in his aspect and manner towards him. The final preparations personal to the latter being speedily brought to an end by two boatswain's mates, the consummation impended. Billy stood facing aft. At the penultimate moment, his words, his only ones, words wholly unobstructed in the utterance, were these: "God bless Captain Vere!" Syllables so unanticipated coming from one with the ignominious hemp about his neck — a conventional felon's benediction directed aft towards the

> *quarters of honor; syllables too delivered in the clear melody of a*
> *singing bird on the point of launching from a twig — had a phenom-*
> *enal effect, not unenhanced by the rare personal beauty of the young*
> *sailor, spiritualized now through late experiences so poignantly*
> *profound.*
>
> > *Without volition, as it were, as if indeed the ship's populace were*
> > *but the vehicles of some vocal current electric, with one voice from*
> > *alow and aloft came a resonant sympathetic echo: "God bless Cap-*
> > *tain Vere!" And yet at that instant Billy alone must have been in*
> > *their hearts, even as in their eyes.*[2]

Melville makes it clear that Billy Budd never intended to kill Claggart. He also paints an admirable portrait of Billy as a person who is in many respects innocent, of good character, honest, gentle, trustworthy, loyal, and deeply sensitive. Melville also depicts Captain Vere as an honest and upright man, a leader profoundly committed to his rank. Yet Vere's concept of duty is strict and unbending. It overrides considerations of sympathy and compassion. Is his position morally justifiable in this context? As we will see, the centrality of duty plays a critical role in the ethics of Immanuel Kant. Is Vere's emphasis upon duty supported by Kant's theory? Is the execution of Billy consistent with Kant's deontology? Does Kant claim that it is morally justified to hold persons accountable for the unforeseen consequences of their actions? Would Kant agree with Vere that motives do not genuinely count in calculating culpability? Let us now examine Kantian ethics more closely.

■ IMMANUEL KANT (1724–1804): ORDER AND REASON

What is truly remarkable about the life of Immanuel Kant is that as unremarkable as his own personal life was, and that although he never left the town of Königsberg, Prussia, his ideas have reached into the farthest corners of Western thought and culture. He was raised in a strict Lutheran milieu and his parents were devout Pietists. Having studied theology at Königsberg University, he later taught logic and metaphysics at the same university. His personal life was anything but extraordinary, yet no other thinker in modern times has had the same enduring influence. His insights have permanently inspired philosophical thought. His three major works, *Critique of Pure Reason* (1781), *Critique of Practical Reason* (1788), and *Critique of Judgement* (1790) remain philosophical classics, respectively, of epistemology (the theory of knowledge), ethics, and aesthetics (the theory of beauty). Along with his additional works in ethics, *Prolegomena to a Future Metaphysics* (1783) and *Foundations of the Metaphysics of Morals* (1785), he helped to fashion a cornerstone in Western philosophy, leaving an indelible impression upon ethical analysis. His ideas in turn became a principal inspiration in law, theology, sciences, and social sciences.

Königsberg is now Kaliningrad, Russia. At the university where Kant taught, there is a pathway that meanders through the university campus known as the "Philosopher's Walk." It was given this name because Professor Kant, popular with his students and well-respected among his colleagues, would take his daily stroll along this path at the same exact time, every day, without fail. His habit was so methodical that when classes heard the tapping of his cane on the pavement as he passed by a window, both students and faculty knew the time of day. His discipline demonstrated itself in his daily routine. He would awaken at the same time, early in the morning, and conduct his day according to the same schedule.

Virtually obsessed with orderliness, he relied on routine and habit. Nearly every detail of his day was according to a strict schedule. He was especially attached to time and to his watch. Philosopher Ben-Ami Scharfstein claims that this may have been Kant's way of compensating for his own insecurity when it came to matters of personal health. Kant, though not sickly, was not a picture of health. Later in his life, he became inordinately hypochondriac and periodically suffered bouts of depression. He was immoderately concerned with his personal hygiene, diet, and medicine. In this manner, he associated order with good health, later preoccupying himself with what he believed to be the connection between health and weather. Ben-Ami Scharfstein writes:

> To remain healthy, Kant ordered his life very rigorously. By the time he had grown old, he took the condition of his health to be a work of art created by himself. His interest in new medical discoveries and theories, which he hoped to apply to himself, was intense . . . for Kant had become quite certain that the condition of his health depended on the weather.[3]

In all of this, we need to be especially careful. We need to allow this great thinker's ideas to stand on their own. That is, whatever biographical sketches we have of Kant, his ideas need to be assessed apart from personal anecdotes. His ideas remain original and profoundly influential. In all fairness to any thinker, his or her ideas need to be evaluated on their own merit. Nevertheless, we can never truly and radically sever what a person thinks from how that person lives his or her life. True, as one reviewer correctly puts it, Kant's ideas must stand on their own. Yet insights into his life do help to at least shed some light on his philosophy. Along these lines, just as the common denominator throughout his life lies in his emphasis upon order, so too we find a similar emphasis in his classic works. And order in the best sense derives from the examination and application of reason. Kant argued that reason provides the basis for any sound approach to an understanding of the various disciplines. Through methodic reasoned analysis, he laid the foundations for the conditions for knowledge. Furthermore, Kant argued that our capacity to reason is what distinguishes us from all other creatures. Reason constitutes our redeeming quality.

This emphasis upon reason is seen in Kant's project regarding morality, a project that must be viewed within the entire context of Kant's philosophy: an attempt to establish the grounds for the possibility of knowledge regarding fundamental philosophical questions through a rigorous application of reason. His classic works demonstrate such rigor in their original and challenging analyses of the conceptual grounds of metaphysics, epistemology, ethics, and aesthetics. Along these lines, despite Kant's strict religious upbringing and education in theology, he was firmly committed to establish a basis for morality that rested upon reason and not faith. In this respect, he followed a long line of philosophers who also sought to arrive at a reasoned foundation for morality. He addresses the perennial question among philosophers: What is the ultimate source of authority for morality? Does the ultimate authority lie in religion or in religious beliefs? Kant responds "no." For Kant, the genuine source of authority for morality lies within our capacity to reason.

To illustrate, in *Billy Budd*, after his trial Billy is confined to a small corner on the deck just hours before his execution, and the ship's chaplain comes to visit. At first, the chaplain intends to instruct Billy in Christian matters and to cull forth the "young barbarian's" repentance of his deed so that he can redeem himself before God his "Savior" as well as prepare himself for the afterlife. While the chaplain speaks, Billy's simple nature and innocence shows itself in Billy's respectful demeanor.

> *Billy listened, but less out of awe or reverence, perhaps, than from a certain natural politeness, doubtless at bottom regarding all that in much the same way that most mariners of his class take any discourse abstract or out of the common tone of the workaday world.*[4]

Recognizing Billy's genuine innocence, the chaplain refrains from any further theology. He knows that Billy is a good person, despite his disinterest in religion and "dogma." The source of morality is deeper than any religious dogma. Melville writes:

> But the Bellipotent's chaplain was a discreet man possessing the good sense of a good heart. So he insisted not in his vocation here. At the instance of Captain Vere, a lieutenant had apprised him of pretty much everything as to Billy; and since he felt that innocence was even a better thing than religion wherewith to go to Judgment, he reluctantly withdrew; but in his emotion not without first performing an act strange enough in an Englishman, and under the circumstances yet more so in any regular priest. Stooping over, he kissed on the fair cheek his fellow man, a felon in martial law, one whom though on the confines of death he felt he could never convert to a dogma; nor for all that did he fear for his future.[5] [emphasis added]

■ THE DRIVING FORCE OF DUTY

For Kant, the most compelling force behind morality lies in duty. Thus, his ethics has been called an ethics of duty, denoted by the term "deontology," which literally means "the study of duty." Duty plays a key role in morality. And when an act is done out of a sense of duty, it is done with a "good will." For Kant, duty and good will are coterminous in that they signify each other. More important, acting with a good will, that is, acting out of duty, essentially means that we act according to *principle* and *not out of concern for the consequences of our actions*. This emphasis upon acting for the sake of principle clearly separates Kantian deontology from the utilitarian position that, as we will see later, stresses acting upon consideration of the consequences of our acts.

Duty plays such a significant role in Kant's ethics that he argues that actions done out of duty rather than out of desire actually carry more moral weight. Suppose that my wife and I care for our aging parent primarily because it is our duty. We do not enjoy doing so, and as our parent becomes older and more ill, it becomes more difficult. Nevertheless, we commit ourselves out of devotion and duty. Suppose our neighbor is similarly caring for her aging parent. However, she does so because she enjoys caring for her mother and it genuinely pleases her. Kant would assert that our action, done primarily out of duty—and a good will—has more moral significance. Dutiful acts are more morally praiseworthy. We act despite how we feel about acting. Whatever we feel, whether pleasure or displeasure, we transcend our feelings by acting primarily out of duty.

In this way, the motive behind our act plays a critical part in the morality of that act. Kant's system requires that we examine the intent as well as the action itself. He reminds us that both components—intent and action—are vital components in assessing morality. Indeed, by stressing the centrality of duty, or good will, he prioritizes intent so that intent actually plays a more significant role than the act itself. In which case we find a problem with Captain Vere's argument to his officers regarding Billy Budd. Vere tells his officers that Billy's intent or motives do not count in deciding his culpability. Vere therefore holds Billy accountable solely on the basis of his deed—he acted in a way that brought about the death of Claggart. Even though Billy did not intend to kill Claggart, this is irrelevant as far as Vere is concerned. But this way of assessing things is not what Kant is saying. For Kant, moral responsibility and accountability has to consider motives and intent. More precisely, acting out of duty is necessary for a moral act to be morally praiseworthy. Given this, what moral judgment can we make regarding Billy's deed? The fact that Billy never intended to kill Claggart necessarily enters into our assessment of his deed. The fact that it was an accident tempers Billy's moral culpability. Surely, he acted in a way that was wrong. Yet Kantian morality requires acknowledging the mitigating circumstances surrounding the act. How about Captain Vere? Was his decision to convict Billy morally justified? Vere was certainly acting out of duty. Although he felt both compassion and friendship toward Billy, as an officer in the King's navy he felt obliged to follow a higher principle of duty to military law.

DUTY VERSUS DESIRE

By appealing to military duty, Vere embodies the tension between sentiment, or "scruples," and duty. Kant is well aware of this ever-present conflict between duty and desire, or, as he puts it, duty and inclination. This conflict surfaces throughout our lives. In many instances, we know what we *ought* to do, but it often conflicts with what we *want* to do. One stirring example of this is the 1992 book by Robert James Waller, *The Bridges of Madison County*. It made the *New York Times* best-seller list for three years and was later made into a film with the same title. In the story, Francesca Johnson (Meryl Streep in the film) leads a quiet life in a small town, Winterset,

Iowa. She's married to a devoted, hardworking farmer, Richard, and they have two children. While her husband and children are away at the state fair for a weekend, Francesca encounters Robert Kincaid (played by Clint Eastwood), a photographer for *National Geographic*. Robert is on assignment to take photos of the old, classic wooden bridges in the area. Immediately drawn to each other, they discover that they are in love with each other. They are "soulmates" to each other and spend the weekend together making love. Francesca's quiet world is now turned upside down. Robert must soon leave for another assignment and wants Francesca to leave with him, and she desperately desires the same. They are both convinced that they are truly meant for each other. As Robert puts its, "This kind of certainty comes only once, and never again."[6] Yet she is naturally torn between her desire for Robert and her feelings of duty toward her husband and children.

Francesca decides that the right thing to do would be to stay with her family. Therein lies her duty, even though her passions pull her in another direction. Her duty to her family is first and foremost. Upon telling this to Robert, he has difficulty accepting her decision, because he knows in his heart that they genuinely love each other. He believes she is not being true to her own heart, her duty to herself.

A few days after her family returns from the fair, she and her husband drive into town for supplies. Outside of the grocery store, she sees Robert, and, standing in the rain, he looks at her. Robert then gets into his truck, and waits at the traffic light. Right behind him are Francesca and Richard. This is her last chance as she touches her door handle, but hesitates. As the traffic light turns so does Robert. That is the last they see of each other. For Francesca, duty wins out. In the story, she embodies the Kantian heroine in that duty supersedes personal happiness since personal happiness tends to be driven by personal desire.

▓ THE CATEGORICAL IMPERATIVE

With all of his emphasis upon duty, Kant tells us that the consequences of our actions play an insignificant role in morality. Contemplating the probable consequences of our choices is not at all the determinant in what constitutes a morally sound choice. In fact, one must act in certain ways regardless of the consequences. Acting out of duty is what really matters. That is, we must act in ways that are consistent with principles. Acting out of duty is acting for the sake of principle. However, we cannot simply act for the sake of just any principle. We need to act in accordance with principles that *can be made universal*. That is, our choices or actions are morally sound only if they are congruent with universal principles. However, how do we know whether or not a principle is universal? Tyrants have often acted out of principle, but we would be hard pressed to assert that their principles were universal. The infamous Donatien Alphonse Francois comte de Sade, known as the Marquis de Sade (1740–1814) believed that we are compelled by "Nature's voice" to murder. He writes in his *Philosophy in the Bedroom*, "The freest people are they who are most friendly to murder."[7] Most of us would intuitively agree that de Sade's personal principle does not qualify as a universal one.

Kant constructs one of the most ingenuous methods for determining the rightness or wrongness of our action. It is a tool for ascertaining universal principles, called the categorical imperative. "Imperative" refers to what we should do. "Categorical" indicates that we should do so without exception; that is, it is absolute. Categorical imperative differs from what he posed as a "hypothetical imperative." A hypothetical imperative refers to what we feel we should do based upon what we may desire to do. It is hypothetical because it is contingent upon each person's individual interests. However, individual interests do not necessarily coincide with universal interests. For example, if I desire to ocean kayak out to Block Island, twelve miles off the coast of Rhode Island, I should learn safety techniques as well as rowing and sea kayaking skills. Otherwise, if I kayak out to the island with others, I risk their safety as well as my own. However, many others may not necessarily share the same desire to kayak out to Block Island. There is therefore no duty or obligation of their part to learn these same skills. In the same way, there is no universal nor absolute duty to do something based upon desire. In contrast, a categorical imperative denotes an absolute duty. In other words, Kant's categorical imperative is a method to more clearly determine the universality of principles. Kant more closely examines this categorical imperative in his short treatise, *Foundations of the Metaphysics of Morals*. A selection from this classic treatise is at the end of this chapter. Here, Kant provides two formulations of the categorical imperative: (1) the rule of universalizability and (2) the rule to treat persons as ends in themselves.

FIRST FORMULATION – UNIVERSALIZABILITY

In Kant's *Foundations of the Metaphysics of Morals* we read:

> *There is, therefore, only one categorical imperative. It is:* Act only according to that maxim by which you can at the same time will that it should become a universal law.

> *Now if all imperatives of duty can be derived from this one im-*
> *perative as a principle, we can at least show what we understand by*
> *the concept of duty and what it means, even though it remains un-*
> *decided whether that which is called duty is an empty concept or*
> *not . . . the universal imperative of duty can be expressed as follows:*
> *Act as though the maxim of your action were by your will to become*
> *a universal law of nature.*[8] *[emphasis added]*

Although Kant states there is "only one categorical imperative," this is his first formulation of it. It is referred to as the rule of universalizability. The term "universalizability" sounds daunting. The idea behind it, however, is not. Note the examples that Kant offers in our selection. Let us add another example—a student who contemplates cheating on an exam. A college student is faring quite poorly in his grades and has a low GPA. He needs to do well on his ethics exam in order to raise his GPA and hopefully have better job prospects after he graduates. The night before his ethics final, he contemplates cheating during the exam.

With this example, let us explain the notion of universalizability. The example's key components are these:

A. The student's contemplated act of cheating.

B. The particular maxim, or rule, behind the contemplated act.

C. Can we universalize this particular maxim?

D. If so, then the student's act is morally warranted. If not, then his act is not morally justified.

Let us examine these components. (A) The student deliberates cheating because he is in rather dire straits gradewise, and he needs to improve his job opportunities. At first, given his circumstances, he believes that cheating in this instance is justified. (B) What would be the specific maxim or rule governing his contemplated act? Such a rule could be phrased in various ways, but it would go something like this: "Since I am experiencing poor grades and need to improve my chances of getting a decent job later on, I am justified in cheating on my final exam." (C) Can this specific maxim become universalized? Is it universalizable? That is, suppose we make this maxim a universal rule so that absolutely everyone, everywhere, anytime adheres by it. What would be the outcome of universalizing this rule?

Consider the phenomenon of "suicide terrorism." In March 2002, a young Palestinian man, dressed in the garb of an ultra-Orthodox Jew, stood outside of a building where guests attended a bar mitzvah in the town of

Beit Yisrael, just outside of Jerusalem. No one noticed him. Packed with hidden explosives, he stood by a group of women with baby carriages. As guests streamed out of the hall, he detonated himself, killing ten people and seriously wounding fifty-nine others. Six of those who died were children. The extremist Islamic group Fatah Al-Aqsa Martyrs claimed responsibility for the attack.[9]

Now if we apply the principle of universalizability to this suicide bombing, we detect the lack of logic with respect to these attacks. The maxim behind the individual attack has to do with calling for such an act based upon perceived injustices to Muslims perpetrated by Jews. If we universalize this maxim, perceptions of injustice anywhere by anyone warrant attacking innocent people. The same logic that justifies the Fatah Al-Aqsa Martyrs in turn justifies an Israeli martyr who murders innocent Palestinians. The logic behind suicide terrorism thus perpetuates a vicious circle of retribution and revenge. This logic cannot be universalized without causing moral chaos. According to this principle of universalizability, the act of the suicide terrorist is utterly unjustifiable.

By the way, John Stuart Mill later criticized Kant on the grounds of this first feature of the categorical imperative. Mill argued that the principle of universalizability calls for at least some consideration of consequences. If this is the case, then deontologists still need to weigh the consequences. To illustrate, Captain Vere certainly acts strictly out of duty. His obedience to military and maritime law compels him to believe that the execution of Billy Budd is the only viable option given the circumstances. However, note that when an officer of the court, the sailing master, proposed the option of convicting Billy while giving him a lenient sentence, Captain Vere felt such an option would result in unfavorable *consequences* for the crew, the ship, and the King's navy in general. He pointed out that this could lead to a lack of rigor and strict discipline and would be counterproductive in the long run. Nevertheless, in fairness to Kant, what Kant underscores is that we consider the *logical* outcome of universalizing a maxim rather than its actual outcome. Yet, Mill's may still be a valid critique.

So, what would be the logical implication of universalizing the student's individual maxim to cheat? To begin with, one logical implication would be that numerous students would feel justified in cheating on their exams. Moreover, it would diminish the meaningfulness of issuing grades. Furthermore, academic integrity would certainly lessen, and potential employers would not know whether students truly earned their grades. All this would essentially produce a sort of moral chaos. Therefore, it makes neither logical nor moral sense to universalize this maxim. This is a maxim that cannot and should not be universalized. (D) Therefore, since this maxim cannot be universalized, the student's particular maxim is morally unwarranted, and, more urgent, acting upon this individual, unwarranted (non-universalizable) maxim would be morally unjustified.

To sum this up, the rule of universalizability means asking this all-important question when pondering an act: What if everyone did that? Thus, we discover an implicit "Golden Rule" in this formulation. Would we consider making deceitful promises if we know that all others can feel equally justified in breaking promises they have made to us? Therein lies the merit of this formulation of the categorical imperative. In its require-ment of universalizability, it demands that we abandon self-interest and parochialism. Morality is thus a matter of universal interests.

This same reasoning lies behind Kant's opposition to suicide. In his se-lection, we read his example of the man who on account of misfortunes is "reduced to despair" and "feels wearied of life." If his circumstances are at their lowest ebb, would this constitute reasonable grounds for his suicide? If we seek to universalize his individual maxim, we find that most if not all of us would also feel suicide to be justifiable because we all tend to experi-ence depression and extreme unhappiness at some points in our lives. For Kant, we therefore have a duty to preserve life at all costs, even when the circumstances are dire. Kant himself underwent bouts of depression. As he admits:

> "Life is a burden to me, I am tired of bearing it. And if the angel of death were to come this night and call me from here, I would raise my hand and say, 'God be praised!' . . . I am no poltroon. I still have strength enough to take my life, but I hold this to be immoral. Who-ever deprives himself of life is a beast. . . ."[10]

If we apply this principle of universalizability in the case of Billy Budd, we see that his action is without moral justification, let alone illegal. Granted, his striking Claggart was without any intention of killing him. His personal maxim would be something like this: "Because I am com-pletely stunned, bewildered, and cannot express myself properly in words, I can hit my antagonist." This maxim cannot at all be universalized. The logical implications of doing so would lead to widespread violence and mass fear. According to the rule of universalizability, what Billy did was morally wrong. However, the essence of the story lies in how we assess his level of responsibility as well as determine his just punishment. Clearly, he did the wrong thing. But was his execution the right penalty? Here we get into some nitty-gritty discussion and debate, especially if we also make a distinction between moral duty and military duty.

Captain Vere believes that hanging Billy is the right punishment. Is his decision morally justified? His personal maxim is "Whenever some sailor breaks military or maritime law, that sailor must be punished according to law, regardless of mitigating circumstances, especially in times of possible strife and mutiny." Can we universalize this maxim? Indeed, it seems reasonable that we can, for the logical implication would be some semblance of order or discipline in the navy. But then this assumes that this order would be the likely logical outcome. Why would we assume this to be the case? Here is where the tension between law and morality becomes most apparent.

SECOND FORMULATION—PERSONS AS ENDS

Later on in his *Foundations of the Metaphysics of Morals*, Kant summarizes his second way of expressing his categorical imperative:

> *Thus if there is to be a supreme practical principle and a categorical imperative for the human will, it must be one that forms an objective principle of the will from the conception of that which is necessarily an end for everyone because it is an end in itself. Hence this objective principle can serve as a universal practical law. The ground of this principle is: rational nature exists as an end in itself. . . . The practical imperative, therefore, is the following:* Act so that you treat humanity, whether in your own person or in that of another, always as an end and never as a means only.[11] *[emphasis added]*

Of the two formulations, this seems much clearer. Without hesitation, Kant reminds us that we should never treat other persons *solely* as means to our own ends. We should never view others as instruments, or objects, for our personal satisfaction. To view other persons in this manner is to objectivize, to dehumanize them.

However, note Kant's caveat when he states that we should never treat others *solely* as means to our ends. That is, he recognizes that in some respects we do tend to view and treat others as means to our end, and we often do so quite naturally. When I would regularly visit with my grandmother, I did so with the intent of pleasing her. I would take her for a drive by the seacoast, around Newport's Ocean Drive, which she loved doing. She also loved sharing a cup of tea with me afterwards. However, at the same time, doing all of this with her gave me great pleasure as well. In a sense, since visiting with her was instrumental to my pleasure, she was a means to my end. At the same time, my pleasure in visiting her was not by any means my *only* aim in visiting her. If it was, then I would certainly be guilty of violating Kant's second formulation. This is an important point. Kant recognizes full well that we often do things out of self-interest. We will also relate to others in ways that enhance our self-interest. However, if we treat others *only* as a means to our own end, that is, strictly out of self-interest (in this case self-centeredness), then we are in essence using these others. This is morally wrong.

Why is this morally wrong? It is wrong because by viewing and treating others as objects, we refuse to recognize them as *subjects*. What does it mean to view another as a subject? It means that we should recognize the other as a rational being. And to recognize another as a rational being is to thereby recognize the other as a person. Moreover, this means recognizing the other, the person, as a moral agent, a being with moral status. To view a rational being in this way, as having moral status, means that we recognize that this rational being, this person, has fundamental moral rights by virtue of being a person. And there is no more fundamental right than the right to exercise one's moral rights. This right to exercise one's moral right is self-determination, what Kant calls "autonomy." Therefore, to view the other as a subject is to respect the other's autonomy. This is precisely what Kant means by treating others as ends.

Human reproductive cloning has not yet been achieved, at least as far as we know, despite wild rumors to the contrary. Whether or not this is scientifically feasible is up for debate. Nevertheless, quite a few scientists believe that it is inevitable. Suppose they are right. Suppose we find ourselves at a time when human reproductive cloning has become common. Let us also suppose that a couple, Jim and Mary, find themselves unable to have their own biological child due to infertility. Mary has already made an all-out effort with fertility drug treatments. Having their own biological child is especially important to Jim because he wants to pass on his own genetic lineage, his blood line. Yet the fertility treatments have not been successful. Jim and Mary decide to attempt reproductive cloning, using the technique of somatic cell nuclear transfer. They decide to have the nucleus of one of Jim's cells transplanted into an enucleated egg from Mary. And Mary has agreed to have this "new" egg implanted into her so that she can carry the fetus to term. As a result, the fetus that Mary will bear will carry Jim's genotype. Once born, the child will be like Jim's identical twin, though with a time lapse.

How does Kant's second formulation apply here? Is Jim's attitude toward his child, his clone, such that he is viewing the child strictly as a means to his own end? To begin with, Kant's notion of what it means to be a person, that is, a moral agent, does not apply to human cells, embryos, or fetuses. Kant claims that to be a person requires the capacity to reason, to be rational. However, once the child is born, it will eventually gain this capacity to be rational as it grows. How will Jim view his child? If he views his child primarily as the carrier of his "blood line," with less regard for the personhood of the child, then he clearly violates this second formulation. In this case, he is essentially viewing his child as a means to his own end, and not as an end in itself.

One of the most prominent arguments offered in support of human reproductive cloning has to do with assisting infertile couples so that they can have their own biological offspring. However, if this becomes their sole motive or principal reason for having a child in this way, then such an action becomes morally problematic. In fact, even if reproduction occurs through the natural sexual way, if the primary reasons for having children have to do with satisfying the self-interest or ends of the couple, then this is still morally suspect. Whether reproduction occurs through sexual or through asexual means such as in vitro fertilization or cloning, if the couple or parent view the child as an instrument for their own end, this raises a moral red flag. Here, others may disagree and argue that having a child out of self-interest is not necessarily a bad thing. What is wrong with wanting to carry on one's own lineage? Still, according to Kant's schema, if the motive is *solely* out of self-interest, then the act is not morally justified. All of this reveals to us how Kant's ideas continue to be immensely far-reaching in their implications.

■ WEAKNESSES IN DEONTOLOGY

Despite its powerfully profound effect, Kant's deontology still has its flaws. One foremost flaw rests with his assertion that we need to act according to universal principles. Even though applying the categorical imperative helps us to determine universal principles, what do we do if there are competing universal principles in the same situation? For instance, Kant claims that truth-telling, such as keeping promises, is a universal principle. In his opinion, so is the preservation of life, which is why Kant argues strongly against suicide. Suppose I find myself in a situation where the two conflict. Suppose, after discussing with my grandfather the Karen Ann Quinlan case and the ensuing questions surrounding euthanasia, he exacts a promise out of me: to see to it that I make every effort to not keep him alive if he is in a similar state in which he has no hope of recovery and he is so incapacitated that he cannot decide for himself. I therefore make this promise to him to relieve him of his suffering. Suppose that dreaded situation comes about. If I keep my promise to my grandfather, the result is his death, and I violate the universal principle of the preservation of life. If I act in accordance with that same principle so that he stays alive, I break my earlier promise to him. How does deontology resolve this conflict?

Though most of us would naturally choose life over death, would this be so in all cases? Intuitively, life is preferable to death. At the same time, intuitively, breaking a promise would seem morally warranted if it meant saving a life. Yet, would it always be so? In the case above, I believe there may be some resolution within Kant's analysis. Keep in mind his second formulation, that of treating persons as ends in themselves. As we said earlier, this means respecting the other as a person, a moral agent, a self-determining, *autonomous* human being. It seems to me that this would entail keeping my promise to my grandfather, since doing so would be honoring his own moral agency, this being what he would choose if he could choose for himself. Yet consider the counterargument to this: Do I know with absolute certainty that this is still what he wants? In any case, it remains generally unclear in Kant's analysis as to how to more precisely decide which universal principle prevails in the case of a conflict.

Another flaw lies in Kant's overemphasis upon duty. A duty-driven morality carves away the role of emotions in general and sympathy in particular. According to Kant, acting out of, say, compassion, has little moral significance, although it is surely of practical value since compassion more easily enables us to demonstrate good behavior. Feeling the suffering of another more naturally compels us to assist the other. Yet, would not acting out of compassion also constitute "good will"? Indeed, as we will see, compassion is a principal virtue in traditions like Buddhism, Confucianism, and Western religions. It certainly plays an important role in Aristotle's virtue ethics. Yet Kant downplays its moral weight. In doing so, he appears to minimize the significance of what makes humans more humane— feelings of sympathy, empathy, love, and kindness. Stressing duty as the key moral prerogative risks disconnecting morality altogether from its genuinely human context, a context enmeshed in passions, feelings, and emotions.

By centralizing duty, he also intensifies human rationality or reason. For Kant, what distinguishes us from other species is our capacity to reason, and to a significant degree he is correct, although animal studies increasingly reveal varying degrees of reasoning in other mammals. Yet, we are also creatures who feel. Our capacity to empathize with another, to feel another's suffering as if it were our own, remains a morally unique trait. Kant's overarching focus on duty divinizes it in a way that can produce a dangerous disconnection between morality and life. His ethics stands in danger of becoming abstracted away from reality.

■ STRENGTHS IN DEONTOLOGY

Nevertheless, we cannot deny Kant's penetrating insights. Kant's belief in the intrinsic worth of rational beings was certainly a revolutionary idea during his time, a time when any moral status was based upon factors such as social worth, gender, age, power, and wealth. Kant directly challenged the idea that human beings can be possessed by other human beings, that classes of human beings, such as slaves, have less moral status than other classes. For Kant, the criterion for moral status rests in the capacity to reason, or, as he put it, rationality. For this reason, Kant's thought has far-reaching implications with respect to considerations regarding human rights.

Furthermore, Kant's emphasis upon the universal principle of integrity is vitally important, today more so than ever. By integrity, he means simple and outright honesty, and this incorporates all those elements of truth-telling and promise-keeping. What he strongly suggests is that a society and culture rises or falls contingent upon the value it places upon integrity. And by virtue of his categorical imperative, he proposes a conceptual methodology that tests the meaningfulness of integrity in the most basic sense, being true to one's principles, so that these same principles can be applied to all.

This leads us to what is perhaps Kant's most important contribution in our quest for a universal ethic. By insisting upon the need to universalize our axioms or rules in order to arrive at justifiable universal principles (another application of the Golden Rule), his ethics demands that we transcend self-interest. Personal desires are not morally relevant. What counts is our capacity to reason. In other words, through both formulations of the categorical imperative he provides a conceptual groundwork for addressing the all-important question of universal human rights. That is, rights that we have as humans should not be abrogated in any way. Let us see more closely how this comes about.

Kant insists that we treat all persons as ends in themselves. And what is it that makes us persons? Our capacity to reason. That is, as humans we are rational beings. Our rationality entitles us to be included in Kant's moral community, Kant's "kingdom of ends." Furthermore, by virtue of being persons, we are moral agents; that is, we possess moral status. This means we have fundamental moral rights. Therefore, to treat persons as ends in themselves essentially entails recognizing their moral status. This is the case regardless of skin color, race, religion, gender, age, social level, income, and power. In this way, Kant lays the foundation for a universal, or global, approach to human rights.

Granted, Kant excluded nonhumans from the category of persons. In more recent times, we have discovered that some species of nonhuman animals do possess the capacity to think and to reason in varying degrees. For this reason, given Kant's standard of rationality, they ought to be included within the moral community. During his own time, such views of nonhuman animals were not prevalent. Instead, Kant was addressing the more pressing concern among humans that many humans—children, women, those on the fringes of society such as the physically and mentally impaired, and so on—were essentially viewed as objects, as means to others' ends. Indeed, human slavery and exploitation continues. Not until the early twentieth century did women in America finally acquire rights such as the right to vote and to hold property. In many ways, we still live in a patriarchal society. For instance, the standards of beauty in our culture are still defined and determined by men. And women submit to these standards. We still find expressions of sexism as well as ageism. And we still find it difficult to accord moral status to nonhuman animals. Nevertheless, we need to extend Kant's moral community to incorporate nonhumans as well.

Scholars point out that Kant himself was not specifically addressing the question of universal human rights. Nevertheless, he does stress that all persons, all rational beings, need to be respected in and of themselves. Kant thereby sets the tone for the question of universal human rights. Although we may disagree with Kant's equating the capacity to reason with moral status, his position forces us to ask the critical question, What makes us persons? And would such criteria for personhood be a viable standard for recognizing universal human rights?

■ **NOTES**

1. Herman Melville, *Billy Budd: Sailor,* ed. Harrison Hayford and Merton M. Sealts Jr. (Chicago: University of Chicago Press, Phoenix Books, 1962), p. 54.

2. Ibid., p. 123.

3. Ben-Ami Scharfstein, *The Philosophers: Their Lives and the Nature of Their Thought* (New York: Oxford University Press, 1989; Blackwell, 1980), p. 219.

4. Melville, p. 121.

5. Ibid.

6. Robert James Waller, *The Bridges of Madison County* (New York: Warner Books, 1992).

7. D. A. F. de Sade, *Philosophy in the Bedroom*, in *The Marquis de Sade* (New York, 1966), p. 333; cited in Philip P. Hallie, *The Paradox of Cruelty* (Middletown, CT: Wesleyan University Press, 1969), p. 37.

8. Immanuel Kant, *Foundations of the Metaphysics of Morals*, trans. Lewis White Beck (Indianapolis, IN: Bobbs-Merrill, Liberal Arts Press, 1959), p. 39.

9. See Bruce Hoffman, "The Logic of Suicide Terrorism," *Atlantic Monthly* 281, no. 5 (June 2003): 40–47.

10. Scharfstein, p. 221.

11. Kant, p. 47.

THE GOOD WILL

■

IMMANUEL KANT

Nothing can possibly be conceived in the world, or even out of it, which can be called good, without qualification, except a Good Will. Intelligence, wit, judgment, and the other *talents* of the mind, however they may be named, or courage, resolution, perseverance, as qualities of temperament, are undoubtedly good and desirable in many respects; but these gifts of nature may also become extremely bad and mischievous if the will which is to make use of them, and which, therefore, constitutes what is called *character*, is not good. It is the same with the *gifts of fortune*. Power, riches, honour, even health, and the general well-being and contentment with one's conditions which is called *happiness*, inspire pride, and often presumption, if there is not a good will to correct the influence of these on the mind, and with this also to rectify the whole principle of acting, and adapt it to its end. The sight of a being who is not adorned with a single feature of a pure and good will, enjoying unbroken prosperity, can never give pleasure to an imperial rational spectator. Thus a good will appears to constitute the indispensable condition even of being worthy of happiness.

There are even some qualities which are of service to this good will itself, and may facilitate its action, yet which have no intrinsic unconditional value, but always presuppose a good will, and this qualifies the esteem that we justly have for them, and does not permit us to regard them as absolutely good. Moderation in the affections and passions, self-control, and calm deliberation are not only good in many respects, but even seem to constitute part of the intrinsic worth of the person; but they are far from deserving to be called good without qualification, although they have been so unconditionally praised by the ancients. For without the principles of a good will, they may become extremely bad; and the coolness of a villain not only makes him far more dangerous, but also directly makes him more abominable in our eyes than he would have been without it.

A good will is good not because of what it performs or effects, not by its aptness for the attainment of some proposed end, but simply by virtue of the volition, that is, it is good in itself, and considered by itself to be esteemed much higher than all that can be brought about by it in favour of any inclination, nay, even of the sum-total of all inclinations. Even if it should happen that, owing to special disfavour of fortune, or the niggardly provision of a stepmotherly nature, this will should wholly lack power to accomplish its purpose, if with its greatest efforts it should yet achieve nothing, and there should remain only the good will (not, to be sure, a mere wish, but the summoning of all means in our power), then, like a jewel, it would still shine by its own light, as a thing which has its whole value in itself. Its usefulness or fruitlessness can neither add to nor take away anything from this value. It would be, as it were, only the setting to enable us to handle it the more conveniently in common commerce, or to attract to it the attention of those who are not yet connoisseurs, but not to recommend it to true connoisseurs, or to determine its value.

WHY REASON WAS MADE TO GUIDE THE WILL

There is, however, something so strange in this idea of the absolute value of the mere will, in which no account is taken of its utility, that notwithstanding the thorough assent of even common reason to the idea, yet a suspicion must arise that it may perhaps really be the product of mere high-blown fancy, and that we may have misunderstood the purpose of nature in assigning reason as the governor of our will. Therefore we will examine this idea from this point of view.

In the physical constitution of an organized being, that is, a being adapted suitably to the purposes of life, we assume it as a fundamental principle that no organ for any purpose will be found but what is also the fittest and best adapted for that purpose. Now in a being which has reason and a will, if the proper object of nature were its *conservatism*, its *welfare*, in a word, its *happiness*, then nature would have hit upon a very bad arrangement in selecting the reason of the creature to carry out this purpose. For all the actions which the creature has to perform with a view to this purpose, and the whole rule of its conduct, would be far more surely prescribed to it by instinct, and that end would have been attained thereby much more certainly than it ever can be by reason. Should reason have been communicated to this favoured creature over and above, it must only have served it to contemplate the happy constitution of its nature, to admire it, to congratulate itself thereon, and to feel thankful for it to the beneficent cause, but not that it should subject its desires to that weak and delusive guidance, and meddle bunglingly with the purpose of nature. In a word, nature would have taken care that reason should not break forth into *practical exercise*, nor have the presumption, with its weak insight, to think out for itself the plan of happiness, and of the means of attaining it. Nature would not only have taken on herself the choice of the ends, but also of the means, and with wise foresight would have entrusted both to instinct.

And, in fact, we find that the more a cultivated reason applies itself with deliberate purpose to the enjoyment of life and happiness, so much the more does the man fail of true satisfaction. And from this circumstance there arises in many, if they are candid enough to confess it, a certain degree of *misology*, that is, hatred of reason, especially in the case of those who are most experienced in the use of it, because after calculating all the advantages they derive, I do not say from the invention of all the arts of common luxury, but even from the sciences (which seem to them to be after all only a luxury of the understanding), they find that they have, in fact, only brought more trouble on their shoulders, rather than gained in happiness; and they end by envying, rather than despising, the more common stamp of men who keep closer to the guidance of mere instinct, and do not allow their reason much influence on their conduct. And this we must admit, that the judgment of those who would very much lower the lofty eulogies of the advantages which reason gives us in regard to the happiness and satisfaction of life, or who would even reduce them below zero, is by no means morose or ungrateful to the goodness with which the world is governed, but that there lies at the root of these judgments the idea that our existence has a different and far nobler end, for which, and not for happiness, reason is properly intended, and which must, therefore, be regarded as the supreme condition to which the private ends of man must, for the most part, be postponed.

For as reason is not competent to guide the will with certainty in regard to its objects and the satisfaction of all our wants (which it to some extent even multiplies), this being an end to which an implanted instinct would have led with much greater certainty; and since, nevertheless, reason is imparted to us as a practical faculty, *i.e.* as one which is to have influence on the *will*, therefore, admitting that nature generally in the distribution of her capacities has adapted the means to the end, its true destination must be to produce a *will*, not merely good as a *means* to something else, but *good in itself*, for which reason was absolutely necessary. This will then, though not indeed the sole and complete good, must be the supreme good and the condition of every other, even of the desire of happiness. Under these circumstances, there is nothing inconsistent with the wisdom of nature in the fact that the cultivation of the reason, which is requisite for the first and unconditional purpose, does in many ways interfere, at least in this life, with the attainment of the second, which is always conditional, namely, happiness. Nay, it may even reduce it to nothing, without nature thereby failing in her purpose. For reason recognizes the establishment of a good will as its highest practical destination, and in attaining this purpose is capable only of a satisfaction of its own proper kind, namely, that from the attainment of an end, which end again is determined by reason only, notwithstanding that this may involve many a disappointment to the ends of inclination.

THE FIRST PROPOSITION OF MORALITY

[An action must be done from a sense of duty, if it is to have moral worth]

We have then to develop the notion of a will which deserves to be highly esteemed for itself, and is good without a view to anything further, a notion which exists already in the sound natural understanding, requiring rather to be cleared up than to be taught, and which in estimating the value of our actions always takes the first place, and constitutes the condition of all the rest. In order to do this, we will take the notion of duty, which includes that of a good will, although implying certain subjective restrictions and hindrances. These, however, far from concealing it, or rendering it unrecognizable, rather bring it out by contrast, and make it shine forth so much the brighter.

I omit here all actions which are already recognized as inconsistent with duty although they may be useful for this or that purpose, for with these the question whether they are done *from duty* cannot arise at all, since they even conflict with it. I also set aside those actions which really conform to duty, but to which men have *no, direct inclination*, performing them because they are impelled thereto by some other inclination. For in this case we can readily distinguish whether the action which agrees with duty is done *from duty*, or from a selfish view. It is much harder to make this distinction when the action accords with duty, and the subject has besides a *direct* inclination to it. For example, it is always a matter of duty that a dealer should not overcharge an inexperienced purchaser; and wherever there is much commerce the prudent tradesman does not overcharge, but keeps a fixed price for everyone, so that a child buys of him as well as any other. Men are thus *honestly* served; but this is not enough to make us believe that the tradesman has so acted from duty and from principles of honesty: his own advantage required it; it is out of the question in this case to suppose that he might besides have a direct inclination in favour of the buyers, so that, as it were, from love he should give no advantage to one over another. Accordingly the action was done neither from duty nor from direct inclination, but merely with a selfish view.

On the other hand, it is a duty to maintain one's life; and, in addition, everyone has also a direct inclination to do so. But on this account the often anxious care which most men take for it has no intrinsic worth, and their maxim has no moral import. They preserve their life *as duty requires,* no doubt, but not *because duty requires.* On the other hand, if adversity and hopeless sorrow have completely taken away the relish for life; if the unfortunate one, strong in mind, indignant at his fate rather than desponding or dejected, wishes for death, and yet preserves his life without loving it—not from inclination or fear, but from duty—then his maxim has a moral worth.

To be beneficent when we can is a duty; and besides this, there are many minds so sympathetically constituted that, without any other motive of vanity or self-interest, they find a pleasure in spreading joy around them, and can take delight in the satisfaction of others so far as it is their own work. But I maintain that in such a case an action of this kind, however proper, however amiable it may be, has nevertheless no true moral worth, but is on a level with other inclinations, *e.g.* the inclination to honour, which, if it is happily directed to that which is in fact of public utility and accordant with duty, and consequently honourable, deserves praise and encouragement, but not esteem. For the maxim lacks the moral import, namely, that such actions be done *from duty*, not from inclination. Put the case that the mind of that philanthropist was clouded by sorrow of his own, extinguishing all sympathy with the lot of others, and that while he still has the power to benefit others in distress, he is not touched by their trouble because he is absorbed with his own; and now suppose that he tears himself out of this dead insensibility, and performs the action without any inclination to it, but simply from duty, then first has his action its genuine moral worth. Further still; if nature has put little sympathy in the heart of this or that man; if he, supposed to be an upright man, is by temperament cold and indifferent to the sufferings of others, perhaps because in respect of his own he is provided with the special gift of patience and fortitude, and supposes, or even requires, that others should have the same—and such a man would certainly not be the meanest product of nature—but if nature had not specially framed him for a philanthropist, would he not still find in himself a source from whence to give himself a far higher worth than that of a good-natured temperament could be? Unquestionably. It is just in this that the moral worth of the character is brought out which is incomparably the highest of all, namely, that he is beneficent, not from inclination, but from duty.

To secure one's own happiness is a duty, at least indirectly; for discontent with one's condition, under a pressure of many anxieties and amidst unsatisfied wants, might easily become a great *temptation to transgression of duty.* But here again, without looking to duty, all men have already the strongest and most intimate inclination to happiness, because it is just in this idea that all inclinations are combined in one total. But the precept of happiness is often of such a sort that it greatly interferes with some inclinations, and yet a man cannot form any definite and certain conception of the sum of satisfaction of all of them which is called happiness. It is not then to be wondered at that a single inclination, definite both as to what it promises and as to the time within which it can be gratified, is often able to overcome such a fluctuating idea, and that a gouty patient, for instance, can choose to enjoy what he likes, and to suffer what he may, since, according to his calculation, on this occasion at least, he has [only] not sacrificed the enjoyment of the present moment to a possibly mistaken expectation of a happiness which is supposed to be found in health. But even in this case, if the general desire for happiness did not influence his will, and supposing that in his particular case health was not a necessary element in this calculation, there yet remains in this, as in all other cases, this law, namely, that he should promote his happiness not from inclination but from duty, and by this would his conduct first acquire true moral worth.

It is in this manner, undoubtedly, that we are to understand those passages of Scripture also in which we are commanded to love our neighbour, even our enemy. For love, as an affection, cannot be commanded, but beneficence for duty's sake may; even though we are not impelled to it by any inclination— nay, are even repelled by a natural and unconquerable aversion. This is *practical* love, and not *pathological**—a love which is seated in the will, and not in the propensions of sense—in principles of action and not of tender sympathy; and it is this love alone which can be commanded.

THE SECOND PROPOSITION OF MORALITY

The second proposition is: That an action done from duty derives its moral worth, *not from the purpose* which is to be attained by it, but from the maxim by which it is determined, and therefore does not depend on the realization of the object of the action, but merely on the *principle of volition* by which the action has taken place, without regard to any object of desire. It is clear from what precedes that the purposes which we may have in view in our actions, or their effects regarded as ends and springs of the will, cannot give to actions any unconditional or moral worth. In what, then, can their worth lie, if it is not to consist in the will and in reference to its expected effect? It cannot lie anywhere but in the *principle of the will* without regard to the ends which can be attained by the action. For the will stands between its *a priori principle*, which is formal, and its *a posteriori* spring, which is material, as between two roads, and as it must be determined by something, it follows that it must be determined by the formal principle of volition when an action is done from duty, in which case every material principle has been withdrawn from it.

---

* Passional or emotional

THE THIRD PROPOSITION OF MORALITY

The third proposition, which is a consequence of the two preceding, I would express thus: *Duty is the necessity of acting from respect for the law.* I may have *inclination* for an object as the effect of my proposed action, but I cannot have *respect* for it, just for this reason, that it is an effect and not an energy of will. Similarly, I cannot have respect for inclination, whether my own or another's; I can at most, if my own, approve it; if another's, sometimes even love it; *i.e.* look on it as favourable to my own interest. It is only what is connected with my will as a principle, by no means as an effect—what does not subserve my inclination, but overpowers it, or at least in case of choice excludes it from its calculation—in other words, simply the law of itself, which can be an object of respect, and hence a command. Now an action done from duty must wholly exclude the influence of inclination, and with it every object of the will, so that nothing remains which can determine the will except objectively the *law,* and subjectively *pure respect* for this practical law, and consequently the maxim that I should follow this law even to the thwarting of all my inclinations.

Thus the moral worth of an action does not lie in the effect expected from it, nor in any principle of action which requires to borrow its motive from this expected effect. For all these effects—agreeableness of one's condition, and even the promotion of the happiness of others—could have been also brought about by other causes, so that for this there would have been no need of the will of a rational being; whereas it is in this alone that the supreme and unconditional good can be found. The pre-eminent good which we call moral can therefore consist in nothing else than *the conception of law* in itself, *which certainly is only possible in a rational being,* in so far as this conception, and not the expected effect, determines the will. This is a good which is already present in the person who acts accordingly, and we have not to wait for it to appear first in the result.

THE SUPREME PRINCIPLE OF MORALITY: THE CATEGORICAL IMPERATIVE

But what sort of law can that be, the conception of which must determine the will, even without paying any regard to the effect expected from it, in order that this will may be called good absolutely and without qualification? As I have deprived the will of every impulse which could arise to it from obedience to any law, there remains nothing but the universal conformity of its actions to law in general, which alone is to serve the will as a principle, *i.e.* I am never to act otherwise than so *that I could also will that my maxim should become a universal law.* Here, now, it is the simple conformity to law in general, without assuming any particular law applicable to certain actions, that serves the will as its principle, and must so serve it, if duty is not to be a vain delusion and a chimerical notion. The common reason of men in its practical judgments perfectly coincides with this, and always has in view the principle here suggested. Let the question be, for example: May I when in distress make a promise with the intention not to keep it? I readily distinguish here between the two significations which the question may have: Whether it is prudent, or whether it is right, to make a false promise? The former may undoubtedly often be the case. I see clearly indeed that it is not enough to extricate myself from a present difficulty by means of this subterfuge, but it must be well considered whether there may not hereafter spring from this lie much greater inconvenience than that from which I now free myself, and as, with all my supposed *cunning*, the consequences cannot be so easily foreseen but that credit once lost may be much more injurious to me than any mischief which I seek to avoid at present, it should be considered whether it would not be more *prudent* to act herein according to a universal maxim, and to make it a habit to promise nothing except with the intention of keeping it. But it is soon clear to me that such a maxim will still only be based on the fear of consequences. Now it is a wholly different thing to be truthful from duty, and to be so from apprehension of injurious consequences. In the first case, the very notion of the action already implies a law for me; in the second case, I must first look about elsewhere to see what results may be combined with it which would affect myself. For to deviate from the principle of duty is beyond all doubt wicked; but to be unfaithful to my maxim of prudence may often be very advantageous to me, although to abide by it is certainly safer. The shortest way, however, and an unerring one, to discover the answer to this question whether a lying promise is consistent with duty, is to ask myself, Should I be content that my maxim (to extricate myself from difficulty by a false promise) should hold good as a universal law, for myself as well as for others? and should I be able to say to myself, "Every one may make a deceitful promise when he finds himself in a difficulty from which he cannot otherwise extricate himself"? Then I presently become aware that while I can will the lie, I can by no means will that lying should be a universal law. For with such a law there would be no promises at all, since it would be in vain to allege my intention in regard to my future actions to those who would not believe this allegation, or if they over-hastily did so, would pay me back in my own coin. Hence my maxim, as soon as it should be made a universal law, would necessarily destroy itself.

I do not, therefore, need any far-reaching penetration to discern what I have to do in order that my will may be morally good. Inexperienced in the course of the world, incapable of being prepared for all its contingencies, I only ask myself: Canst thou also will that thy maxim should be a universal law? If not, then it must be rejected, and that not because of a disadvantage accruing from myself or even to others, but because it cannot enter as a principle into a possible universal legislation, and reason extorts from me immediate respect for such legislation. I do not indeed as yet *discern* on what this respect is based (this the philosopher may inquire), but at least I understand this, that it is an estimation of the worth which far outweighs all worth of what is recommended by inclination, and that the necessity of acting from *pure* respect for the practical law is what constitutes duty, to which every other motive must give place, because it is the condition of a will being good *in itself*, and the worth of such a will is above everything.

Thus, then, without quitting the moral knowledge of common human reason, we have arrived at its principle. And although, no doubt, common men do not conceive it in such an abstract and universal form, yet they always have it really before their eyes, and use it as the standard of their decision. . . .

Nor could anything be more fatal to morality than that we should wish to derive it from examples. For every example of it that is set before me must be first itself tested by principles of morality, whether it is worthy to serve as an original example, *i.e.* as a pattern, but by no means can it authoritatively furnish the conception of morality. Even the Holy One of the Gospels must first be compared with our ideal of moral perfection before we can recognize Him as such; and so He says of Himself, "Why call ye Me [whom you see] good; none is good [the model of good] but God only [whom ye do not see]." But whence have we the conception of God as the supreme good? Simply from the *idea* of moral perfection, which reason frames *a priori* and connects inseparably with the notion of a free will. Imitation finds no place at all in morality, and examples serve only for encouragement, *i.e.* they put beyond doubt the feasibility of what the law commands, they make visible that which the practical rule expresses more generally, but they can never authorize us to set aside the true original which lies in reason, and to guide ourselves by examples.

From what has been said, it is clear that all moral conceptions have their seat and origin completely *a priori* in the reason, and that, moreover, in the commonest reason just as truly as in that which is in the highest degree speculative; that they cannot be obtained by abstraction from any empirical, and therefore merely contingent knowledge; that it is just this purity of their origin that makes them worthy to serve as our supreme practical principle, and that just in proportion as we add anything empirical, we detract from their genuine influence, and from the absolute value of actions; that it is not only of the greatest necessity, in a purely speculative point of view, but is also of the greatest practical importance, to derive these notions and laws from pure reason, to present them pure and unmixed, and even to determine the compass of this practical or pure rational knowledge, *i.e.* to determine the whole faculty of pure practical reason; and, in doing so, we must not make its principles dependent on the particular nature of human reason, though in speculative philosophy this may be permitted, or may even at times be necessary; but since moral laws ought to hold good for every rational creature, we must derive them from the general concept of a rational being. In this way, although for its *application* to man morality has need of anthropology, yet, in the first instance, we must treat it independently as pure philosophy, *i.e.* as metaphysic, complete in itself (a thing which in such distinct branches of science is easily done); knowing well that unless we are in possession of this, it would not only be vain to determine the moral element of duty in right actions for purposes of speculative criticism, but it would be impossible to base morals on their genuine principles, even for common practical purposes, especially of moral instruction, so as to produce pure moral dispositions, and to engraft them on men's minds to the promotion of the greatest possible good in the world. . . .

THE RATIONAL GROUND OF THE CATEGORICAL IMPERATIVE

. . . [T]he question, how the imperative of *morality* is possible, is undoubtedly one, the only one, demanding a solution, as this is not at all hypothetical, and the objective necessity which it presents cannot rest on any hypothesis, as is the case with the hypothetical imperatives. Only here we must never leave out of consideration that we *cannot* make out *by any example*, in other words empirically, whether there is such an imperative at all; but it is rather to be feared that all those which seem to be categorical may yet be at bottom hypothetical. For instance, when the precept is: Thou shalt not promise deceitfully; and it is assumed that the necessity of this is not a mere counsel to avoid some other evil, so that it should mean: Thou shalt not make a lying promise, lest if it become known thou shouldst destroy thy credit, but that an action of this kind must be regarded as evil in itself, so that the imperative of the prohibition is categorical; then we cannot show with certainty in any example that the will was determined merely by the law, without any other spring of action, although it may appear to be so. For it is always possible that fear of disgrace, perhaps also obscure dread of other dangers, may have a secret influence on the will. Who can prove by experience the nonexistence of a cause when all that experience tells us is that we do not perceive it? But in such a case the so-called moral imperative, which as such appears to be categorical and unconditional, would in reality be only a pragmatic precept, drawing our attention to our own interests, and merely teaching us to take these into consideration.

We shall therefore have to investigate *a priori* the possibility of a categorical imperative, as we have not in this case the advantage of its reality being given in experience, so that [the elucidation of] its possibility should be requisite only for its explanation, not for its establishment. In the meantime it may be discerned beforehand that the categorical imperative alone has the purport of a practical law: all the rest may indeed be called *principles* of the will but not laws, since whatever is only necessary for the attainment of some arbitrary purpose may be considered as in itself contingent, and we can at any time be free from the precept if we give up the purpose: on the contrary, the unconditional command leaves the will no liberty to choose the opposite; consequently it alone carries with it that necessity which we require in a law.

Secondly, in the case of this categorical imperative or law of morality, the difficulty (of discerning its possibility) is a very profound one. It is an *a priori* synthetical practical proposition; and as there is so much difficulty in discerning the possibility of speculative propositions of this kind, it may readily be supposed that the difficulty will be no less with the practical.

FIRST FORMULATION OF THE CATEGORICAL IMPERATIVE: UNIVERSAL LAW

In this problem we will first inquire whether the mere conception of a categorical imperative may not perhaps supply us also with the formula of it, containing the proposition which alone can be a categorical imperative; for even if we know the tenor of such an absolute command, yet how it is possible will require further special and laborious study, which we postpone to the last section.

When I conceive a hypothetical imperative, in general I do not know beforehand what it will contain until I am given the condition. But when I conceive a categorical imperative, I know at once what it contains. For as the imperative contains besides the law only the necessity that the maxims shall conform to this law, while the law contains no conditions restricting it, there remains nothing but the general statement that the maxim of the action should conform to a universal law, and it is this conformity alone that the imperative properly represents as necessary.

There is therefore but one categorical imperative, namely, this: *Act only on that maxim whereby thou canst at the same time will that it should become a universal law.*

Now if all imperatives of duty can be deduced from this one imperative as from their principle, then, although it should remain undecided whether what is called duty is not merely a vain notion, yet at least we shall be able to show what we understand by it and what this notion means.

Since the universality of the law according to which effects are produced constitutes what is properly called *nature* in the most general sense (as to form), that is the existence of things so far as it is determined by general laws, the imperative of duty may be expressed thus: *Act as if the maxim of thy action were to become by thy will a universal law of nature.*

FOUR ILLUSTRATIONS

We will now enumerate a few duties, adopting the usual division of them into duties to ourselves and to others, and into perfect and imperfect duties.

1. A man reduced to despair by a series of misfortunes feels wearied of life, but is still so far in possession of his reason that he can ask himself whether it would not be contrary to his duty to himself to take his own life. Now he inquires whether the maxim of his action could become a universal law of nature.

His maxim is: From self-love I adopt it as a principle to shorten my life when its longer duration is likely to bring more evil than satisfaction. It is asked then simply whether this principle founded on self-love can become a universal law of nature. Now we see at once that a system of nature of which it should be a law to destroy life by means of the very feeling whose special nature it is to impel to the improvement of life would contradict itself, and therefore could not exist as a system of nature; hence that maxim cannot possibly exist as a universal law of nature, and consequently would be wholly inconsistent with the supreme principle of all duty.

2. Another finds himself forced by necessity to borrow money. He knows that he will not be able to repay it, but sees also that nothing will be lent to him, unless he promises stoutly to repay it in a definite time. He desires to make this promise, but he has still so much conscience as to ask himself: Is it not unlawful and inconsistent with duty to get out of a difficulty in this way? Suppose, however, that he resolves to do so, then the maxim of his action would be expressed thus: When I think myself in want of money, I will borrow money and promise to repay it, although I know that I never can do so. Now this principle of self-love or of one's own advantage may perhaps be consistent with my whole future welfare; but the question is, Is it right? I change then the suggestion of self-love into a universal law, and state the question thus: How would it be if my maxim were a universal law? Then I see at once that it could never hold as a universal law of nature, but would necessarily contradict itself. For supposing it to be a universal law that everyone when he thinks himself in a difficulty should be able to promise whatever he pleases, with the purpose of not keeping his promise, the promise itself would become impossible, as well as the end that one might have in view in it, since no one would consider that anything was promised to him, but would ridicule all such statements as vain pretenses.

3. A third finds in himself a talent which with the help of some culture might make him a useful man in many respects. But he finds himself in comfortable circumstances, and prefers to indulge in pleasure rather than to take pains in enlarging and improving his happy natural capacities. He asks, however, whether his maxim of neglect of his natural gifts, besides agreeing with his inclination to indulgence, agrees also with what is called duty. He sees then that a system of nature could indeed subsist with such a universal law although men (like the South Sea islanders) should let their talents rest, and resolve to devote their lives merely to idleness, amusement, and propagation of their species—in a word, to enjoyment; but he cannot possibly *will* that this should be a universal law of nature, or be implanted in us as such by a natural instinct. For, as a rational being, he necessarily wills that his faculties be developed, since they serve him, and have been given him, for all sorts of possible purposes.

4. A fourth, who is in prosperity, while he sees that others have to contend with great wretchedness and that he could help them, thinks: What concern is

it of mine? Let everyone be as happy as Heaven pleases, or as he can make himself; I will take nothing from him nor even envy him, only I do not wish to contribute anything to his welfare or to his assistance in distress! Now no doubt if such a mode of thinking were a universal law, the human race might very well subsist, and doubtless even better than in a state in which everyone talks of sympathy and good-will, or even takes care occasionally to put it into practice, but, on the other side, also cheats when he can, betrays the rights of men, or otherwise violates them. But although it is possible that a universal law of nature might exist in accordance with that maxim, it is impossible to *will* that such a principle should have the universal validity of a law of nature. For a will which resolved this would contradict itself, inasmuch as many cases might occur in which one would have need of the love and sympathy of others, and in which, by such a law of nature, sprung from his own will, he would deprive himself of all hope of the aid he desires.

These are a few of the many actual duties, or at least what we regard as such, which obviously fall into two classes on the one principle that we have laid down. We must be *able to will* that a maxim of our action should be a universal law. This is the canon of the moral appreciation of the action generally. Some actions are of such a character that their maxim cannot without contradiction be even *conceived* as a universal law of nature, far from it being possible that we should *will* that it *should* be so. In others this intrinsic impossibility is not found, but still it is impossible to *will* that their maxim should be raised to the universality of a law of nature, since such a will would contradict itself. It is easily seen that the former violate strict or rigorous (inflexible) duty; the latter only laxer (meritorious) duty. Thus it has been completely shown by these examples how all duties depend as regards the nature of the obligation (not the object of the action) on the same principle.

SECOND FORMULATION OF THE CATEGORICAL IMPERATIVE: HUMANITY AS AN END IN ITSELF

. . . Now I say: man and generally any rational being *exists* as an end in himself, *not merely as a means* to be arbitrarily used by this or that will, but in all his actions, whether they concern himself or other rational beings, must be always regarded at the same time as an end. All objects of the inclinations have only a conditional worth; for if the inclinations and the wants founded on them did not exist, then their object would be without value. But the inclinations themselves being sources of want are so far from having an absolute worth for which they should be desired, that, on the contrary, it must be the universal wish of every rational being to be wholly free from them. Thus the worth of any object which is *to be acquired* by our action is always conditional. Beings whose existence depends not on our will but on nature's, have nevertheless, if they are nonrational beings, only a relative value as means, and are therefore called *things*; rational beings, on the contrary, are called *persons*, because their very nature points them out as ends in themselves, that is as something which must not be used merely as means, and so far therefore restricts freedom of action (and is an object of respect). These, therefore, are not merely subjective ends whose existence has a worth *for us* as an effect of our action, but *objective ends*, that is things whose existence is an end in itself: an end moreover for which no other can be substituted, which they should subserve *merely* as means, for otherwise nothing whatever would possess *absolute worth*; but if all worth were conditioned and therefore contingent, then there would be no supreme practical principle of reason whatever.

If then there is a supreme practical principle or, in respect of the human will, a categorical imperative, it must be one which, being drawn from the conception of that which is necessarily an end for everyone because it is *an end in itself*, constitutes an *objective* principle of will, and can therefore serve as a universal practical law. The foundation of this principle is: *rational nature exists as an end in itself.* Man necessarily conceives his own existence as being so: so far then this is a *subjective* principle of human actions. But every other rational being regards its existence similarly, just on the same rational principle that holds for me: so that it is at the same time an objective principle, from which as a supreme practical law all laws of the will must be capable of being deduced. Accordingly the practical imperative will be as follows: *So act as to treat humanity, whether in thine own person or in that of any other, in every case as an end withal, never as only.* . . .

. . . Looking back now on all previous attempts to discover the principle of morality, we need not wonder why they all failed. It was seen that man was bound to laws by duty, but it was not observed that the laws to which he is subject are *only those of his own giving*, though at the same time they are *universal*, and that he is only bound to act in conformity with his own will; a will, however, which is designed by nature to give universal laws. For when one has conceived man only as subject to a law (no matter what), then this law required some interest, either by way of attraction or constraint, since it did not originate as a law from *his own* will, but his will was according to a law obliged by *something else* to act in a certain manner. Now by this necessary consequence all the labour spent in finding a supreme principle of *duty* was irrevocably lost. For men never elicited duty, but only a necessity of acting from a certain interest. Whether this interest was private or otherwise, in any case the imperative must be conditional, and could not by any means be capable of being a moral command. I will therefore call this the principle of *Autonomy* of the will, in contrast with every other which I accordingly reckon as *Heteronomy*.

THE KINGDOM OF ENDS

The conception of every rational being as one which must consider itself as giving in all the maxims of its will universal laws, so as to judge itself and its actions from this point of view—this conception leads to another which depends on it and is very fruitful, that of a *kingdom of ends.*

By a *kingdom* I understand the union of different rational beings in a system by common laws. Now since it is by laws that ends are determined as regards their universal validity, hence, if we abstract from the personal differences of rational beings, and likewise from all the content of their private ends, we shall be able to conceive all ends combined in a systematic whole (including both rational beings as ends in themselves, and also the special ends which each may propose to himself), that is to say, we can conceive a kingdom of ends, which on the preceding principles is possible.

For all rational beings come under the *law* that each of them must treat itself and all others *never merely as means,* but in every case *at the same time as ends in themselves.* Hence results a systematic union of rational beings by common objective laws, *i.e.,* a kingdom which may be called a kingdom of ends, since what these laws have in view is just the relation of these beings to one another as ends and means. . . .

BILLY BUDD (CHAPTER 20)

HERMAN MELVILLE

Full of disquietude and misgiving, the surgeon left the cabin. Was Captain Vere suddenly affected in his mind, or was it but a transient excitement, brought about by so strange and extraordinary a tragedy? As to the drumhead court, it struck the surgeon as impolitic, if nothing more. The thing to do, he thought, was to place Billy Budd in confinement, and in a way dictated by usage, and postpone further action in so extraordinary a case to such time as they should rejoin the squadron, and then refer it to the admiral. He recalled the unwonted agitation of Captain Vere and his excited exclamations, so at variance with his normal manner. Was he unhinged?

But assuming that he is, it is not so susceptible of proof. What then can the surgeon do? No more trying situation is conceivable than that of an officer subordinate under a captain whom he suspects to be not mad, indeed, but yet not quite unaffected in his intellects. To argue his order to him would be insolence. To resist him would be mutiny.

In obedience to Captain Vere, he communicated what had happened to the lieutenants and captain of marines, saying nothing as to the captain's state.

They fully shared his own surprise and concern. Like him too, they seemed to think that such a matter should be referred to the admiral.

21

Who in the rainbow can draw the line where the violet tint ends and the orange tint begins? Distinctly we see the difference of the colors, but where exactly does the one first blendingly enter into the other? So with sanity and insanity. In pronounced cases there is no question about them. But in some supposed cases, in various degrees supposedly less pronounced, to draw the exact line of demarcation few will undertake, though for a fee becoming considerate some professional experts will. There is nothing namable but that some men will, or undertake to, do it for pay.

Whether Captain Vere, as the surgeon professionally and privately surmised, was really the sudden victim of any degree of aberration, every one must determine for himself by such light as this narrative may afford.

That the unhappy event which has been narrated could not have happened at a worse juncture was but too true. For it was close on the heel of the suppressed insurrections, an aftertime very critical to naval authority, demanding from every English sea commander two qualities not readily interfusable—prudence and rigor. Moreover, there was something crucial in the case.

In the jugglery of circumstances preceding and attending the event on board the *Bellipotent*, and in the light of that martial code whereby it was formally to be judged, innocence and guilt personified in Claggart and Budd in effect changed places. In a legal view the apparent victim of the tragedy was he who had sought to victimize a man blameless; and the indisputable deed of the latter, navally regarded, constituted the most heinous of military crimes. Yet more. The essential right and wrong involved in the matter, the clearer that might be, so much the worse for the responsibility of a loyal sea commander, inasmuch as he was not authorized to determine the matter on that primitive basis.

Small wonder then that the *Bellipotent*'s captain, though in general a man of rapid decision, felt that circumspectness not less than promptitude was necessary. Until he could decide upon his course, and in each detail; and not only so, but until the concluding measure was upon the point of being enacted, he deemed it advisable, in view of all the circumstances, to guard as much as possible against publicity. Here he may or may not have erred. Certain it is, however, that subsequently in the confidential talk of more than one or two gun rooms and cabins he was not a little criticized by some officers, a fact imputed by his friends and vehemently by his cousin Jack Denton to professional jealousy of Starry Vere. Some imaginative ground for invidious comment there was. The maintenance of secrecy in the matter, the confining all knowledge of it for a time to the place where the homicide occurred, the quarterdeck cabin; in these particulars lurked some resemblance to the policy adopted in those tragedies of the palace which have occurred more than once in the capital founded by Peter the Barbarian.

The case indeed was such that fain would the *Bellipotent's* captain have deferred taking any action whatever respecting it further than to keep the foretopman a close prisoner till the ship rejoined the squadron and then submitting the matter to the judgment of his admiral.

But a true military officer is in one particular like a true monk. Not with more of self-abnegation will the latter keep his vows of monastic obedience than the former his vows of allegiance to martial duty.

Feeling that unless quick action was taken on it, the deed of the foretopman, so soon as it should be known on the gun decks, would tend to awaken any slumbering embers of the Nore among the crew, a sense of the urgency of the case overruled in Captain Vere every other consideration. But though a conscientious disciplinarian, he was no lover of authority for mere authority's sake. Very far was he from embracing opportunities for monopolizing to himself the perils of moral responsibility, none at least that could properly be referred to an official superior or shared with him by his official equals or even subordinates. So thinking, he was glad it would not be at variance with usage to turn the matter over to a summary court of his own officers, reserving to himself, as the one on whom the ultimate accountability would rest, the right of maintaining a supervision of it, or formally or informally interposing at need. Accordingly a drumhead court was summarily convened, he electing the individuals composing it: the first lieutenant, the captain of marines, and the sailing master.

In associating an officer of marines with the sea lieutenant and the sailing master in a case having to do with a sailor, the commander perhaps deviated from general custom. He was prompted thereto by the circumstance that he took that soldier to be a judicious person, thoughtful, and not altogether incapable of grappling with a difficult case unprecedented in his prior experience. Yet even as to him he was not without some latent misgiving, for withal he was an extremely good-natured man, an enjoyer of his dinner, a sound sleeper, and inclined to obesity—a man who though he would always maintain his manhood in battle might not prove altogether reliable in a moral dilemma involving aught of the tragic. As to the first lieutenant and the sailing master, Captain Vere could not but be aware that though honest natures, of approved gallantry upon occasion, their intelligence was mostly confined to the matter of active seamanship and the fighting demands of their profession.

The court was held in the same cabin where the unfortunate affair had taken place. This cabin, the commander's, embraced the entire area under the poop deck. Aft, and on either side, was a small stateroom, the one now temporarily a jail and the other a dead-house, and a yet smaller compartment, leaving a space between expanding forward into a goodly oblong of length coinciding with the ship's beam. A skylight of moderate dimension was overhead, and at each end of the oblong space were two sashed porthole windows easily convertible back into embrasures for short carronades.

All being quickly in readiness, Billy Budd was arraigned, Captain Vere necessarily appearing as the sole witness in the case, and as such temporarily sinking his rank, though singularly maintaining it in a matter apparently trivial, namely, that he testified from the ship's weather side, with that object having caused the court to sit on the lee side. Concisely he narrated all that had led up to the catastrophe, omitting nothing in Claggart's accusation and deposing as to the manner in which the prisoner had received it. At this testimony the three officers glanced with no little surprise at Billy Budd, the last man they would have suspected either of the mutinous design alleged by Claggart or the undeniable deed he himself had done. The first lieutenant, taking judicial primacy and turning toward the prisoner, said, "Captain Vere has spoken. Is it or is it not as Captain Vere says?"

In response came syllables not so much impeded in the utterance as might have been anticipated. They were these: "Captain Vere tells the truth. It is just as Captain Vere says, but it is not as the master-at-arms said. I have eaten the King's bread and I am true to the King."

"I believe you, my man," said the witness, his voice indicating a suppressed emotion not otherwise betrayed.

"God will bless you for that, your honor!" not without stammering said Billy, and all but broke down. But immediately he was recalled to self-control by another question, to which with the same emotional difficulty of utterance he said, "No, there was no malice between us. I never bore malice against the master-at-arms. I am sorry that he is dead. I did not mean to kill him. Could I have used my tongue I would not have struck him. But he foully lied to my face and in presence of my captain, and I had to say something, and I could only say it with a blow, God help me!"

In the impulsive aboveboard manner of the frank one the court saw confirmed all that was implied in words that just previously had perplexed them, coming as they did from the testifier to the tragedy and promptly following Billy's impassioned disclaimer of mutinous intent—Captain Vere's words, "I believe you, my man."

Next it was asked of him whether he knew of or suspected aught savoring of incipient trouble (meaning mutiny, though the explicit term was avoided) going on in any section of the ship's company.

The reply lingered. This was naturally imputed by the court to the same vocal embarrassment which had retarded or obstructed previous answers. But in main it was otherwise here, the question immediately recalling to Billy's mind the interview with the afterguardsman in the forechains. But an innate repugnance to playing a part at all approaching that of an informer against one's own shipmates—the same erring sense of uninstructed honor which had stood in the way of his reporting the matter at the time, though as a loyal man-of-war's man it was incumbent on him, and failure so to do, if charged against him and proven, would have subjected him to the heaviest of penalties; this, with the blind feeling now his that nothing really was being hatched, prevailed with him. When the answer came it was a negative.

"One question more," said the officer of marines, now first speaking and with a troubled earnestness. "You tell us that what the master-at-arms said against you was a lie. Now why should he have so lied, so maliciously lied, since you declare there was no malice between you?"

At that question, unintentionally touching on a spiritual sphere wholly obscure to Billy's thoughts, he was nonplussed, evincing a confusion indeed that some observers, such as can readily be imagined, would have construed into involuntary evidence of hidden guilt. Nevertheless, he strove some way to answer, but all at once relinquished the vain endeavor, at the same time turning an appealing glance towards Captain Vere as deeming him his best helper and friend. Captain Vere, who had been seated for a time, rose to his feet, addressing the interrogator. "The question you put to him comes naturally enough. But how can he rightly answer it?—or anybody else, unless indeed it be he who lies within there," designating the compartment where lay the corpse. "But the prone one there will not rise to our summons. In effect, though, as it seems to me, the point you make is hardly material. Quite aside from any conceivable motive actuating the master-at-arms, and irrespective of the provocation to the blow, a martial court must needs in the present case confine its attention to the blow's consequence, which consequence justly is to be deemed not otherwise than as the striker's deed."

This utterance, the full significance of which it was not at all likely that Billy took in, nevertheless caused him to turn a wistful interrogative look toward the speaker, a look in its dumb expressiveness not unlike that which a dog of generous breed might turn upon his master, seeking in his face some elucidation of a previous gesture ambiguous to the canine intelligence. Nor was the same utterance without marked effect upon the three officers, more especially the soldier. Couched in it seemed to them a meaning unanticipated, involving a prejudgment on the speaker's part. It served to augment a mental disturbance previously evident enough.

The soldier once more spoke, in a tone of suggestive dubiety addressing at once his associates and Captain Vere: "Nobody is present—none of the ship's company, I mean—who might shed lateral light, if any is to be had, upon what remains mysterious in this matter."

"That is thoughtfully put," said Captain Vere; "I see your drift. Ay, there is a mystery; but, to use a scriptural phrase, it is a 'mystery of iniquity,' a matter for psychologic theologians to discuss. But what has a military court to do with it? Not to add that for us any possible investigation of it is cut off by the lasting tongue-tie of—him—in yonder," again designating the mortuary stateroom. "The prisoner's deed—with that alone we have to do."

To this, and particularly the closing reiteration, the marine soldier, knowing not how aptly to reply, sadly abstained from saying aught. The first lieutenant, who at the outset had not unnaturally assumed primacy in the court, now overrulingly instructed by a glance from Captain Vere, a glance more effective than words, resumed that primacy. Turning to the prisoner, "Budd," he said, and scarce in equable tones, "Budd, if you have aught further to say for yourself, say it now."

Upon this the young sailor turned another quick glance toward Captain Vere; then, as taking a hint from that aspect, a hint confirming his own instinct that silence was now best, replied to the lieutenant, "I have said all, sir."

The marine—the same who had been the sentinel without the cabin door at the time that the foretopman, followed by the master-at-arms, entered it—he, standing by the sailor throughout these judicial proceedings, was now directed to take him back to the after compartment originally assigned to the prisoner and his custodian. As the twain disappeared from view, the three officers, as partially liberated from some inward constraint associated with Billy's mere presence, simultaneously stirred in their seats. They exchanged looks of troubled indecision, yet feeling that decide they must and without long delay. For Captain Vere, he for the time stood—unconsciously with his back toward them, apparently in one of his absent fits—gazing out from a sashed porthole to windward upon the monotonous blank of the twilight sea. But the court's silence continuing, broken only at moments by brief consultations, in low earnest tones, this served to arouse him and energize him. Turning, he to-and-fro paced the cabin athwart; in the returning ascent to windward climbing the slant deck in the ship's lee roll, without knowing it symbolizing thus in his action a mind resolute to surmount difficulties even if against primitive instincts strong as the wind and the sea. Presently he came to a stand before the three. After scanning their faces he stood less as mustering his thoughts for expression than as one inly deliberating how best to put them to well-meaning men not intellectually mature, men with whom it was necessary to demonstrate certain principles that were axioms to himself. Similar impatience as to talking is perhaps one reason that deters some minds from addressing any popular assemblies.

When speak he did, something, both in the substance of what he said and his manner of saying it, showed the influence of unshared studies modifying and tempering the practical training of an active career. This, along with his phraseology, now and then was suggestive of the grounds whereon rested that imputation of a certain pedantry socially alleged against him by certain naval men of wholly practical cast, captains who nevertheless would frankly concede that His Majesty's navy mustered no more efficient officer of their grade than Starry Vere.

What he said was to this effect: "Hitherto I have been but the witness, little more; and I should hardly think now to take another tone, that of your coadjutor for the time, did I not perceive in you—at the crisis too—a troubled hesitancy, proceeding, I doubt not, from the clash of military duty with moral scruple—scruple vitalized by compassion. For the compassion, how can I otherwise than share it? But, mindful of paramount obligations, I strive against scruples that may tend to enervate decision. Not, gentlemen, that I hide from myself that the case is an exceptional one. Speculatively regarded, it well might be referred to a jury of casuists. But for us here, acting not as casuists or moralists, it is a case practical, and under martial law practically to be dealt with.

"But your scruples: do they move as in a dusk? Challenge them. Make them advance and declare themselves. Come now; do they import something like this: If, mindless of palliating circumstances, we are bound to regard the death of the master-at-arms as the prisoner's deed, then does that deed constitute a capital crime whereof the penalty is a mortal one. But in natural justice is nothing but the prisoner's overt act to be considered? How can we adjudge to summary and shameful death a fellow creature innocent before God, and whom we feel to be so?—Does that state it aright? You sign sad assent. Well, I too feel that, the full force of that. It is Nature. But do these buttons that we wear attest that our allegiance is to Nature? No, to the King. Though the ocean, which is inviolate Nature primeval, though this be the element where we move and have our being as sailors, yet as the King's officers lies our duty in a sphere correspondingly natural? So little is that true, that in receiving our commissions we in the most important regards ceased to be natural free agents. When war is declared are we the commissioned fighters previously consulted? We fight at command. If our judgments approve the war, that is but coincidence. So in other particulars. So now. For suppose condemnation to follow these present proceedings. Would it be so much we ourselves that would condemn as it would be martial law operating through us? For that law and the rigor of it, we are not responsible. Our Vowed responsibility is in this: That however pitilessly that law may operate in any instances, we nevertheless adhere to it and administer it.

"But the exceptional in the matter moves the hearts within you. Even so too is mine moved. But let not warm hearts betray heads that should be cool. Ashore in a criminal case, will an upright judge allow himself off the bench to be waylaid by some tender kinswoman of the accused seeking to touch him with her tearful plea? Well, the heart here, sometimes the feminine in man, is as that piteous woman, and hard though it be, she must here be ruled out."

He paused, earnestly studying them for a moment; then resumed.

"But something in your aspect seems to urge that it is not solely the heart that moves in you, but also the conscience, the private conscience. But tell me whether or not, occupying the position we do, private conscience should not yield to that imperial one formulated in the code under which alone we officially proceed?"

Here the three men moved in their seats, less convinced than agitated by the course of an argument troubling but the more the spontaneous conflict within.

Perceiving which, the speaker paused for a moment; then abruptly changing his tone, went on.

"To steady us a bit, let us recur to the facts.—In wartime at sea a man-of-war's man strikes his superior in grade, and the blow kills. Apart from its effect the blow itself is, according to the Articles of War, a capital crime. Furthermore—"

"Ay, sir," emotionally broke in the officer of marines, "in one sense it was. But surely Budd purposed neither mutiny nor homicide."

"Surely not, my good man. And before a court less arbitrary and more merciful than a martial one, that plea would largely extenuate. At the Last Assizes it shall acquit. But how here? We proceed under the law of the Mutiny Act. In feature no child can resemble his father more than that Act resembles in spirit the thing from which it derives—War. In His Majesty's service—in this ship, indeed—there are Englishmen forced to fight for the King against their will. Against their conscience, for aught we know. Though as their fellow creatures some of us may appreciate their position, yet as navy officers what reck we of it? Still less recks the enemy. Our impressed men he would fain cut down in the same swath with our volunteers. As regards the enemy's naval conscripts, some of whom may even share our own abhorrence of the regicidal French Directory, it is the same on our side. War looks but to the frontage, the appearance. And the Mutiny Act, War's child, takes after the father. Budd's intent or non-intent is nothing to the purpose.

"But while, put to it by those anxieties in you which I cannot but respect, I only repeat myself—while thus strangely we prolong proceedings that should be summary—the enemy may be sighted and an engagement result. We must do; and one of two things must we do—condemn or let go."

"Can we not convict and yet mitigate the penalty?" asked the sailing master, here speaking, and falteringly, for the first.

"Gentlemen, were that clearly lawful for us under the circumstances, consider the consequences of such clemency. The people" (meaning the ship's company) "have native sense; most of them are familiar with our naval usage and tradition; and how would they take it? Even could you explain to them—which our official position forbids—they, long molded by arbitrary discipline, have not that kind of intelligent responsiveness that might qualify them to comprehend and discriminate. No, to the people the foretopman's deed, however it be worded in the announcement, will be plain homicide committed in a flagrant act of mutiny. What penalty for that should follow, they know. But it does not follow. *Why?* they will ruminate. You know what sailors are. Will they not revert to the recent outbreak at the Nore? Ay. They know the well-founded alarm—the panic it struck throughout England. Your clement sentence they would account pusillanimous. They would think that we flinch, that we are afraid of them—afraid of practicing a lawful rigor singularly demanded at this juncture, lest it should provoke new troubles. What shame to us such a conjecture on their part, and how deadly to discipline. You see then, whither, prompted by duty and the law, I steadfastly drive. But I beseech you, my friends, do not take me amiss. I feel as you do for this unfortunate boy.

But did he know our hearts, I take him to be of that generous nature that he would feel even for us on whom in this military necessity so heavy a compulsion is laid."

With that, crossing the deck he resumed his place by the sashed porthole, tacitly leaving the three to come to a decision. On the cabin's opposite side the troubled court sat silent. Loyal lieges, plain and practical, though at bottom they dissented from some points Captain Vere had put to them, they were without the faculty, hardly had the inclination, to gainsay one whom they felt to be an earnest man, one too not less their superior in mind than in naval rank. But it is not improbable that even such of his words as were not without influence over them, less came home to them than his closing appeal to their instinct as sea officers: in the forethought he threw out as to the practical consequences to discipline, considering the unconfirmed tone of the fleet at the time, should a man-of-war's man's violent killing at sea of a superior in grade be allowed to pass for aught else than a capital crime demanding prompt infliction of the penalty.

Not unlikely they were brought to something more or less akin to that harassed frame of mind which in the year 1842 actuated the commander of the U.S. brig-of-war *Somers* to resolve, under the so-called Articles of War, Articles modeled upon the English Mutiny Act, to resolve upon the execution at sea of a midshipman and two sailors as mutineers designing the seizure of the brig. Which resolution was carried out though in a time of peace and within not many days' sail of home. An act vindicated by a naval court of inquiry subsequently convened ashore. History, and here cited without comment. True, the circumstances on board the *Somers* were different from those on board the *Bellipotent*. But the urgency felt, well-warranted or otherwise, was much the same.

Says a writer whom few know, "Forty years after a battle it is easy for a noncombatant to reason about how it ought to have been fought. It is another thing personally and under fire to have to direct the fighting while involved in the obscuring smoke of it. Much so with respect to other emergencies involving considerations both practical and moral, and when it is imperative promptly to act. The greater the fog the more it imperils the steamer, and speed is put on though at the hazard of running somebody down. Little ween the snug card players in the cabin of the responsibilities of the sleepless man on the bridge."

In brief, Billy Budd was formally, convicted and sentenced to be hung at the yardarm in the early morning watch, it being now night. Otherwise, as is customary in such cases, the sentence would forthwith have been carried out. In wartime on the field or in the fleet, a mortal punishment decreed by a drumhead court—on the field sometimes decreed by but a nod from the general—follows without delay on the heel of conviction, without appeal.

UTILITARIAN ETHICS

■

Morality must be subdued to the needs of the Revolution.
V. I. LENIN

Alice was shocked when she learned that the car bomb was set to explode with a timer instead of being triggered by an electronic device. This meant that they had no control over who would be victims of the explosion. They were to plant the car in a crowded shopping and dining district in Knights-bridge. The bomb was to explode at the height of rush hour, targeting scores of innocent people.

Alice disagreed with the plan. She was totally committed to the cause of the Irish Republican Army, not only to be rid of British control in Ireland, but to work for a socialist Britain. This acted as her umbrella for other "so-cialist" causes: Greenpeace, Save the Whales, antipollution, the workers' movement. She had long ago donned her socialist cap in her struggle against the righteous and affluent bourgeoisie. She proved her dedication to the IRA in numerous ways. She took upon herself the daunting task of rejuvenating the dilapidated old house on 43 Mill Road for the purpose of using it as a British base for IRA activities under the cover of naming it the Communist Centre Union. She personally oversaw the renovation and made it possible for her comrades to inhabit the house in more humane and comfortable conditions. She stole linen curtains from her mother to be used in the house. She stole over a thousand pounds from her father and the monies went to the house and to the cause. Due to her efforts, the First

National Congress of the Communist Centre Union assembled at 43 Mill Road. Through her nightly sorties spray painting political graffiti using topics ranging from Ireland to sexism to the nuclear submarine *Trident,* she indulged herself in the struggle against the "enemy," Margaret Thatcher, and others.

Alice was ready to bomb unpopulated facilities, but not quite ready to harm innocent civilians. With her group's decision to set off the bomb, everything now became startlingly real. She voiced her protest, and Jocelyn answered that "it's a question of how to make the greatest impact. A few windows in the middle of the night—and so what? But this way, it'll be front page in all the papers tomorrow, and on the news tonight."[1]

The next day arrived. Jaspers would drive the car with Faye in the passenger seat, and Faye would set the timing of the bomb. They were to plant the car as designated, in the heart of the busy shopping area in Knightsbridge. Alice went with Bert near the area, to get a view of what would happen. Suddenly, she felt compelled to get away from Bert, dash into a nearby hotel, and dial the Samaritans. When she heard the "friendly, nonjudging Samaritan voice," she whispered excitedly:

> "Oh, quick, quick, there's a bomb, it's going to go off, come quickly, it's going to be in a car."
>
> "Where is this car?" enquired the Samaritan, in no way discomposed. When Alice did not at once answer, "You must tell us. We cannot get someone there until you tell us."
>
> Alice was thinking: But the car isn't even there yet. How do I know it will get there at all? Then she thought of those people, all those poor people, and she said despondently, "Well, perhaps it will be too late anyway."
>
> "But where? The address, do tell us the address?"
>
> Alice could not bring herself to give the address. "It's in Knightsbridge," she said. She was going to ring off, and added, as an afterthought, "It's the IRA. Freedom for Ireland! For a united Ireland and peace to all mankind!" She rang off.[2]

The explosion took its toll: five dead and twenty-three injured, some seriously, including a fifteen-year-old girl who later died—the price to pay for the cause of Ireland and all mankind. In this way, caring and naive Alice entered the world of ignoble and brutal means to what she and her comrades believed as a "noble end." Bert patched a bandage to their act of terrorism with a quote from Lenin:

"The law should not abolish terror; to promise that would be self-delusion or deception; it should be substantiated and legalised in principle, clearly, without evasion or embellishment. The paragraph on terror should be formulated as widely as possible, since only revolutionary consciousness of justice and revolutionary conscience can determine the conditions of its application in practice."[3]

The explosion and its aftermath no doubt brings widespread attention to the IRA. Does it help its cause? Is it morally justified if the aim is to bring about the greater good for the greater number of people? Is the suffering of a few a worthwhile price to pay for the cause of freedom for all of Ireland? According to the utilitarian theory, we should act in such a way that produces, in the long run, the greatest good for the greatest number of people. In the context of this theory, is the car bombing morally justified? This chapter examines utilitarianism more closely. Let us start by describing utilitarianism's principal founder and proponent, John Stuart Mill.

■ JOHN STUART MILL (1806–1873)

Over himself, over his own body and mind, the individual is sovereign.

JOHN STUART MILL, *ON LIBERTY*

One of the best ways to understand a person's philosophy is to know some key aspects in that person's life. This is certainly the case with John Stuart Mill, the most significant formulator of utilitarian ethics. He is indeed one of the truly major forces in Western intellectual history. He continues to exert a prodigious influence on Anglo-American democracy, and his ideas still carve a deep path in our contemporary, liberal ethos with its emphasis upon personal freedom and self-determination. His was a truly liberal and courageous voice in Victorian England as he celebrated what we now uphold as our innate freedoms of conscience, behavior, and speech. And he was a thinker beyond his time as he upheld the equal dignity and rights of women.

At an early age, John Mill acquired an exceptional education with training in geometry, logic, and philosophy as well as in the classical languages of Greek and Latin. In his *Autobiography*, he pointed out how all of this may have inculcated in him an overly analytical frame of mind, which tended to downplay the significance of feelings and emotions in his life. He admitted that he had succumbed to fits of depression in his twenties. He also admitted that the remedy for his depression lay in the recognition that a balanced life needs to cultivate feelings as well as intellect. He found this balance through music and poetry. His love of poetry was no doubt embodied in his love for Harriet Taylor, the wife of a merchant. Sustaining a Platonic relationship for nearly twenty years, and committing "no impropriety," up until the death of her husband they still managed to cause a scandal of no small proportion in that Victorian era. They married two years after her husband died.[4] And her death seven years later devastated him.

Tuberculosis was an albatross in Mill's life. His father died of it. So too did his father's father and brother. It also took the life of his brother, Henry. It would have also taken another brother, George, had he not taken his own life to elude its last stages. Tuberculosis also claimed the life of his wife and long-time companion, Harriet Taylor.

Mill often stressed how Harriet had an enormous influence on his work. She acted as confidant, advisor, and critic of his writings. He describes her impact upon him especially in his celebrated *On Liberty*, written in 1859:

> The 'Liberty' was more directly and literally our joint production than anything else which bears my name. For there was not a sentence of it that was not several times gone through by us together, turned over in many ways, and carefully weeded of any faults, either in thought or expression, that we detected in it.[5]

We cannot ignore the significance of Mill's affair with the married Harriet Taylor. If there is any doctrine that stands out in Mill it is that of individual human freedom, especially freedom from interference from both the public and authorities. That is, the realm of personal conduct is purely a private matter. This theme of personal freedom is the centerpiece of his *On Liberty*. In this courageous work, Mill remains sensitive to the all-pervading tension between freedom and authority, individual sovereignty and official rule, and Mill shows himself as a defender of personal autonomy. Yet even though he defends the text's underlying philosophy of democracy, he also points out that individual freedom needs to be guarded not only from the "tyranny of the magistrate," but also from the "tyranny of the prevailing opinion and feelings," what we can call the "tyranny of the majority." In other words, even democracy is not immune to a type of persecution. Whereas democracy developed as a path where we can be free from persecution by both church and state, citizens in a democracy can also be *persecuted by public opinion.* Yet, as with any position, public opinion is fallible.

No doubt, as Mill himself admits, Harriet's influence was vital. Nevertheless, the most profound philosophical influence upon his thought came from his father and from Jeremy Bentham. His father, James Mill (1773– 1836), a journalist, met the philosopher Jeremy Bentham (1748–1832) and was introduced to Bentham's principle of utility, the cornerstone of utilitarianism. This meeting turned out to have a long-standing effect as his father turned out to be an ardent disciple of Bentham's doctrine.

Mill's father played a critical role in the development of his son's thought. Philosopher Ben Scharfstein states that "although such deep yet partial faithfulness to a parent's ideals is usual, I find Mill's case interesting because I know of no other in which one recognized philosopher inherited his philosophy, or much of it, from another who was his literal father."[6] In any case, it appears that it was essentially the elder Mill's link with Bentham that was the most prominent influence, and, despite severe criticisms of Bentham, Mill was, to the end, loyal to Bentham's banner.[7]

As to the tyranny of the majority, Mill railed against this sort of limited vision and understanding. He often asserts that we need to take into account the genuine complexity of any issue and to examine it from various perspectives. Taking sides is all too easy. It often represents the path of least resistance. As we said in the opening chapter, this tendency to follow the path of least struggle helps to explain why we uncritically adopt ethical relativism. The public is certainly more prone to uncritically taking sides in a controversy. Yet it is this easy and popular approach that Mill warns us against adopting. Mill tells us that we need to consider and weigh all views, all sides of any issue. In this respect, he urges us to engage in genuine dialogue. Taking sides and slipping into extreme positions is all too simple. Yet, as he persistently reminds us, there are no simple solutions to complex questions.

Growth comes from dialogue, and genuine dialogue welcomes, indeed requires disagreement. Genuine dialogue occurs when we recognize the fallibility of our own positions, when we are open to the challenge of positions contrary to ours. According to Mill, a prerequisite to proper understanding lies in admitting the possibility that postures other than our own may be correct. He makes this clear in his classic work *On Liberty*, a relentless assault on conformity and uncritical thinking:

> *He who knows only his own side of the case knows little of that. His reasons may be good, and no one may have been able to refute*

*them. But if he is equally unable to refute the reasons on the oppo-
site side, if he does not so much as know what they are, he has no
ground for preferring either opinion. The rational position for him
would be suspension of judgment, and unless he contents himself
with that, he is either led by authority or adopts, like the generality
of the world, the side to which he feels most inclination. Nor is it
enough that he should hear the arguments of adversaries from his
own teachers, presented as they state them, and accompanied by
what they offer as refutations. That is not the way to do justice to
the arguments or bring them into real contact with his own mind.
He must be able to hear them from persons who actually believe
them, who defend them in earnest and do their very utmost for
them. He must know them in their most plausible and persuasive
form; he must feel the whole force of the difficulty which the true
view of the subject has to encounter and dispose of, else he will
never really possess himself of the portion of truth which meets and
removes that difficulty. Ninety-nine in a hundred of what are called
educated men are in this condition, even of those who can argue
fluently for their opinions.[8]*

This is no timid attack on conformity. Nor is it a polite censure of our general tendency, as lazy creatures who expend little in the way of critical
thinking and self-questioning, to pursue the path of least resistance and to
engage in bland mediocrity.

*In sober truth, whatever homage may be professed, or even paid, to
real or supposed mental superiority, the general tendency of things
throughout the world is to render mediocrity the ascendant power
among mankind.[9]*

Mill reminds us that no single system, theory, opinion, idea, or belief is
infallible. Yet we tend to consider our positions as containing imperishable
truths. True knowledge comes about only when we open ourselves up
to change and seriously weigh all sides of issues. This takes time, humility, and honesty. In this regard, Mill was also a staunch and original
defender for the equal rights of women and urging women to be free from
the drudgery imposed upon them by prevailing cultural habits and male
dominance.

Keep in mind that Mill was critical of those philosophers, *including utilitarians,* who put too much faith in their intellectualized systems. Mill

himself warned against being enslaved to one's own theory and "trusting too much to the intelligibleness of the abstract, when not embodied in the concrete."[10] For Mill, philosophy had to be anchored in the concrete. His ethics, in particular, had to have practical application. As a result, he put forward one of the most far-reaching of practical moralities. His ethics has had a profound influence in modern and contemporary times.

■ WHAT IS UTILITARIANISM?

Utilitarianism offers us a straightforward, practical prescription in our quest for a universal moral standard. Let us review the major ideas of the two most prominent formulators of utilitarianism: Jeremy Bentham and John Stuart Mill.

JEREMY BENTHAM'S "PRINCIPLE OF UTILITY"

This is also known as the "greatest happiness principle," for it directs us to choose that course of action which will bring about for us the greatest pleasure, or happiness. Bentham particularly measures such pleasure in terms of its intensity and duration. Pleasures therefore differ from other pleasures in these terms and therefore in degree. Note that, for Bentham, pleasure and happiness are synonymous.

Furthermore, it appears that Bentham focuses attention on that course of action which will induce the most pleasure for the individual faced with having to make a moral decision. As he states in his *Principles of Morals and Legislation,* the principle of utility "approves or disapproves of every action whatsoever, according to the tendency which it appears to have to augment or diminish the happiness of the party whose interest is in question."[11]

MILL'S REVISION OF BENTHAM

John Stuart Mill modifies Bentham's above scheme in at least two ways. First, he points out that pleasure and happiness are not the same. In this respect, he echoes Aristotle. In doing so, he also reminds us of the ongoing conflict in our lives between desires and values and proposes a way to reconcile this natural tension. (We examined this more closely in our earlier discussion of Aristotle.) In contrast to Bentham's idea that there are different degrees of pleasure, Mill tells us that there are hierarchies of pleasures, some better than others. In other words, Bentham sees that the differences among pleasures are quantitative, whereas Mill views the differences more qualitatively. For Mill, some pleasures are by their nature better, or more noble, than others. For example, intellectual pleasures are of a higher or-der than physical pleasures. Mill distinguishes between higher and lower pleasures in that higher pleasures involve the use of higher faculties such as reasoning, creativity, and analysis. As Mill puts it, "It is better to be a human being dissatisfied than a pig satisfied; better to be Socrates dis-satisfied than a fool satisfied."[12] Engaging in philosophical discourse is a higher pleasure than drinking beer and watching a football game with my buddies. So is studying the Hindu *Nasadaya* (creation Hymn), or reading about other cultures.

A second point in which he modifies Bentham is that he urges us to take that course of action that will maximize happiness for *most people.* In con-trast to Bentham, the principle of utility must consider the happiness for most people, and not just for the parties concerned. As for the agent who is directly involved, Mill states that "utilitarianism requires him to be as strictly impartial as a disinterested and benevolent spectator."[13]

Mill's version is pretty much what utilitarianism has come to mean. Namely, he offers us a universal moral standard for determining what is right and what is wrong, and that standard centers on an assessment of the consequences of our actions. That is, *we need to act in such a way so that our action brings about the greatest happiness for the greater number of people.* We must therefore behave in order to maximize happiness in the best way that we can.

ACT AND RULE UTILITARIANISM

Utilitarian theory is generally divided into two distinct types: act utilitari-anism and rule utilitarianism. According to act utilitarianism, we need to consider the consequences of our individual actions and decisions and choose that course of action which we believe will bring about the greater good for the greater number of people. This means that whether or not our action is right or wrong depends upon our assessment of the *consequences of that action.* The focus is upon each individual act itself, that is, the indi-vidual act that carries moral weight.

Rule utilitarianism is distinct from act utilitarianism because the con-sideration goes beyond the individual act itself. The rule utilitarian argues that we should choose that course of action which conforms to a specific rule which, if followed, would bring about the greater good for the greater number of people. In other words, when faced with a moral choice, we must determine which rule, when followed, would bring about the greater good. We would then act according to that rule. Therefore, whether an act is right or wrong hinges upon the *consequences of a rule* that requires that the act always be performed in similar situations.

To illustrate the distinction between act and rule utilitarianism, consider a physician who is wrestling with whether or not she should tell her patient that he has been diagnosed with a serious cancer from which he will most likely die within the year. The physician has been treating him and his family for some time. She knows from her past experience with him that he would respond quite unfavorably to such disclosure and would probably suffer severe bouts of depression and may even contemplate suicide. She also knows that he and his wife will soon be traveling to Switzerland—their dream vacation they have been planning for a long time. Should she disclose his condition to him and thereby risk his adverse reaction as well as blemishing their trip to Switzerland?

The utilitarian approach to this is clear. She ought to consider her options:

1. Disclose his condition.

2. Withhold the truth altogether.

3. Postpone disclosure until her patient's return from his vacation.

She should then choose that option which she believes, in her reasoned estimation, will produce the greater good for the greater number of people (or the less harm for the most people) over the long term.

The above distinction between act and rule indicates two separate avenues in this consequentialist approach. If the physician proceeds along the lines of act utilitarianism, *she will assess the consequences of disclosure with respect to her specific patient.* She will address that particular situation regarding her particular patient. On the other hand, if she follows a rule utilitarian approach, she will ask herself, "What rule pertaining to disclosure, in similar cases, if followed, will generally bring about the greater good for the greater number of people?" She will then act according to that rule which sustains the principle of utility.

The act utilitarian is clearly more situational, whereas the rule utilitarian focuses more upon considerations outside of the situation while considering situations that are similar. Moreover, keep in mind that utilitarianism sets a universal standard that is *methodological.* In other words, it is concerned with a particular process and method when faced with moral decisions. *It is not to be identified with any set position.* Not all utilitarians are defenders of IRA terrorist acts. Not all utilitarians support a Muslim's "holy war," or *jihad*. Not all utilitarians are ethical relativists. Not all utilitarians defend a just war theory. And so on. Utilitarianism does not provide us with a specific solution to specific questions. Not everyone who employs the utilitarian process will arrive at the same position.

■ WEAKNESSES IN UTILITARIANISM

The bare bones of utilitarian thinking are clear—*one should choose that course of action which, over the long run, will bring about the greatest good for the greatest number of people, all people being equal.* This directs our attention to the probable consequences of our actions and decisions. In doing so, it appeals to our fundamental common sense. After all, as reasonable persons should we not always consider the effects of our actions?

Upon further inspection, however, we can detect some rather elemental problems that are both practical and conceptual. Let us now review the more prominent of these hurdles, and we can begin by pointing out the pragmatic and logistic concerns that we need to confront in applying utilitarian thought.

TIME

In many situations, time is of the essence in that a decision needs to be made as soon as possible. These are emergency matters in which one does not have the time to delve into considerations of consequences. We see this in emergency medical treatment. Emergency medical technicians are trained to respond immediately and without having the luxury of contemplating and weighing various options with their benefits and risks. The all-pervading principle is to save or sustain life in ways that are medically appropriate. Attention is directed to that individual person and that person's well-being—not to the well-being of the group or society.

Such situations do not by themselves detract from the value of utilitarianism. They simply force us to acknowledge that applying the principle of utility in the most reasoned and deliberate fashion may not always be feasible. Nonetheless, we can detect here an implicit rule utilitarianism at work in these situations. The rule of thumb is to act in such a way that will save and restore some level of well-being to the individual, and when applied across the board, this is in the best interests of most people.

PREDICTABILITY

The second practical difficulty has to do with the fact that we generally cannot predict consequences with absolute certainty. We are imperfect and we do not know the future with certainty. This is our innate condition. The Scottish philosopher David Hume made this clear when he asserted that most of our cherished beliefs rest upon the basis of habit and custom rather than on reasoned proof. For instance, I assume that I will live to see the next day and I act on the basis of this assumption. Yet when pressed, I must admit that I do not know this for certain. Nevertheless, on the basis of past experience and habit, I can reasonably assume this to be the case. Are there any beliefs regarding the future that can be held to be certain, that is, grounded in absolute proof?

In Doris Lessing's *The Good Terrorist*, Alice, Jasper, Faye and others end up targeting a civilian population with their car bomb. Though this was their intent, they had no idea that one of their own group, Faye, would also end up as a victim of the explosion. If there is any certainty in life, it is that life often interrupts us with the "unexpected." Was it John Lennon who said that "life is what happens to you when you've made other plans"? Clinical trials may be conducted on a random group of human subjects to test a drug's effectiveness against viral hepatitis. However, after the drug has been FDA (Food and Drug Administration) approved and now on the market, it may turn out to have dangerous side effects on pregnant women. These unforeseen consequences are often beyond our control in that we cannot know the future with absolute predictability.

As with the above problem concerning time, this in itself does not diminish the value of utilitarianism. It simply forces us to confront some reality checks. When we consider various consequences of an act or decision, we need to make a reasoned judgment as to the probable and likely consequences and assign more weight to these than to consequences that are improbable and less likely. At the same time, consideration of these improbable results also plays into our moral calculus. There are two questions we need to address: How *real* is the consequence? And how *risky* is that consequence? That is, what are the likely benefits and harms? And then, we choose the option that we think, in our reasoned estimation, will bring about, in the long term, the greater good for most people, all people on an equal scale.

These two difficulties—time and predictability—present very little in the way of a serious challenge to utilitarianism. They represent the kind of logistic concern that can be found in any theory, no matter how well constructed. As such, they do not genuinely contest the legitimacy of the utilitarian theory. However, there are some profound challenges that center on the more conceptual issues and that question the theoretical basis of utilitarianism. In doing so, they pose the more serious threat to utilitarian theory.

WHOSE GOOD?

In our opening scene, Alice belongs to a group that believes that the good of Ireland lies in freedom from external rule and in total self-determination. That is the underlying goal of the IRA—to bring about Irish self-rule. This sounds noble enough, at least in principle. We generally applaud the notion of self-rule as well as oppose any form of tyranny. However, we meet a roadblock. As far as the IRA is concerned, self-rule is a legitimate end, a good. Yet, others may have a different view of what constitutes the "good" for Ireland. For many legislators in the British Parliament, ingrained tensions between Irish Catholics and Irish Protestants and a long history of social and economic inequities have produced a situation where self-rule is not feasible. Instead, they see the "good" as maintaining a level of peace and order in Ireland and preventing further forms of internecine violence.

This means that what is construed as the greatest "good" for the greater number of people is viewed differently by different people and different groups. In which case, utilitarianism does not appear to offer us a reasonable enough resolution to quite a few situations, at least reasonable enough to evoke a consensus among all peoples as to certain decisions and actions. For person A and person B can both approach a situation in utilitarian fashion, employing the principle of utility. Nevertheless, they can arrive at completely different decisions due to their own distinct notions regarding the "good" and what constitutes the "greater good."

This problem is especially evident when inconsistent values are at stake. For years, our college has been grappling with the problem of enabling students to more safely cross from one side of the campus to the other. Motorists callously speed and pay no heed to the crosswalk where students literally risk their lives in attempting to cross. Yet local zoning regulations prohibit the placement of a stop sign, a stop light, or a flashing warning light. It is therefore left to the college's own devices to come up with a creative strategy. A walkway, bridge, or tunnel would easily cost the school enormous sums of money. We are therefore weighing two distinct and incommensurable values: safety and cost. In this case, it appears that cost will win out. From a utilitarian perspective, this can only be justified if it is already established that cost-effectiveness is the common denominator or standard with which to measure what constitutes the greater "good."

These sorts of decisions are always being made in matters of risk management and engineering. Consider the fate of the out-of-state woman whose four-wheeler became stuck on a beach in Anchorage, Alaska. A high deposit of silt causes mud flats at low tide that act like quicksand. As her vehicle became stuck in these flats, so too did her legs. And rescuers helplessly watched her drown as they tried to extricate her from the mud as the tide came in. Appalled by her senseless death, citizens demanded that warning signs be posted. Yet city officials ruled that the high cost of designing, placing, and maintaining these signs along with added costs of liability and insurance did not justify the signs.[14] Philosopher James Liszka astutely comments further on this when he points out another problem in this kind of decision making: what he calls the "bureaucratization of moral decision making."[15] Namely, those who are most directly affected by the decision (such as students and unknowing visitors to an Anchorage beach) are themselves not part of the decision-making process.

TYRANNY OF THE MAJORITY

Who is it that determines what constitutes the "greater good" for most people? Since individual views of the "good" may differ, do we put it to a vote and choose the prevailing idea of the "good," so that the majority determines the notion of "good"? Yet why would we accept majority opinion as being any more valid than a dissenting opinion? As we saw in the case of cultural relativism, all sorts of moral minefields exist when we relegate morality to public opinion, such as the public opinion in a Sudanese village that sanctions female genital excision. This tyranny of the majority violates the moral rights of individuals. If most Irish consider their country's self-rule as the highest good, this certainly conflicts with some Irish who simply want to live a peaceful, ordered, and secure life under the protection of the British government. And vice versa. If most Irish want simply to live peacefully, this in turn conflicts with the minority's desire for national autonomy. In this fashion, the Irish struggle continues to be a microcosm of the tension that exists in many conflict areas throughout the world. Are self-rule and peace compatible goods?

DOES THE END JUSTIFY THE MEANS?

Taken to its logical extreme, does utilitarian thinking lead to the conclusion that "the end justifies the means"? If we need to pursue that which is in the best interests of most people, then we may find ourselves in the precarious position of asserting that as long as the good end we seek is in most people's interests, then we ought to pursue it, whatever the means. But this raises the *most harrowing issue in ethics.* Indeed, the plaguing question in morality has to do with this relationship between means and ends. Alice and her comrades are committed to the noble end of freeing Ireland from any form of tyranny and bringing about self-rule. In their eyes, this is a good, and one that will bring about better consequences for most people. Yet, as noble as this end is, must they pursue it at any cost? Are the deaths of innocent bystanders a justifiable means to this end?

The answer to this is a resounding "No." To begin with, the axiom that "the end justifies the means" leads to a logical straightjacket. As we described above, disparate notions as to what constitutes the "good" leads to a state of affairs that is utterly and morally chaotic. Thus the axiom cannot be accepted *carte blanche.* However, a fundamental flaw in utilitarianism appears to be that it could lead to this axiom.

The axiom "The end justifies the means" does not work for the following critical reason. Whatever means are used to achieve an end always color the character of that end. This is because ends and means exist in a mutually symbiotic relationship. They do not exist in isolation from each other. They affect each other in an ongoing way. Murdering innocent Londoners as a means to bring about a unified Ireland perversely affects the so-called noble goal so that it no longer becomes noble. Here is a quintessential point. Focusing all of our energies upon the end, we can easily lose sight of the means to that end. On the other hand, getting caught up in the means may result in neglect of the end. Either vision is myopic. The "good terrorist" is an oxymoron, a contradiction in terms. Although bitter toward her own parents, Alice is essentially a good person, caring for others and compassionate, and she strives for what she feels is good. Yet, like the others, she eventually becomes consumed by this noble end in such a way that she becomes uncritically absorbed in the means. In her mind, she is a freedom fighter. Yet through her actions, she remains a terrorist.

The Naval Blockade of Germany How does utilitarianism apply in the case of war? Consider the British naval blockade of Germany during the Great War, World War I. The blockade squeezed Germany in such a way that the British fleet thwarted Germany from receiving any resources from 1914 to 1919. The blockade was finally lifted in March 1919, months after the Armistice was signed in November 1918. However, though the blockade was militarily effective, it also induced the slow starvation of hundreds of thousands of German civilians. Official estimates after the war indicated that between 700,000 and 800,000 civilian deaths resulted from the blockade.[16] A multitude of Germans—including elderly people, women, and children—died from undernourishment and tuberculosis, rickets, and other illnesses associated with malnutrition. Without a doubt, this left its bitter memory in the hearts of the defeated Germans that lasted long after the war. According to Graf Ulrich von Brockdorff-Rantzau, the senior German delegate at the Versailles Treaty:

> The hundreds of thousands of noncombatants who have perished since November 11 because of the blockade were destroyed coolly and deliberately, after our opponents had won a certain and assured victory. Think of that, when you speak of guilt and atonement.[17]

Within a utilitarian context, this blockade illustrates the perplexing issue of the relationship of ends and means. The blockade indeed resulted in the deaths of civilians, and it was calculated that these deaths would be the consequence. In all fairness, leaders in the Royal Navy may not have directly intended the actual starvation and deaths of German children. The blockade was intended as a means to the end of defeating the Germans. Nevertheless, the deaths of civilians was foreseen as a real and probable consequence. Did the end justify the means, the destruction of civilian populations? According to Jonathan Glover, in his poignant work *Humanity*, the British naval blockade represents an early step in a new pattern in war—the direct targeting of civilians as a means to an end.[18]

Aerial Bombing of Major Cities Another case along these same lines has to do with the aerial bombing of major cities in Germany during World War II. There were three main reasons for the aerial bombing of these major cities: (1) more Allied lives would be saved; (2) Germany industry and war productivity would be severely diminished, and (3) German morale would be seriously impaired.[19] Whether or not these reasons were realistic and were achieved is a matter of debate among war historians. In any case, it was clearly foreseen that civilians would suffer the brunt of the bombings. One expert estimated that if half of the projected bombs hit their targets, this would in turn destroy the homes of 20–40 million Germans.[20]

An exceedingly high price to exact for victory. Consider the words of Sir Charles Snow reflecting back on the aerial bombings of German cities.

> It is possible, I suppose, that some time in the future people living in a more benevolent age than ours may turn over the official records and notice that men like us, men well educated by the standards of the day, men fairly kindly by the standards of the day, and often possessed of strong human feelings, made the kind of calculation I have just been describing. . . . Will they say . . . that we were wolves with the minds of men? Will they think that we resigned our humanity? They will have the right.[21]

Three principal German cities were decimated by aerial bombing: Hamburg, Darmstadt, and Dresden. One survivor describes the hellish scene in Hamburg when bombs generated a firestorm that rapidly spread death throughout the city. At least forty thousand German civilians died in the firestorm. Similar scenes visited Darmstadt and Dresden.

> Women and children were so charred as to be unrecognizable; those that had died through lack of oxygen were half charred and recognizable. Their brains tumbled from their burst temples and their insides from the soft parts under their ribs. How terribly must these people have died. The smallest children lay like fried eels on the pavement. Even in death they showed signs of how they must have suffered — their hands and arms stretched out as if to protect themselves from the pitiless heat.[22]

Hiroshima and Nagasaki The justification for the aerial bombing of cities clearly provided grounds for the later use of atomic bombs on the two Japanese cities of Hiroshima and Nagasaki. This use of the atomic bomb continues to be a sensitive issue, a prolonged debate with heated arguments on both sides. Perhaps the most compelling argument justifying the use of the bombs is that it was the only way to end a war that would otherwise drag out in such a way that countless more lives would be lost. On the other hand, arguments opposing the use of the bomb center upon two primary questions: Was this in fact the only alternative to ending the war? Even if it was, would it in turn justify its use on civilian targets?

As for the first issue, there now seems to be compelling evidence that other options were available to obtain Japan's surrender. The fact that the

United States demanded unconditional surrender, however, preempted the probability of Japanese surrender under terms that would jeopardize the position of their emperor. In any case, there were other ways to bring about Japan's surrender. The more intriguing moral debate lies in the second question. If there were no other means to end the war, would this still justify its use on civilian targets? The bombs that were dropped on the two cities of Hiroshima and Nagasaki caused the deaths of nearly a half million people.

The late philosopher Elizabeth Anscombe voiced an absolute objection to the use of the bomb on the principle that any end, however noble, never justifies the intentional killing of innocent people. In her essay, "Mr. Truman's Degree" (included at the end of this chapter), she raises her objection in view of the proposal that Oxford University award former President Harry Truman an honorary degree. The context of her objection is in itself fascinating since the essential purpose for the Oxford committee, or Congregation, to meet was more to discuss modifications of requirements for the Theology degree than to discuss Truman's eligibility for the award. Even more remarkable is the fact that she along with another Oxford philosopher, Phillipa Foot, were the sole objectors.[23]

Rethinking the Just War Theory According to the just war theory, the deliberate and intentional killing of innocent people is wrong. Interwoven with the theory is what is called the "principle of double effect." In situations such as war, abortion, and euthanasia, two sets of consequences will result from an act: consequences that are directly intended and those that are foreseen but not directly intended. Furthermore, the foreseen yet unintended consequences must not outweigh the good that is aimed at. (One can certainly wonder whether this is still relevant if just wars today are no longer possible.[24]) In the case of war, the deaths of innocent people can only be justified if these deaths are not intended but are instead the foreseen consequences of the act, and if these deaths do not outweigh the good that is aimed at. All this seems sensible enough from a utilitarian perspective. Keep in mind that utilitarianism requires that we consider long-range as well as short-term consequences, and that we make a choice in order to bring about the best consequences for all people in the long run.

Yet there is a sticky point in the just war theory, one that Elizabeth Anscombe eloquently brings to our attention, though it seems to have fallen on deaf ears when it was presented to the Oxford Congregation in 1956. The just war theory appears to assume clear lines of distinction between those consequences that are deliberately intended and those that are foreseen. Yet how clear is this distinction? This question becomes particularly acute when foreseen consequences such as the deaths of innocent people are necessarily linked to intended consequences, the destruction of military targets. In other words, if bombing military targets will necessarily produce the deaths of scores of innocent people, how can we legitimately claim that we *intend* one thing but not the other? What counts as an "intended" consequence? How do we draw the lines in a way to prevent such line drawing from becoming essentially arbitrary?

On an intuitive level, killing innocent people to achieve a good end is abhorrent. How do we stop the train of the dangerous premise "The end justifies the means"? On a practical level, however, if there is no other alternative, *not* pursuing the means will most likely bring about even more deaths of innocent people. It would seem difficult to support the position that it would be better to not pursue the means and instead risk a heavier toll of innocent deaths in the future. Herein lies a plaguing quandary in the utilitarian approach. As a theory, it seems compact. But "the devil lies in the details." As applied, it is extraordinarily complex.

Is Utilitarianism a Justifiable Theory? Do utilitarians offer a strong enough justification for their position? They go to lengths to *explain* their theory and its implications. Yet, as we saw earlier in the chapters on relativism and critical thinking, *explanation* is not the same as *justification*. What needs to be demonstrated is that utilitarianism is a morally sound theory and that we therefore *should* act according to its principle of utility. In other words, what does utilitarianism actually prove? Utilitarianism posits that our happiness is what is good for us. It is good that we be happy. It also posits that we should therefore strive to produce this good for as many people as we can. We should maximize this net happiness. But where is the evidence for this? In other words, I can accept the premise that the good lies in happiness, yet this does not necessarily lead to the conclusion that the good must be maximized. The burden of proof lies with the utilitarian to demonstrate *why* we are thereby required to maximize net happiness, or net good. This is especially important because our efforts to maximize this good may often involve bringing about some manner of harm to individuals so that others may gain. It may make common sense to force ten people off a life raft in order to save thirty people. Yet is it justified? Why would we assume that we have to act in ways to bring about the greater good? Why maximize net happiness?

Utilitarianism is no doubt demanding. It may require us to force ten people off the life boat. It does require that we put all on an equal playing field. This means that we give no special preference to our loved ones, friends and family. Though all of these are hard-hitting requirements, the radical demands utilitarianism places on us do not discredit it as a theory. Nevertheless, because it is so exacting, it needs to be justified more than it has been.

■ STRENGTHS IN UTILITARIANISM

BEYOND THE "I"

The most compelling argument in favor of utilitarianism lies in its egalitarian quality. It forces us to go beyond self-interest. In order to bring about the greatest happiness for the most people, everyone is equal, with no individual or group having more moral weight than others. This requires breaking out of the prison of "I," where self-concern trumps over all others' considerations. This is indeed a first and necessary step in moral awareness—attaching equal importance to the interests of others. It makes utilitarianism a remarkably humane school of thought, since it urges us to strive for the happiness and well-being of all peoples. Because all persons are assigned equal moral weight, this acts as a corrective to partiality and prejudice.

COMMON SENSE

Another argument in favor of utilitarianism is that it makes good common sense in many situations. This is especially the case in emergencies. For example, suppose an earthquake occurs and there are only so many medical resources available to treat survivors. It is sound common sense to use these resources on those survivors who stand to benefit, rather than on those victims who are in such bad straits that treatment will provide no benefit. Or suppose we have forty survivors clinging to a life raft that can only carry thirty. Again it makes sense to act in such a way that will save the most lives. Without a doubt, these are hard choices. Yet, although utilitarianism does not provide us with any comfortable resolution, it does give some practical guidance in terms of its principle of utility.

It also makes good sense in that it is a sign of moral responsibility to assign weight to the consequences of our deeds. After all, proper consideration of the consequences of our actions and decisions is a necessary and vital step in moral development. We realize that our actions produce effects, and that we need to consider these effects before we act.

ECONOMY

There is an appealing simplicity to the utilitarian standard. Though profound in its implications, it is concise and economic. One test of a good theory, traditionally known as Occam's razor, is that it is not overly complex, not encumbered by numerous suppositions, rules, and exceptions. In this regard, utilitarianism is strikingly straightforward and clear.

SITUATIONAL

Another appeal is that utilitarianism recognizes the uniqueness of various circumstances. It counters ethical relativism by offering a universal standard. At the same time, its universal standard is flexible in terms of its application in various situations. It demands that we consider the unique aspects of circumstances and that we weigh their moral relevance in our decision. In this regard, not only does it counter ethical relativism, but it also acts as a necessary corrective to forms of moral absolutism, the imposition of absolute moral rules that are inflexible and without exception.

When we examine utilitarianism, we see that it sets a radically high standard. The notion that each one of us ought to be "as strictly impartial as a disinterested and benevolent spectator" is extraordinarily exacting. It requires that we each place ourselves on an equal footing with all others, and, in attempting to bring about maximal net happiness, that we be willing to subordinate and even forfeit our own interests for the good of the whole. This may be even more demanding when it requires that we also be willing to sacrifice not only self interests, but even the interests of our own family and loved ones. This demands an acknowledgment of a fundamental oneness with all other humans.

Are we naturally disposed to think along these lines? Can we think in terms of this sort of radical parity? This demand reminds us of the Christian precept in the New Testament of loving not only our neighbors, but our enemies. It also brings to mind the Buddhist charge of respecting alike all sentient creatures. One essential difference between the utilitarian and Christian and the Buddhist injunction, however, is that Buddhists, at least in principle, view parity with *all* sentient creatures, not just humans, whereas the utilitarian calculus applies to humans. In this respect, as radical as utilitarianism is, Buddhist ethics is even more so. Nevertheless, the instruction to treat all humans on an equal moral footing places rigorous demands upon us.

■ NOTES

1. Doris Lessing, *The Good Terrorist* (New York: Vintage Books, 1985), p. 426.

2. Ibid., p. 435.

3. Ibid., p. 446.

4. Ben-Ami Scharfstein, *The Philosophers: Their Lives and the Nature of Their Thought* (New York: Oxford University Press, 1980), p. 264.

5. John Stuart Mill, *Autobiography*, in Scharfstein, p. 266.

6. Scharfstein, p. 267.

7. John Stuart Mill's most severe criticism of Bentham seems to be that he charged that Bentham never felt the full range of human experience; more important, Bentham seemed deprived of the world of human feelings. See Scharfstein, p. 266.

8. Mill, *On Liberty*, cited in David Denby, *Great Books: My Adventures with Homer, Rousseau, Wool, and Other Indestructible Writers of the Western World* (New York: Simon & Schuster, 1996), p. 354.

9. Ibid.

10. See J. M. Robson, *The Improvement of Mankind: The Social and Political Thought of John Stuart Mill* (Toronto, London: University of Toronto Press, Routledge, 1968), in Scharfstein, p. 267.

11. Jeremy Bentham, *The Principles of Morals and Legislation*, in William N. Nelson, *Morality: What's in it For Me?* (Boulder: Westview Press, 1991), p. 94.

12. John Stuart Mill, *Utilitarianism*, in Nelson, p. 99.

13. Cited in Nelson, p. 95.

14. James Jakób Liszka, *Moral Competence: An Integrated Approach to the Study of Ethics* (Upper Saddle River, NJ: Prentice Hall, 1999), p. 343.

15. Ibid, p. 343

16. Jonathan Glover, *Humanity: A Moral History of the Twentieth Century* (New Haven: Yale University Press, 1999), p. 65.

17. Cited in Glover, p. 66.

18. Ibid.

19. Ibid., p.73.

20. Ibid., p.75.

21. Sir Charles P. Snow, "Science and Government," in Sir Charles Snow, *Public Affairs* (London, 1971), pp. 126–27, cited in Glover, p. 80.

22. Martin Middlebrook, *The Battle of Hamburg: The Firestorm Raid* (London, 1980), p. 276, cited in Glover, p. 78.

23. See Glover, p. 107.

24. See Mary Kaldor, *New & Old Wars: Organized Violence in a Global Era* (Stanford, CA: Stanford University Press, 1999).

FROM UTILITARIANSIM

JOHN STUART MILL

It is quite compatible with the principle of utility to recognize the fact, that some *kinds* of pleasure are more desirable and more valuable than others. It would be absurd that while, in estimating all other things, quality is considered as well as quantity, the estimation of pleasures should be supposed to depend on quantity alone.

If I am asked what I mean by difference of quality in pleasures, or what makes one pleasure more valuable than another merely as a pleasure, except its being greater in amount, there is but one possible answer. Of two pleasures, if there be one to which all or almost all who have experience of both give a decided preference, irrespective of any feeling of moral obligation to prefer it, that is the more desirable pleasure. If one of the two is, by those who are competently acquainted with both, placed so far above the other that they prefer it, even though knowing it to be attended with a greater amount of discontent, and would not resign it for any quantity of the other pleasure which their nature is capable of, we are justified in ascribing to the preferred enjoyment a superiority in quality, so far outweighing quantity as to render it, in comparison, of small account.

Now it is an unquestionable fact that those who are equally acquainted with, and equally capable of appreciating and enjoying, both, do give a most marked preference to the manner of existence which employs their higher faculties. Few human creatures would consent to be changed into any of the lower animals, for a promise of the fullest allowance of a beast's pleasures; no intelligent human being would consent to be a fool, no instructed person would be an ignoramus, no person of feeling and conscience would be selfish and base, even though they should be persuaded that the fool, the dunce, or the rascal is better satisfied with his lot than they are with theirs. They would not resign what they possess more than he for the most complete satisfaction of all the desires which they have in common with him. If they ever fancy they would, it is only in cases of unhappiness so extreme, that to escape from it they would exchange their lot for almost any other, however undesirable in their own eyes. A being of higher faculties requires more to make him happy, is capable probably of more acute suffering, and certainly accessible to it at more points, than one of an inferior type; but in spite of these liabilities, he can never really wish to sink into what he feels to be a lower grade of existence. We may give what explanation we please of this unwillingness: we may attribute it to pride, a name which is given discriminately to some of the most and to some of the least estimable feelings of which mankind are capable; we may refer it to the love of liberty and personal independence, an appeal to which was with the Stoics one of the most effective means for the inculcation of it; to the love of power, or to the love of excitement, both of which do really enter into and contribute to it: but its most appropriate appellation is a sense of dignity, which all human beings possess in one form or other, and in some, though by no means in exact, proportion to their higher faculties, and which is so essential a part of the happiness of those in whom it is strong, that nothing which conflicts with it could be, otherwise than momentarily, an object of desire to them. Whoever supposes that this preference takes place at a sacrifice of happiness—that the superior being, in anything like equal circumstances, is not happier than the inferior—confounds the two very different ideas, of *happiness* and *content*. It is indisputable that the being whose capacities of enjoyment are low, has the greatest chance of having them fully satisfied; and a highly endowed being will always feel that any happiness which he can look for, as the world is constituted, is imperfect. But he can learn to bear its imperfections, if they are at all bearable; and they will not make him envy the being who is indeed unconscious of the imperfections, but only because he feels not at all the good which those imperfections qualify. It is better to be a human being dissatisfied than a pig satisfied; better to be Socrates dissatisfied than a fool satisfied. And if the fool, or the pig, are of a different opinion, it is because they only know their own side of the question. The other party to the comparison knows both sides. . . .

According to the "greatest happiness principle," . . . the ultimate end, with reference to and for the sake of which all other things are desirable (whether we are considering our own good or that of other people), is an existence exempt as far as possible from pain, and as rich as possible in enjoyments, both in point of quantity and quality; the test of quality, and the rule for measuring it against quantity, being the preference felt by those who in their opportunities of experience, to which must be added their habits of self-consciousness and self-observation, are best furnished with the means of comparison. This, being, according to the utilitarian opinion, the end of human action, is necessarily also the standard of morality; which may accordingly be defined, the rules and precepts for human conduct, by the observance of which an existence such as has been described might be, to the greatest extent possible, secured to all mankind; and not to them only, but, so far as the nature of things admits, to the whole sentient creation. . . .

. . . If by happiness be meant a continuity of highly pleasurable excitement, it is evident enough that this is impossible. A state of exalted pleasure lasts only moments, or in some cases, and with some intermissions, hours or days, and is the occasional brilliant flash of enjoyment, not its permanent and steady flame. Of this the philosophers: who have taught that happiness is the end of life were as fully aware as those who taunt them. The happiness which they meant was not a life of rapture; but moments of such, in an existence made up of few and transitory pains, many and various pleasures, with a decided pre-dominance of the active over the passive, and having as the foundation of the whole, not to expect more from life than it is capable of bestowing. A life thus composed, to those who have been fortunate enough to obtain it, has always appeared worthy of the name of happiness. And such an existence is even now the lot of many, during some considerable portion of their lives. The present wretched education, and wretched social arrangements, are the only real hin-drance to its being attainable by almost all.

In a world in which there is so much to interest, so much to enjoy, and so much also to correct and improve, everyone who has [a] moderate amount of moral and intellectual requisites is capable of an existence which may be called enviable; and unless such a person, through bad laws or subjection to the will of others, is denied the liberty to use the sources of happiness within his reach, he will not fail to find this enviable existence, if he escape the positive evils of life, the great sources of physical and mental suffering—such as indigence, disease, and the unkindness, worthlessness, or premature loss of an affection. The main stress of the problem lies, therefore, in the contest with these calami-ties from which it is a rare good fortune entirely to escape; which, as things are now, cannot be obviated, and often cannot be in any material degree mitigated. Yet no one whose opinion deserves a moment's consideration can doubt that most of the great positive evils of the world are in themselves removable, and will, if human affairs continue to improve, be in the end reduced within nar-row limits. . . .

As for vicissitudes of fortune, and other disappointments connected with worldly circumstances, these are principally the effect either of gross impru-dence, of ill-regulated desires, or of bad or imperfect social institutions. All the grand sources, in short, of human suffering are in a great degree many of them almost entirely, conquerable, by human care and effort; and though their re-moval is grievously slow—though a long succession of generations will perish in the breach before the conquest is completed, and this world becomes all that, if will and knowledge were not wanting, it might easily be made—yet every mind sufficiently intelligent and generous to bear a part, however small and unconspicuous, in the endeavor, will draw a noble enjoyment from the contest itself, which he would not for any bribe in the form of selfish indulgence consent to be without.

And this leads to the true estimation of what is said by the objectors concerning the possibility, and the obligation, of learning to do without happiness. Unquestionably it is possible to do without happiness; it is done involuntarily by nineteen-twentieths of mankind, even in those parts of our present world which are least deep in barbarism; and it often has to be done voluntarily by the hero or the martyr, for the sake of something which he prizes more than his individual happiness. But this something, what is it, unless the happiness of others, or some of the requisites of happiness? It is noble to be capable of resigning entirely one's own portion of happiness, or chances of it: but, after all, this self-sacrifice must be for some end; it is not its own end; and if we are told that its end is not happiness, but virtue, which is better than happiness, I ask, would the sacrifice be made if the hero or martyr did not believe that it would earn for others immunity from similar sacrifices? Would it be made if he thought that his renunciation of happiness for himself would produce no fruit for any of his fellow creatures, but to make their lot like his, and place them also in the condition of persons who have renounced happiness? All honor to those who can abnegate for themselves the personal enjoyment of life, when by such renunciation they contribute worthily to increase the amount of happiness in the world; but he who does it, or professes to do it, for any other purpose, is no more deserving of admiration than the ascetic mounted on his pillar. He may be an inspiriting proof of what men *can* do, but assuredly not an example of what they *should*.

MR TRUMAN'S DEGREE

ELIZABETH ANSCOMBE

I

In 1939, on the outbreak of war, the President of the United States asked for assurances from the belligerent nations that civil populations would not be attacked.

In 1945, when the Japanese enemy was known by him to have made two attempts towards a negotiated peace, the President of the United States gave the order for dropping an atom bomb on a Japanese city; three days later a second bomb, of a different type, was dropped on another city. No ultimatum was delivered before the second bomb was dropped.

Set side by side, these events provide enough of a contrast to provoke enquiry. Evidently development has taken place; one would like to see its course plotted. It is not, I think, difficult to give an intelligible account:

(1) The British Government gave President Roosevelt the required assurance with a reservation which meant "If the Germans do it we shall do it too." You don't promise to abide by the Queensberry Rules even if your opponent abandons them.

(2) The only condition for ending the war was announced to be unconditional surrender. Apart from the "liberation of the subject peoples", the objectives were vague in character. Now the demand for unconditional surrender was mixed up with a determination to make no peace with Hitler's government. In view of the character of Hitler's regime that attitude was very intelligible. Nevertheless some people have doubts about it now. It is suggested that defeat of itself would have resulted in the rapid discredit and downfall of that government. On this I can form no strong opinion. The important question to my mind is whether the intention of making no peace with Hitler's government necessarily entailed the objective of unconditional surrender. If, as may not be impossible, we could have formulated a pretty definite objective, a rough outline of the terms which we were willing to make with Germany, while at the same time indicating that we would not make terms with Hitler's government, then the question of the wisdom of this latter demand seems to me a minor one; but if not, then that settles it. It was the insistence on unconditional surrender that was the root of all evil. The connection between such a demand and the need to use the most ferocious methods of warfare will be obvious. And in itself the proposal of an unlimited objective in war is stupid and barbarous.

(3) The Germans did a good deal of indiscriminate bombing in this country. It is impossible for an uninformed person to know how much, in its first beginnings, was due to indifference on the part of pilots to using their loads only on military targets and how much to actual policy the part of those who sent them. Nor do I know what we were doing in the same line at the time. But certainly anyone would have been stupid who had thought in 1939 that there would not be such bombing, developing into definite raids on cities.

(4) For some time before war broke out, and more intensely afterwards, there was propaganda in this country on the subject of the "indivisibility" of modern war. The civilian population, we were told, is really as much combatant as the fighting forces. The military strength of a nation includes its whole economic and social strength. Therefore the distinction between the people engaged in prosecuting the war and the population at large is unreal. There is no such thing as a non-participator; you cannot buy a postage stamp or any taxed article, or grow a potato or cook a meal, without contributing to the "war effort". War indeed is a "ghastly evil", but once it has broken out no one can "contract out" of it. "Wrong" indeed must be being done if war is waged, but

you cannot help being involved in it. There was a doctrine of "collective responsibility" with a lugubriously elevated moral tone about it. The upshot was
that it was senseless to draw any line between legitimate and illegitimate objects of attack. Thus the court chaplains of the democracy. I am not sure how
children and the aged fitted into this story: probably they cheered the soldiers
and munitions workers up.

(5) The Japanese attacked Pearl Harbour and there was war between America and Japan. Some American (Republican) historians now claim that the acknowledged fact that the American Government knew an attack was impending some hours before it occurred, but did not alert the people in local
command, can only be explained by a purpose of arousing the passions of
American people. However that may be, those passions were suitably aroused
and the war was entered on with the same vague and hence limitless objectives;
and once more unconditional surrender was the only condition on which the
war was going to end.

(6) Then came the great change: we adopted the system of 'area bombing'
as opposed to 'target bombing'. This differed from even big raids on cities, such
as had previously taken place in the course of the war, by being far more extensive and devastating and much less random; the whole of a city area would
be systematically plotted out and dotted with bombs. "Attila was a Sissy", as
the *Chicago Tribune* headed an article on this subject.

(7) In 1945, at the Potsdam conference in July, Stalin informed the American and British statesmen that he had received two requests from the Japanese
to act as a mediator with a view to ending the war. He had refused. The Allies
agreed on the "general principle"—marvellous phrase!—of using the new
type of weapon that America now possessed. The Japanese were given a chance
in the form of the Potsdam Declaration, calling for unconditional surrender in
face of overwhelming force soon to be arrayed against them. The historian of
the Survey of International Affairs considers that this phrase was rendered
meaningless by the statement of a series of terms; but of these the ones incorporating the Allies' demands were mostly of so vague and sweeping a nature
as to be rather a declaration of what unconditional surrender would be like than
to constitute conditions. It seems to be generally agreed that the Japanese were
desperate enough to have accepted the Declaration but for their loyalty to their
Emperor: the "terms" would certainly have permitted the Allies to get rid of
him if they chose. The Japanese refused the Declaration, In consequence, the
bombs were dropped on Hiroshima and Nagasaki. The decision to use them on
people was Mr Truman's.

For men to choose to kill the innocent as a means to their ends is always murder, and murder is one of the worst of human actions. So the prohibition on
deliberately killing prisoners of war or the civilian population is not like
the Queensberry Rules: its force does not depend on its promulgation as part

of positive law, written down, agreed upon, and adhered to by the parties concerned.

When I say that to choose to kill the innocent as a means to one's ends is murder, I am saying what would generally be accepted as correct. But I shall be asked for my definition of "the innocent". I will give it, but later. Here, it is not necessary; for with Hiroshima and Nagasaki we are not confronted with a borderline case. In the bombing of these cities it was certainly decided to kill the innocent as a means to an end. And a very large number of them, all at once, without warning, without the interstices of escape or the chance to take shelter, which existed even in the 'area bombings' of the German cities.

I have long been puzzled by the common cant about President Truman's courage in making this decision. Of course, I know that you can be cowardly without having reason to think you are in danger. But how can you be courageous? Light has come to me lately: the term is an acknowledgement of the truth. Mr Truman was brave because, and only because, what he did was so bad. But I think the judgement unsound. Given the right circumstances (for example that no one whose opinion matters will disapprove), a quite mediocre person can do spectacularly wicked things without thereby becoming impressive.

I determined to oppose the proposal to give Mr Truman an honorary degree here at Oxford. Now, an honorary degree is not a reward of merit: it is, as it were, a reward for being a very distinguished person, and it would be foolish to enquire whether a candidate deserves to be as distinguished as he is. That is why, in general, the question whether so-and-so should have an honorary degree is devoid of interest. A very distinguished person will hardly be also a notorious criminal, and if he should chance to be a non-notorious criminal it would, in my opinion, be improper to bring the matter up. It is only in the rather rare case in which a man is known everywhere for an action, in face of which it is sycophancy to honour him, that the question can be of the slightest interest.

I have been accused of being "high-minded". I must be saying "You may not do evil that good may come", which is a disagreeably high-minded doctrine. The action was necessary, or at any rate it was thought by competent, expert military opinion to be necessary; it probably saved more lives than it sacrificed; it had a good result, it ended the war. Come now: if you had to choose between boiling one baby and letting some frightful disaster befall a thousand people—or a million people, if a thousand is not enough—what would you do? Are you going to strike an attitude and say "You may not do evil that good may come"? (People who never hear such arguments will hardly believe they take place, and will pass this rapidly by.)

"It pretty certainly saved a huge number of lives". Given the conditions, I agree. That is to say, if those bombs had not been dropped the Allies would have had to invade Japan to achieve their aim, and they would have done so. Very many soldiers on both sides would have been killed; the Japanese, it is said—and it may well be true—would have massacred the prisoners of war; and large numbers of their civilian population would have been killed by 'ordinary' bombing.

I do not dispute it. Given the conditions, that was probably what was averted by that action. But what were the conditions? The unlimited objective, the fixation on unconditional surrender. The disregard of the fact that the Japanese were desirous of negotiating peace. The character of the Potsdam Declaration—their 'chance'. I will not suggest, as some would like to do, that there was an exultant itch to use the new weapons, but it seems plausible to think that the consciousness of the possession of such instruments had its effect on the manner in which the Japanese were offered their chance'.

We can now; reformulate the principle of doing evil that good may come: every fool can be as much of a knave as suits him.

I recommend this history to undergraduates reading Greats as throwing a glaring light on Aristotle's thesis that you cannot be or do any good where you are stupid.

I informed the Senior Proctor of my intention to oppose Mr Truman's degree. He consulted the Registrar to get me informed on procedure. The Vice-Chancellor was informed; I was cautiously asked if I had got up a party. I had not; but a fine House was whipped up to vote for the honour. The dons at St John's were simply told "The women are up to something in Convocation; we have to go and vote them down". In Worcester, in All Souls, in New College, however, consciences were greatly exercised, as I have heard. A reason was found to satisfy them: *It would be wrong to try PUNISH Mr Truman!* I must say I rather like St John's.

The Censor of St Catherine's had an odious task. He must make a speech which should pretend to show that a couple of massacres to a man's credit are not exactly a reason for not showing him honour. He had, however, one great advantage: he did not have to persuade his audience, who were already perfectly convinced of that proposition. But at any rate he had to make a show.

The defence, I think, would not have been well received at Nuremberg.

We do not approve the action; no, we think it was *mistake.* (That is how communists now talk about Stalin's more murderous proceedings.) Further, Mr Truman did not make the bombs by himself, and decide to drop them without consulting anybody; no, he was only responsible for the decision, Hang it all, you can't make a man responsible just because "his is the signature at the foot of the order". Or was he not even responsible for the decision? It was not quite clear whether Mr Bullock was saying that or not; but I never heard anyone else seem to give the lie to Mr Truman's boasts. Finally, an action of this sort is, after all, only one episode: an incidental, as it were, in a career, Mr Truman has done some good.

I know that in one way such a speech does not deserve scrutiny; after all, it was just something to say on its occasion. And he had to say something. One must not suppose that one can glean anything a man actually thinks from what he says in such circumstances. Professor Stebbing exposing the logical fallacies in politicians' speeches is a comic spectacle.

II

Choosing to kill the innocent as a means to your ends is always murder. Naturally, killing the innocent as an end in itself is murder too; but that is no more than a possible future development for us:[1] in our part of the globe it is a practice that has so far been confined to the Nazis. I intend my formulation to be taken strictly; each term in it is necessary. For killing the innocent, even if you know as a matter of statistical certainty that the things you do involve it, is not necessarily murder. I mean that if you attack a lot of military targets, such as munitions factories and naval dockyards, as carefully as you can, you will be certain to kill a number of innocent people; but that is not murder. On the other hand, unscrupulousness in considering the possibilities turns it into murder. I here print as a case in point a letter which I received lately from Holland:

> We read in our paper about your opposition to Truman. I do not like him either, but do you know that in the war the English bombed the dykes of our province Zeeland, an island where nobody could escape anywhere to. Where the whole population was drowned, children, women, farmers working in the field, all the cattle, everything, hundreds and hundreds, and we were your allies Nobody ever speaks about that. Perhaps it were well to know this. Or, to remember.

That was to trap some fleeing German military. I think my correspondent has something.

It may be impossible to take the thing (or people) you want to destroy as your target; it may be possible to attack it only by taking as the object of your attack what includes large numbers of innocent people. Then you cannot very well say they died by accident. Here your action is murder.

"But where will you draw the line? It is impossible to draw an exact line." This is a common and absurd argument against drawing any line; it may be very difficult, and there are obviously borderline cases. But we have fallen into the way of drawing no line, and offering as justifications what an uncaptive mind will find only a bad joke. Wherever the line is, certain things are certainly well to one side or the other of it.

---

1. This will seem a preposterous assertion; but we are certainly on the way, and I can think of no reasons for confidence that it will not happen.

Now who are "the innocent" in war? They are all those who are not fighting and not engaged in supplying those who are with the means of fighting. A farmer growing wheat which may be eaten by the troops is not "supplying them with the means of fighting". Over this, too, the line may be difficult to draw. But that does not mean that no line should be drawn, or that, even if one is in doubt just Where to draw the line, one cannot be crystal clear that this or that is well over the line.

"But the people fighting are probably conscripts! In that case they are just as innocent as anyone else." "Innocent" here is not a term referring to personal responsibility at all. It means rather "not harming". But the people fighting are "harming", so they can be attacked; but if they surrender they become in this sense innocent and so may not be maltreated or killed. Nor is there ground for trying them on a criminal charge; not, indeed, because a man has no personal responsibility for fighting, but because they were not the subjects of the state whose prisoners they are.

There is an argument which I know from experience it is necessary to forestall at this point, though I think it is visibly captious. It is this: on my theory, would it not follow that a soldier can only be killed when he is actually attacking? Then, for example, it would be impossible to attack a sleeping camp. The answer is that "what someone is doing" can refer either to what he is doing at the moment or to his role in a situation. A soldier under arms is "harming" in the latter sense even if he is asleep. But it is true that the enemy should not be attacked more ferociously than is necessary to put them *hors de combat*.

These conceptions are distinct and intelligible ones; they would formerly have been said to belong to the Law of Nations. Anyone can see that they are good, and we pay tribute to them by our moral indignation when our enemies violate them. But in fact they are going, and only fragments of them are left. General Eisenhower, for example, is reported to have spoken slightingly once of the notion of chivalry towards prisoners—as if that were based on respect for their virtue or for the nation from which they come, and not on the fact that they are now defenceless.

It is characteristic of nowadays to talk with horror of killing rather than of murder, and hence, since in war you have committed yourself to killing—for example "accepted an evil"—not to mind whom you kill. This seems largely to be the work of the devil; but I also suspect that it is in part an effect of the existence of pacifism, as a doctrine which many people respect though they would not adopt it. This effect would not exist if people had a distinct notion of what makes pacifism a false doctrine.

It therefore seems to me important to show that for one human being deliberately to kill another is not inevitably wrong. I may seem to be wasting my time, as most people do reject pacifism. But it is nevertheless important to argue the point because if one does so one sees that there are pretty severe restrictions on legitimate killing. Of course, people accept this within the state, but when it comes to war they have the idea that any restrictions are something like the Queensberry Rules—instead of making the difference between being guilty and not guilty of murder.

I will not discuss the self-defence of a private person. If he kills the man who attacks him or someone else, it ought to be accidental. To aim at killing, even when one is defending oneself, is murderous. (I fear even this idea is going. A man was acquitted recently who had successfully set a lethal booby trap to kill a thief in his absence.)

But the state actually has the authority to order deliberate killing in order to protect its people or to put frightful injustices right. (For example, the plight of the Jews under Hitler would have been a reasonable cause of war.) The reason for this is pretty simple: it stands out most clearly if we first consider the state's right to order such killing within its confines. I am not referring to the death penalty, but to what happens when there is rioting or when violent malefactors have to be caught. Rioters can sometimes only be restrained, or malefactors seized, by force. Law without force is ineffectual, and human beings without laws miserable (though we, who have too many and too changeable laws, may easily not feel this very distinctly). So much is indeed fairly obvious, though the more peaceful the society the less obvious it is that the force in the hands of the servants of the law has to be force up to the point of killing. It would become perfectly obvious any time there was rioting or gangsterism which had to be dealt with by the servants of the law fighting.

The death penalty itself is a completely different matter. The state is not fighting the criminal who is condemned to death. That is why the death penalty is not indispensable. People keep on discussing whether the point of it is deterrence or vengeance; it is neither. Not deterrence, because nobody has proved anything about that, and people think what they think in accordance with their prejudices. And not vengeance, because that is nobody's business. Confusion arises on this subject because the state is said, and correctly said, to *punish* the criminal, and "punishment" suggests "vengeance". Therefore many humane people dislike the idea and prefer such notions as "correction" and "rehabilitation". But the action of the state in depriving a man of his rights, up to his very life, has to be considered from two sides. First, from that of the man himself. If he could justly say "Why have you done this to me? I have not deserved it", then the state would be acting with injustice. Therefore he must be proved guilty, and only as punishment has the state the right to inflict anything on him. The concept of punishment is our one safeguard against being done 'good' to, in ways involving a deprivation of rights, by impudent powerful people. Second, from the side of the state, divine retributive justice is not its affair: it only has to protect its people and restrain malefactors. The ground of its right to deprive of liberty and even life is only that the malefactor is a nuisance, like a gangrenous limb. Therefore it can cut him off entirely, if his crime is so bad that he could not justly protest "I have not deserved *this.*" But when I say that the sole ground of the state's right to kill him is that he is a nuisance, I only mean that he is a nuisance *qua* malefactor. The lives of the innocent are the actual point of society, so the fact that in some other way they may be a nuisance (troublesome to look after, for example) does not justify the state in getting rid of them. Though that is another thing we may yet come to. But the blood of the innocent cries to heaven for vengeance.

Thus the malefactor who has been found guilty is the only defenceless person whom the state may put to death. It need not; it can choose more merciful laws. (I have no prejudice in favour of the death penalty.) Any other defenceless person is as such innocent, in the sense "not harming". And so the state can only order to kill others of its subjects besides convicted criminals if they are rioting or doing something that has to be stopped, and can only be stopped by the servants of the law fighting them.

Now, this is also the ground of the state's right to order people to fight external enemies who are unjustly attacking them or something of theirs. The right to order to fight for the sake of other people's wrongs, to put right something affecting people who are not actually under the protection of the state, is a rather more dubious thing obviously, but it exists because of the common sympathy of human beings whereby one feels for one's neighbour if he is attacked. So in an attenuated sense it can be said that something that belongs to, or concerns, one is attacked if anybody is unjustly attacked or maltreated.

Pacifism, then, is a false doctrine. Now, no doubt, it is bad just for that reason, because it is always bad to have a false conscience. In this way the doctrine that it is a bad act to lay a bet is bad: it is all right to bet what it is all right to risk or drop in the sea. But I want to maintain that pacifism is a harmful doctrine in a far stronger sense than this. Even the prevalence of the idea that it was wrong to bet would have no particularly bad consequences; a false doctrine which merely forbids what is not actually bad need not encourage people in anything bad. But with pacifism it is quite otherwise. It is a factor in that loss of the conception of murder which is my chief interest in this pamphlet.

I have very often heard people say something like this: "It is all very well to say 'Don't do evil that good may come.' But *war* is evil. We all know that. Now, of course, it is possible to be an Absolute Pacifist. I can respect that, but I can't be one myself, and most other people won't be either. So we have to accept the evil. It is not that we do not see the evil. And once you are in for it, you have to go the whole hog."

This is much as if I were defrauding someone, and when someone tried to stop me I said: "Absolute honesty! I respect that. But of course absolute honesty really means having no property at all. . . ." Having offered the sacrifice of a few sighs and tears to absolute honesty, I go on as before.

The correct answer to the statement that "war is evil" is that it is bad — for example a misfortune — to be at war. And no doubt if two nations are at war at least one is unjust. But that does not show that it is wrong to fight or that if one does fight one can also commit murder.

Naturally my claim that pacifism is a very harmful doctrine is contingent on its being a false one. If it were a true doctrine, its encouragement of this nonsensical 'hypocrisy of the ideal standard' would not count against it. But given that it is false, I am inclined to think it is also very bad, unusually so for an idea which seems as it were to err on the noble side.

When I consider the history of events from 1939 to 1945, I am not surprised that Mr Truman is made the recipient of honours. But when I consider his actions by themselves, I am surprised again.

Some people actually praise the bombings and commend the stockpiling of atomic weapons on the ground that they are so horrible that nations will be afraid ever again to make war. "We have made a covenant with death, and with hell we are at an agreement." There does not seem to be good ground for such a hope for any long period of time.

Pacifists have for long made it a point in their propaganda that men must grow more murderous as their techniques of destruction improve, and those who defend murder eagerly seize on this point, so that I imagine by now it is pretty well accepted by the whole world. Of course, it is not true. In Napoleon's time, for example, the means of destruction had much improved since the time of Henry V but Henry, not Napoleon, was a great massacrer of civilians, saying when he did particularly atrocious things that the French were a sinful nation and that he had a mission from God to punish them. And, of course, really large scale massacre up to now has belonged to times with completely primitive methods of killing. Weapons are now manufactured whose sole point is to be used in massacre of cities. But the people responsible are not murderous because they have these weapons; they have them because they are murderous. Deprived of atomic bombs, they would commit massacres by means of other bombs.

Protests by people who have not power are a waste of time. I was not seizing an opportunity to make a "gesture of protest" at atomic bombs; I vehemently object to *our* action in offering Mr Truman honours, because one can share in the guilt of a bad action by praise and flattery, as also by defending it. When I puzzle myself over the attitude of the Vice-Chancellor and the Hebdomadal Council, I look round to see if any explanation is available why so many Oxford people should be willing to flatter such a man.

I get some small light on the subject when I consider the productions of Oxford moral philosophy since the First World War, which I have lately had occasion to read. Its character can easily be briefly demonstrated. Up to the Second World War the prevailing moral philosophy in Oxford taught that an action can be "morally good" no matter how objectionable the thing done may be. An instance would be Himmler's efforts at exterminating the Jews: he did it from the "motive of duty" which has "supreme value". In the same philosophy—which has much pretence of moral seriousness, claiming that "right-ness" is an objective character in acts, that can be discerned by a moral sense—it is also held that it might be right to kill the innocent for the good of the people, since the "prima facie duty" of securing some advantage might out-weigh the "prima facie duty" of not killing the innocent. This sort of philoso-phy is less prevalent now, and in its place I find another, whose cardinal prin-ciple is that "good" is not a "descriptive" term, but one expressive of a favourable attitude on the part of the speaker. Hand in hand with this, though I do not know if there is any logical connection, goes a doctrine that it is im-possible to have any quite general moral laws; such laws as "It is wrong to lie" or "Never commit sodomy" are rules of thumb which an experienced person knows when to break. Further, both his selection of these as the rules on which to proceed, and his tactful adjustments of them in particular cases, are based on their fitting together with the "way of life" which is his preference. Both these philosophies, then, contain a repudiation of the idea that any class of actions, such as murder, may be absolutely excluded. I do not know how influential they may have been or be; they are perhaps rather symptomatic. Whether influential or symptomatic, they throw some light on the situation.

It is possible still to withdraw from this shameful business in some slight degree; it is possible not to go to Encaenia; if it should be embarrassing to someone who would normally go to plead other business, he could take to his bed. I, indeed, should fear to go, in case God's patience suddenly ends.

FEMINIST ETHICS

■

THE HANDMAID'S DUTY

Nolite te bastardes carborundorum. These were the words etched on Offred's cupboard wall by the room's previous occupant, Moira. Moira may
have written this just before she hung herself from the ceiling light fixture.
And even though Offred did not at first know what the words meant, the
epitaph lingered on in her memory. Only later did the Commander reveal
their meaning: "Don't let the bastards grind you down."

Offred is a "Handmaid," one of the few remaining fertile women in the
Republic of Gilead. Fertile women are a scarce resource. The population has
dramatically dwindled on account of excessive carcinogens and numerous
chemicals that had accumulated in the environment, especially in the water system. As a Handmaid, Offred is assigned to serve the Commander
and his wife, Serena Joy. Her sole duty is quite clear: to bear the Commander's child. And each month, in the presence of his wife, the Commander
perfunctorily performs his duty as well. Through the voice of Offred, author Margaret Atwood describes their "Ceremony":

> The Ceremony goes as usual.
> *I lie on my back, fully clothed except for the healthy white cot-
> ton underdrawers. What I could see, if I were to open my eyes,
> would be the large white canopy of Serena Joy's outsized colonial-
> style four-poster bed, suspended like a sagging cloud above us, a
> cloud sprigged with tiny drops of silver rain, which, if you looked at
> them closely, would turn out to be four-petaled flowers. I would not*

see the carpet, which is white, or the sprigged curtains and skirted dressing table. . . .

Above me, towards the head of the bed, Serena Joy is arranged, outspread. Her legs are apart, I lie between them, my head on her stomach, her pubic bone under the base of my skull, her thighs on either side of me. She too is fully clothed.

My arms are raised; she holds my hands, each of mine in each of hers. This is supposed to signify that we are one flesh, one being. What it really means is that she is in control, of the process and thus of the product. If any. The rings of her left hand cut into my fingers. It may or may not be revenge.

My red skirt is hitched up to my waist, though no higher. Below the Commander is fucking. What he is fucking is the lower part of my body. I do not say making love, because this is not what he is doing. Copulating too would be inaccurate, because it would imply two people and only one is involved. Nor does rape cover it: nothing is going on here that I haven't signed up for. There wasn't a lot of choice but there was some, and this is what I chose.

Therefore I lie still and picture the unseen canopy over my head. I remember Queen Victoria's advice to her daughter: Close your eyes and think of England. *But this is not England. I wish he would hurry up.*[1]

Set in some unknown future in Cambridge, Massachusetts, the story unfolds in the theocracy of Gilead, a region regulated by the Old Testament edict to bear children and to multiply. Under the shadow of extreme right-wing religious fundamentalism, Gilead is a rigid society composed primarily of Commanders and their Wives, Marthas, Aunts, and Handmaidens. Commanders were to impregnate the Handmaidens. Marthas perform the usual household tasks. Aunts indoctrinate the Handmaidens, instructing them in their duty to submit to the Commanders and to reproduce. For this reason, Aunts, as tools of the theocracy, possess the most insidious power. In fact, they are the only women who are permitted to read and write. In Gilead, the sole worth of women lies in their ability to produce offspring. Since the Handmaidens are the only women who are fertile, all others are "defective" by Gilead's standards, standards set in stone by men and enforced by women.

Through the complicity and oppressive power of the Aunts, the Commanders assume total control. Not only Commanders, but also women turn out to be the oppressors. Through the Aunts' indoctrination, most women in this society seem to uncritically accept the value of women solely as child bearers. Handmaidens, except for Offred and a few others, are brainwashed into believing in the absolute power and authority of the Genesis passage they hear repeatedly:

> *And when Rachel saw that she bare Jacob no children, Rachel envied her sister; and said unto Jacob, Give me children or else I die. And Jacob's anger was kindled against Rachel; and he said, Am I in God's stead, who hath withheld from thee the fruit of the womb? And she said, Behold my maid Bilhah, go in unto her; and she shall bear upon my knees, that I may also have children by her. [Genesis 30:1–3]*

And the citizens of Gilead seem willing to accept this strict rule of law even though it means the surrender of individual freedoms. Compared to past civilizations, the totalitarian society of Gilead is safe and secure. Who cares about individual rights and liberties, as long as people are secure?

Thus sexual activity is solely for the purpose of procreating and is uncompromisingly controlled through the threat of severe punishment and the promise of reward. Offenses of "unchastity," adultery, homosexuality, masturbation, and attempted escape are punishable by death. The executions are public. They are called "Salvagings." Salvagings are always segregated, executions for women and those for men. Furthermore, attendance at these Salvagings is mandatory. Margaret Atwood cites one such Salvaging that is presided over by Aunt Lydia at which three women are about to be executed. This Salvaging is unique in that all the women who attend to witness the hangings are not told what crimes are committed, as is the custom. As Offred describes, "A collective murmur goes up from us. The crimes of others are a secret language among us. Through them we show ourselves what we might be capable of, after all."[2]

One crucial feature in these Salvagings is that all of the Handmaidens have a hand in the execution by touching the rope that hangs the victim, as if to indicate a collective sign of approval. Offred continues:

> *I've seen it before, the white bag placed over the head, the woman helped up onto the high stool as if she's being helped up the steps of a bus, steadied there, the noose adjusted delicately around the neck, like a vestment, the stool kicked away. I've heard the long sigh go up, from around me, the sigh like air coming out of an air mattress, I've seen Aunt Lydia place her hand over the mike, to stifle the other*

sounds coming from behind her, I've leaned forward to touch the rope in front of me, in time with the others, both hands on it, the rope hairy, sticky with tar in the hot sun, then placed my hand on my heart to show my unity with the Salvagers and my consent, and my complicity in the death of this woman. I have seen the kicking feet and the two in black who now seize hold of them and drag downward with all their weight. I don't want to see it anymore. I look at the grass instead. I describe the rope.[3]

So with this Salvaging in mind, Offred and the other Handmaidens act out their "duty" with the Commanders each month lifelessly, mechanically. Offred states, "I wait. I compose myself. My self is a thing I must now compose, as one composes a speech. What I must present is a made thing, not something born."[4]

Margaret Atwood wrote *The Handmaid's Tale* in 1985, and she intended her novel to be a "precautionary tale." In no way is it science fiction. It is an extrapolation of what life could become like based upon current realities. It is a warning to the reader about how the future could devolve if present realities follow their logical course. And these present realities have to do with underlying assumptions about and attitudes toward women. The tale bears horrifying resemblances to contemporary views concerning women, power, surrender, and the continuing dominance of a male order. Gilead represents this dystopia.

Is Atwood's vision exaggerated? Distorted? Are women still viewed primarily in terms of reproducing? In terms of sexual objects? Is the notion still current that, as far as women are concerned, biology is indeed destiny? Is her depiction of a male-dominated theocracy far-fetched? Her novel is essentially about power and its abuse. Does it apply today? Or have women generally achieved equal rights, privileges, and status compared to men?

■ THE SPIRIT OF FEMINISM AND ITS LANDMARKS

Today there are so many versions of feminism, from mainstream to radical, that it is easy to lose sight of its original meaning and impetus. It rests upon the long-standing history of control and dominance by men throughout the world, men who have not viewed women as their equals. Indeed, women continue to be treated in many respects as chattel, as property, as objects for use by men. Feminism is a vital movement that developed in

Western societies as a reaction against this pernicious perspective. In its original sense, feminism demands that women be viewed and treated, first and foremost, as persons having equal status, equal rights and privileges, and equal access to various jobs and opportunities. In other words, feminism beckons all of us to respect all women everywhere as persons in the genuine sense of possessing moral status.

Consider the Greek city-state of Athens, the birthplace of Western democracy (c. 510 BCE). Here, each Athenian citizen had a right to cast a vote. Women, however, along with slaves and prisoners of war, were not considered citizens. Not only were women viewed as property, but men believed that women were less capable of acting reasonably. Throughout many cultures, the prevailing view of women was that they were essentially irrational beings prone to allow their passions and feelings to overrule their capacity to reason. One sweepingly embarrassing trait in the history of Western philosophy lies in this bias against women as creatures unable to sufficiently reason and analyze and thus unqualified to philosophize. In his dialogue *Phaedo*, Plato describes Socrates' last day as he is about to drink the poison hemlock. Socrates wants to spend his last few hours doing what he loves doing above all else. He wants to converse with his friends, to philosophize, to pursue truth to the bitter end. Socrates' wife Xanthippe is with him. Yet Socrates requests that his friends escort her out of the prison chamber. Why? Socrates has a dual purpose: He wants to shield her from witnessing his agony and death from the poison; he also wants to conduct his conversation with his friends, all male, uninterrupted by expressions of grief. He desires to pursue matters in the most reasoned fashion without having to deal with any bouts of "hysteria."

The term "hysteria" is revealing. The word comes from the Greek term *hysterus*, which literally means "uterus"! How "uterus" came to be associated with the notion of excessive emotion conveys Western culture's bias. It demonstrates Western philosophy's prejudice against women. To illustrate, histories and anthologies of Western philosophy have consisted almost entirely of male philosophers' contributions. We are familiar with Plato, Aristotle, Aquinas, Kant, Mill, and Nietzsche. Plato's view of women is clear from his scene in *Phaedo*. Aristotle believed that females developed later *in utero* than did males, lending support to their supposed intellectual inferiority. Kant considered persons to be rational beings, yet he also felt that women were less capable of rationality. Of these men, only Mill defended the ability of women to reason and philosophize equally well, if not better, then men. We are familiar with Phintys of Sparta (c. 420 BCE), Marie le Jars de Gournay (1565–1645), Mary Wollstonecraft (1759–

1797), and Simone de Beauvoir (1908–1986), all of whom defended the intellectual equality of women and men.

To counter this ingrained bias, the contemporary feminist philosopher Susan Parsons urges women to raise their level of consciousness so that they transcend the long-standing error that women cannot think rationally as well as men. The problem is that women internalize prevailing perspectives about women, and these perspectives are actually myths, myths such as women are biologically inferior, women cannot think as analytically as men, or women cannot succeed as well as men in the workplace. By internalizing these false perceptions, women consider them as facts. Parsons argues that women need to think of themselves as possessing intrinsic value apart from their biology, apart from how they are viewed as sexual instruments by men. She thus encourages women to transcend their embodiment so that they see themselves as rational, valuable, free, and autonomous moral agents.[5] Nevertheless, the development of feminist thinking in the United States has undergone a long and bitter struggle. In view of this, let us review some key moments in this history of American feminism.

WOMEN'S SUFFRAGE AND THE EQUAL RIGHTS AMENDMENT

The first official public demonstration of feminism in America occurred in 1848 at Seneca Falls, New York. There the Women's Rights Convention had its first meeting and passed an official statement of feminism known as the Declaration of Sentiments and Resolutions. This Declaration primarily called for the equal treatment of women, most importantly the same right to vote as men. In this way, the suffrage movement became a crucial platform for American feminists. This Declaration also motivated the Quaker feminist Alice Paul to establish the National Women's Party (NWP) later on in 1916. Again, the principal focus of the NWP was suffrage, or women's right to vote. The efforts of Alice Paul and Susan B. Anthony paved the way for the passing of the Nineteenth Amendment in 1920, also called the Susan B. Anthony Amendment, which officially gave women across the nation the right to vote.

Alice Paul did not stop there. She then tirelessly struggled for the recognition of equality in all other spheres as well as equal protection for men and women by formulating the Equal Rights Amendment (ERA) in 1920. The ERA, however, faced stiff opposition particularly from women. Many women believed that they themselves had a right to choose to stay at home as housewives. Nevertheless, Paul and other feminists claimed that women should still have the right to work outside of the home and to pursue careers if they desired. Quite a few women entered the workplace purely out of necessity when the United States was engaged in World War II. However, this changed after the war when the troops returned home and entered the workforce, "retiring" millions of women. Add to this the fact that as housewives women were not, nor are they today, paid a salary. This is a key reason why housewives' contributions to the household have never been given fair attention. Within a capitalist and market-driven context, the lack of a salary denotes a lack of value. This motivated feminists all the more to fight for the passing of the ERA. Yet, as Betty Friedan in her 1963 book *The Feminine Mystique* emphasized, many women continue to be obstacles to women's rights.

The National Organization for Women (NOW) was established in 1996. Its primary agenda was not only to support equal rights for women, but especially to eradicate various forms of sexual discrimination in the workplace as well as in society in general. This fight against sexual discrimination later included struggling against sexual harassment. One of the classic landmark cases was the Clarence Thomas–Anita Hill hearings. In 1991, an all-male senate subcommittee found the Supreme Court nominee Clarence Thomas innocent of sexual harassment charges brought against him by former employee Anita Hill. Another primary aim of NOW is to raise the awareness of women to enable them to realize how they continue to be unknowingly victimized through sexual oppression within a patriarchal system.

■ FEMINISMS

The philosophy of feminism has undergone many variations so that it is hard to pin down exactly what feminism today is. Yet one common denominator certainly lies in its ethical relevance. Feminism is, at heart, directly related to issues of equity and the fair treatment of women. At its core, it sees that women's unfair treatment as subordinate to men has sustained a long history of inequity that needs to be remedied. Thus feminism is both descriptive, in that women are not viewed as equal to men, and normative—morality demands that this inequality be eradicated. The philosopher Alison Jaggar gives us a concise formula: "Feminists are united by a belief that the unequal and inferior social status of women is unjust and needs to be changed."[6] She then points to some major areas of dissension among feminists:

> *But they [feminists] are deeply divided about what changes are required. The deepest divisions are not differences about strategy or the kinds of tactics that will best serve women's interests; instead, they are differences about what are women's interests, what constitutes women's liberation.[7] [emphasis added]*

For this reason, feminist writer and activist Nancy Lublin designates "feminisms" as a better term than "feminism." According to Lublin,

> *Feminism is a myth. The existence of a single theory of political, economic, and social equality or a single definition of women's rights and interests is impossible. Since the sexuality, race, class, age, religion, and singing ability of women vary greatly, so our visions and constructions of the feminist utopia are also multitudinous. Furthermore, there are varying views regarding the nature of causes and agents of oppression, corrective measures, and the integrity of the category "women" itself.[8]*

Philosopher Nina Rosenstand gives us one of the clearest summaries of this diversity among feminists. According to Rosenstand, the complex phenomenon of feminism can be divided into four basic types: classical feminism, difference feminism, equity feminism, and radical feminism.[9] Let us examine each type in closer detail.

CLASSICAL FEMINISM

Classical feminism upholds the position that women and men are equal to each other in that they are all fundamentally *persons*. That is, all women are persons in the Kantian sense, so they are moral agents and possess moral status by virtue of the fact that they are persons. They are not objects for each other's use, as in Atwood's *Handmaid's Tale*, where the women in Gilead are not viewed as persons but solely as a means toward reproduction. Indeed, all women are principally subjects of moral worth and ought to be treated as such.

Is anatomy destiny? Are biological differences between men and women appropriate and sufficient grounds for determining how each sex is to be viewed, valued, and treated? Classical feminists respond "No." Anatomy and biology certainly account for the more obvious differences, such as childbearing, between the sexes. But strict gender differences and roles are not derived from biology. Instead, such gender differences are products of acculturation. Cultural beliefs and values and social upbringing have a decided impact upon gender roles. Despite this, the most important consideration is not culture but personhood. Regardless of acculturation, women and men should be viewed and treated equally because both women and men are persons, that is, moral agents and moral subjects.

Classical feminists point out that this has not been the case throughout most of human history. History (note the terms, "his" and "story") past and present proves that women have not been viewed nor treated as persons. Instead, they have been viewed as nonpersons, as beings without the same kinds of moral and legal rights and privileges as men. Women have been estranged from the moral community. One of the most influential voices representing this feminist position is the astute and far-sighted French existentialist philosopher Simone de Beauvoir (1908–1986). A selection from her classic work *The Second Sex* is included at the end of the chapter.

Simone de Beauvoir viewed herself in essentially two ways: as a woman and as a philosopher. Her self-view as a woman comes out clearly in her groundbreaking work *The Second Sex.* Her self-view as philosopher is more precisely that of an existentialist philosopher. She has customarily been viewed by male intellectuals as an associate of the celebrated French existentialist Jean-Paul Sartre (1905–1980) and under the shadow of his fame. She herself admits that Sartre's questions in his *Being and Nothingness* set the stage for her own quest for self-discovery. Her own brilliance and originality now more clearly emerges. She manages to break free from the structures implicit in his way of thinking after she herself awakens to the "astonishing realization" of their difference "because he was a man, and I was *only* a woman"[10] [emphasis added]. In other words, this "astonishing realization," radically profound in the 1950s and completely existential in its implications, consisted in discovering that women, on the whole, are viewed and treated as the Other, as Alien, in a world defined, determined, and controlled by men. And because of this otherness, or *alterité*, women are thereby not treated as equals. De Beauvoir cites the earlier, obscure male French philosopher Poulain de la Barre (1647–1725) who wrote, "All that has been written about women by men should be suspect, for the men are at once judge and party to the lawsuit."[11] Much of Western intellectual and cultural history testifies to this inequity. In her *Second Sex,* she examines this condition of women as Other through historical, psychoanalytical, biological, literary, mythical, and personal lenses. The text offers an explanation as to what conditions led to the "otherness" of women.

While she was writing *The Second Sex,* Simone de Beauvoir was going through some personal tension. She had been a longtime friend of Sartre, his closest intellectual confidant and critic. She was also engaged in an intimate relationship with the American writer Nelson Algren. As her biographer Deirdre Bair writes:

> *Nelson Algren had disturbed her rigidly defined, self-controlled world when he showed her that passion and reason could indeed be present within a single man and offered her the opportunity to be part of the traditional male-female couple she had always scorned as an "impossible contrivance of fools who write romance."*[12]

Despite this tension, she remained fully committed to the critical existentialist creed that there is no innate human nature that one must conform to. She believed that to assume that there is a "male" or "female" "nature" and to then adapt to this nature is a measure of bad faith, *mauvais foi,* a false consciousness. Instead, she upheld the radical notion that *we are who we choose to become.* That is, we are essentially what we decide. Our decisions determine what we become, and we continue to become; we are always in process of becoming. There is no finality in the sense that we now *are.* This existential canon for de Beauvoir is also the philosophical foundation for her feminism, her conviction that as long as women as a group are viewed as the Other, as a subcategory, gender equality remains a myth.

De Beauvoir and other classical feminists claim that one factor that has enabled the subordination of women for so long is that women themselves have refused to acknowledge their subjection. For centuries women have simply accepted their condition as the Other either through ignorance, willful ignorance, or outright denial. Why shake the boat? Otherwise, things become risky. And why risk security? Keep in mind that the republic of Gilead in *The Handmaid's Tale* is much safer and more secure for women. However, they pay a dear price—the price of giving up basic freedoms. Nevertheless, the Aunts, Wives, and Handmaids willingly accept their condition. This is the comfort of the familiar that lulls them into a feigned way of living in which they have managed to convince themselves that all is well because all is safe. As Offred admits, "We lived, as usual, by ignoring. Ignoring isn't the same as ignorance, you have to work at it."[13] "Ignoring" thus hypnotizes them into going about business as usual.

The Handmaid's Tale is a fictional account. Yet this "comfort of the familiar" can seduce us in ways so that in real-life situations of clear injustice we relinquish our freedom. Consider a wife who is constantly abused verbally and emotionally by her husband. As far as he is concerned, she is there to serve him. He offers little support in caring for their children. She may as well be a single parent. Her friends and family are horrified by the way he treats her, and they implore her to leave him. Her therapist insists that her husband seek therapy as well, but he stubbornly refuses. He denies any accountability. She occasionally considers taking her children with her and leaving him. Yet she talks herself out of it, rationalizing to herself: "How can I make it on my own?" "How will the children deal with our divorce?" "Why make matters more difficult?" Faced with the reality that her husband will most likely not change his ways, she decides to stay in the marriage. After all, even though at times it may be "hell," at least it is secure. It is known, familiar. The irony here is that even in making this decision, she exercises her free will. That is, she freely decides to remain in an unfree and oppressive situation. Yet is it the right decision?

DIFFERENCE FEMINISM

Difference feminists point out that despite their fundamental equality, women and men do have different traits, dispositions, and qualities. The ideal is to be able to integrate these differences. This is in contrast to the movement within feminism termed "androgyny." The movement of androgyny is somewhat inspired by classical feminism in that, according to androgyny, the stereotyping of so-called male and female traits is purely that—stereotyping. They are simply acculturated labels that have no bearing in reality. We may be conditioned to think of there being innate differences between male and female as we grow up. Androgynists deny that these innate differences exist. Difference feminists maintain, on the other hand, that there are fundamental differences. In this way, hopefully women and men can gain from understanding each other's differences.

A foremost contemporary representative of difference feminism is the Harvard psychologist Carol Gilligan (b. 1936). Her landmark book, *In a Different Voice*, created a groundswell of interest in the question of whether or not women and men exhibit different tendencies, particularly when it comes to moral decision making. Gilligan argues that there are some fundamental differences between girls and boys, women and men when it comes to matters of ethics and what is perceived as ethically right and wrong. She goes on to assert that men and women tend to approach ethical decision making differently. Gilligan's perspectives thereby have a direct impact upon ethical theory. Her work continues to exert a far-reaching influence upon views regarding the role of gender as it relates to ethics.

Gilligan was inspired by the pioneering work of her colleague, child psychologist Lawrence Kohlberg (1927–1987). In his investigations on the moral development of children, he would include moral cases in order to elicit responses from boys and girls, generally between the ages of ten and thirteen. One such case is the well-known Heinz's dilemma.

> *In Europe, a woman was near death from a very bad disease, a special kind of cancer. There was one drug the doctors thought might save her. It was a form of radium that a druggist in the same town had recently discovered. The drug was expensive to make, but the druggist was charging ten times what the drug cost him to make. He paid $200 for the radium and charged $2,000 for a small dose of the drug. The sick woman's husband, Heinz, went to everyone he knew to borrow the money, but he could get together only about $1,000, which was half of what it cost. He told the druggist that his wife was dying and asked him to sell it cheaper or let him pay later. But the druggist said, "No, I discovered the drug and I'm going to make money from it." Heinz got desperate and broke into the man's store to steal the drug for his wife.[14]*

When Kohlberg posed the question, "Should the husband have done that?" he discovered that boys and girls as groups tended to give rather different responses. Boys tended to answer with a clear "Yes." For these boys, Heinz should definitely steal the drug because in their judgment saving his wife's life is more important that breaking the law. In other words, there is a clear conflict between the principles of saving a life and the rule against stealing, in which case saving a life is of higher value. In contrast, the girls tended to be less black-and-white about the issue. They felt that Heinz should discuss the issue further with the pharmacist to try to persuade him to lower his price. Moreover, they also stressed that what good would Heinz be to his wife later on if he was caught and in jail? Who would then take care of her?

Kohlberg concluded from these responses that the boys' reasoning was more morally mature than the reasoning offered by the girls. This was because their responses had to do with appeals to principles and rules whereas the girls did not focus so much on principles and rules. As a gauge, Kohlberg was using his own hypothesis regarding moral development. He had proposed that moral development from childhood to adulthood occurs according to the following phases:

1. Stage of punishment and obedience

2. Stage of individual instrumental purpose and exchange

3. Stage of mutual interpersonal expectations, relationships, and conformity

4. Stage of social system and conscience maintenance

5. Stage of prior rights and social contract

6. Stage of universal ethical principles[15]

Here we see that, for Kohlberg, appealing to principles (as in stages 4, 5, and 6) is of a higher order in moral development than thinking in terms of interpersonal relationships (stage 3). In their responses, boys demonstrated this appeal to more principled ways of reasoning than girls. Kohlberg's conclusion? Moral maturity generally comes earlier for boys than it does for girls.

Carol Gilligan takes issue with this. She agrees with Kohlberg that boys and girls, as well as men and women, tend to exhibit differences in their moral perspectives. Yet in no way does she agree that this means that girls are less morally mature. Her interpretation of the difference between the moral perspectives of men and women lies in this: Men tend to approach moral conflict in terms of specific rules and principles, whereas women approach moral conflict in view of human relationships. This explains the responses of boys to Heinz's dilemma. Boys were rather clear that the principle of saving a life overrides the prohibition of theft. For many boys, it was a black-and-white solution. For girls, however, it was not so clear-cut. Discussing the matter further with the pharmacist was viewed as an option. And the consequences of Heinz being caught and jailed would certainly make matters worse for both him and his wife. The girls thereby approached the situation's human relationships and dynamics. In this respect, they were looking at the crisis through a wider and more humane lens.

This reminds me of the discussion we had in my ethics classes during the Bill Clinton and Monica Lewinsky affair. When I posed the question as to whether or not the President should be impeached, nearly all of my male students responded with an unequivocal "Yes." They grounded their belief in the simple fact that Clinton perjured himself and violated the implicit moral code of his office. In contrast, almost all of the women in the class seemed to be more disinclined to take a strict position of either impeachment or acquittal. Many of them pointed out the damaging impact this would have upon his marital relationship and his relationship to his daughter. Female students thus tended to underscore the importance of familial relationships, and stressed that these were just as important, if not more important, than legal stipulations and rules.

As to Kohlberg's experiment, Gilligan asserts that this does not at all indicate, as Kohlberg concluded, that the girls' approach to moral decision making is any less developed than that of the boys. Gilligan criticizes Kohlberg for reflecting a twofold bias. First, his position represents the enduring Western philosophical bias against the role of feelings and emotions since it assumes logical analysis and reasoning to be the most important faculty in the human psyche. Second, his position clearly and unfairly affronts women on the premise that they are less apt to think in terms of reasoned rules and principles.

To begin with, Gilligan argues that ruling out the significance of feelings and emotions is a one-sided approach to ethics. A more complete, holistic approach is to give weight to feelings and to the dynamics of humans in their relationships with each other, in which case thinking in terms of human relationships is an essential feature not only of moral reasoning but of being human. It can no doubt complicate moral decision making, but it is necessary. Gilligan urges us to free ourselves from the Western intellectual bias against the role of feelings and emotions. For this reason, women are not at all inferior to men when it comes to moral reasoning. They display more of an "ethic of care." They consider the human interactions, and they are equally capable as men of moral reasoning. Gilligan does not assert that this "ethic of care" is superior to one grounded upon an appeal to rules and principles. She does not claim that women's approach is better than that of men. She asserts that both approaches are necessary, and both approaches need to be integrated for a balanced approach to moral reasoning. Men can learn from the perspectives of women and vice versa. Men need to integrate this caring perspective in their approach, just as women need to implement more of an awareness of rules and principles. Feelings and reason must necessarily complement each other.

EQUITY FEMINISM

Equity feminism counters the extreme version of feminism that emphasizes that women are basically superior in most respects to men. These extremists often engage in various types of "male-bashing." Equity feminists believe this is going too far. They contend that a fundamental level of equity between women and men has now been achieved and point out that women are now freer than ever to pursue various careers of their own choice. Women are just as free to remain at home and care for their families in the traditional sense as they are free to work outside of the home pursuing other professions. Now that some parity has finally been won by women, equity feminists resent those feminists who continue to be harshly critical in ways that polarize women and men. In their estimation, these extremists do not fairly represent the attitudes of most women.

The philosopher Christina Hoff Sommers is a representative of equity feminism. Her work *Who Stole Feminism?* is a clear and concise statement of the equity feminist position. It is included at the end of this chapter. She argues that, now that equity has been achieved, women can exercise their freedoms in whatever ways they feel best suits them, and they should feel free to do so, notwithstanding the critique of the extremists, whom she calls "gender feminists." She wrote her article as a result of gender feminists' censure of comments she made regarding the scene in *Gone with the Wind* when Rhett Butler carries Scarlett O'Hara up the stairs. Whereas certain gender feminists consider the scene as comparable to rape, she finds the same scene innocuous. She reproaches this new breed of "gender feminists:"

> The presumption that men collectively are engaged in keeping women down invites feminist bonding in a resentful community. . . . American feminists are guided by women who believe in what they call the male hegemony or the sex gender system, a misogynous culture that socializes women to be docile and submissive to the controlling gender.[16]

In her article, Sommers demonstrates how gender feminism has been fed on misinformation and skewed research all bent upon vindicating the gender feminists' extreme agenda against males' alleged control. For Sommers, these gender feminists have betrayed the genuine spirit behind feminism, this same spirit as expressed in classical feminism.

RADICAL FEMINISM

When she describes "radical feminism," philosopher Nina Rosenstand does not mean extreme feminists, or gender feminists, who are male-bashers. Instead, she reminds us that the Latin root of the term "radical" is *radix*, which literally means "root." Radical feminists disagree with equity feminists and claim that women are still a long way from genuine equity. Despite the facade of equity, there are strong undercurrents of power and patriarchy that need to be addressed in order for true justice to come about.

For instance, there are numerous double standards when it comes to what is considered socially and morally unacceptable. The free sexual activity of young men is more or less condoned, whereas the same free sexual expression on the part of young women is frowned upon. As for careers, even though more women pursue careers and professions, the careers and professions of men are still assigned more importance than those of women. Men as a class are still paid higher salaries. Even though there is a growing interest in women's professional sports, a similar inequity exists between male and female athletes. Indeed, among young children there seems to be a revitalization of interest in "Ken" and "Barbie" dolls with all of their traditional gender associations.

To further illustrate, note that the standards of "beauty" are still determined by men. Women still fundamentally view themselves are persons *needing to be attractive to men.* They dress in ways that hopefully essentially elicit men's attention. They pamper themselves in order to appear beautiful. For whom? Attractive. To whom? The continued success of the cosmetic and fashion industries clearly demonstrates the willing surrender of women to a male-dominated culture. Philosopher Lisa Parker writes of this cultural construction of "beauty." Though we pretend that female beauty constitutes a "natural endowment," in reality it is a matter of artifice.

> *The fashion and cosmetics industries both feed and feed off of the myth that female beauty is a natural gift. Women who lack the gift practice their beauty secrets in private, compensating for nature's mistakes. . . . Cosmetics advertisements are aimed at women who do not measure up to the supposedly naturally beautiful norm. First they imply that these women should feel insecure about the private and public images; then they provide products to address the need they have helped to create.*[17]

Consider one of the most popular cosmetic procedures among women—breast augmentation. (As an example of this kind of cultural construction, note that, in France, breast reduction is the more common procedure.) Even though health insurance does not cover the costs of breast augmentation for cosmetic purposes, hundreds of thousands of women still resort to this procedure. The radical feminist argues that doing so represents these women's surrender to the social pressures and values essentially established by men. Women who suffer from low self-esteem because they have small breasts have unknowingly assimilated these male values. Consider the advertisement in *US Air Magazine* from the Pittsburgh Institute of Plastic Surgery that says "If enlarging your breasts will help you achieve your personal goals call us at. . . ."[18] In fact, having small breasts is now a medical condition diagnosed as micromastia. Parker notes that "the diagnosis also serves to legitimate the very profitable implantation procedure and elevates the status of those who perform it to that of serving a health need."[19] Women who undergo this procedure desire to be attractive and beautiful in ways defined by others. Yet they have somehow convinced themselves that these are their *own values.* They thus suffer from what radical feminists call a "false consciousness." They have, in effect, sold out their own authenticity through this false consciousness. In a sense, they have willingly or unknowingly adopted what Susan Parsons calls the "phallic morality" whereby men continue their oppression by presuming that they are biologically superior to women.[20] The radical feminist Ti-Grace Atkinson calls this demeaning view of women—a view women themselves have internalized—a "metaphysical cannibalism."[21] That is, it diminishes the personhood and humanity of women by reducing them to sexual and reproductive instruments. In *The Handmaid's Tale,* note the divide-and-conquer strategy of the Commanders. The executioners are not men. Instead, the punishments are doled out by women. The Handmaids demonstrate their participation in the execution as well when they hold on to the same rope that hangs female lawbreakers. Atwood calls this "Particicution."[22] Aunts, Wives, Marthas, and Handmaids end up assimilating the values of the Commanders and of the patriarchal order. As the Aunts become the enforcers and oppressors of their own sex, women in Gilead, in turn, measure their value and that of all women in terms of childbearing. In this way, men remain dominant.

Here is the major difference between radical feminists and equity feminists. The equity feminist will assert that, regarding cosmetic surgery, what this all means is that women now have the freedom to make choices regarding their own body and the way they look. If they choose to have larger or, as in France, smaller breasts, that is still their choice. Parker adds that such choices can indeed be freely made and are thus not necessarily uninformed nor inauthentic given an awareness of the cultural contexts in which these options occur. In contrast, radical feminists point out that these same contexts are still fundamentally determined, defined, and dictated by men.

All of this points to the discrepancy between the rhetoric and the reality of equality. As Offred points out in *The Handmaid's Tale*, "Pearls are congealed oyster spit."[23] According to radical feminists, we still live in a patriarchal culture, a culture dominated by men and by male values, values that, by the way, men have also socially and culturally assimilated. And until we free ourselves from this male dominance, we will continue to be either willing or unknowing slaves of patriarchy. Andrea Dworkin's selection at the end of this chapter succinctly reflects this radical feminist posture.

■ WEAKNESSES IN FEMINIST ETHICS

Carol Gilligan underscores a fundamental difference in moral attitude between women and men: Women tend to consider the human dynamics within particular situations, whereas men tend to think more in terms of specific rules and principles. Thus women exhibit an "ethic of care" as opposed to one based upon principles, what Gilligan has also called an "ethic of justice." Her way of delineating the two seems clear enough:

> *From a justice perspective, the* self as moral agent stands as the figure *against a ground of social relationships, judging the conflicting claims of self and others against a standard of equality or equal respect (the Categorical Imperative, the Golden Rule). From a care perspective, the* relationship becomes the figure, *defining self and others. Within the context of relationship, the self as a moral agent perceives and responds to the perception of need.*[24] *[emphasis added]*

Yet is the distinction between the two approaches that clear? Could not the need to appeal to relationships be itself construed as a principle? After all, a prominent principle is that we should care for those in need. Another principle requires that we attend to those to whom we have imminent responsibilities, namely family members. As we shall see later, this emphasis upon family duties, known as the principle of filial piety, is critical in Confucianism. Furthermore, many Asian cultures tend to view the "self" essentially in terms of relationships, in which case it makes less sense to establish a strict dividing line between self and relationships. Yet Gilligan's theory assumes this distinction. Of course, one can argue that Gilligan is addressing the gender distinction as she finds it in Western, particularly American, culture. Nevertheless, the distinction she offers between justice and care, principles and relationship, still appears vague.

One way out of this confusion may be to assert that when men appeal to principles and rules, they are thinking more abstractly. In contrast, by considering human relationships, women tend to be more concretely grounded in the particular situation. Yet this leans toward a precarious distinction between the abstract and the real, the theoretical and the actual. As suggested above, however, an abstract principle only makes sense because it is applied concretely. In other words, the supposedly abstract principle of saving a life only becomes meaningful within the specific context of saving the life, in this case, of Heinz's wife.

What may be another weakness in feminism, though it is more of a danger than a real flaw, is that feminism may become primarily parochial in perspective. Give the fact that the origin and development of feminism is more or less a Western phenomenon, if it remains typically Western in orientation, then it will become shortsighted. That is, we ought not to assume that all women everywhere share the same sets of problems as women in America. Indeed, the "feminisms" described earlier demonstrate that we cannot even assume that all women in America share similar perspectives. And if we mistakenly think that American feminists' issues are universal, then we, in effect, short-circuit any authentic paths to a global feminism.

Why should we presume to speak for the interests and concerns of all women everywhere? For example, American feminists have often spoken out, rightfully so, against the practice of female genital excision in the Sudan and elsewhere. At the same time, philosopher Rosemarie Tong cites how this focus can also be somewhat myopic. She points out that for feminists in developing nations the moral issues have more to do with social and economic exploitation rather than sexual mistreatment. She cites the Egyptian feminist and writer Nawal el Saadawi's example of the pervasive and abusive power of multinational corporations that, through the exploitation of the local labor force, maintain a situation that subjugates both women and men. Tong writes:

> *As Saadawi sees it, women in developed nations frequently fail to appreciate the extent to which they contribute to the economic and political oppression of women (and men) in developing nations. The same U.S. woman who is willing to attend protests against clitoridectomy might not be willing to attend protests against the multinational corporation that pays its employees in developing na-*

tions meager wages. As a result of this practice, the corporation can pay its employees in developed nations generous salaries.[25]

Tong goes on to point out that women in America, for example, need to make more of a genuine effort to see how women elsewhere, in developing nations such as Rwanda, Ethiopia, Egypt, Pakistan, and Mexico view the concerns of American women. For feminists in developing nations, American feminists have the luxury of addressing pseudo-concerns like reproductive technologies and cosmetic surgery. Tong hits the nail on the head when she asserts:

> *The money some Western women spend on perfecting their bodies could instead be spent on corrective surgeries for the maimed and scarred victims of torture and war throughout the world. Similarly, the money some women in the developed nations spend on diet drugs, "diet doctors," and diet books could instead be spent on much needed food supplies for people in developing nations who would be glad to eat a full meal.*[26]

Here, we are addressing the principle of distributive justice. Tong, along with other feminists, clearly suggests that this principle must be seriously applied in order to bring about a genuine global feminism. Keeping this principle in focus would be a necessary corrective against slipping into the trap of feminist parochialism.

■ STRENGTHS IN FEMINIST ETHICS

The overriding merit in feminist ethics lies in its effort to abolish the prevailing biases that have distorted the way we think of women and men and their relation to each other. Throughout numerous cultures, men's power and dominance have sustained a prolonged history of inequity and abuse. And the recognition of this fact, that women everywhere have suffered from the universal condition of being viewed essentially as Other, as the "second sex," in turn becomes a solid basis for a global feminism. Feminist ethics informs us of women's universal plight: In most cultures, women have been viewed essentially as sexual and reproductive objects for men. Women have been, and in many respects continue to be, second-class citizens. Compared to men, they have experienced diminished moral and legal status and have suffered worse socioeconomic conditions and have been more vulnerable when it comes to health care. On these grounds, a global approach to feminism becomes necessary and feasible. Here we see the particularly rich vision of Simone de Beauvoir. As an existentialist, she reminds us that there is no innate human nature that we mold ourselves into. As de Beauvoir insists, it is our choices every step of the way that determine what we become, not some innate nature.

In this respect, feminist ethics urges us to ask the integral question, What does it mean to be free? The feminist agenda is genuinely liberating. All too often we are tied to our perceptions that are based solely upon images. Feminist ethics demands that we think beyond these images and perceptions. For instance, in our American culture, we often think of others in terms of the way they look. We often judge others by what they wear. When we see a Muslim woman wearing the traditional *hijab,* we may mistakenly infer that this same woman is oppressed. The *hijab,* an Arabic word that means "curtain," is loose-fitting and covers most of the body. Because we may stereotype Muslim women as women who are generally suppressed, as for example they were tyrannized by the Taliban, we may mistakenly think of the wearer of the *hijab* in the same way. Actually, for many Muslim women, wearing the *hijab* represents freedom from having to be slaves to fashion in order to be attractive to men. The *hijab* symbolizes modesty and not necessarily repression. We can rightfully ask, Who is more free? The Muslim woman who chooses to wear her *hijab* or the American woman who chooses to be fashionable in order to be appealing? It is certainly the case that many Muslim women refuse to be viewed as sexual objects.

In light of this issue of freedom, radical feminism in particular goes to the heart of the matter. Radical feminism reminds us that the notion of equal opportunity is extensive, across-the-board. It incorporates equality for women not only outside of the home but also within the home. This is the genuine spirit behind feminist ethics. In other words, even if women do have equal access to various professions, one still needs to ask, What about domestic duties and responsibilities? If women pursue their careers outside of the home and then come home and perform nearly all of the household chores, how has equity been achieved? In effect, these same women are basically working a "second shift."[27] The true spirit of equal opportunity requires that if both partners work outside of the home, they both share the housekeeping and child-rearing duties and responsibilities within the home. Otherwise, as radical feminists remind us, equal opportunity is tokenism. If the male partner does not lift a finger to help with meals or laundry or any of the other household chores that women have been traditionally tethered to, then the notion of parity is a sham, and it cannot help but impair the family's emotional health.

The idea here is that equity is a matter of fairness and justice. However, some, including equity feminists, may argue that what really matters within the home more so than an equal sharing of responsibilities is whether there is real "love and affection." In response, philosopher James Sterba points out that notions of love and justice are not mutually exclusive.

> But a standard of love and affection that requires unfairness and imposes unequal burdens simply because of one's sex or sex socialization is not an adequate standard of love and affection. Love and affection within families can and should go beyond fairness or equal opportunity, but they should not go against them. Where there is proper love and affection, one doesn't need to demand fairness and equal opportunity.[28]

■ NOTES

1. Margaret Atwood, *The Handmaid's Tale* (New York: Ballantine Books, Fawcett Crest, 1985), pp. 120–21.

2. Ibid., p. 354.

3. Ibid., p. 355.

4. Ibid., p. 86.

5. Susan F. Parsons, "Feminism and the Logic of Morality: A Consideration of Alternatives," in Elizabeth Frazer, Jennifer Hornsby, and Sabina Lovibond, eds., *Ethics: A Feminist Reader* (Cambridge: Blackwell, 1992), pp. 38–412.

6. Alison Jaggar, "Political Philosophies of Women's Liberation," in *Feminism and Philosophy*, ed. Mary Vetterling-Braggin, Frederick Elliston, and Jane English (Totowa, NJ: Rowman & Allanheld, 1977), p. 5; cited in Nancy Lublin, *Pandora's Box: Feminism Confronts Reproductive Technology* (Lanham, MD: Rowman & Littlefield, 1998), p. xiii.

7. Ibid.

8. Lublin, p. xii.

9. See the discussion in Nina Rosenstand, *The Moral of the Story: An Introduction to Ethics*, 3rd ed. (Mountain View, CA: Mayfield, 2000), pp. 435–48.

10. Deirdre Bair, *Simone de Beauvoir: A Biography* (New York: Summit Books, 1990), p. 382.

11. In François Poulain de la Barre, *De l'égalité des deux sexes* (Paris: Librairie Arthème Fayard, 1984), cited in Bair, p. 389.

12. Bair, p. 385.

13. Ibid., p. 74.

14. Lawrence Kohlberg, *The Philosophy of Moral Development* (New York: Harper & Row, 1981, 1963), p. 19.

15. See James Rest, Elliot Turiel, and Lawrence Kohlberg, "Level of Moral Development as a Determinant of Preference and Comprehension of Moral Judgment Made by Others," *Journal of Personality* 37 (1969): 738–48.

16. Christina Hoff Sommers, *Who Stole Feminism?* (Washington, DC: American Enterprise Institute for Public Policy Research, Bradley Lecture Series, 1994), p. 3.

17. Lisa S. Parker, "Social Justice, Federal Paternalism, and Feminism: Breast Implantation in the Cultural Context of Female Beauty," *Kennedy Institute of Ethics Journal* 3, no. 1 (March 1993): 70.

18. *US Air Magazine* (November 1993), p. 118; cited in Michael C. Brannigan and Judith A. Boss, *Healthcare Ethics in a Diverse Society* (Mountain View, CA: Mayfield, 2001), p. 627.

19. Parker, p. 71.

20. Parsons, p. 393.

21. Ginette Castro, *American Feminism: A Contemporary History*, trans. Elizabeth Loverde-Bagwell (New York: New York University Press, 1990), p. 71.

22. Atwood, p. 357.

23. Ibid., p. 145.

24. Carol Gilligan, "Moral Orientations and Moral Development," in *Women and Moral Theory*, ed. Eva Kittay and Diana Meyers (Totowa: Rowman & Littlefield, 1987), p. 23; cited in James P. Sterba, *Three Challenges to Ethics: Environmentalism, Feminism, and Multiculturalism* (New York: Oxford University Press, 2001), p. 52.

25. Rosemarie Tong, "Towards a Feminist Global Bioethics: Addressing Women's Health Concerns Worldwide," *Health Care Analysis* 9, no. 2 (2001): 242.

26. Ibid., 243.

27. Sterba, p. 65.

28. Ibid, p. 67.

THE SECOND SEX

SIMONE DE BEAUVOIR

CHAPTER XI: Myth and Reality

The myth of woman plays a considerable part in literature; but what is its importance in daily life? To what extent does it affect the customs and conduct of individuals? In replying to this question it will be necessary to state precisely the relations this myth bears to reality.

There are different kinds of myths. This one, the myth of woman, sublimating an immutable aspect of the human condition—namely, the "division" of humanity into two classes of individuals—is a static myth. It projects into the realm of Platonic ideas a reality that is directly experienced or is conceptualized on a basis of experience; in place of fact, value, significance, knowledge, empirical law, it substitutes a transcendental Idea, timeless, unchangeable, necessary. This idea is indisputable because it is beyond the given: it is endowed with absolute truth. Thus, as against the dispersed, contingent, and multiple existences of actual women, mythical thought opposes the Eternal Feminine, unique and changeless. If the definition provided for this concept is contradicted by the behavior of flesh-and-blood women, it is the latter who are wrong: we are told not that Femininity is a false entity, but that the women concerned are not feminine. The contrary facts of experience are impotent against the myth. In a way, however, its source is in experience. Thus it is quite true that woman is other than man, and this alterity is directly felt in desire, the embrace, love; but the real relation is one of reciprocity; as such it gives rise to authentic drama. Through eroticism, love, friendship, and their alternatives, deception, hate, rivalry, the relation is a struggle between concious beings each of whom wishes to be essential, it is the mutual recognition of free beings who confirm one another's freedom, it is the vague transition from aversion to participation. To pose Woman is to pose the absolute Other, without reciprocity, denying against all experience that she is a subject, a fellow human being.

In actuality, of course, women appear under various aspects; but each of the myths built up around the subject of woman is intended to sum her up *in toto;* each aspires to be unique. In consequence, a number of incompatible myths exist, and men tarry musing before the strange incoherencies manifested by the idea of Femininity. As every woman has a share in a majority of these archetypes—each of which lays claim to containing the sole Truth of woman—men of today also are moved again in the presence of their female companions to an astonishment like that of the old sophists who failed to understand how man could be blond and dark at the same time! Transition toward the absolute was indicated long ago in social phenomena: relations are easily congealed in classes, functions in types, just as relations, to the childish mentality, are fixed in things. Patriarchal society, for example, being centered upon the conservation of the patrimony, implies necessarily, along with those who own and transmit wealth, the existence of men and women who take property away from its owners and put it into circulation. The men—adventurers, swindlers, thieves, speculators—are generally repudiated by the group; the women, employing their erotic attraction, can induce young men and even fathers of families to scatter their patrimonies, without ceasing to be within the law. Some of these women appropriate their victims' fortunes or obtain legacies by using undue influence; this role being regarded as evil, those who play it are called, "bad women." But the fact is that quite to the contrary they are able to appear in some other setting—at home with their fathers, brothers, husbands, or lovers—as guardian angels; and the courtesan who "plucks" rich financiers is, for painters and writers, a generous patroness. It is easy to understand in actual experience the ambiguous personality of Aspasia or Mme de Pompadour. But if woman is depicted as the Praying Mantis, the Mandrake, the Demon, then it is most confusing to find in woman also the Muse, the Goddess Mother, Beatrice.

As group symbols and social types are generally defined by means of antonyms in pairs, ambivalence will seem to be an intrinsic quality of the Eternal Feminine. The saintly mother has for correlative the cruel stepmother, the angelic young girl has the perverse virgin: thus it will be said sometimes that Mother equals Life, sometimes that Mother equals Death, that every virgin is pure spirit or flesh dedicated to the devil.

Evidently it is not reality that dictates to society or to individuals their choice between the two opposed basic categories; in every period, in each case, society and the individual decide in accordance with their needs. Very often they project into the myth adopted the institutions and values to which they adhere. Thus the paternalism that claims woman for hearth and home defines her as sentiment, inwardness, immanence. In fact every existent is at once immanence and transcendence; when one offers the existent no aim, or prevents him from attaining any, or robs him of his victory, then his transcendence falls vainly into the past—that is to say, falls back into immanence. This is the lot assigned to woman in the patriarchate; but it is in no way a vocation, any more than slavery is the vocation of the slave. The development of this mythology is to be clearly seen in Auguste Comte. To identify Woman with Altruism is to guarantee to man absolute rights in her devotion, it is to impose on women a categorical imperative.

The myth must not be confused with the recognition of significance; significance is immanent in the object; it is revealed to the mind through a living experience; whereas the myth is a transcendent. Idea that escapes the mental grasp entirely. When in *L'Age d'homme* Michel Leiris describes his vision of the feminine organs, he tells us things of significance and elaborates no myth. Wonder at the feminine body, dislike for menstrual blood, come from perceptions of a concrete reality. There is nothing mythical in the experience that reveals the voluptuous qualities of feminine flesh, and it is not an excursion into myth if one attempts to describe them through comparisons with flowers or pebbles. But to say that Woman is Flesh, to say that the Flesh is Night and Death, or that it is the splendor of the Cosmos, is to abandon terrestrial truth and soar into an empty sky. For man also is flesh for woman; and woman is not merely a carnal object; and the flesh is clothed in special significance for each person and in each experience. And likewise it is quite true that woman—like man—is a being rooted in nature; she is more enslaved to the species than is the male, her animality is more manifest; but in her as in him the given traits are taken on through the fact of existence, she belongs also to the human realm. To assimilate her to Nature is simply to act from prejudice.

... But a woman hardly has means for sounding her own heart; according to her moods she will view her own sentiments in different lights, and as she submits to them passively, one interpretation will be no truer than another. In those rare instances in which she holds the position of economic and social privilege, the mystery is reversed, showing that it does not pertain to *one* sex rather than the other, but to the situation. For a great many women the roads to transcendence are blocked: because they *do* nothing, they fail to *make themselves* anything. They wonder indefinitely what they *could have* become, which sets them to asking about what they *are*. It is a vain question. If man fails to discover that secret essence of femininity, it is simply because it does not exist. Kept on the fringe of the world, woman cannot be objectively defined through this world, and her mystery conceals nothing but emptiness.

Furthermore, like all the oppressed, woman deliberately dissembles her objective actuality; the slave, the servant, the indigent, all who depend upon the caprices of a master, have learned to turn toward him a changeless smile or an enigmatic impassivity; their real sentiments, their actual behavior, are carefully hidden. And moreover woman is taught from adolescence to lie to men, to scheme, to be wily. In speaking to them she wears an artificial expression on her face; she is cautious, hypocritical, play-acting.

But the Feminine Mystery as recognized in mythical thought is a more profound matter. In fact, it is immediately implied in the mythology of the absolute Other. If it be admitted that the inessential conscious being, too, is a clear subjectivity, capable of performing the *Cogito*, then it is also admitted that this being is in truth sovereign and returns to being essential; in order that all reciprocity may appear quite impossible, it is necessary for the Other to be for itself an other, for its very subjectivity to be affected by its otherness; this consciousness which would be alienated as a consciousness, in its pure immanent presence, would evidently be Mystery. It would be Mystery in itself from the fact that it would be Mystery for itself; it would be absolute Mystery.

In the same way it is true that, beyond the secrecy created by their dissembling, there is mystery in the Black, the Yellow, in so far as: they are considered absolutely as the inessential Other. It should be noted that the American citizen, who profoundly baffles the average European, is not, however, considered as being "mysterious": one states more modestly that one does not understand him. And similarly woman does not always "understand" man; but there is no such thing as a masculine mystery. The point is that rich America, and the male, are on the Master side and that Mystery belongs to the slave.

To be sure, we can only muse in the twilight byways of bad faith upon the positive reality of the Mystery; like certain marginal hallucinations, it dissolves under the attempt to view it fixedly. Literature always fails in attempting to portray "mysterious" women; they can appear only at the beginning of a novel as strange, enigmatic figures; but unless the story remains unfinished they give up their secret in the end and they are then simply consistent and transparent persons. The heroes in Peter Cheyney's books, for example, never cease to be astonished at the unpredictable caprices of women: no one can ever guess how they will act, they upset all calculations. The fact is that once the springs of their action are revealed to the reader, they are seen to be, very simple mechanisms: this woman was a spy, that one a thief; however clever the plot, there is always a key; and it could not be otherwise, had the author all the talent and imagination in the world. Mystery is never more than a mirage that vanishes as we draw near to look at it.

We can see now that the myth is in large part explained by its usefulness to man. The myth of woman is a luxury. It can appear only if man escapes from the urgent demands of his needs; the more relationships are concretely lived, the less they are idealized. The fellah of ancient Egypt, the Bedouin peasant, the artisan of the Middle Ages, the worker of today has in the requirements of work and poverty relations with his particular woman companion which are too definite for her to be embellished with an aura either auspicious or inauspicious. The epochs and the social classes that have been marked by the leisure to dream have been the ones to set up the images, black and white, of femininity. But along with luxury there was utility; these dreams were irresistibly guided by interests. Surely most of the myths had roots in the spontaneous attitude of man toward his own existence and toward the world around him. But going beyond experience toward the transcendent Idea was deliberately used by patriarchal society for purposes of self-justification; through the

myths this society imposed its laws and customs upon individuals in a picturesque, effective manner; it is under a mythical form that the group-imperative
is indoctrinated into each conscience. Through such intermediaries as religions, traditions, language, tales, songs, movies, the myths penetrate even into
such existences as are most harshly enslaved to material realities. Here everyone can find sublimation of his drab experiences: deceived by the woman he
loves, one declares that she is a Crazy Womb; another, obsessed by his impotence, calls her a Praying Mantis; still another enjoys his wife's company; be-
hold, she is Harmony, Rest, the Good Earth! The taste for eternity at a bargain,
for a pocket-sized absolute, which is shared by a majority of men, is satisfied
by myths. The smallest emotion, a slight annoyance, becomes the reflection of
a timeless Idea—an illusion agreeably flattering to the vanity.

WHO STOLE FEMINISM?

CHRISTINA HOFF SOMMERS

Until 1989, I was an academic feminist in good standing. My essays were included in feminist anthologies, I was invited to feminist conferences, and my
philosophy courses were cross-listed with courses in women's studies. But I ran
afoul of the feminist establishment when I published an essay in the *Chronicle
of Higher Education* that said something politically incorrect about the famous
staircase scene in the film, *Gone with the Wind*.

I wrote: "Many women continue to enjoy the sight of Rhett Butler carrying Scarlett O'Hara up the stairs to a fate undreamt of in feminist philosophy."
I meant that to be not just a lighthearted comment, but also a serious warning
to feminist theorists that they were out of touch with many women. My remark, however, incensed an organization within the American Philosophical
Association known as SWIP, the Society of Women in Philosophy. Several
prominent members of SWIP wrote outraged letters to the *Chronicle* and the
Journal of the American Philosophical Association. SWIP felt the need to re-
act more formally to my heresy, so they also arranged a meeting at which feminist philosopher Marilyn Friedman would read a paper showing once and for
all how my views were treasonable to women.

At the meeting, Ms. Friedman told an overflowing crowd that she was
stunned by my flippant reaction to Rhett Butler's rape of Scarlett O'Hara. In
her eyes, there was no doubt whatsoever that Rhett had raped Scarlett that
night. Indeed, Ms. Friedman went on to compare Rhett Butler to a sociopathic
murderer: "The name of Richard Speck, to take one example, can remind us
that real rape is not the pleasurable fantasy intimated in *Gone with the Wind*."

Ms. Friedman also called our attention to Angela Carter's feminist rewrite of the "morning-after" scene in *Gone with the Wind*: "Scarlett lies in bed, smiling the next morning because she broke Rhett's kneecaps the night before. And the reason that he disappeared before she awoke was that he had gone off to Europe to visit a good kneecap specialist." The feminists in the audience found this riotously funny.

I then suggested to them that perhaps they ought to reflect on the difference between being raped and being ravished. The distinction is critical, after all, to millions of women who read authors of romance fiction from Margaret Mitchell to Barbara Carlton. It is behind the common sense conviction that Rhett Butler is in no way akin to Richard Speck. But this audience stared at me in angry incomprehension. I had crossed a divide.

If feminism is a religion, Rhett Butler is the devil. My casual acceptance of the women who find Rhett Butler so attractive was not to be forgiven. I never recovered my reputation as a reliable member of the sisterhood. Why?

A surprising number of clever and powerful feminists share the sincere conviction that American women live in an oppressive patriarchy, a male hegemony, where men collectively keep women down. It is customary for these feminists to assemble to exchange stories and to talk about their anger. Once such conference, "Out of the Academy and into the World," took place at the graduate center of the City University of New York in October, 1992.

The morning sessions were devoted to honoring the feminist scholar and mystery writer Carolyn Heilbrun on the occasion of her voluntary retirement from Columbia University after 32 years of tenure. I had just been reading Marilyn Friedman's *The War Against Women*, which Ms. Heilbrun touts on the cover as a book that lays out women's state in the world. It is a state of siege.

Intelligent women who sincerely believe that American women are in a gender war intrigue me. Since a day with Ms. Heilbrun and her admirers promised to be rewarding, I arrived early—but so did a crowd of more than 500 women. I was lucky to get a seat.

Ms. Heilbrun's theme of siege set the tone for the conference. Jane Marcus, a professor at the City University of New York, called the afternoon "anger" session to order. Professor Marcus introduced herself as an expert on anger, and she urged the conference participants to use their rage in their writing.

She introduced the other panelists as angry in one way or another. Alice Jardine of Harvard University's French Department was "angry and struggling." Brenda Silver of Dartmouth University had been "struggling and angry since 1972." Catherine Stimpson, former vice provost of Rutgers University (and recently selected to head the distinguished MacArthur Fellows Program) was introduced as "an engaged and enraged intellectual."

Sarah Ruddick, a feminist at the New School for Social Research who is known for "valorizing" women as the gentle nurturers of our species, told the assembled feminists that "our anger arouses the patriarchy to disgust." Gloria Steinem took the microphone and explained why she was enraged: "I have become even more angry. The only alternative is depression." To deal with patriarchal schools, she recommended an underground system of education. She explained she had in mind a bartering system, in which a midwife could exchange her services in return for instruction in Latin American history. Steinem believes that things are so bad for contemporary American women that we might have consider setting up centers for training political organizers, where, as she put it, real education will take place.

As each speaker recited her tale of outrage and gave more warnings of male backlash to come, it became clear to me that these privileged women really did feel aggrieved. It was equally clear that the bitter spirits they were dispensing on the American public were unwholesome and divisive. For whom do these enraged and engaged women speak? Who was their constituency? It might be said that as academics and intellectuals, they speak for no one but themselves—but that would be to mistake their mission.

The women at the Heilbrun conference are the new feminists, articulate, prone to self-dramatization, and chronically offended. They see themselves as the vanguard of the second wave of the feminist movement: a moral vanguard, fighting a war to save women. But do American women need to be saved by anybody?

Many of the women on the anger panel were tenured professors in distinguished universities. All had fine and expensive educations. None, as far as I know, got her degree by bartering with a midwife. Yet listening to them, one would never guess that they live in a country where women are legally as free as men or whose institutions of higher learning now have more female than male students.

It was inevitable, I suppose, that such capable, energetic women would find their way into leadership positions. But it is unfortunate that American feminism has been taken over by their ideology. They are diverting the women's movement from its true purposes.

The presumption that men collectively are engaged in keeping women down invites feminist bonding in a resentful community. The spirit of the Heilbrun conference is the spirit of much of contemporary feminism. American feminists are guided by women who believe in what they call the male hegemony or the sex gender system, a misogynous culture that socializes women to be docile and submissive to the controlling gender.

According to feminist theorist Sandra Lee Barkty, the sex gender system is "that complex process whereby bisexual infants are transformed into male and female gender personalities, the one destined to command, the other destined to obey."

Sex gender feminism or gender feminism, for short, is the prevailing ideology among contemporary feminist philosophers. It certainly was prevalent at the Heilbrun conference.

Virginia Held, a professor of philosophy at City University of New York, has written this about the revolutionary effects of the sex gender perspective on feminist thought: "Now that the sex gender system has become visible to us, we can see it everywhere." And indeed, most feminist theorists and spokespersons are sex gender feminists: most do see it everywhere.

I confess that I sometimes envy Held and her sister gender feminists the excitement that they seem to get from seeing the world through the lens of sexual politics. Ms. Held reports that many feminist thinkers are convinced that they are initiating an intellectual revolution comparable to those of Copernicus, Darwin, and Freud. Some feminists, she says, think the latest revolution will be even more profound.

Gender feminism is a beguiling and heady philosophy. And I do sometimes wish I could join in all the fun. On the other hand, I have learned that how these women regard American society is more a matter of temperament than insight into social reality. The belief that American women are living enthralled to men, seems to suit some women more than others. I have found that it does not suit me.

I consider myself a mainstream equity feminist. And I believe most American women subscribe philosophically to the classical, first-wave kind of feminism whose main goal is equity, especially in politics and education. A first-wave mainstream or equity feminist wants for women what she wants for everyone: fair treatment, no discrimination.

Equity feminism got us the suffrage and continues to get us many other needed reforms. The equity agenda may not yet be fully achieved, but by any reasonable measure, equity feminism has turned out to be the great American success story.

By contrast, the women at the Heilbrun conference, the women in the Society of Women in Philosophy, and the other new feminists who view the world through the lens of the sex gender system see little to celebrate. They speak instead of backlash, an undeclared war against women. The stories they have to tell are atrocity stories designed to alert women to their plight.

The gender feminist sincerely believes that our basic social institutions—from families and schools to the state itself—are designed to perpetuate male dominance. Believing that women are virtually under seige, gender feminists naturally seek recruits to wage their side of the gender war. They seek support. They seek vindication. They seek ammunition . . .

. . . I wrote *Who Stole Feminism?* because I believe the new feminism has gone astray and that women who care about women's issues must find their way back to the classical feminism of the first wave. The gender feminists do not represent the vast majority of women. They have given feminism a bad name. We should not let them define what it means to be a feminist. I am an equity feminist, as are many women today who refuse to call themselves feminists.

Speaking with a historian friend of mine last year, I lamented the feminist philosophers' attack on rationality, the flood of misinformation in the media on women's victimization, the anti-intellectualism of the feminist academics, the male bashing, and the witch hunts. "Don't be depressed," my friend said. "After all, most of history has been dominated by superstition, authoritariansim, irrationality. Why should we be any different?"

As a teacher of philosophy, I am committed to the idea that we must do our utmost to be different. As a member of the professoriate, I am mortified that more scholars are not protesting the gender bigotry and the anti-intellectualism that characterizes so much of academic feminism.

My historian friend is right, a democratic culture like ours, in which a respect for reason and open expression have actually taken hold, is rare indeed. All the more reason to promote our freedoms and intellectual standards unstintingly. We are not free to hang back and allow unreason and intolerance to have the last word.

THE POLITICS OF INTELLIGENCE

ANDREA DWORKIN

Why is life so tragic; so like a little strip of pavement over an abyss. I look down; I feel giddy; I wonder how I am ever to walk to the end. . . . It's a feeling of impotence: of cutting no ice.
                    Virginia Woolf, her diary, October 25, 1920

Men hate intelligence in women. It cannot flame; it cannot burn; it cannot burn out and end up in ashes, having been consumed in adventure. It cannot be cold, rational, ice; no warm womb would tolerate a cold, icy, splendid mind. It cannot be ebullient and it cannot be morbid; it cannot be anything that does not end in reproduction or whoring. It cannot be what intelligence is: a vitality of mind that acts directly in and on the world, without mediation . . .

. . .Intelligence is a form of energy, a force that pushes out into the world. It makes its mark, not once but continuously. It is curious, penetrating. Without the light of public life, discourse, and action, it dies. It must have a field of action beyond embroidery or scrubbing toilets or wearing fine clothes. It needs response, challenge, consequences that matter. Intelligence cannot be passive and private through a lifetime. Kept secret, kept inside, it withers and dies. The outside can be brought to it; it can live on bread and water locked up in a cell—but barely. Florence Nightingale, in her feminist tract *Cassandra,* said that intellect died last in women; desire, dreams, activity, and love all died before it. Intelligence does hang on, because it can live on almost, nothing: fragments of the world brought to it by husbands or sons or strangers or, in our time, television or the occasional film. Imprisoned, intelligence turns into self-haunting and dread. Isolated, intelligence becomes a burden and a curse. Undernourished, intelligence becomes like the bloated belly of a starving child: swollen, filled with nothing the body can use. It swells, like the starved stomach, as the skeleton shrivels and the bones collapse; it will pick up anything to fill the hunger, stick anything in, chew anything, swallow anything . . .

. . .Traditionally and practically, the world is brought to women by men; they are the outside on which female intelligence must feed. The food is poor, orphan's gruel. This is because men bring home half-truths, ego-laden lies, and use them to demand solace or sex or housekeeping. The intelligence of women is not out in the world, acting on its own behalf; it is kept small, inside the home, acting on behalf of another. This is true even when the woman works outside the home, because she is segregated into women's work, and her intelligence does not have the same importance as the lay of her ass.

Men are the world and women use intelligence to survive men: their tricks, desires, demands, moods, hatreds, disappointments, rages, greed, lust, authority, power, weaknesses. The ideas that come to women come through men, in a field of cultural values controlled by men, in a political and social system controlled by men, in a sexual system in which women are used as things . . . Men are the field of action in which female intelligence moves. But the world, the real world, is more than men, certainly more than what men show of themselves and the world to women; and women are deprived of that real world. The male always intervenes between her and it.

Some will grant that women might have a particular kind of intelligence—essentially small, picky, good with details, bad with ideas. Some will grant—in fact, insist—that women know more of "the Good," that women are more cognizant of decency or kindness: this keeps intelligence small and tamed. Some will grant that there have been women of genius: after the woman of genius is dead. The greatest writers in the English language have been women: George Eliot, Jane Austen, Virginia Woolf. They were sublime; and they were, all of them, shadows of what they might have been. But the fact that they existed does not change the categorical perception that women are basically stupid: not capable of intelligence without the exercise of which the world as a whole is impoverished. Women are stupid and men are smart; men have a right to the world and women do not. A lost man is a lost intelligence; a lost woman is a lost (name the function) mother, housekeeper, sexual thing. Classes of men have been lost, have been thrown away; there have always been mourners and fighters who refused to accept the loss. There is no mourning for the lost intelligence of women because there is no conviction that such intelligence was real and was destroyed. Intelligence is, in fact, seen as a function of masculinity, and women are despised when they refuse to be lost . . .

. . .A woman must keep her intelligence small and timid to survive. Or she must hide it altogether or hide it through style. Or she must go mad like clockwork to pay for it. She will try to find the nice way to exercise intelligence. But intelligence is not ladylike. Intelligence is full of excesses. Rigorous intelligence abhors sentimentality, and women must be sentimental to value the dreadful silliness of the men around them. Morbid intelligence abhors the cheery sunlight of positive thinking and eternal sweetness; and women must be sunlight and cheery and sweet, or the woman could not bribe her way with smiles through a day. Wild intelligence abhors any narrow world; and the world of women must stay narrow, or the woman is an outlaw. No woman could be Nietzsche or Rimbaud without ending up in a whorehouse or lobotomized. Any vital intelligence has passionate questions, aggressive answers: but women cannot be explorers; there can be no Lewis and Clark of the female mind. Even restrained intelligence is restrained not because it is timid, as women must be, but because it is cautiously weighing impressions and facts that come to it from an outside that the timid dare not face. A woman must please, and restrained intelligence does not seek to please; it seeks to know through discernment. Intelligence is also ambitious: it always wants more: not more being fucked, not more pregnancy; but more of a bigger world. A woman cannot be ambitious in her own right without also being damned.

We take girls and send them to schools. It is good of us, because girls are not supposed to know anything much, and in many other societies girls are not sent to school or taught to read and write. In our society, such a generous one to women, girls are taught some facts, but not inquiry or the passion of knowing. Girls are taught in order to make them compliant: intellectual adventurousness is drained, punished, ridiculed out of girls. We use schools first to narrow the girl's scope, her curiosity, then to teach her certain skills, necessary to the abstract husband. Girls are taught to be passive in relation to facts. Girls are not seen as the potential originators of ideas or the potential searchers into the human condition. Good behavior is the intellectual goal of a girl. A girl with intellectual drive is a girl who has to be cut down to size. An intelligent girl is supposed to use that intelligence to find a smarter husband. Simone de Beauvoir settled on Sartre when she determined that he was smarter than she was. In a film made when both were old, toward the end of his life, Sartre asks de Beauvoir, the woman with whom he has shared an astonishing life of intellectual action and accomplishment: how does it feel, to have been a literary lady? . . .

. . .Virginia Woolf, the most splendid modern writer, told us over and over how awful it was to be a woman of creative intelligence. She told us when she loaded a large stone into her pocket and walked into the river; and she told us each time a book was published and she went mad—don't hurt me for what I have done, I will hurt myself first, I will be incapacitated and I will suffer and I will be punished and then perhaps you need not destroy me, perhaps you will pity me, there is such contempt in pity and I am so proud, won't that be enough? She told us over and over in her prose too: in her fiction she showed us, ever so delicately so that we would not take offense; and in her essays she piled on the charm, being polite to keep us polite. But she did write it straight out too, though it was not published in her lifetime, and she was right . . .

To value "the naked contact of a mind" is to have a virile intelligence, one not shrouded in dresses and pretty gestures. Her work did always go down, with the weight of what being female demanded. She became a master of exquisite indirection. She hid her meanings and her messages in a feminine style. She labored under that style and hid behind that mask: and she was less than she could have been. She died not only from what she did dare, but also from what she did not dare . . .

. . .These three things are indissolubly linked: literacy, intellect, and creative intelligence. They distinguish, as the cliché goes, man from the animals. He who is denied these three is denied a fully human life and has been robbed of a right to human dignity. Now change the gender. Literacy, intellect, and creative intelligence distinguish woman from the animals: no. Woman is not distinguishable from the animals because she has been condemned by virtue of her sex class to a life of animal functions: being fucked, reproducing. For her, the animal functions are her meaning, her so-called humanity, as human as she gets, the highest human capacities in her because she is female. To the orthodox of male culture, she is animal, the antithesis of soul; to the liberals of male culture, she is nature. In discussing the so-called biological origins of male dominance, the boys can afford to compare themselves to baboons and insects: they are writing books or teaching in universities when they do it. A Harvard professor does not refuse tenure because a baboon has never been granted it. The biology of power is a game boys play. It is the male way of saying: she is more like the female baboon than she is like me; she cannot be an éminence grise at Harvard because she bleeds, we fuck her, she bears our young, we beat her up, we rape her; she is an animal, her function is to breed. I want to see the baboon, the ant, the wasp, the goose, the cichlid, that has written *War and Peace*. Even more I want to see the animal or insect or fish or fowl that has written *Middlemarch*.

Literacy is a tool, like fire. It is a more advanced tool than fire, and it has done as much or more to change the complexion of the natural and social worlds. Literacy, like fire, is a tool that must be used by intelligence. Literacy is also a capacity: the capacity to be literate is a human capacity; the capacity exists and it can be used or it can be denied, refuted, made to atrophy. In persons socially despised, it is denied. But denial is not enough, because people insist on meaning. Humankind finds meaning in experiences, events, objects, communications, relationships, feelings. Literacy functions as part of the search for meaning; it helps to make that search possible. Men can deny that women have the capacity to learn ancient Greek, but some women will learn it nevertheless. Men can deny that poor women or working-class women or prostituted women have the capacity to read or write their own language, but some of those women will read or write their own language anyway; they will risk everything to learn it. In the slaveholding South in the United States, it was forbidden by law to teach slaves to read or write; but some slaveowners taught, some slaves learned, some slaves taught themselves, and some slaves taught other slaves. In Jewish law, it is forbidden to teach women Talmud, but some women learned Talmud anyway. People know that literacy brings dignity and a wider world. People are strongly motivated to experience the world they live in through language: spoken, sung, chanted, and written. One must punish people terribly to stop them from wanting to know what reading and writing bring, because people are curious and driven toward both experience and the conceptualization of it. The denial of literacy to any class or category of people is a denial of fundamental humanity. Humans viewed as animal, not human, are classically denied literacy: slaves in slave-owning societies; women in woman-owning societies; racially degraded groups in racist societies. The male slave is treated as a beast of burden; he cannot be allowed to read or write. The woman is treated as a beast of breeding; she must not read or write. When women as a class are denied the right to read and write, those who learn are shamed by their knowledge: they are masculine, deviant; they have denied their wombs, their cunts; in their literacy they repudiate the definition of their kind.

Certain classes of women have been granted some privileges of literacy—not rights, privileges. The courtesans of ancient Greece were educated when other women were kept ignorant, but they were not philosophers, they were whores. Only by accepting their function as whores could they exercise the privilege of literacy. Upper-class women are traditionally taught some skills of literacy (distinctly more circumscribed than the skills taught the males of their mating class): they can exercise the privilege of literacy if they accept their decorative function. After all, the man does not want the breeding, bleeding bitch at the dinner table or the open cunt in the parlor while he reads his newspaper or smokes his cigar. Language is refinement: proof that he is human, not she.

The increase in illiteracy among the urban poor in the United States is consonant with a new rise in overt racism and contempt for the poor. The illiteracy is programmed into the system: an intelligent child can go to school and not be taught how to read or write. When the educational system abandons reading and writing for particular subgroups, it abandons human dignity for those groups: it becomes strictly custodial, keeping the animals penned in; it does not bring human life to human beings.

Cross-culturally, girls and women are the illiterates, with two thirds of the world's illiterates women and the rate rising steadily. Girls need husbands, not books. Girls need houses or shacks to keep clean, or street corners to stand on, not the wide world in which to roam. Refusal to give the tool of literacy is refusal to give access to the world. If she can make her own fire, read a book herself, write a letter or a record of her thoughts or an essay or a story, it will be harder to get her to tolerate the unwanted fuck, to bear the unwanted children, to see him as life and life through him. She might get ideas. But even worse, she might know the value of the ideas she gets. She must not know that ideas have value, only that being fucked and reproducing are her value.

Feminists know that if women are paid equal wages for equal work, women will gain sexual as well as economic independence. But feminists have refused to face the fact that in a woman-hating social system, women will never be paid equal wages. Men in all their institutions of power are sustained by the sex labor and sexual subordination of women. The sex labor of women must be maintained; and systematic low wages for sex-neutral work effectively force women to sell sex to survive. The economic system that pays women lower wages than it pays men actually punishes women for working outside marriage or prostitution, since women work hard for low wages and still must sell sex. The economic system that pun-

ishes women for working outside the bedroom by paying low wages contributes significantly to women's perception that the sexual serving of men
is a necessary part of any woman's life: or how else could she live? Feminists appear to think that equal pay for equal work is a simple reform,
whereas it is no reform at all; it is revolution. Feminists have refused to face
the fact that equal pay for equal work is impossible as long as men rule
women, and right-wing women have refused to forget it. Devaluation of
women's labor outside the home pushes women back into the home and
encourages women to support a system in which, as she sees it, he is
paid for both of them—her share of his wage being more than she could
earn herself.

In the workplace, sexual harassment fixes the low status of women irre-
versibly. Women are sex; even filing or typing, women are sex. The debilitating, insidious violence of sexual harassment is pervasive in the workplace. It is part of nearly every working environment. Women shuffle;
women placate; women submit; women leave; the rare, brave women fight
and are tied up in the courts, often without jobs, for years. There is also
rape in the workplace.

Where is the place for intelligence—for literacy, intellect, creativity,
moral discernment? Where in this world in which women live, circumscribed by the uses to which men put women's sexual organs, is the cultivation of skills, the cultivation of gifts, the cultivation of dreams, the cultivation of ambition? Of what use is human intelligence to a woman? . . .

. . .Right-wing women have surveyed the world: they find it a dangerous
place. They see that work subjects them to more danger from more men; it
increases the risk of sexual exploitation. They see that creativity and originality in their kind are ridiculed; they see women thrown out of the circle
of male civilization for having ideas, plans, visions, ambitions. They see
that traditional marriage means selling to one man, not hundreds: the better deal. They see that the streets are cold, and that the women on them are
tired, sick, and bruised. They see that the money they can earn will not
make them independent of men and that they will still have to play the sex
games of their kind: at home and at work too. They see no way to make
their bodies authentically their own and to survive in the world of men.
They know too that the Left has nothing better to offer: leftist men also
want wives and whores; leftist men value whores too much and wives too
little. Right-wing women are not wrong. They fear that the Left, in stressing impersonal sex and promiscuity as values, will make them more vulnerable to male sexual aggression, and that they will be despised for not

liking it. They are not wrong. Right-wing women see that within the system in which they live they cannot make their bodies their own, but they can agree to privatized male ownership: keep it one-on-one, as it were. They know that they are valued for their sex— their sex organs and their reproductive capacity—and so they try to up their value: through cooperation, manipulation, conformity; through displays of affection or attempts at friendship; through submission and obedience; and especially through the use of euphemism—"femininity," "total woman," "good," "maternal instinct," "motherly love." Their desperation is quiet; they hide their bruises of body and heart; they dress carefully and have good manners; they suffer, they love God, they follow the rules. They see that intelligence displayed in a woman is a flaw, that intelligence realized in a woman is a crime. They see the world they live in and they are not wrong. They use sex and babies to stay valuable because they need a home, food, clothing. They use the traditional intelligence of the female—animal, not human: they do what they have to to survive.

PART THREE

THE QUEST FOR UNIVERSAL MORAL STANDARDS IN OTHER TRADITIONS

HINDU *DHARMA*

■

On the twelfth day following young Roop Kanwar's *sati*, hundreds of thousands of Hindus gathered at the site where she died. They shattered the air with steady chants of *"Mahasati mata ki jai"* ("Victory to Great Mother Sati!"). They watched as the red and yellow ceremonial cloth, the *chunari*, a symbol of the woman who performed *sati*, was offered to the flames just as Roop Kanwar offered herself to the flames on the funeral pyre of her dead husband. Her own family and in-laws actively participated in this *chunari* celebration to honor her memory and remains. Hindu scholar John Stratton Hawley recounts the day of Roop Kanwar's *sati*.

> On September 4 of that year, in the village of Deorala, some 50 miles north of Jaipur, in the Shekhavati region of Rajasthan, a young woman by the name of Roop Kanwar became a sati. Roop, a pretty Rajput girl of eighteen, had eight months earlier married a twenty-four-year-old Rajput man by the name of Mal Singh. The day after Mal Singh's untimely death from acute gastroenteritis or a burst appendix, she mounted his funeral pyre with him; there her body was consumed in the flames along with his. . . .
>
> According to early accounts, Roop Kanwar willed her own death and carried it out with dignity and resolve. In commenting on this fact, sympathetic observers often say that Roop had prepared herself for such an event before she had any inkling that it might

become a part of her own life. She is said to have visited the great
sati temple in far-off Ranchi, Madhya Pradesh, where she spent
much of her childhood because her father Bal Singh Rathore, a busi-
nessman, was employed there.

On the day of her own sati, all this preparation came to fruition.
In the traditional fashion, it is said, she took her husband's head in
her hands as she seated herself on the pyre and submitted calmly to
the flames. Icons issued to commemorate the event — primarily
tableaus composed from photographs taken independently of Roop
Kanwar and Mal Singh while both were alive and healthy — recall
it in just this way. For those who buy them, these serve not only as
mementos but as potentially forceful amulets that carry forward
the inner significance of the event.[1]

What is particularly remarkable about this incident is that it occurred
recently in 1987, nearly 160 years after the practice of *sati* was officially
banned. Even though *sati* never swept throughout India, British colonizers
viewed it as dangerous enough to outlaw it in 1829. And even after India
gained its own independence, the Indian government still considered it illegal. All the same, there have been isolated instances, and Roop Kanwar's
became one of the most well known. To this day, she has numerous followers who regularly journey to Deorala to pray at her death site.

It is abundantly clear that there are conflicting accounts regarding
Roop Kanwar's death. Many critics claim that the young widow was forced
to commit the act. Nevertheless, sympathizers and defenders of the practice of *sati* as well as those who believe that Roop Kanwar genuinely
willed her own death flocked by the hundreds of thousands to celebrate
her *chunari.*

What is the meaning behind *sati? Sati* refers to the traditional Hindu
custom in which a Hindu widow is burned and cremated along with her deceased husband on his funeral pyre. The term *sati* literally means "good
woman" and signifies that her inmost essence and truth reveals itself
through her extreme act of sacrifice. Through this act, she herself becomes
a *sati.* According to believers, if her motives are pure and if she acts out of
true devotion to her husband, then her own inner divine "light" will light
the pyre without outside help. When she bursts forth in flames, her divinity is manifest and she joins the ranks of all other *satis* who preceded her.
The woman who commits *sati* therefore becomes divinized through her
deed and crosses that plane from the human to the divine. And her divine

power now acts to protect her husband during his soul's transmigration as well as all others who believe in her power, including those who witness her offering and assemble to commemorate her *sati*. Because she will protect those who honor her, numerous followers will venerate her act at celebrations such as *chunari*. In Hindu tradition, all this illustrates the protective power that the wife and the mother hold in Hindu culture.

Roop Kanwar's *sati* caused a fiery reaction in contemporary India. Thousands of critics protested the event, many of them claiming that her suicide was not voluntary and that she was coerced into committing the act. They claim that she was drugged and then forced to undergo the immolation by her in-laws who may have perceived her as a financial burden to their family upon her husband's death. Bear in mind that women were generally married young and usually to older men. Therefore it was not uncommon for husbands to die prior to their wives. Upon the death of her husband, a wife traditionally had the choice to remain a widow, a *vidhava*, or else become a *sati*. Most wives chose to remain widows. And in an intensely patriarchal society, this meant practicing all sorts of austerities, being prohibited from remarrying, and relying upon the security and guardianship of her in-laws. As a widow, she becomes in a sense a female ascetic, a *tapasvini*, who seeks through her austerities to purify her soul so that she can be reunited at some future point with her husband after her own death.

However, her *sati* has more than its share of defenders. Very few wives took the route of *sati*. This is considered an immediate passage to purification, and a genuine *sati* would be immediately reunited with her husband. One outspoken group that defends her *sati* calls itself Dharma Raksha Samiti, the "Committee for the Defense of Religion." Note that through the name assumed by this group, the group translates *dharma* as meaning "religion." Yet *dharma* actually means something more distinct. *Dharma* is a critical term in Hindu thought signifying "morality." Though it can mean a number of things, as we shall soon see, it essentially refers to the "right way to act" or "doing the right thing," behaving and living in a morally appropriate way. As far as the Dharma Raksha Samiti is concerned, the idea clearly comes across—the act of *sati* is morally justified.

Is this true? Is the act of *sati* morally acceptable? Without getting bogged down in whether or not her act was voluntary, consider this. *If* her act was voluntary, does her *sati* manifest *dharma*? Dharma is the key ethical precept in Hindu philosophy. What more can we say about it? And would dharma be a suitable universal moral standard?

■ WHAT IS DHARMA?

PRELIMINARIES

Before we examine the meaning of *dharma,* let us consider some initial comments. To begin with, Hindu ethics is intimately integrated with the wider body of Hindu teachings regarding philosophy, religion, and society. There is an innate, organic relationship among all of these elements in Hindu culture. Hindu culture harbors a naturally holistic bond between morality and religious, philosophical, and cultural beliefs. Hindu culture especially embodies the intrinsic relationship between metaphysics (world-views), ontology (views of identity), and ethics. This means that we cannot understand ethics in isolation from these other forces. This also requires that we avoid compartmentalizing the field of ethics.

To repeat, Hindu ethics is especially shaped by its intricate metaphysics. Yet its metaphysics is not a unified creed. This brings us to our second critical observation, namely, Hinduism's extremely complex character. For example, there are numerous strands in metaphysics among the various Hindu philosophical schools, the most important being the Vedanta and the Samkhya, and these strands appear to be inconsistent with each other. Furthermore, Hindu thought has undergone and still manages to experience all sorts of modifications, radical changes, assimilation, and reinterpretations so that we need to avoid categorizing Hindu thought, particularly Hindu ethics, in simplistic terms.

Despite Hindu teachings' diversity and complexity, there is one belief that is common to almost all Hindu schools. All Hindus not only believe in a world order, but they also hold that this order is a moral order. That is, a moral law directs the natural outcome of the world. What is morally good ultimately prevails over all else. Justice, truth, and righteousness will always win out in the face of immorality and apparent chaos. This is evident on India's national emblem, which bears the phrase *Satyameva Jayate,* "Truth Alone Triumphs." Morality, *dharma,* rules supreme over immorality, *adharma.* The authority of *dharma* means that justice prevails so that all evil deeds, thoughts, and desires are inevitably punished, whereas all good deeds, thoughts, and desires are eventually rewarded.

The earliest texts, called the Rig Veda (1500–900 BCE), part of a larger collection called Vedas, gave birth to this notion of a moral order in the world in the principle of *rita. Rita* refers to the moral order that is immanent within the universe. The Rig Veda also asserts that this moral order would be maintained by the proper performance of Vedic rituals. This idea of a moral order played a dominant role in the eventual development of the theory of karma, the law of moral cause and effect, and a theory that emerged from the later writings known as the Upanishads (800–300 BCE). We will examine karma more closely later on. Concerning this relationship of moral order, *rita*, to karma, the Hindu scholar Saral Jhingran states that

> the moral quality of our deeds, thoughts and desires not only condi-
> tions our future character, but also manipulates the natural world
> order, so that we are thrown into external circumstances that are
> most suited to materialize or effect the kind of rewards and punish-
> ments which our moral character deserves.[2]

In view of these preliminary comments, we can assert that Hindu ethics is summed up in the concept of *dharma*. *Dharma* is synonymous with morality. The root term that *dharma* comes from is *dhr*, and it means "to support" and "to nourish." *Dharma* has therefore come to mean morally commendable conduct that nourishes and supports our society and our existence. Let us now see how this meaning evolved in Hindu tradition.

DHARMA AS RITUAL DUTY

The primal meaning of *dharma* comes from the ancient texts, the Vedas. The Vedas defined moral conduct as the proper performance of Vedic rites and prayers. Over time, this concern with the strict performance of ritual became rather excessive so that it probably contributed to the later assigning of supreme importance to the highest class, the *brahmana*, a class that included priests who were in charge of such rituals.

Although the Upanishads provide no systematic account of *dharma*, they do give us some hints. For one, they exhort us to study the Vedas and to conform to proper ritual. But they also add another feature. They advocate the practice of virtues, and they advise us to practice virtue by following the good examples of those who behave virtuously.

DHARMA AS CLASS DUTIES: VARNASRAMA DHARMA

The *Bhagavad Gita* is, without any doubt, the most influential work in Hindu thought. As a key chapter in the time-honored Hindu epic, the *Mahabharata*, it was composed around the fifth century BCE. It echoes the Vedic sentiment of carrying out one's duties. However, it goes beyond ritualistic performance. *Dharma* now means carrying out duties within one's social role and class. Social class is referred to as caste. This view of moral conduct is termed *varnasrama dharma*. Furthermore, the text urges that we carry out these caste duties without being attached to the results of our conduct. This is indeed one of the most important teachings in this epic.

The *Gita's* centerpiece is a conversation between the warrior Arjuna and his charioteer Krishna, who also happens to be a god in disguise. Krishna tries to persuade Arjuna to do his duty as a warrior, a *kshatriya*, and to engage in battle in order to defend against injustice. Carrying out this caste duty constitutes *dharma*. Instead, Arjuna is haunted by the likely consequences of carrying out his duty—namely, numerous deaths and the virtual destruction of both Kaurava and Pandava clans. Krishna warns him against being preoccupied with the results of his action. Instead, Arjuna should act solely for the sake of duty. In this way, the *Gita* introduces the notion of *dharma* as duty within one's class and social status. (See the selection at the end of this chapter.)

These social duties extend to how we interact with family, friends, teachers, and others and are delineated in what Hindus refer to as life's stages, or *ashramas*. The first is the student stage, which involves intense and disciplined learning and spiritual training. The next stage is that of the householder, who is committed to caring and providing for all family members. The third stage is metaphorically called the "forest dweller," one who, upon fulfilling family duties, returns to matters of spiritual self-cultivation. The final phase is the hermit. Ideally, this involves the radical detachment from material concerns in order to achieve spiritual awakening. All these stages involve duties that constitute right conduct. By means of this, *dharma* clearly supports social order, cohesion, and harmony. Thus we see the impetus behind *dharma:* its social sustenance.

The classic Dharmasastras (Studies of *Dharma*) were a collection of works written between 700 and 100 BCE. They had a decisive impact upon the Hindu legal system and offer an explicit description of *dharma*. They reiterate the theme of *dharma* as the correct performance of Vedic rites, prayers, and sacrifices. Furthermore, because a major portion of the Dharmasastras were influenced by Mimamsa, one of the six major Hindu philosophical schools, other aspects of *dharma* become prominent.

First, with all this emphasis on the proper performance of rituals, ritualistic conduct now becomes viewed as an end in itself. That is, they are to be carried out purely out of a sense of duty, which means that *dharma* acquires the characteristic of duty, pure and simple. In other words, *dharma* has little to do with performing a ritual out of a desire for its benefits. Instead, *dharma* means performing rites solely out of a sense of duty without attachment to the results of one's conduct. Here we see similarities with the teachings in the *Bhagavad Gita*. (We see an affinity with the Kantian emphasis upon duty, which we discussed in Chapter 4.)

Second, recall the root of *dharma*, meaning "nourish" and "support." The Mimamsa school gives special metaphysical weight to the notion of *dharma*. In other words, acting according to *dharma* sustains social and personal existence. Living morally is thus living authentically. Furthermore, living morally, acting according to *dharma*, sustains and nourishes the universe. By bestowing this metaphysical meaning to *dharma*, moral conduct therefore becomes a fundamental force in our existence.

The Dharmasastras end up defining *dharma* in various ways:

- Following proper ritual, prayer, and sacrifice as stipulated by the Vedas
- Performing proper social duties
- Following others' good example
- Acting according to individual conscience in the true spirit of Hindu teachings

These applications were especially critical regarding specific duties within one's caste. We will more closely examine the caste system later on.

SEEING THE ONE SELF IN THE OTHER

The *Bhagavad Gita* and the Dharmasastras present us with one of the perennial tensions in Hindu ethics: the ever-present tension between *dharma* as pure duty and *dharma* as a desire for good results. However, in either case, the focal point in *dharma* is not the act itself but the attitude with which the act is conducted. This attitude and interior disposition conveys the real value of *dharma*. The classic epic *Mahabharata*, which was composed between 800 and 500 BCE, gives us perhaps the most profound definition of *dharma* and provides a clue to this inner attitude and disposition.

> *What is harmful to oneself, one should not do to others. This is the quintessence of* dharma. *Behavior which is contrary to this is born of selfish desires.*[3]

Here is a version of the Golden Rule. *Dharma* occurs when we act in such a way that we view all others in the same way we view ourselves. Here is where we see a symbiotic relationship between Hindu metaphysics and Hindu morality. This idea of treating the other as if the other is myself fits in perfectly with Hindu metaphysics and ontology. Each one of us is in essence genuine self, or *atman*. At the same time, this *atman* is in essence the universal Self that lives in all beings, known as *Brahman*. In essence, therefore, *atman* is identical to *Brahman*. In essence we are all one since we share in this universal Self. We are thus urged to see this same Self in all beings just as we discover the self, *atman,* in us. Hindu metaphysics centers on this belief in the one Self in all beings.

DHARMA AS UNIVERSAL DUTIES: SADHARANA DHARMA

It is evident that *dharma* is the most pivotal feature in Hindu morality. The moral ideal of *dharma* refers to duties and virtues with respect to one's class. And the connection between *dharma* and karma demonstrates that *dharma* is exceedingly influential in that how a person acts according to *dharma* affects not only his character but his destiny. This makes perfect sense in a scheme whereby there is an intrinsic moral order, or *rita,* to the universe. We now ask: Are there any Hindu duties and virtues that are universal, applicable to all regardless of class?

Even though the emphasis has generally been on caste and social duties, *dharma* not only pertains to these specific social duties, but also pertains to duties that all persons must perform, regardless of class, social status, and stage in life. These universal duties are known as *sadharana dharma.*

To be sure, the great Hindu texts and traditions do stipulate duties and virtues that hold true for all persons, regardless of caste. The Upanishads do not refer to *dharma* in terms of class distinctions and duties. Its moral teachings are universal, for all persons and for all times.[4] For instance, the *Chandogya Upanishad* stresses the importance of charity, integrity and nonviolence (*ahimsa*). The *Brihadaranyaka Upanishad* points to the need for self-control, compassion, and charity. Even the Dharmasastras, texts that focus especially upon caste duties, manage to uphold certain universal duties and virtues such as truthfulness, self-discipline, and *ahimsa.* According to Jhingran, these universal duties and virtues act to complement the sociospecific caste duties. "They [universal duties] are concerned with the inner spirit of man, while caste duties are concerned with the external acts."[5] She also adds Gautama's "eight excellences of the soul" in his *Nyaya Sutras* (c. 200 BCE) to the list of universal virtues that are more interior and soul-directed.

The great epics, the *Mahabharata* and the *Ramayana,* no doubt advocate caste roles and duties. At the same time, they render magnificent stories of heroes and heroines who depict the ideal person, and the ideal person practices universal virtues that all humans need to emulate. And the *Bhagavad Gita* points out that because the "divine nature," *atman*, dwells in each one of us, we are compelled to exercise the following universal virtues:

> *Fearlessness, purity of heart, steadfastness in knowledge and yoga, magnanimity, self-restraint, study of scriptures, austerity, uprightness, non-violence, truth, absence of anger, renunciation, serenity, absence of enmity, compassion for creatures, non-covetousness, gentleness, modesty, absence of fickleness, energy, forgiveness, fortitude, purity, absence of hatred, absence of pride, these belong to one born of divine nature.*[6]

All in all, if we can summarize the most fundamental and outstanding universal virtues, they are truth, charity, self-restraint, nonviolence, and compassion.[7] Now let us more closely examine the meaning behind *dharma* by considering it within the context of what Hindus believe to be the four major goals in life.

■ DHARMA AND LIFE'S GOALS

Hindu teachings reveal that our action and lifestyle must be oriented toward four fundamental goals. These four goals in life are known collectively as *purusarthas*. The Dharmasastras go into great detail explaining these four goals. The goals are oriented toward the fourth goal and highest aim—self-realization. The ultimate purpose in our lives is to experience self-realization. This aim is intensely spiritual. All of life is therefore a pilgrimage to both *know* what my true self is and to *experience* that true self. My true self is *atman*, or soul. It is eternal, perfect, and unchanging. Realizing this is, however, extremely difficult because we usually mistake our self as being something else. Thus, self-realization, awakening to the truth of *atman*, will only occur after numerous lifetimes through continuous rebirths. Our rebirths will occur on various levels—insect, animal, and human. Until we realize and experience who we are, we remain fastened to the wheel of birth, death, and rebirth, over and over. This ongoing cycle of birth, death, and rebirth is known as *samsara*. While we remain chained to *samsara* in human form, we need to seek four major goals. *Dharma* is one of these four goals. Yet its meaning can be more properly understood by examining the other three: material comfort, pleasure, and self-realization.

PROSPERITY: *ARTHA*

One major goal is to acquire some level of *artha,* or material comfort. *Artha* also refers to security and prosperity. This kind of security is a prerequisite for personal growth and a precondition for the spiritual aim of self-realization. Basic physical and material needs have to be addressed before we can attempt to attain spiritual fulfillment. Even today, in many Hindu homes one comes across the figure of Laksmi, the goddess of good fortune and prosperity. And a popular Hindu prayer declares, "O, Thou, endowed with lordly powers, give me beauty, fame, good luck; grant me sons and riches, and confer on me all desired objects."[8]

There are two qualifiers here. First, *artha* is not an intrinsic good. Recall the distinction we made earlier in our discussion of Aristotle between an intrinsic good and an instrumental good. An intrinsic good is a good in and of itself, a good for no other reason than its own attainment. In contrast, an instrumental good is a good that is sought in order to achieve another good. In Aristotelian terms, *artha* is an instrumental good. It is a good in order to achieve the highest good of spiritual enlightenment, self-realization (*moksha*). Fulfilling our most basic material needs is necessary and instrumental in order to finally achieve this spiritual awakening. If we treat *artha* as an intrinsic goal and thereby view it as an end in itself, we then become obsessed with achieving material and physical comfort at any cost, and we sway off *dharma's* course.

The second qualifier follows from the first, and it gives us a clearer picture of what *dharma* is all about. If we mistakenly view *artha* as an intrinsic good, then we tend to disregard whatever means we use to achieve material and physical comfort. But this pulls us away from the true spirit of *artha. Artha* is only a legitimate goal if we employ proper means to achieve it. This goes back to what we discussed earlier in our chapter on utilitarianism, our perpetual question about the relationship between means and end, or Does the end justify the means? *Dharma* works as a critical standard in that it qualifies the attainment of *artha. Artha* is only a genuine good if we employ *dharma* in achieving it. This means that we need to exercise right conduct and right attitude.

Here is the key. Any means that hinge solely upon *self-interest* and *self-gain* are improper means to achieving *artha.* This therefore rules out means that rely on deceit and manipulation or that center on greed. Only through good conduct and sincere attitude can *artha* make moral sense. The means to achieve material and physical comfort are only justified if they are conducted within the spirit of *dharma.* In this fashion, we arrive at a more specific view of *dharma* as *conduct that avoids self-centeredness.*

PLEASURE: *KAMA*

Kama is closely related to *artha* in that it refers to physical pleasure and enjoyment. Vatsyayana (c. first century) defines *kama* in his classic work, *Kamasutra:*

> Kama *is the enjoyment of the appropriate objects of the five senses of hearing, feeling, seeing, tasting, and smelling, assisted by the mind, together with the soul.*[9]

Although the *Kamasutra* describes *kama* in terms of sexual pleasures, *kama* does have a broader meaning as sensual pleasure and refers to all types of pleasures that derive from the physical senses. As a major goal, *kama* acknowledges our bodiliness. My true essence is *atman,* or soul, yet *atman* dwells in my body. We cannot escape our bodiliness. And the Hindu view of bodiliness is critical. Our bodies are viewed as temples since they house our soul, *atman.* Hindus therefore provide us with a rather positive view of bodiliness and what it means to inhabit a body. Pleasure that is bodily is construed as good, as a fundamental goal in life. However, as in the case of *artha,* there are certain qualifiers.

Again, as with *artha, kama* is an instrumental good, not an intrinsic one. Sensual pleasure is not the highest goal nor should it be sought as an end in itself. Sensual pleasure is a basic need, the fulfillment of which could lead to life's highest goal, spiritual enlightenment, called *moksha.* If we view *kama* as an end in itself, we become attached to our bodiliness. We become enslaved to our physical desires and can never be truly free to experience spiritual enlightenment.

Dharma again acts as a counterweight in that it is the regulating principle of genuine, morally justifiable *kama.* As with *artha,* self-centeredness detracts from the moral legitimacy of *kama.* Consider the metaphor of the chariot. The chariot figures prominently in Hindu literature. The most classic example is Arjuna in the opening scene of the *Bhagavad Gita.* The entire book is a conversation between Arjuna and his charioteer and god in disguise, Krishna.[10] Another timeless example of the use of the chariot is in Plato's dialogue *Phaedrus.* Here, Plato points out that the charioteer needs to be in control of the chariot. For Plato, the charioteer represents reason, the "soul's pilot," in managing to restrain the powerful pull of the horses.

In like manner, the charioteer also represents *dharma* as a regulatory principle. The horses pulling the chariot represent the passions. Thus we see the forceful and compelling pull of bodiliness. We realize that we need bodiliness just as we need passion. Without passion, we go nowhere. Without the horses, the chariot is meaningless. Bodily desire is natural, and physical pleasure is a legitimate goal so long as it is channeled through *dharma*. As Krishna advises Arjuna in the *Bhagavad Gita*, "I am pleasure (*kama*) that is not opposed to goodness (*dharma*.)"[11] Physical pleasure, *kama*, is a legitimate goal as an avenue toward the highest goal, spiritual awakening.

SELF-REALIZATION: *MOKSHA*

The most important goal in all of Hindu thought and culture is to *realize who we truly are.* Each one of us is in essence *atman,* or soul, and as *atman* we are eternal and pure. However, we do not ordinarily know this, and we mistake who we are for other things. For instance, we may identify who we are with what we *own,* or with our *bodies,* or with what we *know.* Our basic condition is such that we are under the cloud of *maya,* illusion, and because of this illusion we generally remain truly ignorant of who we are. Our state of ignorance is called *avidya.*

There is another ingredient to all of this, one that is unquestionably radical and sets Hinduism apart from just about every other major tradition. Not only is my genuine nature *atman,* but, as we learn from the Upanishads, *atman* is also identical in essence to the universal soul, *Brahman. Brahman* refers to the principle of all being. In a sense, we can think of *Brahman* as equivalent to God, the ground of all existence.

Herein we find the most extreme and immoderate of all teachings regarding who we are. In essence, each one of us is *atman,* eternal and pure. At the same time, since *atman* is identical in essence to *Brahman,* each one of us is therefore identical in essence to *Brahman,* to God! The Upanishads sum this up in the famous phrase "*tat tvam asi,*" or "That thou art." *Tat* (That) refers to *Brahman; tvam* (Thou) denotes *atman;* and *asi* (are) points to a relationship of identity, not an identity of attributes or characteristics, but an identity *of essence.*

Yet here is our predicament. As long as we do not realize our true nature, we remain stuck on this wheel of birth, death, and rebirth. We are constantly reborn as our souls journey into various psychophysical forms, depending upon our accumulation of positive and negative karma. (We will examine karma more closely in the next section.) When we are reborn into human form, we are given another opportunity to discover and experience our true self, *atman.* However, for most of us, we are hopelessly chained to an almost endless cycle of birth, death, and rebirth.

When we finally discover and experience who we truly are, we experience *moksha*. Given what we have described above regarding our essence, *atman,* and its essential identity with *Brahman,* the experience of *moksha* thereby occurs when I experience my true self as *atman* and, at the same time, experience my primordial, essential oneness with the universal soul, *Brahman. Moksha* is the supreme goal in all of Hindu thought. It is that to which all human lives are oriented. The term itself means "freedom," "release," and "liberation." Once we experience *moksha,* we are free from the samsaric cycle, liberated from the endless wheel of birth, death, and rebirth. *Moksha* is thereby a genuine spiritual awakening that frees us from any further bondage to this cycle, in which case our death will be our last with no further rebirth.

What does all of this mean regarding *dharma?* Situated within these other goals in life—prosperity, pleasure, and self-realization—*dharma* refers all the more to right and proper conduct, and this means conduct that is driven with the aim of spiritual realization and self-awakening. In the context of life's goals, the highest being *moksha, dharma* is driven by *moksha,* just as *moksha* is the driving force behind all of Hindu culture and beliefs. What do we have here? We have in *dharma* a universal moral principle and standard that is understood within the context of spiritual self-realization or self-discovery. *Dharma* is the operative moral principle that underscores and sustains the ultimate aim of self-realization.

In view of this, what can we assert regarding Roop Kanwar's *sati?* If her *sati* was voluntary, was it a valid and justified expression of *dharma?* As we have described, the underlying purpose in *sati* seems to be spiritual, in that a pure heart acting out of devotion would release the inner truth, *sat,* of the widow. It could be claimed, though this is arguable, that this effort to release the inner truth is an avenue toward *moksha,* self-discovery. Of course, there are numerous critics who claim that she did not at all act voluntarily. Yet, are these critics presuming that if she did act voluntarily, her *sati* is right conduct, *dharma?* There is certainly no consensus that acts of *sati* are in themselves expressions of morally right conduct. Let us now consider a classic example from Hindu literature where there is overwhelming agreement that the principal characters embody *dharma* in its purest form.

DHARMA IN THE *RAMAYANA*

The most beloved Hindu epic tale is the *Ramayana.* Its main characters are Rama and Sita, husband and wife. Rama won the hand of Sita in marriage after bending the powerful and miraculous bow owned by her father, King Janak.

Rama's father, King Dasa-ratha, getting on in years, intends to hand his kingdom over to Rama, his favorite son. Just before he is about to bestow his kingdom to Rama, one of the king's wives, Kaikeyi, reminds him of an earlier promise he had made to her that he would grant her two wishes. King Dasa-ratha, being an honorable man, agrees to grant her wishes. He is soon terrified. Her first wish is for her own son, Bharata, to be appointed king instead of Rama. Her second wish is even worse for Rama. She asks that Rama be exiled to the dark Dandaka forest for fourteen years, and that he "live the life of an ascetic, wearing hides and barkcloth garments and matted hair."[12] Despite the king's anguished pleas, Kaikeyi heartlessly stays her ground and will not change her mind. Because the king is a man of his word, he has no recourse but to grant her wishes. His grief is unbearable, and he faints. Just as he faints, his son Rama enters the scene. (See the selection from *Ramayana* at the end of this chapter.)

This scene reveals Rama, like his father, to be a person of integrity and good character. He puts integrity before his own self-interest. He is also fervently devoted to his father. His devotion to his father entails respecting his father's earlier promise to Kaikeyi. He shows his duty and devotion to his father by honoring Kaikeyi's wishes, even if it exacts the heavy price of exile and hardship. Duty comes first before self-interest. And when Rama dutifully agrees to go into exile and to become an ascetic, he visits his mother one last time and tells her, "My lady, it is not in the hopes of gain that I suffer living in this world." Rama reminds her, "You should know that, like the seers, I have but one concern and that is righteousness." Rama's righteousness, his *dharma*, manifests itself through his duty and devotion to his father.

How this story unfolds is well known to Hindus. Rama goes into exile, and his wife Sita and brother Laksham accompany him. Sita is then kidnapped by Ravan, a demon-king. Actually, the major portion of the *Ramayana* describes efforts to rescue Sita. And only with the aid of the monkey-king, Hanuman, does Rama finally save Sita. After exile, Rama becomes king, and Sita, as queen, must now undergo all kinds of trials in order to prove her virtue and loyalty. Part of her ordeal requires that she retreat back into the forest. In the forest, she gives birth to their two sons, and they are all eventually reunited as a family.

In the final scene, Sita is the central character and the Earth Mother celebrates Sita's virtue, integrity, and loyalty. Sita is then transported to the land of the gods. Indeed, in this Hindu classic, not only Rama, but others embody *dharma* such as his honorable father King Dasa–ratha, his faithful brother Laksham, the steadfast and loyal Hanuman, and most especially, his devoted and virtuous wife Sita.

■ DHARMA, DUTY, AND CASTE

As we said above, a key component in *dharma* lies in performing one's social duties with respect to one's role in society. In India, this means carrying out one's duties in one's class or caste. There is a critical link between right behavior and caste duties and virtues. This compels us to examine the caste system more closely in order to understand the role of *dharma*. The caste system in India continues to be the subject of inveterate criticism. The development of the caste system in India is no doubt complex. The caste system primarily came about as an attempt to bring about social order and cohesion. It manifests an explicit class structure on the basis of specific roles and duties within each caste.

The Hindu social system traditionally consists of four main classes, or castes. We see this division into classes in the classic Hindu poem in the Rig Veda called *Purusasukta*, or Hymn of the Primeval Man.[13] The poem counsels the division of society into four estates. Hindu scholar A. L. Basham claims that this suggestion, although it predates the actual establishment of the caste system, lays the seeds for the caste system as a hierarchy.[14] The four castes are *brahmanas, kshatriyas, vaishyas*, and *shudras*.

The *brahmanas* occupy the highest class in this social hierarchy. They are the spiritual guides and leaders in society. They are the educators, and they teach the principles of the Vedas and all other sacred texts. The *kshatriyas* are the warriors, the guardians of society. They occupy the second highest rung on this social ladder. They enforce the laws and see to it that justice is meted out. They seek to redress injustice, and many of them enter into various positions as legislators and administrators. In the time-honored *Bhagavad Gita*, Arjuna is a *kshatriya*. When he undergoes pangs of conscience about having to fight a battle that will result in countless deaths, Krishna, his charioteer, attempts to persuade Arjuna that he must do his duty as a warrior and rectify the injustice that had occurred when the kingdom was unjustly taken from the warrior's Pandava family. Since *dharma* consists in properly carrying out one's social duties, Arjuna would therefore be abdicating his duty as a *kshatriya* by not leading his soldiers into battle against the Kauravas. The third caste is the *vaishya* class. The *vaishyas* are the merchants, farmers, traders, and those involved with other types of business occupations. The *vaishyas* maintain the economic fabric of the community, and they are responsible for seeing to it that all castes have a basic level of material comfort and prosperity. The fourth class is the *shudra*. The *shudras* are the laborers as well as servants. The laborers do their share of physical work and menial labor.

We need to keep in mind that when the caste system originated in India, the intent was not to repress certain classes such as the *shudras* and to view them as inferior, even though the later Dharmasastras point to a strict distinction between the first three classes, referring to them as the "twice-born upper" classes, and the *shudras* as the "lower class." The castes were originally conceived as interacting with each other in an organic relationship, and not one of power and domination. The idea, at least in principle, was that as long as members of each caste performed their duties diligently, each class contributed to the smooth operation of society. This was viewed as a way to fashion social harmony. Within the context of the caste system, *dharma* means to faithfully carry out one's specific duties in one's caste. Following these caste rules is imperative and represents sound moral action.

These four castes constituted official Hindu society. However, there came about a fifth class that was considered to be outside the margins of official society. This fifth caste was called *panchama* ("fifth"). The *panchamas* were later referred to as "outcastes," being outside the formal Hindu social structure. These "outcastes" performed the most menial tasks and those tasks often associated with pollution such as cleaning sewage and refuse. They were also called "untouchables" because it was forbidden for others to have any contact with them. Today, there continue to be millions of *panchamas* in India. They suffer all sorts of discrimination as a result of a long history of prejudice. Reformers such as Swami Dayananda and Mahatma Gandhi spoke out against the hereditary caste system and especially the discrimination against the untouchables. Today, there is a significant movement under way to empower them with more equal status within Hindu society.

The continued discrimination in India against *panchamas* illustrates how reality often conflicts with principles. The principle of *dharma* is an ideal to strive for. Yet in no way does it guarantee that this principle will be carried out in practice, particularly when religious beliefs are especially susceptible to abuse, as the case is with the Indian caste system. For example, when we review the development of the idea of "caste," we can see the potential for exploitation.

The Sanskrit term for caste is *varna*. However, *varna* literally means "color." At first, "color" referred to skin pigmentation. Yet "color" eventually acquired a different connotation due to the influence of the Samkhya school. According to this school, humans possess three primary temperaments or dispositions called *gunas*. These temperaments are purity (*sattva*), virility and action (*rajas*), and dullness (*tamas*). The Samkhya school pointed out that these three temperaments were represented by certain colors. White represents purity; red is the color of virility; and black symbolizes dullness. Samkhya also taught that each one of us as individuals possesses these three temperaments in varying degrees. In addition, different groups also tended to exhibit these traits in various ways. Keep in mind that in India's early history, all sorts of different races and groups occupied its vast territory. India therefore assimilated various racial groupings such as the indigenous Dravidians, the conquering Aryans, Persians, Greeks, and Huns. All of this most certainly produced an increasing class consciousness accompanied by a growing awareness of distinct, though subtle differences in skin color, and, of all the groups, the conquering Aryans appeared to be the lightest in pigmentation.

Over time, Samkhya teachings stressed that each caste manifested distinct traits. The highest caste, the *brahmanas*, exhibited more purity, whereas the *kshatriyas* possessed more virility and activity. The *vaishyas* demonstrated more dullness. In contrast, the lowest caste, the *shudras*, possessed little of any of these traits so that their *gunas* were less developed.[15]

The notion of *varna* eventually referred to the general character traits of specific castes. What this means is that caste membership was at first determined by character, by the weight of temperament, or *gunas*. Later, class membership was determined by birth. In this light, the doctrine of karma worked as a powerfully effective tool for explaining why people were then born into certain classes. Let us turn now to the Hindu idea of karma and its relationship to Hindu ethics.

■ WHAT IS KARMA?

Karma plays a key role in Hindu ethics. It is a major factor in the Hindu moral system and plays a leading role in determining the next rebirth of the individual soul, or *atman*. *Atman*, the person's essence, transmigrates from one psychophysical entity to the next. The *Bhagavad Gita* compares this transmigration of the soul to a changing of clothes. *Karma* thus plays a leading role in both this life and the transition to the next because an individual's quality and accumulation of karma will decide that individual's next psychophysical form.

The term *karma* literally means "deed" or "act." Karma is the rule of cause and effect with respect to morality. In an earlier work, I call it the "principle of moral causality."[16] Just as the law of physical causality means that for every physical cause there will be an equal physical effect, moral causality works the same way. For my every thought and act that has moral significance, that is, having to do with *dharma*, I will experience a corresponding effect. This effect will unquestionably take place, if not in this life, then in some future life. Every thought and act I have with moral weight will bring about either a positive or a negative effect, that is, positive or negative karma.

My act or thought will actually produce a twofold effect. First, it generates either positive or negative karma. Second, it contributes toward cultivating my moral character. This is similar to Aristotle's idea that repeated actions produce a habit, and repeated habits eventually bring about a condition. Thus, habitual good thoughts and actions, *dharma*, engender a good character along with an abundance of positive karma. Repeated bad thoughts and actions, what is known as *adharma*, produce a bad character with plenty of negative karma.

What is especially striking about karma is that we, in essence, carve out our own fortunes and destinies. With respect to the caste system, this means that the caste we are born into is the result of our karma, and karma, of course, is formed by our *dharma*. In all this, we see that the doctrine of karma not only *explains* our next station in life along with the inequalities doled out among humans. Karma by its nature also *justifies* these circumstances. Karma plays both an explanatory and a justificatory role in Hindu ethics.

Hindus believe that our birth into a specific caste is brought about by our karma. We have to be careful, however, not to assign karma an overly fatalistic quality. In no way does the doctrine of karma mean that everything we experience is the direct result of past deeds and thoughts. Karma is not an uncompromising deterministic principle. There is still room for free will. Despite the heavy influence that karma exerts in our past, current, and future lives, Hindus are strong defenders of free will. In other words, although we face all sorts of circumstances in our lives, these circumstances being the products of our karma, we are still *free to choose how we will respond to these circumstances*. And how we respond produces further karma. Karma is, in effect, a product of our free choices and free will. *Dharma*, that which is morally right conduct, can only be morally sound because it consists of conduct that is freely willed and chosen. *Adharma*, immoral conduct, is immoral because it also consists of freely chosen acts and thoughts. Rather than suppress the notion of free will, karma instead underscores our own individual responsibility for our actions as well as for the consequences of our actions. This indeed represents the special quality of being human, for only humans can exercise *dharma*, morally right conduct. Only humans possess the reason and free will that allow us to act ethically or unethically. Therefore, only humans can generate karma. Nevertheless, we see that the commingling of karma with birth into specific castes stands in danger of spawning a more fatalistic vision of existence.

An unforgettable example of the force of karma is the story of the great warrior Karna. This is depicted in the immortal Hindu epic, the *Muhabharata*. Born into the *kshatriya* class, Karna desired to perfect the art of archery and to learn from the great teacher Parasurama. He did this by deceiving Parasurama. He tricked Parasurama into thinking that he was actually a *brahmana*. One day, while his teacher fell asleep on Karna's lap, an insect bit Karna, drawing blood. Yet Karna did not flinch. Soon Parasurama awoke and, seeing the blood oozing from Karna's leg, knew that only a warrior could bear the pain with such equanimity. He then said to Karna:

> You have deceived your teacher. When your hour comes, your knowledge of the astras [an arrow or weapon driven by a supernatural force] will fail you, and what you have learnt from me through deception will not be useful to you.[17]

In this way, Parasurama predicted that Karna's knowledge of the use of his secret and supernatural weapon in archery would finally be of no avail.

On another occasion, while practicing archery in foolish fashion, Karna accidentally shot and killed a brahmana's cow. Because this was the direct result of Karna's own imprudence, the brahmana told Karna:

> In battle your chariot wheel will get stuck in the mud, and you will be done to death even like this innocent cow which you have killed.[18]

Karna turned out to be one of the most fearless and skilled of all warriors. He was a leader of the Kauravas in the fierce eighteen-day battle with the Pandavas. The Pandavas, led by Arjuna, were fighting to regain their kingdom, which was unjustly seized by the Kauravas. Karna finally met his nemesis, Arjuna, in battle. They charged at each other in their chariots, and just as Arjuna was about to release an arrow, the wheel of Karna's chariot sank into the muddy field and would not budge. Nonetheless, Karna was still able to shoot an arrow at Arjuna and momentarily stunned him with its incredible force. Karna was now on the ground, trying in vain to raise the wheel out of the mud. When Arjuna charged at him once more, Karna then determined to kill Arjuna with his supernatural weapon, a Brahmasastra, a weapon that he could magically invoke by reciting a secret mantra, or special saying. Karna struggled for a moment . . . and gasped. He could not remember his mantra! The *Mahabharata* describes what followed:

> And he [Arjuna] drew his bow Gandiva, *aimed his dart with stifled*
>   *breath,*
> *Vengeance for his murdered hero winged the fatal dart of death,*
> *Like the fiery bolt of lightning Arjun's lurid arrow sped,*
> *Like a rock by thunder riven Karna fell among the dead!* [19]

This was no accident. Because of his earlier two serious offenses of deceit and unnecessary killing, Karna brought upon himself grave negative karma and ultimately suffered his fate at the hands of Arjuna.

■ DHARMA'S WEAKNESSES

IS HINDU ETHICS RELATIVIST?

Certain duties and virtues pertaining to *dharma* are relative to various situations. Therefore, what is it that determines what ought to be done in these situations? Does this mean that *dharma* is basically situational? Is *dharma* essentially relativist? Ancient texts seem to point to both the authority of custom, or customary practices, and the authority of community leaders. In other words, custom and leadership can legitimately determine *dharma*. Here, we see real problems.

First, let us address the standard of customs. How should customs be used as the standard of right conduct? The ancient texts point out the importance of customs that are long-standing and traditional. Is Hindu morality claiming that local custom prevails in the absence of strict scriptural, Vedic instruction? Of course, this flexibility makes sense so long as the prevailing customs do not contradict Vedic and other teachings. But why should we rely on tradition for tradition's sake? In our opening chapter, we saw that one of the most significant reasons for female genital excision is that it conforms to long-standing tradition. This may help to explain the practice, but it does little to justify it. The inherent flexibility of Hindu *dharma* appears to be an attempt—not a philosophically defensible one—to explain *and* justify, just as the law of karma both explains and justifies character and circumstances.

What does this appeal to custom and tradition suggest in the case of *sati*? Is the *sati* of Roop Kanwar justified on the basis of it being a customary practice, albeit a quite rare one, among the Rajputs? Although instances of *sati* are no doubt rare, there are still certain regions, such as the state of Rajasthan, where *sati* may occur more often than elsewhere. Would *sati* anywhere be justified on the basis of its customariness?

When we examine *sati* more closely and view, for instance, the *sati* of Roop Kanwar, we clearly see that this becomes more of an issue of male dominance. And male dominance continues to be customary in India. For example, if a wife chooses to remain a widow, then she becomes the responsibility of her in-laws. Not only must they provide economically for her, but they must ensure that she behave properly as a widow. Remarriage is not even an option. And she must remain pure and chaste while under their roof, otherwise shame and disgrace is wrought upon their entire household.[20]

To further illustrate, there is great importance attached to the bride's dowry. A woman not only marries the bridegroom, but also marries into the bridegroom's family. His family guarantee her support and material comfort for the rest of her life. The dowry is provided in recognition of this support. Thus, a paltry dowry is viewed as an insult to the in-laws. Moreover, there have been instances of what is known as "bride burning," the murder of the bride when the wife's husband and her in-laws are displeased with the wife's dowry. A 1995 statistic cited by the Indian National Crimes Record Bureau recorded an average of seventeen "dowry deaths" each day in India.[21] Although dowry deaths are illegal in India, there remain numerous legal problems surrounding legislation, enforcement, and punishment. Moreover, there is the predominant patriarchal view that wives, in comparison with husbands, are second-class citizens. In the face of this, many Hindu reformers like Ishwara Chandra Vidyasagar, Rao Phule, and M. G. Ranade continue their campaign against the unfair treatment of women as they struggle for the rights of widows to remarry.

A second proposed standard in this flexible application of *dharma* lies in the leadership and example of community leaders who are themselves of sound moral character. But how do we recognize whether they are morally upright? What standards do we as a community utilize in acknowledging the moral leadership of certain individuals?

WHAT ABOUT CONSCIENCE?

Caste duties appear to rule out personally derived duties. This is the case with the *Bhagavad Gita*. If our duties are determined by our class affiliation, and if such affiliation is more or less imposed upon the individual, as in the case with the hereditary caste system, where is there room for individual conscience?

Here is the classic tension between duty and conscience. How do we resolve this tension? Are there any clear solutions in Hindu ethics? Recall that the Dharmasastras point out that *dharma* includes acting according to individual conscience in the true spirit of Hindu teachings. The Dharmasastras also emphasize that *dharma* means performing one's class duties. Yet, the texts provide no clear way to resolve the tension between these two expressions of *dharma*. There are surely instances of individuals who, when faced with this conflict, ultimately followed their conscience. For example, Bhisma was a respected leader in the *Mahabharata*. However, he violated his social duty when he surrendered his formal title and took the vow of celibacy. Yet these are exceptions. How do we resolve this tension for ourselves? Hindu texts seem to provide little in the way of guidance here.

WHAT ABOUT EMOTIONS?

Dharma as duty for the sake of duty, as opposed to acting for desired results, is a key teaching in the *Bhagavad Gita*, perhaps its most important precept. Yet, this emphasis upon duty can be exaggerated. It can certainly downplay the role of emotions in making moral decisions. In the same vein, *dharma* in the context of *moksha* appears rather cold and abstract within the metaphysical context of Hinduism. For example, the first three goals in life may be inconsistent with the fourth and final goal of self-realization. The first three goals are definitely life-affirming, whereas the fourth may be construed as life-negating since *moksha* leads to release from the cycle of *samsara*.

DO CLASS DUTIES TRUMP UNIVERSAL DUTIES?

With respect to the two distinct types of duties and virtues—duties and virtues according to one's class, *varnasrama dharma*, and universal duties and virtues common to all, *sadharana dharma*,—the question is, Which set of duties takes precedent? Do universal duties trump caste duties, or vice versa? Here there seems to be no consensus, though the literature tends to prioritize class duties. Hindu ethics therefore seems to place over-riding weight on *dharma* as associated with its class-related duties. This tends to mask the more moral sense of duty. Granted, Hindu teachings do point out moral conduct that can be applied universally, regardless of caste and ritual. Yet there is very little in the way of systematic exposition of these universal virtues, duties, and applications. If we rely on textual evidence, the general impression seems to be that specific social duties have priority over universal duties.

Consider the example of Arjuna in the *Bhagavad Gita*. His specific duty as a *kshatriya* is to lead his men into battle, restore the rightful rule of the kingdom, and rectify the injustice that had prevailed. Yet, Hinduism also stresses the universal duty of nonviolence, or *ahimsa*. Should Arjuna abide by the universal principle of *ahimsa* or the duty assigned to him as a war-rior? Clearly, the *Gita* stresses the priority of this caste duty over the universal duty of *ahimsa*.[22] If caste duties take precedence over universal duties, does this not weaken the notion of "universal" duty and virtue? How can a duty truly be universal unless it applies to all persons in all circumstances regardless of social status and situation? This problem is compounded because the universal duties and virtues that are mentioned in Hindu texts are not put forth in any systematic or organized fashion.

■ DHARMA'S STRENGTHS

INTEGRATIVE QUALITY

One great benefit of the *dharma* tradition in Hinduism is its congruence with a philosophy of life and self. That is, Hindu morality epitomizes that necessary link that exists between metaphysics, ontology, and ethics. Ethics can only make sense when it is based upon some fundamental views concerning the nature of reality and the nature of self. This is certainly the case in Hindu ethics. And this quality sets Hindu morality apart from other traditions that compartmentalize ethics as a segregated discipline.

Hindu morality can only be understood in terms of its metaphysical edifice in which the drive to realize our genuine nature is all-important. (We will see similarities here with the Buddhist tradition as well. Keep in mind that Buddhism's roots lie in Hinduism and can only be properly understood in terms of Buddhists' reactions to some Hindu teachings. Nevertheless, the affinity between metaphysics and morality still exists in Buddhism.)

NONDOGMATIC

Another strength in Hinduism lies in its nondogmatic character through its flexibility in various situations. Hindu morality can never be claimed as being rigid. Indeed, it adapts to circumstances of both place and time. Hindu moral teachings consistently reproach any unconditional, absolute authority assigned to the scriptures. This caution against blind acceptance of the text is refreshing. Hindu morality is not at all dogmatic, not are its teachings viewed as absolutely infallible. There is a realistic recognition of practical and personal contingencies so that the spirit of Hindu moral teachings rather than the letter of the teachings assumes priority. For example, the ancient Vedas in some instances sanctioned extramarital intercourse, or *niyoga,* in the case of an impotent husband or a childless widow. This was outlawed later on to adjust to differences in time and circumstances.

It is this self-critical spirit within Hinduism that may well be its redemption. Hindu ethics is the antithesis of moral absolutism. Hindu philosophy and religion sustains within itself a self-critical drive that truly makes it truth-seeking in the fullest sense.

CAN *DHARMA* BE A UNIVERSAL STANDARD?

Can the Hindu teaching of *dharma* be an adequate universal moral standard? There is reason to hope for this. Hindu philosophy and religion continues to be one of the most flexible and tolerant major cultural traditions. Its teachings manage to be adaptable to varying circumstances. Its teachings are also dynamic in nature in that they successfully undergo constant change and reinterpretation. This tolerance and adaptability seem to favor Hindu *dharma* as a likely candidate for our universal moral standard.

As attractive as this is, however, there are drawbacks. In addition to the weaknesses cited above, there is one fundamental obstacle to posing Hindu *dharma* as a universally applicable ethical criterion. Here, Hindu morality's great strength also becomes its weakness. Its strength lies in its integral relationship with its metaphysics and religion. These areas cannot be segregated from each other.

Hindu ethics cannot be understood apart from its underlying metaphysical substrate of beliefs regarding *atman, Brahman, tat tvam asi, samsara, moksha, karma,* and others. *Dharma* constitutes morally sound behavior and character in view of these critical components. However, these components are unique to Indian culture. We may find some similar metaphysical views in other cultural traditions such as Buddhism. But in no way can we presume Hindu metaphysics itself to be universally valid. And to take *dharma* out of its religious, philosophical, and cultural context would be to violate its spirit. For thousands of years, Hindu morality has sustained billions of individuals, not billions of individual bodies but individual souls, all identical in essence to the universal soul. And Hindu ethics is undeniably a most profound tradition in view of the belief in the transmigration of souls. This deeply religious and metaphysical undercurrent in Hindu morality remains its great strength as well as its chief obstacle to universalization.

■ NOTES

1. John Stratton Hawley, "Hinduism: *Sati* and Its Defenders," in Hawley, ed., *Fundamentalism and Gender* (New York: Oxford University Press, 1994), pp. 81–82.

2. Saral Jhingran, *Aspects of Hindu Morality* (Delhi: Motilal Banarsidass, 1989), p. 34.

3. *Mahabharata*, cited in Charles A. Moore, ed., *The Indian Mind: Essentials of Indian Philosophy and Culture* (Honolulu: East-West Center Press, University of Hawaii Press, 1967), p. 156.

4. See the excellent discussion of this in Jhingran, pp. 173ff.

5. Ibid., p. 175.

6. *Bhagavad* Gita, XVI, 1–3, cited in ibid., p. 178.

7. Ibid., p. 189.

8. Yajnavalkya Smrti, Book I, v. 291, cited in Saral Jhingran, *Aspects of Hindu Morality* (Delhi: Motilal Banarsidass, 1989), p. 11.

9. *The Kama Sutra of Vatsyayana*, cited in John M. Koller, *Oriental Philosophies*, 2nd ed. (New York: Scribner's, 1985), p. 45, note 7.

10. The chariot is an important symbol in Buddhist literature as well. In the classic Buddhist text *Milindapanha*, the Buddhist sage converses with King Milinda and tries to demonstrate to the king the Buddhist notion that there is neither individual soul nor ego by using the metaphor of the chariot.

11. *Bhagavad Gita*, VII, 11, cited in Moore, p. 155.

12. Cited in Michael Brannigan, *Striking a Balance: A Primer on Traditional Asian Ethics* (New York: Seven Bridges Press, 2000), p. 30.

13. See Rig Veda 10.90.

14. See A. L. Basham, *The Origins and Development of Classical Hinduism* (Boston: Beacon Press, 1989), p. 25.

15. See Moore, pp. 162–63.

16. Michael C. Brannigan, *The Pulse of Wisdom: The Philosophies of India, China, and Japan,* 2nd ed. (Belmont, CA: Wadsworth, 2000), p. 252.

17. T. S. Rukmani, "Moral Dilemmas in the Mahabharata," in Bimal Krishna Matilal, ed., *Moral Dilemmas in the Mahabharata* (Delhi: Motilal Banarsidass, 1989), p. 25.

18. Ibid., p. 24.

19. *The Mahabharata,* Book X, in Romesh C. Dutt, *The Ramayana and the Mahabharata* (London: Everyman's Library, 1910), p. 297.

20. It is interesting to note that most cases of *sati* seem to be performed in areas such as Bengal where wives could inherit the property of their husbands. See Katherine K. Young, "Hinduism," in Arvind Sharma, ed., *Women in World Religions* (Albany: State University of New York Press, 1987), pp. 85–86.

21. Cited by Anshu Nangia, "The Tragedy of Bride Burning in India: How Should the Law Address It?" in Larry May, Nancy E. Snow, and Angela Bolte, *Legal Philosophy: Multiple Perspectives* (Mountain View, CA: Mayfield, 2000), p. 593.

22. It is especially interesting that the great reformer Mahatma Gandhi (1869–1948), or Mohandas Karamchand Gandhi, was a devotee of the *Bhagavad Gita,* yet he practiced the principle of absolute nonviolence. He was also heavily influenced by Tolstoi, the New Testament, Thoreau, and the pacifist Jain tradition in India.

FROM THE *BHAGAVAD GITA*

■

CHAPTER 1

Dhritarâshtra said:

What did my (people) and the Pândavas do, O Sañgaya! when they assembled together on the holy field of Kurukshetra, desirous to do battle?

Sañgaya said:

Seeing the army of the Pândavas drawn up in battle-array, the prince Duryodhana approached his preceptor, and spoke (these) words: 'O preceptor! observe this grand army of the sons of Pându, drawn up in battle-array by your talented pupil, the son of Drupada. In it are heroes (bearing) large bows, the equals of Bhîma and Arguna in battle—(namely), Yuyudhâna, Virâta, and Drupada, the master of the great car, and Dhrishtaketu, Kekitâna, and the valiant king of Kâsî, Purugit and Kuntibhoga, and that eminent man Saibya; the heroic Yudhâmanyu, the valiant Uttamaugas, the son of Subhadrâ, and the sons of Draupadi—all masters of great cars. And now, O best of Brâhmanas! learn who are most distinguished among us, and are leaders of my army. I will name them to you, in order that you may know them well. Yourself, and Bhîshma, and Karna, and Kripa the victor of (many) battles; Asvatthâman, and Vikarna, and also the son of Somadatta, and many other brave men, who have given up their lives for me, who fight with various weapons, (and are) all dexterous in battle. Thus our army which is protected by Bhîshma is unlimited; while this army of theirs which is protected by Bhîma is very limited. And therefore do ye all, occupying respectively the positions assigned to you, protect Bhîshma only.'

Then his powerful grandsire, Bhîshma, the oldest of the Kauravas, roaring aloud like a lion, blew his conch, (thereby) affording delight to Duryodhana. And then all at once, conchs, and kettledrums, and tabor, and trumpets were played upon; and there was a tumultuous din. Then, too, Mâdhava and the son of Pându (Arguna), seated in a grand chariot to which white steeds were yoked, blew their heavenly conchs. Hrishîkesa blew the Pâñkaganya, and Dhanañgaya the Devadatta, and Bhîma, (the doer) of fearful deeds, blew the great conch Paundra. King Yudhishthira, the son of Kuntî, blew the Anantavigaya, and Nakula and Sahadeva (respectively) the Sughosha and Manipushpaka. And the king of Kâsî, too, who has an excellent bow, and Sikhandin, the master of a great car, and Dhrishtadyumna, Virâta, and the unconquered Sâtyaki, and Drupada, and the sons of Draupadî, and the son of Subhadrâ, of mighty arms, blew conchs severally from all sides, O king of the earth! That tumultuous din rent the hearts of all (the people) of Dhritarâshtra's (party), causing reverberations throughout heaven and earth. Then seeing (the people of) Dhritarâshtra's party regularly marshalled, the son of Pându, whose standard is the ape, raised his bow, after the discharge of missiles had commenced, and O king of the earth! spake these words to Hrishîkesa: 'O underbraced one! station my chariot between the two armies, while I observe those, who stand here desirous to engage in battle, and with whom, in the labours of this struggle, I must do battle. I will observe those who are assembled here and who are about to engage in battle, wishing to do service in battle to the evil-minded son of Dhritarâshtra.'

Sañgaya said:

Thus addressed by Gudâkesa, O descendant of Bharata! Hrishîkesa stationed that excellent chariot between the two armies, in front of Bhîshma and Drona and of all the kings of the earth, and said: 'O son of Prithâ! look at these assembled Kauravas.' There the son of Prithâ saw in both armies, fathers and grandfathers, preceptors, maternal uncles, brothers, sons, grandsons, companions, fathers-in-law, as well as friends. And seeing all those kinsmen standing (there), the son of Kuntî was overcome by excessive pity and spake thus despondingly.

Arguna said:

Seeing these kinsmen, O Krishna! standing (here) anxious to engage in battle, my limbs droop down; my mouth is quite dried up; a tremor comes over my body; and my hairs stand on end; the Gândîva (bow) slips from my hand; my skin burns intensely. I am unable, too, to stand up; my mind whirls round, as it were; O Kesava! I see adverse omens; and I do not perceive any good (likely to accrue) after killing (my) kinsmen in the battle. I do not wish for victory, O Krishna! nor sovereignty, nor pleasures: what is sovereignty to us, O Govinda! what enjoyments, and even life? Even those, for whose sake we desire sovereignty, enjoyments, and pleasures, are standing here for battle, abandoning life and wealth—preceptors, fathers, sons as well as grandfathers, maternal uncles, fathers-in-law, grandsons, brothers-in-law, as also (other) relatives. These I do not wish to kill, though they kill (me), O destroyer of Madhu! even for the sake of sovereignty over the three worlds, how much less then for this earth (alone)? What joy shall be ours, O Ganârdana! after killing Dhritarâshtra's sons? Killing these felons we shall only incur sin. Therefore it is not proper for us to kill our own kinsmen, the sons of Dhritarâshtra. For how, O Madhava! shall we be happy after killing our own relatives? Although they have their consciences corrupted by avarice, they do not see the evils flowing from the extinction of a family, and the sin in treachery to friends; still, O Ganârdana! should not we, who do see the evils flowing from the extinction of a family, learn to refrain from that sin? On the extinction of a family, the eternal rites of families are destroyed. Those rites being destroyed, impiety predominates over the whole family. In consequence of the predominance of impiety, O Krishna! the women of the family become corrupt; and the women becoming corrupt, O descendant of Vrishni! intermingling of castes results; that intermingling necessarily leads the family and the destroyers of the family to hell; for when the ceremonies of (offering) the balls of food and water (to them) fail, their ancestors fall down (to hell). By these transgressions of the destroyers of families, which occasion interminglings of castes, the eternal rites of castes and rites of families are subverted. And O Ganardana! we have heard that men whose family-rites are subverted, must necessarily live in hell. Alas! we are engaged in committing a heinous sin, seeing that we are making efforts for killing our own kinsmen out of greed of the pleasures of sovereignty. If the sons of Dhritarâshtra, weapon in hand, were to kill me in battle, me being weaponless and not defending (myself), that would be better for me.

Sañgaya said:

Having spoken thus, Arguna cast aside his bow together with the arrows, on the battle-field, and sat down in (his) chariot, with a mind agitated by grief.

CHAPTER II

Sañgaya said:

To him, who was thus overcome with pity, and dejected, and whose eyes were full of tears and turbid, the destroyer of Madhu spoke these words.

The Deity said:

How (comes it that) this delusion, O Arguna! which is discarded by the good, which excludes from heaven, and occasions infamy, has overtaken you in this (place of) peril? Be not effeminate, O son of Prithâ! it is not worthy of you. Cast off this base weakness of heart, and arise, O terror of (your) foes!

Arguna said:

How, O destroyer of Madhu! shall I encounter with arrows in the battle Bhîshma and Drona—both, O destroyer of enemies! entitled to reverence? Without killing (my) preceptors—(men) of great glory—it is better to live even on alms in this world. But if killing them, though they are avaricious of worldly goods, I should only enjoy blood-tainted enjoyments. Nor do we know which of the two is better for us—whether that we should vanquish them, or that they should vanquish us. Even those, whom having killed, we do not wish to live— even those sons of Dhritarâshtra stand (arrayed) against us. With a heart contaminated by the taint of helplessness, with a mind confounded about my duty, I ask you. Tell me what is assuredly good for me. I am your disciple; instruct me, who have thrown myself on your (indulgence). For I do not perceive what is to dispel that grief which will dry up my organs after I shall have obtained a prosperous kingdom on earth without a foe, or even the sovereignty of the gods.

Sañgaya said:

Having spoken thus to Hrishîkesa, O terror of (your) foes! Gudakesa said to Govinda, 'I shall not engage in battle;' and verily remained silent. To him thus desponding between the two armies, O descendant of Bharata! Hrishîkesa spoke these words with a slight smile.

The Deity said:

You have grieved for those who deserve no grief, and you speak words of wisdom. Learned men grieve not for the living nor the dead. Never did I not exist, nor you, nor these rulers of men nor will any one of us ever hereafter cease to be. As in this body, infancy and youth and old age (come) to the embodied (self), so does the acquisition of another body; a sensible man is not deceived about that. The contacts of the senses, O son of Kuntî! which produce cold and heat, pleasure and pain, are not permanent, they are for ever coming and going. Bear them, O descendant of Bharata! For, O chief of men! that sensible man whom they afflict not, (pain and pleasure being alike to him), he merits immortality. There is no existence for that which is unreal; there is no non-existence of that which is real. And the (correct) conclusion about both is perceived by those who perceive the truth. Know that to be indestructible which pervades all this; the destruction of that inexhaustible (principle) none can bring about. These bodies pertaining to the embodied (self) which is eternal, indestructible, and indefinable, are declared to be perishable; therefore do engage in battle, O descendant of Bharata! He who thinks one to be the killer and he who thinks one to be killed, both know nothing. He kills not, is not killed. He is not born, nor does he ever die, nor, having existed, does he exist no more. Unborn, everlasting, unchangeable, and very ancient, he is not killed when the body is killed. O son of Prithâ! how can that man who knows the self thus to be indestructible, everlasting, unborn, and imperishable, kill any one, or cause any one to be killed? As a man, casting off oilcloths, puts on others and new ones, so the embodied (self), casting off old bodies, goes to others and new ones. Weapons do not divide the self (into pieces); fire does not burn it; waters do not moisten it; the wind does not dry it up. It is not divisible; it is not combustible; it is not to be moistened; it is not to be dried up. It is everlasting, all-pervading, stable, firm, and eternal. It is said to be unperceived, to be unthinkable, to be unchangeable. Therefore knowing it to be such, you ought not to grieve. But even if you think that the self is constantly born, and constantly dies, still, O you of mighty arms! you ought not to grieve thus. For to one that is born, death is certain; and to one that dies, birth is certain. Therefore about (this) unavoidable thing, you ought not to grieve. The source of things, O descendant of Bharata! is unperceived; their middle state is perceived; and their end again is unperceived. What (occasion is there for any) lamentation regarding them? One looks upon it as a wonder; another similarly speaks of it as a wonder; another too hears of it as a wonder; and even after having heard of it, no one does really know it. This embodied (self), O descendant of Bharata! within every one's body is ever indestructible. Therefore you ought not to grieve for any being. Having regard to your own duty also, you ought not to falter, for there is nothing better for a Kshatriya than a righteous battle. Happy those Kshatriyas, O son of Prithâ! who can find such a battle (to fight)—come of itself—an open door to heaven! But if you will not fight this righteous battle, then you will have abandoned your own duty and your fame, and you will incur sin. All beings, too, will tell of your everlasting infamy; and to one who has been honoured, infamy is (a) greater (evil) than death. (Warriors who are) masters of great cars will think that you abstained from the battle through fear, and having been highly thought of by them, you will fall down to littleness. Your enemies, too, decrying your power, will speak much about you that should not be spoken. And what, indeed, more lamentable than that? Killed, you will obtain heaven; victorious, you will enjoy the earth. Therefore arise, O son of Kuntî! resolved to (engage in) battle. Looking on pleasure and pain, on gain and loss, on victory and defeat as the same, prepare for battle, and thus you will not incur sin. The knowledge here declared to you is that relating to the Sinkhya. Now hear that relating to the Yoga. Possessed of this knowledge, O son of Prithâ! you will cast off the bonds of action. In this (path to final emancipation) nothing that is commenced becomes abortive; no obstacles exist; and even a little of this (form of) piety protects one from great danger. There is here, O descendant of Kuru! but one state of mind consisting in firm understanding. But the states of mind of those who have no firm understanding are manifold and endless. The states of mind which consists in firm understanding regarding steady contemplation does not belong to those, O son of Prithâ! who are strongly attached to (worldly) pleasures and power, and whose minds are drawn away by that flowery talk which is full of (the ordinances of) specific acts for the attainment of (those) pleasures and (that) power, and which promises birth as the fruit of acts—(that flowery talk) which those unwise ones utter, who are enamoured of Vedic words, who say there is nothing else, who are full of desires, and whose goal is heaven. The Vedas (merely) relate to the effects of the three qualities; do you, O Arguna! rise above those effects of the three qualities, and be free from the pairs of opposites, always preserve courage, be free from anxiety for new acquisitions or protection of old acquisitions, and be self-controlled. To the instructed Brahmana, there is in all the Vedas as much utility as in a reservoir of water into which waters flow from all sides. Your business is with action alone; not by any means with fruit. Let not the fruit of action be your motive (to action). Let not your attachment be (fixed) on inaction. Having recourse to devotion, O Dhanañgaya! perform actions, casting off (all) attachment, and being equable in success or ill-success; (such) equability is called devotion. Action, O Dhanañgaya! is far inferior to the devotion of the mind. In that devotion seek shelter. Wretched are those whose motive (to action) is the fruit (of action). He who has obtained devotion in this world casts off both merit and sin. Therefore apply yourself to devotion; devotion in (all) actions is wisdom. The wise who have obtained devotion cast off the fruit of action; and released from the shackles of (repeated) births, repair to that seat where there is no unhappiness. When your mind shall have crossed beyond the taint of delusion then will you become indifferent to all that you have heard or will hear. When your mind, that was confounded by what you have heard, will stand firm and steady in contemplation, then will you acquire devotion.

Arguna said:
    What are the characteristics, O Kesava! of one whose mind is steady, and who is intent on contemplation? How should one of a steady mind speak, how sit, how move?

The Deity said:

When a man, O son of Prithâ! abandons all the desires of his heart, and is pleased in his self only and by his self, he is then called of a steady mind. He whose heart is not agitated in the midst of calamities, who has no longing for pleasures, and for whom (the feelings of) affection, fear, and wrath have departed, is called a sage of a steady mind. His mind is steady, who, being without attachments anywhere, feels no exultation and no aversion on encountering the various agreeable and disagreeable (things of this world). A man's mind is steady, when he withdraws his senses from (all) objects of sense, as the tortoise (withdraws) its limbs from all sides. Objects of sense withdraw themselves from a person who is abstinent; not so the taste (for those objects). But even the taste departs from him, when he has seen the Supreme. The boisterous senses, O son of Kuntî! carry away by force the mind even of a wise man, who exerts himself (for final emancipation). Restraining them all, a man should remain engaged in devotion, making me his only resort. For his mind is steady whose senses are under his control. The man who ponders over objects of sense forms an attachment to them; from (that) attachment is produced desire and from desire anger is produced; from anger results want of discrimination; from want of discrimination, confusion of the memory; from confusion of the memory, loss of reason; and in consequence of loss of reason he is utterly ruined. But the self-restrained man who moves among objects with senses under the control of his own self, and free from affection and aversion, obtains tranquillity. When there is tranquillity, all his miseries are destroyed, for the mind of him whose heart is tranquil soon becomes steady. He who is not self-restrained has no steadiness of mind; nor has he who is not self-restrained perseverance in the pursuit of self-knowledge; there is no tranquillity for him who does not persevere in the pursuit of self-knowledge; and whence can there be happiness for one who is not tranquil? For the heart which follows the rambling senses leads away his judgment, as the wind leads a boat astray upon the waters. Therefore, O you of mighty arms! his mind is steady whose senses are restrained on all sides from objects of sense. The self-restrained man is awake, when it is night for all beings; and when all beings are awake, that is the night of the right-seeing sage. He into whom all objects of desire enter, as waters enter the ocean, which, (though) replenished, (still) keeps its position unmoved,—he only obtains tranquillity; not he who desires (those) objects of desire. The man who, casting off all desires, lives free from attachments, who is free from egoism, and from (the feeling that this or that is) mine, obtains tranquillity. This, O son of Prithâ! is the Brahmic state; attaining to this, one is never deluded; and remaining in it in (one's) last moments, one attains (brahma-nirvâna) the Brahmic bliss.

FROM THE *RAMAYANA*

1. Rama saw his father, with a wretched look and his mouth all parched, slumped upon his lovely couch, Kaikeyi at his side.

2. First he made an obeisance with all deference at his father's feet and then did homage most scrupulously at the feet of Kaikeyi.

3. "Rama!" cried the wretched king, his eyes brimming with tears, but he was unable to say anything more or to look at him.

4. As if his foot had grazed a snake, Rama was seized with terror to see the expression on the king's face, one more terrifying than he had ever seen before.

5. For the great king lay heaving sighs, racked with grief and remorse, all his senses numb with anguish, his mind stunned and confused.

6. It was as if the imperturbable, wave-wreathed ocean had suddenly been shaken with perturbation, as if the sun had been eclipsed, or a seer had told a lie.

7. His father's grief was incomprehensible to him, and the more he pondered it, the more his agitation grew, like that of the ocean under a full moon.

8. With his father's welfare at heart, Rama struggled to comprehend, "Why does the king not greet me, today of all days?

9. "On other occasions, when Father might be angry, the sight of me would calm him. Why then, when he looked at me just now, did he instead become so troubled?

10. "He seems desolate and grief-stricken, and his face has lost its glow." Doing obeisance to Kaikeyi, Rama spoke these words:

11. "I have not unknowingly committed some offense, have I, to anger my father? Tell me, and make him forgive me.

12. "His face is drained of color, he is desolate and does not speak to me. It cannot be, can it, that some physical illness or mental distress afflicts him? But it is true, well-being is not something one can always keep.

13. "Some misfortune has not befallen the handsome prince Bharata, has it, or courageous Satrughna,* for one of my mothers?

---

* The fourth son of Dasharatha and close companion of Bharata.

14. "I should not wish to live an instant if his Majesty, the great king, my father, were angered by my failure to satisfy him or do his bidding.

15. "How could a man not treat him as a deity incarnate, in whom he must recognize the very source of his existence in this world?

16. "Can it be that in anger you presumed to use harsh words with my father, and so threw his mind into such turmoil?

17. "Answer my questions truthfully, my lady: What has happened to cause this unprecedented change in the lord of men?

18. "At the bidding of the king, if enjoined by him, my guru, father, king, and benefactor, I would hurl myself into fire, drink deadly poison, or drown myself in the sea.

19. "Tell me then, my lady, what the king would have me do. I will do it, I promise. Rama need not say so twice."

20. The ignoble Kaikeyi then addressed these ruthless words to Rama, the upright and truthful prince:

21. "Long ago, Raghava, in the war of the gods and *asuras,* your father bestowed two boons on me, for protecting him when he was wounded in a great battle.

22. "By means of these I have demanded of the king that Bharata be consecrated and that you, Raghava, be sent at once to Dandaka wilderness.

23. "If you wish to ensure that your father be true to his word, and you to your own, best of men, then listen to what I have to say.

24. "Abide by your father's guarantee, exactly as he promised it, and enter the forest for nine years and five.

25. "Forgo the consecration and withdraw to Dandaka wilderness, live there seven years and seven, wearing matted hair and barkcloth garments.

26. "Let Bharata rule this land from the city of the Kosalans, with all the treasures it contains, all its horses, chariots, elephants."

27. When Rama, slayer of enemies, heard Kaikeyi's hateful words, like death itself, he was not the least disconcerted, but only replied.

28. "So be it. I shall go away to live in the forest, wearing matted hair and bark-cloth garments, to safeguard the promise of the king.

29. "But I want to know why the lord of earth, the invincible tamer of foes, does not greet me as he used to?

30. "You need not worry, my lady. I say it to your face: I shall go to the forest—rest assured—wearing barkcloth and matted hair.

31. "Enjoined by my father, my benefactor, guru, and king, a man who knows what is right to do, what would I hesitate to do in order to please him?

32. "But there is still one thing troubling my mind and eating away at my heart: that the king does not tell me himself that Bharata is to be consecrated.

33. "For my wealth, the kingship, Sita, and my own dear life I would gladly give up to my brother Bharata on my own, without any urging.

34. "How much more readily if urged by my father himself, the lord of men, in order to fulfill your fond desire and safeguard his promise?

35. "So you must reassure him. Why should the lord of earth keep his eyes fixed upon the ground and fitfully shed these tears?

36. "This very day let messengers depart on swift horses by order of the king to fetch Bharata from his uncle's house.

37. "As for me, I shall leave here in all haste for Dandaka wilderness, without questioning my father's word, to live there fourteen years."

38. Kaikeyi was delighted to hear these words of Rama's, and trusting them implicitly, she pressed Raghava to set out at once.

39. "So be it. Men shall go as messengers on swift horses to bring home Bharata from his uncle's house.

40. "But since you are now so eager, Rama, I do not think it wise to linger. You should therefore proceed directly from here to the forest.

41. "That the king is ashamed and does not address you himself, that is nothing, best of men, you needn't worry about that.

42. "But so long as you have not hastened from the city and gone to the forest, Rama, your father shall neither bathe nor eat."

43. "Oh curse you!" the king gasped, overwhelmed with grief, and upon the gilt couch he fell back in a faint.

44. Rama raised up the king, pressed though he was by Kaikeyi—like a horse whipped with a crop—to make haste and depart for the forest.

45. Listening to the ignoble Kaikeyi's hateful words, so dreadful in their consequences, Rama remained unperturbed and only said to her,

46. "My lady, it is not in the hopes of gain that I suffer living in this world. You should know that, like the seers, I have but one concern and that is righteousness.

47. "Whatever I can do to please this honored man I will do at any cost, even if it means giving up my life.

48. "For there is no greater act of righteousness than this: obedience to one's father and doing as he bids.

49. "Even unbidden by this honored man, at your bidding alone I shall live for fourteen years in the desolate forest.

50. "Indeed, Kaikeyi, you must ascribe no virtue to me at all if you had to appeal to the king, when you yourself are so venerable in my eyes.

51. "Let me only take leave of my mother, and settle matters with Sita. Then I shall go, this very day, to the vast forest of the Dandakas.

52. "You must see to it that Bharata obeys Father and guards the kingdom, for that is the eternal way of righteousness."

53. When his father heard Rama's words, he was stricken with such deep sorrow that he could not hold back his sobs in his grief and broke out in loud weeping.

54. Splendid Rama did homage at the feet of his unconscious father and at the feet of that ignoble woman, Kaikeyi, then he turned to leave.

55. Reverently, Rama circled his father and Kaikeyi, and withdrawing from the inner chamber, he saw his group of friends.

56. Laksmana, the delight of Sumitra, fell in behind him, his eyes brimming with tears, in a towering rage.

57. Reverently circling the equipment for the consecration, but careful not to gaze at it, Rama slowly went away.

58. The loss of the kingship diminished his great majesty as little as night diminishes the loveliness of the cool rayed moon, beloved of the world.

59. Though he was on the point of leaving his native land and going to the forest, he was no more discomposed than one who has passed beyond all things of this world.

60. Holding back his sorrow within his mind, keeping his every sense in check, and fully self-possessed he made his way to his mother's residence to tell her the sad news.

61. As Rama entered her residence, where joy still reigned supreme, as he reflected on the sudden wreck of all his fortunes, even then he showed no sign of discomposure, for fear it might endanger the lives of those he loved.

The end of the sixteenth *sarga* of the *Ayodhyakanda* of the *Sri Ramayana*.

8

BUDDHIST ETHICS

■

TERROR IN TOKYO'S SUBWAY

Besides having a special interest in Buddhism, Yasuo Hayashi, later dubbed the "Murder Machine" by the Japanese press, had an impeccable science background and quickly climbed to a top position in Aum Shinrikyo's Ministry of Science and Technology. And on an early Monday morning, March 20, 1995, in the thick of Tokyo's commuter rush hour, he clearly proved his loyalty to Aum. With the sharpened tip of his umbrella, Hayashi neatly pierced through the rolled morning newspaper concealing his three packets of deadly liquid sarin nerve gas as his train rolled into the Akihabara station. He immediately disembarked, exited the underground subway, took an antidote for the poison, and escaped into a waiting car driven by another Aum member. At the same time, the same scenario played itself out at four other stations as Aum members, each on different trains, pierced their bags of sarin and escaped with their designated drivers.

The result. Total confusion and disaster. Passengers spilled out of subway cars choking, vomiting, and blinded. Thousands of commuters clawed their way to fresh air above ground and collapsed. Twelve victims died and over 5,500 were seriously injured. The Tokyo subway system acts as the circulatory system for the working Japanese and carries over 4 million passengers a day. If full-strength sarin had been used, the fatalities would have reached into the tens of thousands. And Japan was still reeling from the Great Hanshin earthquake that devastated the port city of Kobe and claimed over 6,000 lives two months earlier on January 17, 1995.

Aum members were soon linked to the attacks. Confessions revealed the ultimate target: the subway station at Kasumigaseki, the convergence point of the assailants' trains. The station is a short walk to the Japanese Parliament, the Ministries of Finance and Foreign Affairs, the police headquarters, and Emperor Akihito's Imperial Palace. The Kasumigaseki station is also the deepest subway station in Japan and had been built as the government's own atomic shelter. The attack was aimed at paralyzing the Japanese government. Hayashi was eventually arrested in December 1996 on Ishigaki Island, where he was discovered carrying a token in memorial of those who died from the gas attack—a small Buddhist altar.[1]

"Aum Shinrikyo" literally means "the true teachings of Aum," Aum being the hallowed Sanskrit mantra (Om) that represents the sacred sound of the universe and depicting the triune Hindu gods Brahma, Vishnu, and Shiva. When Aum was given official status as a religion in 1989, there were over four thousand members. Now, even after the gas attack, its membership is well over a hundred thousand. Aum's founder and self-proclaimed visionary is the semi-blind Shoko Asahara, whose real name is Chizuo Matsumoto. Matsumoto was born in 1955 in the small village of Yatsushiro on Japan's southernmost island of Kyushu. Nearly two months after the attack, Matsumoto was found in a crawl space less than three feet high at Kamikuishiki, carrying, not a Buddhist altar, but nearly one hundred thousand dollars in cash. He was arrested and eventually charged with the murders of twenty-five people—twelve deaths as a result of his order to gas the subway along with thirteen other related deaths.

Asahara's devotees are young, well-educated, and committed to Asahara, the "new Buddha." Mitsuhara Inaba now knows that Asahara was the mastermind behind the Tokyo nerve gas attacks. Yet he still keeps a photo of Asahara on his *butsudan,* or home altar. He and other members had been desperately searching for a new and transforming Buddhism, one with a more active and practical application for their lives. Among Japanese, Buddhism had often been associated with funerary rites and was thus losing its meaning among the younger generation. Countless followers remain convinced that their master's teachings have a firm footing in the Buddhist tradition. In the words of Inaba: "For me the Master [Asahara] was a spiritual leader. Not a prophet or anything, but the person who would provide the final answer to Buddhist teachings."[2]

Aum Shinrikyo sees itself as unmistakably Buddhist. At the same time, it borrows elements from other traditions like Hindu and Tibetan yoga as well as Christian and Jewish teachings and even smatterings of millenialism and Nostradamus. Asahara not only claimed to be the "new Buddha," but he also viewed himself as the new Christ, the redeemer of humanity. When the police located the cult's secret compound in the little village of Kamikuishiki, on the foothills of the sacred Mount Fuji, they discovered this to be a "death factory" where the bodies of thirty or more victims were incinerated in a giant microwave oven. They came upon a giant statue of the Hindu god of destruction, Shiva, blocking the entrance to a secret door to the chemical laboratory where the deadly sarin nerve gas was produced. How genuinely Buddhist are the teachings of Aum Shinrikyo? What Buddhist teachings could possibly justify the deliberate attack on innocent commuters and passengers?

■ THE THREE SIGNS OF EXISTENCE

The Buddha delivered his first sermon at the village of Sarnath. Here he presented the core of his teachings—the Four Noble Truths and the Middle Way. Despite later disputes as to the proper interpretation of his teachings, all Buddhists believe in the Four Noble Truths and in the Middle Way. Here, the Buddha presents his diagnosis regarding our fundamental human condition, and he offers a cure. Before we examine these teachings, we need to first situate them within the Buddhist three signs of existence. In effect, these signs, along with the core teachings, constitute the Buddhist *dharma*, or "teachings."[3]

FIRST SIGN: *DUKKHA*

The young woman Kisagotami gave birth to a son who died of an illness within a year. Stricken with grief, the mother carried the dead boy from house to house asking for medicine to restore him back to life. She then approached Siddhartha Gautama (the personal and family name of the Buddha). Siddhartha counseled her to go to every home in the village and bring back a mustard seed from each household that has not experienced death. She returned empty-handed, realizing that death stings each and every one of us.

The celebrated fifth-century Buddhist sage Buddhaghosa wrote this story in his *Vissudhimagga*. It poignantly illustrates the first sign of existence, *dukkha*, the universality of suffering. *Dukkha* literally means "dislocation" and denotes a suffering that goes beyond physical pain. Physical pain can be measurable, but suffering is much more intimate and less discernible. *Dukkha* refers to suffering that is profoundly existential, of which death is a stark reminder.

SECOND SIGN: *ANICCA*

The *Buddhacarita* (*Deeds of the Buddha*) tells of young prince Siddhartha, who was born in 623 BCE in Lumbini, on the border of India and what is today Nepal. Siddhartha's father, ruler of the Sakya clan, wanted to shield his young son from the harsh realities of life and prohibited him from going beyond the palace walls. Nevertheless, young Siddhartha bribed his charioteer to take him outside the palace.

On their first journey, they encountered a very old man barely walking along the road. On another journey, they passed by a sick person being attended to by others. On their third journey, they passed by a funeral procession. On their fourth journey, they rode by laborers sweating and struggling while plowing the fields. These experiences left their imprint in young Siddhartha's heart and memory. They laid the groundwork for what he later referred to as the second sign of existence: *anicca*. *Anicca* means "impermanence" and refers to the fact that all of life, without exception, undergoes change. We age. We struggle to make ends meet. And we die. Nothing stays the same. Each moment rises and falls. Each moment in time therefore carries within itself life and death, being and nonbeing. Life is like a never-ending river.

THIRD SIGN: *ANATMAN*

The third sign of existence, *anatman* (*anatta* in Pali), literally means "no-self," or "no-soul." Here, the Buddha takes issue with the Hindu teaching regarding *atman*. As we recall, *atman* is the individual immortal soul or self in each of us. The all-important goal in Hinduism is to realize the truth of our identity as *atman*. For the Buddha, however, there is no empirical evidence to support the idea of an individual, private, independent soul or self. However, we all possess a true nature. Yet this true nature, our Buddha nature, is not some private entity. Buddhists refer to our true nature as *anatman*.

This notion of *anatman* is the most challenging idea in Buddhist thought. We in the West are accustomed to think and speak in terms of an individual, private, and permanent entity we call "self." For Buddhists, what we think of as "self" is actually a continually changing pattern of physical and mental forces. Buddhists essentially break down our experience into five components, or aggregates, called *skandhas:*

- physical form (matter)
- feelings and sensations
- perceptions
- mental activities, particularly that of volition
- consciousness

Together, these five aggregates constitute *nama-rupa,* or "name-form." The "I" that we think exists is actually a composite of these five components, and each component undergoes constant change. In which case, there are no logical grounds for assuming a permanent "I."

When I am playing the piano, what is really happening in light of these five aggregates? First, there is my physical form, my body, in contact with the physical form of the piano. Second, there are the sensations involved in pressing down on the keys, in touching the pedal, as well as feelings evoked by the music. Third, there is the perception of sounds coming from the piano and the sight of the music on the pages in front of me. Fourth, there is the mental construct, or conception, of the sounds constituting music. My mental activity therefore makes some sense out of the sounds, and this includes the will or volition to play the music. Finally, there is an overall awareness of what is happening, an awareness of the piano, the player, the music sheet, and the music itself. This constitutes the consciousness of "playing the piano." Where is this "I" that is independent of these components? Instead of finding an "I," Buddhists discover only the *experience* itself.

As fundamental as this idea is in Buddhist thought, however, from a practical point of view this has little force in ordinary conversation. For instance, Buddhists still believe in some form of continued existence after death. And in many contexts, the term "soul" is still used to refer to this rebirth. We see this in the Japanese practice of *mizuko kuyo,* literally meaning "water children rites," the memorial service offered in Buddhist temples in which parents of an aborted fetus pray for the "soul" of their "baby."[4] For Buddhists, what is reborn is like a "stream of consciousness" that comprises the karma accumulated over numerous lifetimes. In a sense, some sort of "character" is reborn, yet this character is not permanent nor is it private. This question of the relationship between Buddhist rebirth and *anatman* remains one of the most puzzling ideas in Buddhism.

MAKING MORE SENSE OF NO-SELF

Interconnectedness We can situate *anatman* within the Buddhist teaching of dependent origination, called *pratityasamutpada*. What this means is that all things in existence are so intimately connected with each other that all things affect everything else. No events happen in isolation. Existence is an intricate web of mutual and symbiotic cause-and-effect. Once we cast a pebble into a calm lake, it sends out a ripple effect that reaches onto the shore. Yet the stone's ripple effect does not end with the shore. It continues to affect all aspects of the environment in subtle but meaningful ways. As we shall see in our final chapter, all this has profound implications for the environment. Our human actions produce their ripple effects upon our environment and upon all other sentient beings.

The innate interconnectedness of *pratityasamutpada* helps to explain why the idea of individualism and individual rights is foreign in Buddhist cultures. Interconnectedness emphasizes notions of duty and obligation rather than rights and thus subordinates the idea of individual autonomy, a key moral precept in the West that we have seen highlighted through Kant's discussion of the "person" as a moral agent. In this way, *pratityasamutpada* holds us accountable and duty-bound to all sentient beings.

Nirvana According to Buddhists, as long as we remain under the illusion of a separate, permanent self, we will experience countless rebirths. Enlightenment comes about when "I" awaken to the truth that *there is no* "I." This awakening is called *nirvana*, which literally means "extinguishing," as in extinguishing a flame. What is extinguished is the false sense of an individual, private, and permanent self-entity. If and when I experience nirvana, I am then liberated from the wheel of birth, death, and rebirth. Here we see a radical difference from Hindu thought. For Hindus, the highest experience, *moksha*, entails an awakening to one's genuine self, *atman*. In contrast, for Buddhists, because there is no *atman*, the ultimate experience, nirvana, consists in awakening to the fact of the illusion of self.

When Shoko Asahara returned from a visit to India and Tibet in 1986, he publicly announced that he had experienced nirvana while meditating in Tibet. He then proceeded to engage in a full-fledged marketing campaign to tout his alleged nirvana experience. After visiting the Dalai Lama in the following year, he then claimed to be the new Buddha, not only for the salvation of Japan, but for the whole world. This is a far cry from the selflessness experienced in nirvana.

■ THE FOUR NOBLE TRUTHS

The Four Noble Truths remain the pivotal teaching in Buddhism and provide an existential context for Buddhist ethics. Through these truths, the Buddha acts as our physician, first conveying to us his diagnosis of our human condition, and then offering us a way to be healed from our condition.

THE FIRST TRUTH: SUFFERING IS UNIVERSAL

The Buddha describes this first Truth of suffering (*dukkha*):

> . . . *this is the Noble Truth of Sorrow. Birth is Sorrow, age is sorrow, disease is sorrow, death is sorrow; contact with the unpleasant is sorrow, separation from the pleasant is sorrow, every wish unfulfilled is sorrow — in short all the five components of individuality are sorrow.*[5]

Dukkha is ubiquitous. Consider the world scandal of poverty. The celebrated Thai activist and cofounder of the International Network of Engaged Buddhists, Sulak Sivaraksa, reminds us that of the more than forty thousand people who die each day from undernourishment and starvation, at least 75 percent of them are children.[6]

THE SECOND TRUTH: THE SOURCE OF SUFFERING LIES IN CRAVING

What is the cause of our suffering? The root cause of suffering is *tanha* (*trishna* in Sanskrit), which literally means "desire," "thirst," and "craving." "Craving" comes closer to the meaning of *tanha*, for craving represents the extreme manifestation of desire. Recall how Kisagotami literally clung to her dead baby boy. As the Buddha states,

> *this is the Noble Truth of the Arising of Sorrow. It arises from craving, which leads to rebirth, which brings delight and passion, and seeks pleasure now here, now there — the craving for sensual pleasure, the craving for continued life, the craving for power.*[7] *[emphasis added]*

The Buddha singles out three distinct objects of craving: sensual pleasure, continued life, and power. Underlying these three is an even deeper object of our craving—ideas, whether it is an *idea* of what constitutes pleasure, *ideas* regarding continued life, or *ideas* about power and control. Since our minds give birth to our ideas, the driving force in all of this is mind. And when we cling to an idea, we become attached to it. When we become attached to an idea, that idea takes us over. We no longer *have* the idea. The idea *has us*. Witness the opening scene in our chapter on utilitarianism where Alice Melling and her crew of IRA terrorists are ensnared by the idea of "freedom for all Ireland, at any cost."

Shoko Asahara's actions clearly demonstrated his craving for power, privilege, and material comforts. He charged outrageous fees for certain "religious aids" such as his bathwater for ¥100,000 (about $1,000) per liter, calling it "Miracle Pond"! The sect also sold a tiny vial that allegedly contains Asahara's own blood for the incredible fee of ¥1,000,000, or about $10,000. The buyer is supposed to drink the blood in order to acquire some of the "the Master's" powers. There is also the PSI, or Perfect Salvation Initiation, a "telepathy headgear" with all sorts of wiring that can be rented for ¥1,000,000 a month! The device supposedly enables the wearer to be on the same brain wavelength as "the Master."[8]

THE THIRD TRUTH: WE CAN FREE OURSELVES FROM SUFFERING

Note that the source of suffering, our tendency to cling and to grasp, lies within us. We ourselves create our suffering. Thus, there is a window of hope that would not exist if the cause were external and therefore beyond our control. Of the five components we discussed earlier, the mental faculty of volition, or will, generates our tendency to crave or to cling. But volition by its very nature can be controlled. How? It is precisely *through* our mental faculty that we can exert some control over our mental faculty. Ludwig van Beethoven (1770–1827) was virtually stone-deaf by 1817. Yet he managed to compose masterpieces like his string quartets and *Ninth Symphony*, relying on his inner ear as well as sight in order to "hear." My mind can free me from my mind. How is this possible? Only if we can extricate ourselves from the illusion of self. The key lies in uncovering the ontological error of an independent and permanent "I." As long as we sustain the illusion of "I," we will continue to crave. The key lies in waking up to the truth of *anatman*. Yet this is the most difficult course to pursue.

THE FOURTH TRUTH: THE EIGHTFOLD PATH

The Eightfold Path is the centerpiece of Buddhist morality. If we diligently follow this path, we can liberate ourselves from the condition of suffering that we in effect impose upon ourselves. The Buddha shows us the way, but only we can follow it. The Eightfold Path consists in these steps:

• right view	• right livelihood
• right resolve	• right effort
• right speech	• right mindfulness
• right conduct	• right concentration

Not only do these steps impact upon each other, but they incorporate the harmony of mental activity (right view, right resolve, right effort, right mindfulness, right concentration) and bodily behavior (right speech, right conduct, right livelihood), mind and body.

Right View Right view requires that we embrace the Three Signs and the Four Noble Truths. Otherwise, we fall victim to what Buddhists call the Four Perverse Views:

- clinging to permanence
- enjoying another's suffering
- clinging to a self
- having false beliefs about beauty[9]

For example, if we cannot accept *anicca,* our attachment to a false sense of permanence pervades our understanding of things and explains why we can remain attached to an idea of a permanent self, an idea that is for us an anchor in this sea of impermanence.

Right Resolve Right resolve means having the disposition needed to pursue the path and therefore underscores attitude and purity of intention. Right resolve is also called right "thought." Right thought requires having the proper conception of thought itself. Right thought is a sort of critical "self-scrutiny" of *how* one thinks and *what* one thinks about. It is an epistemological critique of our process of understanding, and underlying all this is the need to be free of any notion of a permanent, independent self, or "thinker."

Right Speech Speech indicates character. Right speech is speech that is harmonious. It avoids any negativity such as deceit, cursing, gossiping, and spreading rumors. Right speech ultimately means that we should speak in ways that alleviate suffering. The Buddha lays the groundwork for right speech in his *Discourse to Prince Abhaya* when he asks the prince to consider three fundamental questions regarding speech: Is it true? Is it gracious? Is it useful?[10] According to the renowned German philosopher Martin Heidegger (1889–1976), much of our speech consists of "idle talk." His view comes close to what the Buddha was getting at. In his classic *Being and Time*, Heidegger states:

> *What is said-in-the-talk as such, spreads in wider circles and takes on an authoritative character. Things are so because one says so. Idle talk is constituted by just such gossiping and passing the word along — a process by which its initial lack of grounds to stand on becomes aggravated to complete groundlessness. . . .*
>
> *The groundlessness of idle talk is no obstacle to its becoming public; instead it encourages this. Idle talk is the possibility of understanding everything without previously making the thing one's own.*[11]

Right Conduct Right conduct helps to alleviate the suffering of all sentient creatures. It forbids any behavior that brings about *unnecessary harm* and thus prohibits injuring others, stealing, destroying property, living unchastely, self-debasement, and any other actions that spawn suffering. The *Majjhima-nikaya* describes how, while instructing his son Rahula, the Buddha uses the image of a mirror to show him the vital relationship between behavior and reflection:

> *What do you think about this, Rahula? What is the purpose of a mirror?*
> *Its purpose is reflection, reverend sir.*
> *Even so, Rahula, a deed is to be done with the body [only] after repeated reflection; a deed is to be done with speech . . . with the mind [only] after repeated reflection.*[12]

Especially in light of the interconnectedness of all things, our actions in some way impacts upon all others, and we need to reflect upon this before we act.[13]

Right Livelihood Right livelihood pertains to the life choices we make regarding our careers. First, does our career promote happiness or does it bring about suffering? Buddhists warn against becoming warriors or butchers. The preoccupation of Aum scientists with producing sarin nerve gas at their Kamikuishiki complex unreservedly violates right livelihood. And in 1992, after purchasing a machine factory in Ishikawa Prefecture, Aum members made parts for AK-74 assault rifles. Second, does our career arouse unhealthy attachments? Do we choose careers that reinforce attachments? Expending energies to enhance our material comfort may mean denying or remaining ignorant of the bigger picture, the more global view that exposes worldwide famine, disease, and poverty.

Right Effort The mind can be a wild beast that enslaves us, or it can be our vehicle to attain our goal. It depends upon our volition or will. Volition can be our undoing, or it can be our lifeline. Right effort requires guarding the mind through volition against forces that distract and pull us away from our goal of liberation. We can rationalize to ourselves any action that we take, hence, the power of the mind. This capacity for self-vindication bares itself in the interior conflict between what we desire and what we value. Desires, temporary by nature, can be so powerful that they can drive us to do things we would not do under the rule of reason. To think that I am a passive tool of my mind is wrongheaded. Right effort means realizing our capacity to control our mind. It reclaims for us our proper compass so that we stay on the right track.

Right Mindfulness In the course of day-to-day activities, we generally take for granted our bodies and our minds. Are we aware of our posture, the way we walk, the way we sit, where our hands are, what we do with our bodies while we're doing it? The same can be said for mind. Our minds speed ahead with thoughts of work, deadlines, and meetings, but are we reflecting, or are we simply caught up in our thoughts? Right mindfulness requires that we be fully aware of both body and mind and demands that we keep both in balance. Although this balance is possible, it demands discipline, patience, and proper meditation, or *dhyana*. In Buddhist tradition, the practice of meditation is all-important especially because it seeks to sustain the unity of mind and body.[14]

Right Concentration It is through the mind that we can be free from the mind. When we are free from the mind, we reach a state called *samadhi*, the term for right concentration. This is a state of pure consciousness, a condition of "neither-perception-nor-nonperception," a state that is reached when I have abolished the conventional dualistic tendency to think of a natural difference between the observer and the observed, the "I" and the object. This requires enduring practice and patience and is immensely difficult in our culture, which flourishes on the quick fix and immediate gratification. The Buddhist scholar Walpola Rahula outlines four steps in the attainment of *samadhi*.[15] First, we purge all negative thoughts and keep positive thoughts. Second, we eliminate thoughts altogether in order to release our minds from the hold of intellect. The third step requires that we purge our minds of the feelings of joy and happiness. Finally, we remove from our minds *all* sensations so that we enter a state of pure consciousness, pure awareness, without any thoughts or sensations to distract us. This is a state of pure equanimity, the absence of any dualism between subject and object and of any notion of a distinct and separate "I" or self.

■ THE MIDDLE WAY

Despite having a wife, a son, and all the blessings of family life, Siddhartha Gautama felt a profound discontent in his heart that gnawed away at him so that he decided to leave his family and embark upon his own personal search. He journeyed for many months in the forest and joined a group of wandering Hindu ascetics. In order to attain *moksha*, or spiritual enlightenment, these ascetics practiced all sorts of bodily deprivation including fasting, and to no avail. Siddhartha eventually abandoned the group and journeyed on his own.

According to legend, weary and emaciated, he passed out under a tree. That same day, a maiden, who regularly made a habit of leaving offerings for the gods under the tree, came upon the sleeping figure and believed him to be a god incarnate. She left the food there for him. Upon waking up, Siddhartha discovered the food and, eating portions of it, slowly regained his bodily strength and mental concentration. He then experienced a most profound insight. He realized that the path to enlightenment cannot lie through bodily deprivation, the ascetic path, nor can it lie through bodily indulgence, his former lifestyle at home. The way to enlightenment avoids these two extremes, and this is the Middle Way to salvation. He then committed himself to staying under what is now known as the Bodhi tree, and meditated until he reached his enlightenment.

As the cornerstone of Buddhist ethics, the Middle Way requires that we live a life of balance. Here we see a strong likeness with Aristotle's view of virtue. Recall that for Aristotle, virtue avoids the extremes of excess and deficit. The Buddha knew firsthand that attachment to either extreme embodies an attachment to self, for the illusory self is the driving force behind both the desire for excess and the desire for deprivation. As the Buddha states, "All mortification is vain so long as self remains, so long as self continues to lust after either wordly or heavenly pleasures."[16]

In American culture, excess continues to be the norm in many ways, from fashion to food. A student in my class from the war-torn country of Bosnia expressed amazement at her American roommate's daily habit of showers. Such excess seduces us into mistaking what we *desire* with what we really *need.* And slipping into the other extreme of deficit is equally dangerous. Not only does bodily deprivation endanger health, but it also enslaves one in a prison of self-absorption. Consider our culture's obsession with beauty as thinness. The Buddhist text *Vinaya-pitaka* tells the story of the monk Sona, a lute player before he entered the monastery. Obsessed with seeking enlightenment, he engaged in self-deprivation and practiced walking meditation so strenuously that his feet bled. At one point, the Buddha addressed Sona:

> "Now what do you think, when the strings of your lute became too tight, could you get the right tune, or was it fit to play?"
> "No indeed, Sir."
> "Likewise, when the strings became too slack, could you get the right tune or was it then fit to play?"
> "No indeed, Sir."
> "But when the strings were neither too tight nor too slack but were keyed to an even pitch, then did it give the right tune?"
> "Yes indeed, Sir."
> "Even so, Sona, too much zeal conduces to restlessness and too much slackness conduces to mental sloth." So saying, the Master admonished the young monk to strike a balance between these two extremes and develop an even tempo of spiritual equilibrium.[17]

The Buddha offers us a positive attitude toward material and physical comfort so long as it is in moderation. As he states in his Sermon at Benares, the key is moderation:

> But to satisfy the necessities of life is not evil. To keep the body in good health is a duty, for otherwise we shall not be able to trim the

lamp of wisdom, and keep our mind strong and clear. This is the middle path, O bhikshus, that keeps aloof from both extremes.[18]

The second-century Buddhist philosopher Nagarjuna's landmark work, *Madhyamika Karika* ("Fundamentals of the Middle Way"), is surely one of the most influential works in Buddhist philosophy.[19] Here Nagarjuna gives another twist to the Middle Way by situating it within the context of the Buddhist idea of *sunyata*, or "emptiness." *Sunyata* essentially means that all things and all sentient beings are void of a permanent substance and therefore lack a permanent self-entity. At the same time, things and beings do exist. The Middle Way therefore avoids the extremes of materialism, which claims that only the material matters, and nihilism, which asserts that the material and physical count for nothing.

THE SUPREME VIRTUES AND MIDDLE WAY

Buddhists point to an inseparable link between insight and action, wisdom and morality. As the Buddha tells his disciple Ananda, "So you see, Ananda, good conduct gradually leads to the summit."[20] *Nirvana*, the annihilation of the illusion of self, can only be achieved by living virtuously. Along these lines, these four supreme virtues embody the prescription of the Middle Way:

- compassion, *karuna*
- lovingkindness, *metta*
- sympathetic joy, *mudita*
- impartiality, *upekkha*[21]

Compassion The Theravadist ideal was to become an *arhat*, a person who achieves perfect insight into his or her true nature. Upon experiencing this nirvana, the *arhat* would be liberated from the wheel of birth, death, and rebirth. The *arhat* depicted the virtue of wisdom, or *prajna*, and the Theravada school considered wisdom as the highest virtue. In contrast, the Mahayana ideal was to become a *bodhisattva*, one who achieves nirvana yet decides to reenter the cycle of birth and death in order to help free others from suffering. The *bodhisattva* chooses to do so out of compassion for all sentient beings and therefore embodies both wisdom and compassion.

Eventually, all Buddhists have come to think of compassion as the consummate virtue. As the *bodhisattva* demonstrates, compassion not only means the ability to *feel* the suffering of another, but also requires that we *commit ourselves to alleviating* the suffering of others. In our selection at the end of the chapter, the seventh-century Buddhist Shantideva says of the *bodhisattva*, "He will not lay down his arms of enlightenment because of the corrupt generations of men, nor does he waver in his resolution to save the world because of their wretched quarrels."[22]

This commitment to alleviate suffering is ultimately what Buddhist ethics is all about. It requires us to detach ourselves from the illusion of permanence and self. The metaphysical principle of dependent origination supports this further by underscoring that the "other" is not really "other" but is also "myself." In this way, the suffering of the "other" is also "my" suffering.

This compassion represents the Middle Way. It avoids drawing a clear distinction between myself and the other so that I convince myself that "I" am not the "other." In such a way, I harden my heart to the experiences of the other. Compassion also avoids my identifying totally with the other so that I cannot effectively do anything to remedy the suffering.

Lovingkindness Lovingkindness requires cultivating the inner disposition to seek the well-being of all others. Though it is easier to be concerned about the well-being of those whom we love, those closest to us, Buddhists urge that we foster this same attitude toward *all* beings, even our enemies.

This virtue illustrates the Middle Way. On the one hand, total identification with the other interferes with the perspective necessary to ascertain others' best interests. On the other hand, lovingkindness requires that we avoid indifference to the other, in which case all that matters to me is my own satisfaction. This is challenging in our culture where self-absorption is nearly raised to the level of a virtue.

Lovingkindness is synonymous with the Buddhist and Hindu principle of *ahimsa*, or nonviolence. Shoko Asahara, however, interpreted Buddhist teachings in convenient ways. For instance, the Tibetan Tantra Vajrayana Buddhist notion of *phoa* means that prayers to the dying person can bring about positive karma for the soul of that person and help raise that soul to a higher spiritual level. Asahara gave a perverse twist to this idea. He claimed that killing persons who are evil or who participate in evil systems would release them from their negative karma, and would bring about needed positive karma for their souls. Those who kill these "evil" persons would actually be performing a sort of "mercy killing."[23] At the same time, those who do the killing would bring upon themselves spiritual merit.

In 1989, parents of Aum members claimed that their adult children were being brainwashed into donating monies. They hired a young and energetic lawyer, Tsutsumi Sakamoto, who vigorously spoke out against the cult. Within weeks, he, his wife, and their year-old child were missing from their Yokohama apartment. Six years later, months after the nerve gas attack, their remains were found in makeshift graves far from Yokohama. Confessions by Aum members revealed that six men murdered the family under Asahara's orders. His twisted use of *phoa* and his self-inflation completely contradicts the virtue of lovingkindness. It also runs counter to the virtue of sympathetic joy.

Sympathetic Joy Though it is easy to share in the happiness of those whom we love, can we share in the joy of strangers? Of enemies? This is what sympathetic joy requires. It assumes the deep ontological and metaphysical truth of interconnectedness. Sharing in another's happiness is a natural by-product of this interconnectedness since the so-called "other" is really "myself." *Pratityasamutpada* and *anatman* convey the Buddhist teaching that we are all of the same essence, and we all share the same Buddha nature.

As with the first two virtues, sympathetic joy represents the Middle Way. In the first place, it avoids indulging totally in the happiness of others, for this absorption is actually a disguised form of self-indulgence. In addition, it avoids the other extreme of indifference toward the happiness of another as well as resentment of another's good fortune.

Impartiality The *Visuddhimagga* tells of an encounter between bandits and four monks, or *bhikkus* (literally meaning "beggars").

> *Suppose a person is sitting in a place with a dear, a neutral, and a hostile person, himself being the fourth; then bandits come to him and say, "Venerable sir, give us a bhikku," and on being asked why, they answer "So that we may kill him and use the blood of his throat as an offering," then if that bhikku thinks "Let them take this one, or this one," he has not broken down the barriers. And also if he thinks "Let them take me but not these three," he has not broken down the barriers either. Why? Because he seeks the harm of him whom he wishes to be taken and seeks the welfare of the others only. But it is when he does not see a single one among the four people to be given to the bandits and he directs his mind impartially towards himself and towards those three people that he has broken down the barriers.[24]*

Impartiality means "breaking down the barriers." *Upekkha,* translated as "equanimity" and "neutrality," requires a "steady mind," one not swayed by any ties. This may well be the most difficult thing for us to achieve because we naturally tend to discern differences. Note the Middle Way here in which impartiality avoids the one extreme whereby we become so impartial that we have complete indifference toward all things and all creatures. It also avoids the other extreme of blatant prejudice. Buddhists were the most outspoken opponents of the Hindu caste system. The Buddha believed that this caste separation led to spiritual elitism. The *Brahman* caste, being the highest, may tend to view themselves as more spiritually advanced than the other castes. And the fifth caste, *panchamas,* or *harijans* ("children of God") as Mahatma Gandhi called them, continue to suffer intense discrimination in India.

Asahara at first proclaimed himself to be the new Buddha for Japan. In the late 1980s, he broadened his mission to include the whole world and added an apocalyptic flavor to his role. He viewed all nonbelievers, particularly America, much of Japan, rival Japanese religions, Jews, and Freemasons, as enemies of Aum. This divisive rhetoric provided the rationale for the cult's later terrorist actions. Instead of "breaking down the barriers," Asahara's teachings erected unbridgeable barricades, a far cry from the spirit of impartiality.

These virtues are relevant on a broader, political level. Burma's Aung San Suu Kyi, born in 1945, won the Nobel Peace Prize in 1991 for her defense of human rights against Burma's military regime. In the spirit of Buddhist and Gandhi's teachings regarding nonviolent resistance against corrupt government, she endured hunger strikes and imprisonment. She was finally released in July 1995 after six years in detention. As we see in the selection "In Quest of Democracy," she reminds us that the principles of good government have their basis in Buddhist teachings, as outlined in the "Ten Duties of Kings." These duties embody the supreme virtues. Aung San Suu Kyi remains a living legacy of Buddhist social ethics as she continues in her struggle for human rights.

■ WEAKNESSES IN BUDDHIST ETHICS

Does Buddhism justify acts of violence? It is clearly the case that the Aum Shinrikyo attack violates the principle of *ahimsa* and the prohibition of unnecessary harm. Yet, Buddhism's history is spotted with incidents where violence appeared to be sanctioned. In medieval Japan, there were territorial feuds among Buddhist temples and many Japanese Buddhists were armed for defense. Kofukuji Temple's monk-warriors enabled the temple to acquire control over the region of Nara for hundreds of years. In 1959, a Buddhist monk assassinated the prime minister of Sri Lanka, S. W. R. D. Bandaranaike, on supposedly religious grounds. And armed uprisings by Buddhist monks often led to the overthrow of corrupt governments in Sri Lanka. Buddhists have defended these uprisings as actions against corrupt governments and rulers.[25]

But where does Buddhism draw the line between those acts of violence that are justified and those that are not? Many Buddhists are opposed to any form of violence. The Dalai Lama, for one, prohibits the use of arms, even in cases of self-defense. And Buddhist teachings generally proscribe intentional killing. Yet if one kills in an act of self-defense, is the killing intentional? And what precisely distinguishes necessary from "unnecessary harm"? As we can see throughout this work, this lack of precise delineation exists in other traditions as well.

Another weakness is that the Buddhist virtue of impartiality seems rather naive in view of our human nature. We humans are naturally discriminatory. This is certainly the case from a purely phenomenological viewpoint. My visual perspective of Sanshiro Pond on the University of Tokyo campus is determined by where I am standing in relationship to the pond. My colleague, although he stands next to me, will naturally have a distinct and different visual perspective, even if only slight, since he cannot occupy my standpoint. My perspective and understanding regarding religious terrorism is my own because I am who I am and no one else can be me. It naturally differs from that of a militant member of Aum Shinrikyo.

Along these same lines, Buddhists urge us to assign equal moral weight to all sentient creatures. Is this not counterintuitive and even unnatural? Should we not love our family and friends more so than strangers? Is it not natural and actually more humane to treat those closer to us with greater moral weight?

Here is a third flaw. According to Buddhists, there is no independent self. Combined with *pratityasamutpada*, this notion helps to enhance the belief in our essential connectednes with each other. Yet, this same idea can also generate complete self-effacement. That is, stressing our collective identity could also lead to minimizing the importance of the individual.

A few days after the sarin gas attack, police raided Aum's chemical laboratory and weapons hideout in Kamikuishiki. When they broke into the complex, they came upon at least fifty Aum members who were so emaciated that they needed medical treatment. These members had given up their wordly possessions to the cult, and they also gave up their health, existing on meager provisions. If the Middle Way steers us away from the extreme positions, how does the belief in *anatman* embody this Middle Way? That is, how can we maintain the notion of *anatman* while striking a balance between collective and personal interests? It seems that Buddhist cultures have gone to the extreme in overemphasizing the collective at the expense of the personal.

■ STRENGTHS IN BUDDHIST ETHICS

The Middle Way urges us to live a life of harmony. When we get caught up in extreme positions, we lose sight of perspective. The Spanish philosopher George Santayana once defined a "fanatic" as "one who has redoubled his efforts, but who has also lost his goal." Buddhist ethics fundamentally warns us against falling victim to our own zeal. This message is particularly appropriate now as we continue to witness various forms of militant religious extremism. Groups such as the Palestinian Hamas, the Jewish Hizbollah, and Sikh separatists have justified their use of violence by an appeal to deep-seated religious convictions and moral worldview. In the 2000 report *Patterns of Global Terrorism,* the U.S. State Department listed the most notable international terrorist organizations, more than half of which had religious ties, groups like Aum Shinrikyo, al-Jihad, Hamas, Hizbollah, and al-Qaida.[26] Although group members may not view themselves as terrorists, their zeal may lead to the use of force to achieve their ends. It was their total dedication to their "Master" that led Aum Shinrikyo members to inflict the poisonous sarin gas upon innocent victims. Buddhist ethics, in its genuine sense, strongly cautions us against uncritically slipping into such extremism.

A second strength is that Buddhist ethics underscores the importance of cultivating good character. This is especially stressed through the notion of no-self. There is a natural link between sound insight—insight into our true nature—and good action. Buddhist ethics centers on *being* who we truly are, on getting in touch with our pure Buddha nature. It concerns itself less with *doing* the right thing. Indeed, Buddhist ethics reminds us that we cannot separate *what* we do from *who* we are. Whereas an emphasis upon rules can lead to various types of rule worship, Buddhist ethics' key premise rests upon cultivating good character and is thereby deeply humanistic.

Finally, as in Hinduism, there is a clear link between metaphysics and ethics. For example, *annica* affects how we see the universe—as fleeting and temporary—and thereby impacts upon moral action since the context of our actions is now a reality that we ought not to cling to. Seriously pondering the idea of *anatman* impacts upon how we behave with each other and naturally sustains a more selfless way of being in the world with others. And the notion of *pratityasamutpada* enjoins us to treat others as ourselves and vice versa. All this engenders a more collective, communal vision of both who we in essence are and how we should behave with each other. Furthermore, it provides a sound basis for an ecological ethic. Herein lies a most valuable component in Buddhist ethics. The metaphysical groundwork of interdependence acts as a necessary corrective to our overemphasis upon individualism. It reminds us that the moral community extends beyond self and carries us beyond the private sphere of family and friends. It compels us to think in terms of community and global accountability. And in stressing that all sentient creatures comprise our moral community, it is vitally relevant for a more ecological ethic.

■ NOTES

1. Haruki Murakami, *Underground: The Tokyo Gas Attack and the Japanese Psyche,* trans. Alfred Birnbaum and Philip Gabriel (New York: Vintage International, 2001, first published by Kodansha Ltd. as *Andaguraundo* in 1997), pp. 144–45.

2. Ibid., p. 284.

3. Note that this use of *dharma* is distinct from the Hindu term *dharma* in the last chapter where *dharma* refers to sound, moral conduct. Here, it refers to the Buddha's teachings. The text here uses the more common terms, even though some are in Pali and others are in Sanskrit.

4. There is much controversy in Japan regarding exorbitant rates of these rituals along with criticism that such temples are exploiting the parents' grief.

5. From Samyutta Nikaya, 5:421ff, in William Theodore de Bary, ed., *The Buddhist Tradition in India, China and Japan* (New York: Random House, Vintage Books, 1969), p. 16.

6. Sulak Sivaraksa, *Seeds of Peace: A Buddhist Vision for Renewing Society,* ed. Tom Ginsberg (Berkeley, CA: Parallax Press, 1992), p. 28.

7. From Samyutta Nikaya, in de Bary, p. 16.

8. Brackett, pp. 72–74.

9. See *Anguttaranikaya* 4, 49, 1, in Hans Wolfgang Schumann, *Buddhism: An Outline of Its Teachings and Schools* (Wheaton, IL: Theosophical Publishing House, 1973), p. 69.

10. See the *Abhayar_jakum_ra-sutta* and the discussion in David J. Kalupahana, *A History of Buddhist Philosophy: Continuities and Discontinuities* (Honolulu: University of Hawaii Press, 1992, pp. 50–52.

11. From Martin Heidegger, *Being and Time*, trans. J. Macquarrie and E. Robinson (Oxford: Blackwell, 1967), pp. 212–13.

12. From *Majjhima-nikaya* 1.415, in Kalupahana, p. 106.

13. Ibid.

14. One of the most important Buddhist meditative techniques is *vipassana*, which literally means "insight." This technique cultivates complete awareness of four domains: bodiliness, feelings and sensations, ideas, and mind.

15. Walpola Rahula, *What the Buddha Taught,* 2nd ed. (New York: Grove Press, 1974), pp. 48–49.

16. From the Buddha's Sermon at Benares, in Lucien Stryk, ed., *World of the Buddha: A Reader* (New York: Doubleday, Anchor Books, 1968), p. 50.

17. From the *Vinaya-pitaka*, in Stryk, pp. 211–12.

18. In Stryk, pp. 50–51.

19. He represents the Mahayana school of Buddhism, a school that resulted from a dispute within the early, more conservative school called Theravada. The Mahayana and the Theravada remain the two major Buddhist schools. The Mahayana school purports to be more faithful to the Buddha's genuine teachings and gave itself the name "Mahayana," which literally means "greater vehicle," "vehicle" referring to the Buddha's teachings. Mahayana labeled the original Theravada school "Hinayana," meaning "small vehicle." Nagarjuna was Mahayana's most brilliant apologist.

20. In *Anguttara-nikaya*, V.2, cited in Gunapala Dharmasiri, *Fundamentals of Buddhist Ethics* (California: Golden Leaves, 1989), p. 22.

21. See the discussion in Dharmasiri, pp. 42ff.

22. From Shantideva's *Compendium of Doctrine (Siksasamuccaya)*, in de Bary, p. 84.

23. See Mark Juergensmeyer, *Terror in the Mind of God: The Global Rise of Religious Violence* (Berkeley: University of California Press, 2000), p. 114.

24. From *Visuddhimagga*, 305–07, in Dharmasiri, p. 47.

25. See the discussion in Juergensmeyer, pp. 112–13.

26. See http://web.nps.navy.mil/~library/tgp/tgpndx.htm.

FROM COMPENDIUM OF DOCTRINE

◼

SHANTIDEVA

THE SUFFERING SAVIOR

The bodhisattva is lonely, with no . . . companion, and he puts on the armor of supreme wisdom. He acts himself, and leaves nothing to others, working with a will steeled with courage and strength. He is strong in his own strength . . . and he resolves thus:

"Whatever all beings should obtain, I will help them to obtain. . . . The virtue of generosity is not my helper—I am the helper of generosity. Nor do the virtues of morality, patience, courage, meditation and wisdom help me—it is I who help them.[1] The perfections of the bodhisattva do not support me—it is I who support them. . . . I alone, standing in this round and adamantine world, must subdue Māra, with all his hosts and chariots, and develop supreme enlightenment with the wisdom of instantaneous insight!" . . .

Just as the rising sun, the child of the gods, is not stopped . . . by all the dust rising from the four continents of the earth . . . or by wreaths of smoke . . . or by rugged mountains, so the bodhisattva, the Great Being, . . . is not deterred from bringing to fruition the root of good, whether by the malice of others, . . . or by their sin or heresy, or by their agitation of mind. . . . He will not lay down his arms of enlightenment because of the corrupt generations of men, nor does he waver in his resolution to save the world because of their wretched quarrels. . . . He does not lose heart on account of their faults. . . .

"All creatures are in pain," he resolves, "all suffer from bad and hindering karma . . . so that they cannot see the Buddhas or hear the Law of Righteousness or know the Order. . . . All that mass of pain and evil karma I take in my own body. . . . I take upon myself the burden of sorrow; I resolve to do so; I endure it all. I do not turn back or run away, I do not tremble. . . . I am not afraid . . . nor do I despair. Assuredly I must bear the burdens of all beings . . . for I have resolved to save them all. I must set them all free, I must save the whole world from the forest of birth, old age, disease, and rebirth, from misfortune and sin, from the round of birth and death, from the toils of heresy. . . . For all beings are caught in the net of craving, encompassed by ignorance, held by the desire for existence; they are doomed to destruction, shut in a cage of

---

1. These six, generosity (*dāna*), moral conduct (*śīla*), patience (*kṣānti*), courage or energy (*vīrya*), meditation (*dhyāna*) and wisdom (*prajñā*) are the *Pāramitās*, or virtues of the bodhisattva, which he has developed to perfection. Many sources add four further perfections—"skill in knowing the right means" to take to lead individual beings to salvation according to their several characters and circumstances (*upāyakauśalya*), determination (*pranidhāna*), strength (*bala*), and knowledge (*jñāna*). Much attention was concentrated on these perfections, especially on the Perfection of Wisdom (*Prajñāpāramitā*), which was personified as a goddess, and after which numerous Buddhist texts were named.

pain . . . ; they are ignorant, untrustworthy, full of doubts, always at logger-heads one with another, always prone to see evil; they cannot find a refuge in the ocean of existence; they are all on the edge of the gulf of destruction.

"I work to establish the kingdom of perfect wisdom for all beings. I care not at all for my own deliverance. I must save all beings from the torrent to rebirth with the raft of my omniscient mind. I must pull them back from the great precipice. I must free them from all misfortune, ferry them over the stream of rebirth.

"For I have taken upon myself, by my own will, the whole of the pain of all things living. Thus I dare try every abode of pain, in . . . every part of the universe, for I must not defraud the world of the root of good. I resolve to dwell in each state of misfortune through countless ages . . . for the salvation of all beings . . . for it is better that I alone suffer than that all beings sink to the worlds of misfortune. There I shall give myself into bondage, to redeem all the world from the forest of purgatory, from rebirth as beasts, from the realm of death. I shall bear all grief and pain in my own body, for the good of all things living. I venture to stand surety for all beings, speaking the truth, trustworthy, not breaking my word. I shall not forsake them. . . . I must so bring to fruition the root of goodness that all beings find the utmost joy, unheard of joy, the joy of omniscience. I must be their charioteer, I must be their leader, I must be their torchbearer, I must be their guide to safety. . . . I must not wait for the help of another, nor must I lose my resolution and leave my tasks to another. I must not turn back in my efforts to save all beings nor cease to use my pain. And I must not be satisfied with small successes."
[From Śikṣāsamuccaya, pp. 278–83]

THE LOST SON

A man parted from his father and went to another city; and he dwelt there many years. . . . The father grew rich and the son poor. While the son wandered in all directions [begging] in order to get food and clothes, the father moved to another land, where he lived in great luxury . . . wealthy from business, money-lending, and trade. In course of time the son, wandering in search of his living through town and country, came to the city in which his father dwelled. Now the poor man's father . . . forever thought of the son whom he had lost . . . years ago, but he told no one of this, though he grieved inwardly, and thought: "I am old, and well advanced in years, and though I have great possessions I have no son. Alas that time should do its work upon me, and that all this wealth should perish unused! . . . It would be bliss indeed if my son might enjoy all my wealth!"

Then the poor man, in search of food and clothing, came to the rich man's home. And the rich man was sitting in great pomp at the gate of his house, surrounded by a large throng of attendants . . . on a splendid throne, with a footstool inlaid with gold and silver, under a wide awning decked with pearls and flowers and adorned with hanging garlands of jewels; and he transacted business to the value of millions of gold pieces, all the while fanned by a fly-whisk. . . . When he saw him the poor man was terrified . . . and the hair of his body stood on end, for he thought that he had happened on a king or on some high officer of state, and had no business there. "I must go," he thought, "to the poor quarter of the town, where I'll get food and clothing without trouble. If I stop here they'll seize me and set me to do forced labor, or some other disaster will befall me!" So he quickly ran away. . . .

But the rich man . . . recognized his son as soon as he saw him; and he was full of joy . . . and thought: "This is wonderful! I have found him who shall enjoy my riches. He of whom I thought constantly has come back, now that I am old and full of years!" Then, longing for his son, he sent swift messengers, telling them to go and fetch him quickly. They ran at full speed and overtook him; the poor man trembled with fear, the hair of his body stood on end . . . and he uttered a cry of distress and exclaimed; "I've done you no wrong!" But they dragged him along by force . . . until . . . fearful that he would be killed or beaten, he fainted and fell on the ground. His father in dismay said to the men, "Don't drag him along in that way!" and, without saying more, he sprinkled his face with cold water—for though he knew that the poor man was his son, he realized that his estate was very humble, while his own was very high.

So the householder told no one that the poor man was his son. He ordered one of his servants to tell the poor man that he was free to go where he chose. . . . And the poor man was amazed [that he was allowed to go free], and he went off to the poor quarter of the town in search of food and clothing. Now in order to attract him back the rich man made use of the virtue of "skill in means." He called two men of low caste and of no great dignity and told them: "Go to that poor man . . . and hire him in your own names to do work in my house at double the normal daily wage; and if he asks what work he has to do tell him that he has to help clear away the refuse-dump." So these two men and the poor man cleared the refuse every day . . . in the house of the rich man, and lived in a straw hut nearby. . . . And the rich man saw through a window his son clearing refuse, and was again filled with compassion. So he came down, took off his wreath and jewels and rich clothes, put on dirty garments, covered his body with dust, and, taking a basket in his hand, went up to his son. And he greeted him at a distance and said, "Take this basket and clear away the dust at once!" By this means he managed to speak to his son. [And as time went on he spoke more often to him, and thus he gradually encouraged him. First he urged him to] remain in his service and not take another job, offering him double wages, together with any small extras that he might require, such as the price of a cooking-pot . . . or food and clothes. Then he offered him his own cloak, if he should want it. . . . And at last he said: "You must be cheerful my good fellow, and think of me as a father . . . for I'm older than you and you've done me good service in clearing away my refuse. As long as you've worked for me you've shown no roguery or guile. . . . I've not noticed one of the vices in you that I've noticed in my other servants! From now on you are like my own son to me!"

Thenceforward the householder called the poor man "son," and the latter felt towards the householder as a son feels towards his father. So the house-holder, full of longing and love for his son, employed him in clearing away refuse for twenty years. By the end of that time the poor man felt quite at home in the house, and came and went as he chose, though he still lived in the straw hut.

Then the householder fell ill, and felt that the hour of his death was near. So he said to the poor man: "Come, my dear man! I have great riches . . . and am very sick. I need someone upon whom I can bestow my wealth as a deposit, and you must accept it. From now on you are just as much its owner as I am, but you must not squander it." And the poor man accepted the rich man's wealth . . . but personally he cared nothing for it, and asked for no share of it, not even the price of a measure of flour. He still lived in the straw hut, and thought of himself as just as poor as before.

Thus the householder proved that his son was frugal, mature, and mentally developed, and that though he knew that he was now wealthy he still remem-bered his past poverty, and was still . . . humble and meek. . . . So he sent for the poor man again, presented him before a gathering of his relatives, and, in the presence of the king, his officers, and the people of town and country, he said: "Listen, gentlemen! This is my son, whom I begot. . . . To him I leave all my family revenues, and my private wealth he shall have as his own."
[From Saddharmapuṇḍarīka, 4.101 ff.]

IN QUEST OF DEMOCRACY

■

AUNG SAN SUUKYI

I

Opponents of the movement for democracy in Burma have sought to under-mine it by on the one hand casting aspersions on the competence of the people to judge what was best for the nation and on the other condemning the basic tenets of democracy as un-Burmese. There is nothing new in Third World gov-ernments seeking to justify and perpetuate authoritarian rule by denouncing liberal democratic principles as alien. By implication they claim for themselves the official and sole right to decide what does or does not conform to indige-nous cultural norms. Such conventional propaganda aimed at consolidating the powers of the establishment has been studied, analysed and disproved by political scientists, jurists and sociologists. But in Burma, distanced by several decades of isolationism from political and intellectual developments in the outside world, the people have had to draw on their own resources to explode the twin myths of their unfitness for political responsibility and the unsuitability of democracy for their society. As soon as the movement for democracy spread out across Burma there was a surge of intense interest in the meaning of the word 'democracy', in its history and its practical implications. More than a quarter-century of narrow authoritarianism under which they had been fed a pabulum of shallow, negative dogma had not blunted the perceptiveness or political alertness of the Burmese. On the contrary, perhaps not all that surprisingly, their appetite for discussion and debate, for uncensored information and objective analysis, seemed to have been sharpened. Not only was there an eagerness to study and to absorb standard theories on modern politics and political institutions, there was also widespread and intelligent speculation on the nature of democracy as a social system of which they had had little experience but which appealed to their common-sense notions of what was due to a civilized society. There was a spontaneous interpretative response to such basic ideas as representative government, human rights and the rule of law. The privileges and freedoms which would be guaranteed by democratic institutions were contemplated with understandable enthusiasm. But the duties of those who would bear responsibility for the maintenance of a stable democracy also provoked much thoughtful consideration. It is natural that a people who have suffered much from the consequences of bad government should be preoccupied with theories of good government.

Members of the Buddhist *sangha* in their customary role as mentors have led the way in articulating popular expectations by drawing on classical learning to illuminate timeless values. But the conscious effort to make traditional knowledge relevant to contemporary needs was not confined to any particular circle—it went right through Burmese society from urban intellectuals and small shopkeepers to doughty village grandmothers.

Why has Burma with its abundant natural and human resources failed to live up to its early promise as one of the most energetic and fastest-developing nations in South-east Asia? International scholars have provided detailed answers supported by careful analyses of historical, cultural, political and economic factors. The Burmese people, who have had no access to sophisticated academic material, got to the heart of the matter by turning to the words of the Buddha on the four causes of decline and decay: failure to recover that which had been lost, omission to repair that which had been damaged, disregard of the need for reasonable economy, and the elevation to leadership of men without morality or learning. Translated into contemporary terms, when democratic rights had been lost to military dictatorship sufficient efforts had not been made to regain them, moral and political values had been allowed to deteriorate without concerted attempts to save the situation, the economy had been badly managed, and the country had been ruled by men without integrity or wisdom. A thorough study by the cleverest scholar using the best and latest methods of research could hardly have identified more correctly or succinctly the chief causes of Burma's decline since 1962.

Under totalitarian socialism, official policies with little relevance to actual needs had placed Burma in an economic and administrative limbo where government bribery and evasion of regulations were the indispensable lubricant to keep the wheels of everyday life turning. But through the years of moral decay and material decline there has survived a vision of a society in which the people and the leadership could unite in principled efforts to achieve prosperity and security. In 1988 the movement for democracy gave rise to the hope that the vision might become reality. At its most basic and immediate level, liberal democracy would mean in institutional terms a representative government appointed for a constitutionally limited term through free and fair elections. By exercising responsibly their right to choose their own leaders the Burmese hope to make an effective start at reversing the process of decline. They have countered the propagandist doctrine that democracy is unsuited to their cultural norms by examining traditional theories of government.

The Buddhist view of world history tells that when society fell from its original state of purity into moral and social chaos a king was elected to restore peace and justice. The ruler was known by three titles: *Mahasammata*, 'because he is named ruler by the unanimous consent of the people'; *Khattiya;* 'because he has dominion over agricultural land'; and *Raja*, 'because he wins the people to affection through observance of the *dhamma* (virtue, justice; the law)'. The agreement by which their first monarch undertakes to rule righteously in return for a portion of the rice crop represents the Buddhist version of government by social contract. The *Mahasammata* follows the general pattern of Indic kingship in South-east Asia. This has been criticized as antithetical to the idea of the modern state because it promotes a personalized form of monarchy lacking the continuity inherent in the western abstraction of the king as possessed of both a body politic and a body natural. However, because the *Mahasammata* was chosen by popular consent and required to govern in accordance with just laws, the concept of government elective and *sub lege* is not alien to traditional Burmese thought.

The Buddhist view of kingship does not invest the ruler with the divine right to govern the realm as he pleases. He is expected to observe the Ten Duties of Kings, the Seven Safeguards against Decline, the Four Assistances to the People, and to be guided by numerous other codes of conduct such as the Twelve Practices of Rulers, the Six Attributes of Leaders, the Eight Virtues of Kings and the Four Ways to Overcome Peril. There is logic to a tradition which includes the king among the five enemies or perils and which subscribes to many sets of moral instructions for the edification of those in positions of authority. The people of Burma have had much experience of despotic rule and possess a great awareness of the unhappy gap that can exist between the theory and practice of government.

The Ten Duties of Kings are widely known and generally accepted as a yardstick which could be applied just as well to modern government as to the first monarch of the world. The duties are liberality, morality, self-sacrifice, integrity, kindness, austerity, non-anger, non-violence, forbearance and non-opposition (to the will of the people).

The first duty of liberality (*dana*) which demands that a ruler should contribute generously towards the welfare of the people, makes the tacit assumption that a government should have the competence to provide adequately for its citizens. In the context of modern politics, one of the prime duties of a responsible administration would be to ensure the economic security of the state.

Morality (*sila*) in traditional Buddhist terms is based on the observance of the five precepts, which entails refraining from destruction of life, theft, adultery, falsehood and indulgence in intoxicants. The ruler must bear a high moral character to win the respect and trust of the people, to ensure their happiness and prosperity and to provide a proper example. When the king does not observe the *dhamma*, state, functionaries become corrupt, and when state functionaries are corrupt the people are caused much suffering. It is further believed that an unrighteous king brings down calamity on the land. The root of a nation's misfortunes has to be sought in the moral failings of the government.

The third duty, *paricagga*, is sometimes translated as generosity and sometimes as self-sacrifice. The former would constitute a duplication of the first duty, *dana*, so self-sacrifice as the ultimate generosity which gives up all for the sake of the people would appear the more satisfactory interpretation. The concept of selfless public service is sometimes illustrated by the story of the hermit Sumedha who took the vow of Buddhahood. In so doing he who could have realized the supreme liberation of *nirvana* in a single lifetime committed himself to countless incarnations that he might help other beings free themselves from suffering. Equally popular is the story of the lord of the monkeys who sacrificed his life to save his subjects, including one who had always wished him harm and who was the eventual cause of his death. The good ruler sublimates his needs as an individual to the service of the nation.

Integrity (*ajjava*) implies incorruptibility in the discharge of public duties as well as honesty and sincerity in personal relations. There is a Burmese saying: 'With rulers, truth, with (ordinary) men, vows'. While a private individual may be bound only by the formal vows that he makes, those who govern should be wholly bound by the truth in thought, word and deed. Truth is the very essence of the teachings of the Buddha, who referred to himself as the *Tathagata* or 'one who has come to the truth'. The Buddhist king must therefore live and rule by truth'. The Buddhist king must therefore live and rule by truth, which is the perfect uniformity between nomenclature and nature. To deceive or to mislead the people in any way would be an occupational failing as well as a moral offence. 'As an arrow, intrinsically straight, without warp or distortion, when one word is spoken, it does not err into two.'

Kindness (*maddava*) in a ruler is in a sense the courage to feel concern for the people. It is undeniably easier to ignore the hardships of those who are too weak to demand their rights than to respond sensitively to their needs. To care is to accept responsibility, to dare to act in accordance with the dictum that the ruler is the strength of the helpless. In *Wizjaya*, a well-known nineteenth-century drama based on the *Mahavamsa* story of Prince Vijaya, a king sends away into exile his own son, whose wild ways had caused the people much distress: 'In the matter of love, to make no distinction between citizen and son, to give equally of loving kindness, that is the righteousness of kings.'

The duty of austerity (*tapa*) enjoins the king to adopt simple habits, to develop self-control and to practise spiritual discipline. The self-indulgent ruler who enjoys an extravagant lifestyle and ignores the spiritual need for austerity was no more acceptable at the time of the *Mahasammata* then he would be in Burma today.

The seventh, eighth and ninth duties—non-anger (*akkodha*), non-violence (*avihamsa*) and forbearance (*khanti*)—could be said to be related. Because the displeasure of the powerful could have unhappy and far-reaching consequences, kings must not allow personal feelings of enmity and ill will to erupt into destructive anger and violence. It is incumbent on a ruler to develop the true forbearance which moves him to deal wisely and generously with the shortcomings and provocations of even those whom he could crush with impunity. Violence is totally contrary to the teachings of Buddhism. The good ruler vanquishes ill will with loving kindness, wickedness with virtue, parsimony with liberality, and falsehood with truth. The Emperor Ashoka who ruled his realm in accordance with the principles of non-violence and compassion is always held up as an ideal Buddhist king. A government should not attempt to enjoin submission through harshness and immoral force but should aim at *dhamma-vijaya,*a conquest by righteousness.

The tenth duty of kings, non-opposition to the will of the people (*avirodha*), tends to be singled out as a Buddhist endorsement of democracy, supported by well-known stories from the *Jakatas*. Pawridasa, a monarch who acquired an unfortunate taste for human flesh, was forced to leave his kingdom because he would not heed the people's demand that he should abandon his cannibalistic habits. A very different kind of ruler was the Buddha's penultimate incarnation on earth, the pious King Vessantara. But he too was sent into exile when in the course of his strivings for the perfection of liberality he gave away the white elephant of the state without the consent of the people. The royal duty of non-opposition is a reminder that the legitimacy of government is founded on the consent of the people, who may withdraw their mandate at any time if they lose confidence in the ability of the ruler to serve their best interests.

By invoking the Ten Duties of Kings the Burmese are not so much indulging in wishful thinking as drawing on time-honoured values to reinforce the validity of the political reforms they consider necessary. It is a strong argument for democracy that governments regulated by principles of accountability, respect for public opinion and the supremacy of just laws are more likely than an all-powerful ruler or ruling class, uninhibited by the need to honour the will of the people, to observe the traditional duties of Buddhist kingship. Traditional values serve both to justify and to decipher popular expectations of democratic government. . . .

Where there is no justice there can be no secure peace. The Universal Declaration of Human Rights recognizes that 'if man is not to be compelled to have recourse, as a last resort, to rebellion against tyranny and oppression', human rights should be protected by the rule of law. That just laws which uphold human rights are the necessary foundation of peace and security would be denied only by closed minds which interpret peace as the silence of all opposition and security as the assurance of their own power. The Burmese associate peace and security with coolness and shade.

> The shade of a tree is cool indeed
> The shade of parents is cooler
> The shade of teachers is cooler still
> The shade of the ruler is yet more cool
> But coolest of all is the shade of the Buddha's teachings.

Thus to provide the people with the protective coolness of peace and security, rulers must observe the teachings of the Buddha. Central to these teachings are the concepts of truth, righteousness, and loving kindness. It is government based on these very qualities that the people of Burma are seeking in their struggle for democracy.

In a revolutionary movement there is always the danger that political exigencies might obscure, or even nullify, essential spiritual aims. A firm insistence on the inviolability and primacy of such aims is not mere idealism but a necessary safeguard against an Animal Farm syndrome where the new order after its first flush of enthusiastic reforms takes on the murky colours of the very system it has replaced. The people of Burma want not just a change of government but a change in political values. The unhappy legacies of authoritarianism can be removed only if the concept of absolute power as the basis of government is replaced by the concept of confidence as the mainspring of political authority: the confidence of the people in their right and ability to decide the destiny of their nation, mutual confidence between the people and their leaders and, most important of all, confidence in the principles of justice, liberty and human rights. Of the four Buddhist virtues conducive to the happiness of laymen, *saddha*, confidence in moral, spiritual and first. To instil such confidence, not by an appeal to the passions but through intellectual conviction, into a society which has long been wracked by distrust and uncertainty is the essence of the Burmese revolution for democracy. It is a revolution which moves for changes endorsed by universal norms of ethics.

In their quest for democracy the people of Burma explore not only the political theories and practices of the world outside their country but also the spiritual and intellectual values that have given shape to their own environment.

There is an instinctive understanding that the cultural, social and political development of a nation is a dynamic process which has to be given purpose and direction by drawing on tradition as well as by experiment, innovation and a willingness to evaluate both old and new ideas objectively. This is not to claim that all those who desire democracy in Burma are guided by an awareness of the need to balance a dispassionate, sensitive assessment of the past with an intelligent appreciation of the present. But threading through the movement is a rich vein of the liberal, integrated spirit which meets intellectual challenges with wisdom and courage. There is also a capacity for the sustained mental strife and physical endurance necessary to withstand the forces of negativism, bigotry and hate. Most encouraging of all, the main impetus for struggle is not an appetite for power, revenge and destruction but a genuine respect for freedom, peace and justice.

The quest for democracy in Burma is the struggle of a people to live whole, meaningful lives as free and equal members of the world community. It is part of the unceasing human endeavour to prove that the spirit of man can transcend the flaws of his own nature.

9

CONFUCIAN HARMONY

■

THE FOOTBINDING OF ELDER SISTER

Born in 1884, Chang Mo-chün was twenty-two when she enlisted as a revolutionary with T'ung Meng Hui. She later played a prominent role in China's 1911 Revolution, the uprising that witnessed the downfall of the Qing dynasty and the birth of the Republic of China. After the revolution, she followed in her father's footsteps as a leading administrator in education. In her autobiography, she also admits that she was an activist at an early age as she vividly recalls how horrified she was to discover, when she was seven, that her older sister had to have her feet bound. She describes the event:

> *Fifty years ago, the custom of footbinding was still very strong in our country, and Hunan Province was no exception. In my childhood, I used to sleep in the same bed with my older sister. One night I was awakened by the sound of chirping sobs; I saw her sitting up with the quilt over her shoulders, holding her feet in her hands and weeping, her face streaked with tears. She looked miserable. I asked her what was wrong. She replied in a low voice, "My feet have been bound by Nanny Ho. Although during the day it makes walking difficult, I can still bear the pain. But at night, my feet get hot under the quilt, and I can't sleep with the cutting pain." When she finished saying this, she swallowed her sobbing for fear of waking Mother.[1]*

Upon hearing this, Chang Mo-chün immediately reached out to unwrap the bindings from her sister and to relieve her of her agony. Her sister stopped her, declaring that she had to submit to the binding purely out of respect for custom. "Don't be in such a hurry. Haven't you heard Mother complaining about the difficulty of changing the evil customs of our country? Haven't you often heard our elders say 'Nobody is interested in lotus boats a foot long. . . . '?"[2] The next morning, Chang Mo-chün pleaded with her mother to unbind Elder Sister's feet. Although her mother agreed that the custom was both cruel and pointless, she urged her daughter to wait patiently for the right opportunity before protesting more publicly.

The opportunity came two years later. Chang Mo-chün and her entire family actively supported a campaign by an American missionary, Dr. Gilbert Reid, to eradicate the custom of footbinding. His Society for Natural Feet in Shanghai became a leading force in speaking out against the custom. So, at such a young age, Chang Mo-chün played a dynamic and active role in raising people's awareness of the harmful effects of footbinding and in eventually stamping out the custom. Of course, such a long-standing custom does not die easily, and she encountered many who slandered her and her family. In response to this defamy, she wrote this poem when she was nine:

> Sympathy for natural feet has moved
>   hundreds of spirits,
> Women can be seen rising from the depths
>   of the bitter sea of degradation;
> Nature's ways are best after all,
> The return to dignity begins with
>   emancipating the body.[3]

Footbinding did not originate with Confucianism. Nonetheless, is it congruent with Confucian teachings? Confucian teachings have had a durable effect upon Chinese culture. And during Imperial China, these teachings underscored the subordination of women in that men played a more active public and official role in society. Indeed, it is even alleged that Zhu Xi (or Chu Hsi), the founder and foremost philosopher of the later movement that reaffirmed Confucian teachings known as Neo-Confucianism, required women to have their feet bound when he became governor of Fujian province. He supposedly observed that women demonstrated an excess of sexual freedom, so he imposed a rule that all women bind their feet. After his decree went into effect, many women could only walk with the aid of a cane. Therefore, whenever women assembled at weddings and other celebrations, their presence was marked by the numerous canes lined up at these meetings. This gave rise to the term "forest of canes." Footbinding was intended to keep women in their place and to inhibit their free movement.[4]

Most scholars question whether this account of Xhu Xi is true. Even so, we do know that Zhu Xi sought to resuscitate the teachings of Confucius and that he stressed the dangers of relying upon feelings and passions rather than upon reason. As he writes in his well-known poem, "Self-Warning":

> The body has become light after ten years floating on the sea,
> Yet on the return, one still feels for the dimples on a girl's cheek.
> Nothing is more dangerous than human desire in this world, *Few
> have been spared being ruined once they get here!*[5] (emphasis added)

Zhu Xi wrote these verses after reading the minister Hu Quan's poem admiring the allure of a prostitute. For Zhu Xi, such dangerous passions were linked more so to women than to men. Does Zhu Xi's and the Confucian insistence upon the supremacy of reason do so to the extent of providing some grounds for the extreme oppression of women as demonstrated in footbinding? Is all this consonant with the original teachings of Confucius?

■ THE CONFUCIAN LEGACY

Confucian teachings continue to permeate Chinese civilization and culture. They have also provided for the Chinese an enduring mantle of moral precepts. This has been the case despite efforts such as Mao Zedong's "great proletarian cultural revolution" in 1966 to eradicate such "outmoded" vestiges of tradition. The humanitarian teachings of the great sage Confucius, along with those of his successors like the brilliant Mencius, continue to ring true in Chinese thought. In fact, a sort of Confucian "revival" seems apparent when one considers recent attempts by Deng Xiaoping and Singapore's former prime minister Lee Kuan Yew to restore and refurbish dilapidated Confucian shrines. Moreover, witness the surge of academic conferences devoted to the study of Confucianism and Confucian classics. In 1984, the China Confucius Foundation was established with headquarters in Beijing. In October 1989, Beijing, which is still Marxist-Leninist in ideology, also hosted a conference to celebrate Confucius's 2,540th birthday, months after the Tienanmen Square crackdown. And even though, as Chinese scholar William Theodore de Bary astutely points out, the government's interest in Confucianism may be more cosmetic than substantive, there was at least some public recognition of the Confucian heritage, hopefully opening the door to more sustained renewal.[6] Indeed, rather than cosmetic, the new twist in Confucian interest seems to lean in the direction of appealing to it as an antidote for what many Chinese perceive as the moral decay and corruption associated with Westernization.

CONFUCIUS

This current Confucian revival in order to restore moral and political order somewhat mirrors Confucianism's beginnings. Confucianism took root in times of extreme unrest, in what was called the Warring States Period. During this period, there was tension regarding the role of government and the nature of the relationship between rulers and the ruled. There was fragmentation and conflict in all corners of society. Confucius, or K'ung Fu Tzu (551–479 BCE), appeared at the right time. His insights gave order to the prevailing instability. And considered by Chinese as their greatest teacher, Confucius's lessons had a profoundly far-reaching effect throughout the course of Chinese history.

Confucius himself did not write the three classics that are attributed to him—the *Analects,* the *Great Learning,* and the *Doctrine of the Mean.* These were his sayings and lessons put together by his students after his death. All three classics are deeply humanistic in outlook, emphasizing our human responsibilities to each other in order to bring about and ensure an orderly and just society. Moreover, these responsibilities are moral in nature, and their proper actualization fosters a society that is morally upright. This notion is critical. Confucius's teachings can be viewed within the context of a vital twofold relationship. The first relationship is the inherently dynamic interaction between our character and our conduct. That is, we cannot separate who we *are* from what we *do.* Confucius sets forth the ideal of the "superior person," or *chün tzu.* The superior person, one who is morally upright, sustains an inner harmony between good character and good behavior. How can we bring about this harmony? Through the habitual practice of virtue. Habits produce a condition. The habit of virtuous deeds generates the condition of being virtuous. Here we see a striking similarity to Aristotle. Later, we will examine more closely the unique nature of Confucian virtues. For now, note the ultimate significance of the innate rapport between character and conduct.

The second relationship is equally critical and becomes all the more clear when we discuss the specific Confucian virtues of *jen* (humaneness) and *li* (propriety). When we examine them, we see that Confucian virtues are *social* in nature. They are inherently interrelational, having to do with who we are as individuals and who we are as part of a group. Confucius and his successors repeatedly tell us that we need to recognize the natural bond between the "I" and the "other." Indeed, Confucianism emphasizes that we can only properly understand who we are in terms of our relationships, and, without a doubt, the most fundamental relationship is that of family. This strong notion of relationality permeates Confucian thought. It challenges our Western conventional ontological assumptions. That is, the notion of identity is, for the Confucian, defined in terms of relationships. Suppose we ask a Confucian: Who are you in essence? The response would naturally be in terms of relationships—for example, "I am my wife's husband, my father's son, my mother's son, my brother's brother, my sisters' brother, my students' teacher, my friends' friend, and so on." Suppose we ask an American: Who are you in essence? The response would in turn be more privatized. That is, even though I as an American may recognize that I am imbedded in a web of relationships such as family, I also maintain that at my core, there is a private, independent self, separate from these relationships which I may therefore view as more incidental to my true identity. In contrast, for Confucians, our web of relationships is not peripheral to who we are, but in effect constitutes who we are. This idea of relationality is critical in order to understand Confucian ethics.

MENCIUS

We owe the transmission of Confucius's teachings not only to his students, but particularly to his celebrated successors Mencius (Meng-tzu, c. 372– c. 298 BCE) and Hsün-tzu (c. 313–238 BCE). Mencius, especially, not only reaffirms but elaborates more fully on Confucius's teachings. What we can call Confucianism today is in large measure due to the influence of Mencius. Furthermore, Mencius and Hsün-tzu sow the seeds of tension as to differing interpretations of the "Master." For example, Mencius stressed the innate goodness of human nature, in which case cultivating virtuous character through performing habitual good deeds should come easier for humans. On the other hand, Hsün-tzu argued that human nature is inherently weak and corrupt. This means that moral cultivation comes as a result of deliberate and difficult struggle and effort. Nevertheless, they both pass on Confucius' underlying message: that we can separate neither character from conduct, nor individual from collective. And they reaffirm the key Confucian virtues that we will later discuss, the virtues of *jen* and *li*.

Mencius is responsible for framing much of what the Confucian tradition believes regarding human nature, or *jen hsing*. For Mencius, human nature is not some static, passive entity. Instead, human nature is constantly in process. It is essentially dynamic, continually being remolded throughout our lives by what we do. Our conduct fashions our character, and character affects conduct, all in mutual interaction. And this does not occur in a vacuum. This ongoing mutual fashioning and refashioning of conduct and character takes place within a relational nexus. Human nature develops within the web of various relationships. Our relationships define who and what we become. And we are in constant process of becoming, never fully fashioned.

In order to bring home to us the idea that we are all born with the potential for good, Mencius believes that we have what he calls the "four beginnings," or four seeds that will bring about moral cultivation as long as we properly cultivate these four capacities. He illustrates this innate capacity and the four beginnings through his allegory of Niu Mountain, depicted in the selection at the end of the chapter. The story of Niu Mountain conveys Mencius's teaching that, like the mountain, our natures are essentially pure and good. We need to get back in touch with our original nature. We need to recognize the four beginnings within us and cultivate them throughout our lives.

NEO-CONFUCIANISM AND ZHU XI

Confucius's teachings certainly endured the test of time and the gauntlet of challenges from other doctrines such as Taoism and Buddhism, the increasing popularity of which forced a reassessment of the Master's teachings with special attention to the classics *Great Learning, Doctrine of the Mean,* and the *Book of Changes.* This reevaluation led to the movement known as Neo-Confucianism. Beyond any doubt, the most outstanding philosopher and representative of Neo-Confucianism is Zhu Xi (1130–1200). In revitalizing the spirit of the Master's teachings, he established a school that was later called the School of Principle, so named because of the emphasis he placed upon the idea of "principle," or *li. Li* literally means "order" or "pattern," and refers to the primordial order of the universe, the principle, or essence, of all things. Two earlier philosophers, the Ch'eng brothers, Ch'eng Yi (1033–1108) and Ch'eng Hao (1032–1085), described this *li* as the Principle of Heaven, or *t'ien-li.* Furthermore, they claimed that *li* is thereby inherently divine and good. And since this Heavenly Principle is the principle of all things, all things are also intrinsically good. Zhu Xi elaborated further on this idea, and more systematically examined the relationship between *li*, principle, and its material manifestation in all things, a material force known as *ch'i*.

Zhu Xi's analysis of the relationship between *li* and *ch'i* was to have the most comprehensive impact upon the unfolding of Chinese thought and culture, particularly because he highlighted the primacy of principle, *li*, over all things material. In effect, what this meant was that order or pattern, as the Heavenly principle itself, supersedes all else. Material force, *ch'i*, is subordinate to this principle. In order to discover this principle, Zhu Xi advocated the study and serious investigation of things, especially the primary sources such as the classic Confucian texts. In fact, Zhu Xi wrote leading commentaries on the four classics—*Analects*, *Great Learning*, *Doctrine of the Mean*, and the *Book of Changes*. His commentaries were considered authoritative and were required reading in examinations for all those seeking government posts. At the same time, Zhu Xi's commentaries influenced the development of Confucianism in both Korea and Japan, where Confucianism later became firmly established.

As the selection by Zhu Xi at the end of this chapter makes clear, the proper examination of principle, *li*, can only come about by utilizing reason and intellect. Moreover, reason and intellect supersede emotions and feelings. For Zhu Xi, the level of emotions remains corrupt and fallible, subject to whims. In contrast, the order reflected by *li* is better represented through reason. Bear in mind Zhu Xi's verse, "Nothing is more dangerous than human desire in this world." Confucian scholars then proceeded to link emotions, feelings, and that "dangerous" desire with women. Men, on the other hand, were viewed as being more capable of acting according to reason and principle. Although the story of Zhu Xi requiring women to bind their feet cannot be proven, there is certainly evidence that Neo-Confucians thought of women as more prone by their nature to desire.

Within this patriarchal context, footbinding perniciously stood out as a curious symbol of the oppression of women in China. There also came about a peculiar paradox. The notion of bound feet for woman was no doubt associated with a rigid male-dominated ethos and thereby signified a strict demarcation of women's societal roles and responsibilities. At the same time, this token of oppression became a highly fetishized object in that small feet represented feminine grace, beauty, and aristocracy, as opposed to large feet, which were viewed as ugly and as symbolizing lower-class status. "Golden lotuses" eventually acquired importance as eroticized objects and inspired intense sexual desire.

> It [the bound foot] formed an essential prelude to the sex act, and its manipulation excited and stimulated beyond measure. The eye rejoiced in the tiny footstep and in the undulating motion of the buttocks which it caused; the ear thrilled to the whispered walk, while the nose inhaled a fragrant aroma from the perfumed sole and delighted in smelling the bared flesh at closer range. The ways of grasping the foot in one's palms were both profuse and varied; ascending the heights of ecstasy, the lover transferred the foot from palm to mouth.[7]

In any case, can we conclude that Zhu Xi himself was a proponent of footbinding? Probably not. Particularly when we examine one of the most well known metaphors in Chinese philosophy—Zhu Xi's analogy of the pearl hidden in the mud. Only when the muddy water is cleared away does one come upon this pearl. The pearl in essence is clear and pure. It has been there all along. However, the mud has kept it hidden from us. In this fashion, Zhu Xi tells us that the pearl represents our true nature. And our true nature is pure. Through much of our lives, we think otherwise. Our nature is often hidden within waters of various circumstances and events, and these waters tend to obfuscate what we truly are. We are in essence good. The pearl lies in *all* of us, men *and* women.

Zhu Xi's metaphysics and ethics focus upon three fundamental ideas: *T'ai-chi, li,* and *ch'i. T'ai-chi* is the Heavenly Principle, the principle of all things that come into being and that pass away. It is the principle of the universe, the ultimate principle without which there would be nothing. *T'ai-chi* is necessarily dynamic, continually manifesting itself. This manifestation of the Heavenly Principle is *li.* (Note that this is not the same *li* as the *li* of propriety.) According to Zhu Xi, *li* is the natural self-expression of *T'ai-chi.* This dynamic quality of heavenly principles continues, for *li* in turn also needs to express itself, or rather to actualize itself in physical, material form. When it expresses itself in material form, it does so through material energy, called *ch'i. Ch'i* refers to material force. Physical bodies and matter thereby come about through this material force, *ch'i.*

This brings us to the all-important link among Heavenly Principle, *li,* and *ch'i.* Our essence is *li,* referred to as "principle." Yet in its essence, our essence is identical to Heavenly Principle. Since Heavenly Principle is inherently pure and good, our own essence, like the pearl, is the same. This is perhaps Zhu Xi's most important teaching: *li,* or principle, is identical to

Heavenly Principle. In essence, our true nature is good. *Ch'i*, or material force, however, is not perfect since it is associated with the physical and material. Indeed, physical manifestations by themselves fall short of the ideal that they attempt to reflect.

For example, we may entertain conceptually the ideal, perfect society. However, when we attempt to materialize this ideal, we discover that the society we fashion is less than ideal. Ideal teachings remain ideal because there is an inseparable chasm between the ideal and the real. There will always be a gap between a tradition's ideal teachings and that tradition's lived history. Can we ever physically draw a perfect circle? We may be able to conceptualize it, but physically manifesting it is another story.[8] Is there such a thing as a perfect island? We can imagine it, but cannot actualize it.[9] In like manner, whatever is materialized is, by its nature, imperfect. This means that material force, *ch'i*, contains within itself corrupt elements that act as barriers to perfection. *Ch'i* is symbolized by the muddy waters in which our perfect nature is immersed. Furthermore, according to Zhu Xi, there is no more poignant incarnation of our imperfection than our feelings, emotions, desires, and passions.

How is it possible to minimize the corruptive force of desires? In our selection at the end of this chapter, Zhu Xi advocates essentially two ways to clear up the "muddy water" so that we can discover our pearl. In order to discover our principle, what he refers to as "preserving the mind," we first need to cultivate the habit of sincerity and seriousness. We then need to apply this to the investigation of things. By investigating the nature of things, we hopefully discover their principle, and, in doing so, this will enable us to discover our own principle, our pearl, as well. And again, this pearl lies in women as well as in men.

Though Zhu Xi himself was most likely not a supporter of footbinding, his influence is evident in the Chinese tendency to downplay the expression of emotions. The celebrated anthropologist Francis L. K. Hsu points out how Chinese literature tends to pay less attention to the inner emotional state of characters. Instead, novels like the classic *The Romance of the Three Kingdoms* describe what characters do rather than what they feel.[10] This downplaying of emotions shows itself in the "love" relationship between men and women. Rather than madly falling in love and baring each other's hearts, the Chinese think of intimacy in terms of considering significant others besides themselves, namely, their respective families. Again, this brings us back to the importance of the wider sphere of relationships that, in effect, comprise one's identity for the Chinese. In other words, a pragmatic concern for their parents assumes more importance than how one feels. The American notion of "following one's heart" is strange. Because Chinese highlight practical considerations such as parental and sibling opinion more so than "following one's heart," Hsu goes on to claim that this explains why so-called "crimes of passion" are rare in Chinese society. He states, "Not only are sex crimes rare in China, but all crimes motivated by runaway emotions are equally unusual." [11] The point here is that concern for others, natural enough in a context that is strictly interpersonal, leads to minimizing the importance of expression of emotions. And absent this interpersonal nexus, individual emotions can become intensified.

To further illustrate this downplaying of emotions, consider the Academy Award–winning film directed by Ang Lee, *Crouching Tiger, Hidden Dragon*. It gained popular appeal due to its dazzling martial arts choreography and its story line surrounding the possession of the Green Sword of Destiny, owned by the famous warrior Li Mu Bai. The movie intriguingly depicts how all the main characters must come to terms with their worst enemy—themselves, their hidden desires. There are also two love stories throughout the film: the love between Li Mu Bai and Yu Shu Lien, and between Jen and "Gray Cloud," the desert bandit. The love that Li Mu Bai and Yu Shu Lien have for each other is pivotal. They know in their hearts how they deeply feel. Yet, custom, respect for the memory of a dear friend, and propriety assume precedence over the free display of their feelings. Moreover, reason prevails in their interaction so that they do not openly confess their feelings to each other as well. To do so would lead to "losing face" with each other. They keep their true hearts hidden.

It is only in one of the final scenes, when Li Mu Bai is dying from a poisoned dart, does he admit his feelings and "open his heart" to Yu Shu Lien. While desperately waiting for Jen to return with an antidote to the poison, Yu Shu Lien wisely urges Li Mu Bai to not waste his energies on speaking. Yet, he knows his end is near. He confesses to her, "I have wasted my entire life. I did find enlightenment, when at last I realized that I love you." Dying in her arms, he utters his last words:

> I'd rather be a ghost floating by your side, seven days, and be together, than enter Heaven, without you. My love for you will always keep me from being a lonely spirit.

The scene can be viewed as either tragic or liberating. It is tragic that throughout his life he did not feel free enough to admit his love for her. Only in dying does he do so, and then, it is too late. The scene is also liberating, for at least he did share with her his true heart, and did not die as he lived, keeping his heart hidden from her. In this sense, his dying does bring about an awakening for Yu Shu Lien as well. Li Mu Bai dies calmly in her arms, and she then instructs Jen, the impetuous aristocrat whose marriage was arranged but who truly loves Gray Cloud, to go to the mountain temple of Wu Dun where Gray Cloud is hiding. She tells Jen: "Promise that whatever path you take in this life, you will always be true to your heart."

Indeed, even during his own time, Zhu Xi's authority underwent challenges. The celebrated philosopher, Wang Yangming (1472–1529), claimed that Zhu Xi undermined the most important idea in the classic texts, namely, the fundamental identity of principle and mind. In which case, interior reflection, introspection, is a better path to discovering principle than the study of external things because mind is principle. Wang Yangming went even further with the radical claim that, because mind is in essence principle, genuine knowledge naturally expresses itself in action. He thereby equated knowledge and action. That is, genuine knowledge or insight naturally manifests itself in sincere action.

Wang Yangming's ideas did influence certain circles, particularly in Japan, and was, for a time, extremely popular. In time, however, Zhu Xi's brand of Neo-Confucianism became the dominant school, particularly when the Manchus took over China in 1644. Yet as the Manchu rule buckled in the nineteenth and twentieth centuries, so did Zhu Xi's supremacy. And when the Chinese Republic was officially established in 1912, Confucianism was no longer the official state belief. Confucianism suffered further setbacks during and after Mao Zedong's Cultural Revolution in the 1960s. Despite all this, however, the heart of Confucian ethics—its heralded virtues of *jen* and *li* and its esteemed values of family, filial piety, and loyalty—still prevail throughout China. More important, Chinese thought and culture still manifests the twin relationships we described above: the natural affinity between character and conduct, and the innate rapport between the individual and the collective.

■ CONFUCIAN VIRTUES

HUMANENESS: *JEN*

One of Confucius's most devoted students was Chung-kung. Not clear about the meaning of the virtue of *jen,* he asked his teacher. As we read in the *Analects:*

> Chung-kung asked about perfect virtue [jen]. The Master said, "It is, when you go abroad, to behave to every one as if you were receiving a great guest; to employ the people as if you were assisting

> at a great sacrifice; not to do to others as you would not wish done
> to yourself; to have no murmuring against you in the country, and
> none in the family."[12]

In this striking passage, Confucius stresses the fundamental relational aspect of the virtue of *jen*. *Jen* is the leading virtue in Confucian ethics. It often
translates as "humaneness" or as "benevolence," "human-heartedness,"
"compassion," and "goodness." Whatever term we choose, one thing is
certain: *Jen* embodies the intrinsic relationship between individual and
community. The above passage makes it clear that the genuine meaning of
virtue can only show itself within this relationship. As guests, we should
treat others as if they themselves were guests; employing entails being employed. This switching of roles becomes especially clear with Confucius's
Golden Rule, "not to do to others as you would not wish done to yourself,"
ultimately requiring that we place ourselves in the others' situations. And
this can only be done if we recognize the relational nexus in which we are
constantly engaged.

This becomes all the more clear when we study the Chinese character
for *jen*. It is actually a composite of two characters. The first character, 亻,
represents the individual human person. The second character, 二, represents the number "two." The ideogram for *jen*, 仁, therefore depicts the
notion of "one-being-with-others." This is our human situation. We do
not exist as isolated beings. Existing means interrelating.

Moreover, this interrelationship, this nexus of individual/communal,
means that in no way should individuality supersede community. Individual interests are in effect subordinate to the good of the community. This
is a critical feature in Confucian ethics. And for many contemporary Chinese, this is precisely the feature of Confucianism that sets the Chinese
apart from the Western emphasis upon individualism. One reason why
Confucianism may be witnessing a revival today is that it can be touted as
a healthy alternative to excessive individualism as manifest in the West.
Recall Mencius's teachings regarding the goodness of our original nature.
In light of this, he goes on further to stress that there is no better way to
cultivate our true nature than through exercising the virtue of *jen*. In fact,
Mencius adds a special quality to the meaning of *jen*, and he extends its
meaning into "compassion." For Mencius, the greatest virtue is *jen*. As
compassion, it means our ability to relate to and identify with the other, to
place ourselves in the other's position.

Given this idea of *jen* as humaneness, it is hard to see how the now-
outmoded and outlawed practice of footbinding could have been sanctioned

by Confucian teachings. The practice itself, which endured for over a thousand years, was anything but humane. The practice was often brutally painful and with long-term injurious health consequences. The initiates were young girls usually between five and seven. And it was usually the mother who performed this procedure upon her daughter, whose feet underwent intense inflammation. The young girl's pain would last for over a year until eventually the nerves would be deadened in the feet. And repeated rebindings led to decaying flesh and broken bones so that the end result would be the "golden lotus," an ideally aesthetic foot size of three inches! The scholar Howard Levy describes the process:

> *The success or failure of footbinding depended on skillful application of a bandage around each foot. The bandage, about two inches wide and ten feet long, was wrapped in the following way. One end was placed on the inside of the instep, and from there it was carried over the small toes so as to force the toes in and towards the sole. The large toe was left unbound. The bandage was then wrapped around the heel so forcefully that heel and toes were drawn closer together. The process was then repeated from the beginning until the entire bandage had been applied. The foot of the young child was subjected to a coercive and unremitting pressure, for the object was not merely to confine the foot but to make the toes bend under and into the sole and bring the sole and heel as close together as was physically possible.[13]*

To repeat, *jen* embodies the relational characteristic of Confucian virtue. It is not meant as virtue in a private sense. We can therefore assert that virtue in the Confucian sense is equivalent to social virtue. There is no more poignant example of this relational, social feature of virtue than what Confucians consider to be the Five Relationships: ruler and subject; father and son; husband and wife; elder brother and younger brother; friend and friend. Since these five relationships, in a sense, form the cornerstone of Confucian society and ethical behavior, we will examine these in a separate section. What we need to keep in mind at this point is that these relationships reflect the critical need to recognize and sustain the individual/communal nexus. That is, this urges us all the more to steer clear of viewing the individual solely as individual, as private. This cautions us against overemphasizing the individual at the price of the collective to which the individual belongs.

PROPRIETY: *LI*

The virtue of *li* is perhaps best understood as the other side of the coin of *jen*. That is, *jen*, as humaneness, needs to be made manifest in our actions. *Li* is this concretized expression of humaneness. *Li* literally means "rites," "ritual conduct," and "propriety." Propriety encompasses all of these. The general meaning behind the term, "propriety," is that we act in a decent fashion, with etiquette and good manners, good judgment and discretion. More specifically, how do we do this? Through acting in accordance with the codes of conduct and rules that befit the situation. The classic Confucian text *Li Chi* (*Book of Rites*) outlines in very precise fashion specific rules and codes of behavior for various settings such as family interactions, marriages, festivals, and funerals. All this is critical for social cohesion. As the scholar Roger Ames points out, "Ritual practice is the rhyme and rhythm of society."[14] Furthermore, acting according to these rules and codes should not simply be done perfunctorily. They must be actualized with the proper attitude and disposition. Only with the right interior disposition can they be virtuous. And this is where *jen*, humaneness, enters in. They must be performed in the spirit of humaneness and benevolence. As the Master states, "Fine words and an insinuating appearance are seldom associated with true virtue."[15]

Hsün-tzu was particularly instructive regarding the importance of *li*. Because he downplayed the possibility that we are innately good and argued that we are more prone to corruption, *li* plays a critical role in bringing about societal order and well-being. Social stability depends upon the self-restraint and discipline that *li* demands. There are essentially two functions of *li:* to order, that is, to bring about stability, and, to "ennoble," to enhance and uplift.[16] *Li* brings about order and social stability. More important, it orders, or guides, our desires and emotions. It is important to stress that *li* does not repress or suppress emotions, but instead channels them in a proper way. At the same time, *li* channels our emotions in ways that are creative and enriching. Aesthetics, whether through poetry, calligraphy, painting, music, martial arts, or other forms of creativity, raises our passions to an acceptable and noble level. In this way, desires, feelings, and emotions are creatively transformed.

As with the virtue of humaneness, the virtue of propriety assumes special weight when measured within the context of relationality. This is the case for two reasons. To begin with, acting according to the virtue of propriety requires steadfast discipline. Propriety demands self-restraint. It means behaving appropriately, in the right way, in specific situations. This self-restraint and discipline tempers one's character and thus works to cultivate moral character. Second, this personal discipline and moral development is crucial to bring about social harmony. Personal discipline leads to public symmetry. This is critical. The participation in social cohesion through propriety is an ongoing, creative process and not some static formality. Again, we see that all-important symbiosis between individual and collective embodied in the virtue of propriety. Confucians view individual identity within a collective syntax. And within this syntax, duties and obligations to sustain social harmony are all-important.

Moreover, as we see in the Five Relationships, this collective cohesion is ordered according to hierarchy. The Five Relationships denote the importance of special relationships. Among the five relationships, there is no mention of relationships with strangers. These relationships do not urge us to treat everyone alike as equals. What these Five Relationships convey is that not everyone is equal. Everyone is to be treated with respect, but not equally, for there are hierarchies in relationships. This is why introductions, particularly in Japan, usually require the sharing of business cards. The sharing of business cards is rather formal and almost ritualized. Yet it is an important way to break through the ice and know others' names and occupations and vice versa. Once this ice is broken, then further connections become possible. One thing is certain: Once a relationship has been formed, then expectations of trust and mutual obligations accompany the relation.

This emphasis upon hierarchy is most apparent among Chinese, Japanese, and Koreans, all influenced by Confucianism, with their strict rules regarding the proper ways to speak to and address those in authority, superiors, and family superiors. True courtesy requires abstaining from expressions of familiarity. For instance, by using third-person terms and titles apart from intimates and close friends, a proper decorum is sustained. This decorum is necessary in hierarchical relations. The violation of this "space" is also a violation of "face" among the Chinese, Japanese and Koreans. The notion of "face" is all-important in a culture infused with the importance of relationality. "Face" thereby has to do with how an individual appears before others, these others being those outside of the sphere of family, intimates, and close friends. The expression "saving one's face" means being able to present oneself to the public in a way that is appropriate. As we said, in a relational context, "face" is significant—it focuses upon the manner in which the individual presents him- or herself to others. And in a hierarchical context such as Confucianism, face is also significant. The higher one's status, the more responsive one is to the demands of "saving face," for there is more at stake should one "lose face," or not act appropriately. We see this emphasis upon "saving face" as a central value in Confucian cultures.

Keep in mind this emphasis upon social harmony. Confucius asserted that "The exemplary person seeks harmony rather than agreement; the small person does the opposite."[17] The metaphor of "harmony" is insightful. In music, harmony can only occur with the right combination of different notes. There can be no harmony if all of the notes are B-flat. However, we can play together G, E-flat, and B-flat to both form a chord and produce harmony. The same occurs within the social setting. Each person is, as a distinct note, unique. In cooperating with other unique persons, each person contributes his or her original share to the whole. *Li*, in the proper sense, denotes this social harmony, a community as a constant creative process that unfolds through each person's distinct participation in whatever the situation calls for. Proper participation is what is meant by *li*. As Ames states:

> *The community is a project of disclosure. This inseparability of personal integrity and social integration collapses the means/end distinction, rendering each person both an end in himself or herself and a condition or means for everyone else in the community to be what they are. The model is one of mutuality.*[18]

Li reminds us of the interpersonal quality of who we are. According to Confucians, the human being is not comprised of some sort of static essence, a "being" in the sense of some private entity. Rather than possessing an individual essence, human beings are defined more so by what they *do*, how they *behave*, how they *conduct* themselves. In this respect, we are always in process. This dynamic quality to who and what we are underlies what is meant by character. As we said above, this was an idea more fully elaborated by Mencius in pointing out our potential to come to proper fruition due to our essentially good disposition.

■ FILIAL PIETY AND FAMILY

The most fitting application of both *jen* and *li* lies in the centrality of family. For Confucians, the cultivation of virtue begins with the family. In particular, it lies in the dedication and service of children to their parents. This is the principle of filial piety, which clearly embodies *jen*. Filial piety, a lifetime of devotion to one's parents, is the cornerstone of Confucian society.

Society rises or falls according to the degrees to which respect is demonstrated to one's parents. To this day, the *Classic of Filial Piety* is a time-honored text and advises us:

> Therefore to be without love of parents and to love other men [in their place] means to be a "rebel against virtue"; to be without reverence for parents and to reverence other men means to be a "rebel against sacred customs."[19]

Filial piety is the glue that binds parents and children with each other as well as the basis for the relationship between husband and wife. Moreover, the duties and obligations that are enshrined within the Chinese family tend to even themselves out over a lifetime. That is, the matrix of familial duties remains reciprocal. As a child, one has specific obligations toward one's parents. When that same child later becomes a parent, the same set of duties are afforded him or her. That is, familial duties naturally balance themselves out. This only makes sense because duties and obligations are established due to relationality. The relation defines the individual and how that individual ought to behave. In this sense, filial piety also extends beyond the family borders, affecting how we ought to interact with friends, in the workplace, and in government.

The interpersonal quality of virtue is indeed explicit in how the Chinese construe family. To illustrate, our American culture places more prominence upon the nuclear family than upon the extended family, in which case the parents assume their sole prerogative over their children. Parents therefore tend to resent interference by their parents when it comes to authority over their children. The parents, not the grandparents, have overriding authority over their children. However, within the Chinese family, the web of relations is wider, so that it is not uncommon for grandparents to exercise authority over their grandchildren. What we may think of as outright "interference" is often construed as natural "involvement" by the grandparents. Francis Hsu comments on this interesting familial distinction:

> The more exclusive and omnipresent parental control in America makes the parental image stand out above all else in the mind of the young. A child's attitude, whether of dependence or rebellion, becomes focused upon the parents, since they are the sole sources of reward or punishment. The American family pattern thus nourishes a personality marked by strong emotions and preoccupation with the self.

The diluted and less lineal parental control in China evokes early in life an appreciation of the differences between changing external circumstances. Since parents are not the sole determinants in punishment or reward, they do not become the chief oppressors or only gods. Therefore, there is a less turbulent opposition or paralyzing attachment between parents and children. The parental image in the mind of the individual has its proper place with those of other relatives. The Chinese family pattern is thus the source of a personality characterized by more moderate emotions and a desire for harmony with the external world.[20]

In the family, *li* is expressed through the reciprocity of rights and duties that plays itself out throughout family members' lives. For instance, the parents' commitment to care for their children later pays itself off when grown children assume a similar dedication to care for their aging parents. And the ties of relationality provide the ground for these obligations. In other words, parents do not devote themselves to their children simply out of love, but primarily because it is their duty as parents. In like manner, adult children do not care for their aging parents solely out of reciprocity, that is, because their parents cared for them. They do so out of respect for their parents *as parents.* This sort of familial security is what filial piety is all about. Thus, filial piety glues the family together. In like manner, the Chinese show respect for the elderly *because* they are elders. This is a key value. The Chinese cherish tradition and history. The elderly are living inheritors of history. They are valued intrinsically for being elderly. This same respect for the elderly extends itself into respect for the elder child or sibling. This explains why birth order is especially important in Chinese families.

We see this also in Japan and Korea, cultures that have been heavily influenced by Confucian teachings. There we see this same display of respect for the elderly. Whenever I visit Japan, I am always struck by how seats on crowded trains and busses are often yielded to the elderly. And in Japan, this respect for the elderly shows itself in the respect and deference for those in authority.

■ WEAKNESSES IN CONFUCIAN ETHICS

Let us review again the five cardinal relationships (*wu lun*):

- ruler and subject
- father and son

- husband and wife

- elder brother and younger brother

- friend and friend

These relationships clearly embody the meaning of virtue as essentially social, so that virtue only makes sense within an interpersonal tapestry. On the one hand, the critic can argue that in essence all virtues have social features. Still, in Confucian thought, the defining quality of a virtue lies precisely in its social, interpersonal meaning. Even so, note the strong patriarchal thrust in four of these five relations: ruler, father, husband, and elder brother, so that in marriage, for example, even though husband and wife show their respective deference for each other, the wife's status remains subordinate. As the Chinese saying goes, "The husband sings and the wife harmonizes."

There is still strong evidence of China's long history of lingering patriarchy. Since family-planning policies have restricted the number of children in the home to two, the ideal is still to have sons instead of daughters, and this has certainly been supported and sustained through Confucian teachings. There is a high rate of abortions among women who discover that their fetus is female, and female infanticide is also not uncommon. Nonetheless, would it be fair to consider Chinese, and more particularly Confucian culture, as unjustly patriarchal? China has indeed recently undergone quite a bit of modernization, especially in the past few decades after the failure of Mao's Cultural Revolution. Western forms of capitalism have made significant headway in Hong Kong, Taiwan, Singapore, and Beijing. At the same time, Chinese society has become more exposed to feminist movements, and voices claiming equal rights among women continue to be heard. China today is a far cry from the past when women were raised to acknowledge their "three obediences": (1) to one's father prior to marriage, (2) to one's husband during marriage, and (3) to one's son upon the husband's death. These "three obediences" today are considered archaic and no longer viewed as virtues.

■ STRENGTHS IN CONFUCIAN ETHICS

A most valuable component of Confucian ethics lies in its notion of self as relational. This is extremely vital and acts as a necessary counterweight to the Western idea of self as privatized, individual, and strictly independent. The Confucian, relational idea of self compels us to reassess our own ideas of identity. Furthermore, it reminds us of the necessary link between ontology and ethics in that views of personal identity, or self, naturally affect views of what is construed as right and wrong behavior.

To illustrate, this has far-reaching implications with respect to how we think of human and moral "rights." As long as our fundamental vision of self remains privatized, as is generally the case in many Western traditions, conflicts surrounding the clash of rights between individual entities—for example, the fetus and the mother, or the patient and the physician—remain difficult to resolve. Viewing self within a more relational scale, however, helps to construct such conflicts in a different light. For instance, the Confucian notion of self as relational helps us view environmental issues in a more all-encompassing perspective. The Confucian view of self as relational enables us to realize that the contrary notion of a solipsistic self is fundamentally impoverished. In this fashion, Confucian moral teachings, with their emphasis upon virtue as fundamentally social in nature, informs us of our innately collective situation, one that dynamically involves flesh-and-blood human interaction.

Is the Confucian emphasis upon relationality consistent with the practice of footbinding? Most Westerners view the custom as barbaric, torturous, and certainly a violation of the human rights and dignity of women. Yet if human nature is relational, in what respect can we weigh alleged human rights violations? Reexamining the ontological groundwork of a culture, in the sense of individual or personal identity, thus becomes critical. In Chinese culture, indelibly infused with Confucian ideas of human existence as decidedly relational, notions of personal, individual self-determination, or autonomy, have little place. Instead of underscoring rights, as we do in Western cultures, Chinese stress sets of mutual duties and loyalties and strict divisions of labor. This means that if we are to criticize the practice of footbinding, our critique carries more weight if expressed in terms of the violation of these duties and obligations, rather than as a violation of individual rights.

This does not at all mean that we should think of Confucian ethics as the magic bullet to moral crises. Indeed, Confucian ethics itself can learn from non-Confucian components, such as the Western traditions' respect for individualism. Nevertheless, reassessing our view of self through a Confucian lens could well be a necessary first step to cross-cultural dialogue and understanding.

■ NOTES

1. Chang Mo-chün, "Opposition to Footbinding," in Li Yu-ning, ed., *Chinese Women Through Chinese Eyes* (Armonk, NY: M. E. Sharp, East Gate Book, 1992), pp. 125–26.

2. Ibid., p. 126.

3. This account is described in Chang Mo-chün.

4. Most scholars dispute the idea that Zhu Xi required footbinding. See the account in Wang Ping, *Aching for Beauty: Footbinding in China* (Minneapolis: University of Minnesota Press, 2000), p. 48.

5. Cited in Wang Ping, p. 47.

6. See William Theodore de Bary, "The New Confucianism in Beijing," *The American Scholar* 64, no. 2 (1995, Spring): 175–190.

7. Howard Levy, *Chinese Footbinding: The History of a Curious Erotic Custom* (New York: Bell, 1967), p. 34.

8. The contemporary Chinese philosopher Fung Yu-lan uses this example to illustrate the distinction between *li* and *ch'i.*

9. This example is used by Guanilo of Marmoutier to criticize Anselm's (ca. 1033–1109) ontological argument for the existence of God.

10. Francis L. K. Hsu, *Rugged Individualism Reconsidered: Essays in Psychological Anthropology* (Knoxville: University of Tennessee Press, 1983), p. 61.

11. Ibid., p. 62.

12. James Legge, trans., Analects, XII, 2, in *Confucius: Confucian Analects, The Great Learning, and the Doctrine of the Mean* (Oxford: Clarendon Press, 1893; New York: Dover, 1971), p. 251.

13. Levy, pp. 23, 26.

14. Roger T. Ames, "Rites as Rights: The Confucian Alternative," in Leroy S. Rouner, ed., *Human Rights and the World's Religions* (Notre Dame, IN: University of Notre Dame Press, 1988), p. 200.

15. Legge, Analects, I, 3, p. 139.

16. Antonio Cua characterizes the function of *li* as "ennobling." See Antonio S. Cua, "The Concept of *Li* in Confucian Moral Theory," in Robert E. Allinson, *Understanding the Chinese Mind: The Philosophical Roots* (Hong Kong: Oxford University Press, 1989), p. 218.

17. Legge, Analects, XIII, p. 23.

18. Ames, p. 201.

19. Cited in Michael C. Brannigan, *Striking a Balance: A Primer in Traditional Asian Values* (New York: Seven Bridges Press, 2000), p. 206.

20. Hsu, p. 64.

NIU MOUNTAIN

MENCIUS

6A:8. Mencius said, "The trees of the Niu Mountain[1] were once beautiful. But can the mountain be regarded any longer as beautiful since, being in the borders of a big state, the trees have been hewed down with axes and hatchets? Still with the rest given them by the days and nights and the nourishment provided them by the rains and the dew, they were not without buds and sprouts springing forth. But then the cattle and the sheep pastured upon them once and again. That is why the mountain looks so bald. When people see that it is so bald, they think that there was never any timber on the mountain. Is this the true nature of the mountain? Is there not [also] a heart of humanity and righteousness originally existing in man? The way in which he loses his originally good mind is like the way in which the trees are hewed down with axes and hatchets. As trees are cut down day after day, can a mountain retain its beauty? To be sure, the days and nights do the healing, and there is the nourishing air of the calm morning which keeps him normal in his likes and dislikes. But the effect is slight, and is disturbed and destroyed by what he does during the day. When there is repeated disturbance, the restorative influence of the night will not be sufficient to preserve (the proper goodness of the mind). When the influence of the night is not sufficient to preserve it, man becomes not much different from the beast. People see that he acts like an animal, and think that he never had the original endowment (for goodness). But is that his true character? Therefore with proper nourishment and care, everything grows, whereas without proper nourishment and care, everything decays. Confucius said, "Hold it fast and you preserve it. Let it go and you lose it. It comes in and goes out at no definite time and without anyone's knowing its direction.' He was talking about the human mind."

6A:9. Mencius said, "Don't suspect that the king[2] lacks wisdom. Even in the case of the things that grow most easily in the world, they would never grow up if they were exposed to sunshine for one day and then to cold for ten

---

1. Outside the capital of the state of Ch'i.
2. Probably King Hsüan of Ch'i (r. 342-324 B.C.).

days. It is seldom that I have an audience with him, and when I leave, others who expose him to cold arrive. Even if what I say to him is taking root, what good does it do? Now chess playing is but a minor art. One cannot learn it unless he concentrates his mind and devotes his whole heart to it. Chess Expert Ch'iu is the best chess player in the whole country. Suppose he is teaching two men to play. One man will concentrate his mind and devote his whole heart to it, doing nothing but listening to Chess Expert Ch'iu's instructions. Although the other man listens to him, his whole mind is thinking that a wild goose is about to pass by and he wants to bend his bow, adjust the string to the, arrow, and shoot it. Although he is learning along with the other man, he will never be equal to him. Is that because his intelligence is inferior? No, it is not."

6A:10. Mencius said, "I like fish and I also like bear's paw. If I cannot have both of them, I shall give up the fish and choose the bear's paw. I like life and I also like righteousness. If I cannot have both of them, I shall give up life and choose righteousness. I love life, but there 'is something I love more than life, and therefore I will not do anything improper to have it. I also hate death, but there is something I hate more than death, and therefore there are occasions when I will not avoid danger. If there is nothing that man loves more than life, then why should he not employ every means to preserve it? And if there is nothing that man hates more than death, then why does he not do anything to avoid danger? There are cases when a man does not take the course even if by taking it he can preserve his life, and he does not do anything even if by doing it he can avoid danger.[3] Therefore there is something men love more than life and there is something men hate more than death. It is not only the worthies alone who have this moral sense. All men have it, but only the worthies have been able to preserve it.

Suppose here are a small basket of rice and a platter of soup. With them one will survive and without them one will die. If you offer them in a loud and angry voice, even an ordinary passer-by will not accept them, or if you first tread on them and then offer them, even a beggar will not stoop to take them. What good does a salary of ten thousand bushels do me if I accept them without any consideration of the principles of propriety and righteousness? Shall I take it because it gives me beautiful mansions, the service of a wife and concubines, and the chance gratitude of my needy acquaintances who receive my help? If formerly I refused to accept the offer (of rice and soup) in the face of death and now I accept for the sake of beautiful mansions, if formerly I refused the offer in the face of death and now accept for the sake of the service of a wife and concubines, if formerly I refused the offer and now accept for the sake of the gratitude of my needy acquaintances, is that not the limit? This is called casting the original mind away."[4]

---

3. Cf. *Analects*, 15:8.
4. According to Chu Hsi, this is the original mind of shame and dislike.

6A:11. Mencius said, "Humanity is man's mind and righteousness is man's path. Pity the man who abandons the path and does not follow it, and who has lost his heart and does not know how to recover it. When people's dogs and fowls are lost, they go to look for them, and yet, when they have lost their hearts, they do not go to look for them. The way of learning is none other than finding the lost mind.

6A:12. Mencius said, "Suppose there is a man whose fourth finger is crooked and cannot stretch out straight. It is not painful and it does not interfere with his work. And yet if there were someone who could straighten out the finger for him, he would not mind going as far as to the states of Ch'in and Ch'u because his finger is not like those of others, yet he does not hate the fact that his mind is not like those of others. This is called ignorance of the relative importance of things."[5]

6A:13. Mencius said, "Anybody who wishes to cultivate the *t'ung* and *tzu* trees, which may be grasped by one or both hands, knows how to nourish them. In the case of their own persons, men do not know how to nourish them. Do they love their persons less than the *t'ung* and *tzu* trees? Their lack of thought is extreme."

6A:14. Mencius said, "There is not a part of the body that a man does not love. And because there is no part of the body that he does not love, there is not a part of it that he does not nourish. Because there is not an inch of his skin that he does not love, there is not an inch of his skin that he does not nourish. To determine whether his nourishing is good or not, there is no other way except to see the choice he makes for himself. Now, some parts of the body are noble and some are ignoble; some great and some small. We must not allow the ignoble to injure the noble, or the smaller to injure the greater. Those who nourish the smaller parts will become small men. Those who nourish [the greater parts will become great men. A gardener who neglects his *t'ung* and *tzu* trees and cultivates thorns and bramble becomes a bad gardener. A man who takes good care of his finger and, without knowing it, neglects his back and shoulders, resembles a hurried wolf.[6] A man who only eats and drinks is looked down upon by others, because he nourishes the smaller parts of his body to the injury of the greater parts. If he eats and drinks but makes no mistake of injuring the greater parts of his body, how should his mouth and belly be considered merely as so many inches of his body?"

6A:15. Kung-tu Tzu asked, "We are all human beings. Why is it that some men become great and others become small?" Mencius said, "Those who follow the greater qualities in their nature become great men and those who follow the smaller qualities in their nature become small men." "But we are all

---

5. This interpretation is according to Sun Shih (962–1033), subcommentary on Chao Ch'i's commentary in the *Meng Tzu chu-shu* (Subcommentary and Commentary on the *Book of Mencius*) in the Thirteen Classics Series.

6. The meaning of the phrase is obscure.

human beings. Why is it that some follow their greater qualities and others follow their smaller qualities?" Mencius replied, "When our senses of sight and hearing are used without thought and are thereby obscured by material things, the material things act on the material senses and lead them astray. That is all. The function of the mind is to think. If we think, we will get them (the principles of things). If we do not think, we will not get them. This is what Heaven has given to us. If we first build up the nobler part of our nature, then (the inferior part cannot overcome it. It is simply this that makes a man great."

6A:16. Mencius said, "There is nobility of Heaven and there is "nobility of man. Humanity, righteousness, loyalty, faithfulness, and the love of the good without getting tired of it constitute the nobility of Heaven, and to be a grand official, a great official, and a high official—this constitutes the nobility of man. The ancient people cultivated the nobility of Heaven, and the nobility of man naturally came to them. People today cultivate the nobility of Heaven in order to seek for the nobility of man, and once they have obtained the nobility of man, they forsake the nobility of Heaven. Therefore their delusion is extreme. At the end they will surely lose [the nobility of man] also."

6A:17. Mencius said, "The desire to be honored is shared by the minds of all men. But all men have in themselves what is really honorable. Only they do not think of it. The honor conferred by men is not true honor. Whoever is made honorable by Chao Meng[7] can be made humble by him again. *The Book of Odes* says, 'I am drunk with wine, and I am satiated with virtue.'[8] It means that a man is satiated with humanity and righteousness, and therefore he does not wish for the flavor of fat meat and fine millet of men. A good reputation and far-reaching praise are heaped on him, and he does not desire the embroidered gowns of men."

6A:18. Mencius said, "Humanity subdues inhumanity as water subdues fire. Nowadays those who practice humanity do so as if with one cup of water they could save a whole wagonload of fuel on fire. When the flames were not extinguished, they would say that water cannot subdue fire. This is as bad as those who are inhumane.[9] At the end they will surely lose [what little humanity they have]."

6A:19. Mencius said, "The five kinds of grain are considered good plants, but if they are not ripe, they are worse than poor grains. So the value of humanity depends on its being brought to maturity."

6A:20. Mencius said, "When Master I[10] taught people to shoot, he always told them to draw the bow to the full. The man who wants to learn [the way][11]

---

7. A high official of the Chin state.

8. Ode no. 247.

9. This is Chiao Hsün's interpretation. Chao Ch'i and Chu Hsi, however, interpret *yü* not as "the same as" but as "to help," that is, it greatly helps (encourages) the inhumane.

10. An ancient famous archer.

11. Insertion according to Chao Ch'i.

must likewise draw his bow (his will) to the full. When a great carpenter teaches people, he always tells them to use squares and compasses. The man who wants to learn must likewise use squares and compasses (or moral standards)."

MORAL CULTIVATION

■

ZHUXI

A. HOW TO STUDY

1. *Question:* Does what is called the fundamental task consist only in preserving the mind, nourishing the nature, and cultivating and controlling them?

Answer: Both the effort of preserving and nourishing and that of the investigation of principle to the utmost must be thorough. However, the effort of investigating principle to the utmost is already found within that of preserving and nourishing, and the effort of preserving and nourishing is already found within that of the investigation of principle to the utmost. To investigate principle to the utmost is the same as investigating to the utmost what is preserved, and to preserve and nourish is the same as nourishing what has been investigated. (1:18b–19a)

2. Now there is nothing for the student to do except to examine all principles with his mind. Principle is what is possessed by the mind. Always preserve this mind to examine all principles. These are the only things to do. (1:19a)

3. Although literature cannot be abolished, nevertheless the cultivation of the essential and the examination of the difference between the Principle of Nature (*T'ien-li*, Principle of Heaven) and human selfish desires are things that must not be interrupted for a single movement in the course of our daily activities and movement and rest. If one understands this point clearly, he will naturally not get to the point where he will drift into the popular ways of success and profit and expedient schemes. I myself did not really see the point until recently. Although my past defect of emphasizing fragmentary and isolated details showed different symptoms from these ways of life, yet the faults of forgetting the self, chasing after material things, leaving the internal empty, and greedily desiring the external remain the same. Master Ch'eng said, "One must not allow the myriad things in the world to disturb him. When the self is established, one will naturally understand the myriad things in the world." [12] When one does not even know where to anchor his body and mind, he talks about the kingly way and the despotic way, and discusses and

---

12. I-shu, 6:2a.
13. *ibid.,* 18:5b.

studies the task of putting the world in order as if it were a trick. Is that not mistaken? (1:30a–b)

4. I have heard the sayings of Master Ch'eng I, "Self-cultivation requires seriousness. The pursuit of learning depends on the extension of knowledge."[13] These two sayings are really the essentials for the student to advance in establishing himself in life. And the two efforts have never failed to develop each other. However, when Master Ch'eng taught people to hold fast to seriousness, he meant nothing more than the primary importance of being orderly in clothing and appearance, and by the extension of knowledge he meant no more than to find out, in reading books and history and in dealing with things, where their principles are. The teachings are nothing like the absurd, wild, and unreasonable theories of recent times. (1:37b–38a)

B. PRESERVING THE MIND AND NOURISHING THE NATURE

5. If one can in his daily life and at leisurely moments decidedly collect his mind right here, that is the equilibrium before the feelings of pleasure, anger, sorrow, and joy are aroused, and is the undifferentiated Principle of Nature. As things and affairs approach, the mind can clearly see which is right and which is wrong accordingly. What is right is the Principle of Nature, and what is wrong is in violation of the Principle of Nature. If one can always collect the mind like this, it would be as if he holds the scale and balance to measure things. (2:2a)

6. The mind embraces all principles and all principles are complete in this single entity, the mind. If one is not able to preserve the mind, he will be unable to investigate principle to the utmost. If he is unable to investigate principle to the utmost, he will be unable to exert his mind to the utmost. (2:4b)

7. *Someone asked:* How about guarding against depravity and concentrating on one thing? *Answer:* Concentrating on one thing is similar to "holding the will firm," and guarding against depravity is similar to "never doing violence to the vital force."[14] To guard against depravity merely means to prevent depraved forces from entering [the mind], whereas in concentrating on one thing one protects, it from the inside. Neither should be unbalanced in any way. This is the way the internal and the external mutually cultivate each other. (2:8b)

C. HOLDING FAST TO SERIOUSNESS (CHING)

8. The task of seriousness is the first principle of the Confucian School. From the beginning to the end, it must not be interrupted for a single moment. (2:21b)

---

14. *Mencius,* 2A:2.

9. Seriousness merely means the mind being its own master. (2:22a)

10. If one succeeds in preserving seriousness, his mind will be tranquil and the Principle of Nature will be perfectly clear to him. At no point is the slightest effort exerted, and at no point is the slightest effort not exerted. (2:22a)

11. To be serious does not mean to sit still like a blockhead, with the ear hearing nothing, the eye seeing nothing, and the mind thinking of nothing, and only then it can be called seriousness. It is merely to be apprehensive and careful and dare not give free rein to oneself. In this way both body and mind will be collected and concentrated as if one is apprehensive of something. If one can always be like this, his dispositions will naturally be changed. Only when one has succeeded in preserving this mind can he engage in study. (2:22a)

12. It is not necessary to talk much about the doctrine of holding fast to seriousness. One has only to brood over thoroughly these sayings [of Ch'eng I], "Be orderly and dignified,"[15] "Be grave and austere,"[16] "Be correct in movement and appearance and be orderly in thoughts and deliberations,"[17] and "Be correct in your dress and dignified in your gaze,"[18] and make real effort. Then what [Ch'eng] called straightening the internal life and concentrating on one thing will naturally need no manipulation, one's body and mind will be serious, and the internal and external will be unified. (2:22a–b)

D. TRANQUILLITY

13. In the human body there is only a [combination of] activity and tranquillity. Tranquillity nourishes the root of activity and activity is to put tranquillity into action. There is tranquillity in activity. For example, when the feelings are aroused and all attain due measure and degree, that is tranquillity in activity. (2:38a)

14. About response to things. Things and the principle [inherent] in my mind are fundamentally one. Neither is deficient in any degree. What is necessary is for me to respond to things. Things and the mind share the same principle. To be calm is to be tranquil. To respond is to be active. (2:38b)

15. Ch'eng I sometimes also taught people sitting in meditation. But from Confucius and Mencius upward, there was no such doctrine. We must search and investigate on a higher plane and see that sitting in meditation and the examination of principle do not interfere with each other, and then it will be correct. (2:44a–b)

---

15. *I-shu*, 15:5a.
16. *ibid.*, 15:21a; originally from the *Book of Rites*, "Meaning of Sacrifices."Cf. translation by Legge, *Li Ki*, vol. 2, p. 216.
17. *I-shu*, 15:5a; the first half originally from *Analects*, 8:4.
18. *I-shu*, 18:3a.

E. THE EXAMINATION OF THE SELF AND THINGS

16. There is dead seriousness and there is living seriousness. If one merely adheres to seriousness in concentrating on one thing and, when things happen, does not support it with righteousness to distinguish between right and wrong, it will not be living seriousness. When one becomes at home with it, then wherever there is seriousness, there is righteousness, and wherever there is righteousness, there is seriousness. When tranquil, one examines himself as to whether one is serious or not, and when active, one examines himself as to whether he is righteous or not. Take, for example, the cases of "going abroad and behaving to everyone as if you were receiving a guest and employing the people as if you were assisting at a great sacrifice." [19] What would happen if you were not serious? Or the cases of "sitting as if one is impersonating an ancestor, and standing as if one is sacrificing." [20] What would happen if you were not serious? Righteousness and seriousness must support each other, one following the other without beginning or end, and then both internal and external life will be thoroughly penetrated by them. (3:1b–2a)

17. If the Principle of Nature exists in the human mind, human selfish desires will not, but if human selfish desires win, the Principle of Nature will be destroyed. There has never been a case where both the Principle of Nature and human selfish desires are interwoven and mixed. This is where the student must realize and examine for himself (3:3a)

18. "Thinking alone can check passionate desires." [21] What do you think of the saying? *Answer:* Thinking is the same as examining. It means that when one is angry, if one can directly forget his anger and examine the right and wrong according to principle, then right and wrong will be clearly seen and desires will naturally be unable to persist. (3:3b)

19. To say that one must examine at the point where the feelings are about to be aroused means to be careful when thoughts and deliberations are just beginning, and to say that one must examine after the feelings have been aroused means that one must examine one's words and actions after they have taken place.[22] One must of course be careful about thoughts and deliberations when they begin, but one must not fail to examine his words and action after they have taken place. (3:7a)

---

19. *Analects,* 12:2.
20. *Book of Rites,* "Summary of Ceremonies," pt. 1. Cf. Legge, *Li Ki,* vol. 1, p. 62.
21. Ch'eng I's saying, *I-shu,* 25:3a–b.
22. The question of examination before and after the feelings are aroused was extensively discussed by Chu Hsi and his friends. See *Chu Tzu wen-chi,* 53: 18a–20a.

ETHICS IN AFRICA: TO BE IS TO BELONG

■

ANNA—AND LUCIEN'S OTHER WIVES

Anna Kangombe was eighteen years old when she married Lucien Mubumbyi. Both belong to the Masai people, a large group that inhabits Kenya and parts of Tanzania. Lucien, on the other hand, was forty-one. Nevertheless, despite the fact that her husband was more than twice her age, Anna felt no shame in marrying him. In fact, her own family members strongly encouraged her to marry the successful farmer. Lucien had earned his hard-won reputation as a prosperous entrepreneur and farmer in his village with abundant livestock and more than enough villagers who worked for him. Villagers looked up to him, and he had far-reaching social influence and status. So, encouraged by her mother and sisters, Anna became the fifth of Lucien's current wives. Anna's family repeatedly told her that marrying into Lucien's family would be the highest honor both for her and for them, whereas it would have been a disgrace to be the only wife of a husband.

This arrangement had been set up years ago before Anna was even born. When Lucien was twenty-three, he presented a gift to Anna's mother while she was pregnant with Anna. By that time, the young man had already proven to others in the village that he was a responsible caretaker for his farm. For that reason, Anna's mother and father accepted his gift. And, as was the custom among the Masai, by accepting his gift, they pledged that if they gave birth to a daughter they would consider offering her to Lucien later on to be his wife.

Up until the time she married Lucien, Anna was still a virgin. For the Masai, as well as for many other African ethnic groups, not only is it a social taboo to be unmarried, but to be an unwed mother is extremely offensive. This shames the family, disrupts the order of the entire village, and is particularly problematic regarding matters of inheritance of family properties and land. Upon marrying Lucien, Anna now assumes the duty to bear a child. If she cannot bear a child, this would be a disgrace for her and her family. Nevertheless, because she shares a household with other wives of Lucien, this shame would not lead to loneliness because she would help care for other children within the family.

We see here that polygamy continues to be the common practice in sub-Saharan Africa. Of an estimated 742 ethnic groups in this region, 580 of them still practice polygamy, despite long-standing protests from Christian missionaries.[1] Nevertheless, most Africans are not Christians, and traditional values continue to be the undercurrent of prevailing practices. Is polygamy morally justified? Or is it morally offensive? It is considered immoral as well as illegal according to Western social standards. Yet it is acceptable for many Africans. Are Africans morally misguided? Why is it sanctioned?

■ SHATTERING THE STEREOTYPES

A malignant misconception of African thought is that it is fundamentally primitive and unsophisticated. To label African thought in this way disregards Africa's rich indigenous heritage and traditional ethos, an ethos grounded upon the authority of custom, tradition, and the well-being of the community. And by community, we mean those both living and dead, or "ancestors." Moreover, this wrongheaded thinking fails to consider Africa's ongoing contact with the West, a continuum of contact that also challenges long-held traditional beliefs. Africa with its fifty-three nations and nearly twelve hundred diverse groups is extremely complex. This leads to difficulties in attempting to generalize anything regarding what may be construed as the "African perspective." In this light, we can claim what we have asserted of other cultures, namely, we ought not to view Africa as some monolithic entity. At the same time, we can still ascertain some general tendencies or dispositions in thinking among the African nations.

Some scholars dismiss African thought as being unsystematic and lacking rigid philosophical analysis. One reason for this bias seems to be the complex body of stories and myths upon which African thought is grounded. For instance, philosopher Kwame Anthony Appiah argues that much of African thought is essentially irrational due to its reliance upon folklores and proverbs. Yet this judgment is unfair, for it presumes that Africans themselves are not capable of rational, analytical thinking.

Along similar lines, another stereotype is that African thought cannot have any real system of ethics because behavior is dictated by local customs. Yet this betrays some confusion between custom and morality. Customs refer to social rules, either explicit or implicit. In doing so, these obviously reflect social values. However, not all social values are moral values. For instance, the Akans, the largest ethnic grouping in Ghana, West Africa, place great store on beautiful speech—speech that is logical, rhetorical, nicely delivered, and culminates in a proverb.[2] Failure to deliver such speech, however, is not considered immoral. All cultures value beauty, and beauty is generally determined and assessed in different ways in different cultures. But the lack of beauty does not constitute something immoral.

Matters of etiquette are more complex. Social etiquette reflects social values. And many of these social values do have moral relevance. This is certainly the case in Confucianism, which highlights the virtue of *li*, propriety, or more properly called "etiquette." Nevertheless, we can still generally say that a faux pas in etiquette does not constitute the same degree of moral seriousness as, for example, stealing another's property or telling a deliberate lie. That is, regarding customs, there are gradations of moral gravity.

Others critics bluntly assert that there is fundamentally no moral system in African thought. Yet, we need to rethink this. In quite a few cultures there is less of a need to systematize one's thinking in strict fashion. Furthermore, philosophical and moral thinking can be expressed in various creative ways. Again, we need to be careful to avoid casting a Western standard upon other cultures and traditions in evaluating them. In addition, as many of my African students insist, there is no one African culture. Instead, there are many African cultures. We need, therefore, to refrain from thinking of any nation or tradition as homogenous. Nevertheless, there are some dominant themes, directions, and emphases within certain traditions. We will examine these prevailing themes below.

■ WHAT IS THE BASIS FOR MORALITY?

RELIGION IS THE SOURCE

There are two fundamental positions regarding the decisive source of African moral teachings. One school of thought declares that morality is ultimately based upon religion and religious beliefs. Theologian John Mbiti's selection at the end of this chapter reflects this point of view. Mbiti and others assert from the outset that Africans recognize that they inhabit a religious universe. On the basis of this assumption, religion plays the most prominent role in people's lives. As Mbiti states:

> According to African peoples, man lives in a religious universe, so that natural phenomena and objects are intimately associated with God. They not only originate from Him, but also bear witness to Him. Man's understanding of God is strongly coloured by the universe of which man is himself a part. Man sees in the universe not only the imprint but the reflection of God.[3]

Mbiti asserts that morality is grounded upon the force of religion. He also affirms the moral authority bestowed upon one supreme God. For instance, the Yoruba, the West African ethnic group that mostly inhabits southwestern Nigeria, call this supreme God *Olodumare*. The Ashanti of Ghana call him *Onyankopon Kyeame*, and the Hausa, who live in northern Nigeria and Niger, call him *Allah*.[4]

Africans also recognize minor gods who happen to be emanations of the supreme God. In any case, that which is morally taboo is taboo because it is specifically prohibited by either the supreme God or by minor gods. The gods therefore pose moral standards. For example, among the Yoruba it is taboo to drink palm wine because it forbidden by the minor god *Obatala*.[5] And any sin against a minor god constitutes a sin against the supreme God as well. African scholar Bolaji Idowu claims that for the Yoruba "Man's concept of the Deity has everything to do with what is taken to be the norm of morality."[6] Mbiti and others assert that in all African countries God is the "final guardian of law and order and of the moral and ethical codes." Thus, the moral standard is to avoid offending God.

What is especially noteworthy is that an individual offense also constitutes an offense by the entire group. Mbiti raises the example of the sin of pride. According to the Nuer, it is considered sinful to praise one's own baby. This is viewed as an act of false pride and is an offense against God. And God will not only punish the individual parent but the entire village. All others in the community bear the consequences of an individual's expression of pride.

The basis for morality is so theocentric or centered on the deity, that, as expressed by Mbiti in his selection, it is not the case that an act is wrong in itself. It is wrong because it incurs God's wrath and punishment. "Since the consequences are bad, therefore the act which invites them must be bad."

In other words, any act that impacts negatively upon the group, due to consequences, is wrong. He makes the interesting claim that even adultery is
not wrong in itself unless it is discovered! By being discovered, there are
harmful consequences for various parties. If it is kept secret, and no party
is harmed, then there is nothing intrinsically wrong with the act. This is
why ritual is so vital. Ritual acts as a purgative to alleviate the negative
consequences of incurring God's wrath.

In maintaining that religion is the ultimate source of moral teachings,
African philosophers point out that since God is perfect, his will is also perfect. In turn, the will of humans is derived from this divine will, so that
even if we postulate that human reason, instead of religion, is the source of
morality, this human reason is in effect the reflection of God's will. Philosopher M. Akin Makinde cites evidence for this from the Yoruba culture,
which, along with other African cultures, stresses that primary duties such
as respecting elders, avoiding theft, being repentant, and forgiving others
are all expressions of God's will. Furthermore, for the Yoruba, these primary duties are necessary in order to strive for moral perfection and to
avoid being reborn again in this life. The Yoruba believe that one who
has attained moral perfection will no longer be reincarnated once he or
she dies.[7]

There is also the pivotal belief that when one acts immorally toward another person, he or she is also behaving immorally toward oneself. This is
the injunction to think of others as you think of yourself. Here we see a
striking parallel to the Golden Rule. Among the Akan, this Golden Rule is
stated, "Do not do unto others what you would not that they do to you."
Makinde cites the sacred saying, or *odu ifa*, among the Yoruba:

> *You do it to yourself, you do it to yourself, it is to the person who
> throws ashes at others that the wind directs the ashes. You do it to
> yourself, you do it to yourself. For an evil doer succeeds only in do-
> ing half of an evil deed to others; the other half of evil he invariably
> does to himself.*[8]

RELIGION IS NOT THE SOURCE

On the other hand, others claim that the ultimate source of morality is independent of religion. Kwasi Wiredu is a proponent of this position, and his
selection is at the end of this chapter. According to Wiredu, people are compelled to live morally with or without religion. Even atheists must live
morally. The source of morality exists outside of religious beliefs. Religion

may certainly be a catalyst for someone to act morally, but it is not the true source of morality. For instance, even if we accept the theocentric position and hold that religion is the source of morality, how do we even begin to resolve what seem to be differences among the gods? Philosopher Segun Gbadegesin points out how for some Yoruba, the minor god *Orunmila* does not prohibit palm wine, as opposed to *Obatala*'s prohibition of it.[9] In contrast to a theocentric position, Wiredu argues in his selection that, above all else, morality is deeply humanistic. He demonstrates this by pointing out certain beliefs and moral teachings in Akan society where morality is founded upon elevating human interests. All of this is independent of religious beliefs.

This raises a persistent challenge in ethics. What, more precisely, is the nature of the relationship between morality and religion? This question has been a thorny one in the history of Western philosophy. It merited discussion in one of Plato's early dialogues, *Euthyphro*. Here, Socrates confronts the young man Euthyphro who is on his way to the courthouse to charge his own father with starving to death a household slave. Given the magnitude of the accusation, Socrates coaxes Euthyphro to instruct him as to the true source of morality. When Euthyphro claims that it lies in the will of the gods (polytheism was the prevalent belief in Greece at that time), Socrates poses to Euthyphro—and to us—a profound question: *Is something good because the gods will it, or do the gods will it because it is good?* Socrates then goes on to discredit the belief that the ultimate authority for morality lies in religion.

Along with Plato, many philosophers would assert that the source of morality must transcend religious beliefs, and that religious beliefs are an expression rather than a source of morality. The source of morality lies, for instance, in our common humanity and/or our shared capacity to reason. Along these same lines, many African philosophers contend that we need to be moral even if we do not have a set of religious beliefs.

IDENTITY AND ETHICS

VITAL FORCE

In his classic 1945 work, *Bantu Philosophy*, the Belgian missionary Rev. Placide Tempels concluded from his work in the Congo that an axiomatic principle throughout African thought is that of "vital force." For Africans, the views of identity, what Western philosophers refer to as ontology, center on this vital principle. For Africans, to live requires cultivating this "vital force." This in turn means to live fully, to become strong, to stay healthy. The lack of this force results in all sorts of illness, injury, and particularly moral disorder. This vital force sustains order, growth, prosperity, and moral harmony. Therefore, whatever enhances this vital force is considered worthwhile and good, and whatever detracts from it is to be avoided.[10] This vital force, a key notion in African views regarding identity, certainly impacts directly upon views of ethics. We see this especially in the case of *iwa*.

IWA

One of the most important moral ideas in African cultures is that of cultivating good character. Among the Yoruba, the term for good character is *iwa*. However, it is important to note that the original meaning of *iwa* referred to the plain fact of living.[11] That is, living conveys an intrinsic value to a person. In African thought, a person's life has a sanctity all its own, and this sanctity is all the more sustained through "vital force." Africans are therefore taught to respect human life in all forms. Indeed, within the context of this original meaning, the perfection of *iwa*, or living, entailed living forever, being immortal.

Over the course of time, *iwa* acquired the meaning of good character, and this idea was derived from its original. As we said, living is intrinsically good. Yet character enhances living. *Iwa* as character therefore can perfect *iwa* as existence. Living in itself is good, but living with good character is better. As Gbadegesin puts it:

> Thus an original beauty of existence could be improved upon by adorning it with character. The difference between one form of existence and another would then be located in the quality of its adornment, that is, the quality of its character.[12]

This is the "cosmetic of *iwa*" that needs to be constantly learned and cultivated. According to Gbadegesin, "there is a need for character training from the beginning so that the cosmetic of *iwa* (character) may have time to sink into the core of *iwa* (existence) very early in life."[13] Wiredu supports this all the more in his selection when he points to the home as the "theatre of moral upbringing . . . at parents' feet and within range of kinsmen's inputs."

Of all the virtues, the most fundamental one is patience. According to traditional Yoruba religious beliefs, *Iwa* was born of the goddess *Orunmila* and the god *Suuru*, and *Suuru* symbolizes patience. There are shades of this *iwa* in Wiredu's selection at the end of this chapter, where he states that persons have three components: life, blood, and charisma. The life element comes from the divine. The mother provides the blood principle, while the father provides the charisma principle. Both mother and father provide the elements that lay the foundation within the social nexus.

TO BE IS TO BELONG

Perhaps the most significant principle in African ontology, or views of identity lies in the importance of belonging. That is, "to be" is "to belong." No person exists independently. Each person belongs to a family, a clan, or wider group. Theologian John Mbiti states this clearly:

> Only in terms of other people does the individual become conscious of his own being, his own duties, his privileges and responsibilities towards himself and towards other people. When he suffers, he does not suffer alone but with his corporate group; when he rejoices, he rejoices not alone but with his kinsmen, his neighbours and relatives whether dead or living. . . . Whatever happens to the individual happens to the whole group, and whatever happens to the whole group happens to the individual. The individual can only say "I am, because we are; and since we are, therefore, I am."[14]

Since this relationality is clearly the key to understanding personal identity, ethics centers on the core system of obligations and duties that are a necessary part of this relationality. The well-being of the group is the measure of moral behavior. Whatever enhances group well-being is morally obligatory. Whatever detracts from it is morally prohibited. This means that there are duties to act with kindness and generosity not only toward one's friends and family, but to all in the community, for the community is viewed as the larger family.

Notions of self-determination that are so prominent in Western cultures are certainly less so in Africa. Group welfare and interdependence overrides self-interest. Excessive expressions of self-interest are morally unjustified. Within its context of interdependency, there is little emphasis in African ethics upon individual rights. Instead, African ethics stresses duties, and these duties are to the entire group as one collective body. Duties to family members are also duties to the community. Sharing food with one's neighbor is also sharing food with the whole group.

At the same time, this does not mean that matters of self-interest are totally absent. Indeed, African moral thought supports the notion that each person must think critically for him- or herself. Each person must strive to achieve a level of independence in this respect. Blind conformity to the group is discouraged as antithetical to ethical behavior. Nevertheless, the good of the group supersedes the good of the individual. For instance, for the Masai the ideal person is the *nganyet,* one who lives for others.[15] Whatever will harm the group is prohibited so that intervening with a person's exercise of self-determination is justified if doing so protects the group.

■ THE MORAL AUTHORITY OF THE COMMUNITY

Theologian John Mbiti's classic statement, "I am because we are, and since we are, therefore I am," is a succinct summary of the African view of personal identity. Individual identity makes little sense in and of itself. The person is defined in terms of his or her relationship within the fabric of the community. In turn, the individual contributes to communal identity and well-being. Indeed, what truly matters is the good of the community to which the individual belongs.

This means that moral action is not confined to individual behavior. The person is defined by and defines the group. There is a necessary interrelational rapport between the individual and the community, and this harmony establishes moral standards, principles, and rules. Therefore, ethics is not so much a question of "What should *I* do?" but of "What should *we* do?" This is a fundamental starting point in understanding African morality. Kwasi Wiredu makes this abundantly clear:

> The integration of individuality into community in African traditional society is so thoroughgoing that, as is too rarely noted, the very concept of a person has a normative layer of meaning. A person is not just an individual of human parentage, but also one evincing in his or her projects and achievements an adequate sense of social responsibility.[16]

The community remains at the heart of moral concern. Exaggerating individual interests at the expense of the community is a moral aberration. As we said earlier, African ethics emphasizes duties and obligations within the web of relationships that persons find themselves. Adhering to these duties will promote communal well-being. Along these lines, let us return to our opening scene of polygamy. Theologian and priest Eugene Hillman points out that the Western emphasis upon individualism is especially evidenced through its norm of monogamy. Whereas, in many African societies, emphasizing as they do the interests of the community above all else, polygamy makes better sense in that it contributes to social adhesion by extending the kinship web and, in so doing, further extending the pattern of regulated duties.[17]

Perhaps the most important thing to understand regarding polygamy in Africa is that it is necessarily linked to the African system of kinship. For many Africans, polygamy sustains the value of generational continuity and economic security. Africans consider kinship relations to be the most valuable component in the community. Each individual's sense of self and feelings of duty are delineated in terms of kinship relations. There is thus a symbiotic relationship between the individual and the kinship group to which she belongs. And in this relationship, a reciprocity of obligations is prominent. All of this brings about order within the group. In contrast to much of Western thinking, the individual is not set apart from the group, from the collective. As Hillman puts it, each individual is

> *affirmed and fulfilled only in relation to the good of others; and this is explicitly recognized as normative, to the extent that the individual is expected to follow the socially established patterns. What is good for the larger community is, for that reason, presumed to be good for each of its members. In this sense, each man lives for others; and his personal development is always community-oriented.[18]*

Again, this is not to deny the importance of individuality. Individual persons have an intrinsic value. Individuals are viewed as unique. As we will see below, this is why so much time is spent in assigning the right name for every new baby, a unique individual, yet one who is now also a unique member of the household. There is always this tension between the unique individual and the household. Nevertheless, priority always goes to the community. Individual persons each have their own gifts, talents, and dispositions. And they are to cultivate these in order to contribute to the good of the group.

In describing Akan society and its ethics, philosopher Pieter Coetzee outlines three factors that underscore this community-centered morality. First of all, "Kinship is the highest value." In this way, the "social dimensions of the Akan ethic are rooted in biological relationships (parental, filial)." Second, "To have a moral identity is to be morally constituted through another." Here, he points to the "unity of social and moral identity." Third, "the phenomenon of moral affirmation requires reciprocity." In this case, there is recognition of the interaction between the individual and the group in terms of a set of duties and obligations that, if properly performed, brings about the good of the community.[19]

This community-centered morality is further evident in the strong socialization process that begins at childbirth. For instance, among the Yoruba, elderly women in the household act as midwives and deliver the newborn, and for a period of time after the birth of her child, the mother's only physical contact with her newborn lies in breast-feeding. The baby is physically handled by other females in the household—other mothers, other wives, sisters, and so on. All adult householders act as keepers and guardians of the new child.[20] As the child grows, other wives within the household as well as wives of brothers and cousins play an active role in raising the child. And, more important, there is a shared participation in the moral training of the child. It is imperative for adults in the household to correct the child's misbehavior as soon as it occurs. If the adults do not do so, they abdicate their moral responsibility. As we will see below, elders in particular play a special role in the moral training of the child.

The process of naming is another interesting household event. The baby is not given a name until after the seventh day. This is done rather ceremoniously, with the male members of the household playing key roles. The name is based upon a number of factors: the family's profession, the child's date of birth, any significant events prior to the child's birth such as a death or some other crisis, and the male elder's consultation with an oracle.[21] In contrast to the now-popular American habit of assigning names that are unique and uncommon and that are intended to convey individuality, African cultures assign names that stress membership within the household so that the child acquires a name that signifies its uniqueness within the family. And as the child grows, household members, particularly the mother, often point out to the child the family lineage, reminding him or her of family roots and heritage.

Within this household-centered context, many Africans view polygamy as an arrangement that favorably affects the entire community. The husband pledges to support *all* the families in his household, and this sustains the social order. Along these lines, Hillman describes the custom of "bride-wealth":

> The well-known African custom of "bride-wealth," paid by a man to the parents or guardians of his wife, is not only intended to be a

support to the permanence of marriage and a compensation to the family which gives away a member, but it is also a pledge of a man's ability to provide adequately for his wife and children. This payment signifies, among other things, a man's willingness and ability to help his in-laws; and it shows that he loves his prospective wife more than his hard-earned possessions.[22]

Hillman points out that polygamy fills an important socioeconomic role in ways that sustain kinship continuity and social integration. First, since there is a steady need for a broad-based and dependable labor force for food production, and since there is a high rate of infant mortality, the more offspring the better. Polygamy makes sense here. Second, polygamy brings together different families into the single kinship group so that there is a stable continuity across generations. This produces intergenerational and interfamilial solidarity. These family group alliances lay the groundwork for mutual duties and "assistance patterns." Marriage is not only between husband and wife, but also between respective families.

Polygamy is a function of social solidarity on the level of the extended family, the clan, and the tribal or ethnic community. Each new marriage sets up new relationships of affinity between two different kin groups, that of the husband and that of the wife; and their children are kin to both groups. A variety of new mutual assistance patterns are thus established.[23]

Third, polygamy increases the number of ancestors, and this has a lasting impact regarding the reverence that the living are supposed to have toward their dead ancestors. Fourth, divorce is less likely. The typical ground for divorce, female infertility, would not hold since the barren wife would still have the responsibility of raising the children of other wives in the family. Moreover, there is less of a desire for extramarital relationships. In contrast to polygamy, an imposed system of monogamy may well result in increased prostitution and adultery.[24]

THE MORAL AUTHORITY OF ELDERS

A popular African proverb states: "It is the moral fault of the elder who refuses to admonish a morally straying child, and it is the moral fault of the child who refuses to heed the moral admonishment of the elder."[25] In his selection, Wiredu underscores the importance of constant correction and oversight from adults: "The need for correction is an unending contingency in the lives of mortals." African cultures generally assign special moral weight to the teachings and instructions of the elders within the community. The elders have the moral obligation to educate, hand down, and embody moral teachings to all others.

Why are the elders assigned such prominent moral privilege? As a start, elders have lived life in a fuller sense. They have borne the brunt of experiences both harsh and pleasant. They have gained the wisdom in dealing especially with life's obstacles and moral conflicts. They are thus able to provide for others the kinds of practical lessons that are much more useful than abstract moral principles. It is this real-life, matter-of-fact knowledge that elders in particular possess. African cultures thus place a premium on practical wisdom (what Aristotle called *sophrosune*), and elders, through their own life experiences, have earned the privilege of transmitting this practical wisdom. As philosopher Polycarp Ikuenobe puts it with another proverb: "What a child cannot see while standing on a stool, an elder can see while sitting." [26]

Furthermore, this practical wisdom is inherently dynamic. It is not some static body of unchanging teachings. Elders learn to shape prior teachings according to new circumstances. This flexibility is crucial for it means that practical wisdom refers, in a sense, to unlearning lessons that have been already learned. This natural cultural deference to the elder differs from our fast-paced culture that places more pragmatic value on productivity and mistakenly associates productivity with youthfulness. Moreover, positing elders as a source of moral teachings actually grounds morality in concrete, lived experiences and not in some abstract, transcendent realm. In summary, this emphasis upon the authority of the elders along with that of the well-being of the community situates African morality upon a common humanitarian ground so that communal well-being is what is uppermost.

■ WEAKNESSES IN AFRICAN ETHICS

This dominant emphasis upon group well-being stands in danger of collapsing any value of the individual. We can understand the importance of stressing community rather than viewing each individual as some atomized and isolated entity apart from the group. But does this mean in African thought that the individual person is entirely *defined* by the group? Is there any room at all for individual autonomy, or self-rule? There is an Akan saying that "One tree does not make the forest." [27] True. But there still need to be individual trees to constitute the forest. In like manner, there need to be individual persons in order to make up a community. Yet if the selfhood and identity of the individual is purely dependent on the projects and goals of the group, village, or community, does this not impair individual freedoms and liberties?

A pitfall in this strong community-centered ethic is that it can tend to crush any value to the individual *as individual*. Philosopher Kwame Gyeke points this out in his critique of a radical communitarian interpretation in African thought:

> *A consideration of other aspects of human nature would certainly be appropriate: a person is, of course, by nature a social (communal) being; but he/she is by nature other things as well (i.e. he/she possesses other essential attributes). Failure to recognise this may result in pushing the significance and implications of a person's communal nature beyond their limits, an act that would in turn result in investing the community with an all-engulfing moral authority to determine everything in the life of the individual person. One might thus easily succumb to the temptation of exaggerating the normative status and power of the cultural community in relation to those of the person, thus obfuscating our understanding of the real nature of the person.[28]*

Features regarding the "real nature" of the individual have been described above in the discussion of identity. Nevertheless, there still remains the danger of inflating the authority of the group, in turn deflating any power to the individual.

If so, then this allows little room, if any, for the recognition and exercise of individual rights as well as duties. How can we reconcile the value of the individual with this emphasis upon the collective? We see this with Mbiti's example of adultery. To argue that adultery is only wrong when it becomes discovered because it then incurs the wrath of God and thus brings about negative consequences for the community seems disingenuous. Aside from the objection that adultery could not go undetected by an all-knowing supreme God, the notion of harm in this case seems to be defined solely in a collective sense, that is, in terms of the harm that the group suffers as a result of God's wrath. This leaves little room for harm in the more private, personal sense. But could there not be private harm, particularly with respect to individual conscience? This is especially the case since the individuals engaged in adultery are fully aware of the potential negative repercussions on the community. This exaggeration of collective harm detracts from considerations of individual conscience.

■ STRENGTHS IN AFRICAN ETHICS

We can learn some valuable and much-needed lessons from African cultures regarding the cohesiveness of the family as a moral guide for children. This includes lessons on what it means to raise children. Good parenting requires moral watchfulness and correction. In African culture, the ideal is not to be a "friend" to your child, but to be a guide, an example of good character. We see this clearly in the idea of viewing elders as a source of moral authority. The African household provides a rather clear moral structure for children. Western experts in child psychology such as Robert Coles never tire of reminding us that children need constant and vigilant moral guidance, a clear moral structure. Without it, children fall prey to a sense of aimlessness. To be sure, African parents and elders guide children not only by what they say but by what they do. Furthermore, raising the children in a morally upright manner is not simply a matter for the parents and specific householders, but for all other adults in the community.

If there is any one lesson that African parents and elders continue to impart to their children, it is that through their constant vigilance, children learn the importance of self-restraint. Children learn that their immediate desires often need to give way to the needs of others. This is an invaluable lesson for us in our own culture where thinking first of others is subordinate to self-gratification. Indeed, self-absorption does not lend itself to genuine altruism. In learning that others come first, African children learn their most important moral lesson, and this lesson plants the seeds for the priority of community welfare over personal desires.

African parents and elders embody this lesson by virtue of their ongoing sacrifice of their own desires on behalf of their children. Parents constantly demonstrate this duty to give up their individual desires in order to bring about what is best for the children. Furthermore, the stories that elders pass on to children are often stories of sacrificing individual interests in order to bring about the good of the group. In African communities, we see no professional experts when it comes to moral training. The moral guides are parents, elders, and all other adults within the community. Moral cultivation and guidance is a collective, communal affair, and not one relegated to the state.

The elders in particular hold a high status within the community because, through imparting lessons of wisdom, they provide valuable moral guidance to the youth. This is rather similar to the valuable role played by the elderly in Chinese society. Like the Chinese who are influenced deeply by Confucian teachings, African cultures value history and tradition, and the elderly are the inheritors of this tradition. The elderly are thus looked up to with utmost respect. Moreover, in the African context of mutual interdependence and a system of mutual duties among family members, the elderly are also respected because of the gratitude that the younger members of the household have for them. As parents, the elders made unbounded sacrifices in raising their children. It therefore makes perfect sense to reciprocate with respect and devotion to these parents in their golden years. African cultures respect the elders in the way that the Chinese writer Lin Yutang puts it: "A natural man loves his children, but a cultured man loves his parents."[29]

For these reasons, Africans believe that it is a blessing to grow older, in complete contrast to our culture, which dreads aging. In African cultures, the elders are respected essentially because they are older and thus wiser. In this context of interdependence, where "to be" is "to belong," this makes sense. This is, without a doubt, one of the most valuable lessons we can take with us from Africa.

■ NOTES

1. Eugene Hillman, *Polygamy Reconsidered: African Plural Marriage and the Christian Churches* (Maryknoll, NY: Orbis Books, 1975), pp. 93–94.

2. See the discussion in Kwasi Wiredu, "Custom and Morality: A Comparative Analysis of Some African and Western Conceptions of Morals," in Albert G. Mosley, ed., *African Philosophy: Selected Readings* (Englewood Cliffs, NJ: Prentice Hall,1995), pp. 390–91.

3. John S. Mbiti, *African Religions and Philosophy* (New York: Doubleday, 1969), p. 62.

4. M. Akin Makinde, "African Culture and Moral Systems: A Philosophy Study," in *Second Order: An African Journal of Philosophy* 1, no. 2 (July 1988): 11.

5. Segun Gbadegesin, "Individuality, Community, and the Moral Order," in P. H. Coetzee and A. P. J. Roux, eds., *The African Philosophy Reader* (London and New York: Routledge, 1998), p. 300.

6. Makinde, pp. 3–4.

7. Ibid., p. 16.

8. Ibid., p. 13.

9. Ibid.

10. Placide Tempels, *Bantu Philosophy* (Paris: Présence Africaine, 1959), p. 44.

11. See the discussion in Gbadegesin, 303ff.

12. Gbadagesin, p. 304.

13. Ibid., p. 305.

14. John S. Mbiti, pp. 108–09.

15. Hillman, p. 112.

16. Kwasi Wiredu, "Custom and Morality" note 39, p. 400.

17. See Hillman, chap. 4, pp. 109–38.

18. Hillman, p. 112.

19. Pieter H. Coetzee, "Particularity in Morality and Its Relation to Community," in Coetzee and Roux, p. 284.

20. See Gbadegesin, p. 292.

21. Ibid., p. 292.

22. Hillman, p. 93.

23. Ibid., p. 118.

24. Ibid., pp. 114–25.

25. Polycarp Ikuenobe, "Moral Thought in African Cultures? A Metaphilosophical Question," *African Philosophy* 12, no. 2 (1999): 111.

26. Ibid., 112.

27. Kwami Gyekye, "Person and Community in African Thought," in Coetzee and Roux, p. 321.

28. Ibid., p. 322.

29. From Lin Yutang, *The Importance of Living* (Heinemann, 1931).

THE CONCEPTS OF EVIL, ETHICS AND JUSTICE

JOHN S. MBITI

THE ORIGIN AND NATURE OF EVIL

From previous considerations we have seen that African peoples are much aware of evil in the world, and in various ways they endeavour to fight it. Several views exist concerning the origin of evil. Many societies say categorically that God did not create what is evil, nor does He do them any evil whatsoever. For example, the Ila hold that God is always in the right, and "cannot be charged with an offence, cannot be accused, cannot be questioned . . . He does good to all at all times."[1] One of the Ashanti priests is reported as saying that God "created the possibility of evil in the world . . . God has created the knowledge of good and evil in every person and allowed him to choose his way," without forbidding him or forcing His will on him.[2] From various myths we saw that when God originally created man, there was harmony and family relationship between the two; and the first men enjoyed only what was good.

Some societies see evil as originating from, or associated with, spiritual beings other than God. Part of this concepts is a personification of evil itself. For example, the Vugusu say that there is an evil divinity which God created good, but later on turned against Him and began to do evil. This evil divinity is assisted by evil spirits, and all evil now comes from that lot. Thus, a kind of duel exists, between good and evil forces in the world. There are other peoples who regard death, epidemics, locusts and other major calamities, as divinities in themselves, or as caused by divinities.

In nearly all African societies, it is thought that the spirits are either the origin of evil, or agents of evil. We have seen that after four or five generations, the living-dead lose personal links with human families, and become "its" and strangers. When they become detached from human contact, people experience or fear them as "evil" or "harmful." Much of this is simply the fear of what is strange; but some are believed to possess individuals and to cause various maladies like epilepsy and madness. If the living-dead are not properly buried, or have a grudge, are neglected or not obeyed when they give instructions, it is thought that they take revenge or punish the offenders. In this case, it is men who provoke the living-dead to act in "evil" ways.

We saw in the previous chapter that there are people in every community who are suspected of working maliciously against their relatives and neighbours, through the use of magic, sorcery and witchcraft. As we shall shortly point out further, this is the centre of evil, as people experience it. Mystical power is neither good nor evil in itself: but when used maliciously by some individuals it is experienced as evil. This view makes evil an independent and external object which, however, cannot act on its own but must be employed by human or spiritual agents.

As in all societies of the world, social order and peace are recognized by African peoples as essential and sacred. Where the sense of corporate life is so deep, it is inevitable that the solidarity of the community must be maintained, otherwise there is disintegration and destruction. This order is conceived of primarily in terms of kinship relationship, which simultaneously produces

---

1 Smith & Dale, pp. 199 f., 207, 211.
2 R. A. Lystad *The Ashanti* (1958), p. 163 f.

many situations of tension since everybody is related to everybody else and deepens the sense of damage caused by the strain of such tensions. If a person steals a sheep, personal relations are at once involved because the sheep belongs to a member of the corporate body, perhaps to someone who is a father, or brother, or sister or cousin to the thief. As such it is an offence against the community, and its consequences affect not only the thief but also the whole body of his relatives.

There exist, therefore, many laws, customs, set forms of behaviour, regulations, rules, observances and taboos, constituting the moral code and ethics of a given community or society. Some of these are held sacred, and are believed to have been instituted by God or national leaders. They originate in the Zamani where the forefathers are. This gives sanctity to the customs and regulations of the community. Any breach of this code of behaviour is considered evil, wrong or bad, for it is an injury or destruction to the accepted social order and peace. It must be punished by the corporate community of both the living and the departed, and God may also inflict punishment and bring about justice.

In human relationships there is emphasis on the concepts of hierarchy based partly on age and partly on status. In practice this amounts to a ladder ranging from God to the youngest child. God is the creator and hence the parent of mankind, and holds the highest position so that He is the final point of reference and appeal. Beneath Him are the divinities and spirits, which are more powerful than man and some of which were founders and forefathers of different societies. Next come the living-dead, the more important ones being those who were full human beings by virtue of going through the initiation rites, getting married and raising children. Among human beings the hierarchy includes kings, rulers, rainmakers, priests, diviners, medicine-men, elders in each household, parents, older brothers and sisters, and finally the youngest members of the community. Authority is recognized as increasing from the youngest child to the highest Being. As for the individual, the highest authority is the community of which he is a corporate member. This authority also has degrees, so that some of it is in the hands of the household-family, some is invested in the elders of a given area, part is in the hands of the clan, and part is in the whole nation which may or may not be invested in central rulers.

According to some societies, individuals or the people as a body or through its chief or king, may offend against God. For example, the Barundi believe that God gets angry with a person who commits adultery. The Bachwa believe that God punishes people who steal, neglect ageing parents, murder or commit adultery. The Bavenda say that if their chief offends against God, He punishes the whole people with locusts, floods or other calamities.

Most African peoples accept or acknowledge God as the final guardian of law and order and of the moral and ethical codes. Therefore the breaking of such order, whether by the individual or by a group, is ultimately an offence by the corporate body of society. For example, before the Gikuyu sacrifice and pray for rain, they first enquire from a diviner or seer why God has allowed such a long drought to come upon them. The animal for sacrifice must be of one colour, and be donated by or bought from a person who, is honest, trustworthy and has not committed "murder, theft, rape, or had any connection with poison (witchcraft) or poisoning."[3] In this and the previous examples, we see that murder, theft and the like, are considered offences against God. The guilt of one person involves his entire household including his animals and property. The pollution of the individual is corporately the pollution of those related to him whether they are human beings, animals or material goods. We have considered myths concerning the first men, and seen how the disobedience of the original men involved the rest of their descendants in a corporate offence against God, so that the punishment He executed on them (death, separation from Him, withdrawal of free food, loss of immortality and the like), automatically became the punishment for all their descendants.

Let us take another example from the Nuer. It is thought that a person may offend against God by being proud of his cattle or children if they are many. This causes God to take away the cattle or children. Therefore for the Nuer, "the worst offence is to praise a baby," and one should refer to it as "this bad thing." The people believe that if a person does wrong, God will sooner or later punish him, and the punishment affects not just the individual alone, but the corporate group of which he is only a part. Praising a baby may cause it to die: the offender is not the baby, but the person who is proud before God. The Nuer, like many other African peoples, have different rules of behaviour. Offences arising from the breach of these, whether deliberately or accidentally, bring misfortune both to offenders and other people who are not directly responsible. For them, the evil lies not in the act itself, but in the fact that God punishes the act.[4] By committing a particular offence, a person puts himself and other people in the dangerous situation where God punishes him and other people. Since the consequences are bad, therefore the act which invites them must be bad. The outward manifestations only indicate the bad or evil inside, and the outward misfortune may contaminate other people who are closely related to the offender. Such is the logic of the matter in the sight of the Nuer and, it would seem, many other African peoples. Something is evil because it is punished: it is not punished because it is evil.

There are other societies in which people do not feel that they can offend against God. For example, the Ankore recognize God as the final principle of order, but individuals do not offend Him nor feel guilty towards Him.[5] It is

---

3 Kenyatta, p. 243 f.
4 Evans-Pritchard, II, pp. 14 f., 189 f.
5 F. B. Welbourn conference paper on "The High God," 1964.

held among the Azande, Akan, Swazi, Banyarwanda and others, that God has no influence on people's moral values.

Various types of offences are considered to be against the spirits and the living-dead. We have indicated that the living-dead, and to a less extent the spirits also, act as intermediaries between God and men, and that they are the guardians or police of tribal ethics, morals and customs. Where such spirits were once the founders or forefathers of the nation, it is commonly believed that they delivered many of the laws and customs of their people. Therefore any breach of these customs is an offence not only to the human society but also to the spirits and the living-dead. The offence is most serious when it is against the patriarchs, kings or other noble men. Unless steps are taken to avert it, the offenders and their relatives must be punished. But it is chiefly within the family circles that spirits and the living-dead are likely to be offended. Therefore the pouring out of libation and making offerings of bits of food are done on the family basis so that members of the family may remain on good terms with their departed relatives. This is in addition to strengthening the fellowship and renewing contact between the two groups. When the living-dead make demands or give instructions, these are generally followed immediately and obediently, unless they become excessive.

We have emphasized the corporate nature of African communities which are knit together by a web of kinship relationships and other social structures. Within this situation, almost every form of evil that a person suffers, whether it is moral or natural evil, is believed to be caused by members of his community. Similarly, any moral offence that he commits is directly or indirectly against members of his society. The principle of hierarchy is most helpful here. As a rule, a person of a lower rank, status or age commits an offence against another person or being of a higher rank or age. One may also offend against a person of the same status. Never or rarely does a person or being of a higher status do what constitutes an offence against a person of a lower status. What is considered evil or offensive functions from a low level to a higher level; and if a witch, for example, bewitches a little child, this act puts her on a lower level than the child. That is the philosophical understanding concerning what constitutes evil in the context of relationships. Something is considered to be evil not because of its intrinsic nature, but by virtue of who does it to whom and from which level of status.

According to this principle, God does not and cannot commit evil against His creation. We have already mentioned societies like the Akamba, Herero and others who firmly hold that since God does them no evil, they have no need to sacrifice to Him. When people feel that a misfortune or calamity has come from God, they interpret this not as an offence, but as punishment caused by their misdoings. So also the spirits on the whole do not offend against men; the living-dead do not offend against men, the king or ruler does not offend against his subjects, the elder in the village does not offend those who are younger or under him, and parents do not offend against their children. If parents do something which hurts their children and which constitutes an offence against the children, it is not the children as such who experience it as offence: rather, it is the community, the clan, the nation or the departed relatives who are the real object of offence, since they are the ones in a higher status than the parents. Consequently it is not the children themselves but the offended community or clan or living-dead who punish the parents.

This is the ideal. There are exceptions to it as to any generalizations. For example, if the king departs from the laws and customs established by the founders of the nation, he would be considered as offending against his subjects because he has departed from the established order. Indeed the offence is also against the patriarchs and heroes of the nation and, therefore, it is in effect an offence against beings of a higher status. But if he takes the cow of somebody among his subjects, this may not be regarded as an offence against the owner of the cow: for it is the king who has taken the cow, and he has the right to take it.

Within this tightly knit corporate society where personal relationships are so intense and so wide, one finds perhaps the most paradoxical areas of African life. This corporate type of life makes every member of the community dangerously naked in the sight of other members. It is paradoxically the centre of love and hatred, of friendship and enmity, of trust and suspicion, of joy and sorrow, of generous tenderness and bitter jealousies. It is paradoxically the heart of security and insecurity, of building and destroying the individual and the community. Everybody knows everybody else: a person cannot be individualistic, but only corporate. Every form of pain, misfortune, sorrow or suffering; every illness and sickness; every death whether of an old man or of the infant child; every failure of the crop in the fields, of hunting in the wilderness or of fishing in the waters; every bad omen or dream: these and all the other manifestations of evil that man experiences are blamed on somebody in the corporate society. Natural explanations may indeed be found, but mystical explanations must also be given. People create scapegoats for their sorrows. The shorter the radius of kinship and family ties, the more scapegoats there are. Frustrations, psychic disturbances, emotional tensions, and other states of the inner person, are readily externalized and incarnated, or made concrete in another human being or in circumstances which lay the blame on an external agent.

Here then we find a vast range of occasions for offences by one or more individuals against others in their corporate community. The environment of intense relationship favours strongly the growth of the belief in magic, sorcery, witchcraft, and all the fears, practices and concepts that go with this belief. I do not for a moment deny that there are spiritual forces outside man which seem sometimes to function within human history and human society. But the belief in the mystical power is greater than the ways in which that power might actually function within the human society. African communities in the villages are deeply affected and permeated by the psychological atmosphere which creates both real and imaginary powers or forces of evil that give rise to more tensions, jealousies, suspicions, slander, accusations and scapegoats. It is a vicious cycle. Let us illustrate this by moving from the academic to the practical.

Within this intensely corporate type of society, there are endless manifestations of evil. These include murders, robberies, rape, adultery, lies, stealing, cruelty especially towards women, quarrels, bad words, disrespect to persons of a higher status, accusations of sorcery, magic and witchcraft, disobedience of children and the like. In this atmosphere, all is neither grim nor bright. It is hard to describe these things: one needs to participate or grow up in village life, to get an idea of the depth of evil and its consequences upon individuals and society. A visitor to the village will immediately be struck by African readiness to externalize the spontaneous feelings of joy, love, friendship and generosity. But this must be balanced by the fact that Africans are men, and there are many occasions when their feelings of hatred, strain, fear, jealousy and suspicion also become readily externalized. This makes them just as brutal, cruel, destructive and unkind as any other human beings in the world. By nature, Africans are neither angels nor demons; they possess and exercise the potentialities of both angels and demons. They can be as kind as the Germans, but they can be as murderous as the Germans; Africans can be as generous as the Americans, but they can be as greedy as the Americans; they can be as friendly as the Russians, but they can be as cruel as the Russians; they can be as honest as the English, but they can also be as equally hypocritical. In their human nature Africans are Germans, Swiss, Chinese, Indians or English—they are men.

Ritual matters are another area where offence might be committed. Every African society has regulations and procedures about ceremonies and rituals. When offence is committed here, it is often necessary to perform ritual purification. We may cite an example from the Gikuyu, who perform the ritual of "vomiting the sin," to cleanse a person from ritual evil. For this purpose a goat is slaughtered and its stomach contents taken out. An elder presides over minor occasions, but a medicine-man is necessary for major offences, The stomach contents are first mingled with medicines, Then the officiating elder takes a brush with which he wipes off some of the mixture on the tongue of the offender, enumerating the offences committed. Each time the offender spits out the mixture on the ground. Afterwards the walls of his house are brushed with the same mixture. If the house is not so cleansed, it must be demolished. This rite is full of symbolism which is not hard to see.

RESTITUTION AND PUNISHMENT

The majority of African peoples believe that God punishes in this life. Thus, He is concerned with the moral life of mankind, and therefore upholds the moral law. With a few exceptions, there is no belief that a person is punished in the hereafter for what he does wrong in this life. When punishment comes, it comes in the present life. For that reason, misfortunes may be interpreted as indicating that the sufferer has broken some moral or ritual conduct against God, the spirits, the elders or other members of his society. This does not contradict the belief that misfortunes are the work of some members, especially workers of magic, sorcery and witchcraft, against their fellow men. This village logic is quite normal in African thinking. I do not understand it, but I accept it. The Banyarwanda and Barundi express God's punitive acts in a proverb that "God exercises vengeance in silence."[6] The Nuer link sickness with the fault that lies behind it, and therefore sacrifice in order to stay the punitive consequences. "In the one case the emphasis is on the actions from which one looks forward to the sickness which, when it comes, is identified with them. In the other case the emphasis is on the sickness and one looks backwards from it to faults which might have brought it about, even if one makes no attempt to discover what they were."[7] The same might be said about many other African peoples.

Each community or society has its own set form of restitution and punishment for various offences, both legal and moral. These range from death for offences like practising sorcery and witchcraft, committing murder and adultery, to paying fines of cattle, sheep or money for minor cases like accidental injury to one's companion or when sheep escape and eat potato vines in a neighbour's field. It is generally the elders of the area who deal with disputes and breaches arising from various types of moral harm or offences against custom and, ritual. Traditional chiefs and rulers, where these exist, have the duty of keeping law and order, and executing justice in their areas. Nowadays there are governmental law courts, some of which make use of the services of the elders, and incorporate something from the traditional customary law.

There is one form of justice administered through the use of the curse. The basic principle here is that if a person is guilty, evil will befall him according to the words used in cursing him. By the use of good magic, it is believed, a person can curse an unknown thief or other offender. But most of the curses are within family circles. The operative principle is that only a person of a higher status can effectively curse one of a lower status, but not vice versa. The most feared curses are those pronounced by parents, uncles, aunts or other close relatives against their "juniors" in the family. The worst is the curse uttered at the death-bed, for once the pronouncer of the curse has died, it is practically impossible to revoke it. If the guilty person repents and asks for the curse to be lifted, the person who uttered it can revoke it either automatically or ritually if it is a very serious one. There are many stories in African villages, telling about the fulfilment of curses where a person is guilty. If one is not guilty, then

---

6 Guillebaud in Smith, p. 200.
7 Evans-Pritchard, II, p. 194.

the curse does not function. Formal curses are feared much in African societies, and this fear, like that or witchcraft, helps to check bad relationships especially in family circles.

Formal oaths are used as another method of establishing and maintaining good human relationships. There are oaths which bind people mystically together, the best known being the one which creates what is rather loosely referred to as "blood-brotherhood." By means of this oath, two people who are not immediately related, go through a ritual which often involves exchanging small amounts of their blood by drinking or rubbing it into each other's body. After that they look upon each other as real "blood" brothers or sisters, and will behave in that capacity towards each other for the rest of their lives. Their families are also involved in this "brotherly" contract, so that for example, their children would not intermarry. This oath places great moral and mystical obligations upon the parties concerned; and any breach of the covenant is dreaded and feared to bring about misfortunes. There are oaths taken when people join the so-called "secret societies," when they are initiated in the rites of passage or in professions like divination. Other oaths are taken when secret information is divulged, to guard some knowledge or other secrets. Oaths may also be taken by children before the death of their parents if the latter want very much that their children observe certain instructions or carry out important requests. Oaths range in seriousness: some are meant to bring about death if they are broken, others cause temporary pain or misfortunes of one type or another. The belief behind oaths is that God, or some power higher than the individual man, will punish the person who breaks the requirements of the oath or covenant. Like curses, oaths are feared and many are administered ritually and at great expense.

SUMMARY AND CONCLUSION

African notions of morality, ethics and justice have not been fully studied, and many books either do not mention them or do so only in passing. Idowu is one of the few exceptions here, and he devotes a whole chapter to the question of God and moral values among the Yoruba. He argues that for the Yoruba, moral values derive from the nature of God Himself, Whom they consider to be the "Pure King," "Perfect King," "One clothed in white, Who dwells above" and is the "Essentially white Object, white Material without pattern (entirely white)." Character (*Iwa*) is the essence of Yoruba ethics, and upon it depends even the life of a person. So the people say, "Gentle character it is which enables the rope of life to stay unbroken in one's hand"; and again, "It is good character that is man's guard." Good character shows itself in the following ways: chastity before marriage and faithfulness during marriage; hospitality; generosity, the opposite of selfishness; kindness; justice; truth and rectitude as essential virtues; avoiding stealing; keeping a covenant and avoiding falsehood;

protecting the poor and weak, especially women; giving honour and respect to older people; and avoiding hypocrisy.[8] This can be applied, with additions to the list of what constitutes good character, to many African societies. It pertains to the traditional concept of "good" and "bad" or evil, that is, to the morals and ethics of any given society.

We can here make a distinction between "moral evil" and "natural evil." Moral evil pertains to what man does against his fellow man. There are customs, laws, regulations and taboos that govern conduct in society. Any breach of the right conduct amounts to a moral evil. We find endless examples of that in African societies. It is the opposite of cultivating or manifesting the virtues of good character. Indeed, we can say that good character is "good" because of the conduct it depicts. What lies behind the conception of moral "good" or "evil," is ultimately the nature of the relationship between individuals in a given community or society. There is almost no "secret sin": something or someone is "bad" or "good" according to the outward conduct. A person is not inherently "good" or "evil," but he acts in ways which are "good" when they conform to the customs and regulations of his community, or "bad" (evil) when they do not. To sleep with someone else's wife is not considered "evil" if these two are not found out by the society which forbids it; and in other societies it is in fact an expression of friendship and hospitality to let a guest spend the night with one's wife or daughter or sister. It is not the act in itself which would be "wrong" as such, but the relationships involved in the act: if relationships are not hurt or damaged, and if there is no discovery of breach of custom or regulation, then the act is not "evil" or "wicked" or "bad."

Those who practise witchcraft, evil magic and sorcery are the very incarnation of moral evil. They are, by their very nature, set to destroy relationships, to undermine the moral integrity of society, and to act contrary to what custom demands. Therefore such people are also instruments of natural evil—at least people associate them with it, so that when accidents, illnesses, misfortunes and the like strike, people immediately search for the agents of evil, for witches, for sorcerers and for neighbours or relatives who have used evil magic against them.

Even if, as we have pointed out, God is thought to be the ultimate upholder of the moral order, people do not consider Him to be immediately involved in the keeping of it. Instead, it is the patriarchs, living-dead, elders, priests, or even divinities and spirits who are the daily guardians or police of human morality. Social regulations of a moral nature are directed towards the immediate contact between individuals, between man and the living-dead and the spirits. Therefore, these regulations are on the man-to-man level, rather than, the God-to-man plane of morality. One could draw up a long list of them: don't kill another man except in war, don't steal, don't show disrespect to people of a

---

8 Idowu, pp. 144–68; cf. P. Tempels *Bantu Philosophy*, pp. 75–108, with some odd conclusions.

higher status, don't have sexual intercourse with a wide variety of persons, such as another man's wife, your sister or other close relative or children, don't use bad words especially to someone of a higher status, don't backbite, don't tell lies, don't despise or laugh at a cripple, don't take away someone else's piece of land; keep the many taboos and regulations concerning parts of the body, proper behaviour according to kinship relationships, and activities such as hunting, fishing and eating; observe the correct procedure in ritual matters and so on. In positive language, the list is also long, including items like: be kind, help those who cry to you for help, show hospitality, be faithful in marriage, respect the elders, keep justice, behave in a humble way towards those senior to you, greet people especially those you know, keep your word given under oath, compensate when you hurt someone or damage his property, follow the customs and traditions of your society.

The list of what should and should not be done is so long and detailed that a person is constantly confronted with moral demands throughout his life. This is seriously so in the environment where the individual is conscious of himself in terms of "I am because we are, and since we are, therefore I am." And, as we have seen, within the African communities where kinship makes a person intensely "naked," these moral demands are uncomfortably scrutinized by everybody so that a person who fails to live up to them cannot escape notice. Therefore, the essence of African morality is that it is more "societary" than "spiritual"; it is a morality of "conduct" rather than a morality of "being." This is what one might call "dynamic ethics" rather than "static ethics," for it defines what a person *does* rather than what he *is*. Conversely, a person is what he is because of what he does, rather than that he does what he does because of what he is. Kindness is not a virtue unless someone is kind; murder is not evil until someone kills another person in his community. Man is not by nature either "good" or "bad" ("evil") except in terms of what he does or does not do. This, it seems to me, is a necessary distinction to draw in discussing African concept of morality and ethics. It should also help us to understand something about the belief in witchcraft, magic and sorcery.

This point is connected with the second form of evil, which we have distinguished as "natural evil." By this I mean those experiences in human life which involve suffering, misfortunes, diseases, calamity, accidents and various forms of pain. In every African society these are well known. Most of them are explainable through "natural" causes. But as we saw for African peoples nothing sorrowful happens by "accident" or "chance": it must all be "caused" by some agent (either human or spiritual). If our analysis in the previous paragraph is valid, we can see also that the logic or philosophy behind "moral evil" would not permit "natural evil" to take place purely by means of "natural causes." People must find the agent "causing" such evil. In some societies it is thought that a person suffers because he has contravened some regulation, and God or the spirits, therefore, punish the offender. In that case, the person concerned is actually the cause of his own suffering: he first externalizes the cause, and then inverts it. But in most cases, different forms of suffering are believed to be caused by human agents who are almost exclusively witches, sorcerers and workers of evil magic. We have seen that these are the incarnation of evil viewed socially. They are also "responsible" for "causing" what would be "natural evil," by using incantations, mystical power, medicines, by sending secondary agents like flies and animals, by using their "evil eye," by wishing evil against their fellow man, by hating or feeling jealous, and by means of other "secret" methods. The logic here is that "natural evil" is present because these immoral agents exist; and these are evil because they do evil deeds. Again I confess that I do not understand this logic, but I accept it as valid for our understanding of African religions and philosophy. To say, in African societies, that a person is "good" or "bad" has extremely profound connotations, for it summarizes the whole image or picture of the person in the context of his actions. One does not "love" in a vacuum: it is the deeds which signify that there is love behind them; one does not "hate" in a vacuum, it is the deeds that signify what lies behind them. In such experiences, the world of nature is not divorced from that of man. In the experience of evil, African peoples see certain individuals as being intricately involved, but wickedly, in the otherwise smooth running of the natural universe. This is again another point where we observe that African ontology is deeply anthropocentric.

Our discussion has so far been focused upon the traditional setting. We cannot leave the picture there, without saying something about changes that are taking place all over Africa. These changes certainly have a bearing on traditional religions and philosophy: shaping them and being shaped by them. . . .

THE MORAL FOUNDATIONS
OF AN AFRICAN CULTURE

KWASI WIREDY

INTRODUCTION

Morality in the strictest sense is universal to human culture. Indeed, it is *essential* to all human culture. Any society without a modicum of morality must collapse. But what is morality in this sense? It is, simply, the observance of rules for the harmonious adjustment of the interests of the individual to those of others in society. This, of course, is a minimal concept of morality. A richer concept of morality, even more pertinent to human growth, will have an essential reference to that special kind of motivation called the sense of duty. Morality in this sense involves not just the *de facto* conformity to the requirements of the harmony of interests, but also that conformity to those requirements which is inspired by an imaginative and sympathetic identification with the interests of others even at the cost of a possible curtailment of one's own interests. This is not a demand for a supererogatory altruism. But a certain minimum of altruism is absolutely essential to the moral motivation. In this sense, too, morality is probably universal to all human societies, though most certainly not to all known individuals.

The foregoing reflection still does not exclude the possibility of a legitimate basis for differentiating the morals of the various peoples of the world. This is so for at least three reasons. First of all, although morality in both of the senses just discriminated is the same wherever and whenever it is practised, different peoples, groups, and individuals have different understandings of it. The contrasting moral standpoints of humanism and supernaturalism, for example, illustrate this diversity. Secondly, the concrete cultural context in which a moral principle is applied may give it a distinctive colouring. Lastly, but most importantly, there is a broad concept of morals closely contiguous to the narrow one—which is what the two concepts of morality noted earlier on together amount to—in regard to which the contingencies of space, time, and clime may play quite a constitutive role. This appertains to the domain that, speaking very broadly, may be called custom. What is pertinent here are such things as the prescriptions and proscriptions operative in a community regarding life and death, work and leisure, reward and retribution, aspirations and aversions, pleasure and pain, and the relationships between the sexes, the generations, and other social categories and classes. The combined impact of such norms of life and thought in a society should give a distinctive impression of its morals.

AKAN HUMANISM

But let me start with the matter of conceiving morals. African conceptions of morals would seem generally to be of a humanistic orientation. Anthropological studies need substantial support for this claim. Nevertheless, the accounts are not always philosophically inquisitive, and I prefer, in elaborating on this characterisation, to rely on my own native knowledge of the life and thought of the Akans of Ghana. On this basis, I can affirm the humanism in question with less inhibition. The commonest formulation of this outlook is in the saying, which almost any Akan adult or even young hopeful will proffer on the slightest provocation, that it is a human being that has value: *Onipa na ohia*. The English translation just given of the Akan saying, though pertinent, needs supplementation, for the crucial term here has a double connotation. The word *(o)hia* in this context means both that which is of value and that which is needed. Through the first meaning the message is imparted that all value derives from human interests, and through the second that human fellowship is the most important of human needs. When this last thought is uppermost in his or her consciousness an Akan would be likely to add to the maxim under discussion an elucidation to the effect that one might have all the gold in the world and the best stocked wardrobe, but if one were to appeal to these in the hour of need they would not respond; only a human being will. (*Onipa ne asem: mefre sika a, sika nnye so; mefre ntama a, ntama nmye so; onipa ne asem.*) What is already beginning to emerge is the great stress on human sociality thought, but before pursuing this angle of the subject, let me tarry a while on the significance of Akan humanism.

One important implication of the founding of value on human interests is the independence of morality from religion in the Akan outlook: what is good in general is what promotes human interests. Correspondingly, what is good in the more narrowly ethical sense is, by definition, what is conducive to the harmonisation of those interests. Thus, the will of God, not to talk of that of any other extra-human being, is logically incapable of defining the good. On the Akan understanding of things, indeed, God is good in the highest; but his goodness is conceptually of a type with the goodness of a just and benevolent ancestor, only in his case quality and scale are assumed to be limitless. The prospect of punishment from God or some lesser being may concentrate the mind on the narrow path of virtue, but it is not this that creates the sense of moral obligation. Similarly, the probability of police intervention might conceivably give pause to a would-be safebreaker, though if he or she had any sense of morals at all it would not be thanks to the collective will of the police or even the state.

This conceptual separation of morals from religion is, most likely, responsible in some measure for the remarkable fact that there is no such thing as an institutional religion in Akan culture. The procedures associated with the belief in sundry extra-human beings of varying powers and inclinations, so often given pride of place in accounts of African religions, are in fact practical utilitarian programs for tapping the resources of this world. The idea, in a nutshell, is that God invested the cosmos with all sorts of potentialities, physical and quasi-physical, personal and quasi-personal, which human beings may bend to their purposes, if they learn how. Naturally, in dealing with beings and powers believed to be of a quasi-personal character, certain aspects of behaviour patterns will manifest important analogies to the canons of ordinary human interactions. For example, if you wanted something from a being of superhuman repute who is open to persuasion mixed with praise, pragmatic common sense alone would recommend an attitude of demonstrative respect and circumspection and a language of laudatory circumlocution reminiscent of worship, but the calculative and utilitarian purpose would belie any attribution of a specifically religious motivation. In fact, the Akans are known to be sharply contemptuous of "gods" who fail to deliver; continued respect is conditional on a high percentage of scoring by the Akan reckoning.

In total contrast to the foregoing is the Akan attitude to the supreme being, which is one of unconditional reverence and absolute trust. Absent here is any notion that so perfect a being requires or welcomes institutions for singing or reciting his praises. Nor, relatedly, are any such institutions felt to be necessary for the dissemination of moral education or the reinforcement of the will to virtue. The theatre of moral upbringing is the home, at parents' feet and within range of kinsmen's inputs. The mechanism is precept, example, and correction. The temporal span of the process is lifelong, for, although upbringing belongs to the beginning of our earthly careers, the need for correction is an unending contingency in the lives of mortals. In adulthood, of course, as opposed to earlier stages in life, moral correction involves discourses of a higher level and may entail, besides, the imposition of compensatory obligations (of which more later); but, at all stages, verbal lessons in morality are grounded in conceptual and empirical considerations about human well-being. All this is why the term "humanistic" is so very apt as a characterisation of Akan moral thinking. At least in part, this is why it is correct to describe that ethic as non-supernaturalistic in spite of the sincere belief in a supreme being.

Insofar, then, as the concept of religion is applicable to the Akan outlook on life and reality, it can refer only to the belief and trust in a supreme being. In this respect, Akan religion is purely intellectual. In this respect, too, it is purely personal, being just a level of an individual's voluntary metaphysic, devoid of social entanglements. In truth, most Akans espouse that metaphysic as a matter of course. Akan conventional wisdom actually holds that the existence of God is so obvious that it does not need to be taught even to a child (*Obi nkyere akwadaa Name*). Nevertheless, sceptics are not unknown in Akan society, and a time-honoured policy of peaceful *laissez faire* extends to them as to all others in matters of private persuasion.

DEFINING MORALITY

Morality, too, is intellectual, by Akan lights. Concrete moral situations in real life are frequently highly composite tangles of imponderables, and perceiving them in their true lineaments is a cognitive accomplishment in itself. So, too, is the sure grasping of first principles and their judicious application to the particulars of conduct. Morality is also personal, for in the final analysis the individual must take responsibility for his or her own actions. But surely morality is neither purely intellectual, for it has an irreducible passional ingredient, nor is it purely personal, for it is quintessentially social.

All these insights are encapsulated in various Akan maxims and turns of phrase. Recognition of the intellectual dimension of right conduct is evidenced in the Akan description of a person of ethical maturity as an *obadwenma*. This word means "one possessed of high thinking powers". Literally, it means "child, thinking child", in other words, a thinking child of the species. The Akans are no less emphatic in their articulation of their sense of individual responsibility. According to a very popular proverb, it is because God dislikes injustice that he gave everyone their own name (thereby forestalling any misattribution of responsibility). Along with this clear sense of individual responsibility goes an equally strong sense of the social reverberations of an individual's conduct. The primary responsibility for an action, positive or negative, rests with the doer, but a non-trivial secondary responsibility extends to the individual's family and, in some cases, to the surrounding community. This brings us to the social orientation of the Akan concept of a person. We will not be able to elaborate it fully in the present discussion, but a crucial consideration will be adduced here. It is that, for the Akans, a person is social not only because he/she lives in a community, which is the only context in which full development, or indeed any sort of human development is possible, but also because, by his/her original constitution, a human being is part of a social whole.

The underlying doctrine is this. A person consists of three elements. One of these comes *directly* from God and is, in fact, a speck of the divine substance. This is the life principle. By virtue of this constituent all human beings are one; they are all members of the universal family of humankind whose head and spring is God (*Nipa nyinaa ye Nyame mma: obiara nnye asaase ba*). Literally, all human beings are the children of God; none is a child of the earth. The two remaining elements are more mundane in origin. There is what might be called the blood principle which derives from the mother and, somewhat more specifically, there is what might be called the charisma principle which comes from the father. The blood from the mother is what principally gives rise to a person's body. The biological input from the father is responsible for the degree of personal presence that each individual develops at the appropriate stage (i.e. the individual's degree of charisma). The ontological classification of these elements is not exactly straightforward. Suffice it to say that the physical/spiritual dichotomy is unlikely to be a source of light in this connection. In any case, our interest here is in the social significance of those components.

Both the maternal and paternal contributions to the make-up of a person are the basis of membership in specific social units. The Akans being a matrilineal group, it is the blood principle that situates a person in the most important kinship unit, namely, the lineage, or, more extensively, the clan. Through the charisma principle one is a member of a grouping on the father's side which, although largely ceremonial, is nevertheless the framework of a lot of goodwill.

The point now is that, on this Akan showing, a person has a well structured social identity even before birth. Thus, when an Akan maxim points out that when a human being descends from on high he/she alights in a town (*se onipa siane fi soro a obesi kuro mu*), the idea is that one comes into a community in which one already has well defined social affiliations. But society presupposes rules, and moral rules are the most essential of these. Since all rules have their rationale, a question that challenges the ethical imagination, especially one thoroughly impregnated with visions of the ineluctable sociality of human existence, is: what is the rationale of moral rules? Among the Akans some of the most profound philosophic conceptions are expressed by way of art motifs, and a celebrated answer to this question is offered in one such construct of fine art: a crocodile with one stomach and two heads locked in combat. The lessons are:

1. Although human beings have a core of common interests, they also have conflicting interests that precipitate real struggles.

2. The aim of morality, as also derivatively of statesmanship, is to harmonise those warring interests through systematic adjustment and adaptation. The single stomach symbolises not only the commonality of interests, but also a natural basis for the possibility of a solution to the existential antinomy.

Two levels of solution are distinguishable, corresponding to a distinction foreshadowed in our opening paragraph. There is the level of prudence or enlightened self-interest, and there is that of pure moral motivation. Both species of thought and intention may be equally adapted to securing the social good, the first through cool and calm ratiocination, the second through both rational reflection and human sympathy. But they evoke different appraisals from people of goodwill. There will always be something distasteful about correctness of conduct bereft of passion. A Ghanaian comedian puts it even more strongly. Speaking with a deliberately unidiomatic bombast, he opines: "Ability without sentimentality is nothing short of barbarity." Nevertheless, it appears that teachers of morals everywhere have tended to find prudential considerations more psychologically efficacious in moral persuasion than abstract appeals to goodwill. Certainly, Akan ethical reflection does not stay immobile at this level of ethics, but Akan discourse abounds in prudential maxims, for example:

1. If you do not allow your neighbour to reach nine you will never reach ten. (*Woamma wo yonko antwa nkrong a worentwa edu.*)

2. Somebody's troubles have arrived; those of another are on the way. (*Obi de aba; obi de nam kwan so.*)

3. It is a fool that says, "My neighbour is the butt of the attack, not me." (*Kwasea na ose, "Ye de meyonko, yenna me."*)

4. The stick that was used to beat Takyi is the same that will be used to beat Nyankomago. (*Abaa a yede boo Takyi no aa na ye de bebo Nyankomago.*)

5. One person's path will intersect with another's before too long. (*Obi kwan nkye na asi obi de mu.*)

That Akan ethics transcends this level of moral understanding is evident from other parts of their corpus of moral sayings. I will comment here on one particularly instructive form of moral expostulation. To a person whose conduct betrays obliviousness to the interests of others, it is said, "Sticking into your neighbour's flesh, it might just as well be sticking into a piece of wood" (*Etua woyonko ho a etua dua mu*), than which there can scarcely be a lower rating for a person's moral stature. On this reading of morals, the ultimate moral inadequacy consists in that lack of feeling which is the root of all selfishness. The implied imperative is: "In all inter-personal situations put yourself into the skin of the other and see if you can contemplate the consequences of your proposed action with equanimity." If we call the recommended frame of mind sympathetic impartiality, we may elicit from the Akan maxim under discussion the view that sympathetic impartiality is the first principle of all morals. This principle is the logical basis of the Golden Rule, or the obverse of it that is frequently heard in Akan ethical talk, namely, "Do not do unto others what you would not that they do unto you" (*Nea wo yonko de ve wo a erenye wo de no mfa nye no.*) Or, more literally, what you would not find acceptable if it were done to you by another, do not do to him or her. To be sure, this does not sound, even in our vernacular, as epigrammatic as the normal run of Akan apothegms, but it provides, nonetheless, a solid foundation for the definition of moral worth in its most edifying sense.

ETHICS AND PRACTICE

The foregoing account of the Akan perspective on moral first principles, however brief, must form the basis of our next question, which is: "In what basic ways do the Akans endeavour to translate their ethical understanding into practical fact?" In this regard the single most important consideration concerns the depth of the Akan sense of what we have called the sociality of human existence. Morality is, of course, necessarily social. Hence any group of humans that can be credited with any sense of morals at all—surely, a minimal species credential—will have some sense of human sociality. But in the consciousness of moral humankind there is a finely graduated continuum of the intensity of this feeling which ranges, in an ascending order, from the austerely delimited social sympathies of rigorous individualism to the pervasive commitment to social involvement characteristic of communalism. It is a commonplace of anthropological wisdom that African social organisation manifests the latter type of outlook. Akan society is eminently true to this typology.

What this means, more amply, is that Akan society is of a type in which the greatest value is attached to communal belonging. And the way in which a sense of communal belonging is fostered in the individual is through the concentrated stress on kinship identity already adumbrated in our earlier allusions to the Akan concept of a person. Not only is there what might perhaps be called an ontological basis for this identity in terms of the constituents of personhood, but there is also a distinct normative layer of a profound social significance in that concept. Thus conceived, a human person is essentially the centre of a thick set of concentric circles of obligations and responsibilities matched by rights and privileges revolving round levels of relationships irradiating from the consanguinity of household kith and kin, through the "blood" ties of lineage and clan, to the wider circumference of human familyhood based on the common possession of the divine spark.

In consequence of this character of the Akan concept of a person, habitual default in duties and responsibilities could lead to a diminution in one's status as a person in the eyes of the community. Not, of course, that becoming less and less of a person implies being thought more and more unworthy of human rights. On the contrary, there is a strong sense of the irreducibility of human dignity in Akan thought. However socially inept an individual may be, he/she still remains a being begotten of a direct gift of God incarnated through the intimacy of man and woman. He/she remains, in other words, a human being, and as such is deserving of a certain basic respect and sympathy. Indeed, as soon as confirmed social futility begins to look pathologically chronic, animadversion quickly turns into solicitude, and any previous efforts in hortatory correction or in the application of more concrete sanctions are redirected towards rehabilitation, usually with the aid of indigenous specialists in bodily and mental health.

Nevertheless, any Akan steeped in the culture, or even just sensitive to surrounding social norms, constantly watches and prays lest he/she be overtaken by the spectre of loss of personhood (in any degree). More positively and also more optimistically, every cultivated Akan (*Okaniba*) sees life as a scenario of continual striving after personhood in ever increasing dimensions. The details of this life mission, so to speak, will also be the details of the Akan vision of the ethical life. We must here content ourselves with only broad outlines. But before going on, let us note that our focus has been on ethics or morals in the sense in which morality is a matter of *mores*, rather than of the Categorical Imperative or even of the less hallowed canons of prudence.

What, then, in its social bearings, is the Akan ideal of personhood? It is the conception of an individual who, through mature reflection and steady motivation, is able to carve out a reasonably ample livelihood for self, "family", and a potentially wide group of kin dependants, besides making substantial contributions to the well-being of society at large. The communalistic orientation of the society in question means that an individual's image will depend rather crucially upon the extent to which his/her actions benefit others rather than him/herself, not, of course, by accident or coincidence, but by design. The implied counsel, though, is not one of unrelieved self-denial, for the Akans are well aware that charity further afield must start at home. More pertinently, they are apt to point out that one cannot blow a horn on an empty stomach

(*Yede ayaase na ehyen aben*). Still, an individual who remained content with self-regarding successes would be viewed as so circumscribed in outlook as not to merit the title of a real person.

Opportunities for other-regarding exertions in Akan society were legion in the past and remain so even now. By the very nature of the traditional economy, which was predominantly agricultural and based on individual self-employment, public works had, as a rule, to be done by voluntary communal labour. Habitual absences or malingering or half-hearted participation marked an individual down as a useless person (*onipa hunu*) or, by an easily deduced Akan equation, a non-person (*onye onipa*). In contemporary Ghana (and Ivory Coast), where the Akans live, many of the public works are financed out of mandatory taxes and carried out by professionals with hired labour. Nevertheless, in the villages and small towns a significant portion of such work is still done by way of voluntary communal labour, and a good proportion also through voluntary contributions of money and materials.

SOME CONTEMPORARY PROBLEMS

What follows is a contemporary complication: with the growth of commerce and industry, including the industry of modern politics, a non-negligible number of Akans have become very rich. In the Akan manner, they make voluntary contributions of unprecedented magnitude to their communities; and the communities, for their part, reciprocate in fine eulogistic style and lionise them in other ways too, as is traditional. So far, so good, except for the following circumstance. Some of these rich people are known to have come by their assets through dubious techniques of acquisition. The unfortunate effects of this situation on the ideals of the young constitute some of the more intractable problems generated by the impact of industrialisation on the Akan traditional ethic.

Another aspect of Akan communalism imperilled by modern conditions, through atrophy rather than adulteration, is the practice of neighbourhood mutual aid. This practice has its foundations deep in the Akan conception of values. It is relevant here to recall the Akan adage, *Onipa na ohyia*, quoted earlier in this discussion. It was interpreted as affirming, through the semantic fecundity of the word *hyia*, both that human interest is the basis of all value and that human fellowship is the most important of human needs. The concept of *hyia*, in the context of that adage is, in fact, a veritable mine of ethical meanings. In that context it also bears the seeds of another fundamental thought in the Akan philosophy of life which is made explicit in the maxim, *Onipa hia moa*, meaning, by way of first approximation, "A human being needs help." The intent of the maxim, however, is not just to observe a fact, but also to prescribe a line of conduct. The imperative here is carried by the word *hia*, which in this context also has a connotation of entitlement: a human being deserves, ought, to be helped.

This imperative is born of an acute sense of the essential dependency of the human condition. The idea of dependency may even be taken as a component of the Akan conception of a person. "A human being," says a noted Akan proverb, "is not a palm tree so as to be self-sufficient" (*Onipa nye abe na ne ho ahyia ne ho*). Indeed, at birth a human being is not only not self-sufficient but also radically self-insufficient, if one may be permitted the expression: he/she is totally dependent on others. In due course, through growth and acculturation, acquired skills and abilities will reduce this dependency but will never eliminate it completely. Self-reliance is, of course, understood and recommended by the Akans, but its very possibility is predicated upon this ineliminable residue of human dependency. Human beings, therefore, at all times, in one way or another, directly or indirectly, need the help of their kind.

One very standard situation in Akan life in which this truth was continually illustrated was in traditional agriculture. As hinted earlier, this was generally based on smallholdings worked by individual farmers and their households. In such a mode of production recurrent stages were easily foreseeable where the resources of any one farmer would be insufficient to accomplish a necessary task efficiently—be it the initial clearing of the ground or the scooping out of, say, cocoa beans from great heaps of pods. At such moments, all that was necessary was for one to send word to one's neighbours indicating the time, place, and the nature of the help needed. Very much as day follows night, the people would assemble at the right time at the indicated place with their own implements of work and together help get the job done speedily and with almost festive enthusiasm, in full and warranted conviction that when their turn came the same gesture would be returned in exactly the same spirit. Anybody who availed himself of the benefits of this system and yet dragged his feet when the call came from others was liable to be convicted, at the bar of public opinion, of such fathomless degeneracy as to be branded a social outcast. The type of mutual aid here discussed probably occurs in varying intensities in rural communities all over the world, but in traditional Akan society it was so much and so palpably a part of working experience that the Akans actually came to think of life (*obra*) as one continuous drama of mutual aid (*nnoboa*). *Obra ye nnoboa*: "Life is mutual aid", according to an Akan saying.

In recent times, however, amidst the exigencies of urbanisation and the increasing— if not as yet preponderant—commercialisation of agriculture, the ideology of mutual aid is losing some of its hold; and the spirit of neighbourhood solidarity, though by no means extinguished, is finding fewer avenues of expression. It has not escaped some leaders of opinion that the traditional ethos of mutual aid might profitably be channelled into a strong movement of modern cooperatives, but as yet, organised effort in this direction is halting in momentum and paltry in results.

Nevertheless, in countless small ways the sense of human solidarity continues to manifest itself quite pervasively in the daily life of the Akans and of the peoples of Ghana generally, of whom these moral characterisations remain true, if not to the letter, then at least to the syllable. Happily, too, the threat of individualism posed by urbanisation has not as yet proved unduly deleterious to the Akan's national trait. Thus, even now, whether in the countryside or in a large city, a Ghanaian coming upon another human being, Ghanaian or foreigner, who is in difficulty, will go out of his/her way to help. As far as he/she is concerned, the bad person is exactly the one who would walk off on the excuse of some pressing business. Of course, if urbanisation and other apparent concomitants of modernisation are not controlled with conscious and rational planning based on the humane sensitivities of the communalistic ethic, then this fund of automatic good will dry up and African life will experience increasingly the Hobbesian rigours of a single-minded commercialism.

KINSHIP AND MORALITY

The allusion to foreigners in the last paragraph prompts a further observation. The sense of human solidarity which we have been discussing works particularly to the advantage of foreigners, who, in the deeply felt opinion of the Akans, are doubly deserving of sympathy; this is on the grounds, firstly, of their common humanity, and, secondly, of their vulnerability as individuals cut off for the time being, at any rate, from the emotional and material support of their kinship environment. Accordingly, when, some time ago, an Akan guitarist and lyricist, Kwabena Onyina, sang *Akwantu ma sem: akwantufo ye mmobo* (Think of the woes of travel: the plight of a traveller is rueful) he struck a sympathetic chord in the deepest reaches of the Akan consciousness. Gratified visitors to Ghana have often been quick to acknowledge the benefits accruing to them.

Again, to pursue an allusion in the preceding paragraph: the notion of kinship support just mentioned is of the highest importance in the Akan communal set-up, for it is the basis of the sense of belonging which gives the individual much of his/her psychological stability (this, incidentally, is why a traveller bereft of it strikes the Akan so forcefully as a sad case). It is also, conversely, the basis of a good proportion of the obligations in terms of which the individual's moral standing is assessed. The smallest and most intimate Akan kinship unit is the matrilineal household. This includes a person's mother and his/her mother's children, his/her mother's sisters and brothers, the children of the mother's sisters, and, at the top, the grandmother. It is instructive to observe that the English words aunt and cousin fail to capture the depth of kinship feelings corresponding to the relations of mother's sister and mother's sister's children respectively, in spite of their mechanical correctness as translations. In the Akan language the words for mother and mother's children are the same as for mother's sister and mother's sister's children. Since the relationships noted already comprehend quite a sizeable community, especially if the grandmother concerned has been even averagely fertile, this guarantees that in a traditional setting an Akan child begins life with quite a large sense of belonging and a broad sweep of sympathies.

The next extension of the circle of the kinship relations just described brings us to the level of the lineage. Here the *basic unit* consists of a person's grandmother and her children and grandchildren, together with the grandmother's brothers and sisters and the children and grandchildren of her sisters. This unit quickly swells with the culturally legitimate addition of a grandmother's maternal "cousins" and their descendants. From the point of view of a person's civic existence, this is the most significant circle of relations, for it was through the head of the lineage that, in traditional times, a person had his/her political representation. The lineage, as can easily be imagined, is a quite considerable group of people, but it is small in comparison with the maximal limit of kinship grouping, which is the set of all the people descending from one woman. The latter is the clan. For a quick idea of magnitude, consider that the Akans, now numbering in the region of seven million, trace their collective ancestry to seven women. Patently, individual Akans will never know all their relatives, but they can rest assured that they have a million of them.

For many practical purposes, however, it is the household and (basic) lineage circles of relations that have the most significance in terms of informal rights and obligations. Two illustrations must suffice here. Adult members of the lineage may be called upon to make financial contributions to rescue one of the fold fallen on hard times, say, with threatening insolvency. In view of the group's numbers, this does not necessarily take a heavy toll on individual pockets. Moreover, it is not lost upon the reflective individual that he/she might conceivably have been the beneficiary.

The next illustration has to do with somewhat lugubrious subject matter. Bereavement is one of the severest trials of the human psyche; unfortunately, it is recurrent. By both precept and practice Akan traditional culture engages itself, preeminently one might say, with finding ways to soothe lacerated emotions in such crises. The lineage system incorporates in its arrangements just such a mechanism. In full operation, everyone in the lineage is expected to play his/her part by word, song, dance, and material resource. Nor does the culture leave this to the lineage alone. Friends, neighbours, and even indirect acquaintances can always be counted upon to help in various ways to lighten the burden of sorrows. The framework for all this is the elaborate system of the Akan funeral. In spite of the excesses to which this institution has become subject through the rising tide of commercialism and egotistical exhibitionism, it remains an avenue for the expression of human solidarity at its most heartfelt. Proper participation therein is, in Akan eyes, contributory proof of real personhood.

CONCLUSION

It is clear from the foregoing that socialisation in the broad context of the lineage can be a veritable school for morality in its Akan acceptation. It is through the kinship channels of the lineage set-up that the Akan sense of the sociality of human beings finds its most natural expression. Moral life in the wider community is only an extension of a pattern of conduct inculcated at the lineage level. The fundamental values, some of which we have already outlined above, are the same on the two planes, and may briefly be summarised. A communalistic orientation will naturally prize social harmony. A characteristic Akan, and, it seems, African way of pursuing this ideal is through decision-making by consensus rather than by majority opinion. In politics—traditional African politics, not the modern travesties rampant on the continent—this leads to a form of democracy very different from the Western variety.

A thoroughgoing consensual approach to social issues can be expected to lead to corresponding procedures in other areas of social life too. A particularly interesting case relates to the Akan reaction to wrongdoing. Though the retributive spirit is not totally absent from reactions, especially at the state level, with some forms of wrongdoing the predominant tendency is to seek compensation or reconciliation or, in cases where extra-human forces are thought to be estranged, purification. I abstain advisedly from using the word "punishment" in this context, for, given this last remark, it may well be that there is no unproblematic rendition of this notion in the Akan conceptual framework. I am unable, however, to pursue this question here.

A well-known feature of Akan morals is respect for age. This is intelligible not only from the fact that we are dealing with a society strongly based on kinship relations which are naturally patterned into hierarchies based on age, but also because in traditional societies, which in part Akan society still remains, age is associated with knowledge, experience, and wisdom.

Akan moral thinking with regard to sex and marriage also deserves special mention. Here the humanistic and communalistic aspects of the Akan outlook come into play with interesting results. Because only empirical considerations bearing on human interests are admitted in moral evaluation, such unconditional proscriptions of pre-marital sex as are found in Christian teaching are absent from the moral rules of the Akans. From their point of view, it would be irrational to stop a prospective couple from seeking full knowledge of each other, moral, psychological, sexual, and so on. There is, of course, no sexual free-for-all; but still, a non-furtive relationship between an unmarried man and an unmarried woman need not be restricted to hugging. The only proviso is that it should be above board. On the other hand, the high value placed on reproductive fertility in a communalistic society based on single family unit agriculture will predictably lead to great emphasis being placed on the desirability of marriage and procreation. So much is this the case that being married with children well raised is part of the necessary conditions for personhood in the normative sense. A non-marrying, non-procreative person, however normal otherwise— not to talk of a Casanova counterpart—can permanently forget any prospect of this type of recognition in traditional Akan society. The only conceivable exceptions will be ones based on the noblest of alternative life commitments.

To understand all these facts about the Akan conception of morals is not necessarily to understand the culture in its entirety, but it is to have some sense of its foundations.

ISLAMIC ETHICS

■

THE ASSASSINATION OF ANWAR SADAT

On October 6, 1981, Egypt's President Anwar Sadat stood ceremoniously in the grandstand, dressed in full military uniform. Respected and loved by many, Sadat had recently won the Nobel Peace Prize for his efforts to restore some semblance of peace between Arabs and Jews. The annual parade commemorated the Egyptian army's crossing the Suez Canal and driving back the Israeli forces in 1973. And even though the Israeli army later regained their territories on the west bank of the Suez Canal and the Golan Heights with the help of enormous shipments of American weapons, Egyptians viewed the initial success over the Israelis as a victory, with this parade in the event's honor.

Just then, an armored truck stopped in front of the grandstand, and four armed men leapt from the truck throwing grenades and firing machine guns. Within seconds, Sadat was dead, his uniform splattered with blood, his body riddled with bullets.

The leader of the attack was also the mastermind: twenty-four year-old Khaled al-Islambuli, a lieutenant in the Egyptian army. He and his three accomplices had long considered Sadat as a betrayer of Islam. As they were immediately overpowered by guards, the wounded leader shouted, "I am Khaled al-Islambuli, I have killed Pharaoh, and I do not fear death."[1] Nearly six months later, on April 15, 1982, all four assassins, along with Mohammed Abd al-Salam al-Faraj, were executed.

Who was al-Faraj? During their trial, the assassins justified their action on the basis of Faraj's pamphlet entitled "The Neglected Duty" (*Al-Faridah al-Gha'ibah*). (A selection from this writing is at the end of this chapter.) According to Faraj's text, the Qur'an offers a valid sanction for the assassination. His tract, written in the 1970s, remains a pivotal text for modern militant Muslims and supports the violent overthrow of enemies of Islam, whether soldiers or civilians. In the text, Faraj proposes a sixth pillar of Islam in addition to the five pillars (belief in one God, daily prayers, alms to the poor, fasting during Ramadan, a pilgrimage to Mecca). His sixth pillar exhorts all devout Muslims to conduct a *jihad*, or sacred struggle, against enemies of Islam such as supporters of modern decadence, namely, America and her allies, as well as Muslim leaders like Sadat who betray Islamic law, or *sharia*. This sixth pillar is a call to arms, a religious "neglected duty," for every Muslim. Faraj is now dead, yet his tract lives on as a powerful testament in defense of extreme measures.

Soon after Sadat's death, the highest religious Islamic authority in Egypt, the Mufti, wrote a refutation to Faraj's position, and this was published in the Egyptian newspaper *Al-Ahram* on December 8, 1981, thus reaching a wide audience. Days later, the Cairo newspaper *Al-Ahrar* achieved particular notoriety by publishing Faraj's pamphlet in its entirety. At the same time, the newspaper's editor introduced the tract by warning readers of the pernicious nature of its contents.[2] (Note that Theodore Kaczynski's Unibomber "Manifesto" was also made public, compliments of the *Washington Post*.) Without a doubt, the tract has taken root in the minds and hearts of many Muslims. Is "Neglected Duty" an authentic depiction of Islamic teachings?

■ ISLAM'S IMAGE PROBLEM

Of all the major world traditions, Islam in particular suffers from a serious image problem. Besides misperceptions surrounding the treatment of women in Islam as well as its defense of polygamy, Islam is often linked to the extremely volatile political fabric in Middle Eastern countries. Scenarios abroad of highjackings, American hostages, terrorism, embassies under assault, suicide bombings, the continuing specters of Osama bin Laden and Saddam Hussein, as well as controversies within America surrounding Louis Farrakan, leader of the group Nation of Islam, have all contributed to fashioning a twisted image of Islam. Many Americans have come to think of Islam as a religion of violent fanatics. It is therefore all the more imperative to point to a critical difference between Islamic extremists and those devout Muslims who follow the creed of nonviolence that is espoused in the Qur'an.

The prevailing misconception of Islam is that Islam views itself as conducting a global conflict against the West and all that the West stands for. That is, because Muslims have historically engaged in a dualistic view of the world—the world of true believers (*dar al-Islam*) and the world of heretics (*dar al-Harb*)—this inevitably leads to equating Islam with extremism: Islam = Islamic fundamentalism = Islamic extremism.[3] Such a view is distorted.[4] No doubt, there are pockets of Islamic extremism, just as there are pockets of extremism in other religions. However, Muslim scholar John Esposito points to the dangers of associating Islam with Islamic extremism:

> *To equate Islam and Islamic fundamentalism uncritically with extremism is to judge Islam only by those who wreak havoc — a standard not applied to Judaism and Christianity. The danger is that heinous actions may be attributed to Islam rather than to a twisted or distorted interpretation of Islam. Thus despite the track record of Christianity and Western countries when it comes to making war, developing weapons of mass destruction, and imposing their imperialist designs, Islam and Muslim culture are portrayed as somehow peculiarly and inherently expansionist and prone to violence and warfare.*[5]

Indeed it is unfair to simply link Islam with its extremist elements. At the same time, it would be naïve to deny or downplay the extent of Islamic extremism throughout Islam's complex history and teachings. We find persistent manifestations of radicalism, violence, and outbursts of terrorist acts particularly in modern Islam, from Egypt's outlawed al Gamaa-i Islamiya ("the Islamic Group") to the militant branch of the Palestine Liberation Organization (PLO) to extremist Palestinian factions such as the al-Aqsa Martyrs and Hamas. Egypt's al Gamaa-i Islamiya was spearheaded by Sheik Omar Abdul Rahman, the blind scholar and former Islamic theologian who is now serving a life sentence in the United States for conspiring with eight others to blow up the World Trade Center the first time around on February 26, 1993. Experts believe he may have also been involved in the assassination of Anwar Sadat. The al-Aqsa Martyrs have been responsible for numerous acts of suicide terrorism against the Jews, such as the suicide bombing in Beit Yisrael mentioned in Chapter 4. As for Hamas, the term literally means "zeal" and is an acronym for Harakat al-Muqawama al-Islamiya, "Islamic Resistance Movement." Hamas was born in the late 1980s as a radical faction intended to counter what it perceived to be the weaker, ineffective PLO. Hamas followers take their cause to new heights, believing it to be grounded upon religion, and they chastise the PLO's political compromises.[6] Leaders in the Hamas movement continue to recruit suicide bombers from among its young followers. Although we commonly refer to their actions as "suicide bombings," the term used by Hamas is *istishhadi*, meaning "self-chosen martyrdom."[7] For members of Hamas, these martyrs carry out their actions as part of their religious duty in their ongoing war against Israeli "occupiers" in the Gaza Strip.

Despite this, we should still avoid casting Islam within the mold of its extreme manifestations. Moreover, Islam's complexity becomes even more apparent in that we find disparate expressions of Islam within different political contexts. For example, Libya, under the thumb of the military dictator Muammar Qaddafi who has openly denounced America and its allies, exhibits more radical expressions of Islam. In contrast, Islam tends to be more conservative in the monarchy of Saudi Arabia, which has consistently been America's ally. Thus the notion of a monolithic Islamic threat is unfounded, for the real determinative factors are political and economic forces that shape national interests. As Esposito states, this misperception of Islam is dangerous on a number of levels. Not only does it sustain various forms of repression, but it can actually produce the extremism that we think is the norm.

> *Perception of a global Islamic threat can contribute to support for repressive governments in the Muslim world, and this to the creation of a self-fulfilling prophecy. Thwarting participatory politics by canceling elections or repressing populist Islamic movements fosters radicalization. Many of the Islamists harassed, imprisoned, or tortured by the regime, will conclude that seeking democracy is a dead end and become convinced that force is the only recourse. Official silence or economic and political backing for regimes by the United States and other Western powers is read as complicity and a sign that there is a double standard for the implementation of democracy. This can create the conditions that lead to political violence that seemingly validates contentions that Islamic movements are inherently violent, antidemocratic, and a threat to national and regional stability.[8]*

■ A JOURNEY THROUGH ISLAM

The shattering episode and aftermath of September 11 have indelibly altered the sense of history, destiny, and well-being among Americans. And besides evoking feelings of confusion, anxiety, and anger, they have forced us to reexamine the role of Islam in human history as well as its formidable presence in the modern world. Today there are over one billion Muslims. Indeed, the Islamic faith dominates the entire Arab Middle East. Muslims form a majority in over forty-eight countries, and they are becoming a dynamic minority in America and Europe. For instance, not only is Islam the third largest religion in the U.K. and the U.S., but Muslims also constitute the second-largest religious group in Germany and France. And even though Islam has definitive Arab features, such as the sole use of Arabic in the Qur'an (translations are not used by Muslims), most Muslims actually come from non-Arab cultures. For example, the most populous Muslim country is Indonesia. Let us shed some light on Islamic ethics by highlighting events in Islam's complex history and development.

MUHAMMAD'S MESSAGE OF SUBMISSION

The charismatic prophet Muhammad was born in the thriving commercial city of Mecca around 570. Both parents died while he was still young, and he was raised by relatives. As a young man, he married the wealthy widow Khadijah who had once employed him. Trader by occupation, he was reflective by nature, and would often retreat to meditate in caves. Around 610, the archangel Gabriel appeared to Muhammad in a cave on the mountain of 'Arafat in present-day Saudi Arabia and relayed to the Prophet God's design for the world. Because Muhammad himself was unable to write, his revelations were recorded by his relatives and later put together into a collection called the Qur'an, or "Verses." These "Verses" resonate with power. Written in Arabic, they are intended to be recited out loud in Arabic, for the sound of the verses represents the divine speech of God, or Allah.[9] The message from the angel essentially emphasizes submission to the will of Allah, and thus the term for this message is "Islam," which means "submission." A Muslim is "one who submits." It is a message of both discipline and universal love, as seen in the various names for Allah, such as *al-Qadir* ("the powerful") and *al-Rahman* ("the compassionate").

Because mercantile profit in Mecca depended upon the prevailing polytheism and the sale of popular shrines, Muhammad's message of one true God threatened its commercial success. Muhammad openly chastised the merchants for their greed, reminding them that sooner or later they will all be held to account before Allah. Eventually, merchants threatened Muhammad, and he fled north to Medina. While in Medina, he shared his revelations and helped to unify the city, which had been torn apart by various factions. He finally returned to Mecca with his disciples and waged a holy war, or *jihad*, on nonbelievers and transformed Mecca into a holy city. By the time Muhammad died in 632, his message of submission to the will of Allah had become the dominating belief in that part of the world.

To this day, all Muslims regard Muhammad as their moral ideal. As Allah's messenger, the "Seal of the Prophets," he has conveyed Allah's divine plan. And his life embodies Allah's definitive message. Yet, in no way do Muslims deify Muhammad. To do so would violate the supreme command of Allah—that there are no other gods but Allah. In this respect, by virtue of their worship of money and profit, the Meccan merchants were guilty of idolatry.[10] This injunction to worship only one god and its accompanying condemnation of idolatry has been a major voice through Islamic history. Sadat's assassins equated what they perceived as the blasphemy of modern rulers like Sadat who sway from the message of Allah and who thus worship other gods to Mecca's flourishing idolatry. We find this radical interpretation of Muhammad's mission in Faraj's disturbing pamphlet at the end of this chapter.

RIFTS OVER THE MESSAGE: SUNNIS, SHIITES, AND SUFIS

Disputes as to Muhammad's legitimate successor led to various rifts within Islam, particularly the split between the Shi'i Muslims, or Shiites, and the Sunni Muslims. The Sunni Muslims claim that succession stems from the caliphate or leadership of Mu'awiyah (661–750) and his resulting Umayyad dynasty, whereas the Shiites claim Ali (d. 681) and his son Husain (d. 680), both of whom were assassinated, as the rightful successors. Since Ali was the cousin of Muhammad, Shiites argue that leadership should be hereditary. In any case, the Sunni movement remains the mainstream tradition in Islam and, along with all Muslims, advocates strict submission to the will of Allah. Both Sunnis and Shiites require that Muslims practice the Five Pillars, described below. They demand absolute devotion to the one and only God, Allah, and chastise any form of idolatry, whether it is to another god or whether it lies in making gods of wealth, the body, and the material. And they both require that every Muslim strive to achieve a good and just society.

Shi'i teachings still prevail in Iran and Iraq and a few other countries. Among doctrinal differences from the Sunnis is the Shi'i notion of the *Imam* as the spiritual leader of all of Islam. The term also designates the prayer leader at local mosques. According to the Shi'i, there is a succession of twelve of these spiritual leaders, of whom the last, named Muhammad, has yet to appear. This hidden Imam currently exists in Allah's paradise, and the expectation of his return to earth is profoundly inspiring for Shiites. What is equally inspiring is the martyrdom of the original successors, Ali and Husain. Their deaths have enkindled more extreme expressions of "witness," the meaning behind the term "martyr," among more radical Muslims. And within the Shiites is the Isma'iliya sect, whose practices are even more secretive and extreme. Often flouting mainstream Islamic teachings regarding the law, they sometimes resorted to killing their opponents after taking hashish, and from this use of "hashish" came the Western term "assassin."[11] Therefore, although both Sunni and Shiite share the basic moral teachings, Shiites tend to interpret these teachings in more extreme ways. All Muslims need to strive for a just society, but just *how* this justice is to be achieved remains a constant source of contention among Muslims.

Mainstream Islam, expressed through the Sunni movement, has always had a problem with the Islamic mystical movement of Sufism. The fundamental reason is doctrinal. For orthodox Muslims, there is an irreparable distance between the human and the divine. Any attempt to approximate or identify with the divine is viewed as blasphemous. Sufis, however, claim that humans have an essential oneness with Allah. The famous Sufi Mansur al-Hallaj was executed in 922 for heresy when he expressed his oneness with God by stating, "I am the Real—*al-Haqq.*"[12] Yet the philosopher al-Ghazali (1058–1111) argued that in essence Sufism and mainstream Islam are not antithetical. He claimed that Sufism is the extreme mystical expression of Islam and that such statements as al-Haqq's should not be taken literally but metaphorically, as an ideal to achieve, although in reality there still remains that irreparable chasm between the human and the divine.

Mainstream Muslims are generally critical of Sufis because they see them as more concerned with their own individual salvation than with working actively to establish a just society. That is, they tend to place personal piety above the common welfare. However, it would be unfair to generalize about Sufis in this regard. The great Muslim philosopher Avicenna (980–1037) tends to exhibit this Sufi emphasis upon personal devotion. Yet, as we read in his selection, his mystical leanings do not detract from his emphasis upon the fundamental "partnership" among humans and the primary significance of community. And as opposed to militant extremists such as the assassins of Sadat, for whom the highest display of devotion is through armed struggle against infidels, most Muslim scholars admit that Sufis come closer to the core meaning of devotion, which is spiritual in nature and not at all military or political.

ISLAMIC LAW

Despite these rifts, Islam became the dominant religious power throughout the Arab world on account of military expansions as well as the spread of Islamic learning. It was during the medieval period that Islam witnessed a tremendous growth in learning with the establishment of fabulous teaching centers called *madrasahs* and through conquests later harnessing the Ottoman Empire. Without a doubt, the most eminent was the university at al-Azhar in Cairo, Egypt, whose scholars often provided the definitive interpretations of the Qur'an and Islamic law. These universities produced renowned Islamic scholars such as the philosopher Ibn Rushd (1126–1198), also known as Averroes, who wrote influential commentaries on Aristotle, and the Sufi scholar Ibn al-Arabi (1165–1240), who was especially interested in the more symbolic, rather than literal, interpretation of the Qur'an.

As Islam acquired its powerful status, Islamic law, or *sharia*, became more codified. The law covered all sorts of topics from civil law to morality. And in order to address the many conflicting interpretations of the law, Muslim scholars proposed four criteria for establishing legitimacy:

- First and foremost, the Qur'an
- Tradition, called *sunna,* which often relies upon the works that record the life and statements of Muhammad, called *hadith*
- Use of critical reasoning to arrive at analogies
- Social approval or consensus[13]

To illustrate, consider the wearing of the veil, or *hejab,* by Muslim women. This custom is based upon the two most important criteria: the Qur'an and *hadith.* The Qur'an states:

> And tell the believing women to lower their gaze (from looking at forbidden things), and protect their parts (from illegal sexual acts, etc.) and not to show off their adornment except only that which is apparent (like palms of hands or one eye or both eyes for necessity to see the way, or outer dress like veil, gloves, head cover, apron, etc.), and to draw their veils all over Juyubihinna (i.e. their bodies,

*faces, necks and bosoms, etc.) And not to reveal their adornment ex-
cept to their husbands, their fathers, their husband's fathers, their
sons, their husband's sons, their brothers or their brother's sons, or
their sister's sons, or their (Muslim) women. . . . (24:31)* [14]

The wearing of the veil is deeply symbolic. It signifies that the woman is
Muslim and thus submits to the will of Allah. Furthermore, wearing the
veil embodies her personal decision to follow the teachings and example of
the Prophet, Muhammad, and is thereby an application of the second criteria of *hadith*. The law outlines further specific requirements: the need to
cover the entire body except for face and hands; loose-fitting clothes so that
the woman's shape is not outlined; clothes should not be either transparent
or brightly colored; and no jewelry is to be displayed.

Critics have often pointed out that the wearing of the veil also symbolizes the subjugation of women in Islamic society. If we examine the broader
societal context, we see apparent inequities between men and women
where women seem to be viewed as inferior. For instance, even though
polygamy is rare among Muslims, the Qur'an sanctions polygyny (more
than one wife) for men, yet it does not allow women to have more than one
husband. The Qur'an also permits husbands to inherit twice as much property and possessions as their wives. Moreover, throughout most of Islamic
history, although women learned the basic instructions of the Qur'an, in
contrast to men they were excluded from receiving any further education.
They played virtually no role in public and political affairs. The early practice of veiling, occurring more so among upper-class urban women, eventually led to the seclusion of all women from civic activities. The veil thus
became a symbol of oppression. And as a symbolic gesture of liberation, after the Egyptian feminist Huda Sha'rawi attended an international conference of women in the 1920s, she threw off her veil upon her return to
Egypt. [15]

Nevertheless, even though the veil eventually came to symbolize Muslim women's second-class citizenship, the primary reason for rules regarding the veil concerns modesty. The Qur'an makes it clear that drawing unnecessary attention to oneself, whether man or woman, detracts from the
selfless obedience and submission required by Allah. Clothes and cosmet-
ics for the purpose of enticing men is prohibited, for men then view women
primarily as sexual objects rather than admiring them for their inner
beauty. This is totally different from Western women who dress in ways to
make themselves attractive. But Muslims believe that true femininity and
physical beauty are not one and the same. By requiring that women cover

themselves, the Qur'an suggests that women should be evaluated for their character and intelligence rather than their physical looks and sexuality. Wearing the veil, therefore, is a way for the woman to reveal her femininity while concealing her sexuality. Muslim women are free from the pressures, often felt by women in other cultures, to appear both beautiful and physically attractive to men. By wearing her veil, the Muslim woman chooses to make a statement about her identity, namely that she is a true Muslim, and that means she chooses not to be looked upon as a sex object by others. Even though this notion actually comes close to the core of what feminism is all about, there is a Western misunderstanding regarding the veil. Young Muslim women who wear the veil in the West often face discrimination. The typical Western response is that the wearer must be, on that account, "oppressed." Such response ignores both the fact that many women freely choose to wear the veil and the fact that the veil essentially signifies modesty as opposed to self-absorption.

SETBACK AND RENEWAL

Throughout its complex history, in its confrontation with the West, Islam has manifested an ongoing tension with Western principles. Many of us who are less familiar with Islamic history may view this tension as one that is purely antagonistic. Hence, in view of current crises and sharp frictions particularly after 9/11, an event that has so benumbed us that we have no term for it other than the date, we may mistakenly perceive Islam as an entity that is utterly hostile to the United States. Yet Islam's historic tensions have ranged from being moderate to being extreme. Here are two historic examples: Wahhabi Revivalism and the Muslim Brotherhood. One reviewer insightfully noted that the emphasis here upon Islamic history could take away from considerations of Islamic ethics. The point is well taken. It is also hoped that a more thorough knowledge of Islamic history will help cultivate a better understanding of the current moral, cultural, and political unease within the Muslim world and with the United States.

Wahhabi Revivalism Following the seventeenth century, the Turkish-ruled Ottoman Empire began to crumble through successive European conquests. There came about sustained attempts to revitalize Islamic teachings. For example, the Wahhabi movement (named after Ibn 'Abd al-Wahhab, 1703–1792) in Saudi Arabia reasserted the key Islamic idea of the one, true God, Allah. Wahhabis condemned anything that detracted from this idea, and the movement later denounced atheism, apparent in the former Soviet Union, as well as the prevailing commercialism and material-ism exhibited in America.[16] Wahhabis believed that the corrosion of Arab societies is principally due to the lack of devotion to the Qur'an and insisted upon a return to the basics of the Qur'an, to the fundamentals. In this sense, although the movement viewed itself as reformist, it has also been called "fundamentalist." Wahhabism became tightly affiliated with the Saudi royal family and thus became entrenched as the official state teaching.

Not all Muslims agreed with this strict, fundamentalist approach. Some, like Egypt's supreme judge in Islamic law Muhammad 'Abduh (1849–1905), believed in the need for a reasonable accommodation to modernism and Western science. He opposed an uncritical reliance upon tradition and underscored the use of reason in understanding and inter-preting Islamic teachings, which he still regarded as the highest teachings. This meant accepting the spirit, rather than solely relying on the letter, of the Qur'an.[17]

The Muslim Brotherhood At the close of World War I, Arab nations were under the thumbs of England and France. Western colonialism gen-erated groups such as the Muslim Brotherhood (*al-Ikhwan al-Muslimun*) in Egypt, founded by Hasan al-Banna (1906–1949). In contrast to funda-mentalists like Wahhabis, the group stressed complete freedom from the oppression of foreign control. The Brotherhood played an active part in the tensions between Arabs and the creation of the state of Israel in 1948. And even thought the movement was outlawed during the leadership of Sadat, extremists from the Brotherhood orchestrated his assassination. They be-lieved his peacemaking efforts with Israel were a betrayal of the Arab struggle for independence. It should be noted that many members of the Brotherhood are well-educated and are often professionals in various oc-cupations. The extreme faction of the Brotherhood continues to exert its influence in various countries. They toe a hard line in their effort to re-store the true law, or *sharia*, which in turn incorporates a purely Islamic state.

The ongoing struggle between Palestine and Israel, centered on the settlement of the West Bank along the Gaza strip, continues to be in-tense. And Jerusalem, a holy city to all three religions—Judaism, Chris-tianity, and Islam—remains subjected to ongoing terrorist attacks. While the Jewish movement of Zionism aims to reassert Jewish presence in Pales-tine, Muslims worldwide view the state of Israel as an unjustified en-croachment onto the soil of Islam. Meanwhile, the U.S. support of Israel compounds the tensions and adds to the already existing widespread resentment against America.

Through this brief journey we detect three forceful motifs today in the Muslim world. First, the mainstream tradition, often expressed in fundamentalism, seeks a return to Islam's ancient and classical teachings. This orthodox position, though not openly hostile, still rejects modernism. Next, there is a reformist movement within Islam that strives to revive Islam by coming to terms with modernism instead of simply rejecting it. Finally, there are extremist elements within fundamentalism, many of whom justify terrorist campaigns against "enemies" of Islam. All of this is further complicated due to nationalist and political concerns among the various Muslim countries, stirring the pot with fervent clashes of interest.

■ THE FIVE PILLARS OF ISLAM

The Five Pillars constitute the heart of Islam. Grounded in the Qur'an, they convey the ethical and moral duties of all Muslims, regardless of sect. These duties assume certain undercurrents. To begin with, the most important lies in the term "Islam," advocating complete obedience to the will of Allah. Second, Islam teaches the dignity and worth of all human beings. Everyone is equal in the eyes of Allah. The third current flows from this. It is imperative that every Muslim do good deeds, referred to in the Qur'an as 'amal salih, in order to bring about a just and good society. Islamic morality is not about Muslims simply seeking their own individual salvation. By stressing the critical importance of building a just community, the orientation is collective. That is, Muslims ought to do good deeds and perform religious observances in order to bring about a just society and to enhance the welfare and well-being of all others, particularly those who are most downtrodden and oppressed. It is imperative that Muslims work to bring about a social order that is free from any type of oppression. Indeed, the principle of justice, or adl, plays a prominent role in Islamic ethics. The Qur'an states:

> And what is wrong with you that you fight not in the Cause of Allah, and for those weak, ill-treated and oppressed among men, women, and children, whose cry is: "Our Lord! Rescue us from this town whose people are oppressors; and raise for us from You one who will protect, and raise for us from You one who will help." (Qur'an 4:75)

Moreover, being pious, and therefore just, promises eternal reward to Muslims, whereas impiety means certain misery in the afterlife. In any case, Muslims have the obligation to bring about a good and just society. Avicenna makes this clear in his *Book of Healing* when he prohibits activities such as gambling and usury. Seeking profit as a good in itself cultivates greed and, in turn, diminishes the community's well-being.

This emphasis upon justice is the basis for Islam's defense of polygamy under certain circumstances. We read in the Qur'an:

> *And if you fear that you shall not be able to deal justly with the orphan-girls, then marry (other) women of your choice, two or three, or four but if you fear that you shall not be able to deal justly (with them), then only one or (the captives and the slaves) that your right hands possess. That is nearer to prevent you from doing injustice. (4:3)*

Keep in mind that these verses were revealed to Muhammad after the battle of Uhud in which the deaths of numerous Muslims produced countless numbers of Muslim widows and orphans, so that polygamy was sanctioned as a practical measure. It was not required, nor was it encouraged. Polygamy was merely allowed in the spirit of compassion for widows and orphans and to provide for them in an equitable way. The above verse also clearly mandates fair and equal treatment for wives, as opposed to false notions about "owning" wives and treating them as possessions. Marriage is looked upon as a contract that requires mutual consent. Furthermore, in the case of polygamy, all wives must be treated equitably with identical rights and claims. And if this equity is not provided, a wife has grounds for divorce. Avicenna stresses this need for equity in his selection, and he underscores equity in marriage for the more fundamental purpose of maintaining social stability. His prescriptions for marriage are still in effect in Muslim countries. Finally, Islamic teachings permit polygamy as a defensive measure against adultery and divorce, both of which are serious offenses.

THE FIRST PILLAR: *TAWHID*

The Qur'an states, "There is no god but God and Muhammad is his prophet." Muslims are required to recite this credo in public. This credo expresses *tawhid*, the acknowledgment and devotion to one God and to his prophet. The most serious sin is to worship another god besides Allah. To do so is called *shirk*. The glorification of material comforts and monies is therefore contrary to worshiping the one God and represents *shirk*. Moreover, Islam forbids any concrete representation of God such as in statues and paintings. To capture the image of God in this way is viewed as blasphemous.

If there is any way to make some sense of the resentment that many Muslims feel toward expressions of materialism and commercialism, especially in the West, it is through understanding this idea of the sin of *shirk*. And Faraj's text, the purported theoretical and scriptural basis for the assassination of Sadat, especially chastises those who commit apostasy, those who are Muslims like Sadat yet choose not to live according to Islamic teachings. Instead of living according to Islam, they conspire with "Crusaderism," Communism, and Zionism. Faraj uses the term "Crusaderism" to refer to the materialistic values and idolatry of the Christian West. On the other hand, mainstream scholars, many of whom have issued pronouncements from al-Azhar University, explicitly condemn a militaristic response to this perceived apostasy. According to these scholars, the Qur'an does not sanction such violent measures.

THE SECOND PILLAR: *SALAT*

Muslims are required to pray five times each day: just before sunrise, early afternoon, later afternoon, soon after sunset, and just before retiring. This prayer is called *salat*. When praying they are required to face toward the Kabbah, the holy temple in Mecca. They must also maintain the proper bodily posture and form a line in prayer, regardless of each one's social status. This reminds each Muslim of the fundamental equality of each person in the eyes of Allah.

THE THIRD PILLAR: *SAUM*

Muslims are expected to fast, called *saum*, during the holy month of Ramadan, the ninth month of the lunar year, from sunrise to sunset. During this time, Muslims are also prohibited from smoking and sex. This strict fasting reminds each Muslim of the poor and destitute throughout the world. They become aware of others' hunger and thirst. Here we see the virtue of compassion expressed through this collective participation in others' suffering.

THE FOURTH PILLAR: *ZAKAT*

Muslims are required to give alms each year to the poor and destitute. This almsgiving is in the form of an alms tax and is known as *zakat*. As with fasting, this reminds each Muslim of the poor and destitute who have no financial means to support themselves. There is a universal duty to enhance the welfare of the poor. This entails building a just society and eliminating oppression. Islam recognizes that there are social and systemic roots to poverty. Note these eerily prophetic verses in the Meccan chapter 104 in the Qur'an:

> *Woe to every slanderer and backbiter.*
> *Who has gathered wealth and counted it,*
> *He thinks that his wealth will make him last forever!*
> *Nay! Verily, he will be thrown into the crushing Fire.*
> *And what will make you know what the crushing Fire is?*
> *The fire of Allah, kindled,*
> *Which leaps up over the hearts,*
> *Verily, it shall be closed in on them,*
> *In pillars stretched forth (i.e., they will be punished in the Fire with*
> *pillars, etc.).*

THE FIFTH PILLAR: *HAJJ*

Once during his or her lifetime, each Muslim is expected to make a pilgrimage, called *hajj,* to the holy city of Mecca to the Ka'bah, as long as he or she is physically able and can afford it. Muslims are also encouraged to participate if possible in the annual pilgrimage to Mecca, called *Hajj al-akbar.*

■ DOES ISLAM PROMOTE VIOLENCE?

> *I wanted to know the best of the life of one who holds today an*
> *undisputed sway over the hearts of millions of mankind. . . . I be-*
> *came more than ever convinced that it was not the sword that won*
> *a place for Islam in those days in the scheme of life. It was the rigid*
> *simplicity, the utter self-effacement of the Prophet, the scrupulous*
> *regard for pledges, his intense devotion to his friends and followers,*
> *his fearlessness, his absolute trust in God and in his own mission.*
> *These and not the sword carried everything before them and sur-*
> *mounted every obstacle.*
>
> *Mahatma Gandhi, Young India, 1924*

Islam is essentially a religion that preaches nonviolence. Indeed, Allah is often described with the attributes of Compassion, Mercy, and Pardon. And, as in Buddhism, compassion is a key virtue in Islamic ethics. At the same time, Muslims are also exhorted to bring about a just society and to rid society of all forms of oppression. Therefore, even though Islam upholds nonviolence as an ideal, there may be times when violence is permitted in order to restore injustice and to resist oppression. (This is somewhat similar to the Christian emphasis upon nonviolence, while Christian theorists still uphold a just war doctrine in that war may be sanctioned for purposes of self-defense and if certain criteria are upheld.) In no way does Islam condone violence unless it is absolutely necessary for purposes of defense, to defend the Islamic faith and/or Muslim families. This kind of defensive violence is permitted only under exceptional circumstances and only if it constitutes the absolute last resort.

We see this sanctioning of defensive violence in the case of abortion. Islamic teachings permit abortion only if it means saving the life of the mother. Under no other circumstances is abortion justified. Most important, *permitting* violence in certain contexts in no way replaces the Qur'anic teaching that *encourages* nonviolence. The Qur'an establishes nonviolence as an ideal that Muslims need to strive for. Moreover, in view of the collective emphasis in Islam, killing another individual is not taken lightly, and in effect constitutes an offense against all of humanity. As the Qur'an states, "if anyone killed a person not in retaliation of murder, or (and) to spread mischief in the land—it would be as if he killed all mankind, and if anyone saved a life, it would be as if he saved the life of all mankind" (5:32). Furthermore, in the course of waging a war, Islam categorically condemns the killing of women, children, and elderly people. In this respect, Islamic teachings expressly forbid those techniques of modern war, such as economic sanctions or blockades, whereby innocent populations are unduly harmed and subject to starvation.

What about the teaching concerning *jihad*? *Jihad* happens to be one of the most misunderstood terms in Islam. Westerners often think of *jihad* as a strictly "holy war" between Muslims and non-Muslims, a war that justifies violent and extreme means, such as illustrated in the Crusades in the twelfth century. Using this historical mirror, however, results in misinterpretation. *Jihad* literally means "struggle" and, first and foremost, pertains to the interior, personal struggle within a Muslim to remain true to his and her beliefs. In addition, *jihad* refers to the struggle to apply these beliefs to the social realm with the aim of bringing about a better world. In this respect, *jihad* incorporates a political (as in Aristotle's *polis* or "city-state") ingredient. This stems from the Qur'an's command to struggle against nonbelievers so that these nonbelievers eventually recognize the preeminence of Allah and his message to the Prophet.

Extremists in the Muslim Brotherhood obviously interpreted this version of *jihad* in brutal, literal fashion. As Faraj's text bluntly asserts, *jihad* entails a religious duty to take up arms and fight the enemies of Islam. The text opposes Muslim scholars from the esteemed university of al-Azhar who insist upon *jihad* as representing a spiritual struggle, a struggle that can be resolved through proper knowledge and reflection. According to Faraj and the assassins of Sadat, because al-Azhar has historically backed various ruling regimes in Egypt, it has sold out to Islamic teachings. For the assassins, regimes that defy the message of the Prophet must be overthrown. Faraj's reading of *jihad* is immensely critical for any understanding of the mind-set of contemporary extremists like Osama bin Laden, his al Qaeda network, and others who carry out terrorist acts in the name of Islam. Moreover, these extremists construe *jihad* as either an individual or a collective duty. As an individual duty, a Muslim may therefore decide to sacrifice his or her own life on a suicide mission, in which case, as Faraj's text tells us, young men are not required to seek parental permission. And in countries such as Egypt that place great weight on parental authority, this has far-reaching and insidious consequences.[18]

All this is critical for Westerners to understand. When we examine the history of the spread of Islam, we find a history blotted with military conquests and assassinations. Yet the history of other faith traditions is not without stain. We need to be careful to avoid equating the ideals of Islam with actual practices in specific contexts that are highly politicized. To be sure, Islam does not glorify violence. The overwhelming majority of Muslim scholars, particularly at the pinnacle of Islamic scholarship at al-Azhar University in Cairo, support the mainstream view that *jihad* refers essentially to inner, spiritualized, and thus demilitarized struggle. Nonetheless, there continues to be different interpretations of the role of violence between the mainstream and the more extremist groups. To illustrate, let us review more closely more recent events.

AFGHANISTAN, THE TALIBAN, AND OSAMA BIN LADEN

Before Afghanistan's civil war in 1992, the country reflected a multicultural society with its share of Hindus, Sikhs, Jews, and various Muslim sects, all coexisting with each other with a fair degree of tolerance. The civil war against Soviet rule ripped this solidarity apart. It also provided a booster shot for Islamic extremism. For Muslim extremists, the conquest of the Russian superpower solidified their cause and forged together ideological and strategic links across the Muslim world. In the eyes of these radical Muslims, the defeat of the Soviet troops represented a stunning victory for Islam and meant the possibility of bringing about a "pure" Islamic state. For them, this also meant that the defeat of the other superpower, the USA, was no longer remote.

Before the Taliban rose to power in Afghanistan in 1994, the Wahabbis were the leading Islamic force. Also prior to the Taliban, Islamic radical leaders such as the university-educated Hikmetyar and Masud based their campaigns upon the ideology of bringing about an Islamic society. Their version of Islam was highly politicized—the creation of a true Islamic state in order to counter the corrupt influence of contemporary society and its Western "perversions." At the same time, even though they downplayed the value of diversity among the various ethnic and religious groups and thus sought to homogenize Afghan society, Hikmetyar and Masud held relatively progressive views advocating, for example, a more active role for women in society.

With the takeover by the Taliban, Islamic extremism showed its brutal and oppressive face. The Taliban conducted ruthless campaigns against fellow Muslims who belonged to rival sects, running completely contrary to Islamic teachings, according to most Islamic scholars. Indeed, as the correspondent Ahmed Rashid points out, the Taliban movement represented an anomaly in Islam, lacking any solid basis in Islamic theology:

> The Taliban are poorly tutored in Islamic and Afghan history, knowledge of the Sharia and the Koran and the political and theoretical developments in the Muslim world during the twentieth century. While Islamic radicalism in the twentieth century has a long history of scholarly writing and debate, the Taliban have no such historical perspective or tradition. . . . This has created an obscurantism which allows no room for debate even with fellow Muslims.[19]

The Taliban's interpretation of Islam was so extreme that it set Muslim teachings on a radically different course. This was particularly embodied in the powerful yet dictatorial and secretive leadership of its supreme leader, the one-eyed Mullar Mohammed Omar, who, as of this writing, is still at large. Taliban policies became more brutally oppressive, even to the point of refusing needed humanitarian aid by the UN for the Afghan people. The

Taliban clearly defined their moral universe in strict terms of right and wrong. The Taliban secret "religious" police, known as the *Munkrat*, called themselves the "Department of the Promotion of Virtue and the Prevention of Vice."

Consider the Taliban treatment of women. When the Taliban occupied Kabul in 1996, the Taliban religious police issued the following decrees:

> Women you should not step outside your residence. If you go outside the house you should not be like women who used to go with fashionable clothes wearing much cosmetics and appearing in front of every men before the coming of Islam. . . .
>
> To prevent sedition and female uncovers (Be Hejabi). No drivers are allowed to pick up women who are using Iranian burqa. In case of violation the driver will be imprisoned. If such kind of female are observed in the street their house will be found and their husband punished. If the women use stimulating and attractive cloth and there is no accompany of close male relative with them, the drivers should not pick them up. . . .
>
> To prevent sewing ladies cloth and taking female body measures by tailor. If women or fashion magazines are seen in the shop the tailor should be imprisoned.[20]

The Taliban deliberately intended to oppress women. Women were forced to wear the complete, head-to-toe *burqa*, contrary to the traditional requirement that the face and hands be exposed. Women were no longer allowed to work, unless the work was connected with health delivery. Women were banned from teaching, thus devastating the educational system since most teachers in Kabul were women. With the closure of numerous schools and universities, such ruinous impact upon Afghan youth promises to be far-reaching, especially since the country's literacy level is already one of the lowest in the world. Music was not allowed in public places nor at weddings. Men were not permitted to shave their beards. People were not allowed to keep pigeons or to play with birds. The Taliban abolished the popular sport of kite flying. And the Munkrat even banned displaying photographs and portraits, viewed as a form of idolatry.[21] At first, despite outspoken, worldwide criticism of the Taliban's oppression of women, no calculated effort was undertaken by the UN to prohibit such treatment. Finally, the Taliban's ruthless oppression eventually alerted human rights agencies. Yet the Taliban remained inflexible. Consider Attorney General Maulvi Jalilullah Maulvizada's—one of the Taliban's high-ranking ministers—response to the UN, and note the rhetoric of "Islam" and the "Holy Koran" pitted against the "infidels."

> Let us state what sort of education the UN wants. This is a big infidel policy which gives such obscene freedom to women which would lead to adultery and herald the destruction of Islam. In any Islamic country where adultery becomes common, that country is destroyed and enters the domination of the infidels because their men become like women and women cannot defend themselves. Anybody who talks to us should do so within Islam's framework. The Holy Koran cannot adjust itself to other people's requirements, people should adjust themselves to the requirements of the Holy Koran.[22] [emphasis added]

The Afghan struggle against the Soviets also carved out a reputation for Osama bin Laden, a Yemeni billionaire's son who donated millions to promote the cause of Muslim radicals. Bin Laden was born in 1957, the seventeenth of fifty-seven children. His mother, one of his father's many wives, was from Saudi Arabia. With his six-foot, five-inch stature and his calm demeanor he stands out among his *mujaheddin* (holy warriors fighting in a holy war) comrades. Bin Laden embodies a narrow and wayward interpretation of Islam. He first declared a holy war against Americans in August 1996 while befriending the Taliban regime. Bin Laden was a lavish financial sponsor of Muslim extremist groups throughout the Middle East and Africa, and his monies were channeled into the training of Islamic militants. And, on February 23, 1998, his al-Qaeda network issued a second declaration of holy war against Americans:

> The ruling to kill the Americans and their allies — civilians and military — is an individual duty for every Muslim who can do it in any country in which it is possible to.[23]

In the same spirit as Faraj's "neglected duty," bin Laden and his followers viewed waging war against Americans as a religious duty. He was eventually linked to the bombing of U.S. embassies in Kenya and Tanzania, the killing of American servicemen in Mogadishu, Riyadh, and Dhahran, and the 1993 World Trade Center bombing. And his leading role in the events of September 11 brought about the crumbling of both his Afghan-based al-Qaeda network and the Taliban. As of this writing, he has yet to be apprehended.

REVISIONING ISLAM

There are currently movements in Islam that border more closely on revisionist interpretations that challenge both extremist views and the more traditional perspectives. A case in point is Iran. In 1979 the world took note of the revival of Islam when Ayatollah Ruholla Khomeini's revolution ousted the Shah and replaced him with an Islamic republic ruled by Islamic clerics. Yet the landslide election in 1997 of Iran's president, Seyyed Mohammad Khatami, empowered him to construe Islamic teachings in more progressive ways. To begin with, Khatami defeated a candidate who was primarily backed by Iran's traditional clergy, or *ulema*.[24] The *ulema*, "heirs of the prophets," represent the class of scholars who guard the authority of the Qur'an and bestow a strict, dogmatic, and fundamentally conservative interpretation upon the scriptures. Throughout centuries of Islamic rule, these *ulema* often interpreted Islamic teachings in ways that more or less supported state rulers. However, in recent years, more Muslims have begun to challenge the *ulema's* interpretive authority.

Khatami urges Muslims to confront Western influences not by rejection, as preached by traditional clergy, and not through militant opposition, as espoused by extremists. He argues that Muslims need to face up to scientific advancement. Muslims also need to accept certain premises in democratic societies, such as the defense of human rights, the rule of law, social justice, individual autonomy, and freedom. He asserts that the tide of science and democracy is inevitable, and that it is the duty of every Muslim to adapt Muslim beliefs to changing realities. Moreover, Khatami challenges the interpretive authority of the clergy, and he instructs Muslims to avoid uncritical reliance upon the scriptures as well as any absolutist position that assumes the cloak of infallibility.

> *Given the multiplicity of views of religion over history, we must ensure that we do not think that our view of religion is the only one. . . . True, these are sacred matters, but our interpretations of them are human. Only through this realization will humans open their minds to the experiences and innovations of others.*[25]

This is a far cry from Faraj's "neglected duty." Khatami and others urge Muslims to sensibly recognize Western achievements and to learn from them. He cautions Muslims against slipping into two extremes: complete rejection of the West and all that the West stands for, and total, uncritical adoption of Western values. In a speech at the Organization of the Islamic

Conference, a summit meeting for all Muslim heads of state in Tehran, December 9, 1997, Khatami proposed the following recipe for an authentic Islamic society.

> *In the civil society that we espouse, although centered around the axis of Islamic thinking and culture, . . . personal or group dictatorship or even the tyranny of the majority and elimination of the minority have no place. In such a society, man, due to the very attribute of being human, is venerated and revered and his rights are respected. Citizens of the Islamic civil society enjoy the right to determine their own destiny, supervise the governance and hold the government accountable. The government in such a society is the servant of the people and not their master, and in any eventuality, is accountable to the people whom God has entitled to determine their own destiny. Our civil society is not a society where only Muslims are entitled to rights and are considered citizens. Rather, all individuals are entitled to rights, within the framework of the law and order. Defending such rights ranks among the important fundamental duties of the government.[26]*

Here we have a mingling of Islam with notions of democracy, diversity, tolerance, and individual rights. Is Khatami assuming some universal standard of morality?

■ WEAKNESSES IN ISLAMIC ETHICS

Mainstream Islamic teachings do not support aggressive violence. Nevertheless, can we compartmentalize religious teachings that underlie a society from that same society's intricate political web? Defenders of Islamic nonviolence may draw a strict line between the realist plane that unfolds within Arab states' national-political interests and the morally ideal level that the Qur'an exhorts. Yet, the fact of the matter is that perpetrators of aggressive, including terrorist, violence still justify their actions by appealing to Qur'anic teachings. Simply drawing distinctions between the two levels does not resolve this critical problem of interpretation.

Does any war today make moral sense? There is a thin line between defensive and aggressive violence. Consider the November 13, 2001, *New York Times* section "A Nation Challenged," which carried three eye-riveting photographs during the war in Afghanistan. In the first photo, a Northern Alliance solider was dragging a Taliban prisoner out of a ditch. The second photo showed the prisoner surrounded by soldiers and pleading for his life. His eyes displayed terror and a shocking bolt of awareness of the inevitable—that these were his last moments. The third photo shows him lying dead on the ground, shot in the chest, his head smashed in with rifle butts by the Alliance soldiers. What captures the eye in this visual triptych are the faces of the Alliance soldiers, faces that show amusement and delight. Like a Hieronymous Bosch painting, madness and frenzy constitute the undercurrent, revealing not only the horrors of war but also one of its neverending truths: In war there are no winners. Everyone loses, even the victors, for one can easily lose a sizable chunk of one's humanity in the very process of becoming a victor.

And is there room for individual conscience in Islam? Consider the requirement that Muslim women wear the veil. In principle this should be a free decision undertaken by women. Yet many women are strongly pressured by their families and by their society into wearing the veil. What if the woman herself does not wish to follow the dictates of family and society? Do Islamic teachings support this individual choice? Islamic teachings appear vague here.

Furthermore, feminists point to double standards in applying certain rules. For instance, Avicenna's selection stresses the need for equity within marriage, yet maintains that the wife is more prone to acting irrationally. And while claiming that women should wear the veil because women incite sexual desires, his notion minimizes men's accountability. Furthermore, this "weakness" on women's part can therefore warrant polygamy but not polyandry. Avicenna's position was countered over a century later by the Muslim philosopher Averroes, who defended the idea of strict equality between wives and husbands. However, even though Avicenna's position does not reflect that of all Muslims, many Muslims still adhere to his requirements.

■ STRENGTHS IN ISLAMIC ETHICS

Perhaps the most sterling characteristic of Islamic ethics lies in its simplicity and stark reliance upon its religious teachings. T. W. Arnolds expressed this when he claimed:

> *Islam is a religion that is essentially rationalistic in the widest sense of this term considered etymologically and historically . . . a creed so precise, so stripped of all theological complexities and consequently so accessible to the ordinary understanding might be*

> *expected to possess and does indeed possess a marvelous power of*
> *winning its way into the consciences of men.*[27]

This straightforward quality to Islamic ethics is stressed in the Qur'an: "Surely man is in loss, except for those who believe and do good work, and exhort one another to Truth and exhort one another to patience."[28] Essentially, the ultimate aim in Islamic ethics is to pursue the Truth—Allah and his message constitutes Truth—and doing so with the utmost patience and diligence.

Another significant strength in Islamic ethics is the emphasis upon balance and the avoidance of the extreme positions of materialism and spiritualism. According to the Qur'an:

> *O you who believe! Make not unlawful the Tayyibat (all that is*
> *good as regards foods, things, deeds, beliefs, persons, etc.) which Al-*
> *lah has made lawful to you, and transgress not. Verily, Allah does*
> *not like the transgressors. And eat of the things which Allah has*
> *provided for you, lawful and good, and fear Allah in Whom you be-*
> *lieve. (5:87–88)*

In his selection, Avicenna's emphasis upon moderation is strikingly similar to that of Aristotle's teaching concerning virtue, as he cautions us against slipping into the extreme vices of both excess and deficiency. For Avicenna, genuinely moral laws should cultivate this kind of balance.

Along these lines, Islamic ethics has a harmonious vision of the natural rapport between the individual and the collective. This insight shows itself in the realization that there are social and political factors that generate corruption and exploitation. There is much to be said for the awareness that a cultural and social ethos, or way of thinking, may also lie at the root of oppression. Islamic teachings recognize the organizational and social roots of oppression. This explains why Islamic teachings seek to transform *both* the individual and the society. And this also inspires Muslims to view redemption collectively more so than privately.

■ NOTES

1. In Anthony Shadid, *Legacy of the Prophet: Despots, Democrats, and the New Politics of Islam* (Boulder, CO: Westview Press, 2001), p. 78.

2. Johannes J. G. Jansen offers an excellent analysis of Faraj's pamphlet in *The Neglected Duty: The Creed of Sadat's Assassins and Islamic Resurgence in the Middle East* (New York: Macmillan, 1986), p. 2.

3. This is the position of Reuven Paz, 1998.

4. Clarence Bouchet (1996) cautions us against stereotyping Islam in this way. He points to the various differences among Islamic fundamentalist groups.

5. John Esposito, "Political Islam: Beyond the Green Menace," *Current History* 93, no. 579 (January 1994): p. 24.

6. See the discussion in Mark Juergensmeyer, *Terror in the Mind of God: The Global Rise of Religious Violence* (Berkeley: University of California Press, 2000), pp. 76ff.

7. Juergensmeyer, pp. 72ff.

8. Ibid., p. 23.

9. Muslims believe that the only true Qur'an is written in the original Arabic. All other translations fall short of capturing the sacred sound and quality of the verses.

10. By the same token, Muslims consider the notion of Christ as divine as blasphemous. And since Islam is strictly monotheistic, Muslims are deeply critical of the Christian notion of a triune God, as expressed in the Trinity.

11. Ninian Smart, *The World's Religions* (Englewood Cliffs, NJ: Prentice Hall, 1989), p. 290.

12. Ibid., p. 287.

13. Ibid.

14. *Interpretations of the Meanings of The Noble Qur'an in the English Language*, with comments by Sahih Al-Bukhari, translated by Dr. Muhammad Taqi-ud-Din- Al-Hilali and Dr. Muhammad Muhsin Khan. (Riyadh, Kingdom of Saudi Arabia: Maktaba ar-us-Salam, 1993.)

15. Jane I. Smith, "Islam," in Arvind Sharma, ed.,*Women in World Religions* (Albany: State University of New York Press, 1987), p. 241.

16. Wahhabis consider the Sufi practice of praying to saints at their tomb sites as idolatrous in this sense.

17. Smart, p. 470.

18. See the discussion in Jansen, *The Neglected Duty*, p. 21.

19. Ahmed Rashid, *Taliban: Militant Islam, Oil and Fundamentalism in Central Asia* (Yale University Press, Nota Bene, 2000, 2001), p. 93.

20. Cited in Rashid, pp. 217–19.

21. Ibid.

22. Ibid., pp. 111–12.

23. Ibid., p. 134.

24. Iranian clergy are Shiite Muslims, whereas elsewhere they are mostly Sunni Muslims.

25. Cited in Shadid, p. 215.

26. Ibid., pp. 217–18.

27. Edward Mondet, "Da Propagande chretienne et ses Adversaries Musulmans," (Paris 1890), cited in T. W. Arnold, *The Preaching of Islam* (London 1913), pp. 413–14.

28. See the discussion in Asqhar Ali Engineer, "Islamic Ethic" (Institute of Islamic Studies and Centre for Study of Society and Secularism, posted Jan. 3, 2000) at http://eeumene.org//IIS/esss24.htm, p. 1.

THE BOOK OF HEALING

■

AVICENNA

HEALING: METAPHYSICS X

CHAPTER 2/PROOF OF PROPHECY. THE MANNER OF
THE PROPHET'S CALL TO GOD, THE EXALTED. THE
"RETURN" TO GOD.

We now say: it is known that man differs from the other animals in that he cannot lead a proper life when isolated as a single individual, managing his affairs with no associates to help him satisfy his basic wants. One man needs to be complemented by another of his species, the other, in turn, by him and one like him. Thus, for example, one man would provide another with vegetables while the other would bake for him; one man would sew for another while the other would provide him with needles. Associated in this way, they become self-sufficient. For this reason men have found it necessary to establish cities and form associations. Whoever, in the endeavor to establish his city, does not see to the requirements necessary for setting up a city and, with his companions, remains confined to forming a mere association, would be engaged in devising means [to govern] a species most dissimilar to men and lacking the perfection of men. Nevertheless, even the ones like him cannot escape associating with the citizens of a city, and imitating them.

If this is obvious, then man's existence and survival require partnership. Partnership is only achieved through reciprocal transactions, as well as through the various trades practiced by man. Reciprocal transactions demand law (*sun-*

nah) and justice, and law and justice demand a lawgiver and a dispenser of justice. This lawgiver must be in a position that enables him to address men and make them adhere to the law. He must, then, be a human being. Men must not be left to their private opinions concerning the law so that they disagree, each considering as just what others owe them, unjust what they owe others.

Thus, with respect to the survival and actual existence of the human species, the need for this human being is far greater than the need for such benefits as the growing of the hair on the eyebrow, the shaping of the arches in the feet, and many others that are not necessary for survival but at best are merely useful for it. Now the existence of the righteous man to legislate and to dispense justice is a possibility, as we have previously remarked. It becomes impossible, therefore, that divine providence should ordain the existence of those former benefits and not the latter, which are their bases. Nor is it possible that the First Principle and the angels after Him should know the former and not the latter. Nor yet is it possible that that which He knows to be in itself within the realm of possibility but whose realization is necessary for introducing the good order, should not exist. And how can it not exist, when that which depends and is constructed on its existence, exists? A prophet, therefore, must exist and he must be a human. He must also possess characteristics not present in others so that men could recognize in him something they do not have and which differentiates him from them. Therefore he will perform the miracles about which we have spoken.

When this man's existence comes about, he must lay down laws about men's affairs by the permission of God, the Exalted, by His command, inspiration, and the *descent of His Holy Spirit* on him. The first principle governing his legislation is to let men know that they have a Maker, One and Omnipotent; that *He knows the hidden and the manifest;* that obedience is due to Him since *command* must belong to *Him who creates;* that He has prepared for those who obey Him an afterlife of bliss, but for those who disobey Him an afterlife of misery. This will induce the multitude to obey the decrees put in the prophet's mouth by the God and the angels.

But he ought not to involve them with doctrines pertaining to the knowledge of God, the Exalted, beyond the fact that He is one, the truth, and has none like Himself. To go beyond this and demand that they believe in His existence as being not referred to in place, as being not subject to verbal classifications, as being neither inside nor outside the world, or anything of this kind, is to ask too much. This will simply confuse the religion (*din*) they have and involve them in something from which deliverance is only possible for the one who receives guidance and is fortunate, whose existence is most rare. For it is only with great strain that they can comprehend the true states of such matters; it is only the very few among them that can understand the truth of divine "unicity" and divine "remoteness." The rest would inevitably come to deny the truth of such an existence, fall into dissensions, and indulge in dis-

putations and analogical arguments that stand in the way of their political duties. This might even lead them to adopt views contrary to the city's welfare,
opposed to the imperatives of truth. Their complaints and doubts will multiply, making it difficult for a man to control them. For divine wisdom is not easily acquired by everyone.

Nor is it proper for any man to reveal that he possesses knowledge he is hiding from the vulgar. Indeed, he must never permit any reference to this.
Rather, he should let them know of God's majesty and greatness through symbols and similitudes derived from things that for them are majestic and great,
adding this much—that He has neither equal, nor companion, nor likeness.
Similarly, he must instill in them the belief in the resurrection in a manner
they can conceive and in which their souls find rest. He must tell them about
eternal bliss and misery in parables they can comprehend and conceive. Of the
true nature of the afterlife he should only indicate something in general: that
it is something that "no eye has seen and no ear heard," and that there are
pleasures that are great possessions, and miseries that are perpetual torture.

Know that God, exalted be Hé, knows that the good lies in such a state of
affairs. It follows, then, that that which God knows to be the good, must exist,
as you have known [from the preceding discussion]. But there is no harm if the
legislator's words contain symbols and signs that might stimulate the naturally
apt to pursue philosophic investigation.

CHAPTER 3/ACTS OF WORSHIP: THEIR BENEFITS IN THIS WORLD AND THE NEXT.

Moreover, this individual who is a prophet is not one whose like recurs in
every period. For the matter that is receptive of a perfection like his occurs in
few bodily compositions. It follows necessarily, then, that the prophet (may
God's prayers and peace be upon him) must plan with great care to ensure the
preservation of the legislation he enacts concerning man's welfare. Without
doubt, the fundamental principle here is that men must continue in their
knowledge of God and the resurrection and that the cause for forgetting these
things with the passage of the generation succeeding [the mission of] the
prophet (may God's prayers and peace be on him) must be absolutely eliminated. Hence there must be certain acts and works incumbent on people that
the legislator must prescribe to be repeated at frequent specified intervals. In
this way memory of the act is renewed and reappears before it can die.

These acts must be combined with what brings God and the afterlife necessarily to mind; otherwise they are useless. Remembering is achieved through
words that are uttered or resolutions made in the imagination and by telling
men that these acts bring them closer to God and are richly rewarded. And
these acts must in reality be of such a nature. An example of these are the acts
of worship imposed on people. In general, these should be reminders. Now re-

minders consist of either motions or the absence of motions that lead to other motions. An example of motion is prayer; of the absence of motion, fasting. For although the latter is a negative notion, it so greatly moves one's nature that he who fasts is reminded that what he is engaged in is not a jest. He will thus recall the intention of his fasting, which is to draw him close to God. . . .

The noblest of these acts of worship, from one point of view, should be the one in which the worshiper considers himself to be addressing God, beseeching Him, drawing close to Him, and standing in His presence. This is prayer. The legislator should therefore prescribe for the worshiper in preparation for prayer those postures men traditionally adopt when they present themselves to human kings, such as purification and cleanliness (indeed, he must prescribe fully in these two things). He should also prescribe for the worshipers the behavior traditionally adopted in the presence of kings: reverence, calm, modesty, the lowering of the eyes, the contracting of the hands and feet, the avoidance of turning around, composure. Likewise, he must prescribe for each time of prayer praiseworthy manners and customs. These acts will benefit the vulgar inasmuch as they will instill in them remembrance of God and the resurrection. In this way their adherence to the statutes and laws will continue. For without such reminders they will forget all of this with the passing of a generation or two. It will also be of great benefit for them in the afterlife inasmuch as their souls will be purified in the manner you have known [in our discourse]. As for the elect, the greatest benefit they derive from these things pertains to the afterlife.

We have established the true nature of the afterlife and have proved that true happiness in the hereafter is achieved through the soul's detaching itself by piety from the acquisitions of bodily dispositions opposed to the means for happiness. This purification is realized through moral states and habits of character acquired by acts that turn the soul away from the body and the senses and perpetuate its memory of its true substance. For if the soul continues to turn unto itself, it will not be affected by the bodily states. What will remind and help the soul in this respect are certain arduous acts that lie outside natural habit—indeed they are more on the side of exertion. These tire the body and curb the [natural] animal desire for rest, for laziness, for the rejection of toil, for the quieting of the hot humor, and for avoiding all exercise except that which is conducive to bestial pleasure. In the performance of these acts the soul must be required to recall God, the angels, and the world of happiness, whether it desires to do so or not In this way the soul is instilled with the propensity to be repelled from the body and its influences and with the positive disposition to control it. Thus it will not be affected by the body. Hence when the soul encounters bodily acts, these will not produce in it the propensities and positive disposition that they would normally produce when the soul submits to them in everything. For this reason, the one who speaks truth has said: *Surely the good deeds drive away the bad deeds.* If this act persists in man, then he will acquire the positive disposition of turning in the direction of truth and away from error. He thus becomes well prepared to be delivered unto [true] happiness after bodily separation.

If these acts were performed by someone who did not believe them to be divine obligations and who, nonetheless, had to remember God in every act, rejecting everything else, this one would be worthy of some measure of this virtue. How much more worthy will be the one who performs these acts knowing that the prophet comes from God and is sent by God, that his being sent is necessitated by divine wisdom, that all the prophet's legislation is an obligation demanded of him by God, that all he legislates comes from God? For the prophet was obligated by God to impose these acts of worshiping Him. These acts benefit the worshipers in that they perpetuate in the latter adherence to the laws and religion (sharī'ah) that insure their existence and in that, by virtue of the goodness they inspire, they bring the worshipers closer to God in the hereafter.

Moreover, this is the man who is charged with administering the affairs of men, for insuring their livelihood in this world and their well-being in the world to come. He is a man distinguished from the rest of mankind by his godliness.

CHAPTER 4/ESTABLISHMENT OF THE CITY, THE HOUSEHOLD (THAT IS, MARRIAGE), AND THE GENERAL LAWS PERTAINING TO THESE MATTERS.

The legislator's first objective in laying down the laws and organizing the city must be to divide it into three groups: administrators, artisans, and guardians. He must place at the head of each group a leader, under whom he will place other leaders, under these yet others, and so forth until he arrives at the common run of men. Thus none in the city will remain without a proper function and a specific place: each will have his use in the city. Idleness and unemployment must be prohibited. The legislator must leave the way open to no one for acquiring from another that share of a livelihood necessary for man while exempting himself from any effort in return. Such people he must vigorously restrain. If they fail to refrain from such a practice, he must then exile them from the land. But should the cause here be some physical malady or defect, the legislator must set aside a special place for such cases, under someone's charge.

There must exist in the city a common fund, part of it consisting of duties imposed on acquired and natural profits such as fruit and agricultural produce, part of it imposed as punishment, while another part should consist of property taken from those who resist the law, that is, of war-booty. Thus the fund will serve to meet the exigencies of the common good, to meet the needs of the guardians who do not work in any craft, and those prevented from earning their livelihood by maladies and chronic diseases. Some people have held the opinion that the diseased whose recovery is not to be expected should be killed.

But this is base; for their sustenance will not hurt the city. If such people have relatives enjoying a superfluity of means, then the legislator must impose on these relatives the responsibility for their people.

Just as idleness must be prohibited, so should professions like gambling, whereby properties and utilities are transferred without any benefit rendered in exchange. For the gambler takes without rendering any service at all. Rather, what one takes must always be a compensation given in return for work, a compensation that is either substance, utility, good remembrance, or any other titling considered a human good. Similarly, professions that lead to the opposite of welfare and usefulness, such as the learning of theft, brigandage, leadership of criminal bands, and the like, must be prohibited. Professions that allow people to dispense with warning those crafts pertaining to the association—professions such as usury—must be prohibited. For usury is the seeking of excess profit without practicing a craft to achieve it, even though it does render a service in return. Also those acts—which, if once permitted, would be detrimental to the city's growth—like fornication and sodomy, which dispense with the greatest pillar on which the city stands, that is, marriage, must be prohibited.

The first of the legislator's acts must pertain to marriage resulting in issue. He must call and urge people to it. For by marriage is achieved the continuity of the species, the permanence of which is proof of the existence of God, the Exalted. He must arrange it in such a way that matrimony takes place as a manifest affair, so that there will be no uncertainties concerning progeny causing defects in the proper transfer of inheritances, which are a source of wealth. . . . Through this also—I mean the concealment of marriage—defects in other respects occur: for example, in the necessity that one party should undertake expenditure over the other, in rendering mutual assistance, and in other matters that will not escape the wise person after reflection.

The legislator must take firm measures to assure the permanence of the union so that not every quarrel should result in a separation that disrupts the bond between children and parents and renews the need of marriage for everyone. In this there are many sorts of harm. Also, because what is most conducive to the general good is love. Love is only achieved through friendship; friendship through habit; habit is produced only through long association. This assurance, with respect to the woman, consists in not placing in her hands the right to make the separation. For in reality she is not very rational and is quick to follow passion and anger. But a way for separation must be left open and not all doors closed. To prevent separation under all circumstances results in all kinds of harmful consequences. Of these is the fact that some natures cannot adapt themselves to others: the more they are brought together, the greater the resulting evil, aversion, and unpleasantness. Or again, someone might get an unequal partner, or one who is of bad character, or repellent in nature. This will induce the other partner to desire someone else—for desire is natural—and this in turn leads to many harmful consequences. It also might so happen that the married couple do not cooperate for procreation and if ex-changed for other partners they would. Hence some means for separation is necessary. But the law must be strict about it.

The means for separation must not be placed in the hands of the less ra-tional of the two, the one more prone to disagreement, confusion, and change. Instead, this must be relegated to the judges who will affect the separation when they ascertain the woman's mistreatment by the other partner. In the case of the man, an indemnity must be imposed on him so that he will approach separation only after ascertainment and after he finds it to be the right thing for him in every way.

The legislator must, nevertheless, leave the way open for reconcilation without, however, emphasizing it lest this encourage thoughtless action. On the contrary, he must make reconciliation more difficult than separation. How excellent was that which [Muhammad] the greatest of legislators com-manded—that the man, after thrice pronouncing the formula for divorce, is not allowed to remarry the woman until he brings himself to drink a cup un-surpassed in bitterness, which is, to first let another man marry her by a true marriage and have real relations with her. If such a prospect awaits a man, he will not approach separation recklessly, unless he has already determined that the separation is to be permanent, or unless he is of a defective character and takes perverted pleasure in scandal. But the likes of these fall outside the pale of men who deserve the seeking of their welfare.

Since woman by right must be protected inasmuch as she can share her sex-ual desire with many, is much inclined to draw attention to herself, and in ad-dition to that is easily deceived and is less inclined to obey reason; and since sexual relations on her part with many men cause great disdain and shame, which are well-known harms, whereas on the part of the man they only arouse jealousy, which should be ignored as it is nothing but obedience to the devil; it is more important to legislate that the woman should be veiled and secluded from men. Thus, unlike the man, she should not be a bread-earner. It must be legislated that her needs be satisfied by the man upon whom must be imposed her sustenance. For this the man must be compensated. He must own her, but not she him. Thus she cannot be married to another at the same time. But in the case of man this avenue is not closed to him though he is forbidden from taking a number of wives whom he cannot support. Hence the compensation consists in the ownership of the woman's "genitalia." By this ownership I do not mean sexual intercourse. For both partake of its pleasure and the woman's share is even greater, as is her delight and pleasure in children. But by this I mean that no other man can make use of them.

It must be legislated with respect to the child that both parents must un-dertake his proper upbringing—the woman in her special area, the man by provision. Likewise it must be prescribed that the child must serve, obey, re-spect, and honor his parents. For they are the cause of his existence and in addition have borne his support, something we need not enlarge upon as it is evident.

THE NEGLECTED DUTY

∎

MUHAMMAD AL-SALAM FARAJ

(§16) THE ESTABLISHMENT OF AN ISLAMIC STATE

This is a duty which is rejected by some Muslims and neglected by others although the proof for the obligatory character of the establishment of a state is clear, and made obvious by the (text of the) Book of God—Blessed and Supreme He is,—for God—Glory to Him—says: "and that you must rule between them according to what God sent down," and He says: "Whosoever does not rule by what God sent down, those, they are the unbelievers." He says— Glorious and Majestic He is—in (the first verse of) Surah 24 (of which we quoted verse 55 in the previous paragraph), about the obligatory character of the prescripts of Islam: "a Surah which we sent down and which we made obligatory." From this (verse) (it follows) that the establishment of the Rule of God over this earth (mentioned in verse 55 of this Surah) must be considered to be obligatory for the Muslims. God's prescripts are an obligation for the Muslims. Hence, the establishment of an Islamic State is an obligation for the Muslims, for something without which something which is, obligatory cannot be carried out becomes (itself), obligatory. If, moreover, (such a) state cannot be established without war, then this war is an obligation as well.

(§17) Muslims are agreed on the obligatory character of the establishment of an Islamic Caliphate. To announce a Caliphate must be based on the existence of a (territorial) nucleus (from which it can grow). This (nucleus) is the Islamic State. "Whosoever dies without having taken upon himself (the obligation of) a pledge of allegiance does not die as a Muslim." So, it is obligatory for every Muslim to seriously strive for the return of the Caliphate in order not to fall into the category of people (mentioned in the) Tradition (quoted in this paragraph). By "pledge of allegiance" (the text of the Tradition) means "allegiance to the Caliphate."

(§25) THE RULERS OF THE MUSLIMS TODAY ARE IN APOSTASY FROM ISLAM

The Rulers of this age are in apostasy from Islam. They were raised at the tables of imperialism, be it Crusaderism, or Communism, or Zionism. . . . It is a well-established rule of Islamic Law that the punishment of an apostate will be heavier than the punishment of someone who is by origin an infidel (and has never been a Muslim), and this in many respects. For instance, an apostate has to be killed even if he is unable to (carry arms and) go to war. Someone, however, who is by origin an infidel and who is unable to (carry arms and) go to war (against the Muslims) should not be killed, according to leading Muslim scholars like Abū Ḥanīfah and Mālik and Aḥmad (ibn Ḥanbal). Hence, it is the view of the majority (of the jurists) that an apostate has to be killed, and this is in accordance with (the opinions held in) the Schools of Law of Mālik, Al-Shāfiʿī and Aḥmad (ibn Ḥanbal). (Other examples of this difference are) that an apostate cannot inherit, cannot conclude a legally valid marriage, and to eat from the meat of animals which he slaughtered is forbidden. No such rules exist concerning someone who is by origin an infidel (and has never been a Muslim). When apostasy from a religion is worse than having always been an infidel, then apostasy from the prescripts (of a religion) is (also) worse than having always been an infidel. So, apostasy is worse than rebellion against the prescripts of a religion which comes from someone who has always been outside (this religion).(")

Ibn Taymīyah says on p. 293:

(§26) "It is a well-established rule of Islamic Law that the punishment of an apostate will be heavier than the punishment of someone who is by origin an infidel (and who has never been a Muslim), and this in many respects. For instance, an apostate has to be killed in all circumstances, he does not have the right to profess his new religion against the payment of the head tax, and there can be no Convenant of Protection (between an ex-Muslim and the Muslim authorities) unlike the case with someone who has always been an infidel (non-Muslim, e.g., a Christian or a Jew). For instance, an apostate has to be killed even if he is unable to (carry arms and) go to war. Someone, however, who is by origin an infidel and who is unable to (carry arms and) go to war (against the Muslims) should not be killed, according to leading Muslim scholars like Abū Ḥanīfah and Mālik and Aḥmad (ibn Ḥanbal). Hence, it is the view of the majority (of the jurists) that an apostate has to be killed, and this is in accordance with (the opinions held in) the Schools of Law of Mālik, Al-Shāfiʿī and Aḥmad (ibn Ḥanbal). (Other examples of this difference are) that an apostate cannot inherit, cannot conclude a legally valid marriage, and to eat from the meat of animals which he slaughtered is forbidden. No such rules exist concerning someone who is by origin an infidel (and has never been a Muslim). When apostasy from a religion is worse than having always been an infidel, then apostasy from the prescripts (of a religion) is (also) worse than having always been an infidel. So, apostasy is worse than rebellion against the prescripts of a religion which comes from someone who has always been outside (this religion)."

(§71) THE ANSWER TO THOSE WHO SAY THAT IN ISLAM JIHĀD IS DEFENSIVE ONLY

Concerning this question it is proper that we should refute those who say that *jihād* in Islam is defensive, and that Islam was not spread by the sword. This is a false view, which is (nevertheless) repeated by a great number of those who are prominent in the field of Islamic missionary activities. The right answer comes from the Apostle of God—God's Peace be upon Him—when he was asked: "What is *jihād* for God's cause?" He then said: "Whosoever fights in order to make the Word of God supreme is someone who (really) fights for God's cause." To fight is, in Islam, to make supreme the Word of God in this world, whether it be by attacking or by defending. . . .

Islam spread by the sword, *and under the very eyes of these Leaders of Unbelief who conceal it from mankind. After the (removal of these Leaders) nobody has an aversion (to Islam). . . .*

It is obligatory for the Muslims to raise their swords under the very eyes of the Leaders who hide the Truth and spread falsehoods. If (the Muslims) do not do this, the Truth will not reach the hearts of Men. Read with me the Letter of the Prophet—God's Peace be upon Him—to Heraclius, which is reported on the authority of Ibn 'Abbās in the (Collection of Traditions entitled) *Al-Ṣaḥīḥ* by Al-Bukhārī. Its text runs as follows:

(§72) In the Name of God, the Most Compassionate. From Muḥammad, the Servant and Apostle of God, to Heraclius, the Ruler of the Byzantine Empire. Peace upon whomever follows the (divine) Guidance. I call upon you to accept Islam. Become Muslim and be saved. God will bring you your reward twofold. When you turn away (from this Call), the sins of (your subjects) . . . will be held against you. "Say: 'O people of the Book, come to a word which is fair between us and you, to wit that we serve no one but God, that we associate nothing with Him, and that we do not take one the other as Lords apart from God'; if they then turn away, say ye: 'Bear witness that we are Muslims.'" (Qur'ān 3.64)

We add the text of the Letter of the Prophet—God's Peace be upon Him—to Khosrau as well:

(§73) In the Name of God, the Most Compassionate. From Muḥammad, the Apostle of God, to Khosrau, the Ruler of the Persian (Sasanid) Empire. Peace upon whomever follows the (divine) Guidance and believes in God and His Apostle and testifies that there is no god but God alone, He has no associate, and (testifies) that Muḥammad is His Servant and His Apostle. I call upon you from God, for I am the Apostle of God to all mankind, to warn those who are alive. True is the word to the infidels: Become Muslim and be saved. When you refuse, the sins of (your subjects), will be upon you." (This Tradition is reported) by Ibn Jarīr (Al-Ṭabarī) on the authority of Ibn Isḥāq.

(§74) Al-Bayhaqī quotes the text of the Letter which the Apostle sent to the (Christians) of Najrān:

In the Name of the God of Abraham, Isaac and Jacob. From Muḥammad, the Prophet and Apostle of God to the Bishop and the people of Najrān. Peace upon you. I praise the God of Abraham, Isaac and Jacob. I call upon you to serve God, and not to serve men. I call upon you to let yourselves be ruled by God, and not by men. When you refuse, then a head tax. When you refuse (this, too), be apprised of war. A greeting of Peace.

(§75) (Muḥammad)—God's Peace be upon Him—sent similar Letters to Al-Muqawqis (the Ruler of Egypt), to the King of Yamāmah (in Arabia), to Al-Mundhir ibn Sāwī, the Ruler of Bahrein, to Al-Ḥārith ibn Abī Shimr the Ghassanid (King in Northern Arabia), to Al-Ḥārith ibn 'Abd al-Kalāl, the Ḥimyārī (King of Southern Arabia), to the King of Oman, and to others.

(§76) THE VERSE OF THE SWORD (QUR'ĀN 9.5)

Most Koran commentators have said something about a certain verse from the Koran which they have named the Verse of the Sword (Qur'ān 9.5). This verse runs: "Then when the sacred months have slipped away, slay the polytheists wherever ye find them, seize them, beset them, lie in ambush for them everywhere."

The Qur'ān scholar Ibn Kathīr noted in his commentary on this verse: "Al-Ḍaḥḥāk ibn Muzāḥim said: 'It cancelled every treaty between the Prophet—God's Peace be upon Him—and any infidel, and every contract and every term.' Al-'Ūfi said about this verse, on the authority of Ibn 'Abbās: 'No contract nor covenant of protection was left to a single infidel since (this) dissolution (of treaty obligations) was revealed.'"

(§77) The Qur'ān scholar Muḥammad ibn Aḥmad ibn Muḥammad ibn Juzayy al-Kalbī, the author of (a Qur'ān commentary entitled) *Tafsīr al-Tashīl li-'Ulūm al-Tanzīl*, says: "The abrogation of the command to be at peace with the infidels, to forgive them, to be (passively) exposed to them and to endure their insults preceded here the command to fight them. This makes it superfluous to repeat the abrogation of the command to live in peace with the infidels at each Qur'anic passage (where this is relevant). (Such a command to live in peace with them) is found in 114 verses in 54 surahs. This is all abrogated by His word: "Slay the polytheists wherever ye find them" (Qur'ān 9.5) and "Fighting is prescribed for you" (Qur'ān 2.216).

Al-Ḥusayn ibn Fadl says: "This is the verse of the sword. It abrogates every verse in the Qur'ān in which suffering the insults of the enemy is mentioned." It is strange indeed that there are those who want to conclude from Qur'ān verses that have been abrogated that fighting and *jihād* are to be forsworn.

(§78) The Imām Abū 'Abdallāh Muḥammad Ibn Ḥazm who died in *456* AH says in (his book entitled) *Al-Nāsikh wa-'l-Man-sūkh* (The Abrogating and the Abrogated Passages from the Qur'ān), in the Chapter "On Not Attacking the Infidels": "In 114 verses in 48 surahs everything is abrogated by the Word of God—Exalted and Majestic He is—: 'Slay the polytheists wherever ye find them' (Qur'ān 9.5). We shall discuss this whenever we come across it, if God—Exalted He is—permits." End of quotation.

(§79) The scholar and Imam Abū al-Qāsim Hibbat Allāh ibn Salāmah says on "Slay the polytheists wherever ye find them": "The third verse is indeed the third verse, and it is this verse which is the verse which abrogates. But it abrogates 114 verses from the Qur'ān and then the end of it abrogates the beginning of it, because the verse ends with: 'If they repent and establish the Prayer and pay the Zakāt, then set them free' (Qur'ān 9.5, end of the verse)." (This quotation is taken from) a book (entitled) *Kitāb al-Nāsikh wa 'l Mansūkh.*

(§84) FIGHTING IS NOW A DUTY UPON ALL MUSLIMS

When God—Praised and Exalted He is—made fasting obligatory, he said (Qur'ān 2.183): "Fasting is prescribed for you." In regard to fighting He said (Qur'ān 2.216): "Fighting is prescribed for you." This refutes the view of whoever says that *jihād* is indeed a duty and then goes on by saying: "When I have fulfilled the duty of engaging in missionary activities for Islam (*da'wah*), then I have fulfilled the duty (of *jihād*), because (engagement in missionary activities for Islam) is *jihād* too." However, the (real character of this) duty is clearly spelled out in the text of the Qur'ān: It is fighting, which means confrontation and blood.

The question now is: When is *jihād* an individual duty? *Jihād* becomes an individual duty in three situations:

(§85) First, when two armies meet and their ranks are facing each other, it is forbidden to those who are present to leave, and it becomes an individual duty to remain standing, because God—Exalted He is—says: "O ye who have believed, when ye meet a hostile party, stand firm, and call God frequently to mind" (Qur'ān 8.45) and also: "O ye who have believed, when ye meet those who have disbelieved moving into battle, turn them not your backs" (Qur'ān 8.15).

Second, when the infidels descend upon a country, it becomes an individual duty for its people to fight them and drive them away.

Third, when the Imām calls upon a people to fight, they must depart into battle, for God—Exalted He is—says (Qur'ān 9.38–39): "O ye who have believed, what is the matter with you? When one says to you: 'March out in the way of God,' ye are weighed down to the ground; are you so satisfied with this nearer life as to neglect the Hereafter? The enjoyment of this nearer life is in comparison with the Hereafter only a little thing. If ye do not march out He will inflict upon you a painful punishment, and will substitute (for you) another people; ye will not injure Him at all; God over everything has power." The Apostle—God's Peace be upon Him—says: "When you are called upon to fight, then hasten."

With regard to the lands of Islam, the enemy lives right in the middle of them. The enemy even has got hold of the reins of power, for this enemy is (none other than) these rulers who have (illegally) seized the Leadership of the Muslims. Therefore, waging *jihād* against them is an individual duty, in addition to the fact that Islamic *jihād* today requires a drop of sweat from every Muslim.

(§87) Know that when *jihād* is an individual duty, there is no (need to) ask permission of (your) parents to leave to wage *jihād,* as the jurists have said; it is thus similar to prayer and fasting.

(§88) THE ASPECTS OF JIHĀD ARE NOT SUCCESSIVE PHASES OF JIHĀD

It is clear that today *jihād* is an individual duty of every Muslim. Nevertheless we find that there are those who argue that they need to educate their own souls, and that *jihād* knows successive phases; and that they are still in the phase of *jihād* against their own soul. They offer as proof the doctrine of Imām Ibn al-Qayyim, who distinguished three aspects in *jihād:*

1. *Jihād* against one's own soul

2. *Jihād* against the Devil

3. *Jihād* against the infidels and the hypocrites

(§89) This argument shows either complete ignorance or excessive cowardice, because Ibn Al-Qayyim (only) distinguished *aspects* in *jihād,* he did not divide it into successive phases. Otherwise we would have to suspend the waging of *jihād* against the Devil until we finished the phase of *jihād* against our own soul. The reality is that the three (aspects) are aspects (only) that follow a straight parallel course. We, in our turn, do not deny that the strongest of us in regard to faith, and the most zealous of us in regard to waging *jihād* against his own soul is the one (of us) who is the most steadfast.

Whoever studies the Biography (of Muhammad) will find that whenever (a state) of *jihād* was proclaimed, everybody used to rush off for God's cause, even perpetrators of great sins and those who had (only) recently adopted Islam.

It is reported that (once) a man embraced Islam during the fighting and fell in the battle, thus dying a martyr, and the Apostle—God's Peace be upon Him—said: "A small work, a great reward."

(§90) (There is also) the story about Abū Miḥjan al-Thaqafī (who was guilty of a great sin since he was) addicted to wine, while his bravery in the war against Persia was famous.

Ibn al-Qayyim also made mention that the Tradition: "'We returned from the Small *Jihād* to the Great *Jihād'*—and then someone said: 'What is the

Great *Jihād*, O Apostle of God?'—and then (Muḥammad) said: 'The *jihād* against the soul,'" is a fabricated Tradition, see *(the book by Ibn Al-Qayyim entitled *Kitāb*) *Al-Manār*.

The only reason for inventing this Tradition is to reduce the value of fighting with the Sword, so as to distract the Muslims from fighting the infidels and the hypocrites.

PART FOUR

CAN ETHICS

SAVE THE WORLD?

12

ETHICS AND THE ENVIRONMENT

■

GOLFING WITH SILVERSPOT BUTTERFLIES

Richard Schroeder loved golf and was good at it. As a college student, he won a few local and regional tournaments. He could have turned professional. And even though he entered the securities business after graduation, he never lost his passion for the game. His lifelong dream was to design and build the consummate golf course.

Most people never follow their dreams. Richard did, and he set his sights on where he lived, in Gearhart, Oregon. He left his securities position and became the pro at a local club. He then learned all he could about the golf business and about developing and designing a top-notch golf course, one that would be pristine, picturesque, and challenging.

After ten years of careful planning, he designed a blueprint for a golf resort with both hotels and private residences. And in 1986, with enough financial backing, he now had the green light to move ahead with his $100 million project. He was all set to move ahead, except for one "small" problem—butterflies. The land that he had targeted for his exclusive resort was one of only a few habitats for a rare species, the Oregon silverspot butterfly (*Speyeria zerene hippolyta*). The silverspot was listed as a threatened species under the 1973 Endangered Species Act. This meant that threatening, harming, or collecting listed species could result in severe fines as well as imprisonment.

Richard, conscientious about the survival of the *S. z. Hippolyta*, had no desire to be complicit in eradicating a rare species. He consulted with top-notch experts such as Oregon State University's Paul Hammond, the world's leading authority on the butterfly, and the U.S. Fish and Wildlife Service's silverspot recovery team. The Fish and Wildlife Service is a branch of the Department of the Interior and provides an official listing of both threatened and endangered species. It also penalizes those who violate the Endangered Species Act.

Despite earnest efforts to cooperate with the Service, Richard faced a predicament. He could not promise that his building efforts would not harm a single silverspot. Could he come up with a viable "habitat conservation plan" that would fairly balance his development interests with the interests of the butterfly? Moreover, the costs of any conservation efforts were exorbitant. For one thing, the silverspot caterpillars feed off of the blue violet and lay their eggs near the flower. The golf course would have to be redesigned to avoid wreaking havoc on the blue violets. In addition, because the popular Scotch broom shrub naturally overruns the blue violet, the course would have to be developed in a way that prevents the shrub from threatening the violet. In any case, it would require millions of additional dollars to redirect construction and development sites. Add to this the ever-present problem that the silverspot could easily move its own site, so that predicting these sites was futile at best. Because the entire project would have been well over the $100 million price tag, Schroeder's financial patrons backed out of the scheme. The plight of the silverspot butterfly trumped Richard Schroeder's lifetime dream.[1]

When one considers the economic benefits and opportunities for numerous people in a $100 million resort, one can't help but wonder about the rationale for saving a butterfly at any cost. Schroeder's predicament is not unique. Similar tensions exist between various development projects that benefit humans versus the use of natural resources and the survival of species such as the piping plover, the whooping crane, or the northern spotted owl. But butterflies? There is more public support and sentiment when it comes to dramatic species such as the bald eagle. And though the bald eagle is no longer on the endangered species list, there are many other imperiled species that are less visible. Currently, there are well over 2,500 officially endangered species, these species ranging from plants to fish to birds to reptiles to mammals. So we now habitually face this hard choice: What wins out—a nonhuman species or human economic growth?

■ ECOLOGY, BIODIVERSITY, AND HUMAN LIFESTYLES

The ubiquitous catchword "ecology" derives from two Greek terms: *oikos* ("household") and *logos* ("study of"). This "study of our household" has generated a powerful following. We now even have "deep ecology," claiming to be a more radical investigation of our household and ways to clean it up. Philosopher Arne Naess first coined the term "deep ecology" in 1973 when he launched an attack against the "shallow" ecology that was still thoroughly anthropocentric in that it operated solely within the framework of protecting human interests.

Though most ecologists today share a common ground in that they examine the fundamental causes for our environmental crisis, philosophers like Joseph Desjardins have distinguished three types of ecologists. *Deep ecologists* believe that the root cause of our environmental plight lies in a long-standing worldview that sets nature apart from human concerns and thereby justifies the use of all other species for human design. While agreeing that this worldview needs to be changed, *social ecologists* argue that the causes are imbedded within more specific social and political structures. For social ecologists, the root cause has to do with a long and tainted history of social hierarchy and control that manifests itself in various forms of racism and strict class distinctions. *Ecofeminists* take this one step further by claiming that such control involves patterns of patriarchy and a prevailing oppression of women. While accepting the premise of social ecologists, they point out that the need to dominate nature is closely linked to the need for men to dominate women. Philosopher Karen Warren argues that much of this has to do with the association of woman with nature, and, since nature is viewed as subordinate to the interests of men, women in turn are viewed as inferior to men.[2]

Along these same lines, we humans seem to compete on just about every scale, from the battle with nature, to the battle with other tribes and nations, to battle with the opposite sex. Despite nature's lessons, we still lack humility when it comes to nature's power, promises, and perils. Sebastian Junger's true story about the October 1991 sinking of the swordfishing boat *Andrea Gail* in *The Perfect Storm* is a good example of how nature eventually has the upper hand, whereas human hubris leads to human destruction. Philosopher Alan Watts, in his *Nature, Man, and Woman* claimed that our attitudes toward nature are reflected in our attitudes toward the other sex. And instead of collaboration and harmony, these attitudes are essentially of competition and control.

This chapter concerns not only ecology but also the broader realm of the enduring tapestry of life in its natural forms, what we usually refer to as "nature." Yet nature is an extraordinarily elastic term. Others refer to this tapestry as "environment." When we think of environment, we think of the sweeping range of nature from species of microorganisms, plants, and animals to surrounding ecosystems. Yet environment remains equally vague and does not capture the complexity of the natural world. A more current term given to this complex tapestry is "biodiversity," and biodiversity includes four categories: genetic, species, ecological, and landscape:

> Genetic diversity *refers to the unique combinations of genes found within and among organisms. . . . Genetic variability is an important trait in assuring the long-term survival of most species, since it allows them to respond to unpredictable changes in their environment.*

> Species diversity *encompasses the variety of living organisms inhabiting an area. . . .*

> Ecological diversity *refers to the higher-level organization of different species into natural communities, and the interplay between these communities and the physical environment that forms ecosystems. . . .*

> Landscape diversity *refers to the geography of different ecosystems across a large area and the connections among them.*[3]

What is most important to bear in mind here is that there is an intrinsic interaction among all four categories. All things interact somehow with each other. One slight change in species diversity can affect the broader ecosystem and vice versa. For instance, the freshwater mussel called the orange-nacre mucket, now listed as a threatened species, populates Alabama's Mobile River basin. The mucket is unable to move any significant distance. Yet it has a fascinating way of populating new areas. It sends out a tube-like "lure" that consists of larvae, and fish that bite the lure end up with some released larvae attached to their gills. These larvae then feed off the gills while hitching a ride on the fish, and they eventually drop off somewhere upstream or downstream. Yet the success of this maneuvering depends not only upon the fooled fish but also upon water flow, temperature, and other aspects of the basin.[4]

We are now finally realizing that biodiversity is threatened on many sides, and that the key to preserving this natural legacy lies in sustaining diversity on these various levels. And while we have designated certain high-profile places for conservation, places that are scenically appealing to tourists, such as national parks and wildlife preserves, these efforts by themselves are temporary band-aids to a long-term crisis. Tourist aesthetics ought not to be the defining measure of what counts as important.

As for Richard Schroeder's butterfly problem, we see here the tension between economic growth and moral and aesthetic sensitivity. Building a plush resort with first class hotels and a golf course is an obvious economic payoff. To refrain from developing the land in this or other profitable fashion makes little economic sense. Nevertheless, many environmentalists still cast the key issue in moral and aesthetic terms. This leads us to what seems to be an inescapable equation: Benefiting some species means burdening others. What benefits the human species will thus often burden nonhuman species. This depicts what biologist Garrett Hardin calls the "tragedy of the commons." The medieval commons, or communal pasture, was exposed to various herds of cattle. As more cattle grazed on the land, more land was used up as the owners of the cattle benefited. There were no equal efforts at saving the land. For those who tried, their loss was another's gain. How do we maintain the commons so that a fair level of resources remains available to all? Richard Schroeder's case is rare because, in most instances, our need for golf courses overrides whatever rights other species may have. For that matter, do other species even have rights? If so, rights in what sense? Moral rights? And if we extend moral rights to other living things, are these negative moral rights, that is, the right to noninterference, or positive moral rights, the entitlement to these rights. Are other species members of a moral community?

■ WHO/WHAT BELONGS TO THE MORAL COMMUNITY?

Here's a challenge to all of the ethical theories we have examined in this text. How do we manage to dispose of the millions of tons of toxic waste that we have produced, especially when the toxicity of this waste will outlive us, our children's generation, and their children's generation, lingering on for another hundred thousand years? Do we dump it into the ocean? Antarctica? Alaska? Into space? Onto other planets?

This question becomes especially poignant if we expand our moral community. For far too long, our vision of the moral community, at least in the West, has been anthropocentric. We have limited our moral community solely to human persons who, by virtue of being persons, possess moral status. Our most prominent Western philosophers and theologians have steadily pointed out that humans are naturally superior to all other species by virtue of the capacity to reason. Medieval philosopher and theologian Thomas Aquinas (1225–1274) asserted that this capacity to reason indicates that humans are created in the image of their creator God. Nonhuman animals, on the other hand, lack this capacity and are justifiably subjugated to humans for human use. French philosopher Rene Descartes' (1596–1650) famous formula, *Cogito, ergo sum*, "I think, therefore I am," solidifies this view by positing the primacy of thinking, or reasoning in human life. And since nonhuman animals and other species lack this faculty, humans are necessarily superior. And the great German thinker Immanuel Kant (1724–1804) takes this a big step further when he claims that because humans are superior in this regard, they can justifiably use animals as a means to humans' own ends. That is, we have no direct duties toward animals. (However, we must add to this that for Kant, we do have indirect duties to treat animals with respect, and this indirect duty strictly prohibits us from treating animals cruelly.)

Western cultures have therefore long inherited the notion that nature in and of itself is essentially "disposable." This is underscored by philosopher Carl Becker in his article at the end of this chapter. Whatever benefits there are in our natural environment, they exist for us. However, as Becker poignantly points out, we can no longer afford to maintain this attitude for one very practical reason—our resources have become distressingly scarce. According to Becker, the only way to resolve this crisis in which human needs far outstrip nature's resources would be a complete change in our worldview. For Becker, this is where Buddhist philosophy, particularly its teaching regarding the interconnectedness of all things, is invaluable. Moreover, he reminds us that other living entities are stakeholders in the decisions we make with respect to the environment. Thus, environmental concerns compel us to reexamine our traditional views regarding what constitutes the moral community, and whose interests have priority over other species.

So, here's the big question: What determines moral status so that an entity belongs to the moral community? What enables something to possess moral rights? Some philosophers like Joel Feinberg argue that having some sense of self-awareness entitles one to moral status and respect. If so, then this would exclude plant species and the like from membership in the moral community. Others, like Peter Singer, would hold that the capacity for pleasure and pain, or simple sensation, is a viable criterion for moral status. He shares the view of British philosopher Jeremy Bentham (1748–1832) who wrote:

> The day may come when the rest of the animal creation may acquire those rights which never could have been withholden from them by the hand of tyranny . . . a full grown horse or dog is beyond comparison a more rational, as well as a more conversable animal, than an infant of a day or a week or even a month, old. But suppose they were otherwise, what would it avail? The question is not, Can they reason? nor Can they talk? but, Can they suffer?[5]

In Singer's view, all creatures who have the capacity for sensation are part of the moral community. To hold otherwise is to support the unsupportable, that is, what he calls "specicsism." For others, such as Tom Regan, animals possess intrinsic value irrespective of their capacity for sensation. To view animals as objects or as means to our own ends violates this intrinsic value.

In any case, by assuming a nonanthropocentric view of the moral community, we thereby assign moral status to all living beings, not only with respect to individual living things but to their species as well. Not all would agree. Mark Sagoff, in his article at the end, contends that this emphasis upon respecting individual living beings essentially conflicts with promoting the interests of ecosystems. Despite this tension, however, if the level of our moral concern extends into the bigger ecological picture, incorporating ecosystems, one lesson we can learn from ecology and the study of ecosystems is that nothing acts in isolation. All things are interdependent. Indeed, all that we do, whatever we decide, impacts upon the big picture. Excessive use of motorized watercraft in the bay at Long Beach Island, New Jersey, will no doubt affect marine life in the bay for centuries to come. In like manner, consider the impact of growing commercial and recreational shark fishing upon marine species. Researchers at Dalhousie University in Halifax, Nova Scotia, point out that as a result and because the reproductive rate for sharks is much slower than that of other fish, the shark population is drastically decreasing. The general population of sharks has dropped by over 50 percent, and some species, like the hammerhead and the great white, have dropped by over 75 percent![6] This slow demise of a leading predator will no doubt have a long-lasting adverse effect upon marine life's food chains. To illustrate further, the spraying of DDT in Borneo had far-reaching consequences. First, as intended, it destroyed all bothersome houseflies. Then, because the corpses of the houseflies were laden with the pesticide, gecko lizards that preyed on the insects also died. House cats then ate the dead lizards that were saturated with the same poison. They too died. Soon, rats overran the region, bringing with them bubonic plague. To get rid of the rats, healthy cats were then parachuted into the region![7]

■ WHAT/WHO POSES THE MAJOR THREATS?

How serious is this environmental crisis that we face? There are those, like Rachel Carson in her groundbreaking *Silent Spring* (1962) and Paul Ehrlich in *The Population Bomb* (1968), who forecast a bleak and dismal future for a humanity that has been enslaved by its technologies, a humanity that has become the victim of its own discoveries. In contrast, there are so-called ecorealists like Gregg Easterbrook who acknowledge a serious ecological crisis and yet believe that sound progress has been made. Easterbrook argues that global warming is not a truly serious issue. He also claims that, in contrast to the criticism by developing nations, developed nations are actually more ecologically sound and cleaner.[8] And there are those who claim that our air and our rivers are becoming cleaner and that pollution levels are dropping significantly. On the other hand, other voices, becoming more vocal, decry a profound increase in the use of pollutants accompanied by an equally profound decrease in available resources.

Noted biologist E. O. Wilson singled out four major threats to biodiversity, what he terms the four "mindless horsemen of the environmental apocalypse." These are destruction of the natural habitat (this includes pollution); introduction of alien species; diseases from alien species; and overexploitation.[9] From this list, let us now look more closely at how human activity has become synonymous with human culpability, that is, how human interventions have produced a significant portion of our current environmental crises.

HABITAT RUIN

Habitat ruin is considered to be the most prominent threat to biodiversity. It involves a wide range of activities: agriculture (land and water conversion, fertilizers, pesticides), livestock grazing, mining (oil, gas, and geothermal exploration), logging, infrastructure development (roads and bridges), military activities, outdoor recreation such as skiing and off-road vehicles, water development (dams, reservoirs), pollutants, land conversion for urban and commercial sites, and disruption of fire regimes. Of these, agricultural activities, commercial and urban developments, water developments, and outdoor recreation are the top threats to endangered and imperiled species of plants and animals. Here, humans are directly responsible, for example, when it comes to recreation. Outdoor recreation threatens 27 percent of endangered species, with the use of off-road vehicles (ORVs) threatening 13 percent of these species.[10]

ALIEN SPECIES

Humans are also responsible for introducing species that are not indigenous to the region. What state has the highest extinction of its species? Whatever beautiful and romantic image we may have of Hawaii, more species extinctions have occurred here than in any other state. It is a painful example of how indigenous species were adversely affected by human interference in the name of progress and development. Most of Hawaii's indigenous species of plants and birds are now threatened by the introduction of alien species, species that have been introduced by humans. For instance, a ship's crew inadvertently introduced mosquitoes into Hawaii while dumping water barrel dregs filled with mosquito larvae. These mosquitoes were later responsible for spreading avian malaria and other diseases that eventually obliterated quite a few indigenous bird species.[11]

POPULATION, DEVELOPMENT, EXTINCTION

Moreover, there is a clear interrelationship among population, urban and commercial development, and their impact upon ecosystems. First, consider population growth. Twenty-five percent of the world's population lives in industrialized countries, yet this group also consumes 80 percent of the world's resources. In the next fifty years, the world's population will double, thus bringing about a world population of over 11 billion people! [12]

More people mean more development sites and infrastructure activities. This is bound to have a negative impact upon biodiversity and will no doubt affect endangered and imperiled species. Florida, Hawaii, and California will be especially affected because these areas house quite a few endangered species and, at the same time, their projected population growth far outpaces the rest of the country. For instance, southern California is one of the wealthiest regions in the United States. A prosperous hi-tech business economy continues to lure more and more people into the area, and housing developments sprout up and litter the coastal shoreline. An acre of shoreline can sell for nearly $4 million! Yet the tide of human population gains momentum. This has in turn nearly obliterated the coastal sage shrub that covered most of the shoreline. A number of bird species such as the California gnatcatcher depend upon the shrub for their survival. The gnatcatcher and other bird species are listed as threatened.[13] Again, we face this thorny issue. How do we protect and parcel out lands that are crucial for species survival when these same lands are targeted for building developments?

POLLUTION

Pollution is the most obvious case of human activity adversely affecting our ecosystems. What does pollution say about who we are as humans? And, just as there are various types of human activities, there are various types of pollution, ranging from biochemical waste, nuclear waste, industrial waste, pesticides and other solvents, to smog, and pollution in oceans, lakes, and rivers. Indeed, pollution remains the biggest threat to aquatic species. Moreover, geographic areas of high pollution concentration are often situated close to poor and minority residences. For example, in Richmond, California, the majority of residents are African American. In 1993, soon after the city's General Chemical plant leaked sulfur trioxide, over twenty thousand residents went to nearby hospitals. Even though the leak proved to be the result of negligence, residents must still bear the burden of proof to show that any construction of future chemical sites would harm them. Another example is the enormous amount of waste that is dumped into the Rio Grande from nearby U.S.-operated chemical plants across the border in Mexico. These plants are acting illegally, because they are required to export all waste to the United States. Most of the residents along the Rio Grande obtain their drinking water from the river. The rate of anencephaly in border cities of Brownsville, Texas, and Matamoros, Mexico, is four times the national average in the United States! And still, despite attempted legal suits against these companies, the burden of proof rests with the residents—they must prove the link.[14]

Perhaps the leading question concerning pollution is, What constitutes an unacceptable risk? For example, is a 1 out of 1,000,000,000 exposure to lead in drinking water an acceptable risk? Although research in chemicals has produced enormous benefits such as penicillin, other antibiotics, and contraceptives, there are risks associated with chemical toxins. There is a clear link between cancer and chemical toxins, and a strong connection between industrial chemicals and adverse effects upon the nervous system, which is most volatile because nerve cells do not have the capacity to regenerate. Workers who are constantly exposed to neurotoxins like lead, or solvents like furniture polish, shoe polish, disinfectants, and rubber cement, are thus at risk. And the effect of smog and air pollution on the respiratory system is well documented.[15]

GLOBAL WARMING

Here is another area where human activity has induced perilous consequences for the ecosystem. In the atmosphere, high above the earth's surface, there is the so-called gossamer ozone layer, which filters out harmful rays from the sun. Without this ozone protection, intense heat would cripple the growth of crops and plants, adversely affect life-forms in the ocean, and make us more susceptible to blindness and skin cancer. Yet, due to an increasing amount of chlorofluorocarbons (CFCs) in the atmosphere, this layer is being depleted. These CFCs are released in abundant amounts from human interventions such as insulation, air conditioning, cleaning solvents, and aerosol sprays. The increasing amount of carbon dioxide we have released into the atmosphere has contributed to our global warming and increasing incidences of anomalous, extreme weather patterns. Scientists still disagree with each other regarding how much these greenhouse gases are the direct result of human activities. Nonetheless, human actions such as the burning of carbon-based fossil fuels have definitely contributed to global warming.

Now that we face these critical issues, there are full-fledged international efforts to stem the tide of further greenhouse gases. In 1987, 24 countries signed the Montreal Protocol to eliminate CFCs. Within ten years, 139 more countries added their signatures to the pact. In 1992, there was the earth Summit at Rio de Janeiro, Brazil. And in 1999, 160 nations met in Kyoto, again to address global warming. Even so, enforcing international policies is a problem in itself. If a country adopts strict environmental regulations, industries then move to countries lacking the strict laws. There is a financial incentive for these industries to relocate. The host country therefore finds itself at a disadvantage with respect to its own workforce and may therefore be pressured into lowering its originally stricter standards.[16]

■ SUSTAINABILITY

Is there a solution to our environmental crises? Clearly, we need to bring about what is called a "sustainable" world. By "sustainable" we mean using our resources in wise, balanced, and fair ways within the framework of both present needs and long-range planning. It demands a vision of moral responsibility regarding the future of our planet. This moral responsibility compels us to recognize and act upon two critical assumptions: our spatial, geographic interconnectedness with all other nations and our temporal, historical link to the future based upon decisions that we make in the present. Sustainability envisions a society that "meets the needs of the present without compromising the ability of future generations to meet their own needs." [17] According to leading experts at Massachusetts Institute of Technology, this would require the following:

> In a sustainable society population, capital and technology would be balanced so that the per capita material living standard is adequate and so that the society's material and energy throughputs meet three conditions:
>
> 1. Its rates of use of renewable resources do not exceed their rates of regeneration.
>
> 2. Its rates of use of nonrenewable resources do not exceed the rate at which sustainable renewable substitutes are developed.
>
> 3. Its rates of pollution emission do not exceed the assimilative capacity of the envirnoment. [18]

All of this requires that we recognize two critical distinctions. The first is the distinction between *growth* and *development*. A society that concentrates merely on growth is one that measures progress quantitatively, in terms of size and the abundance of resources. On the other hand, a society that focuses upon development, that is, a society that seeks sustainability, measures progress qualitatively. It would "discriminate among the kinds of growth and purposes for growth. It would ask what growth is for, who would benefit, what it would cost, how long it would last, and whether it could be accommodated by the sources and sinks of the earth." [19] Economist Herman Daly resorts to the same distinction when he speaks of a "steady-state economy" versus a "growth economy":

> Growth is quantitative increase in the physical scale of through-put. Qualitative improvement in the use made of a given scale of

throughput, resulting either from improved technical knowledge or from a deeper understanding of purpose, is called "development." An SSE [steady-state economy] therefore can develop, but cannot grow, just as the planet earth, of which it is a subsystem, can develop without growing.[20]

In this respect, while tackling the plaguing issues of poverty and unemployment, sustainability underscores the notion of "enough" instead of the notion of "more." This requires a radical transformation of worldview, one that measures the good in qualitative rather than material and quantitative terms.

The second critical distinction is that of desires versus needs. In our society we have no doubt confused the two. What constitutes a comfortable lifestyle? With our Big Mac culture, big houses, Starbucks, spacious malls, sports utility vehicles (SUVs), and so on, ours is a culture of great expectations. That is, we have confused what we worry about not having with what we think we need. We have allowed our individual preferences to become desires to such an extent that we then perceive them as being basic needs. The fact of the matter is that although we may prefer a big house, complete with a two- or three-car garage, and although all sorts of forces pressure us into believing that we do desire these things, do we really, in essence, *need* them? If our preferences translate into unlimited wants and desires, then the possibility of a just distribution of scarce resources remains dismal.

ENERGY ALTERNATIVES

In view of the above, a sustainable world must consider alternative sources for energy, for we are overly dependent upon oil for our energy source, and this is exacerbated by our growing population, expanding industrialization and urbanization, and monumental increases in energy consumption. Furthermore, our dependency upon oil from the Middle East and particularly from the Persian Gulf region, which currently has two-thirds of the oil reserves in the world and remains geopolitically unstable, can catapult us into long-term disaster. Note our war on Iraq, even in the face of near-global criticism. All of this points out to us the clear interrelationship among our nation's environmental health, its economic health, and issues of national security.

Although there are currently efforts to utilize oil sources beyond the Middle East, such as in the former Soviet Union, we still need to seek alternative sources for our energy. Yet, we face a giant hurdle. The U.S.

Congress continues to make radical cuts when it comes to funding research and development (R&D) projects that are intended to study viable forms of energy as alternatives. When it comes to so-called hybrid vehicles, Japanese and European researchers may well be outpacing the United States when it comes to improving fuel cells as an alternative to petroleum.[21] For example, Germany's "smart car" is a "smart" effort to produce environmentally reliable cars. Yet Congress continues to make cuts in research along these lines. Allocations for the 1996 "advanced-transportation-technology budget" were sliced by 30 percent, and renewable energy funding has also been cut by 30 percent. As of 2002, the total cuts have amounted to 60 percent.[22]

Experts urge us to look into new technologies such as light-colored, reflective roofing and shade trees as ways to "cool" those "heat islands" we call cities, so named because of their poor air quality. Cities as a rule exude more heat, up to five degrees, and these "heat islands" affect the climate. Here is where smog becomes a noted factor since smog increases with the rise in temperature.[23] Just think of the increase in energy use, particularly with air conditioners during a heat wave, and this no doubt affects the overall health of the residents, particularly the more vulnerable elderly. We cannot afford to turn our attention away from new technologies that could

> help cool the Los Angeles area by five degrees, reducing annual air-conditioning bills by more than $150 million. Since smog formation is very temperature-sensitive, such cooling would reduce smog concentrations by 10 percent, which would be comparable to removing three quarters of the cars on the road. The health-related benefits of that smog reduction would be worth $300 million a year. Applied nationally, the energy savings alone could exceed $10 billion a year by 2015.[24]

Yet all of this requires not only full-fledged federal fiscal support for pollution prevention technologies and R&D, but also a radical change in attitudes. Instead of focusing upon consumption of resources, our society needs to refocus upon pollution prevention. This transformation is critical. Yet, government unwillingness to fund these efforts remains the roadblock.

> Equally remarkably, Congress demonstrates an overwhelming desire to gut the funding for investments by the energy-efficiency-and-renewable-energy program, although it costs Americans only $4.00 per person per year.[25]

WHY SAVE SPECIES?

When the Nixon administration in 1973 established the Endangered Species Act (ESA), its first real test came about five years later when the U.S. Supreme Court forced the closing of the nearly completed Tellico Dam in Tennessee in order to save the tiny, 3-inch snail darter fish.[26] Despite the enormous benefits of hydroelectric power and flood control, the fish won out because it was listed as endangered. In theory, the idea behind the ESA is to save endangered species, but here's the problem. The wording extended itself to *all* species, and the actual number of species is staggering! As Mann and Plummer state:

> *According to E.O.Wilson, a renowned entomologist at Harvard, there are only a few thousand types of the mammals and birds that people like to anthropomorphize, but there may be something on the order of 100 million species, of which only about 1.4 million have been named. Creatures such as fungi, insects, and bacteria form the vast majority of this horde; mammals, birds, and other vertebrates are little but colorful epiphenomena.*[27]

Nevertheless, it is important to save species, and three arguments have been advanced to support why.[28] First, doing so is ultimately beneficial for humans. Many of our foods and medicines are derived from various species. For example, in Washington State, every year the Weyerhaeuser tree company plants hundreds of millions of Pacific yew (*Taxus brevifolia*) seedlings in the hopes of eventually harvesting the tree's roots, bark, and needles. These contain taxol, a promising new treatment for ovarian cancer, highly lethal since it resists chemotherapy. Weyerhaeuser has collaborated with the pharmaceutical company Bristol-Myers Squibb in a combined effort to extract the lifesaving taxol. Also, in central Florida there is the Lake Placid scrub mint that contains chemicals that protect the mint from insects. This repellent could prove very useful to humans as an insect repellent. The scrub mint is now listed by the government as an endangered plant species due to the bustling housing developments throughout central Florida.[29]

Second, saving species is also useful to the order and fabric of earth. It helps to keep our house in order so that we can generate soil, fresh water, and a healthy atmosphere. Third, there is what biologist David Ehrenfield calls the "Noah Principle," the idea that all species have intrinsic worth. Therefore each and every living thing has an inherent right to exist, whether it is the sperm whale, white shark, cockroach, plant, or even microorganisms. And on this global Ark, many would contend that we need to protect as many species as we can. In his selection at the end of the chapter, Mark Sagoff alludes to this species egalitarianism when he points out that such a notion is essentially incompatible with the premise behind animal liberation, which seeks to protect the rights of individual animals.

COSTS AND PRIORITIES

This sounds nice in theory, but reality is another matter. Simply put, we cannot preserve all species. To begin with, the costs of conservation and preservation are outright staggering. In a 1990 federal study (the estimate now is likely higher) recovery plans for species listed as endangered or threatened were expected to be around $4.6 billion over the next ten years.[30] This is because conservation efforts usually come into tension with human development efforts. Human habitats clash with natural habitats. Nonetheless, a necessary condition in conservation would require that we curtail human development projects. E. O. Wilson and Paul Ehrlich put it this way:

> The first step . . . would be to cease "developing" any more relatively undisturbed land. Every new shopping center built in the California chaparral, every hectare of tropical forest cut and burned, every swamp converted into a rice paddy or shrimp farm means less biodiversity . . . ending direct human incursions into remaining relatively undisturbed habitats would be only a start . . . The indispensable strategy for saving our fellow living creatures and ourselves in the long run is . . . to reduce the scale of human activities.[31]

Is this even possible? It is *only* possible if we adopt a new mind-set, a new ethos. In this regard, there is much we can learn from other traditions, such as some of the Buddhist themes we have already discussed.

Next, how do we even begin to decide which species are worth preserving? Would we rate the California condor over the alligator? What about the pesky mosquito? Do we rank what biologist David Marshall calls the "glamour species" over "creepy crawlies"?[32] Note how the names we assign to certain species express a certain sentiment about them as well: "cockroach," "bug," "vulture," as opposed to "butterfly," "panther," and "peregrine falcon." How do we fairly decide the priority of a species as well as the funds allocated to save that species? Thus far, it seems that there has been an unfair distribution of government funds for recovery. Mann and Plummer cite how more monies have been doled out for threatened than for endangered species. Of the three most expensive species in terms of allocated recovery funds, two of them, the northern spotted owl and the grizzly bear, are not endangered but threatened.

We are, without a doubt, at the crossroads. We cannot afford to put off these issues, for we are talking about the long-term future of our planet, and we can only save our planet if we act now.

> But though the asteroid that is headed toward us this time is, figuratively speaking, of our own making, we also have the power to avoid it. To have a chance for success, though, the conservation choreography will have to occur on the very human timescale of the next few decades. Doing so will also require knowledge and commitment to action.[33]

Despite its merits, the traditional approach to conservation is not sound enough, addressing issues with each species as they arise on an ad hoc basis; only when officially listed as endangered or imperiled or threatened does the species obtain protection. Conservationists feel that we need to abandon this incremental approach and look at the long-term picture.

■ WEAKNESSES IN ENVIRONMENTAL ETHICS

Perhaps the most prominent weakness in the vast field of environmental ethics lies in what many would construe to be its fundamental incompatibility with respecting the rights of individual members of various species. Some describe this as the tension between species and individuals. The more appropriate way to think of this tension is that between the concern for ecosystems, with its emphasis upon relationships and balance among all species, and individual members of species. Thus, the interests of ecology, if viewed systemically, appear to override the interests of individual animals.

Philosopher Mark Sagoff addresses this tension in his article at the end of this chapter. He labels the tension as that between environmental ethics and animal liberation. Referring to Aldo Leopold's classic manifesto of ecology in *A Sand County Almanac*, Sagoff argues that the concern for ecological balance, or ecosystem wholeness, operates under principles that conflict with the principles underlying animal liberation. The underlying principle of ecosystem balance requires that we act in ways that preserve the overall balance of our ecosystem. For animal liberationists, the key principle is that we treat all nonhuman animals equally and see to it that individual animals do not suffer needlessly. By incorporating nonhuman animals into the moral community in this way, animal liberationists such as philosopher Peter Singer argue that we have a duty not only to refrain from harming animals, but also to work in ways that would prevent unnecessary harm. That is, the moral rights that we assign to nonhuman animals should be positive and not just negative.

For this reason, the humane orientation behind animal liberation conflicts with the more globally oriented need for ecological wholeness, balance, and harmony. This is especially so since the moral rights that Peter Singer, Tom Regan, and others attribute to animals are positive rights—we have the moral responsibility to protect all living beings from unnecessary harm and to relieve animal suffering whenever possible. Thus, ecology and egalitarianism appear to be incompatible. Consider the case of hunting. As Sagoff points out, Leopold himself was an ardent hunter. Yet Leopold's concern was with environmental balance, with maintaining the "diversity, integrity, beauty and authenticity of the natural environment." According to Sagoff and apparently Leopold, this aim is compatible with hunting as a way of thinning out herds in excess of their habitat.

Another major weakness concerns the overall agenda of environmental ethics. Who sets the agenda? Whose values are most prominent? It appears as if the agenda is being set by environmentalists, ecologists, and animal rights activists primarily in Western cultures. Are they in effect imposing their values concerning ecology to all other cultures? Surely, ecology is a global concern with global impact. Yet are the principles biased? Is this a case of cultural imperialism?

To illustrate, the leading premise in contemporary environmental ethics is that we need to get beyond our long-standing anthropocentric orientation as to who and what constitutes the moral community. This obviously entails extending the community of moral concern to other living beings and, for many ecologists, *all* living beings. Yet, can we feasibly apply this notion in developing countries? In most of these countries, poverty, famine, malnutrition, and inadequate health care are the main concerns. How would conservation efforts such as respect for wilderness areas alleviate these conditions? Critics like sociologist Ramachandra Guha argue that these dire conditions essentially stem from "economic and political structures" as well as "life style choices."[34] Addressing conservationist and preservationist issues will do little to affect these structures of power and inequity.

Guha cites "Project Tiger" as an example. Project Tiger is a system of wildlife parks that is intended to protect the interests of large mammals like the tiger, elephant, and rhinoceros. Yet throughout India's history, there has been an ongoing, cooperative relationship that people, mostly farmers, have had with the surrounding environment. People's relationship with nature had been balanced. However, when conservationists set these wilderness areas aside, this disrupts the prior balance. Not only are resources used to protect the tiger at the expense of the poor laborers and farmers who live near these parks, but these parks, as in Africa, are maintained primarily for the benefit of tourists. The owners of the parks therefore reap the financial gains from tourists while the peasants remain poor and destitute. As Guha puts it:

> Until very recently, wildlands preservation has been identified with environmentalism by the state and the conservation elite; in consequence, environmental problems that impinge far more directly on the lives of the poor — e.g., fuel, fodder, water shortages, soil erosion, and air and water pollution — have not been adequately addressed.[35]

■ STRENGTHS IN ENVIRONMENTAL ETHICS

The crisis that we face awakens in many of us a sense of the sacred with respect to species and spaces. For instance, Native American beliefs remind us that all of nature is holy and should be treated with the utmost respect. Furthermore, this respect goes hand in hand with compassion for all living things. As we have seen earlier, compassion is the predominant virtue in Buddhist ethics. Mahayana Buddhism sets forth the *bodhisattva* as its prototype of both wisdom and compassion. Buddhists contend that a genuine awakening necessitates an ardent commitment to facilitate awakening for *all* beings. As the seventh-century Buddhist Shantideva describes the *bodhisattva's* resolve in his *Compendium of Doctrine:*

> He will not lay down his arms of enlightenment because of the corrupt generations of men, nor does he waver in his resolution to save the world because of their wretched quarrels.[36]

As the incarnate fusion of wisdom and compassion, the *bodhisattva* announces:

> I must not wait for the help of another, nor must I lose my resolution and leave my tasks to another. I must not turn back in my efforts to save all beings nor cease to use my merit for the destruction of all pain. And I must not be satisfied with small successes.[37]

A second strength is that this also reminds us of the interconnectedness of existence. This works temporally as well as spatially. Environmental sensitivity entails a genuine commitment to consider the consequences of our actions and therefore to future generations. In all of this, we transcend both the prison of space that presumes a geographical distance between ourselves and nature, and the prison of time that posits a historical distance among past, present, and future.

This is what the Buddhist teaching of dependent origination, or *pratityasamutpada,* is essentially all about. It means that all things in existence are so intimately connected with each other that everything affects everything else. Nothing occurs by itself. No events happen in isolation. All aspects of existence interpenetrate. Existence is an intricate web of mutual and symbiotic cause-and-effect. There is in the literal sense an ongoing, perennial intercourse. Consider the image of a quiet lake. Once we cast a pebble into the lake, it sends out a ripple effect that reaches the shore of the lake. *Pratityasamutpada* means that the ripple effect from the simple stone does not end with the shore. It continues to affect the land beyond the shore, all of the lake, the lake bottom, the air, and all aspects of the environment in subtle but meaningful ways.

Finally, all of this also exhorts us to reconsider the beauty of simplicity. Sustainability embodies an awareness of the critical distinction between what we truly need and what we do not need. It forces us to examine what we take for granted. How do we measure so-called progress? In terms of monetary success? A nation's GNP? We have this implicit faith in economy, science, and technology as the litmus test for progress. Yet, as Becker points out, the benefits of antibiotics and nuclear energy also have their downside. Scientific, medical, and technological progress is always a two-edged sword. We've reveled in their improvements, welfare, and convenience. Now we feel their shortcomings and flaws. And Becker's "fatal flaws" of Western capitalism essentially have to do with naively equating the "good" with what is fundamentally economic. If we define ourselves and others essentially in economic terms, we fail to discover the intrinsic richness of our human essence, an essence that, rather than being at odds with nature, shares its common ground.

In view of these weaknesses and strengths, the issues raise an incisive caveat with respect to environmentalists' underlying values and principles. It compels us to reassess our own positions. It also entails that we do so in serious and critical fashion so that we do not fall victim to the type of cultural imperialism that cross-cultural sensitivity and understanding, what this book is all about, seeks to avoid. And the ideas in this text are only a starting point. Cross-cultural sensitivity and understanding are necessary first steps to cross-cultural dialogue.

■ NOTES

1. From Charles C. Mann and Mark L. Plummer, "The Butterfly Problem," *Atlantic Monthly* 269, no. 1 (January 1992): 47–70.

2. Karen J. Warren, "The Power and the Promise of Ecological Feminism," in Joseph DesJardins, *Environmetnal Ethics: Concepts, Policy, and Theory* (Mountain View, CA: Mayfield, 1999), p. 543.

3. Bruce A. Stein, Lynn S. Kutner, and Jonathan S. Adams, eds., *Precious Heritage: The Status of Biodiversity in the United States* (New York: Oxford University Press, 2000), p. 8. This work is perhaps the most comprehensive reference work on biodiversity.

4. Ibid., p. 179.

5. From Jeremy Bentham, *An Introduction to the Principles of Morals and Legislation*, in James Rachels, *The Elements of Moral Philosophy*, 4th ed. (Boston: McGraw-Hill, 2003), p. 98.

6. Julia K. Baum, Ransom A. Myers, Daniel G. Kehler, Boris Worm, Shelton J. Harley, and Penny A. Doherty, "Collapse and Conservation of Shark Populations in the Northwest Atlantic," *Science* (January 17, 2003), pp. 299; 389–92.

7. Mann and Plummer, p. 53.

8. See Gregg Easterbrook, *A Moment on the Earth* (New York: Penguin Books, 1995).

9. See E. O. Wilson, *The Diversity of Life* (Cambridge, MA: Belknap Press of Harvard University Press, 1992).

10. See the discussion in *Precious Heritage*, pp. 242ff.

11. Ibid., p. 239.

12. DesJardins, p. 394.

13. *Precious Heritage*, p. 302.

14. Robert D. Bullard, "Justice and Environmental Decision Making," in DesJardins, p. 446.

15 Ann Misch, "Assessing Environmental Health Risks," in DesJardins, pp. 267ff.

16. DesJardins, p. 476.

17. Donella Meadows, Dennis Meadows, and Jorgen Randers, "From *Beyond the Limits*," in DesJardins, p. 89.

18. Ibid.

19. Ibid.

20. Herman E. Daly, "Moving to a Steady-State Economy," in DesJardins, p. 127.

21. Joseph J. Romm and Charles B. Curtis, "Mideast Oil Forever?" *Atlantic Monthly*, 277, no. 4 (April 1996): 62ff.

22. Ibid., pp. 64, 67.

23. Ibid., p. 68.

24. Ibid., p. 58.

25. Ibid., p. 72.

26. See the discussion in Mann and Plummer, pp. 53ff.

27. Ibid., p. 51.

28. See ibid., p. 52ff.

29. *Precious Heritage*, p. 159.

30. Mann and Plummer, p. 55.

31. Ibid., p. 53.

32. Cited in ibid., p. 58.

33. *Precious Heritage*, p. 320.

34. Ramachandra Guha, "Radical American Environmentalism and Wilderness Preservation: A Third World Critique," in DesJardins, p. 591.

35. Ibid.

36. From Shantideva's *Siksasamuccaya*, in William Theodore de Bary, ed., *The Buddhist Tradition in India, China and Japan* (New York: Vintage Books, Random House, 1972, 1969), p. 84.

37. Ibid., p. 85.

ANIMAL LIBERATION AND ENVIRONMENTAL ETHICS

MARK SAGOFF

"The land ethic," Aldo Leopold wrote in *A Sand County Almanac*, "simply enlarges the boundaries of the community to include soils, waters, plants, and animals, or collectively, the land." What kind of community does Leopold re-

fer to? He might mean a *moral* community, for example, a group of individuals who respect each other's right to treatment as equals or who regard one another's interests with equal respect and concern. He may also mean an *ecological* community, that is, a community tied together by biological relationships
in interdependent webs or systems of life.

Let us suppose, for a moment, that Leopold has a *moral* community in
mind; he would expand our *moral* boundaries to include not only human beings, but also soils, waters, plants and animals. Leopold's view, then, might not
differ in principle from that of Christopher Stone, who has suggested that animals and even trees be given legal standing, so that their interests may be represented in court. Stone sees the expansion of our moral consciousness in this
way as part of a historical progress by which societies have recognized the
equality of groups of oppressed people, notably blacks, women and children.
Laurence Tribe eloquently makes the same point:

> What is crucial to recognize is that the human capacity for empathy
> and identification is not static; the very process of recognizing rights
> in those higher vertebrates with whom we can already empathize
> could well pave the way for still further extensions as we move up-
> ward along the spiral of moral evolution. It is not only the human lib-
> eration movements—involving first blacks, then women, and now
> children—that advance in waves of increased consciousness.

Peter Singer, perhaps more than any other writer, has emphasized the analogy between human liberation movements (for example, abolitionism and suf-
feragism) and "animal liberation" or the "expansion of our moral horizons" to
include members of other species in the "basic principle of equality." Singer
differs from Stone and Tribe, however, in two respects. First, he argues that the
capacity of animals to suffer pain or to enjoy pleasure or happiness places
people under a moral obligation which does not need to be enhanced by a doctrine about rights. Second, while Stone is willing to speak of the interests of his
lawn in being watered, Singer argues that "only a being with subjective experiences, such as the experience of pleasure or the experience of pain, can have
interests in the full sense of the term." A tree, as Singer explains, may be said
to have an "interest" in being watered, but all this means is that it needs water
to grow properly as an automobile needs oil to function properly. Thus, Singer
would not include rocks, trees, lakes, rivers or mountains in the moral community or the community of morally equal beings.

Singer's thesis, then, is not necessarily that animals have rights which we
are to respect. Instead, he argues that they have utilities that ought to be
treated on an equal basis with those of human beings. Whether Tribe and
Stone argue a weaker or a different thesis depends upon the rights they believe
animals and other natural things to have. They may believe that all animals
have a right to be treated as equals, in effect, they may agree with Singer that
the interests of *all* animals should receive equal respect and concern. On the

other hand, Tribe, Stone or both may believe that animals have a right only to life or only to those very minimal and basic rights without which they could not conceivably enjoy any other right. I will, for the moment, assume that Tribe and Stone agree that animals have basic rights, for example, a right to live or a right not to be killed for their meat. I will consider later the possibility that environmental law might protect the rights of animals without necessarily improving their welfare or protecting their lives.

Moral obligations to animals, to their well-being or to their rights, may arise in either of two ways. First, duties to non-human animals may be based on the principle that cruelty to animals is obnoxious, a principle nobody denies. Muckraking journalists (thank God for them) who depict the horrors which all too often occur in laboratories and on farms, appeal quite properly to the conviction and intuition that people should never inflict needless pain on animals and especially not for the sake of profit. When television documentaries or newspaper articles report the horrid ways in which domestic animals are often treated, the response is, as it should be, moral revulsion. This anger is directed at human responsibility for the callous, wanton and needless cruelty human beings inflict on domestic animals. It is not simply the pain but the way it is caused which justifies moral outrage.

Moral obligations, however, might rest instead on a stronger contention, which is that human beings are obliged to prevent and to relieve animal suffering however it is caused. Now, insofar as the animal equality or animal liberation movement makes a philosophically interesting claim, it insists on the stronger thesis, that there is an obligation to serve the interests, or at least to protect the lives, of *all* animals who suffer or are killed, whether on the farm or in the wild. Singer, for example, does not stop with the stultifying platitude that human beings ought not to be cruel to animals. No; he argues the controversial thesis that society has an obligation to prevent the killing of animals and even to relieve their suffering wherever, however, and as much as it is able, at a reasonable cost to itself.

I began by supposing that Aldo Leopold viewed the community of nature as a *moral* community—one in which human beings, as members, have obligations to all other animals, presumably to minimize their pain. I suggested that Leopold, like Singer, may be committed to the idea that the natural environment should be preserved and protected only insofar as, and because, its protection satisfies the needs or promotes the welfare of individual animals and perhaps other living things. I believe, however, that this is plainly not Leopold's view. The principle of natural selection is not obviously a humanitarian principle; the predator-prey relation does not depend on moral empathy. Nature ruthlessly limits animal populations by doing violence to virtually every individual before it reaches maturity; these conditions respect animal equality only in the darkest sense. Yet these are precisely the ecological relationships which Leopold admires; they are the conditions which he would not interfere with, but protect. Apparently, Leopold does not think that an ecological system has to be an egalitarian moral system in order to deserve love and admiration. An ecological system has a beauty and an authenticity that demands respect—but plainly not on humanitarian grounds.

In a persuasive essay, J. Baird, Callicott describes a number of differences between the ideas of Leopold and those of Singer—differences which suggest that Leopold's environmental ethic and Singer's humane utilitarianism lead in opposite directions. First, while Singer and other animal liberationists deplore the suffering of domestic animals, "Leopold manifests an attitude that can only be described as indifference." Second, while Leopold expresses an urgent concern about the disappearance of species, Singer, consistently with his premises, is concerned with the welfare of individual animals, without special regard to their status as endangered species. Third, the preservation of wilderness, according to Leopold, provides "a means of perpetuating, in sport form, the more virile and primitive skills. . . ." He had hunting in mind. Leopold recognized that since top predators are gone, hunters may serve an important ecological function. Leopold was himself an enthusiastic hunter and wrote unabashedly about his exploits pursuing game. The term "game" as applied to animals, Callicott wryly comments, "appears to be morally equivalent to referring to a sexually appealing young woman as a 'piece' or to a strong, young black man as a 'buck'—if animal rights, that is, are to be considered on par with women's rights and the rights of formerly enslaved races."

Singer expresses disdain and chagrin at what he calls "'environmentalists'" organizations such as the Sierra Club and the Wildlife Fund, which actively support or refuse to oppose hunting. I can appreciate Singer's aversion to hunting, but why does he place the word "environmentalist" in shudder quotes when he refers to organizations like the Sierra Club? Environmentalist and conservationist organizations traditionally have been concerned with ecological, not humanitarian issues. They make no pretense of acting for the sake of individual animals; rather, they attempt to maintain the diversity, integrity, beauty and authenticity of the natural environment. These goals are ecological, not eleemosynary. Their goals are entirely consistent, then, with licensing hunters to shoot animals whose populations exceed the carrying capacity of their habitats. Perhaps hunting is immoral; if so, environmentalism is consistent with an immoral practice, but it is environmentalism without quotes nonetheless. The policies environmentalists recommend are informed by the concepts of population biology, not the concepts of animal equality. The S.P.C.A. does not set the agenda for the Sierra Club.

I do not in any way mean to support the practice of hunting; nor am I advocating environmentalism at this time. I merely want to point out that groups like the Sierra Club, the Wilderness Society and the World Wildlife Fund do not fail in their mission insofar as they devote themselves to causes other than the happiness or welfare of individual creatures; that never was their mission. These organizations, which promote a love and respect for the functioning of natural ecosystems, differ ideologically from organizations that make the suffering of animals their primary concern—groups like the Fund for Animals, the Animal Protection Institute, Friends of Animals, the American Humane Association, and various single issue groups such as Friends of the Sea Otter. Beaver Defenders, Friends of the Earthworm, and Worldwide Fair Play for Frogs.

D. G. Ritchie, writing in 1916, posed a difficulty for those who argue that animals have rights or that we have obligations to them created simply by their capacity to suffer. If the suffering of animals creates a human obligation to mitigate it, is there not as much an obligation to prevent a cat from killing a mouse as to prevent a hunter from killing a deer? "Are we not to vindicate the rights of the persecuted prey of the stronger?" Ritchie asks. "Or is our declaration of the rights of every creeping thing to remain a mere hypocritical formula to gratify pug-loving sentimentalists?"

If the animal liberation or animal equality movement is not to deteriorate into "a hypocritical formula to gratify pug-loving sentimentalists," it must insist, as Singer does, that moral obligations to animals are justified, in the first place, by their distress, and, in the second place, by human ability to relieve that distress. The liberationist must morally require society to relieve animal suffering wherever it can and at a lesser cost to itself, whether in the chicken coop or in the wild. Otherwise, the animal liberationist thesis becomes interchangeable with the platitude one learns along with how to tie shoestrings: people ought not to be cruel to animals. I do not deny that human beings are cruel to animals, that they ought not to be, that this cruelty should be stopped and that sermons to this effect are entirely appropriate and necessary. I deny only that these sermons have anything to do with environmentalism or provide a basis for an environmental ethic.

In discussing the rights of human beings, Henry Shue describes two that are basic in the sense that "the enjoyment of them is essential to the enjoyment of all other rights." These are the right to physical security and the right to minimum subsistence. These are positive, not merely negative rights. In other words, these rights require governments to provide security and subsistence, not merely to refrain from invading security and denying subsistence. These basic rights require society, where possible, to rescue individuals from starvation; this is more than the merely negative obligation not to cause starvation. No; if people have basic rights—and I have no doubt they do—then society has a positive obligation to satisfy those rights. It is not enough for society simply to refrain from violating them.

This, surely, is true of the basic rights of animals as well, if we are to give the conception of "right" the same meaning for both people and animals. For example, to allow animals to be killed for food or to permit them to die of disease or starvation when it is within human power to prevent it, does not seem to balance fairly the interests of animals with those of human beings. To speak of the rights of animals, of treating them as equals, of liberating them, and at the same time to let nearly all of them perish unnecessarily in the most brutal and horrible ways is not to display humanity but hypocrisy in the extreme.

Where should society concentrate its efforts to provide for the basic welfare—the security and subsistence—of animals? Plainly, where animals most lack this security, when their basic rights, needs, or interests are most thwarted and where their suffering is most intense. Alas, this is in nature. Ever since Darwin, we have been aware that few organisms survive to reach sexual maturity; most are quickly annihilated in the struggle for existence. Consider as a rough but reasonable statement of the facts the following:

> All species reproduce in excess, way past the carrying capacity of their niche. In her lifetime a lioness might have 20 cubs; a pigeon, 150 chicks; a mouse, 1,000 kits; a trout, 20,000 fry, a tuna or cod, a million fry or more; an elm tree, several million seeds; and an oyster, perhaps a hundred million spat. If one assumes that the population of each of these species is, from generation to generation, roughly equal, then on the average only one offspring will survive to replace each parent. All the other thousands and millions will die, one way or another.

The ways in which creatures in nature die are typically violent: predation, starvation, disease, parasitism, cold. The dying animal in the wild does not understand the vast ocean of misery into which it and billions of other animals are born only to drown. If the wild animal understood the conditions into which it is born, what would it think? It might reasonably prefer to be raised on a farm, where the chances of survival for a year or more would be good, and to escape from the wild, where they are negligible. Either way, the animal will be eaten: few die of old age. The path from birth to slaughter, however, is often longer and less painful in the barnyard than in the woods. Comparisons, sad as they are, must be made to recognize where a great opportunity lies to prevent or mitigate suffering. The misery of animals in nature—which humans can do much to relieve—makes every other form of suffering pale in comparison. Mother Nature is so cruel to her children she makes Frank Perdue look like a saint.

What is the practical course society should take once it climbs the spiral of moral evolution high enough to recognize its obligation to value the basic rights of animals equally with that of human beings? I do not know how animal liberationists, such as Singer, propose to relieve animal suffering in nature (where most of it occurs), but there are many ways to do so at little cost. Singer has suggested, with respect to pest control, that animals might be fed contraceptive chemicals rather than poisons. It may not be beyond the reach of science to attempt a broad program of contraceptive care for animals in nature so that fewer will fall victim to an early and horrible death. The government is

423

spending hundreds of millions of dollars to store millions of tons of grain. Why not lay out this food, laced with contraceptives, for wild creatures to feed upon? Farms which so overproduce for human needs might then satisfy the needs of animals. The day may come when entitlement programs which now extend only to human beings are offered to animals as well.

One may modestly propose the conversion of national wilderness areas, especially national parks, into farms in order to replace violent wild areas with more humane and managed environments. Starving deer in the woods might be adopted as pets. They might be fed in kennels; animals that once wandered the wilds in misery might get fat in feedlots instead. Birds that now kill earthworms may repair instead to birdhouses stocked with food, including textured soybean protein that looks and smells like worms. And to protect the brutes from cold, their dens could be heated, or shelters provided for the all too many who will otherwise freeze. The list of obligations is long, but for that reason it is more, not less, compelling. The welfare of all animals is in human hands. Society must attend not solely to the needs of domestic animals, for they are in a privileged class, but to the needs of all animals, especially those which without help, would die miserably in the wild.

Now, whether you believe that this harangue is a *reductio* of Singer's position, and thus that it agrees in principle with Ritchie, or whether you think it should be taken seriously as an ideal is of no concern to me. I merely wish to point out that an environmentalist must take what I have said as a *reductio*, whereas an animal liberationist must regard it as stating a serious position, at least if the liberationist shares Singer's commitment to utilitarianism. Environmentalists cannot be animal liberationists. Animal liberationists cannot be environmentalists. The environmentalist would sacrifice the lives of individual creature's to preserve the authenticity, integrity and complexity of ecological systems. The liberationist—if the reduction of animal misery is taken seriously as a goal—must be willing, in principle, to sacrifice the authenticity, integrity and complexity of ecosystems to protect the rights, or guard the lives, of animals.

A defender of the rights of animals may answer that my argument applies only to someone like Singer who is strongly committed to a utilitarian ethic. Those who emphasize the rights of animals, however, need not argue that society should enter the interests of animals equitably into the felicific calculus on which policy is based. For example, Laurence Tribe appeals to the rights of animals not to broaden the class of wants to be included in a Benthamite calculus but to "move beyond wants" and thus to affirm duties "ultimately independent of a desire-satisfying conception." Tribe writes:

> To speak of "rights" rather than "wants," after all, is to acknowledge the possibility that want-maximizing or utility-maximizing actions will be ruled out in particular cases as inconsistent with a structure of

agreed-upon obligations. It is Kant, not Bentham, whose thought suggests the first step toward making us "different persons from the manipulators and subjugators we are in danger of becoming."

It is difficult to see how an appeal to rights helps society to "move beyond wants" or to affirm duties "ultimately independent of a desire-satisfying conception." Most writers in the Kantian tradition analyze rights as claims to something in which the claimant has an interest. Thus, rights-theorists oppose utilitarianism not to go beyond wants but because they believe that some wants or interests are moral "trumps" over other wants and interests. To say innocent people have a right not to be hanged for crimes they have not committed, even when hanging them would serve the general welfare, is to say that the interest of innocent people not to be hanged should outweigh the general interest in deterring crime. To take rights seriously, then, is simply to take some interests, or the general interest, more seriously than other interests for moral reasons. The appeal to rights simply is a variation on utilitarianism, in that it accepts the general framework of interests, but presupposes that there are certain interests that should not be traded off against others.

A second problem with Tribe's reply is more damaging than the first. Only *individuals* may have rights, but environmentalists think in terms of protecting *collections, systems* and *communities*. Consider Aldo Leopold's oft-quoted remark: "A thing is right when it tends to preserve the integrity, stability, and beauty of the biotic community. It is wrong when it tends to do otherwise." The obligation to preserve the "integrity, stability, and beauty of the biotic community," whatever those words mean, implies no duties whatever to individual animals in the community, except in the rare instance in which an individual is important to functioning of that community. For the most part, individual animals are completely expendable. An environmentalist is concerned only with maintaining a population. Accordingly, the moral obligation Leopold describes cannot be grounded in or derived from the rights of individuals. Therefore, it has no basis in rights at all.[1]

Consider another example: the protection of endangered species. An individual whale may be said to have rights, but the species cannot; a whale does not suddenly have rights when its kind becomes endangered. No; the moral obligation to preserve species is not an obligation to individual creatures. It cannot, then, be an obligation that rests on rights. This is not to say that there is no moral obligation with regard to endangered species, animals or the environment. It is only to say that moral obligations to nature cannot be enlightened or explained—one cannot even take the first step—by appealing to the rights of animals and other natural things.

Garrett Hardin, in his "Foreword" to *Should Trees Have Standing?*, suggests that Stone's essay answers Leopold's call for a "new ethic to protect land and other natural amenities. . . ." But as one reviewer has pointed out,

Stone himself never refers to Leopold, and with good reason; he comes from a different place, and his proposal to grant rights to natural objects has emerged not from an ecological sensibility but as an extension of the philosophy of the humane movement.

A humanitarian ethic—an appreciation not of nature, but of the welfare of animals—will not help us to understand or to justify an environmental ethic. It will not provide necessary or valid foundations for environmental law.

NOTE

Tom Regan discusses this issue in *The Case for Animal Liberation* (1983):

> Because paradigmatic rights-holders are individuals, and because the dominant thrust of contemporary environmental efforts (e.g., wilderness preservation) is to focus on the whole rather than on the part (i.e., the individual), there is an understandable reluctance on the part of environmentalists to "take rights seriously," or at least a reluctance to take them as seriously as the rights view contends we should. . . . A rights-based environmental ethic . . . ought not to be dismissed out of hand by environmentalists as being in principle antagonistic to the goals for which they work. It isn't. Were we to show proper respect for the rights of individuals who make up the biotic community, would not the *community* be preserved?

(*Id.* at 362.) I believe this is an empirical question, the answer to which is "no." The environmentalist is concerned about preserving evolutionary processes; whether these processes, e.g., natural selection, have deep enough respect for the rights of individuals to be preserved on those grounds, is a question that might best be left to be addressed by an evolutionary biologist.

PHILOSOPHY EDUCATING HUMANITY

CARL BECKER

FROM A LINEAR TO A CYCLICAL WORLDVIEW

The Judaeo-Christian-Islamic world-view epitomizes linearity. God creates the world out of nothing and destroys it when he pleases; the world has a beginning and an end. Moreover, the beginning and end of the world are within human memory and anticipation; humans trace their lineage back to Adam and anticipate the end of the world. Recent Christians may argue for a more ancient beginning in the Big Bang, but seem no less convinced of the temporality and linearity of the human project. Humans are born from nothing, live only once on this world, and then return to dust or are judged on another heavenly plane.

The byproduct of this worldview is the notion of disposability. Like actors on a stage, humans have no responsibility to preserve their stage-set for the next season; this season is all that matters. The world is so huge compared to human size and time-frames that humans seem incapable of exhausting its "resources." Material objects are precisely that, "resources" to be used by "resourceful" humans for their benefit or enjoyment. Since the world is materialized from "nothing," we are absolved from contemplating the origins and limitations of the materials we mine and consume.

The 21st century makes painfully clear the fallacy of this use-and-dispose attitude. Humans are likely to outlive our resources, at the rate we consume them. Petroleum will be exhausted in half a century. Fresh water is becoming an increasingly valuable commodity. One after another, Asian countries are changing from food exporters to food importers, and African countries increasingly approach starvation as the deserts expand upon once-arable land. The limitations of food, fuel, and land become painfully evident.

The only viable solution to these crises involves a changing of ideals, from consumptive to sustainable, from linear "use and dispose" to cyclical "reuse and recycle." In practical terms, this means that everything which is mined, manufactured, or produced must be recycled and reused, with a minimum of wasted energy and resources. Land cannot be wasted on raising beef cattle when the same land would feed many times as many people raising soybeans. Petroleum cannot be wasted in pipeline leaks, idling engines, unnecessary trips and empty passenger seats; solar, wind, tidal, and ocean energy must replace fossil and nuclear.

The circularity of human existence is a basic presupposition, not to say realization, of Buddhist philosophy. The consequence of this realization is to treat food, fuel, and the earth with great care: to receive each item with awe and respect. It includes a recognition that human life itself is inescapably predicated upon the consumption of resources and the taking of life. The guilt of our taking of life cannot be fully assuaged by the assurance that it is inevitable; rather, this consciousness gives rise to a deep humility and desire to make the most of one's life, so that the many plants, animals, and minerals sacrificed for each human life will not have been sacrificed totally without meaning. Because life is seen as essentially suffering, it becomes a goal to reduce the suffering of all sentient beings as much as possible.

FROM DIVINE SALVATION TO KARMIC NECESSITY

The conception of human sin or hubris runs deep in Western thought too. But the tendency of the Western religious world-drama is to end in salvation of both world and humankind by supernatural intervention; a deus ex machina resurrects the faithful in a new magically created world even as the material world is destroyed. The population and food supply of heaven is no more a concern than that of earth; both are magically cared for. Since God will terminate the whole human experiment someday soon, we need not care too seriously about how much we bequeath to our great-grandchildren; since God will terminate our bodies anyway, we need not care too seriously about how we pollute them. 19th century American popular thought imagined that the earth and sea would absorb whatever were spat or discarded upon them.

Recently, we are learning to our awe and ultimate peril that neither air nor earth nor sea can absorb the level of waste we are throwing at them. The 21st century painfully portrays the limitation of the ecosystem to absorb wastes and byproducts. A corollary of the circularity of resources is that everything that is "used" goes somewhere and affects something. Nothing is without effect on the environment. In a matter of a generation, our CFC pollution has made a dangerous dent in the ozone hole, and our CO_2 exhaust has created an irreversible rise in global temperature. Decreased polar ice means decreased plankton generation, while increased UV means a decrease in krill, because krill eggs are killed by UVb. So the very basis of the ocean food chain is being eroded by human pollution, even as overfishing taxes its limits at the upper ends of the food chain.

NOx and SOx thrown into the air fall as acid rain, making land and water less suitable for farming. DPEs (and tobacco smoke) lead to lung cancers, while heavy metal wastes lead to Alzheimer's disease. Decades of dumping unsorted garbage leaves our landfills and underground water reserves polluted with heavy metals and carcinogens.

Everything we discard affects us in the future in some way. This notion that every action (karma) has ineluctable future effects, is part and parcel of the Buddhist world view. Ironically, although Western science also preaches cause and effect, its analytic approach makes it all too easy to ignore effects which are not desired or anticipated. This consciousness of limitation, of cause-and-effect, of interdependence runs deep in Taoism and Buddhism, and is now much needed in the modern world. Ultimately, every glass, metal, paper, or plastic that is manufactured must be recycled into other non-polluting forms. Every organic material which is produced must be reduced by bacterial action into combustible gas and solid fertilizer. Waste heat and other emissions must be recovered or minimized wherever possible.

FROM HUMAN DOMINION OVER NATURE TO HUMAN PLACE WITHIN NATURE

The tendency of the dominant Western Christian ethic was to oppose man to nature, civilized man to barbarian, "good" animals and insects to "bad." Man's "destiny" consisted in bringing nature under human control, exterminating or "civilizing" peoples who had not yet adopted (Christian, Islamic, or Enlightenment) Truth, and killing off large mammals, wolves, and "pests" of all kinds. The artificial polarization of "right and wrong" "good and bad" "true and false" not only engenders conflicts as divergent cultures come into Conflict, but often backfires in the ecological sphere.

Killing off one species of insect, for example, leaves a particular plant without its pollinator, and another species without its food. Those species in turn destabilize an ever growing circle of lives in the ecosystem and food chain, until the widespread damage is irreversible. Human introductions of foreign species into the Great Lakes of America and Japan have had equally disastrous results, destroying native populations.

Extermination of species is not only a question of aesthetics, but may be a key to human survival. Of the thousands of varieties of grain cultivated or harvested by humans until the 19th century, only a few dozen remain in wide circulation—and some of these are hybrids with heavy fertilizer-dependence and little ability to reproduce. As desertification, salinification, acid rain and global warming change the climatic parameters for world agriculture, the limited number of highly specialized species now grown may not be able to respond to new conditions as readily as might other strains, ostensibly less productive but in fact more durable or adaptable. Grains harvested in marginal to desert areas, for example, have given way to more productive hybrids which require heavy input of water and chemical fertilizer. Now that it is evident that neither water nor chemical fertilizer will be indefinitely available, there is once again a rising need for grains which can naturally adapt to and survive within marginal conditions—but such gene pools are rapidly disappearing.

Similarly, the promise of cloning is proving to be a hollow dream. Cloned foods have been implicated in lower immunity and resistance within consumers, as well as in tumerogenesis. Cloned laboratory animals promise more consistent statistical results in drug tests—but conversely less applicability of those results to the spread of natural populations. Cloned species which narrow, rather than broadening the gene pool threaten to reduce adaptability. And there is wide agreement that the producing of humans purely for the purpose of organ harvesting violates all moral principles and sensibilities.

The evidence points rather in the opposite direction: that we should prize genetic variety, both for its future adaptability and for its inherent potentials. Here too, the one-cause one-effect billiard-ball thought habits are inapplicable. Genes tending to sickle-cell anemia on the one hand, at the same time provide immunity to malaria; altering a single genome for a single purpose may entail a wide-range of unforeseeable and irreversible consequences.

All of this suggests that humans need to be more humble in the face of nature; and to see themselves less as agents destined to dominate than to live within and in harmony with nature. It is widely understood that Eastern worldviews, from Shinto Animism to Taoist "Dancing WuLi Masters," had an appreciation of the organic interconnection of all "sentient beings;" that Eastern philosophies tend to place man in a not-very-privileged position within the natural world, rather than as the crown of creation above or opposed to the non-human world. While such world-views can also be found among many primitive or developing societies, it was primarily in the East that these world-views were elevated and refined through centuries of debate and cogitation to the levels of world-class philosophies rather than mere attitudes alone.

FROM THE PERFECTIBILITY OF HUMANITY AND THE WORLD THROUGH SCIENCE

The twentieth century was an age of great faith in the ability of science to overcome human problems, typified by the search for cures for everything from plagues to conflicts. There were campaigns to wipe out disease; wars to end wars; people are not crippled or senile, they are "challenged." From antibiotics to nuclear energy, science has changed human life expectancies and lifestyles. However, great expectations have given way to even more challenging problems which these technologies have created. Antibiotics have evolved strains of super bacteria resistant to known antibiotics. Nuclear power has produced megatons of toxic nuclear waste for which no safe disposal method is known. CFCs, DPEs, and dioxins raise cancer levels, while heavy metals threaten large human populations with Alzheimer's.

While sterilization, vaccination, and antibiotics have temporarily stemmed epidemic plagues, they leave us with new diseases for which no cure is known. The same chlorine which kills bacteria leaves PCBs in drinking water or generates carcinogenic trihalomethanes during its journey from the pumping station to the point of use. Cancer, heart, blood, and brain dysfunctions are products not of single invasive bioorganisms, but of years of lifestyle and pollution. Such diseases can rarely be cured by single operations or simple injections.

Western science and medicine, paradigmatically analytic, tend to underestimate the variety of factors which give rise to diseases and immunity impairment. Conversely, Buddhist and Taoist philosophies tend to see causes, not as singular, unique, or operating in vacua, but rather as multifold, interlinked, and dependent on a wide range or causal conditions. (While science also understands this theoretically, it tends to simplification for methodological purposes.) A reduced human hubris and a more holistic understanding of human health as well as environmental integrity is encouraged by a re-reading of Eastern medical models. When medicine is seen as a war on aging and disease, it is doomed to failure, because aging and disease can never be overcome. This is a fundamental insight of Buddhism. Western doctors traditionally fail to provide adequate spiritual care for their terminal patients because they have been trained to rescue the body but not to counsel the soul when the body is irrecuperable. A more humble understanding of the limitations of medicine and technology might lead to a more humane treatment of terminal patients.

FROM ATOMISTIC MECHANISTIC INDIVIDUALISM TO ORGANIC INTERDEPENDENCE

Classical atomic theory suggested that matter acted like billions of independent little billiard balls, bound by natural laws but not by relations to other billiard balls. Enlightenment thinkers like Locke and Rousseau extended this atomistic notion to the human realm, suggesting that men (not women) were essentially free agents whose liberties extended indefinitely as long as they did not infringe upon the liberties of others. Such a philosophy could only have arisen in a substantially underpopulated state, in which almost unlimited resources seemed available for anyone's use and development.

A more Buddhist perspective suggests that nothing could fail to affect others, that our existence itself is inextricably relational and interdependent. Thus, the air I breathe is air you cannot breathe; the food I eat is food (and land and fertilizer and labor and transportation) you cannot use; the time I use a phone or WC are time and space you cannot use it, and the condition in which I leave them affects the feelings of subsequent users.

My existence depends both upon my parents, and upon a host of other factors which affect their relationship and habits in raising me; my existence also depends on farmers and power plant workers and teachers and sanitary engineers, in fact on the whole web of society who in turn are affected by the ways I pay them, respect or disrespect them, thank, curse or ignore them. The illusion of independence may remain possible in certain parts of Alaska or Australia, but in most of the world, population has reached the point where our social interdependence and interrelationships is no longer open to question.

This consciousness of relatedness is deeply embedded in Sino-Japanese culture, visible in Confucius' Rectification of Names; in Buddhist *pratitya samutpada;* in Japanese and Korean languages, where every sentence expresses not plurals and tenses, but distance and levels of relationships between speakers, listeners, and third parties.

FROM COMPETITION TO COOPERATION

Charles Darwin's discovery that species compete for survival and territorial expansion was quickly extended into a Social Darwinism used to justify a wide range of monopolism, sexual and racial discrimination, and the prosperity of the richest. More recently, this extension of this view has led to theories like the Selfish Gene and the Blind Watchmaker, vindicating extended selfishness on biological bases, and the Naked Ape/Killer Ape, which would link male aggressive tendencies to biological bases.

Such theories were theoretically unsound from the beginning for a number of reasons. Darwin's observations were not about individual happiness or success, but rather about traits that enabled whole species to survive in competition with other species. Conversely speaking, Darwin presupposed that unwritten rules within any given family tend to work to keep that family from self-destructive behavior. Ironically, while Darwin recognized that limited resources and territory were one reason for inter-species competition, his emulators who adapted Darwinism to the social sphere tended to focus more upon the values of competition than upon any concern of how this competition ultimately affected the environment itself.

The ultimate challenge, not only to darwinism, but indeed to the human race itself, comes from the glorification of competition. Military competition continues to threaten the thermonuclear destruction of the planet, as nuclear proliferation reaches smaller and more desperate countries outside of the superpowers. Technology can neither safeguard nor harmlessly dismantle all the nuclear, biological, and chemical weapons men have created. At the same time, interethnic rivalries and competition for limited resources elevate the danger that local conflicts will escalate from name-calling into fatal violence. Indeed, humankind must ask itself: can we overcome our tendencies towards violence, and replace them with tendencies to cooperation?

Matrilineal societies in the simian world, and societies which highly regard "feminine" qualities of compromise and mutual support tend to demonstrate that humans can find alternatives to violent competition and lethal force. If humans desire to pass on a livable planet to their progeny for more than a few more generations, they must learn to curb their appetites for sex and violence, and replace them with the joys of nurturing and working together.

It is almost needless to say that these qualities have typified the crowded cultures of East Asia for centuries. The million-peopled cities of Kyoto and Edo, for example, supported their populations not by military empire or far-flung trade networks, but by close cooperation with neighboring areas. Within each town and village, extended families and clans were organized into collective community-help organizations, which helped each other in times of disaster and celebrated together in times of good harvest. Weapons were illegal for most of the population, and conflicts were resolved by negotiation, compromise, and sublimation rather than by joust, contract, or lawsuit.

FROM GLORIFICATION OF WEALTH
TO RESPECT FOR HUMANHOOD

As Max Weber pointed out, the Industrial Revolution in the West overturned the ascetic and chivalric ideals of the Christian Middle Ages with the notion that labor and its rewards were proofs of divine salvation. As capital became portable, and accumulation of capital became acceptable among Christian communities, the acquisition and consumption of resources became equated with human worth. This is ironically reflected today in the measuring of national worth by GDP or GNP, which attribute greater value to expenditures on a war or oil spill than to volunteer work or successful parenthood. This distorted philosophy was made possible by the illusion (not present in original Calvinism, to be sure, but superimposed by the colonialism of new continents) that resources were unlimited; the more one consumed, the more contribution to the national economy. Ironically, Puritan Christianity eventuated in a glorification of wealth, self-satisfaction, and even greed.

Karl Marx argued that wealth was a product of inherently valuable resources and the human labor spent to exhume, shape, and market them; Subsequent Economists (name) demonstrated that prices in a free economy are products of supply and demand. Marxist attempts to regulate supply and demand almost inevitably gave way to capitalist economies, and socialist attempts to provide benefits to less productive segments of society almost inevitably bankrupted their exchequers.

The fatal flaws of Western Capitalism are at least twofold. First, prices fail to reflect the hidden costs of (a) resource recycling or reprocessing when the product is consumed or discarded; (b) recouping the waste heat and byproducts during manufacture; (c) assuring continued availability of the kinds of resources and energy being used to produce the given goods. Prior to the industrial revolution, when populations remained small and most goods were organic by nature, such problems of recycling and waste byproducts seemed insignificant. Today, with populations covering every inhabitable land area, and manufacturers producing goods with materials which will take millennia to biodegrade, it has become essential to build in the cost of recycling and environmental maintenance into the pricing of goods. Such moves are already well begun in the EU, in recycling taxes, carbon taxes, ISO 1400, and similar standards.

The second important reevaluation required of capitalism is a critique of the standards it unwittingly fosters, of valuing all activities and even human beings in primarily economic terms. This has the ridiculous and tragic consequence of valuing child-care, education, and environmental volunteerism less than the money-making activities of pimps, pushers, and stock speculators; it encourages the illusions that "more is better" and "money is the key to happiness." These illusions are ultimately as fatal to the environment as they are to any genuinely sustainable happiness or human-level satisfaction.

Humanity must re-learn the truths, not unique to the Orient, to be sure, that the reasons to respect humans are not primarily economic, not for what they will yet earn, but because they have intrinsic aesthetic value as beings in themselves. In Japanese culture, for example, one is not "born human," but one "becomes" human, or "achieves" adulthood, through self-cultivation. Countless schools of self-perfection, from Zen meditation and tea ceremony, to music, art, physical exercise, calligraphy, poetry, and even cooking give ranks and respect to people demonstrating levels of mastery. These arts are not eroded by age; rather the skills of tea-master as well as of calligrapher are enriched with age and practice. Indeed they confer an honor to the aged which tends to be forgotten in money-oriented Western societies. People are respected for what they know, for what they can do or have done, for their refinement of character, wisdom, and sensibility. This is what makes them truly human as opposed to animal. While the recognition of the Buddhist values of wisdom, compassion, and human-heartedness is possible without ranking them, the Japanese custom of attaching names and ranks to people's talents and characters has the added merit of presenting a public acknowledgment, an alternative to the monetary standard, and a goal to which youth can aspire.

FROM ABSOLUTE CULTURAL VALUES
TO NECESSARY COMMON VALUES

Most isolated cultures tend to absolutize their own values; for others, like the Judaic, Christian, and Islamic traditions, contact with competitors, oppressors, or external challenges foster a petrification of values systems, literally or figuratively carved in stone and sacred books. Discoveries of geology, paleontology, and astronomy tend to cast doubt upon the accuracy of some parts of those sacred books, even while encounters with other cultures and life-styles challenged traditionally-held values. Some people respond with a blind fundamentalism, but the broader Western tendency has been to a relativistic humanism if not nihilism, suggesting that no values are ultimate and perhaps all are ultimately groundless. Ironically, rejection of traditional values has often occasioned a moral vacuum in education, an inability to educate morality because of an inability to exalt one value system over any other.

One solution to moral relativism might be to seek the common values held by the vast majority of successful cultures: restraints against killing, incest, deceit, etc. Another proposal might be to seek the meta-ethical preconditions for successful interaction, as in Habermas' theories about the ideal communication community. In the train of this paper, however, a more fruitful approach were to begin with the common conditions which face humanity and the future of the earth.

If the human project is to be maintained more than a few generations into the future, considerations of population control, biological diversity, sustainability of technologies, and responsibility to future generations become unavoidable. These depend not on cultural tastes or traditions; they become minimum prerequisites for human continuity. The shrinking of the globe and the foreshortening of history demand new common values, not based on the power of one group over another, but based on a consciousness of our organic interlinking with each other. Stripped of their cultural paraphernalia and chauvinisms, some Western as well as Asian religious philosophies may already hold this ideal, but one need not be religious to understand and espouse it. The survival of the planet as we know it demands nothing less than human cooperation in this project.

1 *THE BLACK STORK:*
SCIENCE, FACT, VALUE, AND CULTURE

Dr. Harry Haiseldon shocked the nation when he publicly announced that, between 1915 and 1918, he "permitted" the deaths of six "defective" infants. His story later became the basis for a controversial 1927 film, *The Black Stork.* In one episode of the film, Claude, who has a genetic disease, marries Anne, despite warnings from his doctor that there is a strong likelihood their child would be born deformed. This turns out to be the case. Yet the doctor refuses to perform surgery that would save the child's life. The film raised serious questions not only about what constitutes a life not worth living, but also about what makes for a good life.

This film aired during the beginnings of the eugenics movement in the United States. It also depicted a time when aesthetic values played an increasingly leading role in response to these questions. That is, goodness, health, and beauty were equated. For many people, an attractive appearance counted as the key determinant in notions of health. Furthermore, as *The Black Stork* demonstrated, a link was established between health, aesthetics, and race.

How much has changed? To illustrate, our ongoing research in reproductive technologies and in sequencing the human genome exemplify genetic engineering with the explicit purpose of preventing debilitating diseases. Yet another component of genetic engineering is its full-fledged effort at "selective breeding," to bring about "better" human beings. Are we engaged in an effort to produce the "perfect" baby? Are so-called objective values of health and illness in effect subjective values that reflect both personal and cultural (especially middle-class and white) values and attitudes? Do we as a culture continue to equate physical attractiveness with health? What about the role and moral responsibility of media, since media continue to play a powerful role in framing our views of beauty and ugliness? How does all this square with critical thinking? Can critical thinking enable us to view these issues more objectively? (Historian Martin Pernick raises these questions in his insightful *The Black Stork: Eugenics and the Death of "Defective" Babies in American Medicine and Motion Pictures since 1915,* New York: Oxford University Press, 1996. His account is worth reading.)

2 THE INSANITY PLEA

On the morning of June 20, 2001, Andrea Pia Yates drowned her five young children in their bathtub, one at a time: three-year-old Paul; two-year-old Luke; John, age five; the boys' baby sister, six-month-old Mary; and finally the oldest, Noah, age seven. This led to one of the most publicized cases in recent U.S. history. Although she admitted killing her children, Yates pleaded not guilty by reason of insanity. Nevertheless, on March 13, 2002, a Houston jury found Yates guilty of premeditated murder, charged with the murder of three of her children. The thirty-seven-year-old mother was sentenced to life imprisonment with parole eligibility after forty years. The Texas jury took little time to decide on the sentence, voting against the alternative sentence of lethal injection. Yates now spends her days in solitary confinement at a prison for the mentally ill in Rusk, Texas. She has been placed on suicide watch at least three times after slipping into psychotic states.

The defense attorneys argued that Yates had a personal history of mental illness. She had experienced chronic depression since her early twenties and especially after having her first child. Yates herself claimed that she often had visions of a knife stabbing someone, and that she heard voices in her head, ordering her to kill. Not wanting to live with these visions, she tried to take her own life instead. She attempted suicide just two years before killing her children. Ever since her suicide attempt she had been taking various psychotherapeutic drugs for her depression. Moreover, there was a history of mental illness in her family.

The prosecution did not deny that she suffered from mental illness. They argued that she could still distinguish between right and wrong. They claimed that she still deliberately murdered her children knowing it was wrong. If she knew right from wrong at the time of the killings, then she could not be legally insane at that time. The prosecuting lawyers also implied that there were other motives having to do with getting back at her husband.

How prominent a factor should the insanity plea play in a criminal trial? Is it a legitimate defense for criminal action? What are the moral issues surrounding the use of the insanity plea? Can one suffer from mental illness and still be of sufficiently sound mind to commit such a horrible act as Yates did? In assessing the morality of any act, we consider not only the act itself but also the intent. Yet intent also concerns itself with the state of mind of the actor. Should we place more moral weight on the action or on the intent? What is the relationship between action and intent? How does the distinction between law and morality come into play here? Was Yates's sentence morally justifiable? Should she have received the death penalty? Could there be other more morally justifiable alternatives to Yates's sentence?

3 THE USA PATRIOT ACTS I AND II

Less than two months after 9/11, on October 27, 2001, the U.S. Congress passed the "Uniting and Strengthening America by Providing Appropriate Tools Required to Intercept and Obstruct Terrorism" Act, otherwise called the USA Patriot Act. The act is a critical mandate that takes active measures to secure the country's protection and defense. Moreover, it represents a pivotal step in support of the work of the newly formed Department of Homeland Security. In its effort to secure the defense of the country and its citizens, it provides an unprecedented degree of latitude to the government to conduct and enforce necessary and critical monitoring, surveillance, and search and seizure.

Despite its aim, however, the USA Patriot Act has encountered fierce criticism from various civil rights groups such as the American Civil Liberties Union (ACLU). Many feel that the act gives the federal government far too much power, allowing it to encroach upon our fundamental civil liberties, liberties that are imbedded in our constitution. To illustrate, section 215 of the act bestows nearly complete authority to the Federal Bureau of Investigation to acquire search warrants to investigate any questionable activity that is viewed as having some link to terrorist or potential terrorist conduct. This essentially means that even the slightest suspicion of terrorist activity, without the need for strong and compelling evidence, can be sufficient grounds for search and seizure. Moreover, the same section includes a "gag order" in that those individuals and organizations that are under federal scrutiny and that have been served a search warrant may not make this known to others, including the press.

Despite this gag order, news has leaked out about FBI officers searching through public library records (see Leigh Estabrook, "Public Libraries and Civil Liberties: A Profession Divided," Urbana: University of Illinois Library Research Center, January 2003, www.lis.uiuc.edu/gslis/research/civil_liberties .html). Critics point out that this places librarians in a difficult situation because it counters their primary obligation to ensure the rights of the public who use the library's public information for individual reasons.

Proponents of these measures argue that all this is in the best interests of the country. The provisions appear strict, but serious actions need to be taken in light of the gravity of the threats we face from terrorist groups, many of which may have operative cells within the United States. Moreover, these measures have so far already been effective in preventing further terrorist actions within the country. Defenders go on to claim that these sorts of measures do not target ordinary citizens, but those deemed to be dangerous to the well-being of the nation. Extreme measures are thus justified in these exceptional times.

The Bush administration has recently proposed a second version of the USA Patriot Act. This revision, USA Patriot Act II, formally entitled the

Domestic Security Enhancement Act of 2003, will soon be proposed to Congress for consideration. A government source has apparently leaked out a copy of the proposed document to the Center for Public Integrity. The document appears to expand federal powers even further, allowing the executive branch final control over judicial authority in matters of surveillance, search and seizure, imprisonment, and more. For instance, in some cases, seizure of data may be allowed without any search warrant. Furthermore, notions as to what constitutes potential terrorist activity are more at the discretion of federal authorities (see Nancy Kranich, "Part II: The USA Patriot Act Impacts Free Expression in the U.S.," in Peter Phillips and Project Censored, *Censored 2004: The Top 25 Censored Stories*, New York: Seven Stories Press, 2003, pp. 275–281).

This entire matter is evidently complex, with many ethical and legal issues. What are the most prominent moral issues? In view of the moral theories we have examined, what are the moral justifications for the USA Patriot Act? Are the criticisms of provisions of the act justified? Is there a stronger argument in support of the act than against it? What about the new act about to be proposed? In times of emergency, should the executive arm of the government have the final say? Where does moral accountability enter in? Are there prominent deontological considerations at stake? What about the application of utilitarian theory? In view of the tension between individual liberties and collective well-being, do our circumstances warrant the overriding of individual rights for the good of the country? If so, are there limits? How do we resolve this ubiquitous tension between individual and collective? Are there any morally relevant factors that other moral theories and traditions can offer for our consideration?

4 FERTILITY PILLS AND REPRODUCTIVE RIGHTS

In early October 1997, the world witnessed the birth of the first living septuplets. After thirty weeks of pregnancy and as a result of fertility drugs, Bobbi McCaughey gave birth to seven babies—four boys and three girls. Perinatologists at Iowa Methodist Medical Center in Des Moines dubbed these seven as Babies A through G. The first-delivered baby was Kenneth, nicknamed "Hercules" because of the weight of the other six babies on him. Of the seven, he weighed the most: 3 pounds, 4 ounces. The babies survived after spending months in Blank Children's Hospital's neonatal intensive care unit, and each one went home to their waiting mother, father, and twenty-two-month-old sister, Mikayla, amidst cheers from hospital staff and neighbors.

News of the successful birth along with the promise of fertility treatments spread as the McCaugheys assumed media's center stage. Throughout Iowa and the nation this was a joyous event, a victory for reproductive medicine, family values, and community. Volunteers in Des Moines willingly gave their time in an organized effort to help the McCaugheys in caring for their babies.

Yet in what sense was this genuinely a success? To begin with, fertility drugs such as Metrodin (the drug given to Bobbi McCaughey) and Pergonal can easily disturb a woman's hormonal pattern so that numerous eggs, as many as forty, can be released in a single cycle. The result: a high rate of multiple births. Thus, more and more couples are resorting to fertility treatments. However, this has its share of medical risks. The aggressive use of fertility treatment usually results in premature deliveries, and these babies experience a high mortality rate within the first year. Even if they survive, their long-term health is often compromised due to digestive and respiratory complications. They are especially prone to neurological disorders.

When interviewed about the prospects of having septuplets, the father, Kenny McCaughey, responded that he and Bobbi were "trusting in the Lord for the outcome" (*Newsweek*, December 1, 1997, p. 62). He and his wife even wrote a book about their experience, *Seven From Heaven: The Miracle of the McCaughey Septuplets* (Thomas Nelson, 1998). Bobbi went on to author another book, *Celebrating the Wonder of Motherhood: Intimate Moments with My Daughter Mikayla and the Septuplets* (Thomas Nelson, 1999).

The human female uterus naturally releases one egg per cycle. The uterus is not intended to produce multiple births. Is this aggressive use of fertility drugs a violation of natural law? How does the natural law theory fit into all of this? Moreover, this aggressive use of fertility treatment is not applied globally. Numerous cultures do not have access to these reproductive technologies. For many cultures, the fundamental concerns center not on advanced medical technologies but on basic health care needs. Have fair is our (U.S.) "obsession" with reproductive rights? Are reproductive rights absolute? Again, how does this square with natural law ideas?

5 ZOE WARWICK

Zoe Warwick was a celebrated British female bodybuilder who won a number of European bodybuilding awards. She also regularly ingested performance-enhancing steroids, and eventually paid the price. She died a lingering, painful death after her body shut down as a result of taking thirty times her normal dose of anabolic steroids.

Sally Jones, who interviewed Warwick while she was dying, describes Warwick's terrible ordeal in an article called "Killing Zoe" (*Inside Sport* 51, March 1996: 40–46). Jones describes how Warwick experienced unwavering physical and emotional pain, and that she needed at least seventeen different medications. The side effects of the steroids were distressing as her body became increasingly masculinized and there were radical changes in her voice, genitals, and sex drive. Along with numerous accompanying medical problems, she looked nearly completely "unwomanlike."

Warwick's death came as a shock to England and to the sporting world. It clearly warns us of the dangers involved in the use of performance-enhancing drugs. It also demonstrates the tragic repercussions of a personal as well as cultural obsession with winning at any cost. Yet, on closer inspection, what was the real horror, the real "crime" for many observers, particularly male, of Zoe Warwick's fate? Surely, it concerns the medical risks associated with anabolic steroids. At the same time, did Warwick go beyond the barriers of sexuality? Female athletes are clearly assuming a more prominent role in the world of sports. However, the world of sports is still male-dominated. It is one thing for a female athlete to excel in her sport. It is another thing for her to look less "female," almost to the border of looking "male." Did Zoe's "crime" also lie in this transgression of gender distinction? Scholars Tara Magdalinski and Karen Brooks comment on Warwick's case:

> Warwick is "unwomaned" and "unsexed" through her practices . . . .
> Warwick's body, not her mind, however, is the site at which the fears
> and horror of the social body towards female athletic steroid users is
> mapped out, thus playing out the mind/body dualism where the body
> is signified as feminine and the mind as male. As a female her subjec-
> tivity is located in her body and by altering her body and expressing
> her mind, she challenges social and cultural expectations. Warwick ex-
> ceeds the limits and is thus constructed, in the form of a warning, as
> irrational and her competitive urge as dangerous. (Tara Magdalinski
> and Karen Brooks, "Bride of Frankenstein: Technology and the Con-
> sumption of the Female Athlete," in *Sport Technology: History, Phi-
> losophy and Policy*, ed. Andy Miah and Simon B. Eassom, Oxford:
> JAI, Elsevier Science, 2002, p. 207.)

How has Warwick challenged cultural convictions? Are these convictions reasonable? Are there still certain rules that women must conform to in order to play in the male world of sports? How does a feminist ethic address these sorts of questions?

6 THE JAPANESE AND WHALING

Since 1981, the International Whaling Commission (IWC), which now consists of thirty-nine member nations, had set strict limits on the killing of whales for commercial purposes. It specifically banned the killing of the endangered sperm whale. Nevertheless, despite worldwide suspensions of commercial whaling, some Japanese still manage to violate the moratorium as they continue to kill minke whales. Japan is not alone. Norway and Iceland have also threatened to resume whaling.

Japanese often justify their actions claiming that they are killing these whales for valuable research purposes. Yet many of the whales they kill end up as expensive fare in high-priced restaurants. In Japan, whale meat continues to draw some of the steepest prices, usually costing between 4,000 and 7,000 yen (about $US40 to 70) per pound. The Japanese also argue that there are presently a sufficient number of minke whales (over 700,000) so that the relatively small number they intend to catch would have no negative impact on the total population of these whales. It is estimated that the Japanese kill approximately 300 minke whales annually (Andrew Pollock, "They Eat Whales, Don't They?" *New York Times*, May 3, 1993). Many Japanese also resent the intrusion of other countries' morals on their own. On the other hand, opponents argue that even though minke whales are not yet endangered, they may well become so. Furthermore, due to their impressionable size as well as intelligence, all species of whales deserve full protection.

Are the Japanese justified in the killing of minke whales? Since minke whales are not on the endangered species list, why the fuss? Are there stronger arguments against the killing of minke whales? Is there a double standard at work here? While we Americans protest the killing of whales, we also feel morally justified in killing various other animals for food, such as cattle, chicken, and pigs. In addition, we engage in breeding practices, such as egg factories as well as tiny enclosures for young cattle in order to produce veal, which seem rather cruel. In addition, to what degree should size and intelligence be a factor in how we evaluate the moral status of any animal species? Does a frog have less moral status and protection since it is much smaller and less "impressionable" than a whale? The Japanese feel resentful that other countries are in a sense determining what foods they should not eat, thus interfering in their economies and social systems. How would we feel if the tables were turned? Is this intervention on our part justified?

7 BEIJING, THE OLYMPICS, AND HUMAN RIGHTS

On an international scale, the Olympics comprise the greatest sporting event in the world. In principle, it symbolizes our global unity and community within the context of spirited athletic competition. It represents the highest virtues of our humanity and our commitment to excellence. Citizens of Beijing and all of China were therefore jubilant when it was announced by the International Olympic Committee (IOC) in July 2001 that Beijing would host the 2008 Summer Olympics. Beijing won the decision over four other major cities: Osaka, Istanbul, Paris, and Toronto. Throughout this most populated country in the world (with its 1.3 billion people) Chinese broke into celebrations with fireworks, parades, and other sorts of fanfare.

The Chinese know that this will help to bring world attention to their country, just as when the world watched as the Chinese Republic's president, Hu Jintao, congratulated the country's first astronaut, thirty-eight-year-old Lt. Col. Yang Liwei, before his historic fourteen-orbit mission on October 15, 2003. The Chinese also know that being picked for the Olympics will no doubt boost their economy. Furthermore, many Chinese see it as a critical and necessary step toward world dialogue and as a vital bridge to understanding more of Chinese culture and society.

Not all countries shared China's jubilation. The Dalai Lama, the exiled spiritual leader of Tibet, lives in the small village of Dharamsala in India. When news of Beijing's "triumph" was announced, a spokesperson for the Dalai Lama voiced immediate censure and disapproval. These and other critics of the decision pointed out the ongoing history of human rights abuses in China. They feared that this choice in essence legitimizes these abuses. Amnesty International also sounded a similar warning, claiming that the Chinese government, due to its history and practices, is not entitled to host an event that symbolizes fair play and universal moral principles, the principles embodied in the International Olympic Committee's Code of Ethics.

In the United States, critics also oppose the Bush administration's apparent complicity with the decision. The Bush administration has decided that U.S. athletes will participate and has chosen to remain essentially neutral regarding the International Olympic Committee's decision. Chinese dissidents who have moved to the United States have also voiced their strong opposition. Many critics see comparisons with the 1936 Summer Olympics, which were hosted in Hitler's Germany.

On the other hand, supporters believe that this decision will help to cultivate the seeds of democracy in China. In this way, it would aid in bringing world attention to human rights abuses and would thereby pressure the Chinese to bring them to a halt. Moreover, it would help its lagging economy and spark its health care and educational systems.

Is the comparison with "the Nazi Olympics" a sound one? Since Confucianism continually emphasizes the well-being of the society over that of individual self-interests, this seems a bit like utilitarianism. From a utilitarian perspective, would the IOC's decision bring about more benefits than harms? If the United States remains neutral on the matter, is the U.S. government's official "neutrality" morally justified? Have the Olympics become more a matter of politics than of athletic achievement? What are some Confucian perspectives on these issues? Is the decision to select Beijing a humane one? Should the citizens of China be held accountable for decisions and policies of their leaders? Do so-called universal human rights find a basis in Confucian teachings, or are they more or less incompatible?

8 ASSISTED SUICIDE FOR PSYCHOLOGICAL SUFFERING?

Up until July 1994, euthanasia and assisted suicide in Holland had officially been offered as a possible option for those who were terminally ill and suffering from intractable, unbearable physical pain. Things changed, however, when Dutch psychiatrist Dr. Boudewijn Chabot admitted that he assisted with the suicide of fifty-year-old Hilly Bosscher. When Chabot reported the case afterwards, he referred to her anonymously as "Netty Boomsma."

When she met Chabot, Netty was suffering from depression and intolerable psychological suffering. She was divorced after twenty-five years of an abusive relationship with her husband. Prior to her divorce, her two sons died, both at the age of twenty. One committed suicide. The other son died from lung cancer. Ms. Bosscher wanted to die, and then consulted with the Dutch Voluntary Euthanasia Society. The Society then referred her to Dr. Chabot.

According to Chabot, Netty was not psychotic. Neither was she deterred from making a "competent" decision about her fate as she continually requested that she be allowed to take her own life. On September 28, 1991, Chabot finally acceded to her request, giving her sufficient sleeping pills and a liquid drug mixture. That same day, she took the medication and died. This was the first reported case of a physician assisting a patient who was mentally suffering though otherwise healthy.

The Dutch Supreme Court eventually found Chabot guilty for essentially two reasons. First, he did not have another psychiatrist personally examine his patient. Although he did seek consults, these were conducted without personal interviews with the patient. Next, there was no evidence that this request constituted an "emergency situation" as required by Dutch law. Though he was found guilty, however, the psychiatrist was not punished as the Court ruled that psychological suffering could constitute grounds for requests for euthanasia and assisted suicide. In doing so, the Dutch Supreme Court set a landmark precedent, ruling that euthanasia as assisted suicide may at times be justified for those experiencing severe psychic suffering, even in the absence of physical pain. Thus, mental suffering could be accepted as grounds for euthanasia and assisted suicide.

Critics point out that assisted suicide can never be warranted for a person who undergoes psychological suffering. If it is at all justified, and many critics believe that it is not, it is only for those who are terminally ill and in unbearable physical pain and suffering. In addition, whereas a clear line is drawn when it comes to cases of terminal illness and intractable physical pain, emotional and psychic suffering is much less clear to assess and is thereby subject to the discretion of the physician's interpretation. Furthermore, assisted suicide in such cases minimizes the significance of providing proper palliative care and medical treatment for those who are severely depressed.

In his defense, Chabot and his lawyers claimed that Chabot acted in accordance with official guidelines to ensure the following: that his patient suffered from unbearable pain (in this case, psychological); that Netty genuinely desired to die; and that she freely and competently made the request. His patient showed no evidence of hysteria or psychosis. The patient would not respond medically to antidepressant treatment if this was offered. Since the patient refused outright this medication, imposing this on her without her consent would violate her autonomy.

Should medical treatments such as polypharmacy and electroconvulsive therapies be imposed upon patients to treat their depression, even against their will? What would be some major utilitarian and deontological concerns about this? How much weight should be given to patients' requests for euthanasia and to assisted suicide? Is emotional and psychological suffering just as severe as physical suffering? Are slippery slope arguments legitimate here? That is, would sanctioning this eventually influence how we view those who are mentally ill, elderly, dependent, and chronically disabled? How should notions of "hopelessness" be assessed? What about the court's implied distinction between patients who are considered "psychotic" versus those who are "non-psychotic"? Many of us are at times unhappy. Does our unhappiness ever cross the line so that it becomes grounds for these kinds of requests? If so, when? Does all this blur the boundaries between general unhappiness and psychological illness?

9 STONING FOR ADULTERY

Sixteen months after her divorce, Amina Lawal gave birth to her daughter, Wasila. When her local Nigerian villagers in Katsina State discovered she was pregnant, they had her arrested on the grounds of adultery. On March 22, 2002, the thirty-year-old Muslim woman and single mother was tried before the local Shariah court and, according to an interpretation of Shariah law, was found guilty of the crime of adultery. Shariah refers to Islamic law and extends into nearly every aspect of personal life and behavior. According to the new Shariah penal code, an out-of-wedlock pregnancy was sufficient grounds for the criminal charge of adultery. At the time, Amina admitted that she had engaged in sexual relations with her partner, primarily in order to establish his paternity. She was ignorant of Shariah law concerning adultery. After the court found her guilty, it then sentenced her to be stoned to death. A few months later, in August, a Shariah court of appeals upheld the ruling.

This case became known worldwide due to publicity and pressure from various international human rights and women's rights groups. On September 25, 2003, Amina was finally acquitted of the charges and set free. She was acquitted on legal technicalities: There needed to be four witnesses to her involvement with another man; she had not been allowed to retract her early confession; according to Islamic law, she needed to repeat her confession four times, instead of just the one time; three judges should have presided over the first trial rather than just the one; there was also the "sleeping embryo" possibility (the odd notion that it was quite possible for an embryo to be in gestation for a few years).

There is a clear conflict here between interpretations of Shariah law. There are also major issues surrounding gender equality. Since only women can become pregnant, does this suggest that women are more likely than men to be stoned to death? In this case, Yahay Mohammed, Amina's partner at the time she became pregnant, at first admitted that he fathered the child. He later retracted his statement and denied paternity. His word was taken at face value, and he did not stand trial. According to the Shariah penal code in northern Nigeria, Yahay's personal oath that he never had sexual intercourse with Amina is proof enough of his innocence unless four eyewitnesses can testify to his sexual involvement with Amina. This clearly seems sexist since it implies, for example, that one can get away with rape as long as there are no witnesses, whereas the women who are victims can be subjected to charges of adultery. Though Amina was set free, her cause lingers for there are still others in Nigeria awaiting their execution by stoning.

Certain states in northern Nigeria have introduced very strict Shariah applications of the penal code, including brutal and inhumane punishments such as stoning. Stoning is absolutely inhumane. After the victim is buried up to her waist, fist-sized rocks are thrown at her head and face until the head nearly comes off. According to Amnesty International and other human rights watches, these punishments constitute torture. Nigeria as a country has openly defended the protection of human rights. For instance, the Federal Republic of Nigeria ratified the Convention Against Torture in June 2001. And the president of Nigeria, Olusegun Obasanjo, has clearly opposed capital punishment. Since he took office in 1999, there have been no government executions.

Yet the federal government here is clearly at odds with local government rulings. Moreover, Muslim scholars will point out that how the northern Nigerian states interpret Shariah also conflicts with mainstream tenets of Islam. Many of them claim that the ruling against Lawal in no way represents the major Muslim teachings, which underscore that men and women are to be treated equally before the law. What is at issue is how regional governments, in this case northern Nigerian states, can apply extreme interpretations of Shariah in ways that violate Muslim mainstream teachings as well as principles of international human rights. Furthermore, since the Shariah penal code only applies to Muslims and not to others (there is a strong population of Christians in Nigeria), it can be viewed as discriminatory on the basis of religious beliefs.

How do feminist perspectives and ethics apply here? Does all this lend further weight to arguments opposed to capital punishment? Is it possible to ensure that regional governments implement a system of Muslim law that is consistent with the respect for international human rights? According to international human rights principles, sexual relations outside of marriage between consenting adults are not viewed as criminal offenses. Can we reconcile this tension between views based upon religious beliefs with international perspectives and consensus?

10 DIGITAL ANGEL

A sophisticated application of current technology includes tracking devices that provide twenty-four-hour surveillance and data collection for both humans and pets. An example of this is a monitoring system known as Digital Angel, based in South St. Paul, Minnesota. The system offers a tracking system that locates people, pets, and objects by using sophisticated biosensors and envirosensors and combines wireless telecommunication with GPS (Global Positioning System). It is used in the tracking and recovery of wild and domestic animals. It also enables users to be alerted to emergency situations regarding the elderly. It has proved to be of immense value for family members, professional caregivers, emergency workers, pet owners, and many others.

Despite these obvious benefits, critics see these surveillance technologies as imposing further threats to our privacy. As it now stands, our privacy rights are already seriously jeopardized due to advanced information technologies. Areas of present and potential abuse include medical information, personal history, spending history, financial status, and so on. According to critics, invasive technologies will continue to erode what little privacy remains. What's to stop corporations and governments from using such surveillance technologies as Digital Angel for their own purposes? Many citizens already feel vulnerable to practices like "data mining" and "data shadowing." More strangers know about us each time we use our credit cards, send e-mails, and browse through the Internet.

Proponents point out the clear benefits of tracking systems such as Digital Angel. Families can now know more about the whereabouts and well-being of those they love and for whom they care. The same goes for pet owners. Emergency workers can be alerted to a coworker's distress. Consider the benefits for patients in hospitals as well as in homes, for health care professionals in nursing homes, and for military personnel on the battlefield. Moreover, more businesses are cashing in on privacy management and protection and selling programs designed to protect privacy.

Nevertheless, there is an expected tension between our advanced information technologies and issues regarding personal privacy. As we continue to be bombarded with unsolicited "snail" mail, e-mail, voice mail, and telemarketing, we are facing the two-edged sword (benefits vs. risks) of information technologies. According to Alan Greenspan, chair of the Federal Reserve Board:

> The appropriate balancing of the increasing need for information in guiding our economy to ever higher standards of living, and essential need of protection of individual privacy in such an environment, will confront public policy with one of its most sensitive tradeoffs in the years immediately ahead. (See Toby Lester, "The Reinvention of Privacy," *Atlantic Monthly* 287, no. 3, March 2001, p. 29.)

How should this tension be addressed? Should regulation of these information technologies such as surveillance systems be the province of federal and/or state governments? Or should corporations themselves assume responsibility for proper regulation and control in order to prevent abuse? How would a deontological perspective influence this issue? Namely, how would the two expressions of the categorical imperative—universalizability and treating persons as ends in themselves—be applied to this critical issue of personal privacy? What directions would a utilitarian analysis take in addressing this tension between information technology and personal privacy?

11 HINDU WIDOWS

In India, the filming of Deepa Mehta's *Water* came to a halt early in 2000 after incessant and oftentimes violent protests by Hindu fundamentalists. A few extremists even threatened to commit suicide in order to publicly protest the celebrated Indian movie director's film. The plot centers on a group of Hindu widows who face rigid social barriers and are forced into poverty due to the ongoing restrictions placed upon many widows. This story line has led to riots by extremists. There have even been threats on Mehta's life. Nevertheless, she still plans to go through with the filming, but in an undisclosed location and with a different title.

Of India's 900 million people, an estimated 33 million of them are Hindu widows. Many of them face a rather bleak livelihood. To begin with, upon marriage, Hindu brides marry into their husband's family and thus dissolve relations with their own families. Upon the deaths of their husbands, it is not uncommon for widows to be blamed for the death, for failing to protect their husbands. One way to expiate their "crime" had been through the ancient practice of *sati*, which still occurs in remote areas in northern India. Many widows in the lower classes, or castes, are exploited as servants for their in-laws. Many are also expelled from the family in order to prevent them from inheriting property, especially land. Forced to live ascetic lives, they are often compelled to survive through begging and living in the poorest of conditions.

Many widows in the lower castes appear to embody the "homeless" of India, facing outright discrimination, social stigma, constant eviction, and sexual harassment. Many widows are also forced into prostitution into order to survive. One commentator points out that the Hindi word for widow, *randi*, has almost become synonymous with prostitution (John Burns, "Once Widowed in India, Twice Scorned," *New York Times*, March 29, 1998, sec. 1, p. 1). And even though inheritance laws for widows have been put into place, actual practices circumvent these laws in order to favor the husband's family. Widows are virtually left with very little pension. Some castes ban remarriage. If a widow does remarry, she suffers even greater stigma and loses all rights and possessions.

The holy city of Vrindavan, which houses thousands of Hindu temples, is a haven for these disenfranchised widows. There, many of the estimated 16,000 widows eke out their survival through begging as well as chanting in the city's temples. Despite their dire conditions, widows are often consigned to their fate. For them, this is a result of their karma; that is, through their prior actions they have somehow incurred their lot in life. A way to improve their destiny in a future life is through acceptance, constant prayer, and vigilance.

Keep in mind that many widows in India are also treated well and equitably. It would therefore be unfair to generalize about the plight of Hindu widows. (This is from a personal conversation with a Hindu scholar and friend, Veena

Rani Howard, October 2003). At the same time, Hindu fundamentalists often point out that in certain Hindu texts, such as the *Skanda Purana,* widows are to be viewed as outcastes. Therefore, the situation of many widows in India represents a tension between extreme fundamentalist interpretations of Hindu teachings and claims regarding universal human rights, particularly the rights of oppressed women throughout the world.

How do mainstream Hindu moral teachings address the plight of widows? How can the tension between extremists and the orthodox be alleviated? Note that the Border Security Force of India has enacted a support system for its widows and seems to be successful in enabling widows to be remarried (see "Indian Widows Seek Social Acceptance," http://ccat.sas.upenn.edu/plc/prereading/widremar.htm). Does the sustained caste system in India violate principal Hindu tenets? Is this case a strong argument for or against ethical relativism? How would you apply any of the Western moral theories to the plight of the widows?

465

12 MIZUKO KUYO

Miura Domyo, a Japanese Buddhist priest and abbott of a Tendai Buddhist temple, achieved some popularity after writing *Mizugo,* translated into English as "The Forgotten Child" (trans. Jim Cuthbert, Henley-on-Thames: Ellis, 1983). In his book, he gives readers a rationale for the popular ceremony of *mizuko kuyo,* and he encourages people to practice the ritual. What is *mizuko kuyo?* For well over two centuries, many Japanese women have practiced *mizuko kuyo. Mizuko* literally means "water babies," and *kuyo* means "ritual." This is a ceremony to atone for the untimely death of a child by abortion. The ceremony is generally held in a Buddhist temple where Buddhist priests and priestesses perform rites in order to comfort the spirit of the aborted fetus.

Miura explains how aborting the fetus violates Buddhist teachings regarding the intentional taking of life. Miura then goes on to describe how family members can atone for the abortion by purchasing objects such as an *ihai,* a tablet on which is inscribed the posthumous name of the child. Miura then warns family members that ongoing rituals are necessary, not only to make amends for the death of the fetus, but also to avoid misfortunes such as illnesses, accidents, and financial problems that would result for the family if rituals were to cease.

For reasons such as the above, thousands of families, especially mothers, regularly attend rites at Buddhist temples throughout Japan. Numerous temples also house the remains of aborted fetuses in a special cemetery. Family members often come to these cemeteries to pray to the spirit of their deceased baby. These cemeteries often display the statue of the *bodhisattva* Jizo, assigned to look after the well-being of children. (In Buddhist teachings, a *bodhisattva* is a human being who has achieved enlightenment and is committed to saving the rest of humanity.) Family members can buy statues of this guardian of their child's soul to be placed in the cemetery. They also often purchase these statues for their family altars at home, or *butsudan.* Furthermore, wooden memorial slats, or *toba,* can be bought at the entrance to these temples. These slats have the names of the babies inscribed on them, as well as the names of the family. These are ritually burned at the end of each year, so families feel compelled to buy them for another year. In addition to these ritual objects, the family pays for the ritual itself. Each ritual costs anywhere between US$100 and 300, and families are encouraged to repeat these regularly.

There seem to be a number of Buddhist components in *mizuko kuyo:* the recitation of scriptural prayers during the ceremonies, the use of Buddhist ritual objects, Buddhist memorial tablets such as *ihai,* and Buddhist priests and priestesses officiating. However, sadness can be exploited. In the case of *mizuko kuyo,* it can be commercialized. The ritual is now big business in Japanese Buddhist temples. There can be much money gained from these services. Buddhists who perform these rites claim that the monies go to the temple. Yet many critics, including numerous Buddhists, criticize the commercialization of the ceremony. What would be some Buddhist values that are violated via exploitation and commercialization?

Other critics point out that the popularization of *mizuko kuyo* gives stronger legitimization to abortion, so that abortion can be performed for more self-centered reasons. Abortion was legalized in Japan essentially out of economic necessity. However, critics now view it as representative of a more carefree, irresponsible approach to sexual freedom. How would Buddhist teachings address this? How can religious beliefs be abused? What are ways to address this potential for abuse? Does the purpose behind *mizuko kuyo* have Buddhist roots? Or is the ritual antithetical to Buddhist teachings?

13 AZT RESEARCH IN AFRICA: ETHICAL IMPERIALISM?

We now know that aggressive treatment with azidothymidine, otherwise known as AZT, can lessen the possibility of vertical transmission of the HIV virus from pregnant mothers who are infected with AIDS to their newborn child. An ongoing dosage of AZT during pregnancy can prevent this from happening. However, the cost of this long-term treatment is rather high, certainly too high for most people in Third World countries. Unfortunately, these are the people who are victimized the most by AIDS. In fact, nearly 95 percent of all those who have HIV/AIDS live in the developing world. To illustrate further, there are over 30 million people worldwide who are infected with HIV or AIDS. Twenty-one million of them live in sub-Saharan Africa. Most Africans cannot afford an aggressive AZT regimen. For this reason, researchers have conducted trial studies of less expensive, short-term treatments with AZT. And they have conducted these trials using African women who are already infected with the HIV virus.

The NIH (National Institutes of Health) and the CDC (Centers for Disease Control and Prevention) financed these trials in Abidjan, Ivory Coast, a country of 11 million people. They enrolled HIV-infected women to test the efficacy of short-term, lower-regimen AZT use. In order to assess the treatment's usefulness, researchers also handed out placebos to the women. The women knew they were infected with HIV. They were informed that the results of the testing could benefit them. Yet they themselves did not know whether they were given the AZT or a placebo. This meant that they also did not know whether or not there was a likelihood of transmitting the disease to their children.

Siata Quattara was one of these subjects. After she was informed that she carried the AIDS virus, health workers then explained to her the specifics of the research, including its purpose along with the need to use a placebo. Due to her lack of education, she had little comprehension of what a placebo was as well as its implications. When she was asked why she had taken part in the research, she stated that it was because of "the medical care that they are promising me" (Howard French, "AIDS Research in Africa: Juggling Risks and Hopes," *New York Times*, October 9, 1997, sec. A14, p. 1).

Apparently Siata and the other research subjects, out of desperation upon being informed that they had the AIDS virus, were willing to be a part of the experiment to help their babies as well as themselves. Yet, they as subjects did not know whether they were being treated with the AZT. Many of them were given placebos. Nevertheless, they somehow felt that they were still given some effective medicine. Keep in mind that here, as in many countries in Africa, there is very little access to antiretroviral treatments. For example, in Rwanda, more than 400,000 people are infected with HIV/AIDS. Yet only one thousand of these Rwandans have access to drug treatment that they can afford.

Here's the catch. This type of clinical trial, using placebos and AZT, would not be allowed in the United States. The use of placebos has always incurred much debate. Many would defend their use from a strong scientific perspective, namely, that efficacy can be determined more properly by using placebos. Testing without placebos would be less reliable. Critics argue, however, that this involves deceit and unrealistic expectations as well as anxieties. Moreover, it is already known that AZT reduces transmission.

These trials have also been conducted in Thailand and the Dominican Republic. Nevertheless, they would not be allowed here in the United States. How would we apply Kant's categorical imperative to this, particularly the principle of universalizability? In the same light, how would his respect for persons as ends be applicable? Defenders of the trials argue that the subjects gave their informed consent to participate. That is, they knew what was involved, they freely volunteered, and they competently gave their consent. Is that truly the case here? Does the notion of informed consent have to be readjusted to specific cultural contexts? In light of the complexity of the trials and the subjects' general state of illiteracy, could they knowingly and voluntarily consent? What are some utilitarian considerations? How just would it be to simply provide the aggressive regimen of AZT knowing that most infected women in Africa would not be able to afford it? In view of the high premium in African thought placed upon communal well-being, could this influence how we determine consequences and the greater good?

14 THE SARS VIRUS

Kwan Sui-chu and her family, Canadian citizens, also belong to the rather large population of Chinese in Toronto. She and her husband were visiting Hong Kong when she boarded an elevator at her hotel on February 21, 2003. On the same elevator was a physician from mainland China who had recently been treating a strange new illness. Days later, the physician died. All others on the elevator, including the seventy-eight-year-old Kwan, contracted what was later named the SARS (severe acute respiratory syndrome) virus. Over the next six months, the SARS virus led to a nearly worldwide epidemic, claiming close to nine hundred lives and infecting over eight thousand people.

When Kwan returned home to Scarborough, a suburb of Toronto, she unknowingly passed the virus on to her family. She later died at home, but her son, Chi Kwai Tse, went to the local Scarborough Grace Hospital to be treated for his flu-like symptoms. He and hospital staff were not at first aware that he also had SARS. The chain of contamination spread to health staff and others. Within days, on March 13, Chi died. An administrator at the same hospital, who was Chinese, read about a strange disease in a Chinese newspaper. Noting the symptoms, and aware that many hospital staff were now ill, he then made the connection. By April, there were over two hundred cases of SARS in the region of Toronto. Each case could be traced back to the original case at Grace Scarborough, to Chi Kwai Tse. Outside of Asia, Canada was the country hardest hit with SARS.

For reasons of public health and precaution, the identities of Kwan Sui-chu and her son were disclosed to the public to ensure that those who were in contact with them would be alerted and quarantined. Despite assurances that the risks would be minimal if people were not in contact with the original cases, many people avoided Chinese, Chinese businesses, Chinese restaurants, and so forth. Chinese trade in Toronto took a downward plunge. The Canadian Prime Minister Jean Chrétien even dined at a Chinese restaurant in the city in order to restore some measure of public confidence.

China and Hong Kong have been criticized by public health authorities for not taking quicker steps to prevent the spread of the disease. Critics point out general shortcomings on the part of the health care system including systemic unpreparedness for such an emergency, lack of safeguards, poor planning, faulty transmission of information, and confusion of roles and responsibilities. This slow response also entailed a failure to immediately quarantine. In contrast, Singapore has been singled out for the "exemplary" way it dealt with the crisis, taking prompt measures to quarantine and to prevent the spread of the virus.

Nevertheless, on September 9, 2003, a twenty-seven-year-old Singaporean male doctoral student was believed to have contracted the SARS virus. He was a laboratory technician conducting research on the West Nile virus. His was the first case of the virus since July, when the WHO (World Health Organization) officially announced that the potentially fatal virus (with a 4% mortality rate) had been contained. Immediately upon the discovery of his virus after he exhibited the flu-like symptoms, twenty-five of his coworkers and friends were quarantined and ordered to remain at home in order to prevent the spread of the highly contagious virus.

Scientists believe that the virus originated in China's southern province of Guangdong in November 2002 and by February 2003 had already spread to other parts of the world. Scientists also believe that, although the virus appears to have been contained, further outbreaks are likely. Indeed, more strains of the virus can be mutated and thus more resistant to antivirals and antibiotics. Even after Taiwan was the last country finally taken off the official warning list by WHO, experts indicated that, although it appears that the virus has been successfully contained, more deadly outbreaks could still occur. Thus, Singapore's incident is no surprise.

In view of Toronto's response and disclosure of the identities of the Chinese victims of the virus, was this disclosure morally justified? Considering Confucian teachings that stress the well-being of the community over individual interests, how would this apply to this kind of disclosure? How would Confucian teachings apply to issues of quarantine and isolation? Given our advanced forms of global air travel, where we can now circle the globe in twenty-four hours, how would ethical theories address the need for morally justifiable ways to prevent the spread of lethal and contagious diseases? How would utilitarians and deontologists address the tension between individual freedoms and the common good?

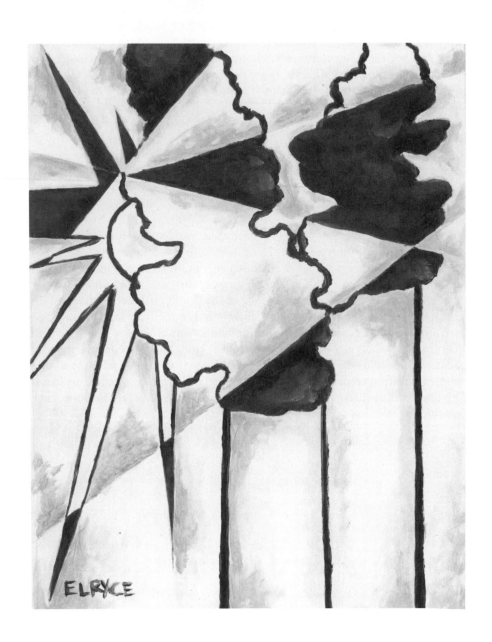

15 HERCULANEUM AND LA OROYA

Lead poisoning is highly toxic and even fatal. Once lead enters the blood-stream, it can lead to kidney failure, seizures, and comas. In the late 1990s, parents in Herculaneum, Missouri, were thus understandably outraged when they learned that the local ten-year-old smelter polluted their town with contaminated substances, including lead. The smelter is owned and operated by the Doe Run Company, based in St. Louis, a company that, according to the EPA (Environmental Protection Agency), is the state's leading polluter. After concerned parents notified the EPA, the Missouri Department of Health and Human Services discovered that emissions from the smelter induced lead poisoning in 30 percent of the children.

In 2000, the EPA ordered Doe Run to clean up its contamination and reduce its levels as well as buy out the homes of the families most affected and pay them to relocate. Although the smelter finally met the official emission standards in January 2002, the level of toxicity due to the lead poisoning still poses a risk to families. Families continue to sue the company claming that Doe Run knew of the risks years ago, yet it did nothing to inform local residents. In any case, pressures from environmentalists, families, and the government finally compelled Doe Run to disclose and make public its emissions data.

Doe Run also owns and operates a smelter in the Peruvian town of La Oroya. Doe Run acquired the smelter from the Peruvian government in 1997. In its purchase agreement, Doe Run also pledged to update the equipment and to maintain Peru's legal environmental standards. However, a decline in profits soon induced the company to forestall its environmental promise and investment. As a result, pollution levels at La Oroya grew to emergency proportions. The smelter emitted high levels of cadmium, sulfur dioxide, arsenic, and lead. According to Peruvian government statistics, nearly 90 percent of the town's children had blood-lead levels above the acceptable standard.

Families were incensed. Yet despite their protests, they met a stumbling block. The Peruvian government had approved Doe Run to hire its own environmental auditing firm. From a legal standpoint, the Peruvian government therefore acted in a way that protected the interests of the company. Attempts are still under way to determine the levels of contamination.

Here we see parallel incidents but with different results due to, on the one hand, disclosure of emissions data from Doe Run in Missouri versus, on the other hand, the lack of disclosure in the Peruvian town. If the same requirement to disclose could have been applied to the Peruvians in La Oroya, there may have been more favorable results. Should the same U.S. standards be applied to Peruvians? What moral theories and principles can address the issue of company disclosure and accountability to the public? What is the relationship between knowledge and empowerment? How do deontological and utilitarian concerns address these issues? What about teleological considerations? What about the virtue ethics of Aristotle?

16 CELL PHONES AND THE DEMOCRATIC REPUBLIC OF CONGO

An indispensable component in cellular telephones is columbite-tantalite, otherwise known as coltan. Coltan is used for many advanced electronic purposes such as fiber optics, night vision goggles, and laptop computers. Due to the increase in demand for cellular phones, there is also an increasing need for coltan. It so happens that the Democratic Republic of Congo (DRC) is not only rich in its supply of diamonds, but has at least 80 percent of the world's supply of coltan. The DRC has an abundant supply of other minerals such as copper, zinc, colbalt, and uranium. Due to the ever-increasing supply of cell phones, prices naturally become competitive and sellers of coltan can exact higher fees. Yet, as rich as the nation is in its share of coltan, the Democratic Republic of Congo remains a poor country.

Coltan mining activities have intensified. At the same time, the DRC is immersed in a civil war. In the DRC's civil war, the rebel army of Tutsis continues to be supported by the Rwandan army. Moreover, the Rwandan militia have taken an active part in the mining of coltan. In fact, armies from both Rwanda and Uganda have penetrated the DRC in order to exact their share of the above minerals ("What Is Coltan? The Link Between Your Cellphone and Congo," on *Nightline*, January 21, 2002, http://abcnews.go.com/sections/nightline/DailyNews/coltan_explainer.html).

All this has resulted in thousands of Congolese miners being displaced. In turn, they and their families have had to move to sites reserved as wildlife refuges and national parks. They have had to resort to coltan mining in these protected areas. In many cases, the coltan mining in these areas has turned out to be unsafe, and there have been a number of mining accidents. In the process, they have also encroached on the habitat of wildlife such as elephants and endangered species such as the eastern lowland gorilla.

Here we see a link among coltan mining, internal war, the displacement of Congolese, and harm to civilians and the environment as well as to endangered species. What moral obligations do governments have to lessen and prevent the violations of the human rights of their citizens like the Congolese miners and their families? What moral obligations rest upon foreign governments like those that sponsor the type of mining that is necessary for the manufacture of cell phones? Knowing what is involved in the production of cell phones, what about the moral obligations upon consumers including cell phone users and potential buyers?

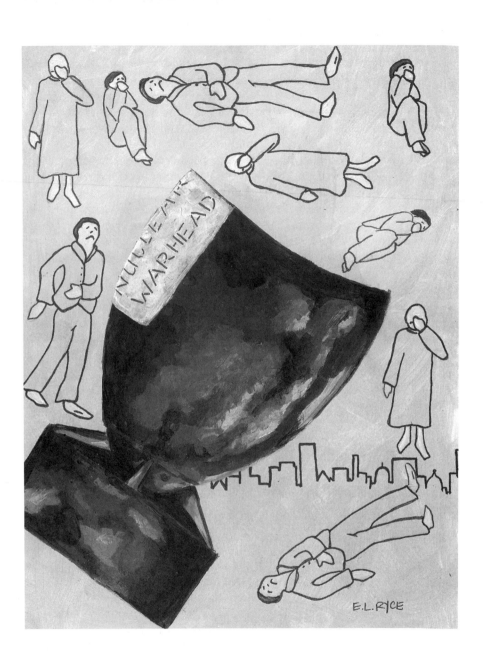

17 CHELYABINSK

A landmark case was decided in a Russian court in 1997. The court ordered that second- and third-generation families be compensated for the emotional and physical distress that resulted from over fifty years of radiation exposure from the northern city of Chelyabinsk's nuclear power plant. This was the first time that Russian courts acknowledged physical and mental harms to victims and their families over later generations.

The area of Chelyabinsk is considered to be the most contaminated region in the world ("Chelyabinsk: The Most Contaminated Spot on the Planet," http://www.logtv.com/chelya). Eighty kilometers outside of the city of Chelyabinsk, a major nuclear weapons site called "Mayak" (meaning "beacon") had been in operation since the late 1940s. The weapons site regularly dumped radioactive waste into the neighboring Techa River, a drainage basin interconnected with many lakes. No less than twenty-four villages depended upon the river as its source of water.

In a series of mishaps, due to an extreme amount of highly toxic chemical and nuclear waste that contaminated the waters, hundreds of thousands of inhabitants have been harmed. The river was first polluted in the early 1950s. Then, in 1957, when a nuclear waste storage unit malfunctioned and exploded, affecting nearly 250,000 villagers, over twenty villages had to be evacuated. Experts claim that the inhabitants were exposed to twice the amount of radiation that was released during the Chernobyl disaster. Finally, in 1967, when Lake Karachay, where much of the radiation had been dumped, virtually dried up, strong winds spread radioactive particles over an area of 23,000 square kilometers.

As a direct result of the exposure, hundreds of thousands of inhabitants suffered cancer, cancer mutations, leukemia, birth defects, circulatory conditions, and sterility. One village in particular, Muslymova, was almost entirely devastated by these diseases. Ever since the accident, the region had been closed off to any foreigners. This tragic contamination exposure was kept a government secret until 1992.

Some of the more prominent issues surrounding the Chelyabinsk catastrophe have to do with the manufacturing of nuclear weapons. What moral issues surround the imposition of nuclear weapons sites? Viewing the issue more broadly in terms of nuclear power plants, what moral obligations do governments have to ensure safety for those who live near nuclear plants? How can we as citizens take measures to ensure protection from nuclear plants and the dangers they pose to surrounding inhabitants? How would deontologists address this issue? Are there convincing utilitarian arguments for maintaining these plants? How about natural law concerns? What Buddhist values address these issues? China is on its way to becoming a nuclear power. How would Confucian values address this? India definitely possesses nuclear weapons. How would Hindu values address this?

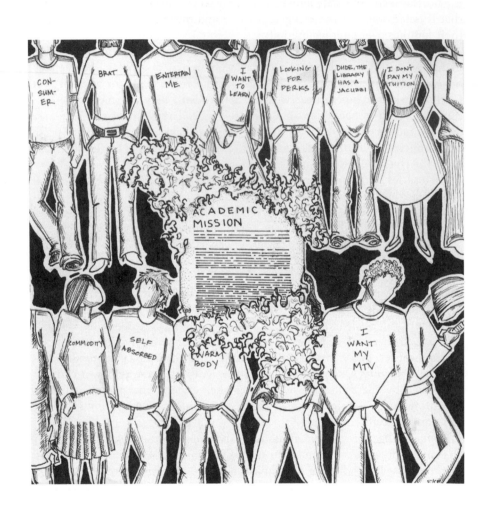

18 THE PERKS OF AN EDUCATION

The University of Rhode Island now has a $54 million sports complex and skating rink. It offers the best in seating with all sorts of plush amenities along with special viewing boxes. The University of Vermont is developing a $70 million student center, replete with an indoor skating pond, theater, and pub. The University of Cincinnati is constructing a $200 million facility with a built-in outdoor mall, shops, and cafes. Ohio State University is constructing a colossal $140 million indoor sports complex offering kayaking, batting cages, climbing walls, and massages. The University of Southern Mississippi is putting plans together for a giant water park with slides and wave pools. Indiana University of Pennsylvania offers virtual golf so that one can play any one of fifty-two world-class golf courses.

Universities throughout the United States are offering perks like these in order to draw more students. The attraction of spas, Jacuzzis, driving ranges, skating rinks, virtual sports, pedicures, massages, and so on is hard for potential freshmen to ignore. Universities are competing with each other to draw high numbers as well as the best and the brightest.

Yet this poses some unsettling questions. Critics point out that these perks draw attention to the entertainment value of what a university has to offer, rather than its academic programs. Has education surrendered to popular culture and its values of entertainment, the easy life, and pampered self-absorption? Critics also point out that these extravagances escalate the costs of tuition and other university expenses. And the ones who pay for these will primarily be the parents of prospective students.

On the other hand, supporters of these marketing strategies argue that these are necessary in order to compete for good students. Rather than excesses, these are viewed as critically necessary, especially in today's consumer-oriented society, with young people being the biggest spenders (see Greg Winter, "Jacuzzi U.? A Battle of Perks to Lure Students," *New York Times*, October 5, 2003).

Do these perks jeopardize the academic mission of the university? Is it possible to use these strategies and still be consistent with academic excellence? Is it fair that parents and future parents have to bear the brunt of these amenities? Is this changing the ways we look at higher education? The ways we look at learning? What are utilitarian arguments that both defend and oppose this kind of marketing? What are some deontological views regarding this issue? Many other cultures regard highly the value of proper education. Furthermore, many students from other countries come to the United States for higher education. How would any of the values of non-American cultures address these issues?

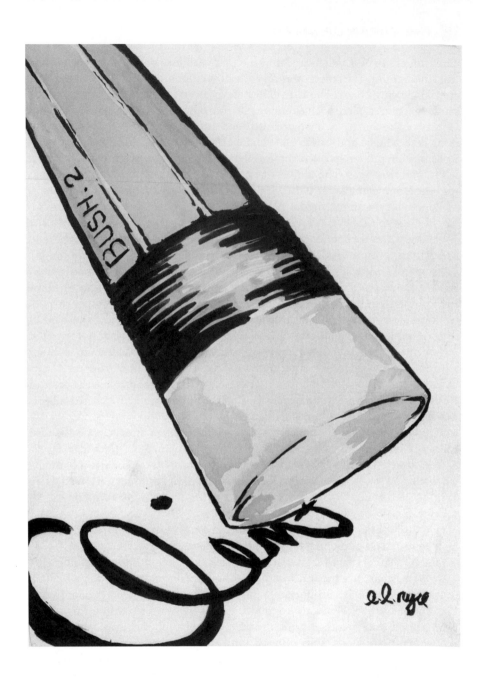

19 THE INTERNATIONAL CRIMINAL COURT

Beyond any doubt, the twentieth century witnessed the biggest toll in the number of human deaths brought about through wars, internal strife, mass torture and executions, and crimes against humanity including outright genocide. We need only consider the recent conflicts in Bosnia and in African countries to realize that international, cross-cultural efforts at addressing and preventing war and genocide is needed now more than ever.

To deal with this on a global level, efforts were made to establish an international criminal tribunal. This international tribunal would act to punish violators of international humanitarian law when countries themselves could not take the appropriate actions. On April 11, 2002, 139 countries voted for the Rome Treaty. The Rome Treaty was invoked years earlier on July 17, 1998, to install an International Criminal Court (ICC). By April 2002, the ICC had received 67 ratifications. One of the signatories was former President Bill Clinton, who signed when he was still in office. The passing of the Rome Treaty thereby formally established the ICC as an official international body.

Less than a month afterwards, on May 6, representatives of the Bush administration, in an unprecedented move, announced that it would "unsign" the earlier signature and thus remove its ratification. It marks the first time that a U.S. president has annulled the signature of an earlier president on a treaty. Furthermore, it was revoking an earlier ratification of a UN treaty. Despite this U.S. opposition to the treaty, there are currently 75 ratifications, and the ICC is now an official reality.

Critics of the ICC claim that its implementation is fundamentally unconstitutional, consisting of an absence of jury trials and lack of due process. Another argument is that rogue countries that have a history of human rights abuse could exploit the ICC for their own purposes, and that there is no built-in mechanism for preventing this. Opponents also point out an apparent absence of accountability on the part of leading judges and prosectors.

Defenders of the ICC refute the above charges and claim that the current administration's stance will have a long-term corrosive impact on U.S. international relations. Furthermore, the Bush administration's actions erode the credibility of any signatures by American presidents. Revoking a UN treaty also weakens the U.S. position in the UN, particularly with respect to the UN Security Council.

The ICC is a significant international instrument. Does the nullification of U.S. support for the ICC weaken global dialogue? Are the arguments for nullification strong enough to morally justify it? What role should the United States play in international efforts to diminish and prevent crimes against humanity? How should the United States exert its power in a morally justified fashion in order to cooperate with other nations and cultures? How does deontology address these issues? What are some utilitarian considerations?

What are other cultural perspectives including African values, Hinduism, Confucianism, and Buddhism? Should the United States essentially look out for itself, its citizens, and its armed forces? What are the moral arguments both opposing and defending the removal of U.S. support for the ICC? (See John B. Anderson, "Unsigning the ICC," *The Nation*, April 29, 2002).

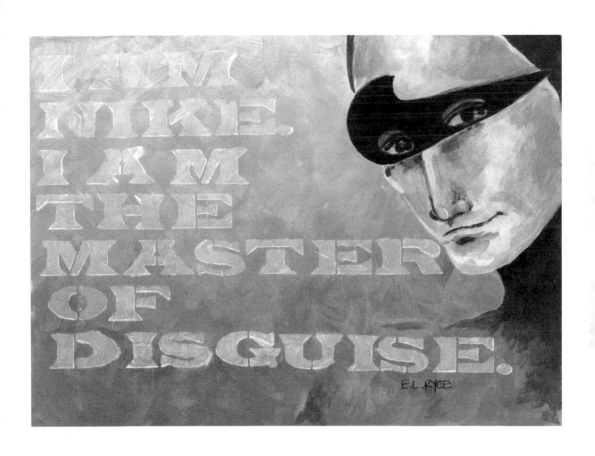

20 NIKE'S RIGHT TO LIE

In the late 1990s, when the mega-billion-dollar corporation Nike was criticized for exploiting foreign labor in developing countries through sweatshops and other oppressive conditions, the kingpin of the athletic market put on a full-court public relations press to counter the accusations. This blitz included advertisement campaigns and even a piece in the *New York Times* by Nike CEO Phil Knight. This campaign essentially denied such exploitation on the part of Nike.

Yet, there seemed to be mounting evidence that the criticism of Nike had solid grounds. In the light of numerous testimonies and a bulk of documentation, it appeared that Nike was deliberately deceiving the public about its overseas practices. For this reason, a leading consumer advocate in San Francisco, Marc Kasky, filed a lawsuit against Nike. He accused Nike of false advertising and deception of the public. When the issue was brought to court, the lawyers for Nike, alluding to former cases, argued that Nike, as a corporation, is also a legal entity known as a "person." As a "person," it thereby possesses, along with all other persons, constitutional rights including a First Amendment right to free speech. And, just as under this right any person has a right to lie and deceive, so does the corporation. The lawyers for Nike claimed that their speech constituted political, and not commercial, speech. Politicians certainly have the constitutional right to deceive in statements they make to the public. In like manner, so does Nike. And lower courts acquitted Nike of the charges.

Kasky persisted, and the issue was taken to California's Supreme Court. In May 2002, the court, by a 4 to 3 majority, overturned the lower court's decision, ruling that the statements by Nike were in effect commercial speech and thus subject to Federal Trade Commission rules. This meant that corporations must make truthful statements about its practices to the public. Nike was stunned by the decision. And so were other giant corporations. Reactions from Microsoft, Pfizer, Monsanto, and ExxonMobile vehemently protested the decision, claiming that corporations are in effect legal persons and should be given the same legal rights.

Nike then took steps to appeal the ruling to the U.S. Supreme Court. Nearly a year later, on April 23, 2003, the U.S. Supreme Court reviewed the case, dismissed the claim by Nike, and sent the case back to California, noting its unique First Amendment issues with respect to the rights of corporations. The case is scheduled to go to court in San Francisco in the fall of 2004.

How valid is the claim that a corporation is a legal person? If it is a legal person and should be treated as such, does it have absolute rights to its constitutional rights? The discussion has occurred along the claims of legal rights. How do moral rights and obligations enter in? How does this demonstrate the tension between legal rights and moral rights? What are some deontological as well as utilitarian considerations in addressing this issue? How are these relevant in determining a sound moral public policy? Since we are dealing here with a huge multinational corporation, should the values and beliefs of other cultures—namely, those directly affected by its corporate practices—be relevant? How should these other cultural values apply? (See Thom Hartmann, "Now Corporations Claim the Right to 'Lie'," *Common Dreams*, January 1, 2003).

CREDITS